Religion, Theologie und Naturwissenschaft /
Religion, Theology, and Natural Science

Edited by
Christina Aus der Au, Dirk Evers, Jan-Olav Henriksen,
Markus Mühling, Gijsbert van den Brink, and Matthias D. Wüthrich

Volume 38

Michael Agerbo Mørch

Systematic Theology as a Rationally Justified Public Discourse about God

Vandenhoeck & Ruprecht

Bibliographic information published by the Deutsche Nationalbibliothek:
The Deutsche Nationalbibliothek lists this publication in the Deutsche
Nationalbibliografie; detailed bibliographic data available online: https://dnb.de.

© 2023 by Vandenhoeck & Ruprecht, Theaterstraße 13, 37073 Göttingen, Germany,
an imprint of the Brill-Group
(Koninklijke Brill NV, Leiden, The Netherlands; Brill USA Inc., Boston MA, USA;
Brill Asia Pte Ltd, Singapore; Brill Deutschland GmbH, Paderborn, Germany,
Brill Österreich GmbH, Vienna, Austria)
Koninklijke Brill NV incorporates the imprints Brill, Brill Nijhoff, Brill Hotei,
Brill Schöningh, Brill Fink, Brill mentis, Vandenhoeck & Ruprecht, Böhlau,
V&R unipress and Wageningen Academic.

All rights reserved. No part of this work may be reproduced or utilized in any form or by any
means, electronic or mechanical, including photocopying, recording, or any information storage
and retrieval system, without prior written permission from the publisher.

Cover illustration: macrovector/Freepik. <a href='https://www.freepik.com/vectors/globe-grid'>Globe grid vector created by macrovector – www.freepik.com</a>

Cover design: SchwabScantechnik, Göttingen
Typesetting: le-tex publishing services, Leipzig
Printed and bound: Hubert & Co. BuchPartner, Göttingen
Printed in the EU

Vandenhoeck & Ruprecht Verlage | www.vandenhoeck-ruprecht-verlage.com

ISSN 2198-4581
ISBN 978-3-525-56871-2

Acknowledgements

Late in his life, Wittgenstein resignedly remarked: "Ich hätte gerne ein gutes Buch hervorgebracht. Es ist nicht so ausgefallen; aber die Zeit ist vorbei, in der es von mir verbessert werden könnte."[1]

And even though it would be haughty to compare myself with this philosophical giant lavishly, his words have resounded in me at the end of this trajectory. It is an immense privilege to work on a topic that matters to you for several years, but the plethora of academic work in modernity has left many – and from time to time, myself included – with a feeling that we write for the shredder. The wisdom seems to be that we work as if the universe depends on our results and, at the same time, relax knowing that this is not the case. As Ludger Jansen says, more optimistically than it may appear here: "Theologen produzieren, so könnte man diesen Komplex prägnant zusammenfassen, Fussnoten."[2] It is not footnotes to Plato (at least not all of it) but to a complex, diverse, and living Christian tradition. As such, maybe this small contribution to the ongoing conversation of Christianity can find its place and become a new, but hopefully not irrelevant, footnote.

"A good thesis is a completed thesis" was the first words I heard in the doctoral program at MF Norwegian School of Theology, Religion and Society (MF), and if I thought that that was embarrassingly unambitious, I later realized that it was profound wisdom. The words were said by the Head of the PhD Program at MF, dr.theol. Nils Aksel Røsæg, who should be praised for joyfully leading all doctoral candidates through troubled waters, stimulating peer discussions and helping with numerous practical details. As my dissertation is now being published in a revised edition, this is the obvious opportunity to thank him for his kind support throughout my doctoral trajectory.

Whether the following book succeeds in reaching its aims is up for the reader to judge. I know for sure, that I have delighted in my effort, repeatedly calming myself with the ancient insight: *Ultra posse nemo obligatur*. I am not self-effacing, though. I have prospered immensely during my doctoral studies, if not economically, then intellectually and socially. I knew my learning curve would be steep but also that

---

1 Ludwig Wittgenstein, *Philosophische Untersuchungen. Philosophical investigations*, ed. G. E. M. Anscombe, P. M. S. Hacker, and Joachim Schulte, Rev. 4th ed (Malden, MA: Wiley-Blackwell, 2009), 4.
2 Benedikt Paul Göcke, ed., *Die Wissenschaftlichkeit der Theologie. Band 1: Historische und systematische Perspektiven*, Studien zur systematischen Theologie, Ethik und Philosophie, 13,1 (Münster: Aschendorff Verlag, 2018), 354.

with fellow travellers and skilled guides, it would be possible if not to move then to climb mountains.

As such, many people – all the way from the bottom to the top of the academic hierarchy – have helped me succeed in the project, and without them, I would not have been able to complete it. No one exceeds the role of my supervisor, professor Atle Ottesen Søvik, who always gave me enough rope but was there to help me when I was about to leave myself hanging. I cannot imagine a better tour guide, and I will remain forever grateful! Also, an extraordinary thanks to my peer and friend, Emil Børty Nielsen, without whom I wouldn't have completed my thesis. An excellent philosopher and talented communicator – lost in traffic, but not in thought. Thanks, Emil!

My doctoral program was financed by Copenhagen Lutheran School of Theology, where my second supervisor, associate professor Jakob V. Olsen is an employee. Stimulating academic freedom and excellence in research, I am immensely grateful for the opportunity and generous support, *sine qua non*. I know the troubles I have cost this institution which makes me humble and pensive.

Sincere thanks to professor Markus Mühling for extensive criticism and encouragement at the 50% and 90% seminars. An erudite and critical scholar with an eye for both detail and scope. And now an additional thanks for inviting me to publish my work in the *RThN Series* at Vandenhoeck and Ruprecht. Therefore, also a varm thanks to Mühling's co-editor of the series, Christina Aus der Au. And a very warm thanks to Jehona Kicaj from Vandenhoeck and Ruprecht for excellent coorperation in preparing the manuscript for publication.

My former colleagues at MF Norwegian School of Theology, Religion and Society should be mentioned since I have received competent and thought-provoking criticism on numerous accounts. From the start, many were critical of the way I framed the discussion, yet with ever-increasing enthusiasm, the faculty engaged in discussions on my research matters. Thanks to (in alphabetical order) Ragnar Misje Bergem, Asle Eikrem, Marion Grau, Terje Hegertun, Harald Hegstad, Jan-Olav Henriksen, Kristin Graff Kallevåg, and Daniela Rapisarda. Also a warm thanks to my doctoral peers John D. Andersen, Filip Rasmussen, and Jo Bertil Rydland Værnesbranden. At the seminars, I have also received critical comments from external professors Werner Jeanrond, Marius Mjaaland, and Knut-Willy Sæter.

A special thanks to professor Gijsbert van den Brink at Vrije Universiteit Amsterdam and professor Frederik Stjernfelt at Aalborg Universitet København. Eminent scholars, gracious conversation partners, and inspiring mentors. Thanks to professor Alan White and MA in intellectual history Benjamin Dalton for upgrading the readability of my school English.

A warm thanks to my family-in-law and my own family for encouragements and timely distractions. To my mother for never lacking support of any conceivable kind!

To Anna, Signe and Eva for not accepting a distant father; for laughing, playing, teasing, kissing, and dancing. Stay curious, girls.

In the Book of Proverbs, we read: "Her children rise up and call her happy; her husband too, and he praises her; 'Many women have done excellently, but you surpass them all.'" (31.28–29). Surpassing words, my dear wife, Elisabeth, has done more than I could have asked for. We shouldn't flatten thanksgivings since "thanks" is a beautiful word. Thanks, Elisabeth – I truly mean it.

A book's life is such that the author ends with writing the acknowledgements, and this is where the reader starts. I hope my book will provide new insights, stimulate further discussions, and hopefully be a little bit of intellectual fun too. I will end here with a quote from Karl Popper, who has been a conversation partner for me for some years now: "I believe that it would be worth trying to learn something about the world even if in trying to do so we should merely learn that we do not know much. This state of learned ignorance might be a help in many of our troubles. It might be well for all of us to remember that, while differing widely in the various little bits we know, in our infinite ignorance we are all equal."[3]

This book is dedicated to the memory of my father, Herluf Emil Mørch (1962–2017).

---

3 Karl R. Popper, *Conjectures and Refutations: The Growth of Scientific Knowledge*, 3rd ed. (revised) (London: Routledge, 2002), 38.

Table of Contents

Acknowledgements 5

Part One: Introduction and Background for the Book

Chapter One: Introduction 17
  1.1 Background for the Book 17
  1.2 The Research Problem 20
      1.2.1 Terminology 25
  1.3 Material 28
  1.4 Method 30
      1.4.1 Outline 32
  1.5 Aim and Relevance of the Book 37

Chapter Two: A Selected Overview of The Historical Background 41
  2.1 Introduction 41
  2.2 Debates in the 20th Century 43
      2.2.1 The Barth-Scholz Debate 43
      2.2.2 The German Debate in the 60s through the 80s 48
      2.2.3 Lund versus Uppsala 52
      2.2.4 Chicago vs. Yale 58
  2.3 Conclusion 63

Part Two: A Scalar Understanding of Systematic Theology

Chapter Three: A Definition of Scientific Systematic Theology 67
  3.1 Introduction 67
  3.2 Level One (Systematic Theology 1) 72
  3.3 Level Two (Systematic Theology 2) 77
  3.4 Level Three (Systematic Theology 3) 81
      3.4.1 Niels Henrik Gregersen's Understanding of
            Systematic Theology 3 81
      3.4.2 Systematic Theology 3 as Normative Ontology 82
      3.4.3 Why Systematic Theology 3 May be Scientific and
            Systematic Theology 1 and 2 Only Derivatively So 87

  3.4.4 The Sources of Systematic Theology 3 89
    3.4.4.1 Thought Experiments as a Source for
       Systematic Theology 3 90
    3.4.4.2 The Natural Sciences 93
    3.4.4.3 The Bible and Tradition 94
  3.4.5 On the Possibility of a Synchronic Constitution of
    Systematic Theology 95
    3.4.5.1 Lorenz Puntel's Structural-Systematic
       Approach to a Theory of Being and God 98
  3.4.6 The Concept of "Truth Candidate" 127
  3.4.7 A Short Introduction to Rescher's Coherence
    Theory of Truth 130
  3.4.8 How to Compare Ontologies. A Puntelian Approach 132
  3.4.9 Conclusion 135

Part Three: Objections to Systematic Theology as Scientific

Introduction 139

Chapter Four: Objection 1—Testability 141
 4.1 Introduction 141
 4.2 Premise 1 142
  4.2.1 Definition of Testability 143
  4.2.2 Testing Single Propositions: Confirmation Theory 145
    4.2.2.1 The Defence of Testing Single Propositions 145
    4.2.2.2 The Critique of Testing Single Propositions 149
  4.2.3 Excursus: Inferences – The Steps from Tests
    to Conclusions 152
    4.2.3.1 Induction 153
    4.2.3.2 Inference to the Best Explanation 158
    4.2.3.3 Conclusion to Excursus About Inferences 167
  4.2.4 Testing Whole Theories: Coherence Theory 167
  4.2.5 Conclusion on Premise 1 173
 4.3 Premise 2 174
  4.3.1 Introduction 174
  4.3.2 Examination of Coherence I 179
  4.3.3 Wolfhart Pannenberg 181
  4.3.4 Alister McGrath 186
  4.3.5 Nancey Murphy 190
    4.3.5.1 Christianity's Crises 196

    4.3.5.2 Naturalism's Solution 197
    4.3.5.3 Naturalism's Crises 198
    4.3.5.4 Christianity's Solution 199
  4.3.6 Examination of Coherence II 201
  4.3.7 Conclusion on Premise 2 203
 4.4 Conclusion 203

Chapter Five: Objection 2—Falsifiability 205
 5.1 Introduction 205
 5.2 Premise 1 206
  5.2.1 What is Falsification? 206
  5.2.2 Karl Popper 207
  5.2.3 Thomas Kuhn 210
  5.2.4 Imre Lakatos 212
  5.2.5 Paul Feyerabend 215
  5.2.6 Larry Laudan 217
  5.2.7 Falsification at Work 1:
    The Hypothetico-Deductive Method 220
    5.2.7.1 The Deductive-Nomological Model 220
    5.2.7.2 The Hypothetico-Deductive Method 221
  5.2.8 Falsification at Work 2: Comparing Degrees of Coherence 224
    5.2.8.1 Falsification as Comparison of Degrees of
      Coherence between Ontologies 228
    5.2.8.2 Systematization 235
    5.2.8.3 Theoretical Framework 237
    5.2.8.4 Scientific Theories must be Falsifiable
      but not Actually Falsified 239
  5.2.9 Conclusion on Premise 1 239
 5.3 Premise 2 240
  5.3.1 Examples of Uses of Falsification 240
  5.3.2 The Concept of Eschatological Verification 244
  5.3.3 Excursus: Falsification at the Level of Systematic
    Theology 2 246
  5.3.4 Recent Attempts at Rendering Ontologies
    Comparable 248
  5.3.5 Conclusion on Premise 2 252
 5.4 Conclusion 253

Chapter Six: Objection 3—Intersubjectivity 255
 6.1 Introduction 255

Table of Contents

- 6.2 Premise 1 257
  - 6.2.1 What is Intersubjectivity? 258
    - 6.2.1.1 Two Major Positions 259
    - 6.2.1.2 What Does Intersubjectivity Presuppose? 261
  - 6.2.2 What is the Best Understanding of the Criterion of Intersubjectivity in Research? 264
    - 6.2.2.1 Methods, Presuppositions, Data, and Results must be Publicly Accessible 265
    - 6.2.2.2 Methods, Data, and Results must be Independent from the Researcher 265
    - 6.2.2.3 The Importance of Criticism for Intersubjectivity 266
  - 6.2.3 What is Gained from Intersubjectivity? 269
  - 6.2.4 Difficulties for a Clear Concept of Intersubjectivity 271
    - 6.2.4.1 Cognitive Biases in Relation to Intersubjective Criticism 272
    - 6.2.4.2 Interpretive Communities and Paradigmatic Thinking as Possible Problems for Intersubjective Criticism 275
    - 6.2.4.3 The Epistemology of Testimony 281
    - 6.2.4.4 Epistemology and Ontology are Related Holistically 283
  - 6.2.5 Conclusion on Premise 1 284
- 6.3. Premise 2 285
  - 6.3.1 Stating the Problem 285
  - 6.3.2 Models for Intersubjectivity in Systematic Theology 286
    - 6.3.2.1 Demarcated Intersubjectivity 287
    - 6.3.2.2 Paradigmatic Intersubjectivity 290
    - 6.3.2.3 Critical Intersubjectivity 293
  - 6.3.3 Complexities in systematic theology in Relation to Intersubjectivity 295
  - 6.3.4 Insecurities in systematic theology in Relation to Intersubjectivity 298
    - 6.3.4.1. Ontology Deals with Comprehensiveness, Which Often Creates Insecurity 299
    - 6.3.4.2 Accepted Insecurities in an Ontological Theory 300
  - 6.3.5 Conclusion on Premise 2 302
- 6.4 Conclusion 303

Chapter Seven: Objection 4—Normativity 307
- 7.1 Introduction 307
- 7.2 Premise 1 310
  - 7.2.1 What is Normativity? 310
    - 7.2.1.1 Short Working Definition of Normativity 311
    - 7.2.1.2 Major Positions 312
    - 7.2.1.3 The Inevitability of Normativity................................ 323
  - 7.2.2 What is Normativity Given the Presuppositions of this Book? 327
    - 7.2.2.1 Normativity and Truth 327
    - 7.2.2.2 Normativity and CUDOS 328
    - 7.2.2.3 Normativity and Revision 330
  - 7.2.3 Conclusion of Premise 1 330
- 7.3 Premise 2 331
  - 7.3.1 Stating the Problem of Strong Normativity in Three Claims 331
    - 7.3.1.1 Strong Normativity Becomes a Problem when it Rests on Questionable Foundations 332
    - 7.3.1.2 Strong Normativity Becomes a Problem When There is a Claim of Truth concerning Supernatural Entities 333
    - 7.3.1.3 Strong Normativity Becomes a Problem When it is Based on Limited Data 335
  - 7.3.2 Models of normativity for Systematic Theology 335
    - 7.3.2.1 As in Religious Studies 336
    - 7.3.2.2 Orthodoxy 336
    - 7.3.2.3 No Normativity—All Theology Is Contextual 337
  - 7.3.3 Strong Normativity in Relation to Coherence in Systematic Theology 338
  - 7.3.4 Conclusion concerning Premise 2 340
- 7.4 Conclusion 340

Chapter Eight: Objection 5—Distinct Discipline with Distinct Research 341
- 8.1 Introduction 341
- 8.2 Premise 1 343
  - 8.2.1 What is Distinct Research? 343
  - 8.2.2 Why is the Criterion of Distinct Research Important? 345
  - 8.2.3 Conclusion on Premise 1.. 347
- 8.3 Premise 2 348
  - 8.3.1 What is the General Problem? 349

        8.3.2 Supposed Problems for systematic theology as
              Distinct Research 350
              8.3.2.1 Systematic Theology Cannot Identify its
                      Object of Study 351
              8.3.2.2 Systematic Theology Cannot Identify its
                      Methods Because of the First Problem 354
              8.3.2.3 Systematic Theology Cannot Explain, Only
                      Describe (Systematic Theology 1) 357
              8.3.2.4 Systematic Theology Builds on a Weak
                      Foundation of Evidence 358
        8.3.3 What Are the Distinctive Marks of
              Systematic Theology 3? 361
              8.3.3.1 Contra Religious Studies 361
              8.3.3.2 Contra Philosophy 362
        8.3.4 Conclusion on Premise 2 366
    8.4 Conclusion 366

Part Four: Conclusion

Chapter Nine 369
    9.1 Summary of the Findings 369
    9.2 Conclusion 372
    9.3 Theses of the Book 372

Bibliography 375

Index 397
    Index of Person 397
    Index of Subjects 401

Part One:
Introduction and Background for the Book

Chapter One: Introduction

This book investigates the discipline of systematic theology and asks how systematic theology can best be construed as a scientific discipline that meets common scientific criteria.[1] The purpose of the first section (1.1) is to give a background for the research question that I present in the next section (1.2). In 1.2.1 I explain four decisions I have made in relation to the terminology used in the text, before I present the material that I have worked with to answer the research question (1.3). In 1.4 I present the proposed method for answering the research question, and I also give a detailed outline of the book (1.4.1). I end this introductory chapter with a presentation of the aim and relevance of the project and I also state the findings of the book (1.5).

1.1 Background for the Book

The discipline of Christian theology consists of a number of subdisciplines that investigate the Christian faith and its sources, theories, history, actuality, problems, etc. Christian theology has been a central part of European universities for many centuries, since the foundation of the University of Paris around 1200.[2] Its presence has been largely uncontested although right from the start, the discipline has given rise to intense discussions about the proper methods, aims, and implications of this field.[3] Especially the question of whether it is possible to study theology like any other topic, i. e., through *unaided* reason, has arisen numerous times.[4] In the Middle Ages and the Renaissance, most universities unquestioningly included theology because everything in the university was organized around the study of theology. But with the growing criticism of Christian metaphysics in the period

---

1 "Systematic theology" is defined in chapter three, but generally in this book it covers the description, discussion, and construction of Christian doctrines. "Scientific discipline" is the name for a defined field of scientific study with a specified subject area (a distinct cluster of data). Often the metaphor of a "branch" on the "tree" of science is used. The subdisciplines in a given field can then be seen as "twigs" or "leaves."
2 Mike Higton, *A Theology of Higher Education* (Oxford: Oxford University Press, 2012), 13–41.
3 Stephen C. Ferruolo, *The Origins of the University: The Schools of Paris and Their Critics, 1100–1215* (Stanford: Stanford University Press, 1985), 47.
4 G. R. Evans, *Old Arts and New Theology: The Beginnings of Theology as an Academic Discipline* (Oxford: Clarendon, 1980), 57–83. See also Ferruolo, *The Origins of the University*, 59.

known as the Enlightenment, this matter was contested.[5] The Bible was thoroughly criticized as a reliable source of truth as were the dogmas, which were historicized and thereby relativized.[6] The consequence was that the philosophical foundation of Christian doctrines was rejected as scholastic speculation and the discipline was largely salvaged only by reference to the practical need for learned clergy.[7] This goes first for Berlin University, which was the starting point for the new research universities, starting in 1810, but the demand for a more scientific understanding of theology spread throughout Europe from there.[8] During the Romantic era, there was a softening of the critique and new attempts were made to understand what theology could be after the philosophical critique had been proposed.[9] But the results of the natural sciences (especially evolutionary theory) and the implications for industrialization and welfare provision called into question the credibility of theology once again. In the beginning of the 20th century, the critique reached a climax with the positivist current in the philosophy of science, which accused all metaphysics,

---

5 The Enlightenment was a disparate stream of thoughts and concerns. Differences between various contexts about how radical the religious critique should be and its institutional consequences for theology can be identified. See further some of the important literature in this field in section 4.3.4, footnote 168.

6 See, e. g., Alister E. McGrath, *Christian Theology. An Introduction*, Fifth Edition (Oxford: Wiley-Blackwell, 2011), 66–69. J. S. Semler was seen as the transition figure between "old" and "new" Protestantism by many in the Enlightenment camp, cf. Thomas Albert Howard, *Protestant Theology and the Making of the Modern German University* (Oxford and New York: Oxford University Press, 2006), 100.

7 Most notable here was Schleiermacher's influential book *Kurze Darstellung des theologischen Studiums* (1811/1830), which has also been very influential in its English translation, see the latest edition: Friedrich Schleiermacher, *Brief Outline of the Study of Theology*, trans. William Farrer (Eugene: Wipf & Stock, 2007). For the context and a description of Schleiermacher's importance, see Howard, *Protestant Theology and the Making of the Modern German University*, 6–8 and 203–210. See also pages 133, 169, and 183 for Schleiermacher's importance to the foundation of Berlin University with his text *Gelegentliche Gedanken* from 1807 (published anonymously in 1808).

8 Howard demonstrates in chapter two of his book that the confessional ties were loosened already at the universities of Halle and Göttingen because of developments in Biblical criticism. However, as he shows in chapter three, the real break in the organization of the university came with the foundation of Berlin University. See especially Howard, *Protestant Theology and the Making of the Modern German University*, 130–131. For a discussion of the spread of the new ideas and theology's new role at the new institution, see ibid. chapter 4, especially page 262. For the development in Germany in the period after Schleiermacher, see Johannes Zachhuber, *Theology as Science in Nineteenth-Century Germany: From F.C. Baur to Ernst Troeltsch* (Oxford: Oxford University Press, 2013) and chapter 5 of Howard's book.

9 McGrath, *Christian Theology. An Introduction*, 69–71.

including theology, of being cognitively meaningless.[10] All these developments have problematized theology as a legitimate discipline at research universities, and there has been extensive debate about how to understand theology in light of all the criticism. More recently, many external (outside the university) factors have influenced the debate, such as secularization, decline in church membership, decreases in funding, decreases in student enrolment, lack of public awareness, etc. But the internal (inside the university) factor, that is, the philosophical critique, has also been severe. Especially with the rise of competing, non-confessional disciplines like religious studies, there has been a struggle over where theology should be situated and how its nature is to be understood.[11] The problems for theology vary depending on the context because different philosophical problems are in focus from country to country,[12] but the 20th century has seen comparable debates among theologians in many Western-European countries about how to respond to the challenges. I give a selected overview of some of these important debates in chapter two. The above is an extremely brief sketch of the last eight-hundred years of academic theology and its increasing crises, but it should give an impression as to why there is a concern for how to construe and sustain scientific theology today.[13] In the next paragraph, I explain why I find it important to contribute to this long discussion.

We do not know whether God exists or not. Many people believe it, many people do not. God's existence is not an obvious fact, and laypeople as well as professional philosophers and theologians believe many different things about God without much agreement. In science, disagreement is widespread in many ways, but it is unusual to have such a degree of disagreement about something so central, including the very existence of the research object, i. e., God. Can theology then be justified as a scientific discipline in the university when the understanding of the most central concept differs so extensively?

Nevertheless, I argue that it is possible to bring the discussion further even within a single book. Numerous questions cannot be answered, of course, nor even

---

10 See, e. g., Peter Godfrey-Smith, *Theory and Reality: An Introduction to the Philosophy of Science* (Chicago: University of Chicago Press, 2003), 25–30. See also Howard, *Protestant Theology and the Making of the Modern German University*, 273.
11 I analyze this conflict in chapter eight.
12 For instance, in the differences between what is traditionally called Anglo-Saxon versus Continental traditions, roughly analytic versus hermeneutic traditions.
13 For a longer and more careful investigation of the historical sources, see Wolfhart Pannenberg, *Theology and the Philosophy of Science* (Philadelphia: The Westminster Press, 1976), 228–96. Note that the focus here has been to sketch the problems for a scientific understanding of theology. I have thus left out many important discussions about the distinctiveness of theology, i. e., the development of different kinds of pietism, the important debate about Dilthey's distinction between *Erklären* and *Verstehen*, Hegel's contribution to the development of a philosophy of religion, and much more. I mention some of these at the beginning of chapter two.

discussed. But some questions can be addressed, discussed, and answered and this will contribute to the necessary debate about the scientific status of systematic theology. In this book I focus on the professionals, on theology as a university discipline, and argue that systematic theology can be construed and sustained as a rationally justified public discourse. It is of importance to systematic theology *internally* to have a continuous discussion of the legitimation of its field, and it is also of importance to systematic theology *externally* to know how to defend, sustain, and develop its field. This book points to more recent ideas in philosophy of science and truth theory as ways to develop a coherent understanding of systematic theology in relation to common criteria.[14]

1.2   The Research Problem

With the background outlined in 1.1 in mind, I can now present the research question that I seek to answer in this book: *How can systematic theology best be construed as a scientific discipline?* By "construe" I refer to how systematic theology is best constituted, undertaken, and substantiated. The answer to the question should include an explication of how researchers do their job, how their theories are tested, and how the scientific status and nature of this work is justified. The answer to the research question obviously also depends on how one understands systematic theology, science, and the notion of a discipline. For this reason, a central contribution of this book is to explicate these notions more carefully in order to give a thorough answer to the research questions. This implies that I am aware that other explications of the notions could lead to different answers to the research question; this is also evident from the many different variations of systematic theology that are available today. I present what I argue is the best understanding of the notions given the chosen presuppositions and then draw a conclusion from this discussion. I describe the chosen method for how to reach a well-founded answer to the research question in 1.4, which includes a detailed outline of the progression.

Philosophers and theologians have not been able to draw a convincing conclusion to the God question despite tremendous efforts over thousands of years.[15] Of course, some are more confident than others in their conclusions, but assessing the vast

---

14 I sum up the findings at the end of 1.5.
15 As mentioned above, what makes this lack of conclusion disturbing is not the fundamental disagreement about basic questions, as is the case in other fields like philosophy of physics. The problematical point is something that neither of these other disciplines struggles with, namely doubts about the very existence of their fundamental material for investigation.

amount of literature on the subject does not enable us to settle the issue.[16] Why is this fundamental question so hard to answer? One reason is, of course, that God – if God exists – is not an empirical object. God has been called an abstract entity, the Absolute, the ground of Being, the totality of existence, among many other things, all intended to emphasize the radical otherness of God. But this characterization of God leaves us with many questions: Where does it leave the scientific study of systematic theology ? Is it even possible to talk about God and, if so, how? Is it possible to count theology as a legitimate part of the academic pantheon? How does systematic theology work scientifically, if at all? These are among the activating questions behind this book even though they are not all addressed and discussed here. They are activating because they point to the curious problem of how systematic theology is to be construed given the radical difficulty of identifying the research subject and dealing with the immense disagreement among its researchers.

The research question can be answered properly only if the presuppositions for the investigation are clearly stated. In order to show how systematic theology can best be construed as a scientific discipline, I need to describe the conditions under which the answer is given. In this book I adopt two standard presuppositions of science, realism and truth. Both these notions are contested and discussed in the philosophy of science, but the debates are so vast that it is impossible to engage fully with them within one book.[17] I nevertheless provide an argument for taking

---

16 Graham Oppy, *Atheism and Agnosticism*, Cambridge Elements. Elements in the Philosophy of Religion (Cambridge: Cambridge University Press, 2018) and Paul Draper, 'Atheism and Agnosticism,' in *The Stanford Encyclopedia of Philosophy*, ed. Edward N. Zalta (Metaphysics Research Lab, Stanford University, 2017) are interesting accounts that acknowledge the openness of the debate even though they state their positions. More confident accounts are given, e. g., by J. L. Schellenberg, *Divine Hiddenness and Human Reason* (Ithaca: Cornell University Press, 1993); Julian Baggini, *Atheism: A Very Short Introduction*, Second Edition (New York: Oxford University Press, 2021) in favor of atheism, and by William Lane Craig, *Reasonable Faith: Christian Truth and Apologetics*, Third Edition (Wheaton: Crossway, 2008) and Richard Swinburne, *The Existence of God*, Second Edition (Oxford & New York: Clarendon & Oxford University Press, 2004) in favor of theism.

17 For good discussions of realism, see, e. g., Evandro Agazzi, ed., *Varieties of Scientific Realism: Objectivity and Truth in Science* (New York: Springer, 2017); Anjan Chakravartty, *A Metaphysics for Scientific Realism: Knowing the Unobservable* (Cambridge: Cambridge University Press, 2007); Michael Liston, 'Scientific Realism and Antirealism,' in *Internet Encyclopedia of Philosophy*, and Stathis Psillos, *Scientific Realism. How Science Tracks Truth*, Philosophical Issues in Science (London: Routledge, 1999). For good discussions of truth theory, see, e. g., Nicholas Rescher, *The Coherence Theory of Truth* (Oxford: Oxford University Press, 1973); Richard L. Kirkham, *Theories of Truth: A Critical Introduction* (Cambridge: MIT Press, 1997); Lorenz B. Puntel, *Wahrheitstheorien in Der Neueren Philosophie. Eine Kritisch-Systematische Darstellung*, Dritte Auflage, vol. 83, Erträge der Forschung (Darmstadt: Wissenschaftliche Buchgesellschaft, 1993).

these notions as presuppositions, because presuppositions should not be arbitrary but must be argued for.

Realism comes in many different forms and there is no standard way to understand the term.[18] I take "realism" to mean the conception of science as making real progress in knowledge, and not just in an instrumental way but gaining real insights into the constitution of reality.[19] Science can describe physical reality accurately, and the objects described by our best methods are approximately as the theories describes them; this also holds for unobservable entities. The best argument for realism is what Hilary Putnam called the "no miracle" argument, which says that it would be a miracle if our best scientific theories turned out to be wrong because there are so precise in both description and prediction.[20] Science is "fallible, partial, and approximate,"[21] but it is our best way to understand the world around us. Realists usually adhere to the notion of a "mind-independent" world, but this is a very complicated matter to capture in a phrase. I presuppose that the world is not dependent on human thoughts and language for its existence, but also that we have no access to the world apart from thought and language, and this puts us in a complicated situation where ontology and semantics are closely related.[22] Here, coherence[23] will be the best tool for assessing the best understandings of the world around us *through* language. There are different kinds of problems with the perspective of realism, especially because the history of science is full of theories

---

18 As Arjan Chakravartty says: "It is perhaps only a slight exaggeration to say that scientific realism is characterized differently by every author who discusses it, and this presents a challenge to anyone hoping to learn what it is." Anjan Chakravartty, 'Scientific Realism,' in *The Stanford Encyclopedia of Philosophy*, ed. Edward N. Zalta (Metaphysics Research Lab, Stanford University, 2017). James Ladyman mentions metaphysical realism, direct realism, causal realism, and scientific realism; semantic realism and structural realism are also important variants. See James Ladyman, *Understanding Philosophy of Science* (New York: Routledge, 2001), 138–42. See also the helpful overview in Jonathan Dancy, *An Introduction to Contemporary Epistemology* (Oxford: Blackwell, 1986), 158.
19 That I do not understand this in a simplified "mirror of nature"-conception is evident from the discussions in chapters four and five.
20 Hilary Putnam, *Mathematics, Matter, and Method*, Second Edition, Philosophical Papers, vol. 1 (Cambridge and New York: Cambridge University Press, 1979), 73.
21 Ladyman, *Understanding Philosophy of Science*, 129.
22 Lorenz B. Puntel, *Grundlagen einer Theorie der Wahrheit*, Grundlagen der Kommunikation und Kognition (Berlin: de Gruyter, 1990), 121–30. See further in 6.2.4.4. In other words, reality exists relatively independent of language and mind. *That* reality exists is assumed, but *what* it is cannot be understood apart from language.
23 "Coherence" is a key term in this book. For a preliminary clarification of the term, see 1.3. For a longer treatment see 3.4.7 and 5.2.8.1.

that were regarded as confirmed but turned out to be wrong.[24] The debate between realism and antirealism is immense, and to contribute to the debate with yet another footnote is not the aim here.[25] I will thus presuppose the standpoint of realism and instead focus on how systematic theology can be understood in relation to this particular perspective in the philosophy of science.

The notion of truth is even more important as a presupposition. There are many theories of truth on the market and there are many attacks on the notion of truth. I presuppose that truth is the aim of science, which means that I reject views that see science as instrumental or pragmatic through and through. It is a truth-seeking enterprise.[26] These notions are important and also legitimate as goals to be pursued, but nevertheless, the practice of science is important because humans care about the truth of reality, and despite the many shortcomings of this kind of work, it is still our best rational tool for investigating reality. So, the proposed understanding of systematic theology is informed by this presupposition in the sense that I am not satisfied with a systematic theology that is *only* pragmatic, existential, spiritual, activistic, etc. All these are relevant for different purposes, but the truth pretention of religious and theological claims is also important to investigate, and I presuppose this for the proposed understanding of systematic theology.[27] The more specific understanding of what truth is, its criteria and definition, will be discussed later, but, briefly, I take coherence, as it is understood by philosophers Lorenz Puntel and Nicholas Rescher, to be the best criterion and definition of truth. I give a short presentation of their understanding of coherence below (1.3) and then more carefully in later chapters. It is possible to proceed otherwise and then end up with other questions, challenges, and possibilities, but that is always the case, hence the justification of a delimited book. The purpose of stating presuppositions is to clarify the conditions of the book so that the reader can assess the arguments on the right premises. The chosen criteria in this book are broadly acknowledged and thus relevant in order to assess whether systematic theology can meet common criteria for science. With the presupposition of realism and truth in hand, I argue that systematic theology can be a science, but I also give substantive arguments for *how* this can be and how this science is best construed. For these reasons, the argument here is that systematic theology does not only meet the criteria for science

---

24 The problem of "pessimistic meta-induction," cf. Larry Laudan, 'A Confutation of Convergent Realism,' *Philosophy of Science* 48, no. 1 (March 1981): 19–49; Nicholas Rescher, *Scientific Realism: A Critical Reappraisal* (Dordrecht: Reidel, 1989), chap. 1.
25 For an introduction see, e. g., Liston, 'Scientific Realism and Antirealism.'
26 Cf. Nicholas Rescher, *The Strife of Systems. An Essay on the Grounds and Implications of Philosophical Diversity* (Pittsburgh: University of Pittsburgh Press, 1985), 186–91.
27 This means that I believe the truth question is important for several pragmatic and life-orienting reasons, but it is *also* important in its own right.

haphazardly but can be sustained as a fruitful investigation of the fundamental structures of reality.[28]

Because systematic theology is understood in many different ways, I provisionally explicate what I argue is the aim of systematic theologians, which also rests on the presuppositions of realism and truth. I define the aim of systematic theology to be presenting *"rationally justified public discourse about God."* Theologians present discourses about God, and this discourse should be both rationally justified and public. *Rationally justified* points to a set of generally accepted criteria for scientific work that theologians try to meet.[29] These criteria occupy a central part of the discussion of this book. The qualifier *public* identifies the arena at which the discourse is aimed, which is the public sphere. More precisely, the public sphere is here understood as the university.[30] Thus, the qualifier has nothing to do with the new field of "public theology" but is a reference to the criterion of intersubjectivity that I later discuss at length.[31] Theologians differ about where to place the emphasis in this triad of university, society, and church, but as is made explicit in chapter six, I take intersubjectivity to be a criterion for scientific work and thus emphasize the context of the university.[32] I do this without thereby diminishing the importance of the other spheres but only reserve an investigation of these to other projects. This also explains why I do not engage with a first-person perspective of belief even though it is relevant to discuss religious epistemology from this angle. If it is possible to give a convincing case for *reformed epistemology*, it could be called *rationally justified private discourse about God*, but, again, I emphasize the public aspect instead.[33] This also explains why I do not discuss the communitarian philosophy and theology that have gained increasing attention in theological circles as

---

28 See further in 3.1.
29 Ladyman, *Understanding Philosophy of Science*, 6.
30 The public sphere also includes church and society at large, but it is not the aim here to integrate these arenas in the discussion. The triad is described and discussed in David Tracy's introductory essay from David Tracy, *The Analogical Imagination. Christian Theology and the Culture of Pluralism* (New York: Crossroad, 1981), 1–31.
31 See, e.g., the *International Journal of Public Theology* that was founded in 2007. It says about its subject: "The idea and practice of public theology has recently emerged as a distinct field of scholarship that proactively engages theology with contemporary public issues. The global project of public theology has expanded the western idea of three audiences – the church, the academy and the public domain – and their inter-relationship to multiple publics. It has now become a global discipline that intersects with the emergence of a world Christianity." See https://brill.com/view/journals/ijpt/ijpt-overview.xml (Accessed 13.12.2021).
32 How I understand intersubjectivity will be explained in chapter six. In other ways, intersubjectivity is also a requirement for the other spheres, church and society, respectively.
33 For a presentation and a defense of the reformed epistemology perspective, see Alvin Plantinga and Nicholas Wolterstorff, eds., *Faith and Rationality: Reason and Belief in God* (Notre Dame: University of Notre Dame Press, 1983).

found in the work of Charles Taylor, Alasdair MacIntyre, Stanley Hauerwas, etc., because, if a convincing case could be made for this approach, that would be to do *rationally justified community discourse about God* and no matter how relevant that may be for the church (something like *fides quaerens intellectum*), it is not the chosen context for this book.[34] *Discourse* can point to different features – in writing or speaking – but in this book it expresses the awareness that all theoretical work is carried out inside a "theoretical framework." The notion of a theoretical framework is explicated below but, briefly, it is an instrument that makes possible "the articulation, conceptualization, and explanation of theoretical contents. A theoretical framework consists of a language, a logic, a conceptuality, and components that constitute a theoretical apparatus."[35] *God* points to the subject that theologians do public discourse about. It is a fact that theologians do not agree on how to understand this subject, but constantly negotiate different explications, yet as a beginning we can broadly state that theologians seek to speak in a rationally justified manner about an entity[36] called "God." It is not a part of this book to discuss the notion of God – that important work is done in many publications every year; instead, I discuss the prolegomena to this discussion and the possibility for situating the discussion in a scientific context (see more below on terminology).

The phrase "rationally justified public discourse about God" appears numerous times in this book because it is a structural principle for the present investigation, which is why it is also the title of the book. The answer to the research question is that systematic theology is best construed as a scientific discipline by being a rationally justified public discourse about God. What this entails and how I argue for it is the content of the book.

1.2.1   Terminology

I define central notions and concepts throughout the book, but there are several terms which need clarification at this point.

---

34 I discuss aspects of communitarian theory, however, in both 2.2.4 and 6.3.2.2.
35 Atle Ottesen Søvik, *The Problem of Evil and the Power of God*, Studies in Systematic Theology 8 (Leiden and Boston: Brill, 2011), 81. This is more or less taken directly from Lorenz B. Puntel, *Structure and Being. A Theoretical Framework for a Systematic Philosophy*, trans. Alan White (Pennsylvania: The Pennsylvania State University Press, 2008), 9.
36 Entity is not to be understood as a "thing" or a "substance." We can call an entity everything that we give a name. Every structure that can be distinguished from other structures is an entity. Thereby, the only thing that is said about God is that not everything is God and we can therefore begin to investigate what characterizes God compared to other entities. On the notion of "structure" see 3.4.5.1.1.2.

Throughout the book the word "God" is used for the Christian God. I have only Christian theology in mind when I discuss suggestions and arguments, but I do believe that much of what I say is applicable to other monotheistic traditions and that fruitful conversations with these traditions would be possible in prolongation of the argument of this book. It is not within the scope of this book to discuss the notion of God, and there is no need to explicate more precisely how I understand the notion of God.[37] It suffices to presuppose a coarse-grained understanding that most researchers at universities can accept, which is a monotheistic conception of God as broadly understood in the Christian tradition.

Two related expressions also need clarification from the beginning. First, I use the term "theism" and especially the adjective "theistic" deliberately, even though they are highly contested in academic theology.[38] In this book, these terms refer to a broad use in the sense of "taking the Christian notion of God seriously." As with the broad use of the notion of God, the use of theism is broad. This implies that when I speak frequently of "theistic ontology" this means an ontology that includes the notion of God no matter how that is articulated more precisely. Second, especially in chapter eight, I use the notion "supernatural entity." *Entity* here is not synonymous with "thing" but refers to a structure that is distinct from other structures. *Supernatural* says that this is an entity not restricted by the natural laws (generalizations).

The words "science" and "scientific" mean different things in different contexts. As a Danish scholar, I use the words as in the German tradition, where *"Wissenschaft"* and *"Wissenschaftlichkeit"* include the human sciences (among them theology)[39] and not as in the Anglophone tradition where science – at least generally – only covers the social and natural sciences.[40] Thus, if I wish to comment on something that separates the natural and/or social sciences from the human sciences, I do this explicitly. In this book, I broadly take the *criteria* for science to be the same in all

---

37 I give a thorough presentation of Puntel's philosophical theology in 3.4.5 that includes a presentation of his argument for a minded, personal God. I do not, however, discuss his understanding of God specifically because I only give the presentation as a subtheme under his larger construction of a synchronic constitution of systematic theology. As such, it is correct to say that I do not discuss the notion of God in this book.

38 See, e. g., Ingolf U. Dalferth, 'The Historical Roots of Theism,' in *Traditional Theism and Its Modern Alternatives*, ed. Svend Andersen, vol. 18, Acta Jutlandica, LXX:1 Theological Series (Aarhus: Aarhus University Press, 1994), 15–41.

39 E. g., Dominikus Kraschl, 'Christiche Theologie als paradigmebasierte Wissenschaft. Ein Plädoyer in wissenschaftstheoretischer Perspektive,' in *Die Wissenschaftlichkeit der Theologie. Band 1: Historische und Systematische Perspektiven*, ed. Benedikt Paul Göcke, Studien zur Systematischen Theologie, Ethik und Philosophie, 13/1 (Münster: Aschendorff Verlag, 2018), 290–91.

40 E. g., Samir Okasha, *Philosophy of Science: A Very Short Introduction*, Second Edition, A Very Short Introduction 67 (Oxford: Oxford University Press, 2016), chap. 1.

scientific fields. Science is *practiced* in various kinds of ways through a great number of different methods depending on the data under investigation. But the criteria for whether the labour in question is scientific are largely the same.[41] I discuss the three most critical criteria for science – testability, falsifiability, and intersubjectivity – in this book and argue for their status in relation to all kinds of scientific work. Hence, as a rule of thumb, I take the differences to be differences in data types; the natural sciences generally work with data that is largely stable whereas the human and social sciences work with data that is stable to a lesser degree (more dynamic).[42] This is because the human and social sciences are occupied with human artifacts and products of human consciousness, which are dynamic objects that are extremely sensitive to change – to a higher degree than natural phenomena, which are often easier to isolate and manipulate in the laboratory, for example.

Often, I use the adjective "best" when I refer to a definition or an argument or something else. This is a normative adjective used within the framework I develop for this book. This means that "best" is equivalent to the highest score given the criteria that I presuppose in this book. When I call a definition of systematic theology the "best," I do not mean to belittle other definitions or approaches, which can be very fruitful or stimulating; rather, I seek to isolate and argue for definitions relative to the theoretical framework as I have stated above. In other words, it is possible to have criteria other than those I have chosen, and it is up for discussion whether other criteria are better. Nevertheless, the criteria are not arbitrary, because I have chosen common, central, and widely accepted criteria for science and philosophical reasoning.

I use "theologian" and "systematic theologian" as well as "theology" and "systematic theology" interchangeably. Different languages use theological terminology differently, but I follow the tradition where "theology" equals the subdiscipline of " systematic theology " and where "exegesis/Biblical studies" and "church history" are used for other distinct subdisciplines. It is sometimes confusing that "theology" is both the name of a discipline and of a subdiscipline, but in the context of the book it will designate the subdiscipline unless something else is stated clearly. I do not define systematic theology here because the understanding of systematic theology is such a focal point in the whole argument that it must be explicated at length. I provide a thorough treatment in chapter three.

---

41 This is in contrast to different important figures such as McGrath. See his *The Territories of Human Reason: Science and Theology in an Age of Multiple Rationalities* (New York: Oxford University Press, 2019) for a different perspective.

42 See further, Rescher, *The Coherence Theory of Truth*, 53–71. Note that Rescher does not talk about the differences between different types of scientific data, but his four examples of data gives an impression of the differences to which data may be subject, even though he largely takes data to consist of propositions.

1.3 Material

In the individual chapters, I introduce representatives of central positions, and throughout I argue for their relevance and importance. It goes almost without saying that I could have selected other figures because most of the discussions in this book have been a part of scientific and theological discourse for centuries. The discussion is systematic/thematic (based on arguments) rather than based on figures and this makes the choice of material important to another degree. Instead of arguing for the relevance of 3–4 figures in answering a specific question, I argue for the relevance of many different figures in relation to arguments for selected themes and questions throughout. This will be done en route in the text because it would be futile to give a comprehensive overview here.

There are, however, three thinkers who play a central role in the development of the argument. The first two are philosophers Lorenz B. Puntel and Nicholas Rescher, who are used for the theoretical framework that I work within, and the third is theologian Wolfhart Pannenberg, who is the most obvious predecessor for this kind of reasoning concerning the research question. I explain, first, why Puntel and Rescher help me answer the research question in the best way, before I, secondly, show how I differ from Pannenberg, with whom I agree in many ways.

The German philosopher Lorenz Puntel and the American philosopher Nicholas Rescher have both written extensively on the question of truth, and because I take truth to be the aim of science they are of interest to me. I argue that they have the most thorough and well-argued understanding of truth with their notion of coherence as the final criterion for truth, and I show their ability to solve problems in philosophy of science on this background. I go much deeper into this below, but I briefly describe their approach here because it is so decisive for the whole argument. Coherence is traditionally understood as a synonym for consistency, but here it is understood as a notion that comes in degrees.[43] This is because coherence in Puntel and Rescher's understanding consists of three components; (1) *consistency,* which means that a theory cannot contain two elements that logically contradict one another, (2) *cohesiveness,* which requires having the optimal number of relations between the data of the theory (the more the better), and (3) *comprehensiveness,* which indicates the number of data points a theory can integrate (the more the

---

43 Puntel, *Wahrheitstheorien in der neueren Philosophie,* 191: "Daraus ergibt sich unmittelbar, daß für jede KH-TW [coherence theory of truth] unter ‚Kohärenz' mehr zu verstehen ist – und immer mehr verstanden wurde – als bloße Konsistenz (Widerspruchsfreiheit)." [From this it follows immediately that for any coherence theory of truth 'coherence' is – and always has been – understood as more than mere consistency (freedom from contradiction). (Translation MAM)]

better).[44] The notion of "data" is vital too, of course, since that is what a theory has to work with. Puntel and Rescher use "data" as a notion for all "truth-candidates." All data are truth candidates, which means that they should be investigated for their possible places in the most coherent theory. No theory can contain all data and still be consistent, thus the quest for coherence is a work in progress that needs constant refinement as new data – e. g., scientific evidence or philosophical arguments – become available. The argument in this book is that this coherence model is the best way to work with scientific data and that it is a model that is the most useful one in the natural, social, and human sciences, systematic theology included. As I have indicated, I go much deeper into this in relation to the questions discussed throughout the text.

The German theologian Wolfhart Pannenberg is a key figure for the argument because he wrote extensively on theology and the sciences/philosophy of science with a vision that is similar to mine.[45] Pannenberg was a colleague of Puntel in Munich and was also inspired by the latter's coherence theory.[46] I argue that much of Pannenberg's work is still of interest today – however much has happened in the meantime in the relevant disciplines and in science in general. This book can thus be seen as aiming to update the theoretical framework of Pannenberg for the 21st century. Pannenberg worked in great detail on the content of Christian theology and gave many excellent examples of how coherence theory works in practice in systematic theology.[47] I focus more narrowly on the criteria for science and develop both the criteria and the response from systematic theology more carefully than Pannenberg did. Another difference is that Pannenberg was an eminent historian who often focused on the historical development of both theoretical debates and doctrinal theories, whereas I focus narrowly on the systematic discussion (except for the historical background in chapter two).[48]

A last note on material: I am aware of the problem of representation in academia in general as well as concerning individual theses. It is fruitful that we have a growing public awareness of diversity and pluralistic representation in various ways, including in academia. Professionally – which is the context here – I am a pluralist, so I seek to hear and consider as many relevant voices as possible before

---

44 These notions are taken from Rescher, because Puntel does not label the ideas but refers to Rescher himself. Rescher, *The Coherence Theory of Truth*, 31–38 and 168–75.
45 Besides a number of interesting articles, two important books have been a continuous inspiration: Wolfhart Pannenberg, *Theology and the Philosophy of Science* and Wolfhart Pannenberg, *Systematic Theology*, trans. Geoffrey W. Bromiley, vol. 1 (Grand Rapids: Eerdmans, 1991).
46 Pannenberg, *Systematic Theology*, 1:21–26.
47 See his *Systematic Theology* vol. 1–3, which collects his views on the broad scope of Christian doctrines.
48 This is seen in Pannenberg, *Theology and the Philosophy of Science*.

making judgments (because I see voices as "data"/"truth candidates"). Pluralism is a benign point of departure (the context of discovery is multifaceted), even though we benefit from clear criteria for our results (the context of justification is critical). All voices are relevant to hear, but not all answers are equally convincing. I am aware that a field as old and diverse field as theology has historical issues with representation and that many voices remain suppressed today. This is critical, and I support the growing awareness of this problem. Still, concerning arguments, I consider it less relevant where something is said (and by whom) and more relevant what is actually said and argued for.[49]

1.4 Method

In the following, I give a detailed presentation of the structure of the book and show how this structure answers the research question presented in 1.2. I do this by stating the construction principle of the book before I give a thorough outline of the individual chapters.

The construction principle of the book is shaped around questions organizing the content of the given chapters. It thus moves from the best definition of systematic theology I have found in part two ("What is the best definition of systematic theology given the presuppositions?") to stating in part three the best objections to this definition in order to find the most problematic aspects ("How can the definition of systematic theology best be challenged?") and the best possible answers to these objections ("How to answer the objections to systematic theology most properly?") before I conclude in part four on whether systematic theology provides sufficient answers to the objections ("Can systematic theology survive the objections given its answers?"). This approach ensures a detailed discussion of these fundamental and urgent questions, which I carry out in a more precise and elaborate way than is usually done in the literature on these questions. After stating the most critical objections to the proposed understanding of systematic theology and showing how systematic theology can answer these objections in a thorough way, I will also have shown how systematic theology is best construed as a scientific discipline because this is the way in which it best meets the objections. Given the presuppositions, I argue that the conclusion explicates the best understanding of systematic theology as a scientific discipline on common criteria for science.

Even though I have some affinities with Karl Barth's famous description of the role of theology – that "Dogmatik ist als theologische Disziplin die wissenschaftliche

---

49 Cf. Alan White, *Toward a Philosophical Theory of Everything: Contributions to the Structural-Systematic Philosophy*, (New York: Bloomsbury, 2014), 14–15.

Selbstprüfung der christlichen Kirche hinsichtlich des Inhalts der ihr eigentümlichen Rede von Gott"[50] – I find it necessary to investigate theology's philosophy of science from a more intersubjective perspective. Even though it seems relevant for the Christian church to examine its doctrines as thoroughly as possible, and the academy is an attractive environment to do this in, I argue that a modern research university must use language, methods, and concepts that are transparent to a broader field of researchers than a particular ideological group. This also implies that Christian theology is perhaps not best treated in a secular research institution and that if a scientific theology does exist, it is not the only kind of theology there is and maybe not even the best one.[51] This should be noted from the beginning. In this book, I am not interested in the types of theology that are not scientific (whether they lack credibility or do not even seek to be understood as scientific); it is irrelevant that these types exist for different reasons and purposes. What I want to investigate is the possibility of explicating a robust notion of systematic theology that meets central criteria in the philosophy of science.

Even though I employ truth theory and assess the best theories and arguments, I adhere to fallibilism as a working condition for all scientific work. Fallibilism means that all our scientific knowledge is vulnerable to future corrections and could turn out to be false.[52] It is not a controversial perspective, but it is an important insight from the history of science that I refer to time and time again – and it becomes especially important when notions such as truth and strong normativity are defended, as I do in the following chapters. I do not track the genealogy of fallibilism or discuss various understandings of how fallibilism works but presuppose it methodologically.[53]

For chapters four through eight I have, for the sake of clarity, used syllogisms as organizing principles for handling the vast material. For each, I formulate two

---

50 Karl Barth, *Dogmatik im Grundriß*, Elfte Auflage (Zürich: TVZ, Theologischer Verlag, 2013). "Dogmatics as a theological discipline is the self-examination of the Christian church with regard to the contents of its peculiar talk about God." Translation MAM.
51 This is also a point made by Karl Popper, *mutatis mutandis*, who in his early critique of psychoanalysis and Marxism pointed to the fact that these two theories could provide valuable insights even though they are not scientific because they cannot be falsified. See Martin Curd and J.A. Cover, eds., *Philosophy of Science: The Central Issues* (New York: W.W. Norton & Company, 1998), 8–9. Later, Popper regulated his critique, cf. Ladyman, *Understanding Philosophy of Science*, 73.
52 See further Nicholas Rescher, 'Fallibilism,' in *Routledge Encyclopedia of Philosophy*, (London: Routledge, 2016). This does not mean that everything we know is likely to be false since all corrections in the history of science has been partial, even when we talk about revolutions. Fallibilism does, therefore, not imply scepticism.
53 See, e. g., Karl R. Popper, *Conjectures and Refutations: The Growth of Scientific Knowledge*, Third Edition (London: Routledge, 2002), 309–13; Susan Haack and Konstantin Kolenda, 'Two Fallibilists in Search of the Truth,' *Aristotelian Society Supplementary Volume* 51, no. 1 (10 July 1977): 63–104.

premises that I investigate in order, and if the premises are sustained, the conclusion follows logically. I introduce the type of syllogism that I use in the introduction to part three.

1.4.1 Outline

In the following, I give a detailed outline of the book and its chapters.

In chapter two, I give, as a background for the own discussion, a selected overview of how the scientific status of theology has been discussed in Western academic theology throughout the 20${}^{\text{th}}$ century. I have chosen four debates that point to important themes in the discussion. I begin with the exchange between Karl Barth and Heinrich Scholz. Scholz demanded that theology should meet the same criteria as all other sciences, and he identified six criteria he found important. Barth replied with a refusal and argued for the acceptability of theology's axiom of God's self-revelation. No external criteria or restrictions could be accepted for theology. Decades later, in the 1970s, the discussion continued in Germany with new voices, and I identify three positions with different views. First is the view of Hermann Diem that theology is a Church discipline and should seek to develop the doctrines of the church (a radicalized Barthian perspective). Second is the view of Pannenberg that accepted Scholz's old challenge and sought to answer it anew with a focus on the coherence of the Christian doctrines. Third is the middle position of Gerhard Sauter, who argued for a theology that was relevant for the church but in ongoing conversation with cultural and scientific voices. The third debate is the Swedish debate between theologians from Lund and Uppsala, a discussion that gained international awareness. These two schools developed new methodologies for theology as a consequence of the growing hostility from the rest of the academia from the 1950s. They sought to understand how theology could be scientific in the way that religious studies is. Anders Nygren from Lund developed a strictly descriptive method with the aim of identifying how the question of the eternal is thematized in the Christian religion. This he called "the fundamental motif." Anders Jeffner from Uppsala pursued a less descriptive method but also sought to identify the demarcation of what theology can hope to thematize. The last debate I discuss is the one between theologians from Chicago and Yale. Essentially, Chicago seeks to do theology that is open for assessment and criticism from everyone. This I show in the writings of Paul Tillich and David Tracy. The Yale school accepts a communitarian epistemology and argues for criteria of theology that are not necessarily open for universal assessment and criticism. I show this in the writings of George Lindbeck and Hans Frei.

In chapter three, I suggest a model for systematic theology that is a revised account of a model presented by the Danish theologian Niels Henrik Gregersen. This model divides systematic theology into three distinct strata that I call systematic theology 1, systematic theology 2, and systematic theology 3. The basic argument is that only systematic theology 3 is scientific in itself but that because it is sustained scientifically, it lends credence to systematic theology 1 and systematic theology 2. Systematic theology 1 is the systematic explication of the religious expressions (semantics) in the lives of Christian believers. Systematic theology 2 is the development of theories of the Christian faith – theories that I suggest are best assessed by their degrees of internal coherence (which resembles the understanding of Pannenberg). Systematic theology 3 is the development and comparison of ontologies which are assessed by their relative degrees of coherence with external alternatives. After the explication of these strata, I present a case for what I call a synchronic constitution of systematic theology as a scientific discipline i. e., I argue that even without the long history of theology that gives us the argument of "cultural proximity" in the study of this religion, it is fruitful to investigate the theories of the Christian faith. This I do with a presentation of Lorenz Puntel's treatment in his book *Being and God*. After this I introduce two important themes for the rest of the book, namely the notion of a truth-candidate and the coherence theory of truth briefly touched upon above in 1.3.

In chapters four through eight, I seek to challenge this understanding of systematic theology by introducing important objections that also work as criteria for science. I devote a chapter to each objection formulated as a syllogism where I discuss the premises in order before concluding. After the following summaries of the individual chapters, I outline the logical progressions between the chapters.

In chapter four, I discuss the criterion of testability through the objection that scientific theories must be testable and that systematic theology theories are not. I first discuss a view of testability that I call "testing single propositions," which was defended thoroughly by various kinds of empiricism. I also explain why this view has failed, with W.V. Quine's criticism as an example. Quine suggested that we instead test whole theories, an approach I support, and I seek to strengthen this view by pointing to coherence theory: we test theories by assessing their degrees of coherence. Between these two versions of testing, I discuss in an excursus the step from hypothesis to conclusion that we call "inference." In other words, inference is about what we can conclude based on the tests. I discuss views of induction here and save a discussion of deductive inferences for chapter five. I conclude that the first premise is sustained, so scientific theories must be testable. In the second part of the chapter, I discuss the second premise, which says that systematic theology theories are not testable. I discuss the view of three theologians – Pannenberg, McGrath, and Murphy – who all seek to defend testability in relation to systematic theology theories. I criticize their suggestions but also seek to develop them by pointing to coherence theory as the best way to test systematic theology theories. I therefore conclude that the second premise is false, and the conclusion of the chapter is therefore that the objection fails.

In chapter five, I discuss the criterion of falsifiability through the objection that scientific theories must be falsifiable and that systematic theology theories are not. This is a systematic progression from the last chapter that says that even though systematic theology theories are testable, they are not testable in the most common scientific way, i. e., falsifiable. I first discuss what falsification is in relation to the major views in the history of the philosophy of science – Popper, Kuhn, Lakatos, Feyerabend, and Laudan – before I investigate two examples of falsification at work. The first is the hypothetico-deductive method, and the second is the comparison of coherence. The hypothico-deductive method is essentially about a hypothesis being formulated, and various observations being predicted from it before an experiment is executed to test whether the predictions hold. If there is a positive result, we have a *weak* verification and can work further with the hypothesis; if there is a negative result, we have falsified the hypothesis. Coherence theory is here understood as a way of testing theories that are relevant alternatives by comparing their degrees of coherence. If one theory is clearly less coherent than another, the first is falsified. I explain various difficulties with this approach, which will be easier to follow when I discuss the arguments in the later chapters, so I will not introduce it further here. On the basis of this discussion, I conclude that the first premise is sustained, so scientific theories must be falsifiable. The second premise says that systematic theology theories are not falsifiable, and I discuss this premise in relation to various attempts at using falsification in systematic theology. I especially discuss the notion of eschatological verification, an idea I am critical of. I also discuss the possibility of falsifying systematic theology 2-theories, where the focus is on internal coherence. However, the main aim is to sustain coherence theory as a tool for falsification in comparing ontologies, and I discuss various attempts to do this in the works of atheist philosopher Graham Oppy and Catholic philosopher Alasdair MacIntyre. The discussion concludes that the second premise fails because it is possible to falsify systematic theology theories, and therefore the objection is rejected.

In chapter six, I discuss the criterion of intersubjectivity through the objection that scientific theories must be testable intersubjectively and that systematic theology theories are not. I first discuss what is understood by intersubjectivity in the philosophical approaches of empiricism and phenomenology. Then I suggest another account by saying that intersubjectivity as a criterion for science means that methods, presuppositions, data, and results must be publicly accessible, and that methods, data, and results cannot be dependent on the researcher. I also argue that criticism is a decisive aspect of intersubjectivity in science. I then discuss what can problematize this understanding of intersubjectivity in terms of cognitive biases, interpretive communities and paradigmatic thinking, the epistemology of testimony, and the holistic relatedness of epistemology and ontology. I defend the developed account of intersubjectivity against these potential objections and argue that a nuanced view of intersubjectivity can serve as a criterion. The conclusion concerning the first premise is that the criterion of intersubjectivity is sustained as a premise. The second premise objects that systematic theology is not intersubjective, and I begin an investigation of this premise by identifying three models for intersubjectivity in systematic theology called demarcated, paradigmatic, and critical intersubjectivity. I defend the last version, which emphasizes standards for criticism that are open to external examination. I end this discussion by arguing that a critical intersubjectivity can deal with complexities and insecurities, which are inevitable parts of theological discourse. I argue that coherence theory once again is the best tool for handling these challenges. The conclusion is, however, that systematic theology can be intersubjective only to a lesser degree than many other disciplines but still in a satisfying way that meets the criterion. The conclusion is therefore that the objection fails.

In chapter seven, I discuss the thesis that scientific theories cannot be normative in a strong sense but that systematic theology theories are so. This objection is closely connected with the debate about what distinguishes religious studies from systematic theology. I first discuss the two major positions in the contemporary debate between those who argue for a separation between descriptive and normative features in research and those who argue against the possibility of such a separation. I argue that much of the debate is confusing because the notion of normativity is imprecise, and I suggest a distinction between a *weak* and a *strong* account. The weak account is shared by all scientific disciplines because it refers to aims of saying something true about natural entities. It is normative for a theory to be proposed, assessed, and defended as the most coherent theory available and therefore the norm for the field. The strong account is contested because it concerns theories that argue for the truth of theories about supernatural entities. I argue that strong normativity is a legitimate part of scientific discourse, and therefore that the first premise is false. The second premise says that systematic theology theories are strongly normative, which is affirmed and unproblematic on the basis of the rejection of the first premise. However, I discuss the notion critically by considering relevant objections to this notion such as the one that strong normativity is problematic because it rests on questionable foundations, because it claims truth of supernatural entities, and/or because it is based on limited data. I then discuss different models of normativity in systematic theology. The first model is the same one discussed in the first part, which sees normativity as weak and thus in relation to religious studies. The second model takes normativity to be the practice of identifying what is authentic Christianity, i.e., orthodoxy. And the third model refuses the notion of normativity because it holds that all theology is contextual. I argue against this relativistic approach. Lastly, I discuss how strong normativity is sustained by coherence theory, which is the critical tool I suggest in assessing theories of strong normativity. I therefore conclude that the second premise is sustained, but because the first premise was false, the objection as such is rejected.

In chapter eight, I discuss the objection that scientific disciplines must do "distinct research," that is, research that is distinct for its discipline yet rationally justified as scientific, but systematic theology is not able to do so. The argument is that when systematic theology is scientific, it is either philosophy or religious studies, and when it is distinctly systematic theology, it is not scientific. I begin by discussing the first premise and argue that identifying the distinctness of a scientific discipline is a valid criterion. There are many overlaps between many disciplines, and this is not a problem, but I argue that something must be identified as distinct and still scientific in relation to a given field. Thus, the first premise is sustained. The critical focus is on the second premise, where I start to identify the supposed problems for systematic theology as distinct research, such as that of systematic theology being unable to identify its object, that systematic theology cannot identify its method because of the unidentified object, that systematic theology cannot explain but only describe, and that systematic theology builds on a weak foundation of evidence. I argue against these supposed problems and then identify what the distinctive marks of systematic theology are in relation to its closest allies, religious studies and philosophy. I argue that the important distinction between systematic theology and religious studies is systematic theology's focus on strong normativity, that is, the truth-pretention of a theistic ontology (this question is not bracketed in systematic theology as it is in religious studies). And I argue that the important distinction between systematic theology and philosophy is systematic theology's commitment to a specific and definite theistic ontology that makes the discipline more fragile but also more precise. I conclude of the second premise that it is false because systematic theology does distinct research that no other field could conduct equally well. Therefore, the fifth and last objection fails.

There is a logical structure to the order of the chapters, which I introduce in the following. The first objection (chapter four) says that systematic theology theories cannot be tested. The discussion in chapter four shows that this objection is wrong because systematic theology theories can indeed be tested. But a new and specified objection can be raised which says that even if systematic theology theories can be tested generally, they cannot be tested against the central criterion of falsification (chapter five). The discussion in chapter five shows that this objection is wrong too because systematic theology theories can indeed be falsified. But, again, a new and more precise objection can be raised which says that even if systematic theology theories can be falsified in principle, the selection and understanding of data and the result of the test is not sufficiently intersubjective (chapter six). The discussion in chapter six shows that this objection is wrong too because the test can indeed be intersubjectively examined. But also to this answer can a new and more precise objection be raised which says that even if systematic theology theories can be tested intersubjectively to a sufficient degree, some of the intersubjective test criteria are problematic because they are normative (chapter seven). The discussion in chapter seven shows that this objection is wrong too because the normativity that is presupposed is actually unproblematic. To this answer a new, more precise, and, for this book, final objection can be raised which says that even if systematic theology can be tested intersubjectively and unproblematically, this only happens when systematic theology takes on the characteristics of another discipline, which is not compatible with regarding systematic theology as a distinct and scientific research discipline (chapter eight). The discussion in chapter eight shows that this objection is wrong because systematic theology can indeed meet the criteria for scientific research and still be a distinct research discipline.

In chapter nine, I conclude on the discussion and present the findings of the book in the form of ten theses. The answer to the research question is that systematic theology is best construed as a scientific discipline by being a rationally justified public discourse about God stratified as a tripartite discipline that meets common criteria for science through the understanding of scientific progression as the upgrading of coherence.

1.5 Aim and Relevance of the Book

The aim of the book is to explicate the best definition of systematic theology that can be judged against the best standard criteria for science in the philosophy of science in order to understand how systematic theology is best construed as a scientific discipline. As stated above, it is irrelevant that there are types of theology that do not meet these standards; the relevant question is whether *any* type does and what a systematic theology that meets the criteria looks like. If theology is to keep its place in the research university, its scientific *character* and *nature* must be argued for. Therefore, I agree with Pannenberg when he writes: "Theology's membership of the class of scientific disciplines cannot, of course, be assumed without discussion."[54] It is such a discussion that is provided here.

The truth value of Christian theories is of great importance to many people, whether professionals or laypeople, believers or unbelievers, and it is therefore also of great importance to know whether systematic theology can be construed as a scientific discipline according to general criteria, since science is usually taken as the highest rational standard humans are able to meet – imperfect, impure, fallibilistic, etc., but nevertheless still largely robust and helpful in our attempts to understand the world we live in.

The aim is also to contribute to the long historical debate about the scientific character of systematic theology. I argue that the way of organizing this book

---

54 Pannenberg, *Theology and the Philosophy of Science*, 5.

provides new insights, enabling us to understand the scientific nature of systematic theology and to argue for its relevance to the aim of science, i. e., to know the truth about reality.

It seems to me that new changes in the secularized research university are once again causing new debates. Decrease in student enrolment, in public funding, job possibilities, church membership etc., leaves the theological faculties in a fragile position.[55] Some theological faculties have merged with religious studies or the humanities; others have been closed or turned into church-affiliated seminaries based on campus.[56] These are primarily external factors that are challenging and interesting. As a reply, one could argue that many excellent universities have theological faculties, that there are publishers, journals, and societies for scientific theologians that present peer-reviewed work in recognized contexts. Given these facts, it could be said that the burden of proof rests on the sceptic and that theology should not be troubled by changing tides.

However, what I aim for, is to start from the opposite end, with the internal debate about the scientific status of systematic theology . The body of scientific knowledge expands all the time, and newly gained insights challenge old presumptions. Thus, we need to discuss whether a scientific theology is possible under criteria accepted in today's intellectual milieu. This is not a simple yes-or-no question, and any given answer will be questioned by many. The ambition is thus to present a detailed study that furthers our discussion given the specific presuppositions that I have stated.

The premise for the whole enterprise of scientific theology at the secular research university is *the intersection of reason*.[57] In the modern period, no religious worldview has any precedence in state universities. This does not make the universities neutral, because their presuppositions (such as secularism, naturalism, methodological agnosticism etc.) are imbued with values. But for the moment it is widely acknowledged that these presuppositions are the most beneficial to the broadest number of citizens, and when we discuss the university as a public institution, it seems impossible to ground its endeavour on other presuppositions.[58] Of course,

---

[55] Miroslav Volf and Matthew Croasmun, *For the Life of the World: Theology That Makes a Difference* (Grand Rapids: Brazos Press, 2018), 35–59.

[56] Michael Agerbo Mørch, ed., *En plads blandt de lærde: Teologiens videnskabelighed til debat* (Frederiksberg: Eksistensen, 2019), 7–12.

[57] This expression, borrowed from the Danish poet and essayist Søren Ulrik Thomsen, points to reason as the common ground in public debate about religious matters, in Danish "fornuftens fællesmængde." See Søren Ulrik Thomsen, 'Pro Ecclesia,' in *Kritik af den negative opbyggelighed*, by Frederik Stjernfelt and Søren Ulrik Thomsen (Valby: Vindrose, 2005), 151–52.

[58] At least for the time being. Of course, if there is a major religious revival and suddenly a majority in society of believers in a given religion, then we will possibly see a revision of the presuppositions for state institutions and thus also universities. At least that is a possibility with which history presents us. Whether this scenario is attractive or not is a discussion reserved for another time.

the foundational values for a university are not given *a priori*; quite the opposite actually. Universities are large, heterogenous, and fragile institutions and thus an obvious battleground for ideological struggle. We have seen this numerous times throughout history to such an extent that we could call it an existential premise for universities. The point is that universities do not have an inherent nature; that they are social constructs that we have to treat with great care. On the other hand, how we organize our universities is not something sacred; it is always up for revision, and thus we have to discuss continuously how to organize these institutions.[59] At present, the *intersection of reason* leads us to a rational, secular, research-based institution. Where does this leave academic theology? If we want to keep theology as a discipline in the secular research university, we have to draw some specific criteria for the work it does. In the ongoing discussion, many academic theologians question the role and place for academic theology in the research university (e. g., Stanley Hauerwas and Gavin D'Costa) and I do understand their concerns.[60] Maybe theology would prosper more if the institutional affiliation were constructed differently? But for the moment, I do think academic theology makes interesting contributions to interdisciplinary conversations and should therefore have a role at the university. But theology must articulate a proper philosophy of science based on general criteria before it is even meaningful to discuss its place within the university. Hence, the aim is to investigate the hypothesis that a carefully explicated understanding of systematic theology can meet the best criteria that provide the foundation for science in the secular research-based university.

Let me end this introduction by stating the findings of the book: (a) I develop the stratified understanding of systematic theology first proposed by Niels Henrik Gregersen, whereby a greater awareness of the different parts of systematic theology comes to sight. (b) I discuss the common criteria of science much more deeply than is usually the case in works on the relation between science and theology and deepen our understanding of the criteria in several ways, e. g., by mapping different positions on intersubjectivity in systematic theology or clarifying the two understandings of normativity. (c) I show how well the notion of coherence puts the criteria to work and gives us a better understanding of how testability, falsification,

---

59 At least it would in the Humboldtian tradition, which is the legacy modern universities are built upon. See Wilhelm von Humboldt, 'Über die Innere und Äussere Organisation Höheren Wissenschaftlichen Anstalten in Berlin', in *Schriften zur Politik und zum Bildungswesen. Werke in Fünf Bänden*, vol. 4, 5 vol. (Darmstadt: Hermann Gentner Verlag, 1993).

60 Hauerwas is a tricky case. He is a severe critic of the Enlightenment tradition and seeks to undermine the secular basis of research institutions. Yet he still thinks his place as a critic is *inside* these institutions because this seems to be the best way to avoid the "sectarian temptation" of (religious) private universities. To me this is close to "having one's cake and eating it," but we will leave this discussion for another time.

and intersubjectivity work in practice. The combination of these findings gives us a more fine-grained defence and substantiation of systematic theology as a scientific discipline than is usually given, and the result is that systematic theology can be seen as a much more robust scientific discipline than is usually the case.

Chapter Two: A Selected Overview of The Historical Background

2.1 Introduction

The aim of this book is to discuss systematically the scientific status of systematic theology. For this reason, a detailed historical study cannot be provided. But the historical background is not forgotten, and with this chapter readers are reminded of some of the most important discussions about the possibility of presenting rationally justified public discourse about God in order to situate the present discussion in its historical and cultural contexts. I cannot examine these discussions in depth here, but I shall at least identify their concerns and questions in relation to the research question.

What theology is and how to do it properly has been discussed for about two thousand years,[1] and the discussion about its scientific status – or more precisely its characteristics in comparison with other academic disciplines – has been intense since the foundation of the first university in Paris around 1200.[2] From 1200 to around 1790 with the French revolution, the discussions were primarily internal with discussions of aided versus unaided reason, the proper tools for studying scripture, the relation between philosophy and theology, and the proper aim of studying theology.[3] With increasing secularization of the universities peaking with the foundation of Berlin University under the direction of Wilhelm v. Humboldt in 1810, theology's scientific status was compromised.[4] Many giants in the history of theology and philosophy contributed to the debate about theology's institutional

---

1 For the hermeneutical questions in the patristic era see, e. g., Werner Jeanrond, *Theological Hermeneutics. Development and Significance* (New York: Crossroad, 1991), 12–26.
2 For the many discussions of theology's nature, method, and status from Paris (c. 1200) to Berlin (c. 1800) see the excellent sources Higton, *A Theology of Higher Education*, 13–41; Evans, *Old Arts and New Theology*; Ferruolo, *The Origins of the University*; Alan Balfour Cobban, *The Medieval English Universities: Oxford and Cambridge to c. 1500* (Aldershot: Scolar Press, 1988); Monika Asztalos, 'The Faculty of Theology,' in *A History of the University in Europe. Universities in the Middle Ages*, ed. Hilde de Ridder-Symoens, vol. 1, 4 vols (Cambridge: Cambridge University Press, 1992), 409–41.
3 For key texts to this period see, e. g., Bruno Niederbacher and Gerhard Leibold, eds., *Theologie als Wissenschaft im Mittelalter. Texte, Übersetzungen, Kommentare* (Münster: Aschendorff, 2006). See also the close examination in Pannenberg, *Theology and the Philosophy of Science*, 228–50.
4 The intense discussions of theology around the foundation of Berlin University is presented in Howard, *Protestant Theology and the Making of the Modern German University*.

affiliation, prominently Kant, Fichte, and Schleiermacher.[5] The 19th century saw increasing pluralization of the field of theology, but to a great extent, liberal protestant theology was accepted as a part of academia.[6] In the late 19th century, new things happened in science in general with new conceptualities for proper science arising through an increasing focus on empirical data and methods (see chapters four and five). The natural sciences made unprecedented leaps in knowledge accumulation, and even though human science scholars tried to identify the inherent difference between, for example, understanding and explanation, they could not escape a growing sense of unease concerning their scientific status.[7] This goes for theology as well, and the debates in the 20th century that is selected for a historical background to the book took place in a cultural climate of growing scepticism towards the scientific status of theology and an ever more insistent call for legitimation of its data, methods, and results.[8]

In the following, four debates in the 20th century are introduced where the focus was on the scientific status of theology. As we will see, most participants argued for the scientific status of theology but in different ways and with different implications. An important recurrent difference is the emphasis on who is to be a part of the rationally justified discourse about God, in other words how "public" it is, in the terminology of the present book. This is therefore one of the marks that I am looking for: not only the defence of theology but also which implications the defence has for a broader conversation about theological themes in the university. This background should make it clear how I take the discussion further in the systematic discussion in chapters three through eight; like most of the authors presented in the following I participate in a discussion about how to understand theology as a

---

5 Cf. Walter Rüegg, 'Theology and the Arts,' in *Universities in the Nineteenth and Early Twentieth Centuries (1800–1945)*, ed. Walter Rüegg, A History of the University in Europe 3 (Cambridge: Cambridge University Press, 2004), 393–458.

6 These developments has been portrayed in both Zachary Purvis, *Theology and the University in Nineteenth-Century Germany*, Oxford Theology and Religion Monographs (Oxford: Oxford University Press, 2016) and Johannes Zachhuber, *Theology as Science in Nineteenth-Century Germany: From F.C. Baur to Ernst Troeltsch* (Oxford: Oxford University Press, 2013).

7 Examples of attempts to draw this line between the disciplines are Wilhelm Dilthey, *Einleitung in die Geisteswissenschaften. Versuch einer Grundlegung für das Studium der Gesellschaft und der Geschichte*, Ninth Unchanged Edition, Gesammelte Schriften 1 (Stuttgart: Teubner, 1990); Heinrich Riekert, *Kulturwissenschaft und Naturwissenschaft* (Tübingen: J.C.B. Mohr, 1921); G. H. von Wright, *Explanation and Understanding* (London: Routledge and K. Paul, 2012). The distinction was influentially commented upon in a short debate book by C.P. Snow that saw the natural sciences and the humanities as two different cultures: C.P. Snow, *The Two Cultures*, Canto Edition (Cambridge: Cambridge University Press, 1998).

8 With his usual zeal in historical studies, Pannenberg traces the development from 1200 until the Barth-Scholz-debate in Pannenberg, *Theology and the Philosophy of Science*, 228–65. I refer to this study for a detailed background.

scientific discipline in comparison with other disciplines, especially philosophy and religious studies, with a focus on criteria and methods. More than most of these authors I identify specific and commonly accepted criteria for scientific work and, by applying coherence theory, show how theology meets these criteria.

I first present the debate between Heinrich Scholz and Karl Barth (2.2.1). Next, I proceed to another debate in Germany with many more participants, taking place from the 1960s to the 1980s. For the purpose I have chosen Hermann Diem, Wolfhart Pannenberg, and Gerhard Sauter as examples from the debate (2.2.2). Third, I turn to Sweden where extensive debate took place between two distinct schools of theology in Lund and Uppsala, respectively. For each school I have chosen a representative, Anders Nygren (Lund) and Anders Jeffner (Uppsala), respectively (2.2.3). I end with a discussion in the US between theologians connected to the respective schools of Chicago and Yale, this time with Paul Tillich and David Tracy (Chicago) and George Lindbeck and Hans Frei (Yale) as representatives (2.2.4).

None of these brief introductions aim at a complete overview or even at assessing or discussing anything anew. The only interest is to situate the present discussion in chapters three through eight, and for this purpose these four debates are found to be helpful. The selection contributes to the systematic discussion and other important discussions are left for another time, e. g., more local debates in Denmark, Norway, and the Netherlands; the debate about the "Death-of-God" theology that gained attention for a few years in the US; the important writings of a number of British theologians (especially T.F. Torrance) that were not as much a part of a defined debate as they were contributions to the discussion of prolegomena in theology; the debates in the Orthodox and Catholic countries in Eastern and Southern Europe with which I only have minimal familiarity. The four examples are thus examples from the West, primarily Europe, and all four are debates that gained international awareness and thus made lasting impressions on the field of theology.

2.2 Debates in the 20th Century

2.2.1 The Barth-Scholz Debate

The debate between Karl Barth and Heinrich Scholz focused on the relation between research object and method. Whereas Barth saw God's revelation as the only possible starting point for theology with the implication that the research methods must take this presupposition seriously, Scholz denied this principle and held that theology must rely on the general scientific methodological standards.[9]

---

9 Pannenberg, *Theology and the Philosophy of Science*, 256–69.

The debate was brief with only three contributions, but all the more conspicuous are their repercussions through history. The initial contribution was an article by Scholz that I introduce here before outlining Barth's reply and Scholz's second article, to which Barth did not respond.

In 1931, Scholz wrote the article "Wie ist eine evangelische Theologie als Wissenschaft möglich?" in *Zwischen den Zeiten*.[10] Scholz' engagement with the question arises from the concern that Kant's old question about a proper metaphysics had not been answered adequately and, more critically, not even discussed satisfactorily.[11] This question also pertains to the possibility or non-possibility of doing theology scientifically, and Scholz discusses several criteria for a rationally justified public discourse about God (in the terminology of this book). He asks the critical and structural question, "Die Frage, die uns beschäftigt, ist die: Welches sind die Bedingungen dafür, dass für eine evangelische Theologie behauptet werden darf, dass diese Theologie eine Wissenschaft ist?"[12] His own answer is a list of six criteria for a scientific discipline. The first three are "minimum conditions" (*Die nichtumstrittenen Mindstforderungen*), the next two are more disputed (*Die umstrittenen Mindstforderungen*), and the last one sums up the first five in one poignant postulate (*Die Höchstforderung*).[13] The six criteria are briefly presented and commented on in the following.

(1) The proposition postulate (*Das Satzpostulat*): Besides questions and definitions, science provides propositions – and only propositions – that are asserted as true.[14] The concern seems to be that science should avoid all arbitrary talk that arises from propositions that are not testable (see the third point) and, of course, avoid propositions that are false.

---

10 A lengthy critical engagement with Scholz's article can be found in Sven Grosse, *Theologie und Wissenschaftstheorie* (Paderborn: Verlag Ferdinand Schöningh, 2019), 21–111. See also Arie L. Molendijk, *Aus dem Dunklen ins Helle: Wissenschaft und Theologie im Denken von Heinrich Scholz* (Amsterdam: Editions Rodopi, 1991).

11 Heinrich Scholz, 'Wie ist eine Evangelische Theologie als Wissenschaft Möglich?', *Zwischen den Zeiten* Vol. 9 (1931): 8–12.

12 Scholz, 'Wie ist eine Evangelische Theologie als Wissenschaft Möglich?', 13. "The question that preoccupies us is this one: what are the conditions for the statement that theology is a science, a statement that evangelical theology could assert?" (Translation MAM)

13 Pannenberg has a helpful summary of the six postulates, Pannenberg, *Theology and the Philosophy of Science*, 270–71.

14 Scholz, 'Wie ist eine Evangelische Theologie als Wissenschaft Möglich?', 19.

(2) The coherence postulate (*Das Kohärenzpostulat*): All propositions must be related to one field of study.[15] The concern here seems to be that the holism of theology makes it impossible to test its propositions and that a more narrow "regional ontology" would be necessary to test the propositions for their truth value (as to the first point).

(3) The controllability postulate (*Das Kontrollierbarkeitspostulat*): All propositions must be testable and not just asserted.[16] Testability does not refer to verification but rather to intelligibility and transparency so that the reader can assess the principles used in the formulations of the propositions.[17] This seems to go somewhat against the first two points but may be included because Scholz as a philosopher wants to reserve an area for metaphysics. What counts as "intelligibility" and "transparency" is not obvious and should have been more clearly explicated.

(4) The independence postulate (*Das Unabhängigkeitspostulat*): The researcher must be independent and without prejudice towards the subject at hand. Additionally, the propositions cannot be stated under pressure from specific presuppositions.[18] This is the first of the more disputed postulates and it is easy to see why. It is impossible to determine whether a researcher is without prejudices, and most philosophers of science accept that this is never the case. It is also the case that all propositions are made in a framework guided by presuppositions. I discuss this in the following chapters.

(5) The congruity postulate (*Das Konkordanzpostulat*): Propositions must agree with all other knowledge, especially restricted by what the natural sciences claim to be physically possible.[19] This is also controversial because it is a presupposition that what is physically possible within current physics is what counts as real. Physics continues to develop, and we do not have a complete understanding of natural reality; thus, this claim could be seen as unnecessarily restrictive.[20]

(6) The formalization principle:[21] This is an Aristotelian principle that classifies all propositions in two categories. The first contains the axioms of a given field,

---

15 Scholz, 'Wie ist eine Evangelische Theologie als Wissenschaft Möglich?', 20.
16 Scholz, 'Wie ist eine Evangelische Theologie als Wissenschaft Möglich?', 21.
17 Scholz, 'Wie ist eine Evangelische Theologie als Wissenschaft Möglich?', 46–48.
18 Scholz, 'Wie ist eine Evangelische Theologie als Wissenschaft Möglich?', 21.
19 Scholz, 'Wie ist eine Evangelische Theologie als Wissenschaft Möglich?', 23.
20 For theology, it is also controversial because the notion of the "miracle" seems to be compromised. This is why this postulate gains such a lengthy discussion by Sven Grosse: Grosse, *Theologie und Wissenschaftstheorie*, 51–111.
21 This is not Scholz' own term but one coined by the editor of Barth's Church Dogmatics, see note on p. 7 of Karl Barth, *Church Dogmatics. The Doctrine of the Word of God. §1–7*, ed. Geoffrey William Bromiley, Thomas F. Torrance, and Frank McCombie, Study Edition, vol. I1 (London and New York: T & T Clark, 2010), 7.

the second encompasses the theorems of a given field. The latter are deduced from the former.[22] This principle seems to go somewhat against the fourth point because it is not obvious why presuppositions are denied while axioms are accepted. But it is probably an awareness of the necessity of axioms in the natural sciences, especially mathematics, that forces Scholz to accept this principle.

Scholz's six criteria for science are not convincing because they spring from a positivistic climate that has since been abandoned. But what interests me here is his call for a justification of theology as a rationally justified public discourse, that is, a type of work that is executed in such a way that it meets commonly accepted standards. His own suggestion may fail, but his concern is close to the one discussed in this book. I will now look at Barth's response to Scholz, which was anything but accommodating.

Barth replied with a complete rejection of Scholz's criteria: "It is still the proper concept of science for our own time. And theology can only say point-blank that this concept is unacceptable to it. Even the minimum postulate of freedom from contradiction is acceptable to theology only when it is given a particular interpretation which the scientific theorist can hardly tolerate, namely, that theology does not affirm in principle that the 'contradiction' which it makes cannot be solved."[23] Or even more poignant: "If theology allows itself to be called, or calls itself, a science, it cannot in so doing accept the obligation of submission to standards valid for other sciences."[24]

But why did Barth refuse Scholz's criticism and his criteria for science? What is at stake for him in the prospect of theology accepting these criteria? I will point to two concerns.

First, the definition of theology. According to Barth, "dogmatics is the scientific self-examination of the Christian Church with respect to the content of its distinctive talk about God."[25] This means that the subject of theology is the Church seeking to understand its object of worship, God and his revelation in Christ. Theology is "no more than human 'talk about God,'" and thus fallible and tentative. But the important point here is that according to Barth, there cannot be an external standard to measure theological work against apart from its "own source and object."[26] Christ is the "basis, goal and content," and all work should be measured by its faithfulness to this event.[27] As mentioned above, this springs from Barth's

---

22 Scholz, 'Wie ist eine Evangelische Theologie als Wissenschaft Möglich?', 24.
23 Barth, *Church Dogmatics*, Vol. I1:7.
24 Barth, *Church Dogmatics*, Vol. I1:8.
25 Barth, *Church Dogmatics*, Vol. I1:1.
26 Barth, *Church Dogmatics*, Vol. I1:2.
27 Barth, *Church Dogmatics*, Vol. I1:4.

insistence that theology has to presuppose God's revelation, an event that cannot be tested but is the positive ground from which everything else springs.

Second, the notion of God in relation to human investigation. God's activity is utterly free, thus making a description of him impossible for standard accounts in science.[28] Science includes three things that cannot be aligned with talk of the Christian God, because if theology accepts to be a "science" it declares: "1. That like all other so-called sciences it is a human concern with a definite object of knowledge, 2. That like all others it treads a definite and self-consistent path of knowledge, and 3. That like all others it must give an account of this path to itself and to all others who are capable of concern for this object and therefore of treading this path."[29] With these words, Barth seems to agree with Scholz's description of science in general but at the same time to maintain that this approach to research does not fit the object of theology, i. e., God and his revelation. With Barth's specific rejection of the contradiction principle, his concern is arguably that he thinks it is impossible to reflect on God and his revelation without accepting paradoxes and thus theology cannot accept the criterion of non-contradictions without qualifications. Thus, their difference is not so much about what counts as science in general as about whether there is a specific and distinct scientific task for the field of theology because of its peculiar research object. If Barth accepted Scholz's criteria for theology, it would lose its ability to talk congruently about its object.[30]

Scholz replied once again in 1936 in a festschrift to Barth with the article, "Was ist unter einer theologischen Aussage zu verstehen?"[31] to which, as mentioned above, Barth did not respond. His main points are the same but strengthened in order to avoid the misconception that the disagreement with Barth is purely semantical.[32] Scholz' central disagreement is with Barth's emphasis on a particular rationality for theology because this will isolate theological statements in irrational circularity.[33] Scholz thus persists in defending the minimum conditions for scientific propositions and insists on the legitimacy and necessity of such conditions for theology too, understood as a rationally justified public discourse about God.

The Barth-Scholz debate is a debate about the nature and method of theology, focusing on what defines the field, the object of study, or the general scientific criteria. These discussions continued decades later when the debate re-emerged in Germany. In the next section I introduce this comprehensive debate.

---

28 Barth, *Church Dogmatics*, Vol. I1:7.
29 Barth, *Church Dogmatics*, Vol. I1:6.
30 Barth, *Church Dogmatics*, Vol. I1:7–9.
31 Heinrich Scholz, 'Was ist unter einer theologischen Aussage zu verstehen?', in *Theologie als Wissenschaft: Aufsätze und Thesen*, ed. Gerhard Sauter (München: C. Kaiser, 1971), 265–77.
32 See the discussion in Pannenberg, *Theology and the Philosophy of Science*, 274–75.
33 Scholz, 'Was ist unter einer theologischen Aussage zu verstehen?', 274–75.

2.2.2 The German Debate in the 60s through the 80s

In the decades following the debate between Barth and Scholz, there was not much discussion of the scientific status of theology in Germany. Hermann Diem wrote an influential three-volume book between 1951 and 1963 called *Theologie als Kirchliche Wissenschaft*, but besides a handful of articles, I have not found much of relevance before 1970. From 1970 to 1980 the debate exploded; at least fifteen books and a couple of articles were published between Helge Siemer's *Theologie als Wissenschaft in der Gesellschaft* from 1970 and Erich Schrofner's *Theologie als positive Wissenschaft* in 1980, and the number would be much higher if we included questions on the nature of theology, the theological encyclopaedia[34] (the relationship between the theological disciplines), theology's institutional location, etc. Even today, in the field of "Fundamentaltheologie," the debate is still prevalent with books and articles being published and a number of ongoing research projects in the area.[35]

In this period, the Barth-Scholz debate about theology's nature, aim, and methods continued in the thought of people like Hermann Diem, Wolfhart Pannenberg, and Gerhard Sauter. The main concern of the theologians was to speak properly about God. Should you speak "about" God, "for" God, "to" God, or neither of the above when you do theology? The clarification of this discourse about God became the axis for the wheel of reflection about the philosophy of science in relation to theology. It involves questions such as (a) what sources should be used? (b) which methods are proper in relation to the sources? (c) how should the concept of truth be defined? and (d) who has the authority to set the terms for theological work? In the following, I introduce the contributions by Diem, Pannenberg, and Sauter because I consider them to be representatives of three distinct approaches that neatly summarize the debate for the purposes here.

Hermann Diem radicalized Barth's dialectical position, built a Great Wall of China between theology and the rest of the disciplines, and emphasized the ecclesi-

---

34 A brief overview of the German discussion is presented in Pannenberg, *Theology and the Philosophy of Science*, 14–20.
35 See footnote 1 in Peter Knauer, 'Ist Theologie eine Wissenschaft?', *Theologie und Philosophie* 93, no. 1 (2018): 81–96. For examples of contemporary German books see, e. g., a broad view from a largely Catholic standpoint in Benedikt Paul Göcke, ed., *Die Wissenschaftlichkeit der Theologie. Band 1: Historische und Systematische Perspektiven*, Studien zur Systematischen Theologie, Ethik und Philosophie, 13/1 (Münster: Aschendorff Verlag, 2018); Sven Grosse, *Theologie und Wissenschaftstheorie* (Paderborn: Verlag Ferdinand Schöningh, 2019); Ulrich Moustakas, *Theologie im Kontext von Wissenschaftstheorie und Hermeneutik* (Hamburg: Kovac, Dr. Verlag, 2017); Ingolf U. Dalferth, ed., *Eine Wissenschaft oder viele? Die Einheit evangelischer Theologie in der Sicht ihrer Disziplinen*, (Leipzig: Evangelische Verlagsanstalt, 2006). Lukas Ohly, *Theologie als Wissenschaft: Eine Fundamentaltheologie aus phänomenologischer Leitperspektive*, (Frankfurt am Main: Peter Lang, 2017).

astical commitment of all theology.[36] Diem's dialectical theology focused on the event of Christ where God reveals himself in Jesus of Nazareth.[37] This truth-claim cannot be assessed on secular premises but must be evaluated by a standard of truth that is ecclesiastical and not by one shared by philosophy.[38] The implications of this view are clearly stated in Pannenberg's critique, which points to Diem's "particular" understanding of the field: "Theologians may envisage such a general concept of science in a different way from other philosophers of science, but these very differences must rest on an assumption of the unity of truth which Diem rejected, for without this assumption all discussion would inevitably cease."[39] The point is not that an external standard for truth should be forced on theology but that a unity of truth must be presupposed if any conversation is to be meaningful. Diem radically opposed this view and refused to embrace any general concept of science to which theology would have to adhere.

But what was Pannenberg's alternative to Diem's view that he rejected? I cannot go into the grand scope of Pannenberg's theology here, although that would be necessary in order to give a more complete answer because almost anything Pannenberg wrote was directly or indirectly an answer to these questions. But for the purpose here, it suffices to look at chapter five of *Theology and the Philosophy of Science*, where Pannenberg presents an outline of his own program for how theology can meet common scientific criteria. As already mentioned, the question about God-talk was central, and Pannenberg emphasized that God was the proper object of theology because the question about God was still open and without conclusion.[40] It is to be considered as a problem, but also as a reference point for all investigations.[41] God is invisible and therefore only possible to investigate indirectly through the implications of God's existence for empirical reality.[42] This, in the terminology of the present book, is equal to the possibility of doing scientific theology as a rationally justified public discourse about God. Pannenberg says, "[b]ecause theology, as an attempt to obtain knowledge, seeks intersubjectivity, it too must direct its attention to this indirect way in which the divine reality is

---

36 I use the term "radicalized" because Pannenberg shows that Barth did not insist on a schism between ecclesiastical science and general science as Diem did. Cf. Pannenberg, *Theology and the Philosophy of Science*, 269; Barth, *Church Dogmatics*, Vol. I1:6–7.
37 Hermann Diem, *Theologie als kirchliche Wissenschaft*, vol. 1 (Munich: Chr. Kaiser Verlag, 1951), 21.
38 Diem, *Theologie als kirchliche Wissenschaft*, 41.
39 Pannenberg, *Theology and the Philosophy of Science*, 19. Note that Diem himself called theology a "particular science" because theology could not accept the common standards at the time.
40 Pannenberg, *Theology and the Philosophy of Science*, 298–299.
41 Pannenberg, *Theology and the Philosophy of Science*, 299.
42 Pannenberg, *Theology and the Philosophy of Science*, 332. Therefore, God cannot be verified as an object both because his being will be disputed as invisible and because verification would be a contradiction of his all-determining reality. See ibid. 331–332.

co-given, to the 'traces' of the divine mystery in the things of the world and in our own lives."[43] This is a consequence of Pannenberg's understanding of God as the all-determining reality, which implies that all objects somehow point to God. Not as singular objects, though, but through the continuity between all things.[44] This points to the importance of history in the thought of Pannenberg. All knowledge is historical, but hence also included in the totality of history such that the singular facts gain their meanings in reference to the absolute: "The reality of God is always present only in subjective anticipation of the totality of reality, in models of the totality of meaning presupposed in all particular experience. These models, however, are historic, which means that they are subject to confirmation or refutation by subsequent experience."[45] To be scientific, theology must be historical because God is only knowable through history. A science of God is then a science of religion which is a science of historical religion. What makes Christianity different from the other religions is that it is not only mythological but also historical.[46] Christianity claims certain things about historical events, such as the life, death, and resurrection of Jesus, that can be investigated through proper historical-hermeneutical tools. Both historically and philosophically, theology relies on common criteria but insists on the relevance of discussing the notion of God in relation to historical experience and in relation to ultimate reality. It is possible to test the truth value of theological propositions, even though the final confirmation cannot be given, because theological – and philosophical – propositions concern ultimate reality, which cannot be surveyed from a historical, particular place but only at the end of history, in theological terms, eschatologically.[47] The legitimation of theological theories is given by comparison to other interpretations of reality; if the theological statement is more subtle and more convincing than present alternatives, it has substantiated itself.[48]

The last example from the extensive German debate in this period is Gerhard Sauter. He is interesting as a middle position between Diem and Pannenberg. His main contribution to the debate is through the edited and commented selection of writings on the subject presented in the book *Theologie als Wissenschaft. Auf-*

---

43 Pannenberg, *Theology and the Philosophy of Science*, 301. I come back to the question of intersubjectivity in chapter six.
44 Pannenberg, *Theology and the Philosophy of Science*, 303.
45 Pannenberg, *Theology and the Philosophy of Science*, 310.
46 Pannenberg, *Theology and the Philosophy of Science*, 314.
47 Pannenberg, *Theology and the Philosophy of Science*, 343.
48 Pannenberg, *Theology and the Philosophy of Science*, 343. Pannenberg also introduces four reasons for judging a theological statement unsubstantiated on pp. 344–345.

sätze und Thesen[49] and the similar compilation *Wissenschaftstheoretische Kritik der Theologie: die Theologie und die neuere wissenschaftstheoretischen Diskussion*.[50]

Sauter rejects Scholz's ambition of finding abstract principles that can serve as the foundation for a unification of science.[51] The characteristic of theology is to make contributions to the development of theology in the cross-field between church and societal context.[52] The aim of theology is not only to reiterate old formulations but also to make of the contemporary context a conversation partner. One difficulty is that theology seeks to say something that is of interest to *everyone*, and this is much more ambitious than the other sciences, which have restricted scopes of address.[53] A consequence of this is that both theology and the other sciences are suspected of ideological import, so the critics of theology say that theology cannot justify its claims if not all presuppositions are accepted, and the theologians accuse the other sciences of having their own dogmas and unjustified axioms or presuppositions.[54] Sauter accepts that theology has difficulty explicating the precise relationship between authority and rationality, especially in relation to its sources, but it is imperative to argue about how theology understands it sources.[55] The objective of theology is the question of "meaning" and this is where the unique contribution theology makes to the sciences lies.[56] Sauter thus suggests that theology is a discipline that focuses on general hermeneutics and that its special focus is to analyse key terms such as revelation, history, church, humanity etc., in themselves and in relation to one another.[57] Sauter proposes that the scientific character of theology relates to its meaning constitution and meaning communication. The question of meaning is universal, and theology seeks to answer this general feeling of unease about reality. The question for theology is to relate totality with what is unique for the individual person. The problem is that there is a need for a notion of totality but that such a notion cannot adequately speak of reality in relation to

---

49 Gerhard Sauter, *Theologie als Wissenschaft: Aufsätze und Thesen* (München: Chr. Kaiser, 1971).
50 Gerhard Sauter, *Wissenschaftstheoretische Kritik der Theologie: die Theologie und die neuere wissenschaftstheoretische Diskussion. Materialien, Analysen, Entwürfe* (München: Chr. Kaiser, 1973). Pannenberg engages primarily with Sauter's short book on method *Vor einem neuen Methodenstreit in der Theologie?* (München: Chr. Kaiser, 1970), which I have not consulted. See Pannenberg, *Theology and the Philosophy of Science*, 289–96.
51 Sauter, *Wissenschaftstheoretische Kritik der Theologie*, 220–22.
52 Sauter, *Wissenschaftstheoretische Kritik der Theologie*, 225–226.
53 Sauter, *Wissenschaftstheoretische Kritik der Theologie*, 213.
54 Sauter, *Wissenschaftstheoretische Kritik der Theologie*, 214.
55 Sauter, *Wissenschaftstheoretische Kritik der Theologie*, 214–217.
56 Sauter, *Wissenschaftstheoretische Kritik der Theologie*, 227.
57 Sauter, *Wissenschaftstheoretische Kritik der Theologie*, 227.

contingent lives.[58] Hence, theology is an open investigation of how these entities can meet and relate.

The German debate in the 60s through 80s was widespread and diverse. The examples from Diem, Pannenberg, and Sauter showed that there were different emphases on the nature, aim, and methods of theology. Diem wanted to integrate the scientific aims of theology with the concerns of the church, Pannenberg argued for a theology on commonly accepted criteria, and Sauter positioned himself somewhere in between with a focus on the concerns of the church but in continuous conversation with the cultural context (science included).

In the next section I introduce a debate in Sweden that attracted international attention. It was a debate especially about methods but still including discussion of the nature and aim of theology.

2.2.3   Lund versus Uppsala

Whereas the two first debates concerned very different understandings of theology and its nature, aim, and methods, this third debate is different. Both perspectives seek to present theology as a rationally justified public discourse, i. e., to show how theology can meet common criteria for science within the university.

The debate in Sweden was initiated by a political reform in 1970 that brought about the foundation of the new disciplines of psychology and sociology of religion, respectively.[59] Religious studies became more separated from theology, and these developments caused new reflections upon what distinguishes theology from other disciplines.[60] This background reminds us of the fact that external factors often serve as instruments for internal reflection and for the assessment of theology's academic status.[61] Another change of circumstances was that the theological faculties were

---

58   Here it becomes clear where Sauter differs from Pannenberg, and why Pannenberg chose to criticize this aspect of Sauter's theology. Pannenberg writes: "He overlooks the fact that history envisaged as an open process contains within itself the contradictions between the future and the present and already at hand, and the contradictions between the various processes and subjects with their different anticipations of the still open future, in such a way that these contradictions are resolved in the process of history itself." Pannenberg, *Theology and the Philosophy of Science*, 291.

59   For the debates in the previous decades that also played a role in the debate in the 1970s and subsequently, I have benefitted from the articles by Arne Rasmusson and Bengt Hääglund: Arne Rasmusson, 'A Century of Swedish Theology,' *Lutheran Quaterly* XXI (2007): 125–62 and Bengt Hägglund, 'Skandinavische Beiträge zur Methodenfrage der Systematische Theologie,' *Theologische Rundschau* 50, no. 4 (November 1985): 364–78.

60   Hägglund, 'Skandinavische Beiträge zur Methodenfrage der Systematische Theologie,' 370–71. I will return to the discussion of the criterion for "distinct research" in chapter eight.

61   See, e. g., Volf and Croasmun, *For the Life of the World*, 35–59.

"de-confessionalized" in 1974,[62] with the effect that the curriculum became open to non-Lutheran students.

The debate between the theological schools of Lund and Uppsala was above all a debate about proper theological methods. For both schools, the scientific nature of theology is based on commonly defined, substantiated, and accepted methods more than on anything else. This often implies a rejection of metaphysics and instead a focus on analysis, explanation, and description of meaning-production.[63]

I begin with an introduction to the Lundensian school with an emphasis on its most influential figure, Anders Nygren. I then turn to the Uppsala school, emphasizing its most influential figure, Anders Jeffner.

The theological faculty in Lund, in the southern part of Sweden, housed the influential Lundensian school of thought. Unusually for Scandinavian theology, it became internationally influential, with translated publications in German and English. Their main concern was to develop a strictly scientific theology based on rigorous objective descriptions purged of valuation and normativity. As with the German debate, the debate in Sweden was primarily apologetic. The theologians sought to argue for the credibility of theology in an increasingly secular climate, and this concern was especially clear in the writings of Anders Nygren.[64]

On the first page of his *magnum opus*, Nygren asks two questions: "How is philosophy as a science possible?" and "How is theology as a science possible?"[65] The answers to these questions depend on how "science," "philosophy," and "theology" are defined. For Nygren, the solution for theology is to see itself as an analytical discipline that objectively explains the religious context of meaning.[66] This is done through a critical assessment of the content of an individual religion in relation to the basic motif that structures the religion: "As it is the task of the philosophy of religion to clarify the presuppositional concepts of religion, so it is the task of theology to clarify the content of an individual religion, and to do so in terms of the central idea of the religion itself. It is this central idea that we call its 'fundamental motif.'"[67] The fundamental motif of a religion is the answer to the basic categorial

---

62 This expression is taken from Rasmusson, 'A Century of Swedish Theology,' 125.
63 Rasmusson, 'A Century of Swedish Theology,' 131.
64 Other important members of the Lundensian school, before and after Nygren, were Gustav Aulén, Gustav Wingren, Per Erik Persson, Bengt Hägglund, and Tage Kurtén among others. See the articles by Rasmusson and Hägglund for analyses and assessments.
65 Anders Nygren, *Meaning and Method*, trans. Philip S. Watson (London: Epworth Press, 1972), 1.
66 Nygren, *Meaning and Method*, 11.
67 Nygren, *Meaning and Method*, 12. Rasmusson says, "The basic method of a scientific systematic theology is the motif research method. It is a main task of systematic theology to determine the basic motif of Christianity. A basic motif is, in this case, the answer of a religion to the basic categorical question, which for religion is the question of the eternal." Rasmusson, 'A Century of Swedish Theology,' 134.

question of how to understand the eternal. For Christianity, the fundamental motif is that the question of the eternal finds its solution in Jesus Christ. This gives us the method of systematic theology, i. e., "motif research" or "motif analysis."[68]

In chapter eleven, Nygren more elaborately presents this idea in relation to the Christian religion. Here he says that the motif analysis is a project of "typological" or "structural" research that seeks to determine the meaning of what is said and not just to describe what is being said.[69] The central motif for Christianity according to Nygren is "the Agape motif," which covers the notion that God loves all of mankind unconditionally in the sense that God does not need any motivation for his love.[70] The Agape motif is one possible articulation of a great religious motif, and it is Nygren's claim that only two alternatives are viable in the history of religions, "the Nomos motif" and "the Eros motif." The former is found in the Judaic religion (primarily the Old Testament) and the latter is exemplified in the Hellenistic religion(s). The former states that human fellowship with God is possible only by keeping the law, the latter states that humane fellowship with God is possible only through a deification of mankind.[71] This way of analysing content in relation to a basic motif is Nygren's suggestion for a scientific theology: "By continually testing the fundamental motif in relation to the factual material, theology has the possibility of strictly objective argumentation, and it is this above all that gives to a theology that works systematically 'the sure progress of a science.'"[72]

Nygren's program was not left without reply. At Uppsala, attempts were likewise made to justify a rational discourse about God on common criteria, but their proposals were different. It is noteworthy that the Uppsala school had a longer prior history than Lund. I take the books by Anders Jeffner to be the climax of the Uppsala school, but Rasmusson shows there was a long development from Nathan Söderblom's ecumenical theology to Jeffner's "life-view" program.[73] I will not go into this development here; instead I stick to Hägglund's general characterization of the program: "Charakteristisch für das neue Programm in Uppsala ist, daß die wissenschaftliche Aufgabe hauptsächlich auf die Vorfragen der systematischen

---

68 Nygren, *Meaning and Method*, 12.
69 Nygren, *Meaning and Method*, 372–73.
70 Nygren, *Meaning and Method*, 374. This is expanded in Nygren's book *Eros and Agape*, published in two parts in Swedish in 1930 and 1936, and as a whole in English in 1953.
71 Nygren, *Meaning and Method*, 374–75.
72 Nygren, *Meaning and Method*, 12.
73 Rasmusson, 'A Century of Swedish Theology,' 143–45.

Theologie beschränkt wird. "⁷⁴ This is seen in the writings of Ragnar Holte, Jarl Hemberg, and especially in Anders Jeffner, on whom I focus in the following.[75]

Jeffner's main concern is to understand the possibility of academic theology in the context of religious studies. His idea was to focus on prolegomenal questions as a way of closing in on theological issues.[76] He included exegetical inquiries, historical interpretations of main texts, correlational reflections between theological concepts and human experiences, but also the analysis of the logical implications of various doctrines and an assessment of the character of the religious metaphors and analogies.[77] In his book *Kriterien christlicher Glaubenslehre*, he discusses the possibility of doing theology in relation to a number of criteria: indirect criterion, criterion of experience, criterion of science, and a logical criterion.[78] The reason for discussing these criteria is related to a concern for establishing the intersubjective character of theology: "Das primäre Kriterienproblem in der Glaubenslehre besteht darin, solche intersubjektiv feststellbaren Eigenschaften von Lehren und sprachlichen Ausdrücken für Lehren anzugeben, an deren Vorliegen man erkennen kann, dass diese Sätze, die diese Lehren ausdrücken, G-Sätze [Glaubenslehraussagen/statements of faith] sind. "[79] According to Jeffner, the criteria justify positive argumentation for faith: "Dieser Terminus steht dafür, (a) dass die explizit argumentativen Teile der Glaubenslehre klare Kriterien für G-Sätze aufweisen oder zumindest enthalten und (b) dass es erlaubt und möglich ist, diese Kriterien auch auf die nicht explizit argumentativen Teile der Glaubenslehre anzuwenden. "[80] To

---

74 Hägglund, 'Skandinavische Beiträge zur Methodenfrage der Systematische Theologie,' 372. "Characteristically for the new program in Uppsala is that the scientific task is mainly confined to prolegomenal questions." (Translation MAM)
75 Before I go into Jeffner, it is worth mentioning that the Uppsala school is still very much alive, as seen in the works of Thomas Ekstrand's non-metaphysical and praxis-oriented theology, in Mattias Martinson's agnostic and unapologetic theology, and also, I believe, in Mikael Stenmark's descriptive approach to worldviews; the latter I think is of note to add to Rasmusson's presentation. Cf. Rasmusson, 'A Century of Swedish Theology,' 147–48.
76 What he in his textbook from 1981 called "roads" to theology (*Vägar till teologi*, Uppsala 1981).
77 Hägglund, 'Skandinavische Beiträge zur Methodenfrage der Systematische Theologie,' 372.
78 Anders Jeffner, *Kriterien christlicher Glaubenslehre: Eine prinzipielle Untersuchung heutiger protestantischer Dogmatik im deutschen Sprachbereich*, Studia doctrinae Christianae Upsaliensia 15 (Uppsala: Almqvist & Wiksell, 1977). As the subtitle says, the book is structured as a critical examination of dogmatic German literature, but it is also a presentation of Jeffner's own program.
79 Jeffner, *Kriterien christlicher Glaubenslehre*, 15–16. [The primary problem of criteria in the doctrine of faith is to specify such intersubjectively ascertainable properties of doctrines and linguistic expressions for doctrines by the presence of which one can recognize that these sentences expressing these doctrines are G-sentences [Glaubenslehr-aussagen/statements of faith]. (Translation MAM)] He restates the demand for intersubjective methods several times, e. g., p. 27.
80 Jeffner, *Kriterien christlicher Glaubenslehre*, 27. "This term stands for (a) that the explicitly argumentative parts of the doctrine of faith have or at least contain clear criteria for G-phrases and (b) that it

be able to give positive arguments for faith content is a prerequisite for theology to be deemed a scientific discipline, and to be able to give positive arguments for a presentation of the Christian faith should not be seen as controversial but evident.[81]

For the purposes here, the most relevant chapters are chapter five on "Wissenschaftskriterien" and chapter seven on "Christlicher Glaube und wissenschaftliche Argumentation." The goal of Jeffner's project is to contribute to a scientific understanding of theology.[82] In chapter five, he identifies the use of a positive, a negative, and a demarcation criterion in the German literature, which are enlightening to investigate, and Jeffner makes the presentation pedagogical by stating a "schema" for each of the criteria:

- The schema of the positive: "Wenn P ein religiöser Satz ist und P mit wissenschaftlicher Methode wahrscheinlich gemacht werden kann, dann ist P ein G-Satz."[83]
- The schema of the negative: "Wenn P in Deutung P1 einer wahrscheinlichen wissenschaftlichen Behauptung widerspricht, dann ist P1 kein G-Satz."[84]
- The schema of the demarcation: "Wenn P ein wissenschaftlich prüfbarer Satz ist, dann ist P kein G-Satz."[85]

Jeffner is very critical of the positive criterion (seen, e. g., in Pannenberg) but open to the other two. Jeffner also reflects on the possibility for making both metaphysical statements and the aligned religious statements hypothetical and then taking the negative and the demarcation criteria as boundary marks by using the schema, "[w]enn P ein religiöser Satz ist und P mit wissenschaftlichen Methoden in Vereinigung mit einer bestimmten Metaphysik wahrscheinlich gemacht werden kann, dann ist P ein G-Satz."[86] I understand Jeffner's proposal as a new formulation of the congruity principle as stated by Scholz (see above). The scientific method sets the boundary for metaphysical proposals, however this is to be understood.

---

is allowed and possible to apply these criteria also to the non-explicitly argumentative parts of the doctrine of faith." (Translation MAM)

81 Jeffner, *Kriterien christlicher Glaubenslehre,* 28.
82 Jeffner, *Kriterien christlicher Glaubenslehre,* 8.
83 Jeffner, *Kriterien christlicher Glaubenslehre,* 87. "If P is a religious proposition and P can be made probable by scientific method, then P is a G proposition." (Translation MAM)
84 Jeffner, *Kriterien christlicher Glaubenslehre,* 89. "If P in interpretation P1 contradicts a probable scientific claim, then P1 is not a G-sentence." (Translation MAM)
85 Jeffner, *Kriterien christlicher Glaubenslehre,* 93. "If P is a scientifically testable proposition, then P is not a G proposition." (Translation MAM)
86 Jeffner, *Kriterien christlicher Glaubenslehre,* 96. "If P is a religious proposition and P can be made probable by scientific methods in union with a certain metaphysics, then P is a G-proposition." (Translation MAM)

This is developed further in chapter seven when Jeffner discusses his "principle of integration." The idea is that the various disciplines should not work in isolation but that each should instead integrate the knowledge of the other disciplines. In theology, we must accept that knowledge produced in other disciplines determines how we understand the age of the universe, the age of the earth, human evolution, the formation of the scriptures, and so on. We must integrate various aspects such as science, moral, aesthetic experience, religious experience etc., into a comprehensive theory.[87] In this way, Jeffner seeks a broader understanding of knowledge than is usually defended in analytic philosophy.[88] Common human experience becomes the critical standard when we read the Bible and when we seek to legitimize statements of faith. But again, it all has to be intersubjectively testable and cannot contradict any accepted scientific knowledge, according to Jeffner.[89]

To sum up, there are many concerns shared between Uppsala and Lund, but they also differ on important points:[90]

- Whereas the object of theology for Nygren was Christianity in its historical manifestation, for Jeffner it was God and God's relationship with man.
- Whereas Nygren had a very narrow understanding of knowledge in the tradition of analytic philosophy, Jeffner sought to broaden the notion of knowledge to include experience and feelings.
- Whereas Nygren sought to purify Christianity by isolating the central motif of the tradition, Jeffner would hear nothing of a pure Christianity.
- Nygren was generally sceptical of the Enlightenment and therefore also of modernity in general. Jeffner on the other hand had a positive approach to these phenomena and sought to integrate them ("science" and "culture") within theological reasoning.

The Swedish debate emphasized the importance of theology as a rationally justified public discourse on commonly accepted criteria. The debate was between different perspectives on how this concern was best met.

In the final example of chosen debates from the 20th century, I introduce the debate between the theological schools of Chicago and Yale. These schools can

---

87 Jeffner, *Kriterien christlicher Glaubenslehre*, 140.
88 I take this quotation to be exemplary: "Man muss mit Hilfe von Gedankengängen, die im Prinzip von allen vernünftigen Menschen akzeptiert werden können, zeigen, dass er vernünftig und erlaubt ist, Erkenntnisansprüche gelten zu lassen, die die empirische Wissenschaft *übersteigen*." Jeffner, *Kriterien christlicher Glaubenslehre*, 141 (italics added). See also the diagram in *Vägar till teologi*, 102.
89 Jeffner, *Kriterien christlicher Glaubenslehre*, 140–142.
90 Rasmusson, 'A Century of Swedish Theology', 146.

also be seen as different attempts to clarify how theology can speak about God in a rationally justified way in line with or polemically against commonly accepted criteria.

2.2.4 Chicago vs. Yale

In this fourth debate, two perspectives again differ in their views of how theology justifies its rationality, how public its discourse is, and which criteria should be used in assessing theological proposals.

As a first characteristic, the Yale school seeks to develop a specific Christian vision for theology, interpretation of texts and community living, whereas the Chicago school seeks to engage in an open-ended conversation with external interests on neutral ground.[91] This is increasingly an important debate because the pluralization of the public sphere in the West is an empirical fact; how Christian academic theology should respond to this development is the theme of an expanding body of literature that can be seen as a continuation of the two American positions.[92]

I start with the Chicago school and describe the main concerns and ideas of its thinkers, and then proceed with the Yale school, focusing of the same topics. Two representatives are selected for each perspective, well aware that others would be of interest as well.

The Chicago school has not been as unified as the Yale School, so this is more of a cluster-term for a pattern of thought where a number of theologians share certain concerns and visions. Contrary to the post-liberalism of the Yale school, these thinkers seek to develop a Christian theology that can meet publicly accepted criteria in a mutual exchange of ideas through critical and self-critical conversation. The approaches to this project are numerous and disparate but they are not the chief concern here. Instead, I focus on how these theologians describe the possibility of making theology a rationally justified public discourse. I first deal with Paul Tillich's suggested solution before I look into one of his main heirs, David Tracy.

Paul Tillich is arguably the most influential voice from the Chicago school. Methodologically, his "method of correlation" has been widely influential in seeking to correlate general human concerns about existence with Christian thought: "The 'situation' to which theology must respond is the totality of man's creative self-interpretation in a special period [...] The following system is an attempt to use the 'method of correlation' as a way of uniting message and situation. It tries to

---

[91] Jeanrond, *Theological Hermeneutics. Development and Significance*, 163.
[92] See, e. g., David F. Ford, *The Future of Christian Theology* (Oxford: Wiley-Blackwell, 2011); Gavin D'Costa, *Theology in the Public Square. Church, Academy and Nation* (Oxford: Blackwell, 2005); Stanley Hauerwas, *The State of the University. Academic Knowledges and the Knowledge of God* (Oxford: Blackwell, 2007); Volf and Croasmun, *For the Life of the World*.

correlate the questions implied in the situation with the answers implied in the message."[93] Tillich's concern is to make Christianity relevant for modern people. This is extremely broad and diffuse, so how does he make it more precise? According to Tillich, the "kerygma" must be re-articulated in such a way as to address the despair experienced by many people today. God as the "ground of Being," the "ultimate concern" of human existence, is what must be brought into contact with humanity.[94] As shown above, what makes theology a *public* concern is the shared problems of a given time that theologians must seek to answer. This is radically different from the postliberal emphasis on tradition that I refer to later. This book has more in common with the general approach of Tillich but differs in the ideas that are proposed as answers. Where Tillich's existential philosophical theology has a therapeutic element at its core, the concern for this book is to emphasize theology's contribution to the quest for truth that I presuppose is central to all scientific work.

I now briefly mention an heir of Tillich's who has been very influential in theological thought and who has contributed substantially to the discussion of what a rationally justified public discourse about God involves.[95] David Tracy presents his own vision for such a discourse in his tome, *The Analogical Imagination*. The new context for theological reflection is the "culture of pluralism," and here theology has to make a contribution to three different publics: society, academy, and church.[96] This is a helpful clarification of the different arenas in which theology must engage, and Tracy's is a perspective I share. In relation to the present book, it is most important to identify Tracy's vision for an academic theology.[97] As he points out, to talk about theology as an academic discipline is often related to a discussion of the nature and validity of theological methods. But the institutional contexts are also important, as is also apparent in the proposals of Anders Nygren and Wolfhart Pannenberg, who explicitly engaged with the institutional debates in Sweden and Germany, respectively. The institutional setting in North America is very different, with a much larger number of private universities than in Germany

---

93 *Systematic Theology*, vol. 1 (Chicago: University of Chicago Press, 1973), 4 and 8.
94 Mary M. Veeneman, *Introducing Theological Method. A Survey of Contemporary Theologians and Approaches* (Grand Rapids: Baker Academic, 2017), 43–49.
95 Werner Jeanrond mentions theologians such as Langdon Gilkey, Hans Küng and Edward Schillebeeckx as heirs of Tillich who have developed the correlational method in various directions and emphasized especially phenomenological questions more properly. See Werner Jeanrond, 'Correlation Theology and the Chicago School,' in *Introduction to Christian Theology. Contemporary North American Perspectives*, ed. Roger A. Badham (Louisville: Westminster John Knox, 1998), 137–53. I also think that diverse theologians such as Gordon D. Kaufman, Karl Rahner, and Bernard Lonergan could be seen as heirs of Tillich.
96 Tracy, *The Analogical Imagination*, 1–31.
97 See especially Tracy, *The Analogical Imagination*, 14–21.

and Sweden, yet the pluralistic North American culture still calls for a clarification of the academic status of theology.[98] This is very important, as I also emphasized in the engagement with the Swedish debate, because the external factors are influential to the configuration of academic theology.[99] One consequence of this is that if theology is supposed to work in a pluralistic university setting, no personal faith can be required. Instead, common criteria for scientific work must be articulated and followed.[100] When Tracy published his book in 1981, many theologians were engaged in this endeavour. Tracy himself mentions Anders Nygren, Gerhard Ebeling, Wolfhart Pannenberg, Schubert Ogden, Van A. Harvey, Hans Küng, Gordon D. Kaufman, Langdon Gilkey, and Johann Metz, and more could have been mentioned. The difficulty for theology is not to accept common criteria, but instead to be "public" and "normative" at the same time (a difficulty that theology shares with philosophy, according to Tracy).[101]

A central problem for Tracy is to understand what kind of discipline theology is. He follows Stephen Toulmin's analysis and differentiates between compact, diffuse, and would-be disciplines.[102] The "compact" disciplines are most often found in the natural sciences; they have agreed-upon collective ideals and a disciplinary locus for the production of reasons, while the "diffuse" and the "would-be" disciplines lack these disciplinary directions and organizations.[103] Theology – together with disciplines such as psychology, sociology, anthropology, etc. – is not a compact discipline because it has a number of fundamental problems pertaining to its activities. Two are especially central: "first, a lack of a clear sense of disciplinary direction and thereby a host of unresolved problems; second, a lack of adequate professional organization for the discussion of new results."[104] This results in two

---

98 Tracy, *The Analogical Imagination*, 14–15. Tracy mentions four different institutions: the seminary, the church-related colleges and universities, the divinity schools of older secular universities, and private or state colleges and universities. (p. 15)

99 As Tracy says, "All proposals for theological method are affected by the particular academic location of a particular theologian." (p. 15)

100 This requirement is very broad and may contain disparate perspectives. A postliberal figure such as Stanley Hauerwas would agree but for very different reasons. See his Hauerwas, *The State of the University. Academic Knowledges and the Knowledge of God*; Stanley Hauerwas, 'Why the "Sectarian Temptation" Is a Misrepresentation: A Response to James Gustafson (1988),' in *The Hauerwas Reader*, ed. John Berkman and Michael Cartwright (Durham and London: Duke University Press, 2001), 90–110.

101 Tracy, *The Analogical Imagination. Christian Theology and the Culture of Pluralism*, 17. I return to the question of normativity in chapter seven.

102 Tracy, *The Analogical Imagination*, 17.

103 Tracy, *The Analogical Imagination*, 17–18.

104 Tracy, *The Analogical Imagination*, 18.

characteristics that Tracy believes are important for contemporary theology: "preoccupation with methodological debate and a tendency to splinter the field into competing 'sects.'"[105] In this regard, the present book is a symptom of an impasse that has held for forty years; nevertheless I intend to present a renewed case for some "agreed-upon standards, criteria and norms for theological performance."[106] Tracy himself mentions Bernard Lonergan's program for theological method as a prime example of a rationally justified public discourse about God.[107] This demand for publicness is mandatory for Tracy, and he is thus in line with the concerns of the Chicago school: "Without that demand for publicness – for criteria, evidence, warrants, disciplinary status – serious academic theology is dead."[108] This poignant statement sums up the concern and vision of the Chicago school. A very different concern and vision is expressed in the Yale school, to which I now turn.

The Yale school – or "postliberal theology" – refers to a number of theologians who were/are concerned to move beyond a liberal worldview without reverting to a preliberal worldview. What this means is a rejection of claims of universal knowledge (often called an Enlightenment value) and claims to common religious experiences (religious liberalism). This gives them a number of presuppositions that Alister McGrath summarizes as basically three: (1) antifoundationalism, (2) communitarianism, and (3) historicism.[109] There is no universal knowledge; instead, the rationality of the community as it is located in a specific tradition is what matters.

The Yale school is closely associated with the names of George Lindbeck and Hans Frei. Therefore, it is indeed the perspective of these two that is introduced in what follows.

As seen in the most important work of this school of thought, George Lindbeck's *The Nature of Doctrine* from 1984, there are a number of important intellectual inspirations that guide the postliberal reflection. Of special importance is (a) the late Wittgenstein's philosophy of language with its emphasis on context and language games,[110] (b) Alasdair MacIntyre's "tradition ethics," where a tradition is claimed to have its own standard of moral reasoning that is historically and socially mediated, and (c) the sociology of culture and religion, primarily in the works of sociologists Clifford Geertz and Peter L. Berger.[111]

---

105 Tracy, *The Analogical Imagination*, 18.
106 Tracy, *The Analogical Imagination*, 18.
107 See Bernard Lonergan, *Method in Theology* (Toronto: University of Toronto Press, 1971).
108 Tracy, *The Analogical Imagination*, 21.
109 McGrath, *Christian Theology. An Introduction*, 92.
110 See also, e. g., Paul L. Holmer, *The Grammar of Faith* (San Francisco: Harper & Row, 1978).
111 George A. Lindbeck, *The Nature of Doctrine: Religion and Theology in a Postliberal Age*, (Philadelphia: Westminster Press, 1984), 7–29.

The implication is that postliberal theology rejects the possibility of a rationally justified public discourse about God (as I have explicated it here) because the criteria and standards cannot be made intersubjective across paradigms. The standard of a tradition will always be "intrasystemic" and there is no possibility of assessing theories from a neutral standpoint. Truth is not an objective category but is seen as a fidelity towards the (doctrinal) tradition. Even though postliberalism has been very influential for decades (and still is), it has had its critics from the beginning. Accusations of lapsing into a Christian ghetto, and of fideism or tribalism, have been widespread.[112] This critique has been vocal from Chicago, where theologians articulated a diametrically opposite vision for theology as a rationally justified public discourse about God.

Lindbeck's colleague Hans Frei is arguably the second most influential postliberal theologian and especially his emphasis on the Christian story or narrative in contrast to propositional dogmatism and liberal philosophy has set the fashion. In works like his masterpiece *The Eclipse of Biblical Narrative*[113] and the late selection of articles *Theology and Narrative*,[114] he develops his understanding of a narrative approach to theology, while in his influential study *Types of Theology*[115] he develops a typology of approaches to Christian theology that he finds both inspirational and problematic.[116] Much of Frei's work is on historical theology but has still been influential for the development of the postliberal program,[117] and his own alignment with the program can be seen in proclamations such as the initial definition of theology in *Types of Theology*: "Theology is an aspect of Christianity and is therefore partly or wholly defined by its relation to the cultural or semiotic system that constitutes that religion."[118]

The two different approaches to theology in the Chicago and Yale schools, respectively, are prevalent and influential in contemporary theology. The Chicago school is very disparate in its ideas and solutions, but its members share a common concern for developing a theology that is a rationally justified public discourse

---

112 McGrath, *Christian Theology. An Introduction*, 92–93.
113 Hans W. Frei, *The Eclipse of Biblical Narrative: A Study in Eighteenth and Nineteenth Century Hermeneutics*, Revised Edition (New Haven: Yale University Press, 1980).
114 Hans W. Frei, *Theology and Narrative: Selected Essays*, ed. George Hunsinger and William C. Placher, (New York: Oxford University Press, 1993).
115 Hans W. Frei, *Types of Christian Theology* (New Haven and London: Yale University Press, 1992).
116 David F. Ford has an accessible summary of this book in David F. Ford, *Theology. A Very Short Introduction*, Second Edition (Oxford: Oxford University Press, 2013) and his presentation of the important focal points of Frei's theology is very helpful: David F. Ford, 'On Being Christologically Hospitable to Jesus Christ: Hans Frei's Achievement,' *The Journal of Theological Studies* 46, no. 2 (October 1995): 532–46.
117 Lindbeck, *The Nature of Doctrine*, 119.
118 Frei, *Types of Christian Theology*, 2.

about God, and thus this stream of thought is a background for the vision of the present book.

Two enlightening quotes from Jeanrond present the differences in their essence: "Lindbeck wishes to explicate Christian faith inside the (actual or potential) Christian movement, while the correlational theologians attempt to develop a public rationality of that faith," and "[w]hile correlational theology emphasizes the need for a global dialogue and all available critical and self-critical strategies to deal with the question of religious truth, postliberal theology has abandoned this kind of search for truth in favour of discussing a given communitarian praxis of narrating and living the Christian story."[119] With the emphasis of the present book on the scientific pursuit of truth and the demand for a rationally justified public discourse about God, it is obvious that it is situated somehow in the tradition of the Chicago school and in opposition to the Yale school without anticipating a specific substantive (regarding content) theology that is similar to that of the Chicago school in all its diversity – its concerns and ideas are related to mine but should not necessarily be conflated with mine.

2.3   Conclusion

The above brief historical overview of some of the important debates on the scientific status of theology in the 20th century has shown that the questions about theology's scientific status are prevalent in theological thought and discussion. The Barth-Scholz debate focused on the questions of what theology is and who is to set the terms for the execution of academic theology. Barth saw theology as a distinct discipline because of the axiom of the revelation of God, while Scholz criticized this approach for being circular. The German debate in (primarily) the 70s was very diverse with many participants, as we saw exemplified in the works of Diem, Pannenberg, and Sauter. Diem saw theology as a servant of the church and radicalized Barth's understanding, Pannenberg was preoccupied with developing a scientific theology that met commonly accepted criteria, and Sauter occupied a middle position with an emphasis on theology's ecclesiastical responsibilities and at the same time argued that it should engage in conversations with contemporary concerns about the meaning of life. As for Sweden, I showed that the schools in Lund and Uppsala – represented by Nygren and Jeffner – shared a common concern for developing a theology that met commonly accepted criteria but that their proposals differed. Nygren developed a strictly descriptive methodology with a focus of the fundamental motif of Christianity as an answer to the question of

---

119 Jeanrond, 'Correlation Theology and the Chicago School,' 148.

the eternal. Jeffner allowed for a broader scope of themes than Nygren, but also demanded that positive arguments for faith content be provided. In the final debate presented, between Chicago and Yale, I showed that Tillich and Tracy emphasized that theology should be developed in close exchange with other disciplines and that the correlation method is the suitable method for this task. The new context of pluralism makes a holistic approach necessary. Lindbeck and Frei disagreed and emphasized instead the communitarian aspects of doctrines, ethics, narrative, and community. There is no universal rationality to adhere to, and thus theology should focus on internal criteria.

The discussion of what science is, what theology is, and how these two should interact, is still prevalent in every context within academic theology. This brief historical overview shows important examples of how the issue was addressed in the 20th century, and it provides the background for the concerns that drive the present book.

In the rest of the book, I focus on a systematic study of the research question, but this historical chapter is not just an appendage to the textual body; it is rather an important way to situate the discussion historically and contextually. From the historical debate I draw a number of concerns that are mirrored in the represented perspectives, especially the concern for how theology can be faithful to its own tasks and aims and still meet commonly accepted criteria. In the following chapters, I suggest different problems and possibilities than those that many of the previous debates focused on, but I share the driving concern to understand what scientific theology is and how it is properly done. Thus, I adopt a number of attitudes and ambitions for theology, but I bring new insights through the developed understanding of what theology is, how this understanding is challenged by objections based on commonly accepted criteria for science, and how responses to these objections could be articulated.

Part Two:
A Scalar Understanding of Systematic Theology

Chapter Three: A Definition of Scientific Systematic Theology

3.1 Introduction

Throughout history many have discussed what theology is – its nature, aim, methods, philosophy, and so on and so forth. It may seem pretentious to try to add anything to this complex debate, both because the history is so intricate and because the terms are so dynamic. Neither "theology" nor "science" is a fixed term, hence they have changed – and still change – through time and according to context.[1] What I aim at in this chapter is to discuss the best version of systematic theology that I have found in the literature, seeking to provide theologians with the conceptual framework they need in order to go do what they aim to do: present a *rationally justified discourse about God*.

I am concerned with the branch of theology called " systematic theology." In theological education, this branch usually includes three distinct fields, namely dogmatics, ethics, and philosophy of religion. From time to time, one also finds practical theology (homiletics, counseling, sociology of religion, missiology etc.) counted as part of systematic theology. As with systematic philosophy, one can understand the adjective "systematic" in two ways: (1) as concerning completeness of scope; the aim of connecting all the various thematic components of theology; and (2) as establishing a counterpart to historical studies.[2]

In an article from 2008, the Danish theologian Niels Henrik Gregersen suggested a stratification of systematic theology into three *distinct* levels[3] which I find stimulating for reflection.[4] That the strata are *distinct* does not mean that there is

---

1 See, e. g., Peter Harrison, who focuses on the terms "science" and "religion" Peter Harrison, *The Territories of Science and Religion* (Chicago: The University of Chicago Press, 2017). But the same goes for "theology" according to McGrath, *The Territories of Human Reason*.
2 Puntel, *Structure and Being. A Theoretical Framework for a Systematic Philosophy*, 1.
3 Niels Henrik Gregersen, 'Dogmatik som samtidsteologi,' *Dansk Teologisk Tidsskrift* 71 (2008): 290–310; see further Niels Henrik Gregersen, 'Samtidsteologiens horisont og fokus,' *Dansk Teologisk Tidsskrift* 74. årg., no. 2 (2011): 167–72. See also the discussion of Gregersen's proposal in Asle Eikrem, 'Dogmatikk som samtidsteologi,' *Dansk Teologisk Tidsskrift* 74. årg., no. 2 (2011): 152–66.
4 Gregersen adopted and developed the tripartition of systematic theology from Hans Frei's stratification in Frei, *Types of Christian Theology*, 20–21. The development is especially in relation to systematic theology 3. There have been other suggestions for a tripartition of systematic theology with different emphases and scopes, e. g., David Tracy who talks about *fundamental, systematic,* and *practical* theology in David Tracy, *The Analogical Imagination*, 54–59 and Gordon Kaufman who talks about

no dynamic relationship between them. There is, and I point to this fact several times and give some examples of the dynamic relationship when relevant. But the strata have different methods and different criteria, and thus they are distinct. But theology is a coherent discipline, thus the distinct and different strata are at the end integrated into theology as such. I discuss these three strata at length in the following, but I shall outline the basic idea here: systematic theology 1 is the explication through "thick" descriptions of the basic expressions of believers' faith (sometimes called "first-order theology"), systematic theology 2 is the systematization of the semantic structures in Christianity aiming at internal coherence (sometimes called "second-order theology"), and systematic theology 3 is then the production and comparison of different semantics, Christian and non-Christian, aiming at external coherence (coherence with knowledge from other disciplines). I take systematic theology 3 to be the most critical aspect of a scientific systematic theology and what gives scientific credibility to the other levels, 1 and 2, and I argue for this claim in the following chapter.[5] The systematic theology that works at the first and second levels is thus derived from the third level, even though inspiration, criticism, elaboration, and much else can move between the strata.[6] I therefore call work on systematic theology 3 "normative ontology," and I explain why in 3.4.2.

There are several reasons for the choice of Gregersen's conceptualization of systematic theology as a starting point for reflection. I think it is fruitful because it recognizes the plurality of the field, is able to incorporate many different approaches and focal points, and differentiates the ambition and scope of different problems and questions. Furthermore, it is analytically productive because it can be used as a research tool for engaging with new questions, as there are basic and urgent questions at all three levels, and there are exchanges between the different strata that make the field coherent. And lastly, the third level is described as a distinct field of research where the strength of theology compared with other semantic traditions can be assessed. It is especially this last point I have in focus in the present book. In the following, I defend an implication of this model that Gregersen does not suggest or even mention: I argue that the credibility of systematic theology 3 justifies the scientific status of systematic theology 1 and 2. Even though fruitful work may still be conducted at the levels of systematic theology 1 and 2 if systematic theology 3 should turn out to be much less coherent than relevant alternatives, a compromised systematic theology 3 would nonetheless be a pivotal blow for the whole field. On the other hand, if systematic theology 3 turns out to be equal or even better than

---

first-order, *second-order*, and *third-order* theology in Gordon D. Kaufman, *An Essay on Theological Method* (Missoula: Scholars Press, 1975), 35–38.
5 Note that this is not Gregersen's argument, as I explain and develop it in the following.
6 I give two examples on how important themes at systematic theology 1 and systematic theology 2 is thematized on the background of a robust account of systematic theology 3 in 3.4.5.1.7.3.

relevant alternatives, this will lend scientific status to systematic theology 1 and 2 and their respective work. Some will undoubtfully find this claim provocative, but the driving motivation behind the endeavour presented here has been to investigate the strength of systematic theology in comparison to relevant alternatives in the academic debate of the 21st century, and I present the most coherent account I have been able to develop.

It is often said that most of the theological disciplines could also be conducted in other research disciplines, and that this should make theology irrelevant as a distinct discipline.[7] I recognize the argument, but while the argument may seem to have some initial plausibility, it fails for several reasons. To name only one: there will always be overlaps between disciplines, e. g., between medicine and biology; sociology, economics and political science; history and philology; literary studies and specific languages; mathematics and computer science; and so on and so forth. Still, in general, I find it unproblematic to say that particular subfields within the field of theology could be re-located to other faculties and disciplines without losing anything essential,[8] e. g., church history to common history, exegesis (OT/NT) to philology or history, etc. Theology is indeed a conglomerate of different vantage points on the vast field of "the Christian tradition," and as a field of study, we need all these different approaches in order to engage properly with the immense amount of data available. Because of the cultural significance of the Christian religion in the West, it seems reasonable to have a specific discipline studying this tradition, but the question remains whether cultural importance and proximity are enough to legitimize the work of systematic theology as a scientific discipline. Because I do a systematic study, I find these pragmatic reasons inadequate in the chosen context but not irrelevant in a broader discussion that takes place all the time in many contexts.

Besides a unified focus (that is, "the Christian tradition") and a cultural proximity principle, is there something distinct about systematic theology that separates it from other fields of study? And is it necessary to exhibit such distinctness in order to be its own discipline? The question is stated poignantly by the Danish philosopher Caroline Schaffalitzky in a recent debate book: "If [theological research] cannot be located in other disciplines – because it is descriptive, unacceptably normative, colored and/or dogmatic – then at the same time this means that it does not live up to the criteria for science and therefore cannot be regarded as scientific research. If

---

7 I return to this objection to scientific theology in chapter eight.
8 Most of these subfields are already in some way or another a part of other disciplines at many universities. Even for universities with separate theology departments, it is not unusual to have other disciplines that address theological questions. Examples are trivial, for example that the study of common history will also engage with church history, studies in classical philology will also deal with the letters of Paul, etc.

what characterizes specific theological research is something else, then we must have an account of what this something else is before we can assess whether it can exist."[9] I will not discuss Schaffalitzky's assessment of systematic theology here,[10] but I want to use it as a springboard to say that I think systematic theology does indeed have something distinct in its nature and that this is important for its role and self-understanding. Thus, I want to offer a proposal of what the *raison d'être* of systematic theology is and determine whether this is enough to qualify it as a legitimate scientific discipline. In the following chapters, I subject this understanding of systematic theology to scrutiny in order to test the strengths and weaknesses of the definition. The aim is thus to identify the best understanding of systematic theology that I have found and to test it against the best objections that I have found in order to assess the scientific credibility of systematic theology.[11]

At the beginning of the discussion of what systematic theology is, I want to state two presuppositions. First, as already stated above, I am not interested in the obvious fact that there are forms of systematic theology that are not scientific. Even though it could be interesting to make a taxonomy of the whole field of systematic theology[12] – e. g., (a) some versions of theology are not scientific and do not want to be so, (b) others are not scientific but claim to be so, etc. – I restrict myself to making a detailed case for a version of systematic theology that could be deemed scientific (presented in this chapter). It is not obvious that it is possible to explicate such an systematic theology using generally accepted scientific criteria, on the contrary it is disputed. Thus, I must emphasize that I do not seek to give a simple yes-or-no answer to a complex question ("is systematic theology a scientific discipline?") but rather to give a detailed presentation of criteria for a robust version of systematic theology as a contribution to the discussion of how systematic theology best can be construed in a proper scientific way (given the framework presented).

Second, because I do not discuss every possible understanding of systematic theology, there may be (plenty of) other versions of systematic theology that should be regarded as scientific (articulated in other theoretical frameworks). This would not be surprising given the fact that theology is still a discipline practiced at many

---

9 Translation MAM. "Hvis denne forskning ikke kan finde sted på andre fag – fordi den er deskriptiv, uacceptabelt normativ, farvet og/eller dogmatisk – så betyder det samtidig, at den ikke lever op til kravene for videnskab og derfor ikke kan betragtes som forskning. Hvis det er noget andet, der kendetegner specifik teologisk forskning, må vi have en redegørelse for, hvad dette andet er, før vi kan tage stilling til, om det kan findes." Caroline Schaffalitzky, 'Findes teologisk forskning?', in *En plads blandt de lærde: Teologiens videnskabelighed til debat*, ed. Michael Agerbo Mørch (Frederiksberg: Eksistensen, 2019), 174.
10 I engage with Schaffalitzky's assessment thoroughly in chapter eight.
11 See chapters four through eight for this discussion.
12 These taxonomies can be found elsewhere, see Frei, *Types of Christian Theology*; Ford, *Theology. A Very Short Introduction*.

acclaimed university institutions. But it is beyond the scope of this work to discuss these other approaches to systematic theology. As stated in the introduction, the way we understand science and the criteria for scientific research provide the conditions for systematic theology. Much theological work accepts some kind of antirealism or scepticism and works from that. This approach can be fruitful in many ways. I seek, instead, to understand how systematic theology can work in a theoretical framework that presupposes realism. Again, a systematic theology that presupposes realism can also be developed in numerous configurations, and mine is only one of these. The reason for presupposing realism is that I take it to be the strongest challenge to systematic theology that, while difficult to engage with, is also stimulating.[13]

Again, the point is not privative – to judge other understandings of systematic theology as unscientific – but heuristically to work with the question: "Given these criteria, how can systematic theology best be construed as a scientific discipline?"

I want to add that standard textbooks on the methods of systematic theology or different typologies of systematic theology reveal the plurality of the field, but this heterogeneity is neither an obvious strength nor a weakness; it is rather a natural result of the complexity of the field and the collapse of foundationalism in epistemology. This is one of the reasons why a transparent methodology, robust and well-described methods, and explicated criteria and theoretical frameworks for scientific work are needed, even though these will always be up for revision and refinement. I am seeking neither essentialism nor exclusivism, but I do aim to present coherent accounts of both science and systematic theology.

In the following, I define and discuss the three levels of systematic theology as I understand them in this book. I proceed from 1 to 3, indicating the increasing importance for the question of the scientific nature of systematic theology, even though, in the proposed account, the legitimacy of levels 1 and 2 derives from level 3, which could thus be addressed first. The point is not the order of the discussion but the maintaining of the three levels as distinct fields of systematic theology. To avoid misinterpretations, I must also add that the numbers 1–3 are heuristic and not qualitative. Level 2 is not more important than is level 1 (or vice versa); it only indicates the structure of the argument for this book' specific purpose. This is also to say that the relationship between the strata is not hierarchical or temporal but logical. In the practice of scientific theology there are transactions between the strata all the time, and much work begins at systematic theology 1 or systematic theology 2 before it proceeds to systematic theology 3 (if not the robustness of

---

13 In other words, I assume that systematic theology could probably meet postmodern criteria for scientific research, but I want to investigate whether systematic theology can meet criteria that are less controversial and also met by other disciplines. Realism is contested or challenged, but hardly anyone argues that disciplines which assume realism (physics, biology, etc.) are not scientific. Thus, I want to assess if systematic theology can meet the same criteria that these disciplines do.

systematic theology 3 is presupposed, which it often is). The logic is that when we clarify what theologians do, the three strata appears as three distinct strata with different criteria and methods, but they are inevitably seen as strata of one coherent discipline.

3.2 Level One (Systematic Theology 1)

At the first level (systematic theology 1), the researcher seeks to explicate the semantics of the different Christian practices, such as liturgical elements, sacraments, prayer, worship, etc. These are elementary expressions of faith and have their natural *Sitz im Leben* in the church as well as in the everyday life of the believer. Gregersen says that the method for systematic theology 1 is *explication* and the criterion is *authenticity*.[14] In the following, I explore this method and this criterion.

The method of "explicating" used towards religious expressions can be understood in different ways. Asle Eikrem clarifies the use of the term in his response article,[15] and I will follow his line of thought because Gregersen agrees that Eikrem adequately qualifies the use of the term by making it more precise.[16] The method of explication arises from the object.[17] The object here is Christianity and Christian semantics as they are understood and practiced today. Systematic theology 1 is not entitled to reinvent Christianity[18] but uses the language and terminology of already existing and practiced Christianity.[19] To listen to and then describe religious discourse is the first task of systematic theology 1. But mere quotations will not suffice;

---

14 Gregersen, 'Dogmatik som samtidsteologi,' 308.
15 Eikrem develops his response in close relation to Puntel, who developed the notion of "explication" in, e. g., Lorenz B. Puntel, *Being and God: A Systematic Approach in Confrontation with Martin Heidegger, Emmanuel Levinas, and Jean-Luc Marion*, trans. Alan White (Evanston: Northwestern University Press, 2011), 209–12.
16 Gregersen, 'Samtidsteologiens horisont og fokus,' 168–69.
17 To be more precise, for Eikrem the method follows from his configurational or structural ontology in line with the thought of Puntel. Here ever more fine-grained explications of structures are needed. I am not convinced that Gregersen's acceptance of Eikrem's understanding of the method of explication implies his acceptance of the ontology behind. Thus, I focus on the shared focus on systematic theology 1's object in the following.
18 It is an open question whether systematic theology 2 and/or systematic theology 3 are entitled to reinvent or revise Christianity for example through new concepts, distinctions, definitions, etc. So here the point is only that systematic theology 1 does not have this ambition but seeks solely to explicate the semantics of the practitioners.
19 Gregersen, 'Dogmatik som samtidsteologi,' 307. Thus, theologians call it baptism, prayer, preaching, mission, scripture etc., even though the explication of the practices may differ in content from how the believer understands them.

systematic theology 1 is devoted to "thick descriptions," to use anthropologist Clifford Geertz' term, borrowed from philosopher Gilbert Ryle;[20] the term means that the whole context with all its intricate intentions, meanings, feelings, values, hopes, desires, etc., is taken into account in shaping our understanding of the discourse.[21] Because human behaviours are not pure actions but semantically structured ones, we need a more sophisticated approach than mere straightforward descriptions.[22]

Eikrem specifies Gregersen's point here, insisting on a third-person perspective on the discourse, because if we rest our case with a description of first-person perspectives, we reduce systematic theology 1 to sociology of religion.[23] Eikrem then defines: "explication means to determine more fully the language in relation to its pragmatic, semantic, and ontological dimension,"[24] and further, "[a] theological exposition of what Christians do is, in other words, a theoretical presentation of Christian meaningful [*meningsbærende*] actions, in which one seeks to determine optimally the pragmatic dimension of the semantic structures which constitute 'Christianity's big universes of meaning.'"[25] The method of explication is to articulate and present ever more refined structural analyses. In other words, we seek to (re)describe what Christians do (pragmatics) but also what they express when they do it (semantics) and the coherence of what is expressed. Gregersen agrees more or less but insists that this explication in systematic theology 1 must be

---

20 Clifford Geertz, 'Thick Description: Toward an Interpretive Theory of Culture,' in *The Interpretation of Cultures. Selected Essays* (New York: Basic Books, 1973), 3–30. See additionally the interesting elaboration of this term in relation to theological hermeneutics in chapter six of Kevin J. Vanhoozer, *Is There a Meaning in This Text? The Bible, The Reader, and the Morality of Literary Knowledge* (Grand Rapids: Zondervan, 1998), 281–350. The point is that the notion of thick descriptions can be applied both from an etic (outsider) and emic (insider) perspective.
21 Researchers themselves are not distanced observers with no commitments either. This makes it more difficult to do research on systematic theology 1 than we may imagine at first. I agree with David Munchin when he writes, "[t]heology's data is massively, necessarily, even exultantly theory-infected. Furthermore, prior commitments of the most sensitive sociological nature – matters of faith, power, authority and money – are clearly absolutely rife within all theological discussion." David Munchin, "'Is Theology a Science?" Paul Feyerabend's Anarchic Epistemology as Challenge Test to T.F. Torrance's Scientific Theology,' *Scottish Journal of Theology* 64, no. 4 (2011): 450.
22 Eikrem, 'Dogmatikk som samtidsteologi,' 155.
23 Gregersen agrees with this correction in his response, Gregersen, 'Samtidsteologiens horisont og fokus,' 168–69.
24 Eikrem, 'Dogmatikk som samtidsteologi,' 156. "Eksplikasjon handler om nærmere å bestemme språket i relasjon til dets pragmatiske, semantiske og ontologiske dimensjon." Italics removed, translation MAM.
25 Eikrem, 157. "En teologisk fremstilling av hva kristne mennesker gjør, er m.a.o. en teoretisk presentasjon av kristne meningsbærende handlinger, der man forsøker optimalt å bestemme den pragmatiske dimensjonen ved de semantiske strukturer som utgjør 'kristendommens store betydningsuniverser.'" Translation MAM.

recognizable to contemporary Christians.[26] This is also his reason to reject Eikrem's demand for coherence concerning systematic theology 1; coherence is also the theoretical term for harmonization of faith expressions, and Gregersen insists that we should avoid harmonizing too soon in our research process (thus, coherence as a criterion is postponed to systematic theology 2).[27] There is a fundamental difference between the respective ambitions of Gregersen and Eikrem that I believe reflects a widespread disagreement among systematic theologians and which concerns the degree to which we should embrace the polydoxy of everyday Christianity. Eikrem – following Puntel – demands that a "fully determined" worldview and thus a coherent explication of the potentially incoherent actions and expressions of believers is mandatory.[28] Gregersen on the other hand wants to listen more carefully to the fractures in contemporary Christianity and accepts that this is a part of our messy world. Pure and clear expressions are rare in real life (e. g., because much of religious language is metaphorical), and Eikrem's demand thus seems utopian.[29] Eikrem's arguments for requiring coherence are strong, but I agree with Gregersen that we will gain more from keeping the different strata distinct. It is valuable and interesting to know the semantics of everyday believers even though their views may be incoherent and fragmented. The researcher will have to choose between attempting to reconstruct the views of the informants as coherently as possible and trying to interpret them in the way that is most probable i. e., as very open and fragmented. The researcher will often have very precise research questions that will prompt very open answers, which the researcher will then have to interpret. And because the answers are vague, this can be done in multiple ways. If we choose to present a coherent reconstruction, we have to say that this is a possible interpretation but that other less coherent interpretations are equally probable.

As mentioned above, Gregersen points to "authenticity" as a criterion for systematic theology 1.[30] But a critical assessment of this criterion may show that we need an exchange between method ("explication") and criterion ("authenticity") because we will see that the criterion we develop for systematic theology 1 will inevitably criticize statements made by believers. In other words, when we explicate

---

26 Thus our description of, e. g., baptism as an action (pragmatics) and of the meaning of baptism (semantics) must be recognizable to church-goers and practitioners; Gregersen, 'Samtidsteologiens horisont og fokus,' 169.
27 Gregersen, 170. Note that Geertz was critical of seeking coherence for the descriptions too, see Geertz, 'Thick Description: Toward an Interpretive Theory of Culture,' 17–18.
28 Eikrem, 'Dogmatikk som samtidsteologi,' 156–57.
29 Gregersen, 'Samtidsteologiens horisont og fokus,' 170.
30 Gregersen develops his understanding of this criterion in his post-doctoral dissertation in relation to Wolfhart Pannenberg. See Niels Henrik Gregersen, *Teologi og kultur: Protestantismen mellem isolation og assimilation i det 19. og 20. århundrede*, Acta Jutlandica, LXV:1 (Aarhus: Aarhus Universitetsforlag, 1988), 236–38.

the expressions of everyday believers, I expect that we will find expressions that may be hard to integrate into an authentic Christianity. This presumed problem will be discussed now.

Because Gregersen accepts and defends the plurality and heterogeneity of the Christian faith[31] at level one, we may ask, what exactly is "authentic Christianity"? We may understand it pragmatically as "faithful Christ-believing" or tentatively as a preliminary concept in a quest to discover what authentic Christianity

is, where we take what we find in churches as prime examples of what Christians believe. We may also approach the question of authenticity more theoretically and use philosopher Edmund Husserl's phenomenological notion of "eidetic variation"[32] to ask, what are the invariant structures that constitute Christianity? This question could be addressed through many subquestions such as, which ideas reconstruct the framework in such a way that we lose the "authentic Christian faith"? By which standards and by whose judgment can we assess this demarcation line?[33] When are the small variations – that are evident in every tradition – accumulated to such an extent that we end up with something different? And is "authentic Christianity" a package with doctrines, rituals, practices, lifestyles, values etc., or is it a doctrinal core focusing, e. g., on the creeds or central Bible verses or something else? Is there a phenomenon in the world that we may call "authentic Christian faith," or is it something more like an academic concept where specialists seek to identify subtle distinctions that believers themselves do not care much about? And what is the antonym for "authentic"? Is it inauthentic, fake, heretical, postulated, or something else? All these questions arise from the attempt to encircle what "authenticity" might mean as a criterion for systematic theology 1.

Is it a viable solution to focus more on the creeds to isolate authentic Christianity? Maybe so. We could say that authentic Christianity is expressed in the three ecumenical creeds of the early Church, so that these symbols are the doctrinal

---

31 E. g., "Men kristendommen eksisterer nu engang ikke I destilleret form, men er et samlebegreb for en række forskellige udformninger af kristendommen, hver med sine traditioner og livsformer." ["But Christianity does not exist after all in a distilled form, but is a collective term for a number of different arrangements of Christianity, each with its own traditions and life shapes."] Gregersen, 'Dogmatik som samtidsteologi,' 297. (Translation MAM) Or, "Ligesom alle andre betydningsuniverser er kristendommen polyvalent, dvs. åben for flere mulige fortolkninger." ["Like all other universes of meaning, Christianity is polyvalent, i. e., open to several possible interpretations."] Ibid., 303. (Translation MAM) This non-essentialism is not well explicated in this article, but, still, it is endorsed by Eikrem, cf. Eikrem, 'Dogmatikk som samtidsteologi,' 159–60.
32 Dan Zahavi, *Husserl's Phenomenology*, (Stanford: Stanford University Press, 2003), 38–39.
33 If we herald a pragmatic point of view, we may say that anyone who understand themselves as a Christian is a Christian, and who is to decide against that? To believe is a life experiment and only in systematic theology 2 do we make this life experiment a thought experiment and test its validity. But where does this leave the criterion of authenticity? Cf. Gregersen, *Teologi og kultur*, 228.

minimum that constitute what Christianity is. Starting from this minimum, the different traditions and confessions are free to have their own practices, rituals, doctrinal emphases, etc. But as the tradition shows, the creeds themselves are open to a broad variety of interpretations, so the mere words of the creeds do not take us far. To give only one example: The opening line of the Apostles' Creed – "I believe in God, the Father almighty, Creator of Heaven and Earth" – is subject to intense discussion and study in contemporary theology. How should we understand the notion of "God"? What does it mean that God is "Father"? What does it mean to be "almighty" and to be "Creator"? The traditional theistic notion of God is contested within a post-metaphysical/post-theistic discourse; the notion of Father is contested in, e. g., feminist theology; the notion of God being almighty is contested due to the problem of evil and the problem of divine hiddenness; and the notion of God as creator is contested due to modern cosmology and evolutionary biology. The point is that the ecumenical creeds are underdetermined and open for continual (re)interpretation.[34]

In his post-doctoral dissertation, Gregersen provides an extensive discussion of three criteria for systematic theology (consistency, coherence, and authenticity). Here he lists two presuppositions for the criterion of authenticity: (1) that systematic theology recognizes that the burden of legitimation rests on novel expressions that differ from traditional expressions;[35] (2) that the Bible has a special status as proto-text for Christianity.[36] But what has appeared since the late 80s is a much more wide-spread scepticism towards such a presupposition as (1). Scholars affiliated with minority studies of all sorts question this "centralism" and ask why the burden is not diametrically opposite; if someone would defend the status quo, it is his job to present a persuasive case for it, as opposed to such a burden resting with those who dissent from the status quo. This is a complicated discussion that I do not address here. Suffice it to note that even though I agree with Gregersen's ambition to let the believers' own semantics be the object of systematic theology 1, the relationship between the method (explication) and the criterion (authenticity) is not easy to handle.

Authenticity in itself is apparently not that useful (it is too diffuse), and it seems better to place it as a sub-criterion under a (main) criterion of coherence. Authen-

---

[34] To counter, we may say that even though the notion of "God" is not given unequivocally, theology still affirms that God exists. To deny that God exists thus falls outside of authentic Christianity. The same could be said about the other statements in the creed. We may not agree what "creator" means, but to deny "creation" is to place oneself outside of authentic Christianity.

[35] Gregersen labels this "the criterion for tradition" [traditionskriteriet], pointing to the great resource of well-tested Christian interpretations throughout history that works both as an inspiration and as a street lamp to light the way forward. Gregersen, *Teologi og kultur*, 238.

[36] Gregersen, *Teologi og kultur*, 237.

ticity is thus a material aspect of the criterion of coherence, and authenticity can be understood as a tool both for selecting the data among which you seek coherence and for choosing which data are most central to integrate in the whole theory.[37] This is something else than Eikrem's suggestion which ultimately harmonizes the heterogeneity of the faith expressions too early in the process; instead it is procedure that sees as authentic those faith expressions that can be incorporated coherently into a viable systematic theology 2 theory. Since there are several of these, it is not too restricted. On the other hand, there is not infinite possibilities which gives us certain boundaries for the task.

3.3 Level Two (Systematic Theology 2)

The second level (systematic theology 2) in Gregersen's account refers to the type of theological work we traditionally call *dogmatics*.[38] Dogmatics seeks to present the Christian faith coherently, focusing on the basic grammar and semantic structures of the Christian faith.[39] The distinct focus here at systematic theology 2 is the demand for *internal* coherence as the broad assessment criterion of the articulation of the Christian faith. Such articulation will often be materialized as versions of different confessions, but it is also important to emphasize that this work can lead to (fundamental) revisions of existing traditions, and systematic theology 2 thus has a kernel of self-reflexive criticism.

But many difficulties arise here. Dogmatics needs to make choices, well aware that no single account of *the* Christian faith is possible.[40] There is no agreement about the understanding of the different *loci*, and thus even though all types of Christian theology seem to accept (e. g.) the notion of the Trinity (judging by the liturgical place of this doctrine in the Church), there is no agreement on how to articulate this doctrine, and it is done in many different kinds of ways.[41] Agreement and consensus are not gateways to truth, and this alleged difficulty for systematic

---

37 Søvik, *The Problem of Evil and the Power of God*, 95–98.
38 The term "dogmatics" is not prevalent in contemporary systematic theology, but I use the term here in agreement with Gregersen's terminology.
39 Gregersen, 'Dogmatik som samtidsteologi,' 308–9.
40 There is no single "true" Christianity, cf. Gregersen, 'Dogmatik som samtidsteologi,' 309. Or stated differently: "Theology is forced [...] into a selective reception of tradition" [*Teologien tvinges ... ud i en selektiv traditionsreception*], Gregersen, *Teologi og kultur*, 230. (Translation MAM)
41 E. g., Karl Rahner, *The Trinity*, trans. Joseph Donceel (London: Burns and Oates, 1970); Fred Sanders, *The Image of the Immanent Trinity. Rahner's Rule and the Theological Interpretation of Scripture*, vol. 12, Issues in Systematic Theology (New York: Peter Lang, 2005); Catherine Mowry LaCugna, *God for Us: The Trinity and Christian Life* (New York: HarperSanFrancisco, 2006); Gijsbert van den Brink, 'Social Trinitarianism: A Discussion of Some Recent Theological Criticisms,' *International Journal*

theology 2 should therefore not be overstated; the point is merely descriptive, to explain why there is such a widespread plurality concerning systematic theology 2. Thus, systematic theology 2 will in practice be a kind of "confessional theology," broadly understood as a type of theological work that cannot take place in hermetic separation from a tradition,[42] but must employ – critically, yet engaged – the resources of a tradition to think things through. The plurality and scope of the Christian tradition makes pure novelty unlikely, and thus new suggestions at different *loci* will in fact be situated within a specific confession.[43] This emphasis reflects Gregersen's description of the task of systematic theology 2: "The task of dogmatics as Theology2 is, then, to formulate well-considered proposals as to how we *could* interpret Christian language today."[44] Systematic theology 2 is then a critical and sober re-description of the Christian semantics articulated as a thought-experiment that systematic theology 2 presents as a possibility for the lived faith to consider. It appears that Gregersen will reserve truth-claims for another stage and instead see the proposals of systematic theology 2 as possibilities and suggestions. I am critical of this defensive understanding of the work of systematic theology 2 and instead suggest that the coherent theories developed by systematic theology 2 be seen as genuine truth candidates for the theological community to consider. This is also to avoid the implicitly relativistic notion that such a tentative strategy of proposals suggests.

Gregersen suggests three methods for systematic theology 2: re-description, systematization, and construction. *Re-description* is what we do when we re-systematize the Christian faith; we describe Christian semantics in a way that seeks to optimize the coherence and scope of our system. *Systematization* is the attempt to formulate a *coherent* account of the Christian faith. *Construction* is the task of systematic theology as it is articulated in the quotation above (footnote 44). Thus, these methods also constitute the criteria for the work at this stratum: internal coherence and

---

of Systematic Theology 16, no. 3 (2014): 331–50; Wolfhart Pannenberg, *Systematic Theology* , trans. Geoffrey W. Bromiley, vol. 1 (Grand Rapids: Eerdmans, 1991), chap. 5.

42 This is a condition for all kinds of thinking and not just theology, as, e. g., Alasdair MacIntyre has shown: Alasdair MacIntyre, 'Epistemological Crises, Dramatic Narrative and the Philosophy of Science,' *The Monist* 60, no. 4 (October 1977): 453–72. We inherit a language, an epistemology, values, etc., and we cannot subject everything to doubt and start with a *tabula rasa*.

43 Thus, even though liberal or postmodern theologians may understand their theologies as "non-confessional," they will always be different variations of for example liberal *Lutheran* theology, postmodern *Anglican* theology, etc. This is inevitable because no one thinks in a vacuum but always in continuation and/or alteration of a specific tradition.

44 Gregersen, 'Dogmatik som samtidsteologi,' 309. "Dogmatikkens opgave som teologi2 er da at formulere velgennemtænkte forslag til, hvordan man *kunne* tolke det kristne sprog i dag." Original italics, translation MAM.

theological scope.[45] This implies that theological theories can be assessed by their degrees of coherence. What *theological scope* implies is vaguer because Gregersen does not explain this metaphor. What I translate as "scope"[46] [da. "rumfang"] is a metaphor that is not developed in Gregersen's account. As I understand it, his point is to resist theological tribalism – we need to be generous in our proposals for dogmatics because Christianity can be systematized in a number of ways.[47] It is not clear precisely what this entails, and for this reason I suggest that the more transparent criterion of internal coherence should gain focus.

As is made explicit in 3.4.5, I am inspired by Lorenz Puntel, who has come into increased focus in Norwegian systematic theology in the last decade or so.[48] Puntel makes coherence the pivotal criterion for truth and meaning, and he develops a fine-grained account of coherence that is very useful for the study of systematic theology. But such a very nuanced philosophy as Puntel's is not mandatory for the definition of systematic theology 2, and I will thus relegate an introduction to Puntel's philosophy to the discussion of systematic theology 3 below. Here it suffices to draw attention to Gregersen's short presentation of coherence as a criterion for systematic theology. According to him, coherence consists of two components: "(1) the interpretation's [*tydning*] degree of inclusivity and completeness; (2) the ability of an interpretation [*tydning*] to connect individual statements coherently and uniformly."[49] Coherence is thus a holistic criterion understood as the integration of as many elements as possible in an optimal way with as many connections as possible between the elements, because the singular possible truth statements strengthen each other by their mutual connections.[50] We can never attain a complete account of reality, but the more coherently we can systematize the Christian semantics, the stronger a truth candidate it is.[51]

Coherence theory could also solve the potential conflict between two versions of the same doctrine; if the one is clearly more coherent than the other, the be-

---

45 Gregersen, 'Dogmatik som samtidsteologi,' 308–9.
46 Another translation could be "capacity."
47 Cf. Niels Henrik Gregersen, 'Den generøse ortodoksi,' in *Den generøse ortodoksi. Konflikt og kontinuitet i Kristendommen* (København: Eksistensen, 2016), 17–49.
48 So has Gregersen, it seems, though indirectly through his admiration and use of Pannenberg. Note, however, that Gregersen is critical towards the Hegelianism of Puntel's philosophy in his response to Asle Eikrem; see Gregersen, 'Samtidsteologiens horisont og fokus,' 172, fn. 6.
49 Gregersen, *Teologi og kultur*, 232. "*1. tydningens grad af inklusivitet eller komplethed og i 2. tydningens evne til en sammenhængende og enhedspræget sammenknytning af de enkelte påstande.*" Original italics, translation MAM. Earlier, Gregersen has pointed to consistency as a criterion for scientific work and with these two points, Gregersen is thus in agreement with Rescher, Puntel, and Pannenberg about the three components of the best theory of coherence.
50 Gregersen, *Teologi og kultur*, 232.
51 On the notion of "truth candidate," see 2.3.7.

liever should affiliate with the first even if the second is the traditional view of her confessional tradition.[52] But the comparison is impeded by the complexity of many doctrines. The complexity springs from the internal relation between the single *loci* so that a low degree of coherence may not appear in the single *locus* but implicate difficulties concerning another doctrine – but then again, the believer should be broadening her systematic reconstruction to include more data and then seek to upgrade the level of coherence so that the internal relation between the *loci* is strengthened. All this for the sake of attaining the goal of systematic theology 2, as Atle Søvik has formulated it: "the goal of a Christian theory is to have an understanding of God's revelation in Christ that is more coherent than alternative understandings."[53]

Here, the point of departure has been to use Gregersen's terminology to encircle the strata of systematic theology 1 and systematic theology 2. Concerning systematic theology 2 we have seen directly above that according to Gregersen, systematic theology 2 focuses on the internal coherence of Christian semantics. I want to add that the theories developed must be seen as truth candidates such that the systematized semantics must be assessed by their implicit truth-claims. I also want to add, and I think this is in line with Gregersen's intention, that "internal" does not restrict systematic theology 2 to the Biblical material but relates to many external data sources such as the natural sciences in the explication of a theological notion of creation. But "internal" refers to a limitation such that the explications are not compared with relevant alternatives in order to judge whether the Christian dogmatics is more coherent than its alternatives. Such comparison of semantics and ontology is reserved for systematic theology 3.

---

52 This is, of course, not as easy as it sounds. The recent debate in Norway between theologians Asle Eikrem and Harald Hegstad about the Cross of Christ shows the many complicated layers of such a discussion, where Eikrem subscribes to a controversial yet strictly coherent notion of Christ's atonement, and Hegstad defends a more traditional Lutheran understanding of Christ's penal substitutionary work where coherence is not the *main* criterion. Harald Hegstad, 'Var korset nødvendig?', *Teologisk tidsskrift* 8, no. 1 (2019): 41–54; Asle Eikrem, 'Korsets gåte?', *Teologisk tidsskrift* 8, no. 3 (2019): 198–204; Harald Hegstad, 'Koherent uten å være autentisk?', *Teologisk tidsskrift* 8, no. 3 (2019): 205–9; Asle Eikrem, 'Mer korsteologi – Ny replikk til Hegstad,' *Teologisk tidsskrift* 9, no. 1 (2020): 52–58; Harald Hegstad, 'Korset som uttrykk for Guds kjærlighet – Sluttreplikk til Asle Eikrem,' *Teologisk tidsskrift* 9, no. 1 (2020): 59–62. Inside a protestant tradition we may say that coherence can work as an instrument for a church that sticks to *semper reformanda*. But maybe this does not solve much. Traditionally, protestants specify this dictum by saying *secundum verbum Dei*, which brings us back to the start, for what if a clearly more coherent explication of a doctrine contradicts Scripture? See Kevin J. Vanhoozer, *Biblical Authority after Babel: Retrieving the Solas in the Spirit of Mere Protestant Christianity* (Grand Rapids: Brazos Press, 2016) for a delicate account.

53 Søvik, *The Problem of Evil and the Power of God*, 97.

3.4 Level Three (Systematic Theology 3)

3.4.1 Niels Henrik Gregersen's Understanding of Systematic Theology 3

Systematic theology 3 in Gregersen's account concerns comparisons between different semantics, Christian and non-Christian. The methods for this type of work are, according to Gregersen, both descriptive (comparisons) and creative (constructions). As with systematic theology 1 and systematic theology 2, the methods are only mentioned and not developed in Gregersen's text, but it is clear that he thinks the comparison between the different semantics in question must take place in relation to a close study of the different practices, texts, rituals, histories, traditions etc., of the respective semantics and, in relation to this, to identify similarities and differences between the semantics. The constructive method(s), on the other hand, concern(s) creative suggestions for how to relate Christianity to other spheres of life in the 21st century.[54] At this level, it is not sufficient to systematize the Christian faith as coherently as possible internally; the coherent account must be externally oriented and thus actually be influenced by and influence contemporary semantics (therefore making "external coherence" the criterion for work at this level). Thus, according to Gregersen, the theologian must work closely with other scholars at this level, especially the philosopher of religion and the ethicist.[55] The comparison is between alternative religions and worldviews that also thematize Being as such and as a whole (to use Puntelian terms; see below).

As we have seen, one of the focal points of discussion between Gregersen and Eikrem are the relationships among the different strata. Eikrem suggests "explication" as a method for systematic theology 3 as well, whereas Gregersen suggests it for systematic theology 1 only (3.2). The reason for this is that Eikrem's structural/relational ontology determines pragmatic, semantic, and ontological conditions as relations and explicating these specific relations is thus programmatic at all levels.[56] To explicate these relations is to both increase the level of detail and to broaden the perspective of the analysis. Gregersen hesitates in his response because it is not obvious what is gained by this work. According to Gregersen, it leads to

---

54 Gregersen, 'Dogmatik som samtidsteologi,' 309–10.
55 Gregersen, 'Dogmatik som samtidsteologi,' 309. In this context, Gregersen does not mention natural scientists as close collaborators, but he does so elsewhere (p. 310). His understanding is that new discoveries in the sciences can become subjects for thematization within systematic theology, e. g., the notion of natural laws that became important in the 16th and 17th centuries and thus important for theology to relate and respond to.
56 Eikrem, 'Dogmatikk som samtidsteologi,' 160. This understanding is developed in relation to Puntel's many works; see especially Puntel, *Grundlagen einer Theorie der Wahrheit*, chap. 2.

too much superfluous work on the one hand, and on the other hand this way of explicating relations at all levels is too abstract and more or less utopian to conduct in its entirety.[57] I place myself somewhere in between these positions because I follow Eikrem's suggestion that explications of relations are important at all strata (systematic theology 1–3), but I also agree with Gregersen that a division of labour between the strata is helpful – even though we should not forget that there are continuous transactions among the strata (as I have emphasized several times). The method can be the same on all three strata, and yet they are kept distinct because it is not the methods but the themes and the tasks that distinguish the strata.

3.4.2 Systematic Theology 3 as Normative Ontology

After the presentation of Gregersen's understanding of systematic theology 3 in 3.4.1, I shall now explicate more precisely how systematic theology 3 is to be understood in this book.

Systematic theology 3 is the focal point of the stratification of systematic theology, since this is where the scientific nature and status of systematic theology is discussed. As stated in the introduction to this chapter (3.1), systematic theology 3 is about "normative ontology," but both these words are contested and therefore need to be explained. By instinct, many are critical toward *normative* claims because they signal a standard that is neither discussed nor argued for but instead simply asserted. This intuition is perhaps especially present in relation to theology and religious studies because of the historical link between academic scholars and religious communities. Normativity, though, should not be taken this way here. Normativity can mean many things,[58] but here I understand the notion in a particular and delimited way: Normativity comes in degrees, and I understand normativity to be the natural outcome of careful research that convinces a researcher of a certain perspective. Even though she should be aware of the fallibilistic nature of human knowledge, she should also boldly present her research with the best arguments she can think of, and as long as others cannot counter the evidence, she should count it as our best current perspective.[59] Stated shortly: *Normativity means judging whether something is true or not given a specific norm or standard.* In this book I take this standard to be that of coherence.[60]

---

57 Gregersen, 'Samtidsteologiens horisont og fokus,' 172.
58 See further in chapter seven on normativity.
59 Mikael Stenmark, 'Science and a Personal Conception of God: A Critical Response to Gordon D. Kaufman,' *Journal of the American Academy of Religion* 71, no. 1 (March 2003): 175–81; MacIntyre, 'Epistemological Crises, Dramatic Narrative and the Philosophy of Science.'
60 At this point I am only dealing with descriptive normativity, which I take to be non-ethical. The notion of normativity in relation to ethics is another field that I do not consider here.

At least since Kant, the notion of *ontology* is considered dubious and problematic by some traditions.[61] Kant aimed to show that our cognitive faculties are not disposed to settle ontological questions in general and that important particular questions about, e. g., cosmology cannot be answered unequivocally.[62] There is still close to no agreement among philosophers about anything in relation to ontology. There are still no "established facts," and "philosophers don't agree about *anything*," as Peter van Inwagen cheekily claims.[63] The reason is that there is "no information" besides the intellectual resources of past thinkers,[64] and thus "[i]f two metaphysical theories are in competition, no experiment will decide between them."[65] The problem is fundamental for van Inwagen; he deems the questions we ask about ontology, or metaphysics, "defective," because they *cannot* be answered.[66] This is because, according to Philip Clayton, there seem to be "subjective leftovers" in many complicated research questions, especially of metaphysics.[67] But is this really a convincing description of the study of ontology? I do not think so. It seems to me that van Inwagen – and Kant for that matter – expects both too much and

---

61 Remember the famous quote from the *Vorrede* of the first edition of *Kritik der reinen Vernunft*: "Dadurch aber stürzt sie sich in Dunkelheit und Widersprüche, aus welchen sie zwar abnehmen kann, daß irgendwo verborgene Irrtümer zum Grunde liegen müssen, die sie aber nicht entdecken kann, weil die Grundsätze, deren sie sich bedient, da sie über die Grenze aller Erfahrung hinausgehen, keinen Probierstein der Erfahrung mehr anerkennen. Der Kampfplatz dieser endlosen Streitigkeiten heißt nun Metaphysik." ["But thereby it plunges into darkness and contradictions, from which it can assume that somewhere hidden errors must lie at the bottom, but which it cannot discover, because the principles which it uses, no longer recognize a touchstone of experience, since they go beyond the limit of all experience. The battlefield of these endless disputes is now called metaphysics."] (Translation MAM) Immanuel Kant, *Kritik der reinen Vernunft. Erster Teil.*, vol. 3, Kant Werke (Darmstadt: Wissenschaftliche Buchgesellschaft, 1968), 11.
62 See the four conflicts (*Widerstreit*) in Immanuel Kant, *Kritik der reinen Vernunft. Zweiter Teil.*, vol. 4, Kant Werke (Darmstadt: Wissenschaftliche Buchgesellschaft, 1968), 409–33. For Kant, the problem arises when our thinking releases its hold on our experience: "Wenn wir unsere Vernunft nicht bloß, zum Gebrauch der Verstandesgrundsätze, auf Gegenstände der Erfahrung verwenden, sondern jene über die Grenze der letzteren hinaus auszudehnen wagen, so entspringen vernünftelnde Lehrsätze, die in der Erfahrung weder Bestätigung hoffen, noch Widerlegung fürchten dürfen ..." ["If we do not merely apply our reason, for the use of the principles of understanding, to the objects of experience, but dare to extend them beyond the limits of the latter, there emerge doctrines that can neither hope for confirmation nor fear refutation in experience..."] Ibid. 410.
63 Peter van Inwagen, *Metaphysics*, Second Edition, Dimensions of Philosophy Series (Cambridge: Westview Press, 2002), 9 and 13.
64 van Inwagen, *Metaphysics*, 9.
65 van Inwagen, *Metaphysics*, 15.
66 van Inwagen, *Metaphysics*, 10.
67 Philip Clayton, *The Problem of God in Modern Thought* (Grand Rapids: Eerdmans, 2000), 40–41.

too little from this field of study.[68] Too much if only final verification can work as a standard for "answered" questions, and too little if he suggests that *everything* is (necessarily) unsettled in the study of ontology. For one thing, as philosophers of science commonly agree today, we can settle for less than final verification,[69] and for another, we need to remember that the distinction between observable and non-observable entities is arbitrary and is adjusted all the time as our knowledge expands. Thus, what we may consider unsolvable today because we lack information in a given field may be solvable tomorrow due to new discoveries.[70] Philosophers of science suggest different strategies for doing work in a stage of research where we lack sufficient information to decide between different hypotheses, one of them being the so-called *Inference to the Best Explanation*, which is a way to choose the hypothesis that best explains the set of evidence we consider. The point against van Inwagen's view is twofold: (1) that philosophers like van Inwagen underestimate our research tools in the field of ontology and also present too stubborn an understanding of what counts as metaphysics. One of the things that has become clear since the critique of Logical Positivism is that metaphysics is inevitable. Kant and his heirs seek to overcome metaphysics, but metaphysics cannot be avoided because metaphysics is about the most fundamental or basic conditions of reality (and therefore exists by definition). Metaphysics may be hidden, but it is possible – if not mandatory – to try to explicate the metaphysical structures that reality consists of. (2) Even though it is correct that many metaphysical questions in themselves (that is, not the empirical implications a metaphysical claim may have, and which can be tested (e. g., with the method of hypothetical deduction)) cannot be answered by experiments in an empirical way, we have good tools to choose between theories. Some metaphysical theories can be more or less falsified through experiments because alternatives explain the data and the results in a more coherent way. But even without empirical tests, we have coherence theory as a helpful tool to assess and choose between theories. I next explain this in greater detail.

I consider the best tool to be the coherence theory of truth and meaning as it is developed by Rescher and Puntel. They have carefully developed an approach to ontology that gives us a comprehensive perspective for analysis and synthesis. What

---

68 As Clayton says, "One may *believe* that metaphysics will never overcome pluralism, that there will always remain vast tracks of unresolved differences, the subjective leftovers of rational debate. But to end rational discourse with one's Thomist or Hegelian (or Buddhist) colleagues based on this expectation is as unjustified as to pretend that one has already refuted their positions through arguments. Not all pluralists must be relativists." (ibid. 41).
69 Ladyman, *Understanding Philosophy of Science*, 129.
70 Ladyman, *Understanding Philosophy of Science*, 175. Think, for instance, of the possibilities of solving the dispute between monism (physicalism) and dualism (mind-body) through research in artificial intelligence.

is most valuable is that we can compare different theories by their respective degrees of coherence and thus choose the most coherent one as our best currently available theory, thereby making actual progress.[71] Thus, when van Inwagen states, "you are perfectly free to disagree with anything the acknowledged expert says – other than their assertions about what philosophers have said in the past or are saying at present,"[72] he is right in terms of not being intimidated by authorities and status symbols in the process of research, but he is far from right regarding the content of theories, because some theories are indeed more coherent, contain more evidence, are better-tested etc., than others. And even though we cannot prove ontological theories, we often have good enough tools to choose among them.

This may sound too idealistic, and it is indeed a challenge that every individual is only able to maintain an overview of a limited amount of data and often does not even know what she does not know (unknown unknowns), let alone whether others have been able to present the most coherent versions of their pools of data for comparison. But these challenges aside, coherence is still a good tool – and the best tool I would argue – that can be used to compare theories and judge between them, and van Inwagen's radical relativism should therefore not be followed.

To sum up: I take systematic theology 3 to involve theories of "normative ontology." Normativity means judging a theory to be true or not, given a specific norm or standard. Ontology, or metaphysics, is "discourse about the fundamental constitution of reality," the articulation of an understanding of reality as comprehensively as possible. This includes all sorts of subtopics (e. g., matter, language, history, knowledge, truth, time etc.) but systematic theology 3 is especially concerned with the role of the notion of the Christian God in its quest for understanding Being as such and as a whole.[73] In this book I take coherence as the best tool for judging something as true (normativity) and for comparing the strength of different ontologies. I take it to be important that systematic theology not only develops fine-grained theories of internal coherence (systematic theology 2) but is also able to show its relative strength compared to other coherent ontologies. As I said in 3.1, there are exchanges between the strata of systematic theology even though I emphasize the distinct division of labour between systematic theology 1, systematic theology 2, and systematic theology 3, and here we have a good example, because the external comparison of ontologies is made urgent by the explication of the understanding of the Christian God in systematic theology 2 as the all-determining reality. If this

---

71 In part three, I discuss how this is done in relation to the themes of falsification, testability, and intersubjectivity.
72 van Inwagen, *Metaphysics*, 12.
73 "Reality" is also emphasized to avoid the objection that theology creates "perfect fictions" where God plays a role without reference to experienced reality.

understanding is to be a viable truth candidate, it cannot be clearly less coherent than relevant alternatives.

Another reason here is that systematic theology 2 includes several theories that are not testable in any common way, such as the presence of Christ in the Eucharist or the reality of being born again in conversion or baptism. Such doctrines must be articulated in ways that are coherent with larger accounts of the Christian faith (systematic theology 2, internal coherence), but they must also cohere with larger theories that are intersubjectively testable (systematic theology 3). Note that the different strata of systematic theology are not isolated from one another but relate as parts of a whole. For this reason, it is also possible to explicate a precise theory of the presence of Christ (systematic theology 2) and then seek to explicate the implications for a larger ontology and compare the latter to alternatives. The point is not that we have to move upwards from level 1 to level 3 but that there are benefits from a division of labour.

Systematic theology 3 is the most important level of this book's argument because this is where the scientific nature of systematic theology (as a distinct discipline) is argued to be located. If systematic theology 3 can be justified, systematic theology 1 and systematic theology 2 will thereby be derivatively justified. The reason for this is twofold. First, the notion of God is widely contested in Western public discourse. This could be due to prejudices, lack of knowledge, a diffuse zeitgeist, or something else, but one of the tasks for systematic theology 3 is to investigate the possibility of a "responsible discourse about God"[74] given what we know in other fields of research and given the standards we currently have for research. If systematic theology 3 is not able to show the legitimacy of this discourse about God in comparison with relevant alternatives, it would compromise the work carried out in systematic theology 1 and systematic theology 2. I elaborate this argument in the following.

Secondly, the notion of God also implies that systematic theology 3 is a kind of research that *only* systematic theology can perform, not because it is esoteric, but because as a discipline it is dedicated to this exact work: to investigate the possibility of a responsible discourse about God, i. e., presenting *rationally justified public* discourse about God. And because it is the ambition here to locate the exact work that *only* systematic theology can perform in order to assess its strengths and weaknesses, this is the apex of the argument (see chapter eight). As indicated above, I am aware that there is no *single* account of systematic theology that every systematic theologian accepts, and there is no single notion of God that every theologian accepts, etc.; thus, what is presented in the present book is *one* take

---

[74] This term is adopted from Gijsbert van den Brink, *Philosophy of Science for Theologians: An Introduction*, Contributions to Philosophical Theology 12 (Frankfurt am Main and New York: Peter Lang, 2009), 159 et passim.

on systematic theology, but it is nevertheless the *best* articulation of systematic theology that I have found given the presuppositions and the theoretical framework of this book.

3.4.3 Why Systematic Theology 3 May be Scientific and Systematic Theology 1 and 2 Only Derivatively So

As stated briefly at the beginning of this discussion, the argument is that systematic theology 3 is what gives scientific legitimacy to the discipline of theology. Thus, systematic theology 1 and systematic theology 2(especially) are only scientific by derivation from systematic theology 3. For this reason, systematic theology 1 and 2 are legitimate and interesting in themselves but from other perspectives. They are scientific disciplines, but their legitimacy rests on the sustainability of systematic theology 3. But why is this? What is it about systematic theology 3 that is different from (especially) systematic theology 2? This important question is addressed in the present section.

The obvious problem for systematic theology 2 is that we do not know whether God exists or not.[75] We have Biblical texts that presuppose God's existence. We have other texts that presuppose it (apocryphal, pseudepigraphic, rabbinic etc.). We have a long tradition that argues for it, claims it, preaches it, worships it (church and theological history). We have contemporaries who claim it and tell of religious experiences (believers, churches, organizations, etc.). We have a rich collection of philosophical arguments, past and present, that sustain and deepen this view. But regardless of this plethora of written and experienced data, we have no final proof of God's existence, and the probability of God's existence may be said to be 0.5.[76] To explicate thick descriptions of church practices (systematic theology 1) or to systematize a coherent theology (systematic theology 2) in a such way as to be scientific is thus dependent on something else, namely a convincing account that belief in God is not wholly fideistic. A way to put it is to say that we must be able to make convincing arguments (e. g., hypothetic deductions) from which to show how God is related to our experienced world. And, further, that we need to show that this theoretical framework is not significantly weaker than available alternatives. This

---

75 Or maybe better: It is not obvious that God exists, because it is not a knowledge that systematic theology 3 has but systematic theology 2 lacks. But systematic theology 2 presupposes God's existence in a more intuitive way than systematic theology 3, where this is the central topic of discussion. It should be noted, further, that other sciences often do not know for sure what they claim but it is at least often more obvious that their entities exist, e. g., H_2O or tectonic plates and so on.
76 Paul Draper, 'Seeking but Not Believing: Confessions of a Practicing Agnostic', in *Divine Hiddenness. New Essays*, ed. Paul K. Moser and Daniel Howard-Snyder (Cambridge: Cambridge University Press, 2002), 197–214. Cf. Oppy, *Atheism and Agnosticism*.

is the reason why a failed systematic theology 3 will have significant implications for the statuses of systematic theology 1 and 2. Yet, this seemingly frictionless distinction between systematic theology 2 and systematic theology 3 is nuanced and complicated when we consider that in order to assess whether God exists, we must be able to make the concept of "God" meaningful. And God cannot be understood meaningfully without the work of systematic theology 2. Thus, we have here an instance of the necessity of systematic theology 2 for systematic theology 3 and see that the transactions among the strata go both ways (as said in 3.1).

But even with this qualification, it is still the argument here that a failed systematic theology 3 would compromise systematic theology 2. An example from another context might be helpful as an illustration. Generally, we don't take "astrology" to be a scientific discipline even though "astrology 1" and "astrology 2" could work properly in stating what practitioners of astrology believe, how they behave, what they perform etc., (a first-order astrology), or coherently describing and developing different systems of astrology (a second-order astrology). We don't even accept constructive astrology, which seeks to "sustain better lives" or promote human flourishing from a pragmatist point of view, as a scientific discipline, and all of this because we do not take astrology to present reliable truth candidates because it is far less coherent than available alternatives.

But can we take systematic theology 3 to be scientific if we are not able to prove God's existence? I think it is possible, because systematic theology 3's legitimacy as a scientific discipline rests on the strength of the arguments for God's *possible* existence as shown by the degree of coherence of a theoretical framework that integrates God (see further 3.4.5).[77] Note that the term "possible" can be misleading here, because it might refer to as little as "not contradictory." In this sense, e. g., astrology is possible even though most scholars would say it is possible to a very low degree. God's existence is contested, but it is much more likely for God to exist than for astrology to be true. For this reason, God's existence is *probable* to a much higher degree than astrology, which is an example of comparison with alternative theoretical frameworks. The point is, therefore, that systematic theology 3 unlike astrology is scientific (not falsified) yet still a distinct discipline conducting work that only systematic theology 3 can execute. This argument is legitimate, however, only if no other ontology is much more strongly corroborated than systematic

---

[77] This is done with rigor in the work of Richard Swinburne. See, e. g., Swinburne, *The Existence of God*. See also the discussion of the distinction between "justification" of positive religious statements and the "truth" of these in Dirk-Martin Grube, 'Justification Rather than Truth. Gotthold Ephraim Lessing's Defense of Positive Religion in the Ring-Parable,' *International Journal for Philosophy and Theology* 66, no. 4 (2005): 357–78.

theology 3 at the moment, i. e., if the basic ontological discussion is still open and ongoing.[78]

As with all other scientific work, I also take ontological theories to be fallible, and the strength of a theoretical framework is thus provisional, but this is not a weakness for systematic theology 3 in particular; it counts as a presupposition for all such reflection. What we can do is make the best possible cases for the different ontologies, compare them, and then judge which one we find most persuasive for the time being.[79] Because the implications of an ontology are substantial (e. g., ethical, concerning value or life-orientation, etc.) we should be cautious in our judgments, which makes it all the more important to have precise criteria for our work, a transparent methodology, and an intersubjective discussion based on precise data and arguments. In the next chapters, I consider whether systematic theology 3 can meet such standards and formal criteria. If not, this would possibly erode systematic theology as a distinct scientific discipline.[80]

3.4.4 The Sources of Systematic Theology 3

A particularly interesting task is to identify the sources of systematic theology 3. The reason is that the approach of coherence could give us a specific approach to the sources that stands in contrast to a more traditional, diachronic legitimation. Within systematic theology 2, I see it as unproblematic to list the four classic sources for the work: scripture, tradition, reason, and experience, also known as the quadrilateral. The different Christian traditions and theological traditions organize the hierarchy among these sources differently, and there is a wide possibility for variations on how they relate to and influence each other. I will not go into this variation here.[81]

Because I take the aim of theologians to be the presentation of "rationally justified discourse about God," the main focus is on reason. But how is "reason" to be understood as a source for systematic theology 3? This challenging question cannot be treated here;[82] instead, I discuss one use of reason that functions as a source

---

78 This brief example of a comparison between systematic theology 3 and astrology is further developed in the discussion of falsification in 5.2.2 and 5.2.7.4.
79 This is a qualified or minimal relativism in line with the thought of Puntel, as I have argued several times already.
80 On condition that the framework of the proposed account satisfies the phenomenon of systematic theology, of course.
81 See other contributions such as Kevin J. Vanhoozer, *Biblical Authority after Babel: Retrieving the Solas in the Spirit of Mere Protestant Christianity* (Grand Rapids: Brazos Press, 2016) and Alister E. McGrath, *Christian Theology. An Introduction*, Fifth Edition (Oxford: Wiley-Blackwell, 2011).
82 For two different views see, e. g., Richard Swinburne, *Faith and Reason*, Second Edition (Oxford and New York: Clarendon, 2005) and Alister E. McGrath, *The Territories of Human Reason: Science and Theology in an Age of Multiple Rationalities* (New York: Oxford University Press, 2019).

for systematic theology 3: thought experiments. These are relevant to discuss in order to understand how coherence theory often works in practice. After this short examination, I discuss the sources provided by the natural sciences (3.4.5.2), and the Bible and tradition (3.4.5.3).

3.4.4.1   Thought Experiments as a Source for Systematic Theology 3

An interesting source provided by reason for systematic theology 3 is thought experiments.[83] The thought experiment is a way to test hypothetical notions and suggestions, not through deductive proofs or inductive probability analysis (quantitative induction) but instead by assessing the coherence of experiments compared to relevant alternatives.[84] Often, thought experiments are given in stories, such as the famous "Gettier Problem" in epistemology, which considers the adequacy of "justified true belief" through a couple of short stories written as thought experiments.[85] Others are fictions used to illustrate fundamental philosophical problems, such as Gilbert Harman's "Brain in a Vat," Nick Bostrom's "Simulation Hypothesis," Bertrand Russell's "Russell's Paradox," or David Hilbert's "Hilbert's Hotel." Still other thought experiments illustrate theories in natural science and have the interesting ability to work as conclusive arguments, e. g., Galilei's "hammer and feather experiment" illustrating the law of falling bodies or Einstein's "accelerating elevator" illustrating general relativity.

When is it useful to construct a thought experiment, we may ask? When we need the tools for constructing crucial experiments, thought experiments seem to be important, according to Niels Henrik Gregersen.[86] Thought experiments

---

[83] The notion of the thought experiment is complex and also controversial. A substantial introduction is given in SEP: James Robert Brown and Yiftach Fehige, 'Thought Experiments,' in *The Stanford Encyclopedia of Philosophy*, ed. Edward N. Zalta (Metaphysics Research Lab, Stanford University, 2019). Note that they do not include types of experiments that I introduce in relation to systematic theology 3, but Nicholas Rescher does, Nicholas Rescher, *What If? Thought Experimentation in Philosophy* (New Brunswick: Transaction Publishers, 2005).

[84] Since the 1990s there has been a debate about the nature and status of thought experiments in science and philosophy. Some argue, as I do, that it is not primarily the argumentative nature of thought experiments that is interesting, but others disagree and say that all thought experiments are deductive or inductive arguments in disguise. The discussion of propositional and non-propositional aspects of thought experiments does not occupy us here, but for a thorough critique of the non-propositional view see, e. g., John Norton, 'Are Thought Experiments Just What You Thought?', *Canadian Journal of Philosophy* 26 (1996): 333–66.

[85] See Edmund L. Gettier, 'Is Justified True Belief Knowledge?', *Analysis* 23, no. 6 (June 1963): 121–23.

[86] Niels Henrik Gregersen, 'The Role of Thought Experiments in Science and Religion,' in *The Science and Religion Dialogue: Past and Future*, ed. Michael Welker, (New York: Peter Lang Edition, 2014), 129.

can thus be both constructive and destructive as well as heuristic.[87] Often minor revisions of one thought experiment turn everything around, such as Niels Bohr's revision of Albert Einstein's thought experiment that ended up convincing Einstein that his critique of Heisenberg's uncertainty principle in quantum mechanics was unsound.[88] A similar example can be found in the philosophy of religion, with John Hick famously arguing for "eschatological verification" in theology as a legitimation of (yet) unprovable dogmas. He imagined two travellers walking a road toward a city. One is convinced of the city's existence, the other is in doubt. Only after the walk is completed will it be determined who was right – likewise with discussions in religion.[89] However, the early Antony Flew argued that this was an unacceptable argument because it is then impossible to falsify theological statements, and all critique of theological statements can be countered with further qualifications that cannot be falsified either.[90]

Thought experiments in systematic theology 3 can be worked out through the formula "given the conditions x, y, z, then a, b, c." Thus, it is a way to think through the consequences of a given theory in light of the information we put into the formula. In other words, to develop a thought experiment is to reflect upon or explicate what the implications of a concept are. Thought experiments makes us capable of having a more precise and coherent understanding of the concept and its relations to other concepts. Brown and Fehige introduce as the most common features of thought experiments the following: "we visualize some situation that we have set up in the imagination; we let it run or we carry out an operation; we see what happens; finally, we draw a conclusion."[91] I take thought experiments to be one of the great contributions of analytical or philosophical theology to the field of theology in general because they enable us to discuss both abstract and hypothetical theories intersubjectively and rationally.

---

87 Brown and Fehige, 'Thought Experiments.' See also Karl R Popper, *The Logic of Scientific Discovery* (New York: Routledge, 2002), 464–80, who uses similar categories though not as fine-grained as Brown and Fehige.
88 Yiftach Fehige, 'Theology and Thought Experiments,' in *The Routledge Companion to Thought Experiments*, ed. Michael T. Stuart, Yiftach Fehige, and James Robert Brown, Routledge Philosophy Companions (London and New York: Routledge/Taylor & Francis Group, 2018), 189–90.
89 John Hick, *Philosophy of Religion*, Second Edition, Foundations of Philosophy Series (Englewood Cliffs: Prentice-Hall, 1973), 90–92.
90 Anthony Flew, R.M. Hare, and Basil Mitchell, 'Theology and Falsification. The University Discussion,' in *New Essays in Philosophical Theology* (London: SCM Press, 1955), 96–130. I discuss these texts at length in 5.3.2.
91 Brown and Fehige, 'Thought Experiments.' See also the list of six of what Gregersen calls "recurring features" of thought experiments: Gregersen, 'The Role of Thought Experiments in Science and Religion,' 131.

To give only one example: a controversial theory in theology is the idea of an afterlife (*post mortem*). No matter how this is more precisely understood, most agree that the notion remains, at this point, hypothetical. What we can do is outline the conditions that must be met if the doctrine is to be possibly true. These could include an almighty God (able to resurrect mortals), the notion of a soul (something that is "alive" when the body decays), a linear view of time (also called A-time), and probably more. The speculation can include even more controversial elements such as "proleptic eschatology" pointing to the notion that eternity is already a part of earthly time, especially for Christians who have been born again into relationships with Christ.[92] The argument is not based on the specific ideas in this example, though, because all of them are discussed intensely in contemporary theology,[93] but on the methodological point that we are able to test hypotheses by outlining the conditions for a given doctrine. Thought experiments are necessary tools for many specific *loci* in Christian theology, but they can also fruitfully contribute to dogmatics as a whole (systematic theology 1–3). To mention one recent example, the Dutch theologian Gijsbert van den Brink has conducted an analysis of what would happen to classic Reformed theology if evolutionary theory were accepted as correct. van den Brink thinks it is indeed correct, but this is controversial among conservative Reformed Christians, and he thus seeks to think through how much of classic Reformed theology could stand and how much needs to be reworked in light of evolutionary theory.[94]

We gain a lot of knowledge about reality when we construct fine-grained thought experiments, from considerations of the fine-tuning of the universe over contrafactual speculation in the study of history to computer models and simulations in many different fields.[95] Philosophy in general is rife with thought experiments that often clarify concepts or even solve conceptual problems. The same is also the case in systematic theology 3 (as well as in systematic theology 2), I would argue.

As with coherence theory in general, we may say that thought experiments in systematic theology 3 that integrate empirical data will be more substantiated than theories that do not. Any reference to empirical data makes a thought experiment

---

[92] See, e.g., Wolfhart Pannenberg, *Systematic Theology*, trans. Geoffrey W. Bromiley, vol. 3 (London and New York: T&T Clark International, 2004), 532–45.

[93] An almighty God is possibly necessary for human afterlife, but how is this connected with our awareness of pain and suffering in the world? A soul may be a popular solution to mind-body dualism and a solution to post-mortem experiences, but how is this connected to the natural sciences' growing understanding of physicalism and/or monism? A linear view of time may be most intuitive in relation to eternity, but how is this connected to physical theories of multiverse(s)?

[94] Gijsbert van den Brink, *Reformed Theology and Evolutionary Theory* (Grand Rapids: Eerdmans, 2020).

[95] Cf. Gregersen, 'The Role of Thought Experiments in Science and Religion,' 130 and 135–38.

stronger even though empirical data will often not be decisive or conclusive in a thought experiment (we would not need the thought experiment if it was). The point is that thought experiments gain in persuasive power when they integrate as much direct correspondence to reality as possible through empirical data because this guards against speculative "as if" philosophy.[96]

3.4.4.2 The Natural Sciences

Some would probably say that the natural sciences should not control the field of systematic theology or set the terms for the work of systematic theology. That goes for the use of the natural sciences in philosophy as well. Time and again we hear theologians and philosophers complain about the "reductionism" of the natural sciences and their latest passing vogues, whether it be neuroscience, evolutionary biology, theoretical physics, etc., etc. Presupposing a stratified understanding of the world, I fully understand the hesitation to let one perspective from the natural sciences hijack an entire field,[97] but the opposite view, a more isolationistic or segregated one, is not better or more helpful. I agree with Lorenz Puntel's vision for philosophy – and thereby also theology – when he writes, "the development of the natural sciences contributes to philosophy an invaluable process of clarification, because that development facilitates determination of the theoretical status of the theoretical enterprise that continues to bear the name 'philosophy' […] At present, it would be simply senseless to pursue philosophy while ignoring the immense

---

[96] As Hans Vaihinger wrote in his 1925 book *The Philosophy of "As If": A System of the Theoretical, Practical and Religious Fictions of Mankind* (New York: Harcourt, Brace and Company). See further Clayton, *The Problem of God in Modern Thought*, 26. This is also to say that thought experiments generally must meet "the sceptical challenge," according to Kathleen Wilkes, who insists that "a legitimate thought experiment must not violate the known laws of nature." Cf. Brown and Fehige, 'Thought Experiments.' See also Rescher, *What If?*, 9–14. Note that Brown and Fehige are critical of Wilkes's challenge and say that thought experiments produce genuine knowledge even when natural laws are violated (e. g., what would have happened after the big bang if the law of gravity had been an inverse cube instead of an inverse square?). But this is unconvincing because the example introduced by Brown and Fehige intends to give us a more qualified notion of the actual universe and thus the violation of laws has a specific purpose that does not end with a theory that violates the known laws of nature.

[97] See, e. g., Roy Bhaskar, *A Realist Theory of Science*, Radical Thinkers 29 (London and New York: Verso, 2008); Roy Bhaskar, *The Order of Natural Necessity. A Kind of Introduction to Critical Realism*, ed. Gary Hawke (Unspecified: Unspecified, 2017); Alister E. McGrath, *A Scientific Theology. Vol. 2. Reality* (Edinburgh: T & T Clark, 2002); Gijsbert van den Brink, *Philosophy of Science for Theologians: An Introduction*, Contributions to Philosophical Theology 12 (Frankfurt am Main and New York: Peter Lang, 2009).

significance and indisputable achievements of the natural sciences."[98] The natural sciences are valuable sources for systematic theology 3,[99] their results making it possible to integrate the most well-sustained knowledge into a coherent worldview. If the findings of the natural sciences should shake the foundation of systematic theology 3, a resistance towards the result would be easy to understand, but not acceptable (without saying that the results of the natural sciences are infallible; the principle of fallibilism is as important in the natural sciences as in all other sciences). But I do not think that such a resistance is prevalent in contemporary theology. Even though some atheistic philosophers claim that there is a reason why almost all theoretical physicists are atheists, their argumentation for this claim is not convincing because much seems to depend on the theoretical framework that the data are interpreted within.[100] That science almost automatically leads us to a materialistic worldview is wrong for a number of reasons (the relation is usually the other way around, incidentally), but I do not discuss this question here.[101]

3.4.4.3 The Bible and Tradition

The Bible and the theological tradition are obvious sources for systematic theology 3, but the question is in what way. I take both to be supreme collections of data for theology, indicating a number of starting points for discussion but not determining the answers. In the history of the Christian faith, both scripture and the doctrines of the Church have been understood as providing final truths and still are so understood by some churches. In academic work, however, this is often not regarded as a viable option. In research, truth is not our starting point but our destination,[102] and the many voices in scripture and in tradition can thus only

---

98 Puntel, *Structure and Being*, 251. I see this quote as a correction of Gregersen's critique of Puntel – that Puntel's metaphysics seems to resist being affected by concrete content, cf. Gregersen, 'Samtidsteologiens horisont og fokus,' 172, fn. 6. But on the other hand the critique is understandable because Puntel does not integrate much concrete science into his published volumes. Cf. the critique of Atle O. Søvik, 'A Theoretical Framework for Talking Seriously about God,' in *Talking Seriously About God. Philosophy of Religion in the Dispute between Theism and Atheism*, vol. 4, Nordic Studies in Theology (Zürich: Lit Verlag, 2016), 55–76.

99 And, of course, also for systematic theology 2, as established above, but our focus here is the sources for systematic theology 3.

100 E. g., Sean M. Carroll, 'Why (Almost All) Cosmologists Are Atheists' (God and Physical Cosmology: Russian-Anglo American Conference on Cosmology and Theology, Notre Dame, 2003).

101 See instead the discussion in Alvin Plantinga, *Where the Conflict Really Lies: Science, Religion, and Naturalism* (New York: Oxford University Press, 2011). For the opposite perspective – that science do lead us to a materialistic worldview – see, e. g., James Ladyman et al., *Every Thing Must Go. Metaphysics Naturalized* (Oxford: Oxford University Press, 2007).

102 Which also goes the other way around: As Bonhoeffer says in his *Nachfolge* – referring to Faust and Kierkegaard – the statement that "I now do see that we can nothing know" is only trustworthy after a

be used as conversation partners for contemporary work and not for protecting an already accepted truth. Pluralism, instead, should be an ideal at the point of departure, even though our end goal is to isolate the best candidates for truth. Maybe Biblical content and/or viewpoints from the theological tradition turn out to be among the best available truth candidates, but that is not given in advance. The consequence of this approach is that systematic theology 3 can work transparently with methods and gain results that can be intersubjectively tested, i. e., that the results are not dependent on the researcher's presuppositions. And as I discuss in chapter six, intersubjective testability is mandatory for scientific research.

3.4.5 On the Possibility of a Synchronic Constitution of Systematic Theology

With this short reflection of the sources for systematic theology 3 I now ask: in light of this book' insistence that theologians aim to present rationally justified public discourse about God, *what are the constitutional conditions for the discipline of theology?* This question is incited by Heidegger's statement in *Sein und Seit:* "Alle Ontologie, mag sie über ein noch so reiches und festverklammertes Kategoriensystem verfügen, bleibt im Grunde blind und eine Verkehrung ihrer eigensten Absicht, wenn sie nicht zuvor den Sinn von Sein zureichend geklärt und diese Klärung als ihre Fundamentalaufgabe begriffen hat."[103] To elucidate the meaning of Being – or I could also say the fundamental constitution of reality – is what is discussed in systematic theology 3 and what is sought to be investigated in the light of the hypothesis about God.

In philosophy of science, constitutional conditions for a discipline are something different from causational conditions.[104] Causational here points to diachronic conditions (tracking the traces through time that lead up to today's discipline), whereas constitutional points to synchronic conditions (which contemporary arguments are there for the discipline's legitimacy?).[105] If we bracket the history of theology

---

long life of research and reasoning ("pursuit of knowledge") and should not be an acceptable excuse from the lazy freshman in a university course to cover his indolence. See Dietrich Bonhoeffer, *The Cost of Discipleship*, Unabridged Edition (New York: Macmillan, 1980), 55.

103 "All ontology, no matter how rich and firmly clamped a system of categories may be, remains basically blind and a reversal of its own intention, if it has not first sufficiently clarified the meaning of Being and understood this clarification as its fundamental task." Martin Heidegger, *Sein und Zeit* (Tübingen: Max Niemeyer Verlag, 1967), 11. Italics removed.

104 These terms are used in the excellent discussion of the historical disciplines by Adrian Currie, Adrian Currie, *Rock, Bone, and Ruin: An Optimist's Guide to the Historical Sciences* (Cambridge: The MIT Press, 2018), 88 and 155–56.

105 Such that when a former president of Harvard University said that if Harvard was "founded today, it wouldn't have a divinity school" he is saying that theology exists for diachronic reasons and

and of theology as a university discipline for a moment and ask, "What would motivate the foundation of a theological scientific discipline today?", what is then the outcome? Note that I am speaking here about the *ontological* level of systematic theology, that is, the question of God's existence. A reference to the historical disciplines in theology or the sociological disciplines is thus not in sight here. I argue this consideration is pressing due to a cultural situation such as the contemporary one in Western Europe where increasing secularization is occurring.[106] Here it seems impossible for theology to just assume God's existence, as has been done in most of theology's history. As Philip Clayton states: "Not to put too fine a point on it: the context for treating the question of God today must be scepticism. Propositional language about God can no longer pass as unproblematic."[107] Or as Ronald F. Thiemann says even more forcefully in *Theology and Revelation. The Gospel as Narrated Promise* from 1985: "Modern theologians seek to assert God's prior reality in an intellectual and cultural atmosphere in which that reality is no longer assumed. No [sic] only has the theistic consensus collapsed but powerful non-theistic alternatives have been proposed. Modern theologians are confronted not only by the logical possibility of atheism, but by its apparent instantiation in those who claim, with Pascal's interlocutor, 'I am so made that I cannot believe.'"[108] From this cultural situation and this point in history, it is necessary to ask what could currently legitimize – i. e., synchronically constitute – systematic theology as a scientific discipline?

Naturally, a synchronic constitution will be multifaceted, as a minimum with robust accounts of epistemology and ontology. This may be done in a number of ways, but in the following I present Lorenz Puntel's theoretical framework for doing what I call "rationally justified public discourse about God," with which I find it stimulating to engage.[109] I take Puntel's explication of God within the context of a comprehensive theory of Being to be a test case for the possibility of a synchronic constitution of systematic theology and therefore ask, what are the main components of his approach to presenting rationally justified public discourse

---

that there are no convincing synchronic reasons for its existence because the "general sense is that theology isn't producing any genuine knowledge that accomplishes anything, that it trades with the irrationality of faith and is useless." Volf and Croasmun, *For the Life of the World*, 43–44.

106 I still find the most stimulating work on secularization to be Charles Taylor, *A Secular Age* (Cambridge: Belknap, 2007). For a short account see Charles Taylor, 'The Meaning of Secularism,' *The Hedgehog Review* 12, no. 3 (Fall 2010): 23–34.

107 Clayton, *The Problem of God in Modern Thought*, 3.

108 Ronald F. Thiemann, *Revelation and Theology. The Gospel as Narrated Promise* (Notre Dame: University of Notre Dame Press, 1985), 5. See also Lars Sandbeck, *Den gudløse verden. Ateisme og antireligion i en postkristen æra* (Frederiksberg: Eksistensen, 2020), Foreword and chap. 1.

109 Puntel, *Being and God*, chap. 3; White, *Toward a Philosophical Theory of Everything*, 168–76. Besides, see also Søvik, 'A Theoretical Framework for Talking Seriously about God.'

about God? Note that because I argue that Puntel's contribution to the discussion is important, the presentation of his argument is relatively detailed and thorough; yet it is not exhaustive, and many technicalities are left out.[110]

Another way to state the question is to ask, "Can we elevate the God-talk from regulative ideas to constitutive ones?" In *Kritik der reinen Vernunft* Kant introduced "the blindness thesis": "Ohne Sinnlichkeit würde uns kein Gegenstand gegeben, und ohne Verstand keiner gedacht werden. Gedanken ohne Inhalt sind leer, Anschauungen ohne Begriffe sind blind."[111] Without empirical content there are only empty knowledge claims, and since God is not an empirical thing, how can we refer to and "express actual positive content" about God?[112] Kant said that it is impossible, and that the notion of God can only be *regulative*, which means an idea that guides our quest for knowledge but of which we cannot achieve knowledge: "Ich behaupte demnach: die transzendentalen Ideen sind niemals von konstitutivem Gebrauche, so, daß dadurch Begriffe gewisser Gegenstände gegeben würde […] Dagegen aber haben sie einen vortrefflichen und unentbehrlich notwendigen regulativen Gebrauch, nämlich den Verstand zu einem gewissen Ziele zu richten, in Aussicht auf welches die Richtungslinien aller seiner Regeln in einen Punkt zusammenlaufen…"[113] We could call the regulative ideas "useful fictions"[114] and then ask, "How can the notion of God ever be more than such a fiction?" Puntel has developed a theoretical framework that he argues takes us beyond Kant, and in the following presentation of Puntel's systematic philosophy we will see how this argument develops.[115] If he succeeds it is a good indication that it is possible to

---

110 As said, a synchronic constitution of systematic theology could be done in a number of ways, and it is not necessary to accept all of the technicalities of Puntel's theory to see how a synchronic constitution could be developed. His proposal is chosen for its level of precision and comprehensiveness.
111 "Without sensuality no object would be given to us, and without understanding none would be thought. Thoughts without content are empty, views without concepts are blind." (Translation MAM) Immanuel Kant, *Kritik der reinen Vernunft. Erster Teil.*, vol. 3, Kant Werke (Darmstadt: Wissenschaftliche Buchgesellschaft, 1968), 98 [B75].
112 Clayton, *The Problem of God in Modern Thought*, 5.
113 "I therefore maintain: the transcendental ideas are never of constitutive use, so that thereby concepts of certain objects would be given […] But on the other hand they have an excellent and indispensably necessary regulative use, namely to direct the understanding to a certain goal, in prospect of which the lines of direction of all its rules converge into one point." (Translation MAM) Immanuel Kant, *Kritik der reinen Vernunft. Zweiter Teil.*, vol. 4, Kant Werke (Darmstadt: Wissenschaftliche Buchgesellschaft, 1968), 565 [B672].
114 Clayton, *The Problem of God in Modern Thought*, 19. As Kant also said in Immanuel Kant, *Prolegomena to Any Future Metaphysics*, trans. James W. Ellington, Second Edition (Indianapolis: Hackett, 2001).
115 Neither Puntel nor I make the presentation in discussion with Kant. Kant's argument is just the background and Puntel's focusses on his own contribution and so do I. Puntel's fundamental criticism of Kant's philosophy is presented in *Structure and Being*, chapter 2.

establish a synchronic constitution of systematic theology as rationally justified public discourse about God.

Before we investigate Puntel's philosophy, note that Puntel develops what he calls "a theory of Being as such and as a whole." This is something different from the *metaphysica generalis* known in the tradition of, e. g., Christian Wolff and Kant, concerning the predicates shared by all beings: "Metaphysics has traditionally sought statements that are true not only as a contingent matter of physical law but necessarily, and true not just of physical being but of all being whatsoever."[116] Thus Puntel's theory of Being as such and as a whole is a "comprehensive systematics," that is, a "deep metaphysics."[117] This is important for many reasons, as is made clear in the following discussion. In Puntel's account, general metaphysics makes a mess of the relationship between absolute Being and contingent beings (a distinction that is not always even evident) and thus he needs to emphasize the very different architecture of his own ontology, where this relation is a key point to develop.[118] This procedure is of interest for theology because if Puntel is successful in his articulation of a coherent theory, it will strengthen the notion of systematic theology 3.

3.4.5.1 Lorenz Puntel's Structural-Systematic Approach to a Theory of Being and God

In *Being and God*, Puntel develops his comprehensive systematic philosophy around seven "steps" that are tightly connected and together govern the development of his deep metaphysics. Note that Puntel understands philosophy as theory (and philosophical activity as pure theoreticity) and the pragmatic, sapiential, educational, therapeutic, etc., aspects of philosophy are not given any attention here,[119] which is an oft-repeated premise for Puntel's work.[120] Of course, it is possible to proceed differently, and it is open for debate whether other approaches would be

---

116 Clayton, *The Problem of God in Modern Thought*, 21.
117 Puntel, *Being and God*, 145.
118 Note that the important thing is to understand the distinction between Being as such and being as a whole. Puntel sometimes uses "einailogy" for Being as such and "ontology" for Being as a whole. Sometimes he makes the same distinction between metaphysics and ontology. I use the terms more liberally, but most often I use ontology for both perspectives. The qualification of the term is clear in the context. For Puntel's distinction between ontology as theory of being and einailogy as theory of Being, see his newest book from 2021, *Sein und Nichts: Das ursprüngliche Thema der Philosophie*. Tübingen: Mohr Siebeck.
119 Puntel, *Being and God*, 146. To choose to do theoretical work is for Puntel to choose to leave subjectivity out of account. Pragmatic concerns are thus relevant in other contexts but not in theoretical work where subjectivity cannot play a part in determining the content.
120 E. g., Puntel, *Structure and Being*, 27.

more fitting for the synchronic constitution of systematic theology.[121] But Puntel presents a carefully considered and coherent account and is thus a good choice for reflection and investigation.[122]

3.4.5.1.1 First Step: The Theoretical Framework

I have already briefly touched upon the notion of theoretical frameworks and will not repeat myself here (see 1.2). Instead, I emphasize the importance of this notion for Puntel's work by pointing to the unavoidability of the concept in all theoretical work.[123] This is clear from the following quotation: "[The theoretical framework's] centrality is clarified by the thesis that every theoretical questioning, every theoretical sentence, argument, every theory, etc., is intelligible and evaluable only if situated within an adequately determined or determinable theoretical framework."[124] As mentioned above, every theoretical framework needs several components such as a language (syntax and semantics), a logic, an ontology, and a conceptuality, and the large theoretical framework thus consists of multiple subframeworks; this makes the work of explicating the individual theoretical frameworks extremely complex and demanding.

It is possible to construct different subframeworks coherently; this implies that "a *plurality* of theoretical frameworks is potentially and indeed even actually available."[125] This is important to recognize because it emphasizes the openness of theoretical work and explains its evident pluralism. When we see multiple theological theories of God, for example, we should not be surprised, because there are

---

121 Two of the other books referred to in the past pages – Volf & Croasmun and Clayton – are examples of other approaches: "We believe the purpose of theology is to discern, articulate, and commend visions of flourishing life in light of God's self-revelation in Jesus Christ." Volf and Croasmun, *For the Life of the World*, 11. And "If language about God is to be constitutive, it must evidence some explanatory value vis-à-vis human experience." Clayton, *The Problem of God in Modern Thought*, 5. As for Volf and Croasmun, I might ask whether they assume God's existence without qualifications (the exact traditional position I seek to avoid). As for Clayton, I might ask if there are no preliminary steps to be taken, before human experience is considered, that could also substantiate constitutive God-talk.
122 A bibliographic note: I do not make cross-references to *Structure and Being* though this volume is the groundwork for *Being and God*. One reason is that *Being and God* is a clear account in itself, another – and more important one – is that Puntel himself makes cross-references and interested readers can thus follow his own explicit intertextuality.
123 As is evident in the third chapter of *Being and God*, the description and explanation of the first step, the theoretical framework, is by far the longest section. Thus, proportionally, it will also take up the most space in the following, even though the specific theological content is most explicitly stated in the final steps.
124 Puntel, *Being and God*, 147.
125 Puntel, *Being and God,* 147. Original italics.

several ways of explicating the notion of God and several ways to integrate the explications into larger systems in a coherent way and to compare these systems with other systems for their degrees of coherence. What we seek – to present rationally justified public discourse about God – is then *expected* to be possible in a number of ways. Whether we find this to be actually so will depend on our scrutinizing the frameworks one by one.

Further, this does not just lead to pluralism; instead, Puntel even emphasizes a special "moderate, non-contradictory relativism"[126] where "[s]entences are true only relative to (that is, within) their own theoretical frameworks."[127] We could define a stronger, contradictory relativism where two propositions that mutually exclude each other are said to be correct because everyone has their own truths (P and not P are true at the same time and with regard to the same), but Puntel's theoretical view does not allow this. His point is that propositions do not float in empty space but are instead always articulated within linguistic (syntactical and semantical) frameworks and that we cannot judge the validity of propositions without assessing the frameworks within which they are uttered.[128] Puntel points to his own variation of the "context principle"[129] – "Only within the context of sentences do linguistic terms have semantic values"[130] – as the fundamental insight for this thought, and he thereby also points to the interconnectedness of the different subframeworks (such as semantic, ontological, logical frameworks) within the larger theoretical framework.

---

126 Puntel, *Being and God*, 148.
127 Puntel, *Being and God*, 147–148. This is also the point of the late Wittgenstein to whom Puntel does not refer: "All testing, all confirmation and disconfirmation of a hypothesis take place already within a system. And this system is not a more or less arbitrary and doubtful point of departure for all our arguments: no, it belongs to the essence of what we call an argument. The system is not so much the point of departure, as the element in which arguments have their life." Ludwig Wittgenstein, *On Certainty*, ed. G.E.M. Anscombe and G.H. von Wright, trans. Denis Paul and G.E.M. Anscombe (Oxford: Basil Blackwell, 1969), 16, §105. Cf. ibid. p. 52, §410: "Our knowledge forms an enormous system. And only within this system has a particular bit the value we give it."
128 This is not identical to widespread notions of constructivism or perspectivism even though it may resemble it. I take it to be obvious that the multiple contexts – personal, social, cultural, and historical – of which every theoretician is a part do influence her, but I do not think that theoretical work can be reduced to these factors. Cf. Clayton, *The Problem of God in Modern Thought*, 8–10.
129 As Michael Dummett calls it with reference to Gottlob Frege, according to Puntel, *Being and God*, 163.
130 Puntel, *Being and God*, 163. In Frege, the formulation is "… it is only in the context of a proposition that words have any meaning." Gottlob Frege, *The Foundations of Arithmetic. A Logico-Mathematical Enquiry into the Concept of Number*, trans. J.L. Austin, Second Revised Edition (New York: Harper & Brothers, 1960), 73, §62.

3.4.5.1.1.1 Datum

From the notion of the theoretical framework, we can proceed to a discussion of what is to be considered relevant for our particular theoretical framework. The central notion here is that of a "datum" – which I discuss more later with reference to the concept of truth candidates (3.4.6) – understood as "any linguistically articulated *candidate* for inclusion in the structural-systematic philosophy."[131] The adverb "linguistically" can be misunderstood since it is used in a peculiar way to cover "propositions expressed by sentences,"[132] but propositions here include mathematical sentences, pictorial expressions, diagrammatical reasoning, etc. It is thus a very wide notion of linguistics and propositions.[133] At the outset, we do not discriminate within the pool of data but instead want to keep as much relevant information as possible available to ourselves. From this, "[t]he task is to determine which of the truth candidates are to be incorporated into the structural-systematic philosophy."[134] If we want to present rationally justified public discourse about God, which data are then to be considered? This is what the discussion of the sources for theology is about (see 3.4.5): Biblical, traditional/historical, philosophical, empirical, and scientific sources are all relevant because the explication of Being as a whole concerns all of reality. We are thus interested in the largest possible amount of relevant data to explicate the most comprehensive account of reality possible. We must determine whether a theological-theoretical framework is possible, convincing, and at least as coherent as relevant alternatives, and if this is indeed the case, then the integration of data has been successful.

3.4.5.1.1.2 Structure

Previously, I have left Puntel's expression "structural-systematic philosophy" unexplained, but now I introduce his notion of "structures," which is one of the most important components of his theoretical approach to philosophy. A structure is a "differentiated and ordered interconnection or interrelation of elements or parts or aspects of an entity, a domain, a process, etc."[135] Three types of structure are the most central: the logical, the semantic, and the ontological structures.[136] These structures are in themselves abstract but become concretized when data are explained

---

131 Puntel, *Being and God*, 149. I explain what Puntel means by structural-systematic philosophy in the next section (3.4.5.1.1.2).
132 Puntel, *Being and God*, 149.
133 In this way it has resemblance with C.S. Peirce's notion of "dicisign," or as Frederik Stjernfelt translates it, "natural propositions." Frederik Stjernfelt, *Natural Propositions. The Actuality of Peirce's Doctrine of Dicisigns* (Boston: Docent Press, 2014).
134 Puntel, *Being and God*, 149.
135 Puntel, *Structure and Being*, 27.
136 Puntel, *Being and God*, 149–50.

and restructured in accordance with the structures. The data are then "elevated" and integrated into the structures that give them the highest possible degree of intelligibility.[137] The relationship between data and structure is not analogical to that between *a priori* and *a posteriori*; instead, structures are the architectonic of actuality, of Being as a whole.[138] The explication of these structures is then the precondition for the integration of the thematized data.

If we follow Puntel here, a synchronic constitution of systematic theology as a rationally justified public discourse about God needs to explicate the logical, semantic, and ontological structures that make this discourse possible. It is also relevant to note that the semantic structures are the most central in that they mediate between the logical and the ontological levels: "Ontological structures are nothing other than semantic structures whose status is determined definitively. Differently stated: ontological structures are *realized* prime propositions."[139] A prime proposition determines theoretically the sentences used, or more precisely what the verb of the sentence expresses. When the status of a prime proposition is fully determined, we have a prime fact. This means that for any semantic prime proposition that has a clear truth-status, there is an ontological structure that corresponds to it. This correspondence is known as a prime fact in Puntel's terminology, which gives us his identity thesis that says that when a proposition is true it is identical to a fact (see further 3.4.5.1.1.5).[140] The connection between the semantic structures and the ontological structures is made by the theoretical operator (see 3.4.5.1.1.4), which seeks to maximize the determination of the semantic structures for the primary facts.[141] The theoretical operator thus shows that there is full identity between the semantic and the ontological structures when the semantic structure is fully determined.

3.4.5.1.1.3 The Four-Stage Method
This is still very abstract. How does Puntel imagine that we might restructure the relevant data and integrate them into the new theory? He proposes a four-stage method. This four-stage method is an *idealized* method for philosophy, working as a *regulative* principle. It is impossible to achieve in full scope, but the regulatory guidelines it provides are helpful.[142] Often, Puntel seems to suggest – and even demand – the impossible (to articulate Being as a whole), and it is thus important

---

137 Puntel, *Being and God*, 150.
138 Puntel, *Being and God*, 150.
139 Puntel, *Being and God*, 165. Original italics.
140 See further, Puntel, *Structure and Being*, 203–214.
141 Puntel gives an example to this complicated idea in *Structure and Being*, 213–215.
142 Puntel, *Being and God*, 151.

to take notice of these qualifications. Let us have a look at what each of the four stages entails.

The *first* stage restructures the available data. This is done in such a way that we end up with an informal articulation of a theory. The scope can be anything from an individual event to the unrestricted universe of discourse.

The *second* stage puts the informal theories produced at the first stage into strictly theoretical form. We have here the constitutive stage, where theories are formulated in a genuine sense with the highest form of precision, we are able to attain.

The *third* stage integrates the theories produced at the second stage into a network of theories or a systematic whole. As I understand it, the criterion at stage two and three is coherency, so that the structuration at the second level[143] seeks to organize the data as coherently as possible and this is repeated at the third level but with a much more demanding set of data (different systematic theories in their own right).

The *fourth* stage seeks to determine whether the systematic theory and its constituent theories are theoretically adequate. This is similar to being true in Puntel's terminology and is what all theoretical work seeks to achieve.[144] I would add that at the fourth stage we compare and then discriminate between the theories according to their degrees of coherency, because this comparison is made possible by the work at the fourth stage and selection among competing theories is central to theoretical work. This resembles Clayton's opinion when he writes, "the driving force in this discipline [metaphysics] is always to unify, to select the best theory from among competing alternatives."[145] I return to this in the next chapters, especially in relation to *testability* (chapter four) and *falsification* (chapter five), where it is made clear that I think Puntel's method is helpful because it makes both explication *and* comparison of theories possible, a twofold advantage I find very important.

3.4.5.1.1.4 The Theoretical Operator

From this brief introduction to the four-stage method, I turn now to a central aspect of Puntel's structural-systematic philosophy: the theoretical operator.[146] The point of the operator is to have a non-arbitrary linguistic criterion for theoretical

---

143 Puntel distinguishes between axiomatic and coherentist methods for stage two. Only the second type is relevant here (because the larger a theory is, the less axiomatic it becomes, cf. p. 153) and defined as follows: "Coherentist and network method theories are structured wholly differently: they are structured as totalities of inferential interrelations of the theories that are made explicit by the method's second stage." Puntel, *Being and God*, 152.
144 Puntel, *Being and God*, 151.
145 Clayton, *The Problem of God in Modern Thought*, 10. Note that according to Puntel, this comparison always takes place within a larger and more encompassing framework, cf. Puntel, *Structure and Being*, 51–52.
146 The full presentation by Puntel is given in *Structure and Being*, chapter two.

work. With the operator, it is possible to exclude modalities and stick to indicatives, which is an implication of the understanding of truth involved here. Something is true when it is fully determined within a coherent theme. To do theoretical work is to present something that is fully determined. Something is fully determined when the relevant connections between the structures has been clarified.[147] Puntel incorporates Wittgenstein's notion of a theoretical operator from the *Tractatus*, "it is the case that," a structure that all indicative and theoretical sentences can be arguments of (e. g., "[it is the case that] the Earth revolves around the sun").[148] A central aspect of this operator is the impersonal pronoun "it." "It" is not the subject of the sentence but indicating the primordial dimension of Being.[149] As such, "it" includes implicitly all prime sentences that can be thematized for theoretical work. Puntel gives an example: "It's redding." This prime sentence "indicate something generally determinate, that is, the spatiotemporal location wherein it says that redding is ongoing. The meaning of the prime sentence, so interpreted, is: redding is happening here and now."[150] By the operator, this prime sentence is linked to all possible happenings where it is "redding." But what is the implication of this linguistic criterion? It makes it possible to do universal *theoretical* work with no reference to subjects, contexts, and/or situations: "theories *as such* are fully independent of any attitude connecting any subject to them."[151] Of course, Puntel is aware that this goes against the mainstream of modern epistemology and hermeneutics, and he deliberately calls his approach "radical" and insists that language (logic, semantics, syntax, etc.) can decentralize the subject from *theoretical* work.[152] On the one hand, it is important to underline the centrality of this notion to his work, on the other hand, it is equally important to remember that Puntel is after all a mild relativist (due to his emphasis on theoretical frameworks).[153]

---

147 Cf. Puntel, *Structure and Being*, 141–154.
148 Puntel, *Structure and Being*, 154. The translation of Wittgenstein's original phrase is, "such and such is the case," an attempt to translate the German "Es verhält sich so und so." Ludwig Wittgenstein, *Tractatus Logico-Philosophicus*, trans. C.K. Ogden (London: Kegan Paul, Trench, Trubner & Co., 1922), 54–55, §4.5. Puntel is aware of these challenges in the English translation, and also of the fact that Wittgenstein probably meant something else by the phrase than what Puntel uses it for: *Being and God*, 154, fn. a and 5.
149 Puntel, *Being and God*, 184.
150 Puntel, *Being and God*, 184.
151 Puntel, *Being and God*, 154–55.
152 Puntel, *Being and God*, 155. Thus, Puntel strongly opposes the late Wittgenstein's emphasis on ordinary language in philosophy presented in Ludwig Wittgenstein, *Philosophische Untersuchungen. Philosophical Investigations*, ed. G. E. M. Anscombe, P. M. S. Hacker, and Joachim Schulte, Revised Fourth Edition (Malden: Wiley-Blackwell, 2009). See Puntel, *Being and God*, 153.
153 In an informal exchange, Asle Eikrem added to this point and emphasized to me that it is important to notice that it is the subject itself who opens up the discursive dimension by using the theoretical operator. And by doing so, the subject recognizes that its own perspective cannot determine

As stated above, the operator establishes full determination once the theoretical work is complete. It cannot be determined in advance, hence the structural-systematic philosophy is "radically anti-foundationalist."[154] We can make various kinds of determinations (e. g., pragmatic) but when something is fully determined, we call it true.[155] Note that it is not the words that matter but the theory behind them. The operator makes the theory linguistically clear, hence we can assess whether the theory succeeds in presenting the facts.

As stated above, the operator is constructed according to the formula "it is the case that …" This is a strictly theoretical expression that is formal and artificial.[156] But it is necessary, according to Puntel, because ordinary, everyday languages are built up around the subject-predicate scheme, which implies that we naturally think in the same way. Implied in our language is therefore a substance ontology, which is highly problematic because substance ontology is fundamentally unintelligible.[157] Puntel's criticism is, briefly, that substance ontology does not make any sense: it seeks to understand something through its attributes, but what is behind the attributes? What connects them? It must be some kind of a substratum, but it is unintelligible what is left when the attributes are removed.[158] If all the properties of a chair are removed – it's form, colour, function, etc. – what is then left? Everyday language communicates effectively and successfully, also about chairs, but it is incapable of gaining enough precision to be useful as a theoretical tool. For this we need a more precise tool, which is the theoretical operator.[159]

---

the theoretical status of its own proposition(s). I hereby thank him for this important comment. Another point is that Puntel's idea of the "intentional coextensiveness of the human mind" (see 3.4.5.1.3.1 below) makes him emphasize the impossibility of becoming a *tabula rasa*; the human mind always already contains concepts, ideas, convictions, etc. See Puntel, *Being and God*, 275. What the philosopher must do with this is two things. First, not to guard anything against theoretical investigation; two, to minimize the influence of these inherent concepts, ideas, convictions, etc. by using the operator.

154 Puntel, *Being and God*, 156.
155 We call it true via the truth operator ("it is true that …"), see Puntel, *Being and God*, 173.
156 Puntel, *Structure and Being*, 77.
157 At a coarse grained level we understand it, but the problem arises when we begin to explicate the structures more fine-grained.
158 As Atle Søvik explains it: "[Puntel] is very critical to substance ontology in all its forms, because they all have the same root problem: the substance is an unintelligible entity. A substance is most often understood as a substrate of attributes (properties and/or relations), but when the attributes are removed, what is left (the substance) is unintelligible." Søvik, *The Problem of Evil and the Power of God*, 88. Cf. Puntel, *Structure and Being*, 194.
159 Puntel, *Structure and Being*, 85. The little word "it" has the potentiality of avoiding the subject-predicate scheme and is thus used for the operator. "It's raining" refers to no subject but is noting that rain is occurring at the moment. This makes the theoretical language more precise, even though it also makes it artificial and awkward (and Puntel therefore avoids it most of the time).

3.4.5.1.1.5 Language, Semantics, and Ontology

Let me end this first account of the theoretical framework with another word on language and ontology. Theoretical work aims for truth, and truth has syntactic, semantic, and ontological aspects.[160] I have already mentioned the tight connection between semantic and ontological structures in the philophy of Puntel, and this is what is now to be developed. Semantics, according to Puntel, has truth as its central issue, and because language is the central subject for semantics in its quest for truth, much of the discussion in connection with semantics is about language.

To Puntel, language must be – and is – determined pragmatically, which means we know how to use it and we understand each other when we use it.[161] There is also an undetermined concept of language, an abstract or general notion, but that seems less relevant here. The determination of language comes in three forms. The *lifewordly* form;[162] the *pragmatic* form;[163] and the purely *semantic* form, where we determine the semantics of language, and as such, this is also where truth is located.[164] The second level (the pragmatic) depends on the third level (the semantic), because the second level presupposes the determination of the third level,[165] thus making the third level decisive.[166] It is possible to determine language in different ways and to different degrees; what is important here it to note that to say something is true is to fully determine it, i. e., to determine its place in a coherent whole, which happens at the third level.

On this basis, Puntel formulates a general and informal formulation of the central idea of truth: "The word 'true,' understood by way of its appearance in the operator 'it is true that ...,' accomplishes both the transition of language from an un- or underdetermined status to a fully determined status and the result of that transition: fully determined language."[167] This means that a "truth-bearer" – a proposition,

---

Ideally, Puntel would, for example, not say "the cat is white" but instead "it's catting white" to show that there is no subject that has a predicate but a structure that takes place. It can be schematized as "it's such-and-suching," cf. White, *Toward a Philosophical Theory of Everything*, 32–33.

160 Puntel, *Being and God*, 168–179.
161 Puntel, *Being and God*, 168. This implies that even though everyday language is often equivocal, we understand each other well enough to coordinate our actions etc., see ibid., 169.
162 Puntel, *Being and God*, 169.
163 Puntel, *Being and God*, 169–170.
164 Puntel, *Being and God*, 170–171.
165 Puntel, *Being and God*, 173. This does not imply that something has to be fully determined semantically in order to be fully pragmatically determined. Even though large parts of our communication are fully determined, not everything is, but this does not compromise our ability to successfully communicate in many different contexts.
166 Which of course is a bit awkward numerically but has the same logical structure as the division of systematic theology 1–3 has.
167 Puntel, *Being and God*, 173. That is, fully theoretically-semantically determined language.

sentence, or utterance – from a given language "qualifies as true" because it has accomplished the transition to "a fully determined status" within the theoretical language.[168] As I understand this, Puntel simply means that the intelligibility (i. e., pragmatic determination) of ordinary language rests on the intelligibility (i. e., theoretical determination) of the semantic structure, which underlines the dependence between the levels of language that I referred to above.

But what about ontology? What is the relationship between ontology and truth, or between ontology and the semantic structures that are fully determined? In much contemporary philosophy, the ontological dimension of truth is understood with the aid of "the identity *theory*," which states that "truth is identical with reality."[169] Puntel instead suggests an "identity *thesis*": "a true proposition '*is* nothing other, nothing less and nothing more, than a constituent of the actual world.'"[170] This means that true propositions (semantics) are identical to facts (ontology).[171] What is attempted here is to take the best part from the correspondence theory, which is concerned with the correspondence of two non-identical relata, and develop the identity thesis: "This core is preserved in that identity can be understood as a *limiting case* – one might also say highest or perfect case – of correspondence."[172] The problem is that the ontological ground of the identity theory is opaque, and Puntel demands clarity here: "Any truth theory that includes an ontological import remains vague and ultimately incomplete until the ontology on which it relies, or which it presupposes, is made explicit."[173] The explication of the ontological structures is therefore mandatory for making a theory intelligible. This is the focus of the second step.

3.4.5.1.1.6 To Sum Up

To sum up on this broad category of "theoretical framework": Every truth is relative to its theoretical framework, which includes a plurality of subframeworks, most importantly semantical, logical, and conceptual frameworks. Inside a theoretical framework, we seek to integrate the largest amount of relevant data made explicit

---

168 Puntel, *Being and God*, 173. Note that Puntel is sometimes unsatisfied with the term "truth-bearer" because it points to truth as a predicate of something. Since Puntel is very critical of all instances of substance ontology he wants to replace it with a relational or structural ontology. For this, the truth-operator "it is true that …" is a better expression. See, e. g., Puntel, *Structure and Being*, 226–227.
169 Puntel, *Being and God*, 177.
170 Puntel, *Being and God*, 177. Original italics. Puntel here quotes from *Grundlagen*, 325.
171 Puntel, *Being and God*, 177. Not that this gives Puntel his "configurational" ontology. Things in the world are not substances but configurations of primary facts (see *Structure and Being*, 410). This goes for humans as well (*Structure and Being*, 262–265).
172 Puntel, *Being and God*, 177. Original italics.
173 Puntel, *Being and God*, 178. Italics removed.

through different structures with the aim of raising the data to systematic intelligibility. To do this, we use the four-stage method. The theoretical framework is mainly concerned with language because all theoretical work is articulated in language, and this makes the category of semantic structures focal.

3.4.5.1.2   Second Step: The Unrestricted Universe of Discourse

The second step investigates the central concept of the "unrestricted universe of discourse." This notion implies that there are "restricted universes of discourse" as well, such as those of the sciences (apart from philosophy). The other sciences have *restricted* discourses; they focus on delimited areas.[174] They necessarily have a limited focus, often on an aspect of empirical reality or on conceptualities in relation to empirical reality.

The deliberate restrictedness of the other sciences entails that if the *unrestricted* universe of discourse can be examined at all, this job cannot be done by any restricted discipline, but *must* be done by philosophy, which by nature is unrestricted.[175] As Puntel's collaborator Alan White puts it: "If the unrestricted universe of discourse is or can or must be a subject matter for theoretical inquiry, it is a subject matter that non-philosophical sciences, which are individuated by their restricted universes of discourse, must leave to philosophy."[176] The unrestricted universe of discourse is comprehensive because it basically includes everything, and not just in principle. This, however, does not imply that the pool of data is static – quite the opposite: it is dynamic, it changes, and it evolves through time, thus keeping the theoretical endeavour alive and alert all the time.[177] This is important, because it underlines the notion of the structural-systematic philosophy as an "open system,"[178] which I find important to acknowledge due to the immense ambition of the project. As we will see in the next chapter, the awareness of openness is important if it is to live up to an important criterion for scientific work, namely the ability to compare the strengths of given theories using such criteria as "testability" and "falsifiability." It is an important claim of the structural-systematic philosophy

---

174 This is, of course, challenged by other theoreticians, for example by some philosophers of physics who claims that physics, at least potentially, has the explanatory power to become a theory of everything. See, e. g., Sean Carroll, *The Big Picture. On the Origins of Life, Meaning and the Universe Itself* (London: Oneworld, 2016) or Brian Greene, *Until the End of Time: Mind, Matter, and Our Search for Meaning in an Evolving Universe*, (New York: Alfred A. Knopf Books, 2020).

175 In *Being and God*, the uniqueness of philosophy as an unrestricted investigation of Being seems to ground the work. This could imply that theology is at most a subbranch of philosophy. But as I pointed out earlier, Puntel sees these two disciplines as aligned in thematizing the absolute, cf. Puntel, 'Der Wahrheitsbegriff in Philosophie und Theologie.'

176 White, *Toward a Philosophical Theory of Everything*, 6. Italics removed.

177 White, *Toward a Philosophical Theory of Everything*, 29.

178 Puntel, *Structure and Being*, 20.

that it is capable of this kind of comparative work: "This yields one sense in which the SSP [structural-systematic philosophy] remains an *open* system: it is *open* to the arising of new theoretical frameworks and new theories, and *capable, as they arise*, of examining them,"[179] and of being examined by them itself, I would add. How this is supposed to be done is outlined partly in the four-stage method described in 3.4.5.1.1.3 and partly in the seven steps as a whole.

3.4.5.1.2.1 Being as Such and as a Whole

Puntel also uses another term for "the unrestricted universe of discourse," namely "Being as such and as a whole." This terminology should be understood as follows: "Being as such" is Being in itself,[180] which is shared by all beings (otherwise they would not be). This is an absolute dimension. "Being as a whole" is the sum of all individual beings. This is a contingent dimension; it includes everything that exists, which means the full set of contingent individual beings. Hence, "Being as such and as whole" is all beings plus the absolute dimension that all the individual beings share. Hence, this is a holistic theory because the whole is more than the sum of its parts: when something is connected, relations arise that make the whole something more than just a list of particulars. The project is then to articulate the most coherent theory that integrates the largest amount of data (comprehensiveness) with the most optimal connections between them (cohesiveness).[181]

The contingent dimension (all individual beings understood as a group) is described in this way: "being as a whole is, as explained below, the comprehensive configuration of facts identical to true propositions expressible by true sentences."[182] In the metaphysical tradition – and especially in the thinking of Heidegger – the emphasis has been on Being as such, but Puntel insists on a dual focus, which he calls "the new task": "developing a theory whose subject matter is this universal

---

179 White, *Toward a Philosophical Theory of Everything*, 29. Original italics.
180 In a prefatory note, Puntel distinguishes between Being/Sein/esse and being/Seiendes/ens. Since English has only one word to use for a distinction that German and Latin have two words for, Puntel distinguishes by with writing a capital B for Sein/esse. See Puntel, *Being and God*, xxi. See also *Sein und Nichts* where Puntel develops the terminology further.
181 Rescher, *The Coherence Theory of Truth*, 169.
182 White, *Toward a Philosophical Theory of Everything*, 24. We have to differentiate between theoretical ideal and practical realism here. The scope of the project seems too immense to be doable, but of course Puntel and White are aware of this: "To be sure, no presentation of the SSP could include all of those sentences (and thereby those propositions and those facts), but that is not because any of those facts are somehow beyond or outside of its scope. It is instead because human finitude precludes the possibility of any human being developing a comprehensive account of everything that is within the SSP's scope, and because the subject matters of the non-philosophical sciences are within its scope only in that those sciences themselves are within its scope." Ibid. 24.

dimension itself."[183] Some might say that such a comprehensive task is futile *per se*, but to say so in advance would be dogmatic according to Puntel; instead, we need to investigate the requirements for the execution of such a task. It should be obvious that this is in alignment with the present quest for the possibility of synchronically constituting a rationally justified public discourse about God. Where many would claim that such a task is futile – e. g., in relation to a Kantian criticism – I suggest that we investigate the requirements for such a task and then discuss whether it can be effectively undertaken.[184]

3.4.5.1.2.2 God

With reference to the question of rationally justified public discourse about God we can ask, is God included in this task of explicating the absolutely universal dimension? Here we need to be aware of a distinction in Puntel's terminology. Traditionally, much ink has been spilled on the question of God's possible existence, but we should not understand Puntel's discussion of the absolute universal dimension as a discussion of existence. Puntel sharply distinguishes between "existence" and "Being." Existence is narrower and relates to "objective being" which means to be "a constituent of the world."[185] It is beings that exist, not Being as such, which is the absolute aspect of all contingent beings, as explained above. God must be connected with Being as such and be the all-encompassing Being of everything else. In this sense, God does not exist, and it would be nonsense to claim that he did, because if all beings die or vanish, God will cease to exist too – a thought that gives a host of other problems as will become clear in the following sections. Being goes beyond existence, and thus the question of whether God exists is "extremely unclear and misleading."[186] Obviously, this is a matter of terminology, but the fundamental distinction between beings vs. Being, existence vs. Being as such, and other pairs is a commonly accepted one in the literature.

As Puntel's collaborator Alan White further says: "Any conception of 'God' that is not situated within an explicitly presented or implicitly presupposed theory of Being as such and as a whole – and hence, obviously, any such conception presented in conjunction with the rejection of such theories – can only be a conception of something or other, an X, that putatively does or does not 'exist' beyond the world familiar to us and somehow separately from it, but that cannot ultimately be made either intelligible or reasonable."[187] I understand this to imply that an assessment of

---

[183] Puntel, *Being and God*, 193.
[184] See, e. g., Clayton, *The Problem of God in Modern Thought*, 18–49.
[185] Puntel, *Being and God*, 193. See further "The Architectonic of the Structural-Systematic Theory of Being" on page 190 and Puntel, *Structure and Being*, 415.
[186] Lorenz B. Puntel, *Being and God*, 173.
[187] White, *Toward a Philosophical Theory of Everything*, 169.

the God-hypothesis is closely connected with an assessment of the intelligibility of the absolute dimension of Being. If "Being as such" is a convincing notion, then God is a convincing notion. If not, God is also compromised. But we need to take some additional steps before we can reach the conclusion of the structural-systematic philosophy. Puntel returns to the question of God more explicitly in the final steps, and I thus withhold the remaining discussion at this point.

3.4.5.1.2.3   To Sum Up

To sum up, the point of the second step is to raise awareness of the *unrestricted* universe of discourse as a legitimate domain to be investigated. This can only be done by philosophy, according to Puntel. In opposition to mainstream thought, Puntel does not think it is a futile endeavour, because we *can* indeed investigate the unrestricted universe of discourse and, therefore, we are obligated to do so. This is the proper task of philosophy, i. e., to present what is also called the most coherent theory of Being as such and as a whole. This complex and comprehensive task is the focus of the structural-systematic philosophy.

3.4.5.1.3   Third Step: Theory of Being as Such

The third and fourth steps deepen our understanding of the double dimensionality of Being: "as such" and "as a whole." The third step is devoted to "as such" and the fourth step is devoted to "as a whole."

Both in relation to "as such" and "as a whole," Puntel uses the term "explication"[188] as a label for the method he deploys, making it a central term in his presentation of the structural-systematic philosophy.[189] To recapitulate: Explication means to clarify relations that are not yet fully settled as by definitions. Explication is therefore a multifaceted strategy: "explication is an analytic/argumentative/disclosive procedure"[190] – the slashes might be taken to indicate synonymity among the three words, but they are actually different factors of the explication procedure.[191] To explicate is to bring characteristics forward and to at least partly clarify them in relation to others without presenting a full and total understanding of them. To

---

188 In *Grundlagen einer Theorie der Wahrheit*, Puntel gives a long and detailed discussion of what explication is in relation to associated words like analysis and definition. See part 2.1 (p. 63–98) but especially the outline in the sections 2.1.4.4 [1]-[2] "Grundmotivation und Grundgedanke der rational-systematischen Rekonstruktion (= RSR)" (p. 90–92). See also *Being and God*, 209–212.

189 As it was for the debate between Gregersen and Eikrem that I discussed at length in relation to the stratification of systematic theology, see 3.2 and 3.4.3.

190 Puntel, *Being and God,* 211. The word "disclosive" is not immediately clear to me. In Danish, we have several options for translation according to the standard dictionary such as "oplyse" [enlighten], "offentliggøre" [publish], "fremlægge" [present], "meddele" [inform], "åbenbare" [reveal].

191 Puntel, *Being and God*, 212.

explain something through explication is thus not an either-or, but a scale between more or less fully explicated relations. Puntel develops this understanding of the method at the third and fourth step in a central passage from *Grundlagen*:

> Auf der Basis solcher und ähnlicher Überlegungen erscheint es sinnvoll, zwei und nur zwei *Stufen* einzuführen und anzuerkennen: ein sozusagen *mittlere* und eine *endgültige*. Auf die mittlere sollen die Aufgaben und Leistungsmöglichkeiten all jener Verfahrungsausdrücke *reduziert* werden, die *diesseits* der durch (positive und negative) Vollbestimmtheit charakterisierten Stufe verbleiben. Für diese letzte durch semantische Vollbestimmtheit gekennzeichnete Stufe des Bestimmungsprozesses soll der Ausdruck *Definition* (=D), für diese andere mit Nicht-Vollbestimmtheit behaftete Stufe der Ausdruck *Explikation* (=E) verwendet werden. Der Ausdruck *Erklärung* (=ER) soll den ganzen semantischen Bestimmungsprozeß *undifferenziert* bezeichnen; das heißt: *Erklärung* wird verwendet, wenn es bei der Charakterisierung des semantischen (B-Bestimmungs-)Prozesses nicht auf die Unterscheidung zwischen den Stufen der *Explikation* und der *Definition* ankommt. Eine *Erklärung* ist also gegeben, wenn eine *Explikation oder* eine *Definition oder beides* vorliegt. Identifiziert man Erklärung, Explikation und Definition mit jeweils einer Menge von prozeduralen Schritten oder von Strukturmomenten, so ist Erklärung die Vereinigungsmenge, bestehend aus Explikation und Definition: ER = E *the union of* D. Hingegen ist die *rational-systematische Rekonstruktion* das *geordnete Paar*, bestehend aus Explikation *und* Definition: RSR = <E, D>.[192]

This is not the place to further discuss Puntel's elaborate outline of analysis, explication, and definition, because for the purpose of the task here it is sufficient to unpack the quotation and elaborate somewhat on it. Puntel wants to distinguish

---

192 "On the basis of such and similar considerations it seems reasonable to introduce and recognize two and only two *levels*: a so to speak *middle* one and a *final* one. To the middle one the tasks and performance possibilities of all those procedural expressions are to be *reduced*, which remain *on this side* of the stage characterized by (positive and negative) full-determinacy. For this last stage of the determination process, which is characterized by semantic fullness, the expression *definition* (=D) shall be used. For this other stage, which is characterized by non-fullness, the expression *explication* (=E) shall be used. The expression *explanation* (=ER) is to denote the whole semantic process of determination in an *undifferentiated* way; that is: *explanation* is used when the characterization of the semantic (B-determination) process does not depend on the distinction between the stages of *explication* and *definition*. Thus, an *explanation* is given when there is *explication or definition or both*. If one identifies explanation, explication, and definition each with a set of procedural steps or of structural moments, explanation is the union set consisting of explication and definition: ER = E *the union of* D. On the other hand, *rational-systematic reconstruction* is the *ordered pair* consisting of explication *and* definition: RSR = <E, D>." (Translation MAM) Puntel, *Grundlagen einer Theorie der Wahrheit*, 92. Original italics.

between a full definition, where the *definiendum* has clarified relations, and explication, where we state connections without having a full definition. The point is that we do not have either a complete definition or none but instead that we can have gradual clarification deepening through successive explications (an ever more refined analysis of the structural relations). To explicate is then to clarify connections, which means I can explicate by presenting a number of characteristics of something (such as consciousness) and partly make clear what it is without offering a complete understanding of it. Almost all scholars agree that we do not fully understand consciousness, but that does not mean that we are at a loss for insight, because many connections can be explicated. Thus, explication is a matter of degree; it is something we can do again and again with increasing precision and elaboration. It is not an either-or, but a gradual process.

What should an explication of Being include? "It should include the immanent structural characteristics of Being or of the dimension of Being."[193] As a starting point, Puntel rejects Plato's influential understanding of being (a form from which immanent characteristics could be derived) and says: "Instead, the dimension of Being is the configuration that includes the dimensions of thinking/mind/language and of word/universe/Being as interrelated."[194] Step 1 in the explication of Being "begins with the explication of Being as such."[195] Puntel states that this procedure has five characteristics, which I present in the following.

3.4.5.1.3.1 First Characteristic: The Intelligibility of the Absolutely Necessary Dimension of Being

As limited and contingent creatures, how can we explicate Being as such? To even make this project feasible, we need to insist that a characteristic of Being as such is the "absolute universal *intelligibility* of the dimension of Being."[196] That it is intelligible makes it accessible to the human mind, but how? Because the sphere of the mind is intentionally[197] coextensive with this dimension of Being, such that "it *is* understandable, knowable, articulable, etc."[198] – though not in all its specificity,

---

193 Puntel, *Being and God*, 212.
194 Puntel, *Being and God*, 215. And further: "The dimension of Being and therefore Being as such is the absolutely comprehensive configuration that includes the entire dimension of thinking/mind/spirit; it therefore cannot be outside the sphere of thinking/mind/spirit. Because this sphere is coextensive with this dimension, this dimension is accessible to it." (ibid.)
195 Puntel, *Being and God*, 215.
196 Puntel, *Being and God*, 215.
197 I do not clarify the notion of "intentionality" here, but it refers to some of the basic configurations of the human being that Puntel identifies, i. e., thinking, willing, and being-conscious. Especially the last two are "unambiguously *intentionally* structured," see *Structure and Being*, 276–282.
198 Puntel, *Being and God*, 215. Original italics. Compare with Tim Maudlin's view: "The world and our senses need not have been constructed in such a way that every physical fact can be settled by

of course, and not to any singular finite mind, but Being as such is accessible to us. This seems to dissolve the famous distinction in Kantian terminology between *das Ding an sich* and *das Ding für mich/Erscheinungen*, which has been a major obstacle for systematic theology in the last 200 years.[199] It also seems to take steps beyond the project of critical realism, which also avoids the pitfall of the Kantian critique but does so with some concessions, admitting limitations to our epistemological abilities even though it insists on an ontological realism.[200]

Puntel instead says that the dimension of thinking/mind/language and the dimension of world/universe/being-in-the-objective-sense come together under the auspices of "a single, primordial dimension, the dimension of Being."[201] The point is that we can grasp "segments" of Being as a whole in a real sense because the relationship between language and reality is internally logical – the one cannot be thought of without the other.

3.4.5.1.3.2 Second Characteristic: The Universal Coherence of the Dimension of Being

The universal coherence of the dimension of Being does not just entail consistency (as in classical logic), but also "positive interlinkings" or configurations.[202] According to Puntel and in contrast to a constructivist understanding, coherence is not a systematicity we create but an inherent quality of Being that we discover: "The coherence is intrinsic to the dimension of Being rather than somehow added to it by its being thought"[203] – this seems to be very important, because it is then possible

---

observation. Indeed, it is more of a miracle that we can reliably discover anything about the world by interacting with it than that we can't discover everything about it." Tim Maudlin, *Philosophy of Physics: Space and Time*, Princeton Foundations of Contemporary Philosophy (Princeton and Oxford: Princeton University Press, 2012), 43.

199 See, e. g., the contention of Clayton in *The Problem of God in Modern Thought* (p. 25): "The Kantian challenge to God-language represents the most serious threat to theology in the modern era." Of course, not all agree, and some even question the use of Kant due to his obscure style of thinking and writing, e. g., Andrew Chignell, "'As Kant Has Shown.'" Analytic Theology and the Critical Philosophy," in *Analytic Theology: New Essays in the Philosophy of Theology*, ed. Oliver Crisp and Michael C. Rea (Oxford: Oxford University Press, 2011).

200 Bhaskar, *A Realist Theory of Science*; Garry Potter and José López, 'After Postmodernism: The New Millennium', in *After Postmodernism: An Introduction to Critical Realism*, ed. Garry Potter and José López (London and New York: Bloomsbury Academic, 2005), 3–16.

201 Puntel, *Being and God*, 215.

202 Or, what I – with Rescher – call *cohesiveness*.

203 Puntel, *Being and God*, 217. This cannot mean, though, that we discover concepts; we create these and try to explicate how they arise inductively or deductively from other concepts, and we seek to strengthen our interpretations by raising the degree of precision (making the theory more fine-grained). Our concepts can then be more or less coherent with things we discover about the world. I suspect Puntel agrees on this clarification.

to reject the accusations that coherence is a fictional system forced upon the world. Coherence is systematicity, and Puntel thus adheres to a coherence theory of meaning. Coherence is not just a structure, but also what makes something intelligible to us as humans: "The universal coherence of the dimension of Being is derivable from its universal intelligibility in that to understand, explain, etc., anything whatsoever is to articulate the configuration and thus the coherent structure within which it is situated."[204] Or as he says: "Intelligibility has an ontological as well as an epistemic status [...] If a conception or theory attains a higher intelligibility in this sense, the result is a specific form of inference to the best explanation."[205] In other words, Puntel's is a coherence theory of truth *and* meaning. I think this is a very helpful duality, and it synthesizes different methodological aspects of the philosophical literature that I find compelling for theological work (more on this below). Note that this is another way of saying what Rescher has termed "inference to the best systematization," a notion I consider in greater detail below.[206]

3.4.5.1.3.3 Third Characteristic: The Universal Expressibility of the Dimension of Being

Expressibility is a technical term covering all modes of articulation. This follows from the first two characteristics, that the dimension of Being is both intelligible and coherent. As we will see soon, it is an important point for Puntel that this dimension of Being is expressible and that as linguistic subjects with the capacity for knowledge, we always experience this dimension of Being as expressed through language.

The last two characteristics are not developed that much in Puntel's work, and they are not important for the discussion here, so I only mention them briefly for the sake of completeness. *Fourth* characteristic: whereas characteristics 1–3 refer to the intellect, this fourth relates to the will. This is the metaphysical quality of *goodness* in the philosophical tradition.[207] The *fifth* characteristic is the metaphysical quality of *beauty* in the philosophical tradition. Characteristics 4 and 5 are not relevant in this context, but in a larger theological program they are evidently important.[208]

---

204 Puntel, *Being and God*, 217.
205 Puntel, *Being and God*, 234.
206 Nicholas Rescher, *Philosophical Reasoning: A Study in the Methodology of Philosophizing* (Malden: Blackwell Publishers, 2001), 138–40.
207 Puntel, *Being and God*, 217.
208 Even though characteristics four and five – goodness and beauty – are not relevant in the present context, they are, of course, in a larger theological program. Where ethics is a golden oldie in systematic theology, aesthetics is experiencing a revival in modern theology with important works by scholars such as Hans Urs von Balthasar and David Bentley Hart.

3.4.5.1.3.4 *To Sum Up*

In the third and fourth steps, Puntel explicates Being "as such" (step 3) and "as a whole" (step 4). This is done by explicating the immanent structural characteristics of Being as such, of which there are five. First, the intelligibility of the dimension of Being; second, the coherence of the dimension of Being; third, the expressibility of the dimension of Being. These three characteristics makes it possible to explicate the dimension of Being. Now we see the contours of a constitutive metaphysics. Next, we move on to Puntel's description of the explication of Being as a whole, which forms the second central part of his ontology.

3.4.5.1.4 *Fourth Step: Theory of Being as a Whole*

From "Being as such" we move to "Being as a whole." Note that in *Being and God* Puntel says that "as a whole" does not mean "as a totality" as it does in much contemporary philosophy.[209] But in *Structure and Being* Puntel makes a programmatical distinction, basically saying that "as a whole" equals totality: "being must be conceived *both* with respect to what constitutes itself [Being as such], *and* in its totality, as encompassing anything and everything, thus all entities of any sort whatsoever."[210] Is this not self-contradictory? Puntel builds on the discussion of the problems involved in talking about "totality" in semantics, logic, and philosophy, and accepts the criticism, because "totality" here equals a closed or finite set.[211] He therefore needs to explain the concept without this reference. What is "as a whole" then? According to Puntel, it is all the fundamental structures – formal, semantic, and ontological – that are made explicit in the structural-systematic philosophy: "these structures simply exhibit the intelligibility and the coherence (in the sense explained above) of anything and everything, of all domains of being, and indeed of the dimension of Being itself."[212] As I understand it, he avoids the problematic notion of "totality" by not referring to a set cluster of facts but instead building from the bottom up in the open system of the unrestricted universe of discourse. Many of these structures that are explicated are contingent, and this raises the question whether *everything* is contingent.

3.4.5.1.4.1 *Contingent versus Absolute*

Puntel denies that everything is contingent. There is something absolute and thereby necessary ("Being as such"). Puntel – like much of the philosophical tradition – as-

---

[209] Puntel, *Being and God*, 220.
[210] Puntel, *Structure and Being*, 416.
[211] The discussions are quite complex, and it would take too much space to assess each aspect. See Puntel, *Structure and Being*, 421–30. Instead of seeing totality as a closed or finite set, Puntel again and again emphasizes the discourse is *unrestrictedly* open.
[212] Puntel, *Structure and Being*, 439.

cribes "absolute necessity" to Being as such and "contingency" to beings, repeating a fundamental distinction in ontology.[213] The installation of the absolute into the structural-systematic philosophy may seem rash; where is the argument? But Puntel gives a simple *modus-tollens* argument for the old view that shows that many peoples' intuition – that there are only contingent beings – cannot be correct: "[Premise 1] If everything – that is, Being as such and as a whole – were contingent, then absolute nothingness would be possible; [Premise 2] but absolute nothingness is impossible; [Conclusion] therefore, not everything is contingent."[214] Why is Premise 2 correct? Puntel gives three reasons: (a) *absolute nothingness* is a non-concept; (b) the concept *"possibility of absolute nothingness"* is radically self-contradictory, because *possibility* is *possibility of Being*; (c) the all-is-contingent thesis entails not only the *possibility of absolute nothingness,* but also the *additional* assumption that the dimension of Being, and – with it – beings, could have arisen by some sort of spontaneous generation so as to have replaced absolute nothingness.[215] The consequence is that Puntel believes to have proved that Being includes an absolutely necessary dimension.[216] *Necessary* is not the same as *absolute*, but the absolute status of Being follows from the necessary status of Being. "Necessary" means that Being is fully independent, and also that everything else is totally dependent on Being. Both notions make Being absolute. "Absolute" means that necessary Being is "not conditioned" in any way and thus not relative to anything other.[217]

---

213 Puntel, *Being and God*, 225. Being as such and as a whole has an absolutely necessary dimension (Being as such) but also a dimension of contingently actual beings (like myself, cats, horses, chairs, etc.) and a dimension of contingently non-actual beings (like fictional characters). But these distinctions only complicate the introduction and are not discussed here. See White, *Toward a Philosophical Theory of Everything*, chap. 8.
214 Puntel, *Being and God*, 228. This *modus-tollens* argument only structures the old view. The argument in itself can be found in many authors, such as Thomas Aquinas. See further in Markus Mühling, *Post-Systematic Theology I: Ways of Thinking – A Theological Philosophy* (Paderborn: Wilhelm Fink at Brill, 2020), 436–42.
215 Puntel, *Being and God*, 229–230. Which would be too strong an understanding of emergence, I suppose.
216 Puntel, *Being and God*, 230. Note that a non-relational understanding of the modalities (e. g., necessity and contingency) has been questioned by other philosophers, for example the German philosopher Nicolai Hartman. See Markus Mühling, *Post-Systematic Theology*, 346. Later, Mühling works through the implications for the notion of God if Hartman's critique of absolute necessity in non-relational terms is convincing, which are essentially that necessity without relations becomes randomness and therefore actually contingent, see pp. 436–442.
217 Puntel, *Being and* God, 230. The German idealists introduced the term *the Absolute* as a technical designation for God, and it has remained common terminology in Christian theology ever since. Puntel does not draw this conclusion at this stage, however, and the term "Absolute" is still purely theoretical and not a synonym for God.

3.4.5.1.4.2 To Sum Up

According to Puntel, the term "as a whole" does not refer to the problematic notion of "totality" in contemporary philosophy. Instead, it is the fundamental structures explicated in the structural-systematic philosophy that include anything and everything inside the open system. Most of these structures are contingent, but there is something that is both necessary and absolute, which is revealed by a short *modus tollens*-argument – showing the impossibility of absolute nothingness. The relationship between the absolutely necessary dimension of Being and these contingent beings is the focus of the next step.

3.4.5.1.5 Fifth Step: The Relationship Between Absolutely Necessary Dimension of Being and the Dimension of Contingent Beings

What is the relation between absolute Being and contingent beings? Traditionally, two answers have been provided: One, the bottom-up-answer, starting from a particular phenomenon and then working up towards the absolute Being; two, the analogy-answer, where an investigation of a worldly phenomenon by analogy says something about absolute Being.[218] As an alternative to these answers, which many find unwarranted today,[219] the structural-systematic philosophy seeks to explicate the relationship as one between the absolute Being and contingent beings, also called the "two dimensions of Being."[220] Not from the bottom up, not as a derivation from the universal to the particular, but as a two-dimensionality that needs precise explication. As might be clear by now, the explication of both dimensions is complex and comprehensive, and the task is immense. What I do, therefore, is focus on the aspect relevant for systematic theology, which I take to be "How to get from absolutely necessary Being to a minded God?"

3.4.5.1.5.1 Coextensiveness Leads to Minded Being

According to Puntel, this is only possible if the human mind is coextensive with Being as such and as a whole, as he argues it is.[221] The reason is that the effect (mind) must have a cause, and the dimension within which minds can be realized cannot itself be without mind (see next section on the principle of ontological rank). Included in the coextensiveness of the human mind with Being is the absolutely necessary Being that ultimately gives rise to the human mind.[222] From this it follows that absolutely necessary Being is a minded Being, involving intelligence, will, and

---

218 Puntel, *Being and God*, 231.
219 Clayton, *The Problem of God in Modern Thought*, 4 and 38.
220 Puntel, *Being and God*, 232.
221 Puntel, *Being and God*, 232.
222 This seems to refer to consciousness with a mind which is something else or more than mere ability to thought.

freedom.[223] This seems like an astonishing claim, so why does this follow according to Puntel? It follows because of the coextensionality of the human mind with the necessary Being, because if not, we would have a "bizarre juxtaposition"[224] between contingent minds that are coextensive with Being as such and as a whole and a "purely abstract or simply non-minded" Being.[225] It is a more coherent theory if there is a match between Being and beings in mindedness, if there is an intentional coextensiveness. And according to Puntel there is because this follows from the explication in the previous steps of Being as such and the absolutely necessary Being.[226]

3.4.5.1.5.2 Greater Intelligibility

This brings us to the following thesis: "the thesis that the absolutely necessary dimension of Being is minded provides *incomparably greater intelligibility* than does the thesis that this dimension is not minded."[227] Why is this so? Because the logical relationship between contingent beings and necessary Being is one of *total dependency* (asymmetrically understood, contingent beings are totally dependent on necessary Being but not vice versa), and this total dependency could not be intelligible if necessary Being were non-minded – or did not at least have the potentiality for mind (which seems to be a coherent possibility as well). It further implies that "[b]ecause the relation between the two must be a *positive* one, a denial that the absolutely necessary dimension of Being is minded results in a simply inexplicable metaphysical gap."[228] Remember that Being as a whole, according to Puntel, is *universally expressible*. If the absolutely necessary Being were non-minded, it would be universally expressible but not able to express itself, which seems odd – and, more importantly, inadequate because contingent beings are *ontologically* dependent on the absolutely necessary Being and thus could have the ability of being expressible and self-expressing (as they are) if absolutely necessary Being is not.[229] According to Puntel, it thus follows that absolutely necessary Being is minded and able to express itself and be expressed.

Puntel introduces an ontological principle that he calls "the *principle of ontological rank*." It says that "[s]omething of a higher ontological rank cannot arise

---

223 Puntel, *Being and God*, 232–233. Becoming an "absolutely necessary personal Being".
224 Puntel, *Being and God*, 234.
225 Puntel, *Being and God*, 234.
226 This is a controversial claim of Puntel's, but it is not relevant to discuss alternatives at this step of the argument.
227 Puntel, *Being and God*, 234. Original italics.
228 Puntel, *Being and God*, 235. Original italics.
229 Puntel, *Being and God*, 235. There could be other options, though, e. g., if the absolute Being expressed itself by producing beings that could express it somehow.

exclusively from or be explained exclusively by anything of a lower ontological rank."[230] The principle of ontological rank does not presuppose grades of being, as if the higher should be more real than the lower. Instead, it thematizes that there cannot be anything in the effect that is not in the cause. If you have, e. g., consciousness in the cause you must have (at least the potential for) consciousness in the effect. If not, we would not know where consciousness came from. Therefore, if the absolutely necessary Being were non-minded, it would have a lower rank than minded humans, and this cannot be the case if contingent beings are asymmetrically (totally) dependent on absolutely necessary Being (which they are). It is the principle of ontological rank that explains why the intentional coextensiveness of the human mind with Being is an argument for the minded absolutely necessary Being. Something worth noticing is that the principle of ontological rank does not conflict with natural-scientific theories like evolutionary theory – because it is reasonable to say that evolution had the potential for mind – though it may conflict with metaphysical and/or philosophical extrapolations of evolutionary theory or other theories in the natural sciences.[231]

3.4.5.1.5.3   To Sum Up

Puntel seeks to understand the relationship between absolutely necessary Being and contingent beings in a novel way. He focuses on the two-dimensionality of Being as such and as a whole and seeks to explicate the relationship. Focus has been on the argument for *minded* Being, which is substantiated by (a) coextensionality between Being and beings, (b) greater intelligibility as to total (asymmetric) dependency, (c) the positive relationship of universal expressibility, (d) the principle of ontological rank; higher ontological ranks cannot arise exclusively from lower ranks. From these arguments for minded Being we then arrive at another central aspect of the relationship between Being and beings, i. e., that of creation.

3.4.5.1.6   Sixth Step: Absolutely Necessary Being as Minded and as Creator

In the recent history of metaphysics and philosophical theology, there has been much discussion of Heidegger's severe critique of what he calls "onto-theology."[232] In simplified form, Heidegger accuses traditional theology of making God a being

---

230 Puntel, *Being and God*, 236. This seems to be an emergentist principle at the ontological level because it rejects reductionism.
231 Puntel, *Structure and Being*, 455. A consideration could be that absolutely necessary Being could also only have the potentiality for mind instead of an actualization of it.
232 The term originated in Kant's first critique where it refers to a notion that has no relation to experience (B659–660). Heidegger – like modern post-theists – uses the term as a critique of all metaphysics that ignore the putative "ontological difference" that is claimed to be between Being (ontologically) and beings/the being (ontic).

rather than Being, albeit the first or highest one, which he finds problematic.[233] How is absolutely necessary *minded* Being related to this criticism? According to Puntel, absolutely necessary minded Being is immune to Heidegger's critique because it is not a being, not an additional being, not even the first or the highest being. It is Being. Puntel, instead, connects with Aquinas' notion that God[234] is *ipsum esse per se subsistens* [subsisting in and by itself], that God must be articulated verbally, not nominally.

Puntel shows that contingent beings owe their existence to absolutely necessary Being, because the existence of contingent beings can only come from a totally independent source; in theological terminology, absolutely necessary Being has *created* contingent beings, brought them into existence from their non-being: "This means that the total dependency of contingent beings on absolute Being is the dependency articulable as Being-created."[235] Creational activity is thus, according to Puntel, a characteristic of absolutely necessary Being as explicated by the structural-systematic philosophy: since contingent beings are, absolutely necessary Being who creates must be.

3.4.5.1.6.1 Causation or Posits?

Puntel states rather broadly that creation is traditionally understood with the aid of metaphysics by the notion of *causality* and causation is understood by analogy, but this is vulnerable to postmodern criticism, and Puntel therefore seeks another way that is not dependent on Aristotelean concepts.[236] What is this way? He develops the understanding of the explication of Being presented above (absolutely necessary Being and contingent beings). Contingent beings might not have been (because they are contingent); thus, the question arises, where do they come from? The answer can only be that absolutely necessary Being is responsible, due to the absolute difference between them. Absolutely necessary Being has chosen the existence of contingent beings in true freedom because its non-dependency on everything else makes it truly free. But we still need an explanation for what happens between A – a universe with only absolutely necessary Being – and B – a universe with contingent beings. Puntel avoids the causal explanation and uses the term "posit" instead: "free, absolutely necessary Being *posits* the contingent dimension of Being *into Being*, and does so *absolutely* in the sense that the positing does not presuppose anything

---

233 As do many others, see, e. g., Clayton, *The Problem of God in Modern Thought*, 38.
234 Though Puntel still withholds the term God. It is first introduced in the seventh step.
235 Puntel, *Being and God*, 237.
236 Puntel, *Being and God*, 242. This is too broad a statement because there are other traditions of creation than causality and also because causality can mean different things. On the postmodernist criticism of the use of analogy here, see Puntel's discussion of Jean-Luc Marion in *Being and God*, 387–388.

prior or anything underlying or anything of the sort. This is creation."[237] What does this mean? It emphasizes the asymmetrical dependency between beings and Being, but not as isolated, particular, singular cases – instead absolutely necessary Being "posits the contingent dimension of Being as a whole."[238] This solves the problem with causality, which is a mistake stemming from the bottom-up-strategy of much traditional metaphysics.[239] Creation is a "singularity" without any analogy in mundane life.[240] This is Puntel's reformulation of the classic understanding of creation in Christian theology from Irenaeus to Aquinas. It is not the reformulation in itself that is interesting in this book' context but the inference from steps 1 through 5 to this sixth step where a focal notion in Christian theology is explicated in philosophical terms.

3.4.5.1.6.2 To Sum Up

First, Puntel seeks to overcome the Heideggerian criticism of onto-theology by pointing to absolutely necessary minded Being, as the absolutely necessary dimension of Being. Being is therefore logically the source of existence for all contingent beings; contingent beings are totally dependent on absolute Being. In theological language, this is creation, and thus absolutely necessary Being is minded *creator*. This creation is carried out in absolute freedom, thus making absolutely necessary Being both minded and free. Puntel rejects the causal explanation of creation and instead uses the word "posit" because absolutely necessary Being does not cause every individual – as a potter makes vases – but instead posits the contingent dimension of Being as a whole, wherein beings can evolve as explained by evolutionary theory and other empirical sciences.

3.4.5.1.7   Seventh Step: An Integral Theory about God

Finally, Puntel now comes to the place in his investigation where the term "God" can be properly uttered and used. He writes, "[t]he thesis is that only after the

---

237 Puntel, *Being and God*, 243. This change in terminology might be unnecessary for Puntel because it is possible to understand and apply the notion of causality in non-Aristotelian terms (as hinted at in the previous footnote), but this might be a consequence of Puntel's Catholic background where Aristotle is still widely influential.

238 Puntel, *Being and God*, 243. Here we can see clearly why the concept(s) of evolution is not threatened by Puntel's concept of creation. What develops inside the dimension of contingent beings is *not* created in this technical sense: "The reason for this is that *everything* that emerges *within* the contingent dimension of Being (the world, the universe) emerges *from* something, however this 'something' may be designated." (Ibid. 243).

239 Puntel, *Being and God*, 244–245.

240 Puntel discusses the solutions of modern physics in relation to the Big Bang (the singularity), especially that of Stephen Hawking but must reject their conclusions even though he does not confront the content of the physical/cosmological theories. See Puntel, *Being and God*, 247–251.

primordial, universal dimension of Being has been explicated as including the absolutely necessary dimension of Being, and the latter as absolutely necessary free or personal Being and then as absolute creating, is the point reached at which it is appropriate to introduce the word 'God'."[241] God is not assumed or taken as an axiom here but explicated carefully through the seven steps of the metaphysical investigation. I assess that Puntel succeeds in this trajectory and hence makes a convincing case for the division of labour between systematic theology 2 and systematic theology 3. Given the results of this investigation by Puntel, we can proceed after the seventh step to explicate a more positive notion of God by developing and comparing coherent theories about God in systematic theology 2. I return to these reflections below (3.4.5.1.7.2).

In the history of theology, God has been – and is – understood in numerous ways, but still, Puntel has not yet undertaken the project of determining whether an adequate understanding of the Christian God, however this may be expressed, can be aligned with structural-systematic philosophy's theory of Being. The focus here is on creation – absolute creating – not on the full range of divine attributes, not because they are irrelevant but due to the scope of the discussion.[242]

3.4.5.1.7.1 God's Transcendence

Two important questions in relation to God and creation are discussed in Puntel's text: (1) How is God's transcendence to be understood? (2) Is it possible to proceed beyond the previous analysis? As for (1), two variants arise: The extreme, apophatic view and the moderate view. Puntel rejects the apophatic way as nonsense because negation is always grounded on some kind of affirmation and the extreme way is thus self-contradictory. Puntel adopts this critique from Aquinas, as is seen in a quotation that encloses Aquinas' understanding very precisely: "Understanding negation is always grounded in an affirmation; therefore, if the human intellect could not know anything positive about God, it could not deny anything of God."[243]

The moderate view has more to it, and it relies on analogical thinking of the kind found in the theology of Aquinas. It moves from the bottom up, from the finite to the infinite, from the imperfect to the perfect, from the contingent to the absolute. But Puntel is unsatisfied with this variant because it separates Being from beings. Therefore, he proposes a third variant focusing on *configurations*: "identifying increasingly comprehensive configurations up to the point of the disclosure of the absolutely comprehensive configuration."[244] With this approach he seeks to

---

241 Puntel, *Being and God*, 252.
242 Puntel, *Being and God*, 254.
243 Thomas Aquinas, 'Quaestiones Disputatae de Potentia, Q.7, a.5.' Quoted from Puntel, *Being and God*, 256.
244 Puntel, *Being and God*, 258.

avoid the consequence in analogical thinking that ultimately separates Being from beings, which would compromise the fact that beings are in Being and Being is in beings;[245] as Puntel expresses it in the following thesis: "There is *no* absolute transcendence of absolutely necessary, personal Being as absolute creating in relation to the contingent dimension of Being, in the following sense: God's transcendence in relation to the contingent dimension of Being occurs *completely within* the total self-immanence of absolutely necessary personal Being as absolute creating."[246]

How is this to be understood? Puntel supports a kind of panentheism expressed in the following quotation: "The transcendence of God in relation to contingent beings occurs *within God* as the consequence of God's own free act. In that God, by creating, posits contingent beings within Being, God creates within God the internal distinction by means of which God transcends contingent beings."[247] Panentheism has gained growing attention in the last decades[248] as a way to conceptualize, theologically and philosophically, the Pauline expression in Acts 17.27 (the *locus classicus* of panentheism): "In Him we live, and move, and have our being."[249] "Pan-en-theism" is different from pan-theism, for instance in its strong emphasis on freedom: God is free and thus distinct, as humans are free and thus distinct from God and each other, but still, God as creator and sustainer is in everything and everything is in God. Many have argued that God's transcendence and immanence are *inversely proportional* (the greater God's transcendence, the lesser God's immance), but Puntel instead maintains that they are *directly proportional* (the greater God's transcendence, the greater God's immanence).[250] I take it to be an open discussion whether the structural-systematic philosophy requires panentheism or whether it is possible to reconstruct the doctrine of creation in another way that is as coherent as this one. This is not discussed further here.

3.4.5.1.7.2 *The Possibility of Proceeding from the Previous Analysis*
As for (2), is it possible to go further in the designation of Being? Puntel's answer is affirmative, but he emphasizes that it is not possible within the current theoretical

---

245 Puntel, *Being and God*, 260.
246 Puntel, *Being and God*, 260. Italics removed, but emphasis on "no" and "completely within" is added.
247 Puntel, *Being and God*, 261–262. Original italics. As such, God's transcendence is here understood relationally (between God and creation) and not as an attribute of God.
248 Panentheism was not invented recently, of course, but has been a part of theological reflection for a long time. I am only pointing to the growing discussion of the concept and the use of the term.
249 See further Philip Clayton and A. R. Peacocke, eds., *In Whom We Live and Move and Have Our Being: Panentheistic Reflections on God's Presence in a Scientific World* (Grand Rapids: Eerdmans, 2004).
250 Puntel, *Being and God*, 263.

framework, that an additional and expanded framework is required[251] because he has reached "a methodological watershed."[252] Why is an expanded framework required? Because "the *absolute freedom* of necessary Being as absolute creating"[253] cannot be explicated in the current framework. The aspect of freedom can only be discovered through history because there cannot be given any a priori argument for or against such freedom; because absolutely necessary Being is free, it suffers no restraints or compulsions.[254] The implication of this for research is that no restraints can apply to the investigation of reality either because if any did, they would compromise the relation between object and method. Puntel states this in the following way: "In pursuing this investigation, the philosopher cannot acknowledge or respect any restrictions of any sort, particularly those imposed by religious communities and above all those imposed by Christian churches."[255] This implies that the traditional doctrinal systems and symbols cannot be a preestablished list of results that we now only seek to substantiate and defend. Philosophy – and systematic theology 3 – needs to be a free endeavour if the framework is to be explicated in a rationally justified way.

Puntel, therefore, rejects traditional understandings of the relationship between philosophy and theology, where philosophy is either only the handmaiden of theology, or theology is somehow a discipline that works with subjects that are reasonable but external to philosophy.[256] Instead, "[p]hilosophy and theology together constitute a *single universal science*, not in the sense of a simple identification, but in the sense that the *thematic domain* that is the traditional concern of Christian theology is also the domain that philosophy investigates following the methodological break

---

251 Puntel, *Being and God*, 264. "Additional determinations of absolute creating beyond absolute intelligence, absolute (and absolutely free) will, and personhood are not explicable or derivable within the theoretical framework with which the just-named determinations emerge."
252 Puntel, *Being and God*, 264.
253 Puntel, *Being and God*, 264. Original italics.
254 Puntel, *Being and God*, 265.
255 Puntel, *Being and God*, 266. Why the "above all those imposed by Christian churches" is a necessary qualification is not immediately clear to me. Later, Puntel discards all constraints from the philosopher's work. However, I doubt that it is possible to the extent Puntel demands it – if it is possible, it is only attainable as a result of intersubjectivity (collective trial and error) and not by a single author. See his statement on page 273. And yet, he seems to moderate his view on page 275. But the whole point is to uphold the distinction between the *practical* and the *theoretical* (278). And yet it appears that he forgets to distinguish between context of discovery and context of justification when he writes, "A person of faith can engage in such questioning while retaining that faith, but not while drawing inspiration, motivation, or – especially – premises from it." (281). Notwithstanding these notes, I support Puntel's aspiration for an unrestricted investigation of Being. This is captured by the phrase of C.S. Peirce, who said, "Don't block the way of inquiry." See Charles Sanders Peirce, '§4. The First Rule of Reason,' in *The Collected Papers, Vol. 1: Principles of Philosophy*, 1931.
256 Puntel, *Being and God*, 266–270.

described above and when that break is effectively respected and the philosopher proceeds in accordance with it."[257] The framework needed for the analysis of God to proceed is thus a framework that must be developed in cooperation between philosophy and theology.[258]

To elaborate on Puntel, I shall give two examples on themes that could be thematized at the level of systematic theology 1 and systematic theology 2 as examples on how the development of a theistic ontology makes it possible to present scientific theology at the other strata.

As to systematic theology 1, the notion of religious experiences can be an example. When believers describe their feelings of divine presence, e. g., when they receive the holy communion or the forgiveness after absolution, it is possible for the theologian to give a thick description of this that integrates God as really effective in these experiences, because it has been argued in systematic theology 3 that divine presence in the world (and in relation to created beings) is a possibility. Systematic theology 1 can therefore also explicate the structures between the experiences and the dogmatics behind the church practices to deepen the understanding of what is happening.

As to systematic theology 2, the notion of revelation comes to mind. This concept is central to the work at systematic theology 2, and the credibility of the term is established with the conclusion of Puntel's synchronic constitution. Because Absolutely Necessary Minded Being is free, we can argue that revelation (the identification of special divine agency with a climax in Jesus of Nazareth) is possible. And since there are lots of data in history that is related to the claim of revelation, we can begin to organize these data in coherent systems and compare these with alternatives. Puntel has shown that systematic theology 3 can work without the notion of revelation, but also that it is a natural implication to investigate the concept of revelation on the background of systematic theology 3 at the level of systematic theology 2.[259]

3.4.5.1.7.3 *To Sum Up*

Puntel thinks that a rationally justified public discourse about God (step 7) is possible within the structural-systematic philosophy (step 1–6). The argument for absolutely necessary, minded, free, creating Being has been made, and the term for Being as creator is "God." Puntel argues for an understanding of God's transcendence

---

257 Puntel, *Being and God*, 271.
258 Stated otherwise: Because philosophy gives us a notion of a free God, it leads us to the history of religions to see if or how God has used his freedom. This relation is explicated like this in both Puntel's and Pannenberg's works, respectively.
259 This is arguably also what Pannenberg has done. He has developed a model of revelation that focuses closely on God's free acts in history, especially in the incarnation of Jesus of Nazareth. See Pannenberg, *Systematic Theology*, 1:189–257.

such that the relationship between transcendence and immanence is explicated through configurations; this points to the fact that Being and beings are within each other, respectively (yet asymmetrically). This is often called "panentheism," all-in-God.

Puntel discusses the possibility of designating God further within the proposed framework, and he concludes in the negative; we need an additional and expanded framework for such designation, a framework that he does not provide. He only says that the methodological watershed calls for something more because God's freedom must be identified in history, and this is not possible to explicate within the framework employed so far. If it is to be done in a rationally justified way, theology and philosophy have to work together under the headline of free inquiry as a single universal science. What Puntel has done is, he says, is to explicate the fundamental framework for theology and make it available for further theoretical work.

The extended analysis of Puntel's theoretical framework for the God hypothesis has been presented as an attempt to determine whether a synchronic constitution of systematic theology is possible. Given the structural-systematic philosophy, it does indeed seem possible. This is not to claim that this is the only possible way to do it, or even the best way, but only to establish that this way is rationally warranted. I do argue, though, that the introduction to and discussion of the structural-systematic philosophy has shown it to be an especially precise and thought-through version of the synchronic constitution of systematic theology. Thus, Puntel has given us the possibility of continuing the work of this book.

A question arises, however, which will be discussed further in chapter eight, namely whether the synchronic constitution is theology proper and not just a branch of philosophy. To respond briefly, demarcating a discipline becomes possible when we have enough data to work with. Christianity contains more than enough data to grant it its own field. But what Puntel's philosophy has shown is that even if we discarded Christianity, a fundamental or natural theology could still be interesting to work with and this would in itself be enough to establish a distinct discipline. The argument is not that Puntel's philosophy should be taken as the framework for a specific discipline but only that it shows that a synchronic constitution of systematic theology 3 is possible.

In the next section, I introduce and discuss the notion of truth candidates, an important notion for both Rescher and Puntel. I have touched upon this term several times, but I need a more precise understanding in order to present coherence theory adequately.

3.4.6   The Concept of "Truth Candidate"

A helpful concept to introduce is the notion of "truth candidate" worked out by Nicholas Rescher. It is bound up with his version of the coherence theory of truth, which is a systematic approach to the search for truth (see 3.4.7). Due to the shortcomings of human cognitive faculties, our theories are fallibilistic, which calls for a regulatory notion of coherence. Truth is not the starting point but the terminus (and *telos*) of inquiry.[260] When we begin, we have a list of propositions that qualify as *truth-candidates* because, seen in isolation, they meet our standards for propositions. These propositions are also called "data," and the sum of them is a body of *prima facie* truths.[261] Data are always theory-dependent and should not be understood as pure or given. A problem with data is that taken as a totality, they are inconsistent, and we must thus develop a criterion for selecting from among the truth candidates. According to Rescher, our best available criterion for such selection is *coherence*, which "becomes the critical *test* of the qualifications of truth-candidates for being classed as genuine truths."[262] But a classical objection to coherence is the danger of stating a fiction as truth, stemming from the fact that reality cannot claim a monopoly on coherence. To avoid this, coherence has to be *with* something, which makes the notion of "data" important; it cannot be *mere* coherence that counts as truth, but only coherence with data, according to Rescher.[263] Individual data are further recognized by Rescher as propositions that have a "logico-epistemic bite," which means they must be plausible and well-founded (thus avoiding truth *ex nihilo*).[264] The best truth-candidates are therefore not merely theoretically possible but reasonably held as such, which warrants an epistemic hierarchy where empirical data are given priority.[265] This is very important because it incorporates the correct intuition of the correspondence theory, which emphasizes that truth has to do with reality, but at the same time maintains that there is not an exact correspondence between propositions and reality.[266] I find that Hugh Gauch's important note fits quite well with this particular understanding of the relationship between correspondence

---

[260] Rescher, *The Coherence Theory of Truth*, 39. This is one of the problems with Richard Rorty's pragmatic account of a consensus theory of truth: it takes consensus to be the point of departure. Nicholas Rescher, *Pluralism. Against the Demand for Consensus* (Oxford: Oxford University Press, 1993), 15.

[261] Rescher, *Philosophical Reasoning*, 181.

[262] Rescher, *The Coherence Theory of Truth*, 39.

[263] Rescher, *The Coherence Theory of Truth*, 65. This includes both propositional and empirical data.

[264] Rescher, *The Coherence Theory of Truth*, 56.

[265] In *Philosophical Reasoning*, Rescher states that "coherence *with the data of experience*" (p. 190, original italics) is mandatory, thus embracing some version of empiricism as basic for systematic philosophy. It seems, though, that Puntel disagrees with my interpretation, when he writes, "[d]ata in this sense are not 'sense data' or anything of the sort; instead, they are the linguistically/logically given starting points for any scientific (philosophical) undertaking." Puntel, *Structure and Being*, 43. But it strikes me that Puntel may be reading his own view into Rescher's given the quote at the beginning of this footnote.

[266] Rescher, *Philosophical Reasoning*, 185. "Now there is – in any event – merit in the correspondence theory's insistence that relations among propositions cannot tell the *ultimate* story because an

and coherence: "As the correspondence theory of truth is elaborated, it is clear that meaningfulness and coherence are necessary preconditions for truth and that truth has practical implications and value. To abandon the correspondence theory and to substitute coherence, pragmatism, or anything else as the core concept or the entirety of truth would be disastrous. If the definition of truth becomes defective or vague, science languishes."[267] Gauch probably supports a stronger version of correspondence than Rescher does, but they seem to agree in emphasizing the necessity of understanding the two views as mutually beneficial. Rescher emphasizes the centrality of empirical data for coherence theory, but he still takes coherence to be the critical criterion for our scientific theories. An advantage of this is that Rescher's perspective gives us the possibility of being scientific realists even though we should be aware of the difficulties in this position with a carefully explicated understanding of the complex relations between language, mind, and reality.[268]

Empirical data have the advantage that they are usually easy for most people to observe (if they know how and where to look) and that they have a more stable nature than non-empirical data. The observation of empirical data will result in many couplings between data, which makes it difficult to find coherent alternatives to the immediate interpretation of the experience. For example, if I, and thousands of others, claim that the historical building *The Round Tower/Stellaburgis Hafniens* ("Rundetårn" from 1642) is located in Copenhagen, this observation connects many sorts of data, and alternative explanations are probably much less coherent. But what, then, about important non-empirical data such as feelings, sensations, memories etc.? How are these to be assessed? Rescher says that we cannot find a "uniform general principle" to determine these but have to make "*ad hoc* considerations."[269] To put it differently, non-empirical data are less stable than empirical data because they are often more strongly delimited (in the mind) and thus give others fewer reasons to trust them. But from the beginning of an investigation, we should not discriminate in considering the data (and that is not Rescher's point of view either). All data are to be judged by their coherence with other data in the larger systematization of theories.

---

appropriate consonance must obtain between 'the actual facts of the matter' and a proposition regarding them to qualify those propositions are [sic] true."

267 Hugh G. Gauch, *Scientific Method in Practice* (New York: Cambridge University Press, 2003), 34.
268 Compare with his statement: "That theory does not hold that any and every system is true, no matter how abstract and limited; it holds that one system only is true, namely the system in which everything real and possible is coherently included." Rescher, *The Coherence Theory of Truth*, 66. See further his exploration in Nicholas Rescher, *Scientific Realism: A Critical Reappraisal* (Dordrecht: Reidel, 1989) and also in Nicholas Rescher, *Reality and Its Appearance*, Continuum Studies in American Philosophy (London and New York: Continuum, 2010).
269 Rescher, *The Coherence Theory of Truth*, 63. Original italics.

The following quote states the notion of the truth-candidate in Rescher's coherence theory:

> Acceptance-as-true is in general not the starting-point of inquiry but its terminus. To begin with, all that we generally have is a body of *prima facie* truths, i. e., propositions that qualify as potential – perhaps even as promising – *candidates* for acceptance. The epistemic realities being as they are, these candidate-truths will, in general, form a mutually inconsistent set, and so exclude one another so as to destroy the prospects of their being accorded *in toto* recognition as truths pure and simple. The best that can be done in such circumstances is to endorse those as truths that best "cohere" with the others so as to "make the most" of the data as a whole in the epistemic circumstances at issue. Coherence thus affords the criterial validation of the qualifications of truth-candidates for being classed as genuine truths.[270]

What does this imply for systematic theology 3? If we take religious experiences or feelings as *data*, we can understand this in a number of ways according to the theoretical framework within which we assess the experiences or feelings. And these understandings can be integrated into different coherent theories. That people have different kinds of religious experiences seems to be a relatively stable phenomenon throughout history and across the globe, but what to make of them? Are they subjectivist fictions, or is there a referentiality pointing to a spiritual reality not visible? We cannot decide based on the experiences alone but have to make judgements based on a more elaborated account. To go from a private to a public justification of these experiences is to let the experiences be assessed through a comparison of different theories that either include or exclude the possibility of religious experiences and then determine whether any of the theories are clearly more coherent than the others. As long as a theory that convincingly includes genuine religious experiences in a coherent way is not clearly less coherent than relevant alternatives, the experiences are to be seen as viable truth candidates.

3.4.7   A Short Introduction to Rescher's Coherence Theory of Truth

In the final two sections of this extensive discussion of systematic theology 3, I first give a short introduction to the coherence theory of truth as it is understood by Rescher (3.4.7). The reason is that I take Rescher's development of this theory to be an intriguing articulation of coherence as a criterion for truth and the best tool

---

270 Nicholas Rescher, *Cognitive Systematization. A Systems-Theoretic Approach to a Coherentist Theory of Knowledge* (Totowa: Rowman and Littlefield, 1979), 67.

for assessing and comparing ontologies. The task of comparing ontologies is the subject of the last subsection of the discussion of systematic theology 3 (3.4.8).

What is required for a coherence theory of truth according to Rescher? He lists what he calls "six conditions," which I shall quote in full length:

1. The truth of a proposition is to be assessed in terms of its 'coherence' with others: whether or not it is to be classed as true depends largely or exclusively on its relationships of compatibility or conflict with others. Correspondingly,
2. The issue of the truth of a proposition is a *contextual* matter in the sense that one cannot in general determine whether or not a proposition is true by inspecting it in isolation, but only by analysing it in the setting of other propositions. Accordingly,
3. The truth of propositions is crucially dependent on matters of *systematization*, that is, of their logical linkages with other propositions together with which they form a connected network. Thus
4. Truths must constitute a *system* that is *consistent* and whose members are appropriately *connected*: they must be interrelated so as to form a single cohesive unit, whose very cohesiveness acts to exclude other possibilities.
5. Moreover, this systematic unit must be sufficiently large to embrace the domain of real facts; it must exhibit a certain completeness – nothing can be omitted without due warrant. Accordingly, the domain of truth is determined through contextual considerations of compatibility and conflict and must be 'systematic' in being consistent, comprehensive, and cohesively unitary. These several systematic facets must be predominant in the coherence determination of truth.
6. However, a coherence theory will be such that certain laws of the classical theory of truth cannot be accepted in their traditional form. In general – outside the boundaries of special circumstances – the Law of Bivalence and of Excluded Middle can in particular be maintained only in a restricted, weakened form, and not their classical strong versions.[271]

What we gain from this is the possibility of collecting a number of theories with the highest level of coherence possible and then comparing these theories for their respective degrees of coherency, thus inferring to the best systematization, which we should count as provisional truth.[272] In sum, this is the proposed suggestion for how theologians can do what they aim to present, namely rationally justified public discourse about God. I elaborate on this account when I discuss the gains

---

271 Rescher, *The Coherence Theory of Truth*, 43–44.
272 Puntel, *Structure and Being*, 43. Cf. Rescher, *Philosophical Reasoning*, 132–41.

of comparing ontologies (see 5.2.8.1). I shall now look more closely into how this comparison is to be accomplished.

3.4.8 How to Compare Ontologies. A Puntelian Approach

As mentioned in 3.4.5.1.1.3, Puntel develops an "idealized four-stage philosophical method" for the work of systematic philosophy. The reason is that we want to be able to compare different systems, different ontologies, but to execute this comprehensive and complex task we need a *modus operandi*. The four-stage method is a helpful step-by-step approach to this task, so I discuss it further here.

The *first* stage is basically the same as Rescher's coherence methodology, which means that we here begin to identify and structure the different truth-candidates relevant for our work.[273] A problem for this kind of work is that the sum of all the data is incoherent and thus our work entails the aim of finding the most coherent theory that integrates as many relevant data as possible. To do this, Puntel suggests that we organize the information gathered into sets that are then scrutinized one by one for consistency. We start by identifying the *maximally consistent subsets* formed out of our collection of inconsistent sets. Set theory works by symbols that may be foreign to some readers, so I give a relatively simple example to introduce Puntel's thought. In the following equation, S = set, and p and q are different data that are parts of the set. Thus, we can have a set that says:

$$S = \{p, p \to q, \neg q\}$$

This set is inconsistent, because it says that p is, and if p is, then q is, but q is not. Therefore, p is not either, although we began by positing p. But we do not just stop here at the inconsistent set. Instead, we form three subsets from the set, and these are called the "maximally consistent subsets" because with the data we have at hand

---

[273] Note that Puntel is very critical of Rescher's use of the term "truth-candidate," which he does not specify precisely enough: "[i] Rescher ultimately fails to clarify the status of the datum. He takes this term as a technical one in a purely methodological sense: for him, 'datum' is simply that X that can and/or should be brought into a coherence nexus. He speaks of the datum as a 'proposition,' but he does not make explicit whether he means that in the usual technical sense (i. e., as the *expressum* of a sentence) or in some other possible sense. He also fails to specify its semantic or ontological status. [ii] At the other extreme, Rescher never specifies just what he means by the 'coherence' or 'whole' to which he ultimately aspires." Puntel, *Structure and Being*, 44. Puntel's charges are interesting, but they are also preposterous. Rescher does, as I have shown, make the semantic status specific, and there is an explicit reason for not making the ontological status specific *yet*. I also do not find the charges that Rescher fails to determine what he means by "coherence" or "whole" convincing. At the end of the day, his account may simply be more straightforward and transparent than Puntel's sometimes wordier and more elusive account.

in the example, this is the highest number of subsets that we can make that are still consistent. The different subsets are numbered as S_1, S_2, and S_3.

$S_1 = \{p, p{\to}q\}$ (equivalent to p q, i. e., "p and q")
$S_2 = \{p{\to}q, \neg q\}$ (equivalent to ¬p ¬q, i. e., "not-p and not-q")
$S_3 = \{p, \neg q\}$ (equivalent to p ¬q, i. e., "p and not-q")

This simple case shows that at the first stage of our investigation, we cannot avoid logic because it is a strong tool for organizing the possibilities into coherent subsets. But it also shows us that pure logic cannot take us much further, because the first stage only isolates the logical status of the truth candidates, but we need extra-logical resources to discriminate among them. The reason is that formal logic – as we use it in set theory – is without positive content because it only explicates the relations among the different elements. The structural sentences we now have at hand are general/universal sentences, but these are not yet constituted as theories, a step that is taken at the second stage.

The *second* stage Puntel calls "constitution of theories" for this very reason. Puntel has a relatively long discussion of different notions of what a theory is, describing the two most substantial forms, the axiomatic and the network forms, respectively,[274] but here it suffices to say that the basic difference between these two is that the axiomatic form has a strict "hierarchical-linear" structure that the network form does not.[275] The axiomatic form is widespread in the formal sciences, but Puntel argues for the use of a network structure in general, arguing that the totality of interrelations must be made explicit and then assessed for coherence. The reason is that in most cases, the "web of relations" cannot be understood in a hierarchical-linear way, but instead requires a more holistic understanding. At this second stage, we therefore need to understand the nature of what we are investigating, and, in most cases, a coherentist/network approach will be the most suitable.[276]

The *third* stage Puntel calls "systematization of theories," which covers the difficult work of creating coherent "networks of theories."[277] At stage one and two, single

---

274 Puntel, *Structure and Being*, 44–50.
275 "The only fundamental difference is that axiomatic systems and/or the axiomatic form of theory (at least in the sense of the first three forms introduced above) have an exclusively *hierarchical-linear* structure, whereas the form of theory relying on the network method does not." Puntel, *Structure and Being*, 48.
276 Note that, where philosophy is concerned, Puntel points to an ideal case at the second stage. "Nevertheless, at least in philosophy it is neither requisite (nor realistically practicable) to accomplish explicitly what the second stage requires; such accomplishment would occur only in the ideal case." Puntel, *Structure and Being*, 50 (under 1.4.4., the third stage).
277 Puntel, *Structure and Being*, 50–51.

theories have been isolated and developed, but now we need to integrate them into a larger whole, a theoretical network. How is this work done? Puntel mentions two steps of the "system-constituting method": "First, it develops a structure of structures that it presents as a network of theories, and second, this network of structures proves to be holistic – to be a whole (in a sense that must, of course, be clarified)."[278] Puntel does not describe this trajectory closely here, but he emphasizes that the network is, obviously, complex and comprehensive. Puntel himself presents an elaborated account of this in his own comprehensive systematic philosophy, especially chapter three of *Being and God,* which I have discussed thoroughly in 3.4.5.1.

The *fourth* stage regards the evaluation of the holistic systems with respect to "theoretical adequacy and truth-status."[279] Because Puntel argues for coherentism instead of foundationalism, we need a fourth stage that at the end of the investigation not only evaluates but also compares the different holistic systems and infers (approximate) truth to the best systematization. In addition to a comparison of the degree of coherence, Puntel lists two criteria for comparison of theories: Their degree of depth and their degree of grainedness. The deeper the structures are, the more fundamental and universal they are, and the finer grained the structures are explicated the higher degree of detail and precision our explication have.[280] The assessment of the comparison can only be provisional, hence there is only an asymptotic approximation to ideal truth because of the contingency of human rationality.

The steps of Puntel's program are thus: (1) identify → (2) constitution → (3) systematization → (4) evaluation and comparison. This is of course an "extraordinarily complex" task, but the argument with Puntel is that it is our best tool for developing coherent theories from the incoherent set of all data available.[281]

An important difficulty is that because foundationalism is unacceptable (because it is considered dogmatic in Puntel's philosophy), the question of "grounding" is salient. According to Puntel, every comprehensive system-grounding is relative to the comprehensive system framework, but the subsystematic theories (stages one and two) are doubly relative because they are relative to their particular frameworks *and* to the comprehensive framework.[282] There is no way to avoid this complexity, and the consequence is that comparison of coherence is the best tool we have for judging the strength of both theories and networks of theories.

---

278 Puntel, *Structure and Being,* 50–51.
279 Puntel, *Structure and Being,* 51–52.
280 Puntel, *Structure and Being,* 408–411.
281 Puntel, *Structure and Being,* 51.
282 Puntel, *Structure and Being,* 52.

To compare ontologies – which I suggest is the ultimate goal of systematic theology 3 – is thus to work at the fourth level. The different ontologies are developed and systematized at levels one through three, and at the last level we seek to evaluate on the best available systematization. This model can work heuristically, critically, and intersubjectively, which are all important features of genuine scientific work.

3.4.9   Conclusion

In this chapter I have discussed the model of a three-level stratification of systematic theology. The aim has been to strengthen the proposed argument that systematic theology 3 – the development and comparison of ontologies understood as comprehensive systematizations of reality – makes it possible for theologians to do what they aspire to do: to present rationally justified public discourse about God. If the work in systematic theology 3 is convincing, it lends credence to the scientific status of the work in systematic theology 1(where the religious expressions of believers are explicated) and systematic theology 2(where internal theories of Christian theology are developed, assessed, and compared). I see the levels as distinct due to a deliberate division of labour even though data, methods, presuppositions, and results can be shared among the strata.

The claim is that systematic theology 3 seeks to develop a *theistic* ontology and then compare this ontology to other relevant alternative ontologies developed in other theoretical frameworks. The test case for systematic theology 3 is thus theism, but it also implies – or hints at – a more elaborate explication of the doctrine of God that is developed in systematic theology 2. In the end, the theories developed in theology will be organic and reflexively interdependent, but there is a deliberate division of labour in order to support the scientific status of the theories, not least in conversation with non-theistic views.

In the next chapters (chapters four through eight), I investigate the main objections to the notion of systematic theology that have been developed in this chapter. The aim is to determine how robust and convincing the theory is when I assess it in relation to central and common criteria for science found in the philosophy of science.

Part Three: Objections to Systematic Theology as Scientific

Introduction

In this third part of the book, I discuss five objections to the proposed understanding of systematic theology as scientific. The five objections are selected from a longer list of possible objections, but I have chosen these five because they pertain to critical criteria for scientific work according to the proposed understanding.[1] Hence, I do not claim that these five objections are the only relevant objections to discuss but that they are the five most relevant for the proposed definition of systematic theology and thus for the scope of this project. The objections discussed are: testability, falsifiability, intersubjectivity, normativity, and distinct research. Each of the five is defined and discussed at length in the following chapters, with one chapter devoted to each objection.

From the outset, I emphasize that I take these five objections to be closely connected but not interchangeable. The investigation therefore carries an element of complexity in that even if systematic theology manages to meet one objection, another objection can still undermine the notion of systematic theology that I have developed. How the objections are connected, and which challenges remain for systematic theology after meeting a given criterion, is explained in the individual chapters.

Before I begin the investigation, I remind the reader how I understand the objections:[2]

- The objection from testability (chapter four) says that systematic theology does not have a criterion for testing.
- The objection from falsifiability (chapter five) says that even if systematic theology can be tested, it cannot use the most common criterion for testing, that is, falsification.

The objection from intersubjectivity (chapter six) says that even if systematic theology can operate with acceptable criteria for testing and even meet the best one, that of falsifiability, there is no agreement on what the criteria says about data.

---

1 There could be other relevant objections than these five, and other researchers may have selected other objections as the most problematic for systematic theology. But based on my understanding of systematic theology and my understanding of science – the two notions that structure the conversation – I argue that these five are the most critical for systematic theology as a scientific discipline.
2 These points were also stated at greater length in the introduction (1.4.1).

- The objection from normativity (chapter seven) says that even if systematic theology can meet criteria for testing and find agreement on what the criteria says about, as a discipline it sets a problematic type of criteria for testing and selection of data.
- The objection from distinct research (chapter eight) says that even if the criteria of systematic theology for testing are not problematic, it does not meet with accepted criteria that would distinguish the discipline from other disciplines in a legitimate way.

These chapters seek to challenge and discuss the thesis that systematic theology 3 is scientific. To make the account as clear as possible, I have written the objections as classic syllogisms and discuss the premises before I assess whether the conclusion is sound or not. The logical form of the syllogism is *modus tollens*: $P \rightarrow Q$, $\neg Q$, $\neg P$ (If P, then Q. Not Q, therefore not P).[3] They are all "T-arguments," which means that all premises must be true if the conclusion is to be true. Taken individually, the premises are not strong enough to uphold the conclusion. On the other hand, if the premises are true, the conclusion follows unconditionally.[4]

Throughout these chapters, systematic theology refers to systematic theology 3 as defined in chapter three if nothing else is stated. As I argued in chapter three, the legitimacy of systematic theology 1 and systematic theology 2 in a research context rests on the legitimacy of systematic theology 3, and therefore it is primarily the proposed understanding of systematic theology 3 that I challenge and defend in these chapters.

---

[3] Note, however, that for the sake of readability and the structure of the chapters, two of the arguments are stated in simplified versions that are not strictly *modus tollens*-arguments. The correct arguments are stated in footnotes in the respective chapters.

[4] See, e. g., Stephen Toulmin, *The Uses of Argument* (Cambridge: Cambridge University Press, 1958), 94–145 and William Hughes and Jonathan Lavery, *Critical Thinking. An Introduction to the Basic Skills*, Canadian Edition, Seventh Edition (Peterborough: Broadview Press, 2015), 161–77.

Chapter Four: Objection 1—Testability

Premise 1. Scientific theories must be testable.
Premise 2. The theories of systematic theology are not testable.
Conclusion. Therefore, the theories of systematic theology are not scientific theories.[1]

4.1 Introduction

The criterion of testability is very broad and imprecise, and it is therefore closely related to the next criterion, discussed in chapter five, the criterion of falsifiability, which I take to be the most widespread understanding of testability.

Scientists test their theories in various ways depending on the subject matter. They measure, weigh, count, calculate, observe, etc. if the subject matter is empirically testable, and they analyse, compare, systematize, argue, etc. when the subject matter is non-empirical or conceptual. That science is under the obligation of testing its claims is almost a truism, and hardly anyone tries to refuse this criterion. Thus, it is not testability as such that is the key question or difficulty for the philosophy of science but two related questions that are also discussed in this chapter. The first is the question *what* must be testable – single propositions or whole theories? The first part of the chapter is devoted to a discussion of the view that science requires the testing of single empirical propositions (4.2.2). The third part of the chapter is devoted to a discussion of the opposite view, namely that testing applies to whole theories (4.2.4). I argue for the latter perspective and want to strengthen this view with an integration of coherence theory in this holistic view of testability. Between these two parts is a relatively long excursus about inferences (4.2.3) because this is the second question of ubiquitous debate in the philosophy of science: which consequences can we draw from our tests? In other words, what is the step from the test to the conclusion? How confident can we be about the results, and which generalizations can we draw from them? Usually, two types of inferences are discussed – induction and deduction – but I restrict the discussion here to induction, because I return to the notion of deduction in relation to the discussion of falsifiability (5.2.7). In this chapter, I discuss the problematic notion of induction

---

1 The correct *modus tollens*-argument says: Premise 1: If theories of systematic theology are scientific, the theories of systematic theology must be testable. Premise 2: Theories of systematic theology are not testable. Conclusion: Theories of systematic theology are not scientific.

and introduce the main arguments for and against this kind of inference (4.2.3.1). The aim here is to show that the standard critique in the tradition from Hume to Popper is valid, but that newer attempts to qualify induction are also interesting and convincing. Next, I discuss two alternatives that contemporary philosophers discuss to refine induction. The first is Inference to the Best Explanation, which has also gained attention in the field of systematic theology (4.2.3.3), and the second is Bayesian Inference, which is an attempt to use probability theory as a tool for induction which is also used by some theologians (4.2.3.3.1). In the present book I take Bayesian Inference to be a version of the Inference to the Best Explanation because the point of Bayesian Inference here is that scientists should infer to the most probable theory available. I suggest an alternative introduced by Nicholas Rescher called Inference to the Best Systematization, which is a convincing model in itself but also a useful bridge to the discussion of the testing of whole theories, where systematicity is essential.

Testability is an essential and useful criterion for science because we believe all sorts of things about the world and express these beliefs to others. Some are harmless or trivial whereas others, such as political, ideological, and religious claims, have potentially significant consequences. If other persons have views fundamentally different from ours, many are hesitant to adopt these beliefs and will probably only consider doing so if they feel deeply persuaded by rational, emotional, or experiential reasons or arguments. This is a truism. So, the question here is whether and how science works differently, and this I shall investigate in the following.

4.2 Premise 1

In science, we try to find rational tools to test the various hypotheses, postulates, arguments, theories etc. we are presented with. In sum, we want to be able to *test* the validity of a given statement by seeking "maximal informativeness and testability."[2] The reason for this is that testing of theories is our best tool for criticism, making it the indispensable tool for judging the claims of a theory: "testing is arguably the most effective organon of criticism in science. Theories can be criticized by testing them against observations or experiments."[3] But it is not without problems. Testability is uncontested as a criterion for science, but it is also one of the most problematic notions.[4] One challenge is that scientists have always referred to "untestable entities,

---

2 Rescher, *Scientific Realism*, 57.
3 Stathis Psillos and Martin Curd, eds., *The Routledge Companion to Philosophy of Science*, Routledge Philosophy Companions (London: Routledge, 2010), 60.
4 As Rosenberg says, "[a] statement which can figure in a scientific explanation must be testable by experience. This requirement, that the claims of science must be testable, is both the most widely

processes, things, events and properties" when they have sought to explain anything, and this seems unavoidable.[5] But perhaps it is not a devastating problem but instead an inevitable condition for fallible humans with limited cognitive capabilities. In this chapter I present a discussion of this criterion and try to push our understanding of testability further. First, I define the term provisionally to demarcate the notion for the following investigation, and then I discuss in detail how testability has been and is to be understood as a scientific criterion – this change in understanding is essentially a move from the testing of single propositions to that of whole theories.

4.2.1   Definition of Testability

Provisionally, I understand the criterion of testability as requiring that it be possible to test scientific theories through a well-described and transparent method. This method can be either empirical or conceptual depending on the research subject. Testability is not a demand for final verification of theories but merely the requirement that it be possible for one researcher to assess, test, and evaluate the results arrived at by another.

From the outset, it is helpful to distinguish between testability as a principle and testability as an umbrella term for methods, i. e., testability can refer either to the demand (a) that theories must be testable, or (b) that it must be possible to test them by this or that method. Merely to state that something must be testable is not very helpful if no one can explain how to do so. For example, when Wesley Salmon discusses scientific inferences and says that they involve three different matters – (1) thinking of the hypothesis, (2) plausibility considerations, and (3) testing or confirmation – we need to know more precisely what (3) covers.[6] To take one example: in line with Bruno Latour and Agent-Network-Theory it is now popular to talk of the "agency of things" and try to analyse the relationship between human agency and the agency of artifacts. But how do we test results arrived at by application of this theory? For one thing, it is not obvious how to do an empirical test. For another thing, even just developing a proper conceptuality leaves us with interpretations that are hard to sustain. As Ronald Giere says, "[t]he first thing to

---

  accepted conclusion and the source of the most intractable problems in the philosophy of science." Alexander Rosenberg, *Philosophy of Science: A Contemporary Introduction*, Third Edition (New York: Routledge, 2012), 65.
5 Rosenberg, *Philosophy of Science*, 84. "Untestable" must here refer to "empirically impossible to test," which is only one way of testing, because there are other ways to test, for example by determining whether the theory leads to inconsistencies. I return to this in 4.2.5.
6 Wesley C. Salmon, *The Foundations of Scientific Inference*, 50th Anniversary Edition (Pittsburgh: University of Pittsburgh Press, 2017), 114.

realize is that applying concepts associated with human agency (mind, consciousness, intentionality) to extended entities involving both humans and artifacts, or to inanimate entities themselves, is a matter of fairly high-level interpretation. One cannot even imagine an empirical test of Clark's claim that his man's notebook is part of the man's mind."[7] The point is that the criterion of testability is only useful if we are able to determine how to execute the test. If a theory is not testable it may not be counted as a scientific theory, but it can nonetheless be valuable for other reasons (e. g., emotive, existential, political, aesthetical, etc.). I can therefore say that it is a legitimate criterion for scientific work that its theories be testable, but *how* testability is practiced, and the validity of the methods, must be discussed carefully.

We have different ways to do this in the natural, social, and human sciences, respectively, and there is an ongoing discussion about how much overlap there is between these approaches. Some state very broadly that we can have the same kind of confidence in all scientific investigations because all explanatory success whether in physics or in political science is rooted in our confidence that human judgment is rational and trustworthy.[8] All explanatory success is said to be rooted in "the cognitive basis" of humans and for this reason there are resemblances between the different scientific fields.[9] Scientific theories are of various kinds in different fields, but the ability and fragility of human rationality is a condition shared by all, so explanations play similar roles in different fields. We can strive toward objectivity, but the observer/theorist inevitably affects the observed/the theory. Others are more confident and self-aware about the possibilities and type of results in their specific discipline and emphasize the differences between the disciplines in this regard. This is obviously due to the major achievements in the natural sciences in the last five hundred years. But the recent history of the philosophy of science – which includes many philosophers who also work in the natural sciences – has nuanced the picture to a significant extent.[10] We have to hold together two streams that flow in different directions: On the one hand it seems problematic to try to downplay the achievements of the natural sciences, but on the other hand, the philosophical critique of positivistic views of science is so detailed and convincing that we cannot but accept it. How then to proceed?

As stated in the introduction, this chapter begins with a discussion of the view that scientific testing concerns single propositions that scientists seek to confirm or verify. This will largely be an overview of a historical discussion because the view

---

[7] Ronald N. Giere, *Scientific Perspectivism* (Chicago: The University of Chicago Press, 2006), 110.
[8] Paul L. Allen, 'Is There Verification in Theology?', *Open Theology* 3 (2017): 429.
[9] Allen, 'Is There Verification in Theology?', 429.
[10] See, e. g., Thomas S. Kuhn, *The Structure of Scientific Revolutions*, Second Edition, Enlarged (Chicago: Chicago University Press, 1970) or James Ladyman, *Understanding Philosophy of Science* (New York: Routledge, 2001), chap. 4.

is not often defended by philosophers of science today, but it is still important to integrate in the discussion because it is part of the background for the contemporary discussion of testing holistic theories that I return to later (4.2.4).

4.2.2   Testing Single Propositions: Confirmation Theory

This section begins with a description of Rudolph Carnap's view of testing and confirmation theory, which was very influential at the beginning of the 20th century. I then discuss more broadly how Logical Positivism understood testing and why the oft-critiqued Verification Principle was defended within this school of thought, before I discuss a premise for much scientific work that is both a condition and a problem, i. e., the idealization of conditions in experimentation (4.2.2.1). I end this section with a discussion of one of the key texts in the criticism of the view of single-proposition testability, namely, W.V. Quine's article "Two Dogmas of Empiricism" (4.2.2.2). Quine's text is a key for understanding why the view of Carnap and Logical Positivism became unsatisfactory for many philosophers of science.

4.2.2.1   The Defence of Testing Single Propositions

Initially, testability was an important criterion for the demarcation between natural science and metaphysics within the school of empiricism.[11] Hardly anyone was more influential in the explication of the term than Rudolph Carnap, who was an ardent defender of the connection between testability and observation throughout his career. As he wrote in 1937 in the second part of his important essay, "Testability and Meaning," "As empiricists, we require the language of science to be restricted in a certain way; we require that descriptive predicates and hence synthetic sentences are not to be admitted unless they have some connection with possible observations, a connection which has to be characterized in a suitable way."[12] Empiricists aimed at certainty, and certainty could only be attained through analysis (*a priori* justification primarily through logic) or observation (*a posteriori* confirmation of "synthetic sentences," as Carnap labels them) of single propositions. Thus, meaningful sentences (or propositions) that were not tautological (that is, had actual content and not only legitimate relations) had to be testable by experiments, because expressions were meaningful only if it was possible to state how to *confirm* them.[13]

---

11   This can still be claimed, see, e. g., this statement from Ladyman: "the sciences differ from the arts in being subject to testing by experience and this must be the final arbiter of any scientific dispute." Ladyman, *Understanding Philosophy of Science*, 75.
12   Rudolf Carnap, 'Testability and Meaning–Continued,' *Philosophy of Science* 4, no. 1 (1937): 33.
13   Ladyman, *Understanding Philosophy of Science*, 95.

Carnap's philosophy is closely connected with an attempt to overcome Hume's argument that scientific research is inductive but irrational. According to Carnap it is both inductive and rational. This ambition to counter Hume is one he shared with a number of scientists and philosophers in Vienna, and I here briefly introduce their philosophy, which has dominated much discussion in the philosophy of science ever since with both heirs and critics. Logical Positivism arose in the 1920s in the famous *Vienna Circle* under the leadership of Moritz Schlick.[14] The Vienna Circle was strongly influenced by the empiricism of Ernst Mach, an epistemological position that states that all non-analytical sentences are justifiable only by sensory experience.[15] Logical Positivism then developed an analytical language with the purpose of distinguishing between cognitively meaningful and cognitively meaningless statements. According to Logical Positivism, all cognitively meaningful statements can be verified empirically (if they are not analytic), which means by observations and experiments: "a statement has empirical meaning iff it is verifiable."[16] This epistemology is well reflected in Carnap's immensely influential article "Empiricism, Semantics, and Ontology," for example in the following central quotation: "… Are unicorns and centaurs real or merely imaginary? […] These questions are to be answered by empirical investigation […] The concept of reality occurring in these internal questions is an empirical scientific non-metaphysical concept."[17] This gives us "the verification principle," which became a popular criterion for meaning at the beginning of the 20th century. "The verification principle was thought to be a way of making precise the empirical observational, or experimental component of science. Obviously, the positivists, following in the empiricist tradition, thought that the basis of science lay in observation and in experiment. These were the tests that made science reliable, the foundation that distinguished science from other types

---

14 Ladyman has a good discussion of Logical Positivism's views and summarizes their philosophy neatly in seven points on page 151 of *Understanding Philosophy of Science*.

15 Rosenberg, *Philosophy of Science*, 196. *Logical positivism* and *logical empiricism* are often used as synonyms, but specialists have discussions about their nuances. If a difference is argued for, then *positivism* is associated with the philosophy of Carnap and *empiricism* with that of Reichenbach. Godfrey-Smith notes some of the nuances within the empiricist camp: Empiricism is "a diverse family of philosophical views, all asserting the fundamental importance of *experience* in explaining knowledge, justification, and rationality. A slogan used for traditional empiricism in this book is 'Experience is the only source of real knowledge about the world.' Not all empiricists would like that slogan. There are also empiricists theories of language, which connect the meaning of words with experience or some kind of observational testing." Godfrey-Smith, *Theory and Reality*, 235.

16 Dancy, *An Introduction to Contemporary Epistemology*, 87.

17 Rudolf Carnap, 'Empiricism, Semantics, and Ontology,' *Revue Internationale de Philosophie* 4 (1950): 21.

of knowledge claims."[18] The Verification Principle was already heavily discussed before the Second World War, but the criticism arose after the war with influential books and articles that undermined the program (see 4.2.2.2).

In order to understand why many philosophers of science grew uneasy with the confirmation theory, it is important to understand a particular working condition for much scientific work. A large amount of scientific work is idealized, which means that researchers isolate their objects and remove many factors that could disturb the measurement or observation.[19] In other words, they change the open system of reality and make an idealized closed system with the hope of understanding a specific aspect of reality in relation to these precise conditions.[20] This is very productive and has been a fruitful procedure for centuries, today, e. g., seen in the prevalent use of computer simulations in many different fields of research. However, when discussing testability, it is important to note that testability – even in an empirical sense concerning single propositions – is not easily done, as Imre Lakatos says emphatically: "The first versions may even 'apply' only to non-existing 'ideal' cases; it may take decades of theoretical work to arrive at the first novel facts and still more time to arrive at *interestingly testable* versions of the research programmes, at the stage when refutations are no longer foreseeable in the light of the programme itself."[21] Lakatos's point is on the one hand that a simple trial-and-error progression through single inductive empirical experiments is not how science works, and on the other hand that these idealized settings make the results underdetermined (see further 5.2.4). Idealization is often necessary because it is the only way to set up theories for empirical testing, so it should be accepted as an inevitable part of modern science, but all the more should we be aware of the pitfalls of this procedure.[22] Idealization is less relevant in conceptual thinking, but an analogous approach might be the tool of creating thought experiments, a procedure that is prevalent in both philosophy and theology (3.4.5.1).

Before I look deeper into this criticism of Logical Positivism and its understanding of testing, it is worth noting that many philosophers and scientists worked to refine the Verification Principle, and this gradually led to a distinction between *strong* and *weak* verification as, e. g., A.J. Ayer already states it in the foreword to *Language, Truth, and Logic* from 1936: "For I require of an empirical hypothesis,

---

18 Peter K. Machamer and Michael Silberstein, eds., *The Blackwell Guide to the Philosophy of Science*, Blackwell Philosophy Guides 7 (Malden: Blackwell, 2002), 3.
19 Currie, *Rock, Bone, and Ruin*, 249.
20 Bhaskar, *A Realist Theory of Science*, 118–26.
21 Imre Lakatos, *The Methodology of Scientific Research Programmes*, Philosophical Papers 1 (Cambridge: Cambridge University Press, 1999), 65. Original italics.
22 See Currie's excellent account of idealization in relation to testing in the historical sciences: Currie, *Rock, Bone, and Ruin*, 249–273.

not indeed that it should be conclusively verifiable [i. e., *strong verification*], but that some possible sense-experience should be relevant to the determination of its truth or falsehood [i. e., *weak verification*]."[23] This understanding of *weak* verification is still present in contemporary science, as I show when dealing with James Ladyman's upgrading of induction (4.2.3.1.2),[24] but as a criterion for all scientific work, it does not have many heirs today. The testing of single propositions is often replaced by a view of testing as concerned with testing whole theories, as we will see in 4.2.4. It is relevant, however, to note that the history of the discussion is more complex than standard textbooks often indicate. Godfrey-Smith among others has noticed that logical positivists already accepted some notion of holism *before* Quine published his article, and that the debate is more about the implications of this insight and how the Verification Principle is actually affected than about some kind of naïve atomism.[25] Notwithstanding this point, Rosenberg sums up the state of the majority of philosophy of science since the mid-20th century in the following clear text: "A statement is testable if definite consequences for observation can be inferred from it and compared to observations. Logical positivists demanded that all meaningful statements be testable. Post-positivist philosophers have accepted that no single statement is testable by itself."[26] The labelling is less interesting than the content, and many philosophers of science today agree with some variant of holism.

Logical Positivism deserves a more careful discussion, but for the purposes here, the above will suffice as a background for introducing one of the main critics of Logical Positivism, W.V. Quine. In the following, his critique given in his article on the two dogmas of empiricism is presented in order to show how it contributed to the overcome of the focus on testing singe propositions by Logical Positivism. This

---

23 Alfred J. Ayer, *Language, Truth and Logic* (Harmondsworth: Penguin, 1983), 9. Jonathan Dancy unfolds the distinction a bit differently: "Strong verification is conclusive verification; a statement is conclusively verifiable if, once we have the best possible evidence for it, there remains no possibility that the statement be false [...] A weakly verifiable statement is not itself strongly verifiable, but is confirmable or disconfirmable by appeal to other statements which are conclusively verifiable; that is, strongly verifiable statements can count as evidence for or against it." Dancy, *An Introduction to Contemporary Epistemology*, 88. It appears that Dancy holds strong verification to be a positive possibility, but this seems to be what Ayer denies.

24 See also Gerhard Schurz, *Philosophy of Science: A Unified Approach* (New York: Routledge, 2014), 26: "The fourth methodological feature: Science attempts to *test empirically* its general and hypothetical sentences by comparing the predicted (potential) observation sentences with the currently known (actual) observation sentences. If the latter are in agreement with the former, the prediction was successful (it then becomes a successful explanation) and the hypothetical sentence (law or theory) is *confirmed* or *corroborated*. If there is a contradiction between the latter and the former, the prediction was without success and the law or theory is *falsified*, or in the case of a merely statistical prediction, *weakened*." See also p. 32.

25 Godfrey-Smith, *Theory and Reality*, 32–33.

26 Rosenberg, *Philosophy of Science*, 201.

is an important example for understanding why the notion of testability turned from the testing of single propositions to the testing of whole theories.

4.2.2.2   The Critique of Testing Single Propositions

In his critique of Carnap's and Logical Positivism's understanding of testing, Quine criticized two dogmas of empiricism that he called "the dogma of analyticity" and "the dogma of reductionism." I present his critique in the following to give one example from the literature that explains why many philosophers of science have left the Verification Principle of single propositions.

The dogma of analyticity is understood in relation to Kant's philosophy, especially a central sentence from the first critique. Kant writes, "Solche allgemeine Erkenntnisse nun, die zugleich den Charakter der innern Notwendigkeit haben, müssen, von der Erfahrung unabhängig, vor sich selbst klar und gewiss sein."[27] Quine argued that Kant (implicitly) presupposes his concept of meaning in his philosophy, and it is thus this concept of meaning that is the object of discussion in Quine's text. Quine states, "[m]eaning is what essence becomes when it is divorced from the object of reference and wedded to the world."[28] Meaning concerns ideas but the concept is so weak that Quine regards it as futile to try to make science rest on meaning. A central problem is the concept of synonymy because ideas are so vaguely determined that often it is not possible to decide whether we are talking of one linguistic form or two.[29] Whether we speak of synonyms or not must be decided by defining the words. Take for instance the word "bachelor". In one use of the term, it is defined as an "unmarried man," thus these two terms are synonyms. But how do we know that? From the dictionary.[30] But the lexicographer is an empiricist working only with descriptive methods, so his definitions are not analytic. Therefore, "[j]ust what it means to affirm synonymy […] is far from clear."[31] Quine's argument is that in almost all cases – "except in the extreme case of the explicitly conventional introduction of new notations"[32] – the definitions rest on synonymy instead of explaining how the terms are related, and the

---

27 "Now such general cognitions, which at the same time have the character of inner necessity, must, independent of experience, be clear and certain before themselves." (Translation MAM) Kant, *Kritik der reinen Vernunft. Erster Teil*, 3:48. Cf. W.V.O. Quine, 'Two Dogmas of Empiricism', *The Philosophical Review* 60, no. 1 (January) (1951): 20–21.
28 Quine, 'Two Dogmas of Empiricism', 22.
29 Quine, 'Two Dogmas of Empiricism', 22.
30 A dictionary is, therefore, a good example of a circularity that is not vicious. We cannot explain and define any word without using other words.
31 Quine, 'Two Dogmas of Empiricism', 25.
32 Quine, 'Two Dogmas of Empiricism', 27.

definitions can therefore not be the key to analytic judgments. In the third section of the article, Quine examines the possibility that the interchangeability between two concepts explains what synonymy is. If that operation is valid, the concepts must be exchangeable with one another in all contexts while the truth value stays identical. The question, however, is whether interchangeability can save synonymity if it is possible to interchange nonsynonymous words or expressions. According to Quine, we cannot make this claim analytically because we need to relativize the words to specific languages and contexts.[33] Another possibility is that semantic rules could solve the problem, as Carnap suggested, but semantic rules are helpful only in clarification of the concept "analyticity" if we already know what this word means.[34] In sum, Quine's argument against the dogma of analyticity is that every attempt to explain and ground analyticity actually presupposes it and thus does not succeed in explaining it. The consequence is that Kant's distinction between analytical and synthetic statements cannot be upheld, and this was a presupposition for the philosophy of Logical Positivism and its view of testing.[35]

The second dogma, *the dogma of reductionism*, concerns reductionism in language and can be treated much more briefly because Quine's assessment builds systematically on his previous exposition. The dogma of reductionism is the view that the truth of a statement has two components, a *linguistic* and a *factual* one. The linguistic component equals analyticity (and thus the problems discussed above return), and the factual component concerns the smallest units of thought that can be verified in experience. But this also presupposes analyticity because we need language to describe the smallest units of thought. The consequence of these arguments is that it is not possible, according to Quine, to treat statements individually, but *only* in conjunction.[36]

Quine thus discards both dogmas of empiricism as myths, but what is left of empiricism then? According to Quine, a more holistic and metaphysical empiricism is needed. As he poignantly states, "[t]he unit of empirical significance is the whole of science."[37] The point is that we do not test isolated statements but always whole units, and we can *eo ipso* make adjustments everywhere we need to in the theory to make it work.[38] Another implication is that Quine's holism is a holism not only about

---

33 Quine, 'Two Dogmas of Empiricism,' 29.
34 Quine, 'Two Dogmas of Empiricism,' 34.
35 Quine, 'Two Dogmas of Empiricism,' 34. "But, for all its a priori reasonableness, a boundary between analytic and synthetic statements simply has not been drawn. That there is such a distinction to be drawn at all is an unempirical dogma of empiricists, a metaphysical article of faith."
36 Quine, 'Two Dogmas of Empiricism,' 38.
37 Quine, 'Two Dogmas of Empiricism,' 39.
38 Quine says: "Any statement can be held true come what may, if we make drastic enough adjustments elsewhere in the system." (p. 40). He even says, "no statement is immune to revision" and that the

testing, but also about meaning.[39] If only the testable has any cognitive meaning, as the positivists say, and we can only test theories holistically, then it follows that meaning is holistic as well. This causes a lot of trouble for the positivists who – in the tradition from Frege and Russell – sought an atomistic notion of meaning. Now we also see why this paper from Quine is so influential in the discussion of testability. The holistic account of testability rests on the critique of the insufficiency of the atomism espoused by Logical Positivism and empiricism. This view is the important background for the proposal of a revised account of testability that is presented in 4.2.4, where I discuss the view of testing as testing of whole theories.

I should add here that there are other implications of Quine's critique – and that of others – that problematize the view of testing as the testing of single propositions. One is the insight that there is no obvious relation between language and objects. This makes our observations theory-laden because we cannot study anything without prior knowledge of and prior expectations about what we will find. Another consequence is the underdetermination of theory, i. e., the fact that we can always form competing hypotheses about why something is the case, and this problematizes the view that single propositions are the important parts of scientific theories.[40] The reason for the problem of underdetermination is that a theory will always say more about reality, than what can be tested empirically. And this data-background can always be understood in many different ways. These two consequences are discussed more closely below.

To sum up, I ask, why was Quine's critique such a devastating attack on Logical Positivism's view of testing? The answer is that Logical Positivism sought to test everything according to sensory experience and thereby to verify individual statements/propositions and that, because Quine showed that conceptual reductionism is not possible and individual statements cannot be tested as such, this procedure simply cannot work.[41] Or to put it differently, there are no "brute facts," no "pure data," because all must be interpreted as parts of systems, "[a] theory can be tested only by means of another theory; a physical system can never be compared with the 'exact' data of observation if we wish to discover its truth value but only with another system, with a whole set of theoretical principles and theorems."[42] As such,

---

fundamental laws of logic could be up for revision (ibid.); but he withdrew this controversial claim in his later writings such as W.V.O. Quine, *Philosophy of Logic*, Foundations of Philosophy Series (Englewood Cliffs: Prentice-Hall, 1970).

39 Godfrey-Smith, *Theory and Reality*, 33.
40 Note that underdetermination is primarily a theoretical problem. In practice, we are able to choose between competing theories, otherwise we would have more competing models than we have.
41 I engage further with this in the discussion of falsification in chapter five.
42 Ernst Cassirer, *The Problem of Knowledge. Philosophy, Science, and History since Hegel*, trans. William H. Woglom and Charles W. Hendel (New Haven: Yale University Press, 1950), 113. And further:

there is a circularity between a linguistic hypothesis and empirical research, because language shapes what we understand in experiments and observations, and the empirical evidence shapes how we understand the meaning of words/linguistic expressions.[43]

The reception of Logical Positivism since Quine (among others) has been harsh, for example in the words of Hilary Putnam: "All the formal algorithms proposed for testing, by Carnap, by Popper, by Chomsky, etc., are, to speak impolitely, *ridiculous*: if you don't believe this, program a computer to employ one of these algorithms and see how well it does at testing theories! There are *maxims* for discovery and maxims for testing: the idea that correct ideas just come from the sky, while the methods for testing them are highly rigid and predetermined, is one of the worst legacies of the Vienna Circle."[44] Putnam's refusal is an example of a complete rejection of the atomism of Logical Positivism's understanding of testability. I agree with this rejection, but before a revised account is suggested, I make an excursus in order to discuss an important aspect of testability, which is that of which inferences can be made from tests. Or, in other words, how do philosophers of science argue for the steps from test to conclusion?

4.2.3   Excursus: Inferences – The Steps from Tests to Conclusions

Quine was one of the leading critics of Logical Positivism, and his arguments were central contributions to the dissolution of its influence in the philosophy of science. The point for the purpose here is that Quine's arguments showed that testing singular statements is not the most important thing, which is rather the testing of whole theories. But before examining the holistic view more closely (4.2.4), I shall now discuss various important instances of inference as they are discussed in the contemporary literature in the philosophy of science (4.2.3). I first discuss the notion of induction and various critiques thereof (4.2.3.1) before giving an introduction to more recent attempts to upgrade induction as seen in Inference to the Best Explanation (4.2.3.2), including Bayesian Inference (4.2.3.2.1). I end with a conclusion to the discussion (4.2.3.3).

"Physical science is a system that must be accepted as a self-contained whole, an organism of which no single part can be made to work without all the others, even those farthest removed, becoming active – or – some more, some less, but all in some precise degree."

43   This is one of the reasons why I find coherence to be so useful in scientific research. With this circularity between language and empirical evidence, coherence can work both as the best tool for clarifying our terminology and for our understanding of empirical evidence.

44   In "The 'corroboration' of theories" in Hacking, *Scientific Revolutions*, New York: Oxford University Press, 1981, 60–79, quoted from Edward G. Slingerland, *What Science Offers the Humanities: Integrating Body and Culture* (Cambridge: Cambridge University Press, 2008), 68.

4.2.3.1 Induction

Induction is here an umbrella term for various kinds of inferences that argue for a relation between particular cases and generalizations. It is understood in a number of ways both historically and in the contemporary literature, and I introduce some of them in the following.[45]

James Ladyman distinguishes between two types of inductivism, a naïve[46] and a sophisticated[47] variant, respectively. The *naïve* inductivism is rooted in Francis Bacon's *Novum Organum*.[48] Bacon proposed that through experiments and observation, it was possible to attain reliable knowledge of the world and thus to infer from single instances to general laws. Moreover, it was possible to gain *new* knowledge of the world as opposed to merely deepening accepted knowledge or rediscovering ancient truths.[49] But since David Hume published his thorough critique of induction[50] in *A Treatise of Human Nature* from 1739 and again in a shortened version in *An Enquiry concerning Human Understanding* from 1748, most philosophers of science have rejected naïve inductivism. Hume's critique was brief, but poignant. It states that it is not possible to gain completely certain knowledge formulated as generalizations because these are always based on a move from past observations to future predictions. And no matter how many times one has observed something – e. g., that the sun rises every morning or that water boils at 100 degrees Celsius – it is not given by logical implication that the same thing will happen the next time.[51] Hume dissolves the link between cause and effect and argues that there is no connection at all between these moments if we examine

---

45 For a good introduction, see Godfrey-Smith, *Theory and Reality*, chapter three (pages 39–56).
46 Ladyman, *Understanding Philosophy of Science*, 27–29.
47 Ladyman, *Understanding Philosophy of Science*, 89–90 et passim.
48 Francis Bacon, *Novum Organum* (Frederiksberg: Anis, 2007).
49 Ladyman, *Understanding Philosophy of Science*, 18. Hence, we can see that Bacon's method is closely related to what we later came to know as the epistemological philosophy of empiricism. Locke, Berkeley, Hume, and Mill are usually listed as founding fathers of this philosophy, which holds two particular doctrines in opposition to rationalism: (1) All concepts are derived from sensory perception. (2) Every proposition which articulates knowledge about the actual world is founded in sensory perception.
50 A very good introduction to Hume's problem and a discussion hereof is given in Leah Henderson, 'The Problem of Induction,' in *The Stanford Encyclopedia of Philosophy*, ed. Edward N. Zalta (Metaphysics Research Lab, Stanford University, 2019). Hume does not use the term "induction" but several other terms that circle around the modern notion of induction.
51 "… and that all our experimental conclusions proceed upon the supposition, that the future will be conformable to the past" and "For all inferences from experience suppose, as their foundation, that the future will resemble the past, and that similar powers will be conjoined with similar sensible qualities." David Hume, *An Enquiry concerning Human Understanding*, ed. Peter Millican, Oxford's World Classics (Oxford: Oxford University Press, 2007), 26–27.

them *a priori*. "In a word, then, every effect is a distinct event from its cause."[52] We only know the connection between cause and effect through experience, and experiences are always contingent. Thus, we cannot put forward laws of nature because that would demand a link between observation and prediction that we cannot establish.[53] This presentation of Hume's problem of induction is well-known and decisive for many. But not everyone agrees. There is still a lively and interesting debate about Hume's arguments.[54] Before I present James Ladyman's modern defence of sophisticated induction, I discuss a very controversial but influential thought experiment – known as the "new riddle of induction" – as an example of how also the critique of induction is carried out in interesting ways in modern philosophy of science.[55]

4.2.3.1.1 Goodman's New Riddle of Induction

In 1953, the American philosopher Nelson Goodman delivered three lectures in London under the title "Fact, Fiction, and Forecast." When these lectures were published the following year, a widespread discussion immediately arose, especially concerning a particular thought experiment which Goodman, with an astute sense of rhetoric, called "The New Riddle of Induction."[56] It concerns the problematic relationship between theory and observation; since we need a language to record and describe our observations, how do we know in advance that our language is correct?

---

52 Hume, *An Enquiry concerning Human Understanding*, 21.
53 There is a large debate about what "laws" actually are in science. I take them to be "established generalizations," which means that the laws in themselves are hypotheses that are tested against their predictions, and when researchers have tested these in a variety of circumstances, we take them to be trustworthy and approximately true. The strength of the generalization is of course dynamic, scalar, and always fallible. Other synonyms could be "regular effects" or "tendencies". See, e. g., Ladyman, *Understanding Philosophy of Science*, 152; Bhaskar, *A Realist Theory of Science*, 107–13; Nancy Cartwright, 'Do the Laws of Physics State the Facts?', in *Philosophy of Science: The Central Issues*, ed. Martin Curd and J.A. Cover (New York: W.W. Norton & Company, 1998), 865–77.
54 See, for example, Tom L. Beauchamp and Thomas A. Mappes, 'Is Hume Really A Sceptic About Induction?', *American Philosophical Quarterly* 12, no. 2 (April 1975): 119–29; Robert Lantin, 'Hume and the Problem of Induction,' *Philosophia* 26 (March 1998): 105–17; Samir Okasha, 'What Did Hume Really Show About Induction?', *The Philosophical Quarterly* 51, no. 204 (July 2001): 307–27.
55 Another strange puzzle for induction is called "the ravens problem" and was formulated by C.G. Hempel. But because the ravens problem is not as widely discussed today as Goodman's riddle, I leave it out of this discussion. For a concise introduction see Godfrey-Smith, *Theory and Reality*, 46–50. Goodman also famously commented on the ravens problem, Nelson Goodman, *Fact, Fiction, and Forecast*, Fourth Edition (Cambridge: Harvard University Press, 1983), 70–71.
56 Goodman, *Fact, Fiction, and Forecast*, 59–83. A good introduction is given here: Daniel Cohnitz and Marcus Rossberg, 'Nelson Goodman,' in *The Stanford Encyclopedia of Philosophy*, ed. Edward N. Zalta, (Metaphysics Research Lab, Stanford University, 2019). See section 5.3.

Goodman suggests that, instead of focusing solely on Hume's old problem concerning the possibility of predicting the future based on past observations and regularities, we should be focusing on the problem of defining confirmation. Goodman provides a conceptual analysis and shows that our terms are time-dependent. His example is an analysis of the statement, "all emeralds examined before a certain time t are green."[57] Through time and in varied contexts, our observations to date have confirmed this hypothesis. But Goodman then introduces the neologism "grue," which he defines as "all things examined before time t just in case they are green but to other things just in case they are blue."[58] The troublesome situation is then that we now have two statements supported by equal evidence, but when we want to make predictions from our observations, our conclusions must be inconsistent, because the first emerald observed after time t will be either green or blue. It must be blue to confirm the definition of "grue", and it must be green to confirm the definition of "green." In other words, our chosen predicates matter to the validity of inductive inferences.

An additional problem is that "green" is a qualitative term unlike "grue," because qualitativeness depends entirely on which term we choose to start with: "qualitativeness is an entirely relative matter and does not by itself establish any dichotomy of predicates."[59] Therefore, "green" is not a more basic term than is the artificially constructed "grue." The point is that what we thought was a simple and basic hypothesis easily confirmed by successive observations is relative to the terminology we use; this points to the complicated relationship between theory and observation. And this is the problem of induction, according to Goodman: it concerns the problem of how we predict anything justifiably, so that "[t]he problem of induction is not a problem of demonstration but one of defining the difference between valid and invalid predictions."[60] Goodman's critique of induction has been discussed widely in recent decades but the above introduction suffices here to show why many think that induction is not a proper method for relating tests and conclusions.[61] Yet, some philosophers of science defend a more sophisticated account of induction, so I end this discussion of induction with an introduction to Ladyman's defence.

---

57 Goodman, *Fact, Fiction, and Forecast*, 73.
58 Goodman, *Fact, Fiction, and Forecast*, 74.
59 Goodman, *Fact, Fiction, and Forecast*, 80. This is the response to the so-called "disjunctive objection," which argues that "grue" is a more complex term than "green" and therefore less probable.
60 Goodman, *Fact, Fiction, and Forecast*, 65.
61 See Douglas Stalker, ed., *Grue! New Riddle of Induction* (Chicago: Open Court, 1992) and Catherine Z Elgin, ed., *The Philosophy of Nelson Goodman: Selected Essays* (New York: Garland, 1997) for an overview of the literature with many important contributions and expanded bibliographies. Especially the replies by Carnap, Quine, and Swinburne have been instructive for many philosophers in this debate.

4.2.3.1.2 Ladyman's Defence of Induction

James Ladyman's strongest argument for induction is that we have many examples of scientists making many different observations under different circumstances and none of them contradict the generalization but rather constitute additional instances of it.[62] As Ladyman says: "our inductive reasoning is more complex than Hume suggests and usually when we infer a causal connection it is because we have tested a regularity in various circumstances and found a certain stability to the behaviour of things."[63]

This may be true, but new difficulties could arise from the fact that much of modern science concerns non-observable entities. Is it possible to infer inductively to non-observable entities? Ladyman thinks so and presents a list of ten theses that strengthen induction even in the case of non-observables. For the sake of the argument, I name them all here, because not many – if any – philosophers support them all, the majority subscribing either to one or some of them:

1. Induction is rational by definition.
2. Hume asks for a deductive defence of induction, which is unreasonable.
3. Induction is justified by the theory of probability.
4. Induction is justified by a principle of induction or of the uniformity of nature.
5. Hume's argument is too general. Since it does not appeal to anything specific about our inductive practices, it can only be premised on the fact that induction is not deduction.
6. Induction is really (a species of) inference to the best explanation, which is justified.
7. There really are necessary connections that we can discover.
8. Induction can be inductively justified after all, because even deduction can only be given a circular (in other words, deductive) justification.
9. Retreat to probable knowledge.
10. Agree that induction is unjustified and offer an account of knowledge, in particular scientific knowledge, which dispenses with the need for inductive inference.[64]

Ladyman says that various combinations of 1, 5, 6, 7, 8 and/or 9 are most popular among philosophers of science today.[65] Especially 5 is important because it points to the fact that scientific behaviour has developed since Hume's day and

---

62 Ladyman, *Understanding Philosophy of Science*, 38.
63 Ladyman, *Understanding Philosophy of Science*, 46.
64 Ladyman, *Understanding Philosophy of Science*, 41–52.
65 Ladyman, *Understanding Philosophy of Science*, 51. If we were to make a survey among non-specialists, I would expect (10) to gain a high score. The tradition from Popper is still strong outside the camp

has become finer-grained, making scientific reasoning more complex. As for (9), it is interesting that Ladyman is sceptical about the use of probability – because we have no knowledge of the total number of circumstances we observe, probability is impossible to calculate and cannot be a sufficient solution to Hume's problem.[66] I discuss attempts to use probability in science in the next section on Inference to the Best Explanation, where Bayesian Inference has drawn a lot of attention recently (4.2.3.2.1).

Ladyman will not accept Hume's critique because "[o]ur scientific knowledge is fallible, partial and approximate, but usually it is the most reliable means we have for predicting phenomena in the world around us."[67] In sum, his case is that scientists make "many observations […] under a wide variety of circumstances, none of which contradict the generalization but all of which are instances of it."[68] The case is, after all, that the most mature and well-tested theories have stood up to immense scrutiny in an impressive number of ways. Remembering the commitment to fallibilism, this does not verify scientific theories in more than a weak sense, but it does make a good case for the robustness of our best theories.

4.2.3.1.3 Conclusion on Induction

The present short introduction to induction (inductive inferences) has focused on Hume's and Goodman's different critiques of induction, with their focus on the impossible move from observation to prediction and the problem of establishing the terminology for our observations. I also focused on one defence of inductivism in the philosophy of Ladyman. His defence is that induction is not perfect – and cannot be so because Hume is generally correct in his critique – but we can work with it nonetheless. When we have propositions that are very detailed and precise, we have good reasons to believe that they are true, because it would be a miracle if a faulty proposition could be correct in so many different cases.[69] I discuss the notion of the "no-miracle" argument in relation to coherence in 6.3.4, but for now I leave induction as such and turn to two attempts to upgrade the notion of inductive inferences.

---

of philosophers of science: "Popper's falsificationism is probably now more popular among scientists than it is among philosophers." (ibid., 65)

66 Ladyman, *Understanding Philosophy of Science*, 50–51. This is also Popper's – and Lakatos's – criticism of probability.
67 Ladyman, *Understanding Philosophy of Science*, 129.
68 Ladyman, *Understanding Philosophy of Science*, 38.
69 Cf. Putnam, *Mathematics, Matter, and Method*, 73. "I believe that the positive argument for realism has an analogue in the case of mathematical realism. Here too, I believe, realism is the only philosophy that doesn't make the success of the science a *miracle*."

4.2.3.2   Inference to the Best Explanation

The term "inference to the best explanation" was coined by philosopher Gilbert Harman,[70] and it has gained prevalence in the literature, but some prefer to use the Peircean term "abduction."[71] Like induction, Inference to the Best Explanation makes non-deductive inferences (non-conclusive), but instead of inferring from single observations to generalized conclusions, this method infers to the best possible explanation for a set of data. If Inference to the Best Explanation is understood more broadly, it collects all kinds of testing, methods, and inferences that in any way confirm, verify, or falsify a theory and then identifies the best overall explanation. Thus, it is both a method and a criterion. In what follows, however, I restrict myself to an understanding of Inference to the Best Explanation as a way of upgrading inductivism. Inference to the Best Explanation is important for the discussion here both because it is a popular method of inference and because it has become influential in theology, as I show in the last part of this section.

In one of the most influential books on the subject, Peter Lipton approaches a definition by writing, "[a]ccording to [Inference to the Best Explanantion], our inferential practices are governed by explanatory considerations […] Far from explanation only coming on the scene after the inferential work is done, *the core idea of [Inference to the Best Explanation] is that explanatory considerations are a guide to inference.*"[72] Therefore, "[a]ccording to [Inference to the Best Explanation], then, we do not infer the best actual explanation; rather we infer that the best of the available potential explanations is an actual explanation."[73]

---

[70] Gilbert Harman, 'The Inference to the Best Explanation,' *Philosophical Review* 74, no. 1 (1965): 88–95.

[71] Igor Douven, 'Abduction,' in *The Stanford Encyclopedia of Philosophy*, ed. Edward N. Zalta (Metaphysics Research Lab, Stanford University, 2017). Note, however, that Peirce used the concept differently himself. Even though he developed and described the notion throughout his long career, the core of his notion is that abduction is a creative method to find new and interesting hypotheses in the context of discovery, whereas the modern notion is the "qualified judgment" in the context of justification, making it more or less the same as IBE. I follow the modern notion here but am aware of the deviation from Peirce's own account. See further 'Abduction > Peirce on Abduction,' (Stanford Encyclopedia of Philosophy) accessed 15 February 2021. See also the following on the difference between Peirce's notion of abduction and Inference to the Best Explanation: "Even if 'making a given fact a matter of course' can be read as 'giving a satisfactory explanation of that fact,' it is remarkable that there is no reference in Peirce's writings on abduction to the notion of *best* explanation. Some satisfactory explanations might still be better than others, and there might even be a unique best one. This idea is crucial in all recent thinking about abduction. Therein lies another main difference between Peirce's conception of abduction and the modern one." Ibid.

[72] Peter Lipton, *Inference to the Best Explanation* (New York: Routledge, 2004), 56. Italics added.

[73] Lipton, *Inference to the Best Explanation*, 58.

The notion of "best" is of course a matter of great controversy. Lipton introduces two qualifiers – likeliest and loveliest – to explain what "best" refers to. "Likeliest," naturally, refers to probability so that the most warranted explanation among our candidates is the one that is most probably true. This variant explains why many philosophers who are fond of Inference to the Best Explanation combine it with Bayesian Inference (see 4.2.3.3.1).[74] "Loveliest," on the other hand, qualifies the hypotheses that provide us with the most comprehensive understanding, such that "[l]ikeliness speaks of truth; loveliness of potential understanding."[75] According to Samir Okasha, "best" equals "simple" or "parsimonious" for many contemporary philosophers,[76] but even though parsimony often is a very helpful tool, especially to avoid ad hocness and superfluous explanations, there is no guarantee that the truth is simple. I will later suggest that coherence is the optimal qualifier of "best" because it integrates both probability and understanding and because Inference to the Best Explanation works in simple inductive cases (single propositions) while coherence works better overall in connection with systematicity.[77] But before making this suggestion, I shall turn briefly to the use of Inference to the Best Explanation in theology.

As mentioned earlier, Inference to the Best Explanation has become influential in many disciplines, and this is also the case with theology (broadly understood). One reason is that central events in the life of Jesus Christ are described in the Bible as unique or even miraculous and thus, if true, break our common notions of how the world works. The most controversial example is the resurrection, where we have the claim that Christ rose on Easter morning after three days in the tomb. Many agree that the grave was empty, but what is the explanation for the empty tomb? There are various live options here such as the claims that his body was stolen or removed or that the tomb in question was the wrong one. Other claims such as the appearances of the resurrected Christ to the disciples can also be explained in a number of ways, appealing to everything from real appearances over mass hallucinations to pure fabrications. The effects of the alleged meetings such as the eager evangelism and the death-defying testimonies of the disciples even under extreme torture can be explained as results of the life-changing meeting with a resurrected Messiah or as religious extremism (the disciples went from sceptics to convinced fanatics despite the impossibility of the postulated events). There are even more data to consider, but the point is that it has become popular among apologetic theologians to point to Inference to the Best Explanation in saying that a bodily resurrection of Jesus of

---

74 Douven, 'Abduction.'
75 Lipton, *Inference to the Best Explanation*, 59.
76 Okasha, *Philosophy of Science*, 25.
77 Rescher, *Philosophical Reasoning*, 134.

Nazareth provides the best explanation for the many data we have in the ancient sources even though the alleged events are highly extraordinary.[78]

Also in systematic theology, Inference to the Best Explanation has become important for some, as seen for example in the many publications by Alister McGrath. The concept plays an important role in his massive three-volume *A Scientific Theology*.[79] I return to McGrath in 4.3.4, so for now I only provide a short comment on his application of Inference to the Best Explanation to theological matters. McGrath introduces the term in relation to his defence of scientific realism (in the version of critical realism),[80] but what is of interest here is that he insists on the compatibility of the concept with Christian theology (the "explanatory dimension" of Christian theology) and hence rejects different versions of non-explanatory religion such as Wittgenstein's or D.Z. Phillips's. The reason is that theology seeks to be a part of the human endeavour that seeks to explain reality as precisely and coherently as possible, for example, in terms of existence or the order of the universe: "The world displays phenomena which 'cry out for explanation'; part of the coherence of Christian theism is its (alleged) ability to offer an explanation for what is observed."[81]

As stated above, I want to add a final bit of nuance to this discussion because I draw upon it in the discussion of testing whole theories in 4.2.4. Nicholas Rescher has presented an alternative view to Inference to the Best Explanation, called "Inference to the Best Systematization."[82] A problem for Inference to the Best Explanation, according to Rescher, is that explanation is in general a local phenomenon while truth as a concept is more global and independent of divergent contexts. On a local, inductive level (single propositions), there is no problem at all, but holistically, Inference to the Best Explanation does not work.[83] A central difficulty for Inference to the Best Explanation is that there will often be several explanations available and how, then, to identify the best (the problem of underdetermination of theory)? Rescher points to coherence as the optimal solution, because the best available solution need not be true. The problem is the word "explanation," which indicates

---

78 There are numerous books and articles arguing in this manner. A popular and representative book is Craig, *Reasonable Faith*, 333–400, especially pp. 359–360.
79 See especially Alister E. McGrath, *A Scientific Theology. Theory*, vol. 3 (Grand Rapids: Eerdmans, 2003), 133–236.
80 Alister E. McGrath, *A Scientific Theology. Reality*, vol. 2 (London and New York: T&T Clark, 2006), 157–60.
81 McGrath, *A Scientific Theology*, 2:296.
82 Rescher, *Philosophical Reasoning*, 132–141.
83 Rescher, *Philosophical Reasoning*, 134.

that the result is conclusive or final.[84] An explanation can be correct or incorrect, but often such a judgment cannot clearly be made.

Often, we have to rely on approximation. This is because we often have conflicting data and need criteria for selecting among them. The alternative, according to Rescher, is systematization: "A proposition that is part of our best available systematization of all the relevant facts we can determine is not thereby necessarily true, but it indeed is thereby qualified to count as our best available *estimate* of the truth."[85] To anticipate the discussion in 4.2.4, this seems promising for the integration of theological statements at the systematic theology 2 level into holistic theories at the systematic theology 3 level because the (often) controversial claims of systematic theology 2 can be carefully explained and argued for only in light of the coherent ontological systematization of systematic theology 3. Hence, systematization in Rescher's account reverses the process so that instead of inferring a system from the data, we construct it from the given data.[86] Consequently, explanations are parts of the system, not competitors to it: "But any thesis – explanatory ones included – that forms part of the optimal (available) *systematization* of the facts-in-general must for that very reason square with our best understanding of the overall situation."[87] This is an auspicious elaboration of the concept and is considered further in the argument for testing whole theories in 4.2.4. To sum up, Rescher gives a more proper definition of what "best" means by referring to coherence, and he broadens the scope of the method by replacing "explanation" with "systematization."

In the following subsection, I introduce a way of upgrading induction that has gained increasing attention in the field of philosophy of science, i.e., Bayesian Inference. After this subsection, I draw a conclusion to the excursus on inference (4.2.3.4).

4.2.3.2.1 Bayesian Inference

In this subsection, I focus on Bayesian Inference only, even though there are other probability theories that could be considered (such as chance theory, prequential theory, propensity theory, etc.[88]), and I do this for two reasons. First, as mentioned above, it is the version of probability theory that is most often combined with

---

84 Rescher says that the difference between explanation and systematization is that explanation is "a retail commodity," explaining one fact at the time, while systematization is "a wholesale commodity," comprehending and balancing all relevant facts at the same time. See page 139
85 Rescher, *Philosophical Reasoning*, 138. Original italics.
86 See more on systematization in the discussion in 3.4.7.
87 Rescher, *Philosophical Reasoning*, 140.
88 See for example the helpful survey article by Colin Howson for an overview of the field. Colin Howson, 'Theories of Probability,' *The British Journal for the Philosophy of Science* 46, no. 1 (1995): 1–32.

Inference to the Best Explanation, and second, Bayesian Inference has been used with promising results in modern philosophical theology and therefore deserves a focal place in this discussion.[89]

Bayes' theorem, which is the rule behind Bayesian Inference, refers to Thomas Bayes, who described the probability of an event based on the prior knowledge of conditions in relation to the event. The rule is given in different versions in the literature, but the simplest account is:

$$P(H|E) = \frac{P(E|H)*P(H)}{P(E)}$$

The letters of the equation is to be understood as:

P	=	Probability
H	=	Hypothesis
E	=	Evidence
P(H|E) and P(E|H)=		conditional probability, meaning "the probability for H given that E occurs" and vice versa.

Because this is often difficult to grasp for uninitiated readers, I now give an example of how Bayesian Inference works. Let us say that yesterday I attended a family get-together, and afterwards I was informed that my uncle had Covid-19. Today, I feel uncomfortable and have respiratory distress. I am anxious that I might have been infected with the coronavirus and thus take a test at the hospital. Sadly, the test comes out positive. But then I ask myself, what is the probability for me having Covid-19 given that I received a positive test result from the health services? To determine this, I can use Bayes' Theorem, where H will stand for me having Covid-19, and E will stand for the positive test result.

My background knowledge provides me with some information that makes it possible for me to calculate the probability that I have the decease. I anticipate that 3% of the population gets Covid-19, which is thus the so-called *prior probability*. Ideally, P(H) is a fact, but often, we do not know the probability of H and have to make a guess, which is the case in this example. I also know that the chance of a positive test result given that I actually have Covid-19 is 96%. This means that I also know that there are 4% with false negatives. If 3% have Covid-19, we know that 97% do not. But we also know that 1% are subject to false positives. With all this background information, we can get an overview of the situation:

---

[89] See, e. g., the many publications of Richard Swinburne. In *Epistemic Justification*, Swinburne gives a general introduction to Bayesian Inference, avoiding most of the technicalities. These are instead treated in the anthology *Bayes' Theorem*. In *The Existence of God* and *Faith and Reason,* he combines Bayesian Inference with Christianity. Thanks to my colleague Emil B. Nielsen for pointing me to these references.

P(H) =	P(Covid-19)	= Probability of having Covid-19	=	3%
P(E|H)=	P(yes|Covid-19)=	Probability of positive test result for people with Covid-19	=	96%
P(E) =	P(yes)	= Probability of positive test result (for anyone)	=	?

We do not yet know P(E), but given the background information, we can calculate it. It is often the case that we will have to find P(E) using the following equation: P(H) x P(E|H) + P(-H) x P(E|-H). We already know P(H) and P(E|H); and the probability that the hypothesis that I have Covid-19 is false is 97%, because 3% have the disease, i. e., P(-H). The probability of a positive test result if I do not have the disease (false positive) is 1%, i. e., P(E|-H). We can now find P(E) by plugging in the following numbers: P(E) = 0.03 x 0.96 + 0.97 x 0.01 = 0,0288 + 0,0097 = 0,0385 (3,85%).

With P(E) at hand, we can calculate the probability of my having the disease:

$$P(H|E) = \frac{0.03 * 0.96}{0.0385} = 0.748 \, (74.8\%)$$

Thus, there is a 74.8% probability that I have Covid-19 if I have a positive test result from the health services. What this kind of testing shows is that the best explanation for my respiratory distress is that I have Covid-19, but also that this is not so strong a conclusion that all other options are excluded. It would be helpful for me to update my knowledge by gaining more evidence, e. g., through an additional test or getting checked for asthma or other ailments.[90]

Bayesian Inference is a simple and helpful tool when we have relevant background information. The strength of the rule is also that it allows us to make experiments to gain new knowledge and that it allows for working in more difficult epistemic situations.[91] It allows us to upgrade our epistemic situation all the time, and this was also Thomas Bayes' original idea: we are fallible, but we can make epistemic progress with continuously higher probability of our hypotheses as results of our tests.[92]

---

[90] I have constructed my own example of the Bayesian approach because of the current salience of the Pandemic. But other examples show even more clearly the surprising fact that there is quite a low probability of having a disease even with a positive test result if only few people in total have the disease. A standard example is positive test results from mammography scans that are far from resting the case concerning breast cancer; see, e. g., Judea Pearl and Dana Mackenzie, *The Book of Why: The New Science of Cause and Effect* (London: Penguin Books, 2019), 105–8.

[91] Cf. Carroll, *The Big Picture*, 75–83.

[92] James Joyce, 'Bayes' Theorem,' in *The Stanford Encyclopedia of Philosophy*, ed. Edward N. Zalta (Metaphysics Research Lab, Stanford University, 2021), sec. 4.

There also have been, however, many objections to Bayesian Inference in the philosophy of science. A central problem is that Bayesian Inference often takes it to be easy to collect evidence and data with precise values: Bayesian Inference "is the most widely accepted recent alternative to received accounts of theory testing [...] But many effects calculated from data which investigators accept as good evidence fail to meet this test, as do most of the data investigators rely upon."[93] We have the same kinds of difficulties here with Bayesian Inference as with all other kinds of observation and experiments: we make theory-laden observations, and our data is underdetermined.[94]

As mentioned above, Bayesian Inference has been used in the philosophy of religion and in apologetics as an instrument for adding up the evidence for God's existence. It is neither 100% certain that God exists, nor 100% certain that God does not. Instead, theologians can try to find evidence that could support the hypothesis that God exists. Unlike the Covid-19 example and the Bayesian approach in modern statistics, we cannot enter specific numbers into the equation when we use it on abstract matters. But we can get a sense of the strength of our hypothesis by integrating theory, background knowledge, evidence, and the criteria for our work. One of the most prominent defenders of this type of Bayesian Inference is Richard Swinburne, and I briefly discuss his use of this kind of testing in philosophy of religion.[95]

The main difference between Swinburne's use of Bayes' Theorem and the already-introduced one is that Swinburne sees it as a formalization of the relationships between evidence, hypothesis, and background knowledge. The result is that he uses the theorem as an organizer for reflection more than as a tool to find exact numbers.[96] Hence, his equation looks a bit different because it allows him to adjust the relationship between evidence and background knowledge since the line between the two is somewhat blurred. Swinburne's equation is therefore the following:

$$P(h|ek) = \frac{P(e|hk)*P(h|k)}{P(e|k)}$$

---

93 Machamer and Silberstein, *The Blackwell Guide to the Philosophy of Science*, 138.
94 Rosenberg, *Philosophy of Science*, 141.
95 In a more popular book on the subject by Stephen Unwin, the author calculates God's existence to be 67 pct. probable. Stephen D. Unwin, *The Probability of God: A Simple Calculation That Proves the Ultimate Truth* (New York: Crown Forum, 2004). Unwin is transparent in his method and aware of the contingency of the results given the subjectivity of the numbers applied (cf. p. 129). Skeptic Michael Shermer subsequently used the spreadsheet in the book and found the probability of God's existence to be 2 ptc., see Michael Brant Shermer, 'God's Number Is Up', 1 July 2004.
96 Swinburne, *The Existence of God*, 68. See also p. 123.

P is still probability, and h and e are still hypothesis and evidence, respectively. K is background knowledge, which is the new factor added. Swinburne has a detailed introduction to his understanding of Bayesian probability, but what is of interest here is how it helps him to discuss God's existence. To put it simply, Swinburne's interest is in the existence of God, so the hypothesis is that God exists. Now he wants to know whether the evidence – often observational – we have is best explained by the hypothesis being true or not. Therefore, we now have two hypotheses, h_1 and h_2, where the first is the affirmation of God's existence and the second is the rejection. The topic of God's existence is tricky, hence "[t]he theist argues from all the phenomena of experience, not from a small range of them."[97] The idea is that if we can explain the evidence better by taking God's existence into account, also assuming that our background knowledge is reliable, then God's existence is more probable than God's non-existence: "The probability, based on the evidence, of God's being will depend on how well the hypothesis of God's being is able to explain the occurrence of phenomena that would otherwise be highly unlikely."[98] Applying the equation, this gives us the following:

$$P(e|k) = P(e|h\&k) \, P(h|k) + P(e|{\sim}h\&k) \, P({\sim}h|k)$$ [99]

To the right of the addition sign we have the measure of the probability that some evidence is better explained without God. Swinburne comments that the resulting "number" will be low "if it is not probable that any other cause would bring e about or that e would occur uncaused," without explaining what "causation" precisely means, except that its absence means that we "have no explanation."[100] This seems strange, though, since there are instances where we have a profound explanation seemingly without causality. Take dissipative adaption in non-equilibrium thermodynamics as an example. The point here is that the ability to absorb and dissipate energy might be the factor that changes inanimate things into living organisms. Or stated

---

[97] Swinburne, *The Existence of God*, 71.
[98] Swinburne, *The Existence of God*, 71–72. Note that the simpler a theory is, the more probable it is, and this is also one of the philosophical reasons why Swinburne accepts classical theism and its emphasis on divine simplicity, cf. Richard Swinburne, *The Coherence of Theism* (Oxford: Clarendon Press, 1977). The literary critic James Wood, reviewed Swinburne's book *Is there a God?* and said that this is exactly the problem: Swinburne's God mirrors Swinburne himself, so that Swinburne's God is a rational, mathematical, philosophical God, fitting nicely into a logical scheme. For an interesting, modern Feuerbachian, critique, see James Wood, 'Child of Evangelism,' *London Review of Books*, 3 October 1996.
[99] I have corrected the last parenthesis in the equation where Swinburne writes "(P~h|k), which makes no sense. Swinburne, *The Existence of God*, 72.
[100] Swinburne, *The Existence of God*, 72. I suppose this means that Swinburne thinks of a causal explanation.

otherwise: biophysics can understand life as uncaused.[101] The point is simply that "uncaused" and "we have no explanation" are not the same thing.

In chapter 6 of *The Existence of God*, Swinburne makes more explicit what he takes to be better explained by the existence of God, thereby raising the probability of the hypothesis. Swinburne makes clear that P(h|k) may be low, but he also emphasizes that it is higher than any alternatives to the hypothesis. This means that there is a stronger relation between our background knowledge and God's existing than between our background knowledge and God's non-existence. This may be surprising, but there are at least two reasons for it. First, the notion of God is arguably acceptable as a *brute fact* such that the chain of explanation can legitimately end with God. This is a more satisfying brute fact than the alternatives, and the reality is that we will have to stop at some point.[102] Secondly, we have evidence in the world that we can coherently explain in relation to God's being, and when we compare these explanations with the alternatives, the latter are much less satisfying, according to Swinburne. The evidence he has in mind is the existence of anything at all, as well as the constitution of the world (such as the moral order, the free will of creational agents with bodies, etc.) and the universe (such as natural laws, the fine tuning of the physical constants, etc.). Again, we do not end up with specific numbers, but Swinburne's argument is that it is *more* likely for God to be than not when we take these matters into account.[103]

Many questions come to mind, especially about how to find reliable intersubjective knowledge to "calculate" with. We get a formalization of the relations among the various units of input, but how does this help us in testing? Relative to a given theoretical framework, there may be many possibilities for using this instrument, but I question its applicability for conversation across frameworks. While Bayesian Inference is an interesting way to make inferences from single propositions to conclusions, there are also difficulties as described above, and the overall critique of induction applies to Bayesian Inference.

---

[101] Jeremy England, *Every Life Is on Fire: How Thermodynamics Explains the Origins of Living Things*, (New York: Basic Books, 2020). England is an esteemed physicist and an orthodox Jewish rabbi, so his point is not that dissipative adaption makes God irrelevant or that science has argued God away, but only that it is possible to explain the evolutionary jump from no life to life in physical terms.

[102] Swinburne, *The Existence of God*, 110–11. The notion of "brute fact" is complicated. Some prefer very simple brute facts and take God to be too complex, while Swinburne takes God to be an example of a simple brute fact. Others again will say that brute facts are arguably complex and that God as a complex being can thus still be a brute fact.

[103] Swinburne, *The Existence of God*, 123.

4.2.3.3   Conclusion to Excursus About Inferences

In this excursus on inferences, I have discussed the relation between hypotheses and conclusion through induction, including Inference to the Best Explanation and Bayesian Inference. The discussion showed that these approaches are less stable, less clear, and less conclusive than we could hope but that they are still valid tools for providing sound scientific knowledge about single propositions through weak verification.[104] But in general, the investigation has showed that science is not primarily about testing single propositions but rather about testing whole theories. This argument is strengthened in the next section. So far, the main issue in the excursus has not been *testing* but rather the conclusions we are able to draw based on testing, that is, the degree of confidence we can have in the inference from test to conclusion. We test theories in all sorts of ways depending on the research objects and the tools at hand, but the interesting philosophical question is how good our theories of inference are, which is why this problem has been in focus here.

In the next subsection, I discuss testability as testing of whole theories. I draw on Rescher's inference to the best systematization and point to coherence theory as the best criterion for testing. I argue that this account qualifies the criterion of testability and makes it fruitful in relation to all kinds of scientific activity.

4.2.4   Testing Whole Theories: Coherence Theory

Even though testability does not relate primarily to single propositions, it is important for at least two reasons: The first reason is that science aims for truth and to assess the truthfulness of a given proposition or theory, we need to be able to test its validity. But there is also another reason for its importance. Science has significant implications for our lives, technologically, medically, ethically, philosophically, and more. Thus, philosopher Anjan Chakravartty writes as follows:

> Of course, realists regard observable consequences as furnishing important tests of the truth of theories, but I intend something different here. It is also the case that in scientific practice, one is often primarily concerned with whether and to what extent theories, models, procedures, tests, etc. *work* – to enable us to cure diseases, send space shuttles to space stations, and to complete successfully the astounding variety of more humble tasks associated with laboratories and fieldwork across the globe on a daily basis. Success in practice is assessed by means of observable consequences.[105]

---

104   Ladyman, *Understanding Philosophy of Science*, 50–51.
105   Chakravartty, *A Metaphysics for Scientific Realism*, 231. Italics added.

This kind of simplistic instrumentalism is of course crude, but it reminds us of the everyday reality that science is a human tool for living in the world, a certain kind of practice. This does not entail an antirealist understanding of science as Chakravartty indeed says, but it reminds us of the fact that science works regardless of our ability to support the results philosophically. This is also in line with a basic Peircean attitude that combines pragmatism with realism. Even though it is valuable to question and discuss our epistemological foundations, it is also important to ask why and how we get real information from nature that we can use, manipulate, elaborate, and amend. One of the shortcomings of antirealist critiques of science is that they tend to make it too easy to just discard empirical knowledge before engaging carefully with it. To question whether there is a cat on the mat is not very helpful from a pragmatic point of view, and it is much more challenging and fruitful to discuss how we can know that this is actually a cat (e. g., phenomenologically, semiotically, semantically, etc.).[106] Testability, then, is important for both philosophical and pragmatic reasons, and I need to investigate the second possible type of testing – testing of whole theories – more closely now.

Testability is an important criterion because it ensures that experiments may be repeated if needed, and this is probably the reason why all scientists accept the necessity of being willing to put their theories to the test.[107] The discussion in 4.2.2 pointed to severe problems with a simplistic empiricist account that restricts testing to single propositions. Logical Positivism sought to remove all metaphysics from science, but there is no way around metaphysical argumentation, i. e., for example, a precise description of the theoretical framework that provides the ground for doing the actual experiments.[108] Conceptual scrutiny is central,[109] and Laudan was therefore on the right track when he pointed to a duality of "empirical" and "conceptual" problems in the philosophy of science.[110] There is a deep connection between these two, and often problem-solving in one sphere relies on input from the other, meaning that empirical problems can sometimes be solved through

---

[106] As John R. Searle said in the discussion following his presentation at the 23rd International Wittgenstein Symposium in Vienna in 2001. The discussion has not been published, but the paper presented is John R. Searle, 'The Classical Model of Rationality and Its Weaknesses,' in *Rationality and Irrationality. Proceedings of The 23rd International Wittgenstein-Symposion*, ed. Berit Brogaard and Barry Smith, Schriftenreihe Der Wittgenstein-Gesellschaft 29 (Vienna: ÖBV & HPT, 2001), 311–24. Thanks to Frederik Stjernfelt for sharing this anecdote with me.

[107] Sven Ove Hansson, 'Science and Pseudo-Science,' in *The Stanford Encyclopedia of Philosophy*, ed. Edward N. Zalta (Metaphysics Research Lab, Stanford University, 2017).

[108] Puntel, *Grundlagen einer Theorie der Wahrheit*, 121–130. See also van den Brink, *Philosophy of Science for Theologians*, 173.

[109] Machamer and Silberstein, *The Blackwell Guide to the Philosophy of Science*, 322.

[110] Larry Laudan, *Progress and Its Problems*, chap. 1 and 2.

conceptual amendments and vice versa.[111] This is also the case with the concept of testability; I argue that testability is a good criterion, and next I try to clarify the concept and make it more operational. Hence, I ask which components should be a part of a robust account of testability. I am interested in an account of testability that can be used in *public scientific discourse* because the concept of systematic theology discussed in this book aims to present rationally justified public discourse about God. This means that the concept of testability must work intersubjectively and cannot be only private. But how can we make testability a public affair given the difficulties we know from history and from the philosophy of science? At least three steps are important to make testability work intersubjectively. (1) A clear and consistent methodology[112] (2) which can be tested intersubjectively (3) to reproduce the postulated results of the method that was used.[113] I argue that these three steps are the minimum required for something to be counted as scientific and that they are an auspicious impetus for developing a criterion that may be fruitful in the social and human sciences as well. Note that these three steps do not mention empirical testing because it is not necessary to restrict the notion of testability to empirical matters. This broadens the perspective and the applicability of the concept. In the following, I expand on the three steps one by one.

(1) *A clear and consistent methodology*. Scientists should state their methodology as clearly as possible for several reasons. First, the methods themselves must be evaluated, and this is most easily done if they are stated clearly and accessibly. To hide the method behind opaque or diffuse words is not helpful. Second, because scientific theories are often complex it is necessary to be able to assess the coherence of the arguments involved and here a detailed description of the procedure from beginning to end is of immense help for the peers.[114]

(2) *That can be checked intersubjectively*. Here I refer to the point that the use of the method must be testable. From (1) we know what the scientist wanted to do, and now we need to know whether this was what she actually did. We need to

---

111 To give only one example out of a vast pool: The concept of evolution is inundated with conceptual difficulties, and the philosophical work done to clarify the concepts is making the empirical work much more useful and understandable. See, e. g., Samir Okasha, *Evolution and the Levels of Selection* (Oxford and New York: Clarendon and Oxford University Press, 2006).
112 Here we lack a precise term in English. "Methodology" literally means "the theory or doctrine of method," but what is intended in this context is to cover the notion of "*fremgangsmåde*" (Danish), "*framgangsmåte*" (Norwegian), "*Verfahren*" or "*Vorgehensweise*" (German). The word "procedure" or "logical procedure" is maybe more precise, but "methodology" is the standard term in academic English covering this notion of a precise description of the coherent structure that takes us from A to Z.
113 Cf. Peder Gravem, *KRL – et fag for alle? KRL-faget som svar på utfordringer i en flerkulturell enhetsskole* (Vallset: Oplandske bokforlag, 2004), 5.
114 I have given an example of this in 1.4.1.

be able to assess whether the method is used precisely, carefully, and fruitfully, or imprecisely, carelessly, and doubtfully.

(3) *To reproduce results of the used method.* The simplest way to evaluate the method and check its use is to try to reproduce the results. From the reproduction we get better understandings of the strength and sufficiency both of the method and of the results.

This is a simplified overview, but as a minimal criterion, the three-step procedure is strong. In many cases points (2) and (3) will either be identical or overlap, making the reproduction and the intersubjective checking refer to the same task. Peder Gravem shows that the hermeneutical concept of "systematic reconstruction" can work very well in line with this scheme. His idea is that we can have a pool of data that we want to reconstruct in a systematic way to make it say something more precisely than it does prior to the reconstruction. When the work is done, we can judge the quality of the reconstruction and also try to do the reconstruction ourselves in order to either support the reconstruction or amend it (or even discard it).[115] How unequivocal the results will be depends on the data and it will thus always be a matter of degree how definitive we take the results to be. In literary studies – e. g., interpretation of the Bible – we will have definite results to a lesser degree than in biochemistry, which is an implication of the relative degree of instability in the data set and not a weakness for the operative understanding of testability itself. Since all scientific work is relative to the theoretical framework in which we produce it, this is also the case for testability. Thus, the central point is that the method and the results should be reproducible in such a way that the process and the results are not dependent on the subjective perspective of the individual scientist but instead attached only to the theoretical framework.

One of the gains from this change of perspective is that we end up with a broader and more sustainable account of testability that fits with the reoriented focus on whole theories instead of single propositions. For this reason, the notion of testability is a good criterion for science if it is understood as applying to whole theories. But even though this kind of testability is a *necessary* scientific criterion, I argue that it is not a *sufficient* one, because it is not enough to be able to test a theory, it is also important *what* the test reveals. A theory can have a consistent and clear method that we can use intersubjectively and of which we can reproduce the results, but time and time again we see that the result is negative. Thus, this theory is not only testable but false, which is an important difference. Therefore, this criterion leads to the notion of falsification that I discuss in the next chapter.

Here the argument is that the broader understanding of testability is more useful in a broad scientific context and that this broader perspective also includes meta-

---

115 Gravem, *KRL – et fag for alle?*, 5–8.

physical theories. When it is stated that "[e]ven though metaphysical doctrines are not testable [empirically, MAM], they too can be criticized to see if they have heuristic power, if they are fruitful and free of contradictions,"[116] we can take "are fruitful" and "free of contradictions" not only as indicating their heuristic powers but also as criteria for their validity. We should not underestimate the differences among the disciplines – that will not help in the practice of science – but we are still able to find commonality among the disciplines (here, that theories need to be testable).[117]

Further, testability is not just a demarcation criterion between science and pseudoscience but also a fruitful heuristic tool. And this is important. As stated above, we need to take the pragmatic aspect of scientific work into account, and our notion of testability must thus be philosophically consistent *and* operational. Hence, I argue that it is fruitful to follow the broader notion of testability described by Godfrey-Smith both because of its pragmatic nature and because it is a theoretical description that is closely connected with how scientists actually work. Godfrey-Smith's description is worth quoting in full:

> Testing in science is typically an attempt to choose between rival hypotheses about the hidden structure of the world. These hypotheses will sometimes be expressed using mathematical models, sometimes using linguistic descriptions, and sometimes in other ways. Sometimes the "hidden structures" postulated will be causal mechanisms, sometimes they will be mathematical relationships that may be hard to interpret in terms of cause and effect, and sometimes they will have some other form. Sometimes the aim is to work out a whole new kind of explanation, and sometimes it is just to work out the details (like the value of a key parameter). Sometimes the aim is to understand general patterns, and sometimes it is to reconstruct particular events in the past; I mean to include attempts to answer questions like "Where did HIV come from?" as well as questions like "Why do things fall when dropped?[118]

This shows the pluralism of scientific activity, the many different approaches we seek to include in our notion of testability. I find the proposed three-step account of testability to be philosophically both robust and flexible, allowing for improving

---

116 Psillos and Curd, *The Routledge Companion to Philosophy of Science*, 64.
117 Cf. Psillos and Curd, *The Routledge Companion to Philosophy of Science*, 178. "It is uncontroversial that explanatory practice – what is accepted as an explanation, how explanatory goals interact with others, what sort of explanatory information is thought to be achievable, discoverable, testable, etc.—varies in significant ways across different disciplines."
118 Godfrey-Smith, *Theory and Reality*, 211. The confusing shift from singular "hidden structure" to plural "hidden structures" is original and not explained. The point of the passage of the quotation is still clear, though.

our scientific practices and for the differences among the disciplines. And further, it seems obvious that systematic theology 3 can work in fruitful ways with this understanding and make actual scientific progress. I argue for this in 4.3 on the discussion of Premise 2.

We need to let the question and the object of our investigation determine the tools we use. If you want to talk about God's relation to his creation you do not use a seismograph. Hence, I concur with Gary Potter and Jose López' apt statement, "[t]here are objects of natural scientific knowledge for which experimentation is not possible or where it is limited in its potential application. There are vast areas of natural science where prediction is of very limited utility in arriving at explanations. The realist understanding of science does not demand a single scientific method. Rather it demands that scientific methods be *appropriate to their objects*."[119] The present book presupposes realism (see 1.2), but as the quote says, this does not entail uniformity of methods. Different methods are needed in our investigation of the world; the basic criterion is that these methods be stated clearly and transparently so that we can test the use of them intersubjectively and – if needed – reproduce the results.

I want to add an important level to this three-step model. Thus far it seems to work on an elementary level where we have singular accounts to test, e. g., a specific systematic reconstruction of a given pool of data. But this is not all we want to do regarding testability; we also want to know how the results fit in with our (broader) theories. Do they raise the degree of coherence, or do they reveal the incoherence of our theories? In the following, I investigate the exchange between singular instances and holistic theories to see how they could relate in practice in systematic theology.

Going back to the example of the systematic reconstruction, we can say that such reconstruction once provided adds another point to the cluster we want to make as coherent as possible. To test the result is then also to see how it fits in with the overall theory. If we take a case from systematic theology 2 as an example, let us say the notion of eternal conscious punishment of the unfaithful, we take as our pool of data a systematic reconstruction of the Biblical texts and the treatment of this notion in the main texts in ecumenical theological history. Let us say we end up with a reconstruction that supports an understanding of the judgment as eternal conscious punishment; we then want to know if this notion strengthens or weakens our theory of God. In our web of belief, we have such notions as creation (*imago Dei* of all humans), of faith as an undeserved gift, of God universally willing the salvation of all mankind, of the infinite love of God, and so on and so forth. At this second level of testability, we then have to determine whether our result at the first level (the degree of persuasion from the reconstruction) can be integrated into

---

119 Potter and López, 'After Postmodernism: The New Millennium,' 13. Original italics.

our theory or if it is supported better by another theory – or if we have to discard the result because there are better solutions to the problem at hand that are not included in the reconstruction.

A pragmatic understanding of science reminds us of the facts that on the one hand we can always approach a higher level of testing of any research question so that we end up testing our total worldview or conception of reality, whereas on the other hand we usually (for pragmatic reasons) stick to the outlined presuppositions and then test alternatives inside these presuppositions. We normally use the Carbon-14 method to test the age of geological items without discussing whether this test works or whether we can trust our ability to use it, etc. This is the premise for fallible humans who want to gain knowledge of reality, and this only emphasizes the usefulness of coherence theory. Coherence is a powerful parameter for testing at both levels and something that we can also use with benefit at the level of systematic theology 3. As Pannenberg poignantly wrote, "[c]oherence provides the final criterion of truth. It can serve as such a criterion because it also belongs to the nature of truth: Whatever is true must finally be consistent with all other truth, so that truth is not only one, but also all-embracing. It is thereby closely related to the concept of the one God."[120] I discuss this more at length in 4.3.3.

4.2.5   Conclusion on Premise 1

The above discussion of Premise 1 – "Scientific theories must be testable" – has confirmed the premise, but only if testing is related to whole theories and not to single propositions. The aim has been to investigate the premise but also to find the best version of testability. I argued that the best version of testability as concerned with whole theories is coherence theory. This version is broader than empirical testing, and the argument is that it fits many more disciplines in fruitful ways, and in the end best serves our aim of finding truth.

Not all scientists test their theories in the same ways, neither inside a given discipline nor across disciplines, but this eclecticism is a result of the diverse data of reality that call for different modes of engagement. This was the reason for the longer excursus on inferences in science, because testing in itself is so diverse that a unified account cannot be given. But what is a key philosophical question is to understand what we are able to conclude after the test has been executed. Here, I discussed different kinds of induction and argued that they are all problematic, but that a notion of weak verification is still used in science, and for good reasons.

---

120   Wolfhart Pannenberg, ed., 'The Task of Systematic Theology in the Contemporary University', in *Theology and the University. Essays In Honor Of John B. Cobb, Jr.* (Albany: State University of New York Press, 1991), 83.

But our best inferences are related to systematizations, and with this I argued that scientific testability is not simply testing, but instead testing with a clear and well-argued method that makes it possible for other researchers to repeat the test and then to integrate the result into a broader theory, thereby raising the degree of coherence.

The question related to the next premise is whether systematic theology can meet the criterion of testability as it is explained in 4.2.

4.3 Premise 2

4.3.1 Introduction

Testability is a good criterion for scientific work, and there are thus no obvious excuses for systematic theology not to accept it if it wants to be a scientific discipline.[121] This gives me reason to discuss the second premise, "The theories of systematic theology are not testable." Of course, we could accept the objection and then instead insist that systematic theology – like a great variety of other activities – contributes to human well-being and flourishing in other ways than by providing scientific knowledge.[122] This option – rejecting the scientific nature of theology but accepting its value for human lives – is common for, e. g., positivistic accounts of science. One of those taking this position is Schurz: "This identification [of theology as science] is unacceptable, because empirically vacuous sentences such as 'God exists,' or fundamental norm sentences like 'Help your neighbour' may nevertheless be *understood*, and so have a communicable *meaning*. Second, we do not devalue such sentences; we denote them as non-scientific, simply because there is no way to test them empirically."[123] But if theologians seek to carry out a rationally justified public discourse about God and succeed in providing arguments for this, then it is natural to conclude that systematic theology is a scientific discipline as are many other less controversial disciplines.[124]

---

121 As I take the aim of theologians to be the presentation of rationally justified public discourse about God, this is a given, but as the historical overview showed, theologians always discuss internally whether it is relevant and possible to be a scientific discipline by satisfying general criteria. See chapter two.
122 I see Gavin D'Costa's contribution to the discussion as an example of this. See his D'Costa, *Theology in the Public Square. Church, Academy and Nation*.
123 Schurz, *Philosophy of Science*, 45.
124 Pannenberg, *Theology and the Philosophy of Science*, 25–28; Pannenberg, 'The Task of Systematic Theology in the Contemporary University,' 91–93.

The discussion above of Premise 1 identified problems with Logical Positivism's understanding of testability as concerned with testing single propositions (including underdetermination of theory and theory-laden observations) and identified Quine's notion of the holism of testing as the stronger alternative that was both stronger philosophically and more dynamic pragmatically. In this section I argue that systematic theology should meet the criterion of testability and embrace it as a proper mark of robust scientific work, despite the difficulties it creates in everyday scientific practices.[125] Of course, everything rests on how we explicate testability, but if we accept the outline from 4.2.4, it is possible for me to show why Premise 2 fails. This is the aim of 4.3. Whether this premise is true can be judged only on the background of a careful discussion of what it implies for the theories of systematic theology to be testable. How have theologians understood this criterion, and how can it be understood in relation to the holistic account? These are the orienting questions of this section.

There is a lot of fruitful work in systematic theology that could broadly be called "secondary literature," referring to the hermeneutical discipline of critical readings of both historical and contemporary sources. Some are basically philological (e. g., "What did Luther mean by 'justification' in his dispute with Latomos?"); others seek systematic reconstruction (e. g., "How to reconstruct the notion of justification in the work of Augustine and Luther?"). All this important work is not considered here. I regard the conventional tools for testing this kind of work as fitting for their task; basically, the task is simply one of comparing the interpretations with the primary literature seen through the chosen hermeneutical method. This meets (1) – (3) above. This is done fruitfully in theology as well as in all the human and social sciences all the time, and I take this to be the unproblematic basis or foundation for these disciplines in the university today.

What is more controversial but also critical is to assess the possibility of testing claims in theology when theologians argue ontologically. Relevant themes could be the existence of God, the notion of creation and/or history (past, present, future), anthropological claims, and much more. Can we test such claims? And what are the consequences for theology when it accepts an understanding of testability that was largely developed outside the discipline itself? Theologians may want to test their claims and be transparent about method(s), terminologies, and presuppositions,

---

125 In recent years there has been a growing awareness and critique of the lack of reproducibility of results in natural science, especially in health studies such as medicine. But this pervasive problem does not lead to the conclusion that reproducibility should be abandoned as a subcategory of testability, and for good reasons. See, e. g., the homepage of the journal *Nature,* which has collected articles and columns on this issue: https://www.nature.com/collections/prbfkwmwvz/ (accessed 13.12.2021). Wikipedia also has a long page on the problem: https://en.wikipedia.org/wiki/Replication_crisis (accessed 13.12.2021).

but this does not automatically reveal the proper tools for testing. What does it mean to test theological-metaphysical claims about reality? The task of this section is to investigate such questions in order to assess the second premise of the objection.

Before I proceed with the discussion of Premise 2, I shall make four introductory comments that are important to keep in mind. First, we need to be aware that systematic theology 3 can be said, broadly, to deal with the Absolute/the common ground of Being/Being as such and as a whole and that this orientation makes it a discipline different from most others (some kinds of philosophy, e. g., the philosophy of physics may be exceptions). Thus, it could be the case that it is possible to test systematic theology 3 propositions and theories but that this testability will be of a kind different from those required in other disciplines, and perhaps (exceptionally) difficult to provide. I therefore argue that testability comes in degrees. As 4.2 showed, there are tests of single propositions with possible weak verification that are very helpful in many instances, and then there are the more critical tests of whole theories where we assess the degree of coherence. Theories also vary in complexity and comprehensiveness, and there is thus variable difficulty in testing them. Because systematic theology works with a theory of Being as such, it is a kind of discipline that does not grow more comprehensive, but this ontological orientation also makes systematic theology theories extremely complex and hence difficult to test. However, the scalar notion of testability that I have here hinted at should not be held against the disciplines as such but should instead be seen as a consequence of the type of data we are investigating.

Secondly, I have stressed the distinction between systematic theology 2 and systematic theology 3, and this is also important in relation to testability. At the level of systematic theology 2, theologians make much more particular claims about God, the world, etc., and the testability of these claims could thus be different from that of claims at the level of systematic theology 3. It could be the case that systematic theology 2 propositions and theories are easier to test because the claims are more particular, e. g., that a believer is reborn in the baptismal act. But the opposite could also be the case, i. e., that it is more difficult because the particular propositions at the level of systematic theology 2 rest on their integration into the larger theoretical framework provided by systematic theology 3. An immediate impression is that the latter is the case, and that theologians can accept non-testable elements into the larger coherent framework if they can be shown to fit with more central elements that are testable. This resonates with the view of Curd and Cover in their comment on Popper's philosophy: "But even if a theory includes some elements that are true by definition or untestable for some other reason, it hardly follows that the theory as a whole or specific versions of it are untestable."[126] The larger theory ("the theory

---

126 Curd and Cover, *Philosophy of Science*, 65.

as a whole") is not compromised by non-testable elements as such, but there is still the requirement that the larger theory as such be susceptible to testing. An example from another discipline could be cosmology, where the theory of the Big Bang is widely accepted even though, empirically speaking, there is a non-testable element in the specific starting point (because of its singularity). This theory is still accepted as scientific because as a whole it explains so many data and integrates them into a comprehensive and cohesive systematization, and many of the other data can be adequately tested.

Thirdly, I find it important to note that there is an ever-refining development of conceptual knowledge and that this also leads to a higher degree of testability. "The *more finely* graduated a concept is, the *sharper* the information we express with it, and the *stricter* the tests to which the hypotheses using it can be subjected."[127] There is normally a period of ripening for scientific concepts, and in this period, there will be much discussion, revision, elaboration, and criticism. This is helpful, and we need to be aware of it so that we assess the most profound account of a theory available. For example, it would be neither relevant nor helpful if creationists argued against evolutionary claims from Darwin's own works alone instead of engaging with the most advanced contemporary work, where genetics plays a central role (something that Darwin could not even know of); and, to give another example, it would be neither relevant nor helpful if religious sceptics did not engage with the best accounts in the philosophical theology or systematic theology and instead only read polemical literature or outdated works.[128] In philosophy of science, there is a problematic tradition of discussing "icons" and making very general claims on the basis of such discussions, using for example the caloric theory of heat or the optical theory of luminiferous ether to argue against correspondence theory or against realism,[129] but it is very possible that we would have very different discussions if, in dealing with general matters in philosophy of science, we were to dispense with the icons and employ other illustrations of the problems.[130] The point is that both actual science and our conceptual tools for understanding why and how science works

---

127 Schurz, *Philosophy of Science*, 99. Original italics.
128 This is a central argument in Wolterstorff's book *Religion in the University*. Many are simply unaware of the developments in philosophical theology and natural theology over the last 40–50 years and thus discuss irrelevant accounts of arguments of which much better versions are available from today's theoretical work, such as the cosmological and ontological arguments for God's existence. See Nicholas Wolterstorff, *Religion in the University* (New Haven: Yale University Press, 2019), 74–77.
129 Larry Laudan, 'A Confutation of Convergent Realism,' *Philosophy of Science* 48, no. 1 (March 1981): 19–49; Stathis Psillos, *Scientific Realism. How Science Tracks Truth*, Philosophical Issues in Science (London: Routledge, 1999), 110–39.
130 This is a central and thought-provoking argument made by Andrew Currie in Currie, *Rock, Bone, and Ruin*, 309–21.

are being continuously refined, and thus our discussions within the philosophy of science must not stagnate at any specific level.[131] Here I take Puntel's understanding of the theoretical framework to be a helpful aid with his emphasis on fine-grained explication of structures.[132] This type of work helps us to get the best possible understanding of a given structure at any given time, and our knowledge is thus constantly updated. In relation to the question of testability and systematic theology 3, we could say that even though we could be convinced that theology has not lived up to the criteria of testability in the past, we still need to know whether this is still the case given the developments in both philosophy of science and theology. We should not abandon the engagement with the historical records, but just as it is helpful to know the strength of a synchronic constitution of systematic theology (see 3.4.5), it is also helpful to know the actual status of testability in relation to theological claims. This justifies the following discussion, where I argue that the stratification of systematic theology and the revised account of testability gives us a coherent and strong notion of how theology meets the criterion of testability.

Fourthly, in this paragraph, I discuss the notion of testability in relation to theoretical frameworks. The aim is to understand theology as rationally justified public discourse about God in relation to the criterion of testability. In relation to the understanding of systematic theology in this book, the aim is not to safeguard theological positions under the shield of relativism, but to take insights from the notion of theoretical frameworks seriously and investigate the possibility of rational testability in their light. In this discussion, Puntel's notion of theoretical frameworks takes the central place, but there are other philosophers who have worked with similar notions, such as Thomas Kuhn with his notion of "paradigms" or Ronald Giere with his notion of "perspectivism."[133] Kuhn's account leans towards relativism whereas Giere's account is more associated with realism. What they share – together with Puntel – is an understanding of scientific work as taking place within certain limitations because we do not have a God's-eye point of view on reality.[134] These paradigms/perspectives/theoretical frameworks are not themselves

---

131 This was also the argument for a more updated discussion of induction, because a number of contemporary philosophers of science who are aware of the Humean-Popperian criticism still argue in favor of it. Why and how do they do it, and what is their new contribution to the field? This more curious approach is more promising than a simple dismissal on historic grounds.
132 Puntel, *Structure and Being*, 408–11.
133 Kuhn, *The Structure of Scientific Revolutions*; Giere, *Scientific Perspectivism*.
134 To give just one example of the inevitability of theoretical frameworks in relation to testability, I refer to Rescher's comment on Moritz Schlick: "In his 1932 paper 'Positivism and Realism,' Moritz Schlick saw the claim that 'something exists independently of us' as having an empirically testable meaning because the independent existence of atoms, cells, stars, historical events, etc., is to be seen as fully testable empirically because we can state the experiential conditions under which such hypotheses are confirmable. But the fact remains that if we did not precommit ourselves to

open for observation or testing in any traditional sense: "Claims about the truth of scientific statements or the fit of models to the world are made within paradigms or perspectives. Here, a comparison with data or an observational perspective can be decisive. On the other hand, claims about the value of paradigms or perspectives themselves are not subject to anything like decisive observational tests."[135] The point is that other philosophers besides Puntel find fruitful insights in this landscape, but I engage with Puntel because I find his approach the most stimulating for a discussion of systematic theology as rationally justified public discourse about God.[136]

After this lengthy introduction, I now proceed with a discussion of testability in relation to coherence. If theological work, as rationally justified public discourse about God, is to be tested, the hypothesis that testing should be concerned with coherence is quite promising. I break the argument into two parts, the first in the following (4.3.2) and the second after a discussion of how contemporary theologians have understood the criterion of testability (4.3.6). Between these two sections on coherence, I discuss the notion of testability in the works of theologians Pannenberg (4.3.3), McGrath (4.3.4), and Murphy (4.3.5).

4.3.2 Examination of Coherence I

I said above that testability comes in degrees, which means that epistemic warrant and possibility are relative to the subject matter. For example, in relation to reproducibility, some propositions and theories are empirically reproducible while others are not. This implies that the "critical test" of a given proposition or theory will vary. Empirical reproducibility roughly separates the natural sciences from the social/human ones, but even within a given field, this type of variation may be relevant. Take theoretical physics as another example where creative suggestions such as string theory might be empirically testable in principle, but where it is made practically impossible by the enormous amount of energy needed for a particle accelerator to locate the strings.[137] The point is that theoretical physics develops other

---

taking empirical experience as indicative of objective facts, we could validate no factual claims whatsoever." (Quoted from Rescher, *Scientific Realism*, 164.)
135 Giere, *Scientific Perspectivism*, 82.
136 In the German anthology *Die Wissenschaftlichkeit der Theologie* edited by Benedikt Paul Göcke, both Ruben Schneider and Christiana Schneider develop their accounts in relation to Puntel whereas Dominikus Kraschl develops his in relation to Kuhn – all three with important results: Ruben Schneider, 'Struktural-systematische Theologie: Theologie als Wissenschaft vor dem Hintergrund der transzendentalen und der linguistischen Wende,' 33–83; Christina Schneider, '"Gott" als theoretischer Term?,' 315–36; Kraschl, 'Christiche Theologie als paradigmebasierte Wissenschaft. Ein Plädoyer in wissenschaftstheoretischer Perspektive,' 277–314.
137 Psillos and Curd, *The Routledge Companion to Philosophy of Science*, 298–99.

criteria than empirical ones for testing theories – such as mathematical precision and coherence with well-tested physics – and we should see something similar in the discipline of theology.

The suggestion here is that testability in relation to ontological theories is to be understood as the careful examination of the coherence of a given (theological) theory both internally and externally. Since science aims for truth, the same goes for theology as a scientific discipline, and because coherence is the final criterion for truth in this book, systematic theology theories should be tested for their degree of coherence.[138]

To clarify this, *internal* coherence refers to the degree of coherence within the theological system, i. e., systematic theology 2. Does a specific proposition or theory increase or decrease the consistency, cohesiveness, and comprehensiveness of our system? *External* coherence on the other hand relates to coherence with knowledge procured outside the theological system, i. e., systematic theology 3. This is important given the all-encompassing and all-embracing nature of the notion of God: "Theological systematics must therefore integrate the wealth of insight gained by all the secular disciplines of the university into the mysteries of nature, human life, and history."[139] In other words, does a specific theory increase or decrease the coherence of the theological system when external knowledge is integrated? What is the degree of coherence of the work in question compared to other ontological theories?

Both the internal and external notion of coherence is critical to theological work, and each relies on the other to some degree. The division of labour between the two approaches is that the scientific nature of theology is justified by the ability to integrate external knowledge to a higher degree than other ontologies; this lends credence to the work done at the level of systematic theology 2. This is not a division of labour that is forced upon the field but a natural distinction evolving from a theological notion of Being (see 3.4).

As I said in the introduction, I return to a deeper examination of coherence in relation to testability in 4.3.6, but I pause for now to assess other proposals for understanding testability in relation to systematic theology. I discuss Wolfhart Pannenberg (4.3.3), Alister McGrath (4.3.4), and Nancey Murphy (4.3.5), who all add important nuances to the questions. I have chosen this particular set of material – Pannenberg, McGrath, and Murphy – because these authors explicitly engage with the notion of testability and thus seek to work constructively with the criterion rather than simply discarding it. I start with Pannenberg, not just

---

138 This resembles Pannenberg's understanding: "The reason is that truth itself is systematic, because coherence belongs to the nature of truth." Pannenberg, 'The Task of Systematic Theology in the Contemporary University,' 84.
139 Pannenberg, 'The Task of Systematic Theology in the Contemporary University,' 92.

4.3.3   Wolfhart Pannenberg

Wolfhart Pannenberg is arguably the single theological author who has written most about the concept of testability. With impressive confidence, he has advocated a strong notion of testability for theological propositions and also showed how it could be deployed honestly.[140] The rationale behind this notion is that "[a] proposition that, in principle, cannot be tested cannot be a proposition."[141] Thus, systematic theology would be conceptually empty if it were impossible somehow or other to test the truth of its propositions. As we saw in 4.2, this is also the position taken by the present book. Hence, Pannenberg hits the mark when he says, "[t]heology can be taken seriously only if, within its foundational context, it accepts that its assertions must be tested against reality."[142]

As mentioned in 4.2.2.1, Logical Positivism entailed that metaphysical propositions, for example about God, were cognitively meaningless. Pannenberg did not agree with the position of Logical Positivism in this regard, but he agreed that scientific statements should be testable. How, then, did he understand the testability to be required of theological statements? As a very demanding task: "Only when the intentions of religious texts and life forms are interpreted appropriately and the religious candidates for truth analysed correspondingly can ideas of God be tested. There exist no direct God experiments, though. Nonetheless, the hypothesis of the pervasive reality of God can and should be *indirectly* tested, that is, via the *implications* of religious truth-claims for worldly realities."[143] The qualifier "indirectly" is the controversial element in this understanding, for how can we bridge the gap between the "implications" and the proposed source, i. e., God?

It is well known that Pannenberg was inspired by Puntel's notion of coherence,[144] but what is even more interesting in this context is that Pannenberg uses coherence in explicit relation to testability: "How can the claim to coherence with all sorts of

---

140 Niels Henrik Gregersen, 'Introduction. Wolfhart Pannenberg's Contributions to Theology and Science,' in *The Historicity of Nature. Essays on Science and Theology* (West Conshohocken: Templeton Foundation Press, 2008), xiv.
141 Wolfhart Pannenberg, *The Historicity of Nature. Essays on Science and Theology* (West Conshohocken: Templeton Foundation Press, 2008), 13.
142 Pannenberg, *The Historicity of Nature*, 21.
143 Gregersen, 'Introduction. Wolfhart Pannenberg's Contributions to Theology and Science', xvi. Original italics.
144 Pannenberg, *Systematic Theology*, 1991, 1:18–24.

human experience of the world ever be tested or confirmed? The answer is that this can be done in the form of a systematic presentation of the Christian doctrine of God, of creation, and of human history in terms of a history of salvation. Such a systematic presentation must be not only consistent within itself and consonant with the biblical witness but also coherent with regard to all matters that have to be taken into account in such a presentation."[145] In the present terminology, this implies that Pannenberg saw systematic theology 1–3 as a united whole that is to be tested against reality, which is different from the proposed case for the rationality of systematic theology as built on the relative strength of systematic theology 3.

Of course, there is a difference due to the non-empirical status of systematic theology's object and also due to the object not following recurring and repeatable rules which can be investigated, manipulated, and repeated. This is because God is not a being among beings – as we saw in 3.4.5 – but, in the words of Pannenberg, "the all-determining reality."[146] Investigating the relation between God and the (indirectly empirical) implications of his alleged being is, therefore, the task of systematic theology: "Propositions about God, his actions and revelations, can, therefore, not be tested directly against their object. But that is not to say that they cannot be tested at all. One can, after all, test propositions in terms of their implications. Propositions about divine reality or divine action can be tested according to their implications for our understanding of finite reality, insofar, that is, as God is asserted to be *the all-determining reality*."[147] Pannenberg does not explicate whether he argues that God determines absolutely all foundational structures of reality or if his view can be understood as a determinism at the deepest levels of reality with this determinism implying an indeterminism at higher levels. And because of this vague explication, it is not easy to understand Pannenberg's notion of "implication" and what it precisely refers to. We may test the implications somehow, but how do we falsify the claim that God, as the all-determining reality, relates to finite reality? From Popper we know that positive confirmations (or "weak verification,"

---

145 Pannenberg, *The Historicity of Nature*, 7. Or as he puts it in his systematic theology: "Claiming that the content of Christian doctrine is true in detail, proclamation implicitly presupposes its inner coherence and its coherence with all that is true." Pannenberg, *Systematic Theology*, 1991, 1:19.
146 Pannenberg, *Theology and the Philosophy of Science*, 301–26. This notion is adopted from Rudolf Bultmann, who stated that, "Gott [...] die Alles bestimmende Wirklichkeit sei." [God is the all-determining reality] Rudolf Bultmann, *Glauben Und Verstehen*, vol. 1, Gesammelte Aufsätze (Tübingen: J.C.B. Mohr (Paul Siebeck), 1966), 26. But whereas Bultmann developed his understanding of this term within a traditional subject-object epistemology, regarding the all-determining reality as beyond this distinction, Pannenberg models the term in correlation with the historical totality of the world.
147 Pannenberg, *The Historicity of Nature*, 16. Original italics. See also page 20: "Statements about God can be tested only against the implications of the *idea* of God, to the extent that God is posited as the all-determining reality." Original italics.

according to Ayer) are commonplace and therefore not always helpful. So when for example a physicist such as Brian Greene says that however a God might possibly be, he would have to agree with "our mathematical laws,"[148] does this imply an ever greater limitation of the Christian God, a kind of "God of the Gaps" where God's explanatory power steadily decreases, leaving it for theology to point to a mere compatibility between the Christian notion of God and the observed universe? If Pannenberg's idea is to work, we must understand it as a process by which we compare our increasingly fine-grained theories about God with our increasingly fine-grained theories about the world. For example, if a theory about God and God's creation becomes very detailed, including God's relation to time, free will, possible life after death, answers to prayer, miracles, etc., then it is either strengthened or weakened by findings about determinism/indeterminism, life/death, soul/body, temporally infinite/finite universe, etc.

Let me go a bit further into the question and ask whether the implications of God's existence can be inferred deductively or only inductively, that is, whether fact X logically implies God's existence or only makes God's existence more or less probable. Take a standard case from natural theology, the fine-tuning of the universe. Physicists are able to calculate the constitution of the physical laws of the universe all the way back to very shortly after the Big Bang, circa 13.8 billion years ago.[149] Even minor deviations from these constants would have made life impossible and would probably have made the universe implode. This fine-tuning makes it very improbable that life would have arisen in other universes, which makes any alleged contingency of the universe very unlikely. On the other hand, we expect life to arise in the case that an omnipotent and loving God wants to share the intra-trinitarian life and have relationships with others. Thus, our notion of God makes us expect life; fine-tuning problematizes contingency as an explanation; and fine-tuning thus points to God as the creator of the universe. This is how natural theology often argues.[150] But is the existence of God *necessary* for the fine-tuning or does fine-tuning only make God's existence *possible* – or better: more or less

---

148 Brian Greene, *Until the End of Time*, 344. The full point is enlightening: "The closest I come to such literalism is acknowledging that some or other god may exist. I recognize that no one can ever rule out this possibility. As long as a purported god's influence does not in any way modify the progression of reality that is well described by our mathematical laws, then that God is compatible with all we observe. But there is an enormous gulf between mere compatibility and explanatory necessity." The last point resembles my question regarding Pannenberg's framework.
149 Steven Weinberg, *The First Three Minutes: A Modern View of the Origin of the Universe*, Updated Edition (New York: Basic Books, 1993).
150 Richard Swinburne, *The Existence of God*, Second Edition (Oxford & New York: Clarendon & Oxford University Press, 2004); William Lane Craig and J.P. Moreland, eds., *The Blackwell Companion to Natural Theology* (Oxford: Wiley-Blackwell, 2012), 202–81; Alister E. McGrath, *A Scientific Theology: Theory* (Grand Rapids: Eerdmans, 2003), 3:195–98.

likely? Many reject the necessity of God's existence because the universe could have come from nothing even if there is no God.[151] God is not needed in a satisfactory explanation of the origins and continuous existence of the universe.[152] The laws of nature and the fundamental constants work with no need for an added creator.[153] Life could have evolved spontaneously by dissipative adaptation, a combination of entropy and certain chemical processes.[154] There are many ways around the conclusion that God is needed for the universe to be, and the question is then how satisfied theology should be with pointing to mere compatibility. I will say that the ideal for theology should be higher probability, which is a more demanding but also more interesting case to investigate.

The point is to insist that we combine Pannenberg's program with actual science, as he would himself have urged, and see how far we can go in testing the claims of theology. As I argued concerning the terminology of "testability," it is not helpful to have a principle if you do not have the methods to apply it. The same goes for Pannenberg's claim that we can test theological propositions indirectly against their implications. We should bear in mind that this cannot be done once and for all. Because general knowledge expands every day, theology has a persistent task in sustaining these implications and keeping them valid. And not just for apologetic reasons, which would be conservative, but also for the constructive task of upgrading our understanding of reality as coherently as possible, integrating all accessible knowledge to the highest degree that is humanly attainable.

One difficulty will be that the very notion of a transcendent and invisible God implies an unsolvable ambiguity when we seek to explicate the implications. An ambiguity will always be present when we seek to describe the implications of the hypothesis of the Christian God because of the relationship between transcendence and immanence. If the transcendent God were to make his being fully visible in the immanent, he would be swallowed up by immanence and thus cease to be God, and so an ambiguity is implied in the very notion of transcendence.[155] This is seen both in the paradox of Christology (e. g., that Jesus according to Paul had to "empty" himself in the act of incarnation, cf. Phil. 2.7) and in the relation between Creator and creation. If ambiguity is inevitable, this reveals the problematic

---

151 Lawrence M. Krauss, *A Universe from Nothing: Why There Is Something Rather than Nothing* (London: Simon & Schuster, 2012). But Krauss' argument has received important criticism by, for example, Alan White; see White, *Toward a Philosophical Theory of Everything*, 158–61.
152 Carroll, *The Big Picture. On the Origins of Life, Meaning and the Universe Itself* or Greene, *Until the End of Time*.
153 Peter William Atkins, *Conjuring the Universe: The Origins of the Laws of Nature* (Oxford: Oxford University Press, 2018).
154 England, *Every Life Is on Fire*.
155 Cf. 3.4.5.1.7.1 and Puntel, *Being and God*, 255–63.

nature of Pannenberg's view of indirect implications, but at the same time, it reveals the importance of increasing the cohesiveness of our theories, because this is argumentatively stronger than vague or underdetermined notions of implication.

In 3.4.5, I discussed the possibility of a synchronic constitution of systematic theology and found that the theoretical framework of Puntel was one that outlines such a possibility in a coherent way. But to bracket history is not usual for theologians and not very helpful in the actual work. The reason – according to Pannenberg – is that Christianity is a historical religion through and through: "Christian doctrine is from first to last a historical construct. Its content rests on the historical revelation of God in the historical figure of Jesus Christ and on the precise evaluation, by historical interpretation alone, of the testimony that early Christian proclamation gives to this figure."[156] But in order to avoid developing a religious myopia, it is important to notice that Pannenberg included the history of the religions, plural, as material for the systematic construction of coherent theological theories: "A testing of theological statements will, therefore, have to hold to religions and their changing history because the total meaning of reality against which the truth of theological statements must be tested is already thematic in religions."[157] The explication and comparison of developments in the different religions are therefore of great value to systematic construction.

To sum up: Pannenberg regards testability as a central requirement for scientific work, including work in theology. Because God is not an empirical object but the all-determining reality, we can only test the notion of God implicitly against its implications for reality. According to Pannenberg, we should also seek to test systematic theology propositions on a smaller scale, which implies testing the hermeneutical correctness of our interpretations (of scriptural, historical, and other religious sources) and the validity of our systematic presentations (all of which I understand as equal to the terms internal and external coherence). A task for theologians is to assess the historical sources of earlier suggestions and then choose the most coherent theories for further development.[158] Note that Pannenberg also sees history as a judge of religious truth-claims – when a religion goes extinct, it is

---

156 Pannenberg, *Systematic Theology*, 1991, 1:x. See also Pannenberg, 'The Task of Systematic Theology in the Contemporary University,' 84.
157 Pannenberg, *The Historicity of Nature*, 18. Puntel also argues that if God is free, we must include history in a coherent theory of who God is and what God has done in history, and Rescher also argued for the coherent integration of history in *Philosophical Reasoning*. This is especially relevant if the important theological notion of revelation is to be discussed in a scientific way.
158 Wolfhart Pannenberg, *The Historicity of Nature*, 9. The complicated subject of hermeneutics is not discussed in the present book, but it is certainly decisive for the work of systematic theology. See, e. g., Pannenberg, *Theology and the Philosophy of Science*, chap. 2 and 3.

not a candidate for truth anymore because the overall assessment has been that its truth-claims about reality were not convincing.

Pannenberg's view has been very influential over the last fifty years, but there have also been constructive criticisms and attempts at improvement. I now turn to two figures who are both sympathetic and critical towards Pannenberg's notion of testability, namely Alister McGrath and Nancey Murphy. I discuss them in this order.

4.3.4 Alister McGrath

Alister McGrath is one of the single authors who has written most extensively on the relationship between theology and science. It is not easy to treat his work briefly, but for the purposes here, I restrict the engagement with his thinking to the issues of testing and explanation. His main understanding of a scientific test is that it makes an *abduction* to the best explanation.[159] I have already touched upon Inference to the Best Explanation in 4.2.3.2 and in the following I expand on it. McGrath often writes with broad strokes, organizing and synthetizing an enormous body of literature, but this also makes his own argument vague and imprecise. Broadly, though, he focuses on Inference to the Best Explanation and its utility for theology.

McGrath is positive towards Pannenberg's insistence on the public nature of theology, and he discusses his respective understandings of revelation and history in several places.[160] He is more reluctant to embrace the neutrality of the context of justification and criticizes Pannenberg for missing the "tradition-embedded character of the intellectual frameworks through which the natural order is viewed, and on the basis of which it is interpreted."[161] What this implies for the testability of theological propositions I discuss in the following. What needs to be said here is that McGrath shares Pannenberg's vision of a public theology but finds sufficient difficulties in his position to try to establish an alternative.

At the end of the second volume of his trilogy on a scientific theology, McGrath insists that such a theology has an explanatory aspect, but he does not explain this aspect in detail.[162] In the third volume on "Theory," he writes that a "scientific theology is motivated by the quest for a unified explanation of reality."[163] Thus, the notion of explanation is very important for McGrath's philosophy of science, which

---

159 The close relation between testing and inferences (here explanation) is thus quite explicit in McGrath's account.
160 E. g., McGrath, *A Scientific Theology*, 1:300–304.
161 McGrath, *A Scientific Theology*, 2:54.
162 McGrath, *A Scientific Theology*, 2:294–96.
163 McGrath, *A Scientific Theology*, 3:133.

is evident from the following representative quotation: "The very idea of 'explanation' denotes the highly significant notion that the world is possessed of a rationality and coherence which may be grasped and understood, and thus ultimately affirms the intelligibility of reality by its beholders."[164] This reflects McGrath's scientific realism in which he follows the tradition of critical realism. The world exists independently of the human mind – there is a way "things are" – and humans seek to understand this reality and explain it however limited and fragile our cognitive abilities may be.[165]

According to McGrath, the context for this quest for explanation is always a given tradition, and a tradition has a triple task to carry out: (1) "A tradition must be able to offer an account of its own specific form and contents, and explicate their interconnection." (2) "A tradition must be able to offer an account of why alternative traditions exist." (3) "A tradition must be capable of seeing the world through theoretical spectacles."[166] I next comment briefly on these three points.

The *first* is "common to most approaches," as McGrath says, and it is hard to imagine a convincing version of systematic theology that presents no defence of its own form and content.[167] So this is a truism but still important to explicate.

The *second* point is more controversial because it rests on the view that the notion of "universal rationality," stemming from the Enlightenment, has collapsed. This is a very general critique both because "universal rationality" can mean many things and because "the Enlightenment" was not a monolithic movement but a very disparate stream of thoughts.[168] In this context the most problematic notion is

---

164 McGrath, *A Scientific Theology*, 3:134.
165 McGrath follows the philosophy of Roy Bhaskar here, see especially Bhaskar, *A Realist Theory of Science*.
166 McGrath, *A Scientific Theology*, 3:137. Nancey Murphy argues for the same kind of explanatory task, claiming that this is a view she has developed in relation to the thinking of Alasdair MacIntyre, and even if McGrath does not refer to MacIntyre's important article, I take McGrath and Murphy to be in general agreement. Nancey C. Murphy, *A Philosophy of the Christian Religion for the Twenty-First Century* (London: SPCK, 2018), 80–101; MacIntyre, 'Epistemological Crises, Dramatic Narrative and the Philosophy of Science.'
167 Even those who reject the systematic character of systematic theology or want a theology without dogma need to explain their choices of form and content (data). Cf. Mattias Martinson, *Perseverance without Doctrine: Adorno, Self-Critique, and the Ends of Academic Theology*, European University Studies. Series XXIII (Frankfurt am Main and New York: Peter Lang, 2000).
168 In the last twenty years, the discussion of the Enlightenment has been vast. A very influential categorization stems from Dutch-American historian Jonathan Israel, who identifies three major groups, the *moderate*, the *radical*, and the *counter*. The point here is that McGrath shows no awareness of this intense debate, and this makes his simplified claim concerning *the* Enlightenment superfluous. See, e. g., Jonathan I. Israel, *Radical Enlightenment: Philosophy and the Making of Modernity 1650-1750*, Illustrated Edition (Oxford: Oxford University Press, 2002); Jonathan I. Israel, *Democratic Enlightenment: Philosophy, Revolution, and Human Rights, 1750-1790*, Illustrated

the refusal of a "universal rationality" because McGrath's own project is articulated as a version of universal rationality. Not in a naïve, simplified way so that he should argue that we can attain empirical proofs or pure interpretation of data, but the widespread awareness that we make theory-laden observations, that all data is underdetermined, that nature can be accessed only through language, and so on, are accepted as *rational* arguments for a more nuanced philosophy of science, and these arguments are almost universally accepted. A more sympathetically reading of McGrath would be to interpret him as saying that the actual scientific work is always done within a tradition, a paradigm, or a theoretical framework, but this is also a truism these days. The interesting point is that even though we inevitably do science in some tradition, we can communicate, compare, discuss, and access results across traditions, and it is hard to see why we could not call this "universal rationality."[169] It is possible that our criteria will be replaced by other and better ones in the future, or that our overall criterion of coherence will turn out to be problematic in a compromising way, but as assessed here and now, universal rationality should not be discarded as such.

The point, however, is that McGrath takes it to be mandatory for a tradition not only to explain the validity of its own existence but also to give a qualified account of the existence of other traditions. If I understand him correctly, this is meant to strengthen the credibility of a tradition and give it wider validity.

The *third* point is again an internal vision for the rationality inside the tradition itself. The explanations that a tradition offers must be convincing to those who accept its presuppositions. This also seems truistic.

The Christian tradition spans many concepts, theories, and systems organized under the headline of Christian belief. As an example, McGrath points to the explanatory work in the Christian tradition concerning "revelation." This complex category has multiple layers – or stratifications, as McGrath prefers it – and includes texts, worship, ideas, and experiences, among other things.[170] The task is to *clarify* the nature of revelation and to maintain a continuity with this "revelationally constituted" tradition.[171] By explicating the different levels and their contents it is possible to reason abductively, which McGrath describes as "arguing backwards from what is accessible and may be observed in the present to what may be argued

---

Edition (Oxford: Oxford University Press, 2013); Jonathan I. Israel, *The Enlightenment That Failed: Ideas, Revolution, and Democratic Defeat, 1748–1830* (New York: Oxford University Press, 2020).

169 McGrath explains his view more carefully later in the text, but the impression is still that he agitates more than he argues, especially because he omits precise references to proponents of this dismissed universal rationality. See McGrath, *A Scientific Theology*, 3:164.
170 McGrath, *A Scientific Theology*, 3:146–48.
171 McGrath, *A Scientific Theology*, 3:146–48.

to lie behind it."[172] McGrath gives an example of a religious experience, which is the *explanandum*, and the stratified concept of revelation, as the *explanans*. The *explanans* points back to the life, death, and resurrection of Jesus Christ, which is the event that can explain the present experience. Strangely, McGrath refuses to call it the "best explanation" and only states that it is legitimate to debate it, but I read him as saying that the Christian tradition has such a fine-grained account of the relation between contemporary religious experiences and the life, death, and resurrection of Jesus that the latter is the best explanation of the former.

Broadening the discussion once again, McGrath now insists that the example is an illustration of a distinct approach to reality, where reality is understood as "crying out for explanation," and theology insists that its own "explanatory competence extends to every aspect of reality."[173] This can only mean that theology is able to incorporate all sorts of evidence into a larger framework, because theology is not a key that magically unlocks the treasure trove of reality.

There is more to say, but McGrath's notion of abduction to the best explanation should be clear enough. The next task is to understand the second point from above, i. e., how the explanation of other traditions is to be developed. This is of special relevance to the present book because of the emphasis on the importance of the comparability of different ontologies. To recapitulate, McGrath says that a tradition should be judged by its ability to explain its own distinctive features and "something" of its rivals.[174] Unfortunately, McGrath does not give a comprehensive account of this, and instead he develops a more nuanced account of how a tradition works according to points 1 and 3.[175] But this is not just unfortunate; it is also very problematic, because point 2 is the controversial part of his undertaking and the one that is less obvious. What is required in order to be able to explain other traditions, and how does comparison make any tradition more valid? McGrath does not answer either question. In the next section I show how this job is done by Nancey Murphy, who provides the details and examples that McGrath's account lacks.

To sum up on McGrath, he primarily sees testing as an abduction to the best explanation, both generally and in theology. His standpoint within critical realism makes him positive toward the natural sciences, but he does not regard these disciplines as neutral. In this regard he disagrees with Pannenberg, whom McGrath understands as more willing to accept findings in the natural sciences as brute facts. McGrath takes a scientific theology to be the best tradition to explain the intelligibility and coherence of nature and history, i. e., the two most important

---

172 McGrath, *A Scientific Theology*, 3:149.
173 McGrath, *A Scientific Theology*, 3:193.
174 McGrath, *A Scientific Theology*, 3:194.
175 McGrath, *A Scientific Theology*, 3:194–236.

components of the contingently actual dimension of being. This does not mean that a tradition provides irrefutable evidence for anything, but that the abductions are consistent with a theistic worldview, that the results can be accommodated with this worldview, and that they reinforce the probability of the worldview for those who accept the tradition.[176]

Now I turn to the second figure who elaborates on Pannenberg's vision, i. e., Nancey Murphy.

4.3.5   Nancey Murphy

The American philosopher of religion Nancey Murphy has unfolded her philosophy of science in relation to systematic theology in two central volumes, *Theology in the Age of Scientific Reasoning* from 1990 and *A Philosophy of the Christian Religion for the Twenty-First Century* from 2018.[177] In the first volume, Murphy is critically engaged in developing a theological account of Imre Lakatos's philosophy of science. In Lakatos' thought, a scientific theory is understood as a research program with three components: a hard core, an auxiliary belt, and a positive heuristic.[178] Murphy's claim is that Lakatos's philosophy is the most sophisticated view available and that it fits very well with theological reasoning, thereby substantiating the arguments for a scientific understanding of theology. Of special interest for the discussion here is the fact that she develops her Lakatosian account in explicit contrast to Pannenberg's program. I briefly sketch Murphy's critique before I examine her own alternative more carefully.

According to Murphy, Pannenberg's sophisticated philosophy of science for theology ultimately fails because it cannot integrate the amount of data it is claimed to integrate. That means, despite the sympathetic ambition for developing a scientific theology in relation to the best theories outside of the discipline, it fails because the program is inconsistent at its core. In her outline of Pannenberg's philosophy of science, Murphy sums up his account as follows: "Pannenberg proposes that theories are to be criticized on the basis of how well (coherently, parsimoniously, and accurately) they account for all the available data."[179] This is presented as an alternative

---

176 McGrath, *A Scientific Theology*, 3:198.
177 Nancey C Murphy, *Theology in the Age of Scientific Reasoning* (Ithaca: Cornell University Press, 1993); Murphy, *A Philosophy of the Christian Religion*.
178 Lakatos, *The Methodology of Scientific Research Programmes*. See further in 5.2.4.
179 Murphy, *Theology in the Age of Scientific Reasoning*, 27. On page 33–34 she gives eight points in propositional form that concisely summarize Pannenberg's complex account.

to David Hume's sceptical approach,[180] but Murphy says that Pannenberg's theory must prove itself to be preferable to Hume's and not simply as an alternative. How might Pannenberg achieve this? According to his own position, he must take "all the available data" into account, and then he must show how Hume's theory can be "encompassed within and interpreted by" his own.[181] But when the two are compared, it becomes evident that Hume's theory "suspends Pannenberg's fact-constituting principles;" this shows that the two accounts are "incommensurable."[182] The point is that even though Pannenberg is able to interpret and incorporate much from Hume, he cannot incorporate Hume's epistemology, upon which all the actual content of Hume's thought is based, because if he did so, he would either change the content of Hume's thought into something non-Humean or destroy the epistemological foundation of his own philosophy. Hume's knowledge theory is atomistic, based on sense impressions of concrete things, whereas Pannenberg's theology is holistic, based on placing all data in relation to other data within the totality of history, past, present, and future. Murphy's conclusion is poignant: "Thus Pannenberg has indeed offered an alternative to Hume but, if I am right about the incommensurability of the two systems, he cannot offer any reason *consistent with his own system* why we should choose his in preference to Hume's, because such superiority (by his own account) depends on the possibility of incorporating Hume's system into his own. They are both comprehensive, well-argued systems that give meaning to the entire historical process."[183] I am not convinced of this interpretation of Pannenberg, because Pannenberg – like Rescher – understands data as truth candidates, which implies that not all data can be included in a coherent theory because there is an overdetermination of data (no theory can include all data as true). The most coherent theory will therefore have to assess some data as untrue (interpret them as untrue). For this reason, Pannenberg does not need to integrate Hume into his theory in any other way than to say that Hume was wrong by showing that his own theory is more coherent.[184]

As noted above, Murphy develops a Lakatosian alternative to Pannenberg (and Hume), and she does so with good examples from the history of theology. Instead

---

180 Developed in the first chapter. Hume's rejection of references to authority and his insistence on sensory impressions in scientific work has been a double challenge for theology ever since, according to Murphy. See Murphy, *Theology in the Age of Scientific Reasoning*, 1–18.
181 Murphy, *Theology in the Age of Scientific Reasoning*, 44.
182 Murphy, *Theology in the Age of Scientific Reasoning*, 44. Italics removed.
183 Murphy, *Theology in the Age of Scientific Reasoning*, 47. Original italics. Murphy also briefly argues for a second reason to dismiss Pannenberg's account, namely that it is unworkable on its own premises. Pannenberg tried to find a neutral or objective starting point for history, primarily to assess the Resurrection story, but he ultimately failed because it is possible to write history from an entirely different point of view, as Hume showed. See ibid., pages 48–50.
184 Cf. Pannenberg, *Systematic Theology*, 1:56–59.

of following these examples, however, I discuss her more recent alternative to Pannenberg, because it clarifies many of the rough points made by McGrath.

In *A Philosophy of the Christian Religion for the Twenty-First Century*, Murphy takes a broader approach than she did in 1990, and she presents concrete studies of themes in philosophy of religion as well as unfolding a nuanced philosophy of science as such. As mentioned in the discussion of McGrath, Murphy develops her account in relation to MacIntyre's theory of traditions. Traditions and practices are closely related in MacIntyre's philosophy, as is evident from the following central definition: "By a 'practice' I am going to mean any coherent and complex form of socially established cooperative human activity through which goods internal to that form of activity are realized in the course of trying to achieve those standards of excellence which are appropriate to, and partially definitive of, that form of activity, with the result that human powers to achieve excellence, and human conceptions of the ends and goods involved, are systematically extended."[185] This dense definition deserves some unpacking, which I will have to neglect here in order to focus instead on the implicit notion of "history," because as MacIntyre later says, every practice has a history, a genealogy that gives it authority and legitimacy for its community of practitioners. Such practices are of course not immune to criticism and revision but there are standards of excellence and rules to follow if you want to learn the game of the practice.[186] Science is obviously a practice in this regard with a history, standards of excellence, rules to learn and follow, a systematic account of the activity, and so on.

Traditions are not static but always undergoing processes of development or decline. MacIntyre takes it to be a central contribution of Thomas Kuhn that his historicism made clear the fallible character of all human knowledge, and this perspective leads to MacIntyre's claim that scientific reasoning always rests on historical reasoning within a tradition.[187] History shows us that traditions can experience internal epistemological crises, and when this happens, it is the ability to constructively and creatively survive this crisis that is the litmus test of a given tradition. When a tradition replaces another as a result of insurmountable

---

185 Alasdair MacIntyre, *After Virtue: A Study in Moral Theory*, Second Edition (London: Duckworth, 1985), 187.

186 MacIntyre, *After Virtue*, 190. Nancey Murphy helpfully condenses MacIntyre's view: "Traditions are something like worldviews extended over time; they become mature when the original authority upon which they are based is called into question and a methodology for going forward is developed. They are embodied in social practices and institutions. In his historical accounts he shows that variations develop over time, and thus the tradition comes to be made up of subtraditions." Murphy, *A Philosophy of the Christian Religion for the Twenty-First Century*, 266.

187 MacIntyre, 'Epistemological Crises, Dramatic Narrative and the Philosophy of Science,' 464 and 470.

difficulties, it is critical that the newer tradition be able to explain why the older tradition failed and why it, the new tradition, solves the crisis in a more satisfying manner: "The criterion of a successful theory is that it enables us to understand its predecessors in a newly intelligible way. It, at one and the same time, enables us to understand precisely why its predecessors have to be rejected or modified and also why, without and before its illuminations, past theory could have remained credible."[188] This explicates the successive element better than does McGrath's account. For example, astrology is discarded and replaced by astronomy because the latter is able to explain why the former is insufficient and why the latter gives more satisfying explanations of the evidence available. But if we have two contemporary theories, say (1) humans have both bodies and souls versus (2) humans only have bodies, it is less clear how one tradition could explain the other better than the other explains itself *and* provide a convincing account of itself, as MacIntyre and Murphy say it must. If coherence were the standard, it would suffice to show that (1) is more coherent than (2) without needing to explain additionally why the less coherent theory fails. But Murphy's point is that McGrath seems to miss how the synchronic assessment of traditions concerns the acknowledged failures of a tradition, and if these failures are better explained by another tradition this gives the latter the upper hand.[189]

How does Murphy use MacIntyre's program? First of all, as a crowbar in the epistemological barrier against religious reasoning. Her argument is that 20th century developments in the philosophy of science have showed that we do not have tools sophisticated enough for justifying scientific theories, and since this is the case, all the more do they fail to explain religious beliefs.[190] When we want to assess Scripture, (church) history, today's religious experiences in churches, and believers' lives as scientific data, we need a proper framework within which to situate the assessment.[191] The proper framework will only be a "large-scale tradition" inside which we can test the validity of a given theory or proposition. Such traditions have their own standards of testing, methods, criteria, etc., and for this reason they are incommensurable with other traditions. However, they are not immune to criticism – especially self-criticism – and they are therefore dynamic. If I understand Murphy's idea, the central standard of testing is the comparison of traditions at

---

188 MacIntyre, 'Epistemological Crises, Dramatic Narrative and the Philosophy of Science,' 460. Later he says, "It is more rational to accept one theory or paradigm and to reject its predecessor when the later theory or paradigm provides a stand-point from which the acceptance, the life-story, and the rejection of the previous theory or paradigm can be recounted in more intelligible historical narrative than previously." (page 467)
189 Murphy, *A Philosophy of the Christian Religion*, 81.
190 Murphy, *A Philosophy of the Christian Religion*, 80.
191 Murphy, *Theology in the Age of Scientific Reasoning*, xi–xii.

the level of systematic theology 3, and much of the work on the levels of systematic theology 1 and systematic theology 2(which she calls first- and second-order theology, respectively) does not require testing in the same way, because the views expressed on these levels are often *properly basic* (in the words of Alvin Plantinga, even though Murphy rejects the foundationalist connotations of this term, a connotation that Plantinga would of course deny). There can be an epistemic crisis inside the tradition, e. g., in reference to a certain dogma or a specific reading of a Biblical text. Murphy mentions the clash of her own feminism with the Last Supper, where only men were said to be present. In such a case, a tradition progresses by arguing for better ways to interpret its formative texts.[192]

If the central way of testing a tradition consists in such comparison, a major difficulty is that very few have the cognitive faculties and emotional empathy needed to understand other traditions in depth.[193] But how then compare? In chapter ten, Murphy provides an extensive example: the comparison of naturalism and theism. This is relevant in two ways. First, because naturalism is arguably the most widespread tradition in science today and thus the most obvious conversation partner for a theology with scientific aspirations. Second, because our epistemic situation is still such that we cannot provide sufficient evidence for the Christian tradition to convince opponents, and for this reason, the best arguments for the existence of God are "arguments *against* non-theistic traditions."[194] I consider next Murphy's use of MacIntyre's idea of large-scale traditions with both a presentation and a critique.

It is central for Murphy that there is no neutral point from which to compare traditions. Hence, every comparison is done from within a perspective, and the task is to give fair accounts of crises and possible solutions of one's own and of the rival tradition. Murphy sums up this task in a precise way:

> taking up this topic in the last chapter offers a chance to take stock of the responses Christians have provided to their own *internal* crises, because a part of what is needed to vindicate one tradition over against an *external* competitor is, in fact, to provide a narrative of the crises it itself has encountered and a judgment regarding its success in overcoming them. Further steps in the justificatory process are, first, to provide a *sympathetic* account of the rival's crises and an estimation of its successes *or failures* in its attempts to overcome them. Finally, the best defense of one's own tradition would be

---

192 Murphy, *A Philosophy of the Christian Religion*, 93. This is also the case in philosophy of science, as I have tried to show by pointing to figures such as Stathis Psillos and James Ladyman as sophisticated developers of positivistic-leaning realism and induction, respectively.
193 Murphy, *A Philosophy of the Christian Religion*, 91.
194 Murphy, *A Philosophy of the Christian Religion*, 93. Original italics.

to show that it has resources, as the rival does not, to explain why the rival should be expected to fail, and to fail specifically at the point(s) it does.[195]

Even though it is a stimulating discussion overall, here I am only interested in how Murphy does the actual comparison, which is what I have been unable to identify so far in McGrath's and MacIntyre's descriptions.

There are four steps in the process of comparison, according to Murphy: First, one has to provide an account of one's own tradition and its crisis plus how it has overcome the crisis (or failed to do so). Second, one must judge the other tradition's crisis and assess as sympathetically as possible how well its crisis has been met. Third, one must explain why the crisis has not been met satisfactorily and even why we should not expect the tradition to be able to meet it satisfactorily in the future. And lastly, fourth, one should ideally be able to either avoid or overcome the opponent's crisis using resources from one's own tradition, which would establish the latter as superior to the former.[196]

Murphy undertakes a lengthy discussion of the comparison of the two traditions, naturalism and Christianity. Of course, both are disparate and multi-layered traditions in themselves, but she takes a coarse-grained approach in order to get the discussion going.[197] So, which problems does she identify in the traditions, how do they solve them (or fail to do so), and how does each solve the opponent's crisis?

In sum, there are two major crises, one for each, that in a way bring about further difficulties:

1. How can one be justified in claiming to know of a God, especially if there are no obvious signs of divine action in the world?
2. If (for the Moral Naturalist) there is no God, then what is the source of moral knowledge?[198]

What Murphy calls the moral crisis of naturalism is often presented as the Euthyphro Dilemma (from Plato's dialogue *Euthyphro*[199]), which asks whether something is pious because God wants it or whether God wants it because it is pious. This may not be the best-chosen example to support Murphy's point, but because she uses it, I consider it.

---

195 Murphy, *A Philosophy of the Christian Religion*, 252. Original italics.
196 Murphy, *A Philosophy of the Christian Religion*, 274–75.
197 She develops a definition of naturalism by examining its roots on page 252–74, but the precise characterization is not important for the argument here.
198 Murphy, *A Philosophy of the Christian Religion*, 284.
199 The dialogue can be found in Plato, 'Euthyphron,' in *Werke*, vol. 1, 8 vols (Darmstadt: Wissenschaftliche Buchgesellschaft, 1977), 351–97.

The epistemological crisis of Christianity and the moral crisis of the naturalist tradition are unfolded in her discussion. In the following, I condense the discussion in order to provide an overview of how Murphy applies her comparative method. To recapitulate, she mentions four steps: (a) provide a narrative of one's own tradition's crises, (b) consider the rival's crises sympathetically, (c) show why the rival fails to meet its own crises, (d) show that one's own tradition is superior in being successful on its own terms *and* in providing an explanation, internally inaccessible to the rival tradition, of the rival's crisis.[200] I begin by investigating Christianity's crisis (4.3.5.1) and naturalism's solution to the crisis (4.3.5.2) before considering Murphy's account of naturalism's crisis (4.3.5.3) and Christianity's solution to it (4.3.5.4).

4.3.5.1   Christianity's Crises

Murphy mentions seven crises for Christianity that are all connected to epistemological issues.[201] In mentioning them, she also briefly addresses them and not surprisingly (her perspective considered), she finds them relatively easy to meet.

1. *The modern epistemological crisis.* The epistemological development from authority to empirical methods has been called an insurmountable crisis for theology. If this was ever true, it was only so when the understanding of empirical methods was coarse and unsophisticated, and nowadays, we have more fine-grained tools that are commensurable with the Christian tradition (i. e., MacIntyrian tradition-constituted rationality).
2. *Biblical criticism.* Like number 1 above, this crisis has been adjusted to an updated epistemology. Earlier higher criticism of the 18th and 19th century was too crude and simplistic, for example in claiming modern historiographical standards for ancient texts. Taking the Canon to be a lens "through which to interpret the world,"[202] it is relatively unproblematic to accept historical criticism.
3. *The problem of religious pluralism.* This issue Murphy leaves open because the debate is still unsettled concerning how to account for the differences among the religious traditions, their accounts of rationality, and how they are embodied.
4. *The problem of special divine action.* This problem is controversial. Murphy seeks to find a way to re-install God in nature, and she pleads for a theory of "quantum divine action."[203] Her concern is that without such a theory, it

---

200 Murphy, *A Philosophy of the Christian Religion*, 274–75.
201 Murphy, *A Philosophy of the Christian Religion*, 275–77.
202 Murphy, *A Philosophy of the Christian Religion*, 275. Italics removed.
203 See further Robert John Russell and Nancey Murphy, eds., *Quantum Cosmology Laws Of Nature: Scientific Perspectives on Divine Action*, (Berkeley: University of Notre Dame Press, 1993).

becomes meaningless to speak of revelation, and theology is left without epistemological warrant. She admits that this is possibly only a notion that can work apologetically within the Christian tradition, but she maintains that it could still be significant (without explaining how and why more precisely).

5. *The problem of evil.* Murphy sees a defence of human free will and of human moral limitations as reasonable alternatives to determinism. From this perspective, both natural evil and moral evil seem to be understandable by-products of human free will and moral limitations.

6. *Science versus Christianity.* Conflicts between science and Christianity have been few and short-lived. There are of course many ways to understand the relationship between science and Christianity (Murphy refers to Robert John Russell's eight-point typology on pages 297–298), but the concrete results produced by science do not challenge Christianity as such. Theoretically, scientific results that support empiricism and thereby desacralize nature have indirectly challenged Christianity (which takes us back to point 1).

7. *Neuroscientific monism versus Christian dualism.* This conflict could be challenging, but Murphy is a defender of an interpretation that points to Christian monism as a viable option even though it goes against the majority within theology.

4.3.5.2   Naturalism's Solution

How could naturalism respond to the crises of Christianity?[204] If naturalism is correct, points 1 and 2 are self-evident. If no God exists, it is not surprising that we lack the resources to know God, and then religious ancient texts cannot be subject to other – or higher – standards (e. g., clarity, insight, scope, infallibility, etc.) than any other texts. As to point 3, the degree of religious pluralism seems somewhat damning for religious truth-pretention; God's existence ought to result in a bit more of a consensus.[205] As to point 4, if God does not exist, there is no problem in explaining (lack of) divine action, even though naturalists then have to explain the many instances of religious experiences around the globe. As to point 5, naturalists can point to the problem of theodicy, but without God and without sin, it might be difficult to explain why we have a moral standard and why suffering is so unevenly distributed. As to point 6, naturalists would probably point to various power plays between science and Church throughout history, but then there are arguably as many struggles within science itself, and we are left with no forceful explanation of

---

204 Murphy, *A Philosophy of the Christian Religion*, 277–78.
205 Think for instance of John Schellenberg's argument against theism from divine hiddenness. Cf. Schellenberg, *Divine Hiddenness and Human Reason.*

why science has prevailed in one form and not in another. As to point 7, naturalists will not have a problem with physicalism, but there might be difficulties with a monistic view of life that are trickier to explain (Murphy does not mention them explicitly here, but she has written extensively on them elsewhere).[206]

4.3.5.3 Naturalism's Crises

Let me now turn to the other side and see which crises Murphy finds in the naturalist tradition.[207] She points to three. These are interesting because here Murphy has to be able to meet her own standards in explicating the views of her opponents.

1. *Self-referential incoherence.* In the strong form, naturalism holds that science is the only genuine way to attain knowledge, but this is a philosophical theory that cannot be argued for scientifically. It is thus self-refuting. In a weaker form, it might be said that methods and explanations should be commensurable with scientific results. But there is still the theoretical problem that the job of the (natural) sciences is to study the natural world "naturalistically" (with specific questions and methods which exclude other distinct perspectives) and thus inevitably can only find the natural world. Stated poignantly: there are questions that the natural sciences cannot possibly answer. Thus, in the strong form, naturalism is self-refuting, whereas in the weakened form it is insufficient.
2. *Inadequate account of the origins and persistence of religions.* Because Murphy addressed Hume so extensively in *Theology in the Age of Scientific Reasoning*, she primarily engages with the newer position of "cognitive science of religion" in her 2018 book. Two main problems with cognitive science of religion are mentioned. First, is there enough scientific evidence to support these theories? Often the bibliographies are circular within the field, which reveals that it is an immature field of research. Second, do these theories provide adequate explanations for the persistence of religions?
3. *Loss of the moral ought.* The enormous plurality of ethical views today seems to undermine the naturalist assumption that an adequate explanation for moral "oughts" can be given without God. All attempts to give a theoretical rationale for traditional morality have failed, according to Murphy. If morality is autonomous, there is no way to judge which theory of moral reasoning is superior to others – and Nietzsche's claim that Christian morality is a slave morality

---

[206] Such as Nancey Murphy, 'Nonreductive Physicalism,' in *Personal Identity in Theological Perspective*, ed. Richard Lints, Michael Scott Horton, and Mark R. Talbot (Grand Rapids: Eerdmans, 2006).
[207] Murphy, *A Philosophy of the Christian Religion*, 279–83.

has made references to universal concepts such as altruism impossible without argument. And so we are back at the same problem.

In all three cases, Murphy's identification of crises within naturalism seem to miss the mark. I hold that (1) only compromises a very limited number of naturalists, because most scientists seem to acknowledge that (natural) science is not the only source of genuine knowledge. Supporting Murphy's account seems to attack a straw man. As for (2), it also seems to be a minor crisis because the field of cognitive science of religion is relatively new and still has only coarse-grained theories of religion. It is too early to definitively evaluate their explanatory strength. As for (3), the plurality of moralities could also be a case against God as a moral authority – that there is no *ought* after all – and this alleged crisis of naturalism is thus not sustained.

4.3.5.4   Christianity's Solution

Next, Murphy seeks to show that the Christian tradition can give a better account of the problems in the naturalist tradition *and also* give reasons why these problems arise in the naturalist tradition.[208]

1. If it is correct that the epistemology of the naturalist tradition is self-refuting, then no further explanation is needed. But is the Christian tradition more coherent with respect to self-referentiality? Murphy believes so, if it is understood in the MacIntyrian way. She actually combines Lakatosian philosophy of science with MacIntyrian tradition theory and says that theories make progress by small reformulations of present theories and in this way seek to overcome difficulties while protecting the hard core of the theory. Conceived like this, MacIntyre's notion of large-scale traditions seems to support the coherence of Christianity.
2. How to account for the shortcomings of the cognitive science of religion? Besides being an immature scientific research program, it has two downsides that also work as gifts for theists. (a) Cognitive science of religion explains the plurality of religions, a plurality which *prima facie* is a problem for theists, but the cognitive science of religion cannot immediately give an account of the Christian belief because it leaves God out of the picture. With God out of the picture (as a presupposition), we would have a new problem, i.e., whether God is needed in order to explain religion, a question the cognitive science of religion cannot answer; (b) it is easy to incorporate the cognitive science of religion into a

---

[208] Murphy, *A Philosophy of the Christian Religion*, 285–300.

theistic program, and it is thus not exclusively a naturalistic approach (even though it intends to be).[209]

3. Murphy devotes a number of pages to addressing the question of a place for ethics. The naturalist tradition is confused because of the lack of a moral authority, but how should theology then understand ethics? In short, Murphy understands it as a part of the human sciences and maintains that this branch of disciplines is the one most closely connected to theology. The hierarchy of the disciplines splits into two branches after physics, chemistry, biology and ecology, i. e., into the natural (astronomy, cosmology) and human sciences (psychology, cognitive science, social sciences, ethics), before they are both embraced by theology, which may be seen as the discipline that answers boundary questions from both ethics and the natural sciences.[210] Without a concept of Ultimate Reality in some form, the question of moral disagreement will not be answered.

With this example, Murphy has provided a carefully structured argument for a philosophy of science for theology that enables us to compare theories across traditions/perspectives/paradigms and in this sense test them. The elaborated comparison between Christianity and Naturalism provides a fine illustration for how the comparison of tradition-constituted rationalities works in practice, and at the same time, Murphy's own suggestions seem to exemplify how difficult it is to actually provide this kind of argument because her own case for the superiority of Christianity is not convincing.

Pannenberg's account was challenged in different ways by McGrath and Murphy, but what unites them is an emphasis on contextual dependency and dependency on tradition. The aim of both McGrath and Murphy is to test theological theories against relevant alternatives, but I suggest that coherence theory provides better tools for this task. Therefore, in the last section of this chapter, I elaborate on the discussion and show that coherence theory is a valuable tool when seeking a way to test theological theories. It might already be clear that the proposals in 4.3.3, 4.3.4, and 4.3.5 show that Premise 2 fails, but the aim is now to show that we can make the conclusion even stronger by understanding the relevance and *modus operandi* of coherence theory.

---

[209] Murphy shows this by a comparison of Catholic modernist George Tyrrell and cognitive scientist Pascal Boyer, but it is not necessary to follow this discussion here, see pages 291–293.

[210] This is a very stimulating model with careful explications. See Murphy, *A Philosophy of the Christian Religion*, 286–87.

4.3.6 Examination of Coherence II

As I said in 4.3.2, the suggestion is that testability in relation to ontological theories is the careful examination of the coherence of a given (theological) theory both internally and externally. Because science aims to discover truth, so does theology as a scientific discipline; and because coherence is the final criterion for truth in this book, systematic theology should be tested for the degree of coherence of its theories. In 4.3.2 it was also said that the requirement of external coherence for systematic theology is entailed by the notion of God as the all-encompassing and all-determining reality. This claim is maintained, but at this point I have the insights of McGrath and Murphy at hand, and I may therefore add that the specific notion of God involved is not decisive for the requirement that systematic theology 3 cohere externally. The requirement might be strengthened by a specific notion of God, but regardless of the particular theology in question, it is still the claim in this book that a theology must exhibit external coherence with evidence from other fields in order to be a coherent scientific theory and thus a viable truth candidate. This is an argument that distances me from Pannenberg because he would start with a careful explication of the notion of God and then test the implications of this notion in comparison with alternatives.

The contribution of coherence theory at this point of the discussion is to provide a strong tool for comparing ontological theories and thus testing the theories. Because coherence comes in degrees, there will often be a kind of safety margin that allows for indeterminable conclusions. But if one theory is much less coherent than another, we can say that it has failed the test. If no single theory is clearly more coherent than the alternatives, we have an open situation with more than one viable option, and it will often be the case that more than one theory or paradigm is a part of the scientific conversation. This is especially the case in the field of theology, as Gijsbert van den Brink explains: "there is evidently more paradigmatic plurality in economics than in biology. Perhaps we might say that theology reaches the limit in this regard. This means that theological hypotheses are often very complex, and far less amenable to precise formulation than hypotheses in for example the natural sciences."[211] Hence, the nature of the discipline – the subject of the field, the methods, the best developed frameworks, etc. – is much more complex in the case of theology than in many other fields. Physics is, for example, straightforward if you know your mathematics; what is challenging and demanding is the immense amount of data we have collected; the social sciences, the humanities, and theology are much more complex, and this makes consensus, progress, clarity, and transparency much more difficult than in some natural sciences. As I have stressed a number of times, the

---

211 Brink, *Philosophy of Science for Theologians*, 205.

data in the different fields vary in kind, and we have a continuum from relatively stable to relatively dynamic data, which is important to note.[212]

In her hierarchization of the disciplines, Murphy has based her position on three premises that are very helpful: "first, the higher-level science must be consistent with the findings of the ones below. Second, the higher level is underdetermined by the lower. Third, lower-level sciences often raise what Ian Barbour calls 'boundary questions': questions that can be formulated at one level but cannot be answered without insights from a higher-level science."[213] When we seek external coherence, these three points are highly relevant. The ontological theory that does this three-step job best will have the upper hand. If we follow Murphy and take Christianity and naturalism as our rivals, we can ask: which one is able to integrate the findings of the other disciplines most coherently? "The findings" must refer primarily to well-established facts that are agreed upon by a large group of scholars, because findings inside the disciplines are affected by the theoretical framework that the scientist works within and are thus not neutral.[214] This also points to Murphy's third point, i. e., that certain questions are boundary questions and need a higher-level discipline to assist in answering them. Here again we can say that the ontological theory that provides the most coherent answer to the boundary question will be the strongest truth candidate at any given time. This third point is also a good example of the fine-grained coherence theory of Rescher and Puntel, because the integration of data from other disciplines and the answers to boundary questions can be measured according to the notions of cohesiveness and comprehensiveness which, together with consistency, are the marks of coherence.

There is an additional benefit to using coherence theory as a way of testing ontological theories. We can use it to discriminate between good and bad theological theories internally (in systematic theology 2). There are evidently many theologies on the market, and the plurality might be seen as evidence for the impossibility of saying anything with confidence in the area of theology. In order not to end up with this conclusion, we have to find a tool by which to discriminate between theories, and I suggest that coherence is the appropriate tool (in line with Pannenberg). Internally, systematizations of the theological *loci* can be compared with regard to their degrees of coherence, and externally they can be compared with regard to their ability to integrate findings in other disciplines.

---

[212] There is, of course, also a continuum within the specific disciplines themselves, and this seem to make the epistemic warrant local and dynamic, which is not a failure but a pragmatic necessity. Cf. Currie, *Rock, Bone, and Ruin*, 21.
[213] Murphy, *A Philosophy of the Christian Religion*, 287.
[214] This is the central argument stated again and again in McGrath, *A Scientific Theology*, vol. 1–3.

4.3.7 Conclusion on Premise 2

Premise 2 states that it is not possible to test theological theories, but the present discussion has showed that it is possible to test them in a number of ways. Pannenberg argued that theological statements are tested implicitly by their implications. McGrath argued for Inference to the Best Explanation as a tool to test theological statements because it is well suited to dealing with historical and natural claims in theology and can work productively in constructing a scientific theology. Murphy argued for a combination of Lakatosian research programs and MacIntyrian tradition-constituted rationality that works on large-scale traditions which can in turn be compared to other traditions with regard to their ability to solve internal crises and explain the crises of other traditions. I suggested that the coherence theory of Rescher and Puntel can work as a way of testing theological propositions and theories by examining their degrees of coherence internally and externally. In this way, it is possible to identify the best theories in the theological camp and compare them to the best available alternatives.

4.4 Conclusion

As a conclusion to this lengthy discussion, I can conclude that Premise 1 stands but Premise 2 does not. The best understanding of testability is that testing concerns whole theories and that whole theories should be tested for their degrees of coherence. This makes it possible to test theological theories as well as theories in other disciplines. I argued that testability can be taken in a rough sense that is unproblematic if we take testability to imply that a transparent methodology can be followed to the same conclusions by anyone who accepts the presuppositions. I also argued that if we broaden the notion of testability from concerning tests of single propositions to dealing with tests of whole theories, we have a finer-grained tool to use on all sorts of scientific theories in general. By using coherence theory, we are also able to compare the degrees of coherence among different ontological theories and thus also to test and compare their strengths. Of course, there is no way around presuppositions in metaphysics, and every theoretical framework is relative to its own presuppositions, but because this is not a specific problem for systematic theology, the criterion of testability does not undermine systematic theology but instead works in its favour.

In the next chapter, I discuss a subbranch of testability, namely falsification. As I said in the introduction to this chapter, the notion of falsifiability is often taken to be the most prevalent notion of testing and can thus be seen as strongest concretization of the criterion of testability.

Chapter Five: Objection 2—Falsifiability

Premise 1.   If systematic theology is a science, then the theories of systematic theology must be falsifiable.
Premise 2.   The theories of systematic theology are not falsifiable.
Conclusion. Systematic theology is not a science.

5.1   Introduction

In chapter four I discussed the first objection to the proposed understanding of systematic theology, the objection that systematic theology cannot be tested. In this chapter, I deepen the discussion of testability by focusing on the most important version of testability, namely falsifiability. Can systematic theology meet the criterion of falsifiability to a satisfactory degree? This question is not covered by the conclusion to chapter four and thus requires a careful discussion.

The procedure follows the construction principle from chapter four. I first give an introduction to the discussion here in 5.1. Then I proceed with a discussion of the criterion of falsifiability, which has a long history in the philosophy of science (5.2). After an explication of what falsification is and how is has been understood by central philosophers in the past (5.2.1–5.2.6), I give two examples of falsification at work, first, in the hypothetico-deductive method for inference (5.2.7) and second, by comparing degrees of coherence (5.2.8). I then conclude with regard to the first premise (5.2.9) before I proceed with a discussion of the second premise (5.3). The more elaborated description of the procedure regarding Premise 2 follows in due course.

The term "falsification" is closely related to its originator, the Austrian philosopher Karl Popper, who in a couple of influential books described his understanding of scientific activity.[1] Popper's falsification is still popular among natural scientists, yet philosophers of science in general are more reserved about it.[2] Popper's context was primarily the natural sciences, and thus much of the discussion has focused on the compatibility of falsification and natural-scientific praxis. I maintain, however,

---

1 It is the standard account to ascribe the term to Popper, yet van den Brink points to a possible refinement of the genealogy of the term: the Groningen philosopher and psychologist Michel ter Hark argues in his Ph.D. dissertation, *Popper, Otto Selz and the Rise of Evolutionary Epistemology*, Cambridge 2004, that Popper appropriated the core of his falsification thesis from the German-Jewish psychologist Otto Selz, see Brink, *Philosophy of Science for Theologians*, 40.
2 Ladyman, *Understanding Philosophy of Science*, 65.

that falsification is also a useful term regarding other scientific disciplines and especially in ontology, a claim that is somewhat controversial because Popper was repeatedly sceptical towards disciplines like psychology, philosophy, theology, and political science. But subsequent developments in philosophy in general and philosophy of science especially give me opportunity to revise Popper's understanding through the notion of coherence. The central claim here will be that if coherence is the main criterion for truth, as I have argued earlier, then the most coherent theory will be taken as provisionally true. The appropriate procedure is then one of performing comparisons between various relevant ontologies concerning their degrees of coherence. If one theory is clearly less coherent than another, then the former can be said to have been falsified (see further 5.2.8). This is something different from what Popper understood by falsification, but as we will soon see, Popper's narrow understanding of falsification has been criticized convincingly by other philosophers, which leaves room for a revised account.

The progression of the following discussion of Premise 1 revolves around two questions: (1) What is falsification, and what does it mean for propositions and theories to be falsifiable? (2) Are the theories of systematic theology falsifiable? I focus more or less exclusively on systematic theology theories instead of systematic theology propositions because the aim is to assess the proposed understanding of systematic theology wherein systematic theology 3 is the focal stratum. Thus, if systematic theology 3 theories are falsifiable to a satisfactory degree, it is less problematic that singular propositions at the level of systematic theology 2 are not. As I said in chapter three, I am aware that the proposed stratification of systematic theology focuses on a division of labour that may blur the organic exchange between the various theories in systematic theology, but as I have said above, it is helpful to keep the strata distinct when a defence of systematic theology's scientific status is at stake.

5.2   Premise 1

5.2.1   What is Falsification?

Falsification in its most simple form is an organized trial-and-error procedure in science. A very common way to apply falsification is through the hypothetico-deductive method (see further 5.2.7). This means that a hypothesis is proposed, a way of testing the hypothesis is suggested, and then the test is executed. If the test result is positive, the theory is still a truth candidate, but if the result is negative, it is falsified.[3] There are many nuances to every step of this short description, but it suffices as a preliminary description of what I discuss here. I will now engage with the major figures of the debate concerning falsification, starting with Karl Popper.

5.2.2 Karl Popper

Karl Popper's theory of falsification is, as already mentioned, the central part of his general understanding of scientific activity. His more general approach is often called "critical rationalism," where *critical* expresses the attitude of regarding all our knowledge as fallible and provisional and thus to be scrutinized without compromise, and *rationalism* expresses the point that rationality plays a decisive role in all scientific endeavor, as opposed to more questionable approaches such as revelations, feelings, intuitions, or pure sensory data.[4] This regards only the context of justification and not that of discovery, where Popper allows the widest range of inspirations possible.[5] For Popper it was a central deficit with the logical positivists that they stuck to a "structural *incompleteness* of science"[6] because almost all scientific theories include metaphysical views and would thus have to be counted as meaningless, which would make all science useless. But regarding the context of justification, Logical Positivism was misguided as well, because it advocates the thought that final verification of theories was possible. Popper's early work *Logik der Forschung* from 1935 was an attack on this kind of thought.[7] Popper's critique was closely related to his discontent with the method of induction, which he believed David Hume had undermined once and for all.[8] There is no logic to induction because it relies on premises we cannot account for. Thus, it cannot be the "confirmation of theories" that demarcates science from other activities because final proofs of theories are impossible. We can corroborate theories but not prove them;[9] we only attain approximate truth, updating our probabilistic confidence in a theory.[10] Another central issue for confirmationism is that pseudoscientific

---

3 Godfrey-Smith, *Theory and Reality*, 69. See also Popper, *The Logic of Scientific Revolutions*, 9.
4 Popper, *Conjectures and Refutations*, 34.
5 Ladyman, *Understanding Philosophy of Science*, 75.
6 Brink, *Philosophy of Science for Theologians*, 38. Original italics.
7 In his autobiography, *The Unended Quest*, Popper takes full credit for the fatal blow to Logical Positivism. This claim may need to be nuanced because an internal critique among other logical positivists had already been presented, but Popper's critique was surely decisive, see Gijsbert van den Brink, *Philosophy of Science for Theologians*, 37.
8 Popper, *The Logic of Scientific Discovery*, 3–7.
9 Popper, *The Logic of Scientific Discovery*, 248–282 et passim; Popper, *Conjectures and Refutations*, 76–78 et passim.
10 Popper would not use the term "probabilistic," which he heavily criticizes when he speaks of the "probability of events." I understand probability in a Bayesian sense that I find very helpful in this

theories are also confirmed all the time because it is relatively easy to come up with a theory that fits observations. Of course, this does not convince critics of the soundness of a single theory (think of astrology, which is also Popper's pet aversion[11]); instead of confirmations, it is the possibility of disproving a theory by testing that makes it scientific, according to Popper. Falsification is thus the mark of scientific activity, because scientists state how their theories could be tested and possibly refuted, i. e., falsified.[12]

Falsification can be understood in a narrow sense as well as a broad one.[13]

- The *narrow* sense is equal to Popper's proposal of falsification as a solution to the demarcation problem, that is, how we are to distinguish true science from pseudoscience.[14] In Popper's view, theories from astrology through Freudian psychology to Marxist theory are pseudoscientific because they can integrate any possible observation into their theories and no possible observation seems to contradict the theory. Real science on the other hand takes risks by stating which observations would falsify the theory, and then the researcher goes looking for this piece of counterevidence.[15]
- The *broad* sense could also be called "anti-confirmation," because the idea is that any final confirmation of scientific theories is impossible and that the aim for scientific work is instead to try to reject a certain theory by experiments and observations. In this way, the concept of falsification is not applied negatively as a demarcation between science and pseudoscience but instead as an indication of how to positively conduct scientific testing.

According to Karl Popper, the problem of demarcation (the "narrow" sense) between science and pseudoscience is at the heart of the philosophy of science: "… I believe that its [the problem of demarcation's] solution is the key to most of the fundamental problems of the philosophy of science."[16] And elsewhere: "The criterion of falsifiability is a solution to this problem of demarcation, for it says that

---

context as well. Cf. Popper, *The Logic of Scientific Discovery*, 133–208. For views similar to mine, see, e. g., Carroll, *The Big Picture. On the Origins of Life, Meaning and the Universe Itself*, 75–83; Richard Swinburne, *Epistemic Justification* (Oxford and New York: Clarendon Press, 2001), 56–128.

11 Popper, *Conjectures and Refutations*, 44–49.
12 Popper, *The Logic of Scientific Discovery*, 57–73.
13 Godfrey-Smith, *Theory and Reality*, 57–74. In the chapter, Godfrey-Smith does not use these terms, but he does so in his summary in the glossary, see p. 235.
14 For example, "*I wished to distinguish between science and pseudo-science*; knowing very well that science often errs, and that pseudo-science may happen to stumble upon truth." Popper, *Conjectures and Refutations*, 44. Original italics.
15 Popper, *The Logic of Scientific Discovery*, 17–20.
16 Popper, *Conjectures and Refutations*, 55.

statements or systems of statements, in order to be ranked as scientific, must be capable of conflicting with possible, or conceivable, observations."[17] To Popper, the scientific status of any given theory equals its degree of falsifiability, testability, or refutability. Note that the awareness of differences in degree appears here – a critical element that I elaborate on several times throughout the present book. The degree of falsifiability increases in proportion with how risky the proposed theory is, i. e., the more risky the predictions a theory makes, the more likely it is to fail, and thus the more scientific is the theory because it exposes itself to the danger of being refuted.[18] From this we get the two keywords of the late Popper: conjectures and refutations.[19] Conjectures are qualified guesses that works as hypotheses, and refutations – which are falsifications – are the only possible final results of research. If we test a theory and fail to reveal its inadequacies, we have not verified our theory, but we have contributed "corroborating evidence" because the theory *in this particular case* resisted our attempt to undermine it.[20] Using the word "corroborate," Popper seeks to integrate positive confirmations into his philosophy in a sense that is less conclusive than "confirmations" are usually conceived to be.

A characteristic of pseudoscientific disciplines, then, is that of guarding their theories from testability understood in terms of falsification. It is, therefore, the litmus test of a theory whether it is testable: "One can sum up all this by saying that *the criterion of the scientific status of a theory is its falsifiability, or refutability, or testability*."[21] Popper's favourite example is astrology, where soothsayers predict the future fortune of an individual but in terms so vague that it is almost impossible to test the predictions, much less refute them. On the other hand, astrologists themselves are often impressed by the many instances of verification of their predictions. But like psychoanalysis (Freud, Adler) or Marxist theory, the many instances of verification ("the incessant stream of confirmations"[22]) do not count in favour of a theory because they are too easy to collect.[23] A large number of confirmations may seem convincing as support for a theory, but if the theory cannot be refuted, it cannot claim to be scientific.[24] Another characteristic problem of pseudoscience,

---

17 Popper, *Conjectures and Refutations*, 51.
18 For Popper, Einstein was eminent in this respect, relentlessly critical of his own solutions, constantly testing the soundness of his theories. See Brink, *Philosophy of Science for Theologians*, 40.
19 See chapter one of Popper, *Conjectures and Refutations*, 43–78.
20 See point 6 in his seven-point program in Popper, *Conjectures and Refutations*, 47–48.
21 Popper, *Conjectures and Refutations*, 48. Original italics.
22 Popper, *Conjectures and Refutations*, 46.
23 Point 1 of his program: "It is easy to obtain confirmations, or verifications, for nearly every theory – if we look for confirmations," Popper, *Conjectures and Refutations*, 47.
24 "A theory which is not refutable by any conceivable event is non-scientific. Irrefutability is not a virtue of a theory (as people often think) but a vice." Popper, *Conjectures and Refutations*, 48.

according to Popper, is its tendency to cover failure with *ad hoc* arguments.[25] These adjustments make anomalies fit the theory even though the observation at first seemed to contradict the book.[26] Popper made this critical observation during conversations with psychologist Alfred Adler, who was good at making his observations of children's behaviour fit to his framework.[27] Why are ad hoc arguments deficient? Because they are not independently testable, and thus we get a lower degree of testability by reducing the precise empirical content of the theory and raising its number of superfluous propositions.[28]

To sum up, falsification in Popper's understanding is meant to supersede verificationism because theories cannot be finally proved but only disproved. Falsification is thus a bulwark against pseudoscience, which, conversely, may be confirmed but cannot be properly tested (and thereby refuted). And when we test such theories, they cover anomalies up by illegitimate *ad hoc* reasoning. Thus, we end up with Popper's definition of falsification: Falsification means "that statements or systems of statements, in order to be ranked as scientific, must be capable of conflicting with possible, or conceivable observations."[29]

Popper's understanding of falsification has been very influential, but it has also been challenged by other philosophers. In the following, I present the most relevant criticisms from four philosophers: Thomas Kuhn (5.2.3), Imre Lakatos (5.2.4), Paul Feyerabend (5.2.5), and Larry Laudan (5.2.6). This order is both thematic and chronological, and because I draw on important insights from all four in the elaboration in 5.2.7 and 5.2.8, I consider each in some detail.

5.2.3 Thomas Kuhn

A major shift in the discussion of philosophy of science came about with Thomas Kuhn's landmark book *The Structure of Scientific Revolutions*.[30] Kuhn's work has

---

25 Popper, *The Logic of Scientific Discovery*, 59–61. The principle of avoiding *ad hoc* hypotheses leads to the principle of simplicity or parsimony in the elaboration of a scientific theory. I will not go into this here, but see ibid. 131.
26 See Popper, *Conjectures and Refutations*, 48 et passim. "Some genuinely testable theories, when found to be false, are still upheld by their admirers – for example by introducing *ad hoc* some auxiliary assumption, or by re-interpreting the theory *ad hoc* in such a way that it escapes refutation. Such a procedure is always possible, but it rescues the theory from refutation only at the price of destroying, or at least lowering, its scientific status."
27 Popper, *Conjectures and Refutations*, 45–46; Brink, *Philosophy of Science for Theologians*, 38.
28 Psillos and Curd, *The Routledge Companion to Philosophy of Science*, 60.
29 Popper, *Conjectures and Refutations*, 51. An excellent explanation of falsification is given in Ladyman, *Understanding Philosophy of Science*, 77.
30 Kuhn, *The Structure of Scientific Revolutions*.

been enormously influential with over a million copies sold; it has been translated into over twenty languages and has been among the ten most cited works in academia for more than thirty years.[31] Kuhn was a physicist and used his knowledge of the history of physics to propose a theory of the *historical* and *sociological* nature of scientific work. Kuhn's book is well-known: Scientific work always takes place within a paradigm, a framework that sets the boundaries for legitimate theories, experiments, and interpretations.[32] Much of the work in science – called 'normal science' – consists in puzzle-solving within the paradigm.[33] This makes normal science conservative as it focuses on the cumulative acquisition of knowledge. But every now and then, anomalies show up, and if these anomalies are impossible to avoid within the existing paradigm, the discrepancy between paradigm and results will eventually lead to a revolution whereby the old paradigm is replaced by a new one.[34] And then the process starts over again. There is thus no objective progress in science because its work is relative to the prevailing paradigm. This led Kuhn to his controversial proposal that any two paradigms are incommensurable and that a shift from one paradigm to another has an analogy in religious conversions (he also labelled this "changes in world view").[35] The paradigms simply do not speak the same language. It is the nature of any given paradigm to monopolize the resources for intellectual work, especially the categories that are entrusted to the

---

31 Steve Fuller, *Kuhn vs. Popper: The Struggle for the Soul of Science* (Cambridge: Icon, 2003), 1.

32 "These [paradigms] I take to be universally recognized scientific achievements that for a time provide model problems and solutions to a community of practitioners." Kuhn, *The Structure of Scientific Revolutions*, viii. In the initial debate in the early 60s, Margaret Mastermann identified no less than 21 different uses of the term "paradigms" in Kuhn's book, which led him to revise his use in the postscript to the second edition. Margaret Masterman, 'The Nature of a Paradigm,' in *Criticism and the Growth of Knowledge*, ed. Alan Musgrave and Imre Lakatos (Cambridge: Cambridge University Press, 1970), 61–65. See also the helpful critique in Dudley Shapere, 'The Structure of Scientific Revolutions,' *The Philosophical Review* 73, no. 3 (July 1964): 383–94. Yet Kuhn still maintained that only two different uses could be identified: first, "the entire collection of beliefs, values, techniques, and so on shared by the members of a given community." And second, "one sort of element in that constellation, the concrete puzzle-solutions which, employed as models or examples, can replace explicit rules as a basis for the solution of the remaining puzzles of normal science." Kuhn, *The Structure of Scientific Revolutions*, 175.

33 As I understand Kuhn, his assessment of puzzle-solving work oscillates between description and polemics. On the one hand, he explains the nature of this kind of work, i. e., that the paradigm points to the significant problems that scientists then seek to solve. On the other hand, he seems displeased with this uncreative type of work, e. g., "[o]ne of the reasons why normal science seems to progress so rapidly is that its practitioners concentrate on problems that only their own lack of ingenuity should keep them from solving." (ibid. 37).

34 Kuhn, *The Structure of Scientific Revolutions*, 52.

35 Kuhn, *The Structure of Scientific Revolutions*, 94; 112; 148; 151. See especially the more thorough treatment of this problem in the Postscript, Kuhn, *The Structure of Scientific Revolutions*, 198–204.

next generation of scientists.[36] Kuhn's historical attack on the cumulative nature of science, however, has proven resilient to scrutiny because even central claims of his argument are quite vague. He does not, for instance, specify when the number of anomalies is great *enough* to undermine a paradigm, and – as Feyerabend among others has shown – Kuhn's notion of "normal science" is unconvincing.[37]

As for falsification, it is obvious that we cannot have falsification as a criterion in Kuhn's perspective if falsification is understood as falsification of single statements. This is not how science works because if it did, all theories would be constantly falsified.[38] Instead, we have to look for another use of falsification that aims at paradigms or frameworks instead. This is a central point for theology and a point I develop further in 5.2.8.

In sum, Kuhn's argument is that normal science is a puzzle-solving activity, but if falsification is put to work with regard to this activity, it would be futile to see science as an accumulation of knowledge. Therefore, falsification is not the procedure that scientists actually follow in practice. This criticism is deepened by another influential philosopher of science, Imre Lakatos, who also criticized Kuhn, however.

5.2.4   Imre Lakatos

The Hungarian philosopher Imre Lakatos criticized both Popper and Kuhn but for very different reasons. On the one hand, as mentioned above, he criticized Popper's falsification theory for being artificial – it is simply not how scientists work. Scientists are tenacious workers.[39] No scientist discards a theory the moment they see an anomaly, and this is a good thing: "They do not abandon a theory merely

---

36 Fuller, *Kuhn vs. Popper*, 37. Yet one of Kuhn's more relativistic points is that the conversion analogy implies that the "hold-outs" of the old paradigm need to die before the new paradigm gains dominion. Consensus then moves and is reestablished again in a different context, cf. Kuhn, *The Structure of Scientific Revolutions*, 151 and 53. The charge of relativism displeased Kuhn, and he responded to it in the Postscript, pp. 186 and 205–7.

37 See Paul Feyerabend, 'Consolations for the Specialist,' in *Criticism and the Growth of Knowledge*, ed. Alan Musgrave and Imre Lakatos (Cambridge: Cambridge University Press, 1970), 197–230. Cf. Laudan, *Progress and Its Problems*, 74. I agree with Laudan when he writes, "[v]irtually every major period in the history of science is characterized both by the co-existence of numerous competing paradigms, with none exerting hegemony over the field, and by the persistent and continuous manner in which the foundational assumptions of every paradigm are debated within the scientific community." It is in this regard that Kuhn's concept of "normal science" is unconvincing.

38 Kuhn, *The Structure of Scientific Revolutions*, 146: "As has repeatedly been emphasized before, no theory ever solves all the puzzles with which it is confronted at a given time; nor are the solutions already achieved often perfect [...] If any and every failure to fit were ground for theory rejection, all theories ought to be rejected at all times."

39 Lakatos, *The Methodology of Scientific Research Programmes*, 4.

because facts contradict it. They normally either invent some rescue hypothesis to explain what they then call a mere anomaly or, if they cannot explain the anomaly, they ignore it, and direct their attention to other problems."[40] As mentioned in the examination of Popper's philosophy, this is exactly what Popper warned against (i. e., ad hoc hypotheses). But Lakatos's point is that Popper's account describes a utopia, an unattainable ideal that no actual scientist would subscribe to in practice.

Another problem for Lakatos was that Popper's argument for falsification was based on an unconvincing conception of probabilities. According to Popper, evidence does not add anything to a theory's probability – the probability is always zero. This claim is the core of Popper's argument against what he calls "probability of events," and it is a consequence of his critique of induction. We do not have a specific number of events to calculate the degree of probability with and hence it will always be arbitrary to conclude on probabilities.[41] But according to Lakatos, the implication of this argument is that a theory with no evidence corroborating it can still count as scientific, and conversely, a theory with all available evidence corroborating it could still be called pseudoscience.[42] At the end of the day, this means that facts are irrelevant to the question of scientific status, which seems ludicrous.

On the other hand, Lakatos criticized Kuhn's interpretation of history, disagreeing that paradigm changes are largely irrational affairs, which he understood to be Kuhn's view.[43] Lakatos, by contrast, views paradigm changes as rational.[44]

But let me take a look now at Lakatos's own suggestions for understanding the method of science. According to him, scientific theories have three components. First, there is a 'hard core' that is the focal element of a theory.[45] This is often a substantiated claim (law, proposition, etc.) that scientists therefore only reluctantly discard. Second, there is a protective belt around the hard core consisting of a number of auxiliary hypotheses.[46] These are more or less well-supported and, therefore, if an anomaly arises, the scientist will probably try to identify a weak link in the chain of auxiliary hypotheses and exchange this element with another. Third,

---

40 Lakatos, *The Methodology of Scientific Research Programmes*, 4.
41 Popper, *The Logic of Scientific Discoveries*, chapter 8.
42 Lakatos, *The Methodology of Scientific Research Programmes*, 3.
43 It is difficult to get a clear understanding of Kuhn's view. In chapter 8 of *The Structure of Scientific Revolutions* he seems to say that anomalies and new discoveries can lead to new paradigms and that these changes are rational. But in chapter 10, where he describes scientific revolutions as worldview changes, he seems to describe them as irrational choices. Lakatos focuses on the second aspect in his critique.
44 Lakatos, *The Methodology of Scientific Research Programmes*, 6.
45 Lakatos, *The Methodology of Scientific Research Programmes*, 4.
46 Lakatos, *The Methodology of Scientific Research Programmes*, 4.

a scientific theory needs to have a positive heuristic. This means that the theory must tell the researcher how to solve problems and respond to anomalies.[47]

No theory is ironclad, and Lakatos therefore suggested that we view theories as "historically extended research programmes."[48] A theory develops over time in the sense that it responds to anomalies by revising its protection belt (rather than discarding the whole theory, as Popper demanded). But a theory can be discarded if a competing research program is more successful in predicting novel observations and is thus stronger than the first program. Lakatos calls the stronger candidate a "progressive" theory and the weaker a "degenerating" one.[49] Most scientists will subscribe to the progressive theory and thus a scientific discipline can shift its research program (which amounts to a scientific revolution).[50]

Even though Lakatos is critical of Popper's solution to the demarcation problem, he joins Popper in rejecting verificationism. Because it is not possible to *prove* any theory, proof cannot be a criterion of demarcation between scientific and pseudoscientific theories. Simple verifications do not entail empirical progress.[51] The reason is simple: it is not possible to develop a proof from a given observation; one cannot make the jump from "some *Fs* are *Gs*" to "all *Fs* are *Gs*." Laws of nature, universalized generalizations that they are, cannot be proved *in toto* because the number of our observations, no matter how large (and over how much time), will always be finite. Thus, there is always the possibility that the next observation will shake the whole system.[52]

Now, Lakatos's solution seems both convincing and useful. We acknowledge that final verification is not possible, but we still find certain theories more promising and convincing than others. This is due to the three components that I described above

---

47 Lakatos, *The Methodology of Scientific Research Programmes*, 4. Lakatos gives the example that, "[f]or instance, if a planet does not move exactly as it should, the Newtonian scientist checks his conjectures concerning atmospheric refraction, concerning propagation of light in magnetic storms, and hundreds of other conjectures which are all part of the programme. He may even invent a hitherto unknown planet and calculate its position, mass and velocity in order to explain the anomaly." (ibid.)
48 Curd and Cover, *Philosophy of Science*, 71.
49 Lakatos, *The Methodology of Scientific Research Programmes*, 5. "Thus, in a progressive research programme, theory leads to the discovery of hitherto unknown novel facts. In degenerating programmes, however, theories are fabricated only in order to accommodate known facts."
50 Lakatos, *The Methodology of Scientific Research Programmes*, 6. "Now, how do scientific revolutions come about? If we have two rival research programmes, and one is progressing while the other is degenerating, scientists tend to join the progressive programme. This is the rationale of scientific revolutions. But while it is a matter of intellectual honesty to keep the record public, it is not dishonest to stick to a degenerating programme and try to turn it into a progressive one."
51 Lakatos, *The Methodology of Scientific Research Programmes*, 6.
52 Lakatos, *The Methodology of Scientific Research Programmes*, 2 et passim. On the discussion of induction, see further in 4.2.3.1.

(hard core; protection belt; a positive heuristic). These encapsulate the rationality of the scientific endeavour and humbly recognize the tentative aspect of all scientific work. But all is not said with Lakatos. As I show in the next two sections, there are important adjustments to make to his account.

5.2.5 Paul Feyerabend

The Austrian philosopher Paul K. Feyerabend is widely known for his anarchistic theory of philosophy of science, presented in *Against Method* from 1975, which originated as a collaborative project with Imre Lakatos who unfortunately died the year before Feyerabend published the book.[53] Feyerabend's scepticism toward methodological reductionism, where a single feature such as falsification is heralded as *the* scientific method,[54] is regularly mentioned as a precise criticism, but his own claim that science *really* works according to the principle that "anything goes" has left him with few heirs among philosophers of science.[55] Though many aspects of Feyerabend's philosophy are interesting, for example his epistemological theories, I am only interested here in his criticism of falsification.

Feyerabend elaborates on Lakatos's aforementioned critique. If we present falsification as *the* method, we run into the problem that no actual scientist works this way: "Methodologists may point to the importance of falsifications – but they blithely use falsified theories, they may sermonize how important it is to consider all the relevant evidence, and never mention those big and drastic facts which show that the theories they admire and accept may be as badly off as the older theories which they reject. In *practice* they slavishly repeat the most recent pronouncements of the top dogs in physics, though in doing so they must violate some very basic

---

53 Paul Feyerabend, *Against Method*, Third Edition (London and New York: Verso, 2010), vii. A large part of their private correspondence has been published, though, and it reveals their agreements and differences. See part three of Imre Lakatos and Paul Feyerabend, *For and Against Method: Including Lakatos's Lectures on Scientific Method and the Lakatos-Feyerabend Correspondence*, ed. Matteo Motterlini (Chicago: University of Chicago Press, 2000), 119–373.

54 Feyerabend gives the example of the "Copernican revolution" where no single principle can be said to be decisive on its own, Feyerabend, *Against Method*, 146: "We see very clearly how misguided it is to try reducing the process 'Copernican Revolution' to a single principle, such as the principle of falsification. Falsification played a role just as new observations played a role. But both were imbedded in a complex pattern of events which contained tendencies, attitudes, and considerations of an entirely different nature."

55 David Munchin has worked on a topic similar to mine but with a narrower focus on combining the philosophical insights of Feyerabend with the theological works of Thomas F. Torrance. See David Munchin, *Is Theology a Science? The Nature of the Scientific Enterprise in the Scientific Theology of Thomas Forsyth Torrance and the Anarchic Epistemology of Paul Feyerabend* (Leiden and Boston: Brill, 2011).

rules of their trade."[56] Popper's critical rationalism was presented before historical and sociological theories appeared in the philosophy of science, and Feyerabend's critique may thus be justified: there is a basic irrationalism to much scientific work because it is a human endeavour. I still think it is vital, however, to remember that Popper never claimed that there is an inner logic in falsification that protects us from bad science or irrationalism at a psychological level. To compare, I strive to make a coherent account of the topic of this book, but even though I think of the questions as deeply as I can, this does not prevent me from making mistakes. I may think the present systematization is robust and coherent, yet a shrewder scholar may see some inconsistency or error in the final product. I may even stick to theories, schools of thought, and authorities that are controversial or regarded as incoherent by the larger community of scholars because I have theoretical, emotional, practical, or institutional reasons to do so (or unknown biases). So, Feyerabend's critique may be precise, but it also seems brutal to write off all "methodologists" because they do not follow their own rules. To do so, he must analyse every single instance of a methodologist who holds on to a "falsified theory" and argue that they do so on purpose even though the falsification is final and convincing. He must prove that they "never mention" the problems facing their favourite theories and that they uncritically repeat their favourite scholars' pronouncements. As a broad and general criticism, Feyerabend seems to have a convincing case, but based on the fact that he mentions very few cases from actual science, I think he paints his picture with too broad a brush.

That said, Feyerabend's argument continues with an emphasis on the unsettled relationship between facts and theories. Falsification is not a viable tool, and instead we need a different tool that "must enable us to choose between theories which we have already tested *and which are falsified*. To proceed further. Not only are facts and theories in constant disharmony, but they are never as neatly separated as everyone makes them out to be."[57] Thus, according to Feyerabend, the underdetermination of theories is a justification for continuing to work on falsified theories, and in continuation of this, the historical situatedness of the scientist relativizes the methods, observations, results etc., thus rendering a final falsification impossible.[58]

---

56 Feyerabend, *Against Method*, 44–45. Original italics. On page 157, Feyerabend quite clearly rejects the compatibility of critical rationalism (and thus also falsificationism) and actual science as we know it: "[I]s it possible to have both a science as we know it and the rules of a critical rationalism as just described? And to *this* question the answer seems to be a firm and resounding NO." (Original italics).
57 Feyerabend, *Against Method*, 45. Original italics.
58 Feyerabend, *Against Method*, 45–46.

In spite of their concurrent criticisms of falsification, Feyerabend also proposes a critique of Lakatos's theory of research programs[59] especially regarding the so-called degenerating programs: If there is a time limit for the pursuit of degenerating research programs – Lakatos nowhere states such a limit – we do not know whether they would have proven fruitful if more time had been given to investigating them.[60] On the other hand, if there is no time limit, there is no distinction between Lakatos' methodology and Feyerabend's methodological anarchism, and thus no theory should be excluded from the scientific endeavour.[61]

Feyerabend's relevance for the present book lies in his radicalization of Lakatos's contention that falsification in relation to single statements cannot, as Popper proposed, be the single criterion for scientific work. Feyerabend thus provides the final stepping stone needed for proposing a revised account of falsification that instead refers to whole theories through coherence and that is thus a more relevant account for systematic theology (5.2.8). But before I proceed to this own discussion, I need to engage with one last figure – Larry Laudan – who has developed a sophisticated account of scientific methodology that absorbs the insights from the above four figures.

5.2.6 Larry Laudan

In his book *Progress and Its Problems* from 1993, the American philosopher Larry Laudan seeks to develop the proposals of Kuhn and Lakatos.[62] Laudan also claims that the history of science should play a decisive and regulatory role in the philosophy of science, and he thus generally seems to applaud Kuhn's and Lakatos's contributions; yet he also wants to adjust important details. Instead of "paradigms" or "programmes," he speaks of "research traditions".[63] Laudan defines a research tradition as "a set of general assumptions about the entities and processes in a domain of study, and about the appropriate methods to be used for investigating

---

59 Feyerabend, *Against Method*, 166–67. See also footnote 11 on page 161.
60 Feyerabend, 'Consolations for the Specialist,' 215. See also Murphy, *A Philosophy of the Christian Religion for the Twenty-First Century*, 75.
61 But see Alan Musgrave's response in Alan Musgrave, 'Method or Madness?', in *Essays in Memory of Imre Lakatos*, ed. R. S. Cohen, Paul Feyerabend, and Marx W. Wartofsky, Boston Studies in the Philosophy of Science 39 (Dordrecht and Boston: Springer, 1976), 477–79. The main point is that even though Feyerabend is correct in his point on the arbitrariness of a precise time limit for degenerating programs, this does not leave us without any guidance from our best current knowledge: "The fact that our judgements of past performance may be reversed in the light of future developments is no reason not to base advice upon them." (p. 478).
62 I find Laudan's engagement with Kuhn and Lakatos stimulating. See especially Laudan, *Progress and Its Problems*, 73–78.
63 Laudan, *Progress and Its Problems*, 70–120.

the problems and constructing the theories in that domain."[64] This is closely linked to Laudan's view of scientific activity as "problem-solving,"[65] which involves both empirical[66] and conceptual[67] problems. Laudan's notion of research traditions is thus a pragmatic account of scientific activity, which is also apparent in his appraisal of historical theory changes: "Most of the past theories of science are already suspected of being false; there is presumably every reason to anticipate that current theories of science will suffer a similar fate."[68] Laudan does not deny that scientific theories *may* be true or approximately true, or that they may bring us – asymptotically – closer and closer to truth, but only that we do not have the theoretical resources for assessing this.[69] Research traditions are very flexible and contingent, not ideally but in practice. Thus, Laudan is yet another philosopher of science who seeks to ground his proposal in how science is actually performed.

I find it fruitful to compare Laudan's and Lakatos's proposals because they are similar yet distinct in important ways. They share a common criticism of Popper's simplified understanding of falsification, and this I need in order to legitimize the revised account presented in 5.2.8. But they also differ, especially in their understanding of the core of a theory, as we shall see shortly. This question is essential to theology because Laudan's account is more sensitive to just how much theories often change without scientists abandoning them.

As already mentioned, the main difference between Lakatos and Laudan is that Laudan allows for *the hard core* of a tradition to change over time whereas Lakatos does not. This may seem like a trivial adjustment, but when we remember that the whole of Lakatos's proposal depends on the immutability of this core, it becomes clear that it is a big deal. According to Laudan, everything in a tradition is up for revision, even though he still takes something in the tradition to be sacrosanct (the core).[70] But the core can also change, and the core of the tradition is therefore dynamic. The changes within an on-going research tradition can take two forms, of which the second one is the more pivotal. The first is obvious; changes in a tradition here take place through "a modification of some of its subordinate, specific theories."[71] This corresponds to adjustments in the auxiliary belt in Lakatos's

---

64 Laudan, *Progress and Its Problems*, 81. Italics removed.
65 Laudan, *Progress and Its Problems*, 11.
66 Laudan, *Progress and Its Problems*, 11–44.
67 Laudan, *Progress and Its Problems*, 45–69. Laudan's awareness of conceptual issues is interesting and important to my engagement with his views. I support his emphasis on the dual stress of this pair of problems.
68 Laudan, *Progress and Its Problems*, 126.
69 Laudan, *Progress and Its Problems*, 126–27.
70 Laudan, *Progress and Its Problems*, 99.
71 Laudan, *Progress and Its Problems*, 96. Italics removed.

philosophy. The second type of change is what distinguishes Laudan from Lakatos (and Kuhn): "a change of some of its most basic core elements,"[72] Laudan writes, and this clears the way for a whole new flexibility in the understanding of how scientific theories evolve. Laudan is well known for listing a number of failed scientific theories that were once considered "verified,"[73] but as I understand him, he argues against positivism, realism, and correspondence theory (and the like) more than he heralds relativism. However, some have read him as a relativist because his "pessimistic meta-induction" leads him to believe that even our best-corroborated theories of today will be rejected at some time in the future.[74] I, for one, do not think that relativism is his goal. His point seems to be that there is a "natural evolution in the research tradition,"[75] even though most of its problem-solving techniques are sustained. But the link between Laudan's historical descriptions and a more normative philosophy of science is not obvious. I understand him as saying that the "natural evolution" of theories that we can identify in the past leads to an "expected evolution" of theories in the future. Hardly any theory is static but will become elaborated – or degenerate – on the basis of further research. Even though we do not know the future, our historical assessment relativizes contemporary research; we should focus on the problem-solving nature of scientific work and not stick with notions of truth or probabilities.[76] This seems to be a version of instrumentalism, but this is not of interest here. What is interesting is that Laudan's account closes his investigation of the past discussion off with the conclusion that a revised account of falsification is needed – an account that does not see falsification only in relation to single statements but also in relation to whole theories. It is also interesting that Laudan's notion of expected evolution has much in common with the theoretical framework of coherentism that I rely on in the present book. It is a central argument of mine that systematic theology works by revising its theories again and again as new evidence is advanced or as alternative theories develop and call for comparisons. But before I discuss falsification at work as the comparison of degrees of coherence (5.2.8), I shall now discuss another version of falsification at work, the hypothetico-deductive method (5.2.7).

---

72 Laudan, *Progress and Its Problems*, 96. Italics removed.
73 Larry Laudan, 'A Confutation of Convergent Realism,' *Philosophy of Science* 48, no. 1 (March 1981): 19–49.
74 Cf. Godfrey-Smith, *Theory and Reality*, 178. But as Godfrey-Smith also mentions, we have seen an impressive development of theories for testing and evidence in the last fifty years, and even though we still have much work to do as a scientific community there is real progress happening. Ibid. 231.
75 Laudan, *Progress and Its Problems*, 98. Italics removed.
76 Laudan, *Progress and Its Problems*, 125–26.

5.2.7 Falsification at Work 1: The Hypothetico-Deductive Method

In the excursus in 4.2.3, I discussed various versions of induction. There I postponed the discussion of deductive inferences to the present context because it is often closely related to falsification. A prevalent way of relating a hypothesis to a conclusion or result is to make deductions. Starting from a hypothesis, we suggest which observations will confirm the theory and then we see whether we can make these suggested observations. This method is called the hypothetico-deductive method. Before discussing this model, I briefly present another model of deduction that is an important part of the discussion in the philosophy of science, even though it is usually regarded as wrong.

5.2.7.1 The Deductive-Nomological Model

In the 20th century, another version of deduction was discussed intensely, namely the so-called deductive-nomological model developed by the German philosopher Carl Gustav Hempel in the influential book *Philosophy of Natural Sciences* from 1966.[77] Hempel also termed it "the covering law model," a term also used commonly in the literature by both adherents and critics.[78] The basic idea was that every scientific explanation must include a deductively valid argument, contain at least one law, and be empirically testable.[79] According to the deductive-nomological model, a theory requires the following four aspects: 1) The explanation must be a valid deductive argument. 2) The *explanans* must contain at least one general law needed in the deduction. 3) The *explanans* must be empirically testable. 4) The sentences in the *explanans* must be true.[80] The third criterion is a demarcation criterion that is relevant to emphasize in the present discussion: "The third condition, *testability*, is supposed to exclude non-scientific explanations that make reference to explanatory factors that cannot be subject to confirmation or disconfirmation by observation, experiment or other empirical data. It reflects the epistemological commitment of empiricism about scientific knowledge: the requirement that the *explanans* be

---

[77] A general introduction to this model is provided by Okasha, *Philosophy of Science*, 37–44.

[78] The model was first developed by Hempel in cooperation with Paul Oppenheim in the paper, Carl Gustav Hempel and Paul Oppenheim, 'Studies in the Logic of Explanation,' *Philosophy of Science* 15, no. 2 (April 1948): 135–75. The term itself was coined by Hempel's critic, William Dray, in *Laws and Explanation in History* (Oxford: Oxford University Press, 1957), 1. Cf. Wright, *Explanation and Understanding*, 11.

[79] What van Fraassen sums up as "explanatory relevance" and "testability," Bas C. van Fraassen, *The Scientific Image*, Clarendon Library of Logic and Philosophy (Oxford and New York: Clarendon Press, 1980), 104.

[80] Adopted from Rosenberg, *Philosophy of Science*, 30–31. Note that Okasha leaves (3.) out of his description, Okasha, *Philosophy of Science*, 37.

testable is meant to exclude non-scientific and pseudo-scientific explanations, such as those offered by astrologers for example."[81]

In Hempel's own words: "Deductive-nomological explanations satisfy the requirement of explanatory relevance in the strongest possible sense: the explanatory information they provide implies the explanandum sentence deductively and thus offers logically conclusive grounds why the explanandum phenomenon is to be expected [...] And the testability requirement is met as well, since the explanans implies among other things that under the specified conditions, the explanandum phenomenon occurs."[82] Despite the clear and creative description of this model with several good examples, Hempel's model has been criticized in the literature, for example, in terms of "the problem of symmetry," which concerns the possibility of providing perfectly well-orchestrated explanations, according to Hempel's scheme, while still being forced to admit that the explanation is odd.[83] This is because even though it is the case that A explains B, given the relevant laws and additional particulars, fact B does not (necessarily) explain A. Therefore, "[e]xplanation is an asymmetrical relation."[84] Another problem for the deductive-nomological model is "the problem of irrelevance." Hempel's model allows for irrelevant information to answer why-questions. As Okasha says, "a good explanation of a phenomenon should contain information that is *relevant* to the phenomenon's occurrence,"[85] but an explanation can satisfy Hempel's model even though the explanation is insufficient or even wrong. Following Hempel's model, one might conclude of a man that he fails to be pregnant because he takes birth control pills, but this is irrelevant because the real reason that he fails to be pregnant it that he is a man.

The deductive-nomological model was popular in the 20th century, but it is almost completely discarded now: "The view is now dead," as Peter Godfrey-Smith laconically writes.[86] Thus, I turn to the hypothetico-deductive method.

5.2.7.2   The Hypothetico-Deductive Method

Another version of deduction is the "hypothetico-deductive method". This method progresses by proposing a hypothesis from which some predictions are deduced

---

81 Rosenberg, *Philosophy of Science*, 31–32. Original italics.
82 Carl Gustav Hempel, *Philosophy of Natural Science*, Foundations of Philosophy Series (Englewood Cliffs: Prentice-Hall, 1966), 52.
83 See for example Godfrey-Smith, *Theory and Reality*, 193. See also the critique in Sylvain Bromberger, 'Why-Questions,' in *Mind and Cosmos. Essays in Contemporary Science and Philosophy*, ed. R.G. Colodny (Pittsburgh: University of Pittsburgh Press, 1966), 105–7.
84 Okasha, *Philosophy of Science*, 42.
85 Okasha, *Philosophy of Science*, 44.
86 Godfrey-Smith, *Theory and Reality*, 191.

and then executing a test to determine whether the predicted phenomena actually occur.[87] This approach seeks to develop a non-trivial understanding of the relationship between theory and data. Even in the natural sciences, most theories include non-empirical, non-observational matters, and the scientist thus first articulates a theory and then deduces various experiments that can implicitly confirm or reject the theory.[88]

Considering the hypothetico-deductive method, we make a distinction between *the context of discovery* and *the context of justification*. The hypothetico-deductive method has (at least) two phases: the first where we develop the hypothesis, and the second where we test it by observation. Every source is legitimate in the first part, the context of discovery, but not in the second, the context of justification. What counts in the context of justification depends on the applied variant of the hypothetico-deductive method. Some argue that positive results confirm a theory, i. e., an inductive variant; others deny this, i. e., a falsification variant.[89]

Even though the hypothetico-deductive method is a very popular method, it has also been criticized. The criticism concerns the kind of situation where we compare different hypotheses by deducing them from the premises and try to assess which one is approximately true. This is often called "crucial experiments," and the history of science is full of examples. The problem is that it is not possible to test isolated elements of a theory.[90] We always test "bundles," as Pierre Duhem famously said.[91] This means both that all scientific theories rest on a large amount of background knowledge that is just presupposed by the theories and that we therefore test theories and "auxiliary assumptions" as a bundle,[92] and that, in order

---

87 Rosenberg, *Philosophy of Science*, 197. Another precise description is given here: "If, a particular sentence was deduced before the fact was observed, it was a prediction, and then later if it was verified, the theory from which it was deduced was said to be confirmed. This was the hypothetico-deductive model because the law was considered a hypothesis to be tested by its deductive consequences." Machamer and Silberstein, *The Blackwell Guide to the Philosophy of Science*, 4. See also Godfrey-Smith, *Theory and Reality*, 69.
88 Rosenberg, *Philosophy of Science*, 76. This model is obviously applicable to theology, *mutatis mutandis*, so that we can have a theory such as "God is the creator" and then deduce from that what we would expect to find, such as the universe having a beginning, the universe being fine-tuned, the universe being organized, creation being contingent, life being complex, etc. I briefly touched upon aspects of this in the discussion of Pannenberg in 4.3.3.
89 Ladyman, *Understanding Philosophy of Science*, 266.
90 Slingerland, *What Science Offers the Humanities*, 66.
91 Ladyman, *Understanding Philosophy of Science*, 77. "However, in reality it is never possible to deduce any statement about what will be observed from a single hypothesis alone […] This feature of the testing of scientific theories was recognised by Duhem who said: 'an experiment in physics can never condemn an isolated hypothesis but only a whole theoretical group.'"
92 Machamer and Silberstein, *The Blackwell Guide to the Philosophy of Science*, 20. See also Ladyman, *Understanding Philosophy of Science*, 13.

to do a decisive experiment, we would have to test every possible alternative, and for obvious reasons, it is not possible to know all the alternatives that remain to be discovered.[93] This "holism of testing" – including the experimenter's regress,[94] the place of skill in testing, and more – is inevitable in scientific activity.[95] As Godfrey-Smith eloquently puts it, "whenever you think of yourself as testing a single idea, what you are really testing is a long, complicated *conjunction* of statements; it is the whole conjunction that gives you a definite prediction."[96] Whether this constitutes a problem or is an acceptable circumstance that does not hinder actual progress is a theme for extensive discussion.[97] In chapter six on intersubjectivity, I discuss the importance of agreement among scientists about what is tested in experiments on a given occasion.[98] I also discuss this more carefully in section 5.2.8 in the discussion of falsification theory and coherence.[99]

Another problem with the hypothetico-deductive method is that we always end up with (too) many hypotheses that explain our observations.[100] We therefore need a more delicate tool in order to select from among possible inferences. How this is done differs from discipline to discipline, so the point here is that we need additional tools to select among the pool of explanatory hypotheses. A third problem is that "theories are typically formulated in terms of universal generalizations. But it is impossible to derive a testable prediction from a universal generalization without specification of the initial conditions obtaining in the domain to which the generalization applies."[101] This is another way to articulate the problem of idealization (4.2.2.1). The context varies, and prediction can therefore often not be generalized. Note also that in practice it is difficult for many disciplines to identify testable consequences for theories and models. Often, the hypothetico-deductive method is applied as a trial-and-error-process, and the discovery is often "postponed" to the context of justification.[102]

---

93 Machamer and Silberstein, *The Blackwell Guide to the Philosophy of Science*, 143.
94 This refers to a sceptical argument presented by Harry Collins that says that we can only get facts if we use good instruments, but we only know that it is a good instrument if it produces facts. For a discussing, see Benoıt Godin and Yves Gingras, "The Experimenters' Regress: From Skepticism to Argumentation," *Studies in History and Philosophy of Science. Part A* 33, no. 1 (1 March 2002): 133–48.
95 Machamer and Silberstein, *The Blackwell Guide to the Philosophy of Science*, 298.
96 Godfrey-Smith, *Theory and Reality*, 31.
97 An extended defense of the more progressive stance is given in Psillos, *Scientific Realism*, 76.
98 Ladyman, *Understanding Philosophy of Science*, 80.
99 For a concise discussion see Ladyman, *Understanding Philosophy of Science*, 76–77.
100 Salmon, *The Foundations of Scientific Inference*, 115.
101 Psillos and Curd, *The Routledge Companion to Philosophy of Science*, 251.
102 Psillos and Curd, *The Routledge Companion to Philosophy of Science*, 446.

Even though some disciplines struggle to find testable consequences for theories and models, the hypothetico-deductive method has a prevalent popularity especially within the natural sciences. It has proved fruitful in many instances, for example, when Einstein predicted the visibility of bent light during solar eclipses, or experiments like Alain Aspect's that seek to verify quantum mechanics (Bell's inequalities tests with pairs of entangled photons). It is also often the method applied in palaeontology and evolutionary biology when predicting both *where* to find fossils and *which* fossils – for example transitional forms between terrestrial even-toed ungulates and whales etc. – will be found.

To sum up, the hypothetico-deductive method is a method that proposes a hypothesis, makes predictions from the hypothesis, and then tests by observation to determine whether the predictions can be either confirmed or falsified. If they are confirmed, the hypothetico-deductive method works like an inductive argument (as weak verification), and if they are falsified, it works like a deductive argument (though not as a final falsification because of Duhem's critique). Despite its problems, the hypothetico-deductive method is still a popular and prevalent method, especially in the natural sciences.

In the next section, another way of applying falsification is discussed, namely the comparison of degrees of coherence.

5.2.8 Falsification at Work 2: Comparing Degrees of Coherence

The critiques of Popper from Kuhn, Lakatos, Feyerabend, and Laudan have called for a revised account of falsification. Instead of focusing on individual statements, we should focus on whole theories. This is not a novel perspective; it has been emphasized by philosophers such as Duhem and Quine. In the following, I integrate their views of falsification with Laudan's pragmatic focus on problem-solving activity. I argue that the organization of data in coherent systems can be seen as attempts to solve conceptual problems and that comparison among theory proposals is a way of testing them by trying to falsify whole theories.

Note an important difference between the present account and Laudan's. Because I take truth as a central aim of scientific work, I do not simply accept his pragmatic instrumentalization of science. It is Laudan's historical studies that lead him to his view of pessimistic meta-induction (that present and future theories will also eventually prove wrong), but he underestimates the accumulation of knowledge because even though individual theories may prove wrong, we do not start from scratch every time but instead build on past ideas, experiments, concepts, theories, etc. Coherence as found in Rescher's and Puntel's configurations is very helpful in this kind of work.

There are also direct ways that Laudan's view can be applied to the proposed taxonomy for systematic theology; for example, Laudan's pragmatic account is easily understood in relation to systematic theology 1 and systematic theology 2. Various kinds of problems arise in the church (systematic theology 1) and in confessional theology (systematic theology 2), and theologians can see their work on these levels as a problem-solving activity concerning topical problems.[103] From a pragmatic point of view, this counts as scientific work, but the argument in this book is that the scientific status of this kind of problem-solving activity gains credence from systematic theology 3. Therefore, it is the possibility of falsifying whole theories at the level of systematic theology 3 that is the crucial question in this perspective.

One of the most promising aspects of Laudan's proposal is the integration of conceptual problems in his analysis. In the quoted works, Popper, Kuhn, Lakatos, and Feyerabend restricted their notions and/or criticism of falsification to empirical problems (singular statements), and even though the ensuing insights are certainly important, it is not a satisfying restriction for at least two reasons. First, our understanding of empirical problems and solutions rests *in extenso* on our conceptualization of the world, and our scientific activity is not a pure endeavour but is dependent upon a number of metaphysical views and decisions, especially concerning language. Thus, falsification is a more complicated method, as the Quine-Duhem thesis shows. Second, as a consequence of the first point, many problems within science are not empirical through and through but also conceptual, and solutions are thus to be found not only in experiments but also in the development of ideas and theories. Laudan has an eye for this, which makes him a valuable sparring partner for the present section. The interest here is hence to broaden the notion of falsification to include concepts and non-empirical theories and frameworks. If we are to make the notion of falsification work, such a broadening is necessary.

In the following, I therefore introduce Laudan's understanding of conceptual problems. According to Laudan, "[c]onceptual problems are characteristics of theories and have no existence independent of the theories which exhibit them, not even that limited autonomy which empirical problems sometimes possess. If empirical problems are first order questions about the substantive entities in some domain, conceptual problems are higher order questions about the well-foundedness of the conceptual structures (e. g., theories) which have been devised to answer the first order questions."[104] Conceptual problems are thus more fundamental because unsolved conceptual problems will compromise a theory in a devastating way. But there is also a variety of conceptual problems, and especially the critical distinction between *internal* and *external* conceptual problems is important to explain.

---

103 As I understand Niels Henrik Gregersen, this is also what he suggests. Cf. Niels Henrik Gregersen, 'Dogmatik som samtidsteologi,' *Dansk Teologisk Tidsskrift* 71 (2008): 309.
104 Laudan, *Progress and Its Problems*, 48.

Internal conceptual problems can, for example, include inconsistency (contradictions), vagueness, and ambiguity. Whereas inconsistency is an either-or issue, ambiguity is a matter of degree.[105] As for internal conceptual problems, progression lies in clarification: "The increase of the conceptual clarity of a theory through careful clarifications and specifications of meaning is [...] one of the most important ways in which science progresses."[106] Laudan mentions the emergence of the theory of special relativity and the development of behaviouristic psychology as examples of this kind of clarification.

External conceptual problems regard conflicts between different theories. Laudan names these "tensions" and categorizes three distinct types. Type-1 problems concern "logical inconsistency or incompatibility."[107] This is straightforwardly understood as a situation where theory A claims P about X, and theory B claims not-P about X. Both cannot be correct, and thus we have a type-1 situation that must be clarified. The second type, type-2 problems, concern situations where two theories are logically compatible, yet "jointly implausible,"[108] which is the case with late seventeenth-century theories of physiology and Newtonian physics, or with seventeenth- and eighteenth-centuries theories of heat (kinetic theory) and fluid theories of electricity. A third type is type 3, where a theory was thought to reinforce another theory but failed to do so and turns out to be "merely compatible with it."[109] In the seventeenth century, various theories of physics were claimed to strengthen Christian theology but in fact only appeared to do so. In Laudan's words, "[...] in many cases, compatibility, as opposed to positive relevance, between two theories is quite rightly viewed as a major drawback to the acceptance of the theories in question."[110] This leads Laudan to a taxonomy for the various relationships between different theories with five different kinds of relations:

1. *Entailment* – one theory, T, entails another theory, T_1.
2. *Reinforcement* – T provides a "rationale" for (a part of) T_1.
3. *Compatibility* – T entails nothing about T_1.
4. *Implausibility* – T entails that (a part of) T_1 is unlikely.
5. *Inconsistency* – T entails the negation of (a part of) T_1.[111]

---

105 Laudan, *Progress and Its Problems*, 49.
106 Laudan, *Progress and Its Problems*, 50.
107 Laudan, *Progress and Its Problems*, 51. Italics removed.
108 Laudan, *Progress and Its Problems*, 52. Italics removed.
109 Laudan, *Progress and Its Problems*, 53. Italics removed.
110 Laudan, *Progress and Its Problems*, 54.
111 Laudan, *Progress and Its Problems*, 54.

2–5 cause conceptual problems *in increasing order*, and their differentiation is an important task for the philosophy of science. But what may be even more interesting here are the various contexts that cause these external problems. Laudan lists three: (1) a conflict caused by different domains being involved, i. e., scientific difficulties; (2) a conflict caused by methodological differences, i. e., normative difficulties; (3) a conflict caused by conflicting worldviews (or components thereof), i. e., worldview difficulties.[112] Even though (1) indicates weaknesses in one or both of the theories compared, we may not give up on either of them. The temporal aspect of science often results in the maintenance of theories because solutions may show up later. In the nineteenth century, biologists, geologists, and physicists disputed the age of the earth, but in the end, thermodynamics, uniformitarian geology, and evolutionary biology could be maintained thanks to the discovery of radioactivity.[113] As for (2), work in the history of science has shown that methodological inclinations effect research profoundly. This makes conceptual problems a potent force in scientific evolution, with the change from inductivist to the hypothetico-deductive method as a prime example.[114] As for (3), this concerns accepted, but "*prima facie* nonscientific beliefs."[115] Why is this important? Because "there has never been a period in the history of thought when the theories of science exhausted the domain of rational belief."[116] The conceptual problem thus arises when we discover an inconsistency between science and extra-scientific belief, where science here equals the natural sciences. According to Laudan, the extra-scientific sphere covers diverse areas such as ethics, theology, and metaphysics.[117] Laudan mentions an example that is still shattering: the possibility of racial differences. Due to our egalitarian social and political frameworks, even to consider racial differences is unacceptable, no matter what empirical data might suggest.[118] Other examples could be research in biochemistry, the development of lethal viruses, or in pharmacy, where we do not fund the development of drugs that disturb our minds. The point is that science can determine neither which problems we should prioritize nor which ones we should refuse to even consider.[119]

---

112 Laudan, *Progress and Its Problems*, 55.
113 Laudan, *Progress and Its Problems*, 57.
114 Laudan, *Progress and Its Problems*, 59–60.
115 Laudan, *Progress and Its Problems*, 61. Original italics.
116 Laudan, *Progress and Its Problems*, 61.
117 Laudan, *Progress and Its Problems*, 61.
118 Laudan, *Progress and Its Problems*, 63.
119 A more recent case for the same arguments is presented in Antonio Damasio, *The Strange Order of Things: Life, Feeling, and the Making of Cultures* (New York: Vintage, 2017). The conspicuous fact here is that Damasio is a natural scientist, which makes him an interesting conversation partner concerning topics like feelings and values in research.

Conceptual problems, and worldview problems especially, are generally harder to solve than empirical problems, and a conceptual problem will thus be critical to a scientific theory. Laudan's general procedure is to accept the theory that solves the most problems, and this is his solution when he compares theories and when he assesses the strength of a theory. I want to suggest that comparisons of theories that are conceptually inconsistent with each other can be done even more beneficially if we compare the degrees of coherence of the theories. In short, the proposal is that the theory that is clearly less coherent than the other is falsified. "Clearly less" is not an exact measure, but it refers to how the comparison is executed in praxis where a high number of researchers must agree that one theory is evidently weaker (less coherent) than another. This also explains why theories that some find less coherent than their alternatives are still viable: the discrepancy of coherence is not great enough (yet). An example could be the problem of evil in theology, where you could say that this problem falsifies theology as such, but both because there are sophisticated attempts to meet this objection and because there is more complexity to theology than merely the issue of theodicy, theology is not clearly less coherent because of this problem. In sum, I suggest that falsification can be a useful tool in comparing non-empirical theories – even ontologies – and that this version of falsification can apply to systematic theology 3 as well. This both legitimizes systematic theology 3 as a scientific field and works positively as a heuristic within the field. The suggestion both defends theology and makes it a promising field for future research.

5.2.8.1   Falsification as Comparison of Degrees of Coherence between Ontologies

With Laudan's notion of conceptual problems I have taken a first step into developing a revised account of falsification. In the following four sections (5.2.8.1–5.2.8.4) I make the account finer-grained. The aim is to show that falsification is still a very useful concept when it is applied to whole theories and that ontologies are not an exception to this. As stated in the introduction, I take it as a presupposition for the thesis that science aims for truth. But even though it is a presupposition, it will be helpful here to explicate how truth is understood. After a brief description to this effect, I turn to an elaborated presentation of coherence theory and connect it with falsification.

Science aims for truth, which is therefore a basic scientific virtue and value.[120] But what is truth? In philosophy, several different "theories of truth" have been offered

---

120 Not everyone agrees, obviously. Besides Kuhn, Feyerabend, Laudan, and the like, such an influential writer as Bas van Fraassen says that science aims at empirically adequate descriptions but not truth. His "constructive empiricism" is an important contribution to the philosophy of science, but I

throughout history – such as correspondence theory,[121] coherence theory, semantic theory,[122] pragmatic theory, consensus theory etc. – but none has achieved the singular status of being most prevalent or acclaimed.[123] In the following, I discuss the coherence theory of truth and argue that it presents the finest-grained option and thus the most convincing theory of truth. This theoretical proposal has been described and developed primarily by Nicholas Rescher and Lorenz Puntel. These two authors discuss at length the important distinction between a *definition of* and a *criterion for* truth. For both, coherence seems to be the best criterion for truth, but it is not obvious that it is also the best definition, and Rescher and Puntel disagree here. Rescher argues that a definition of truth must be formulated in terms of correspondence theory, while Puntel argues that coherence delivers both definition and criterion.[124]

The most common critique of coherence theory is that it seems possible to fabricate a whole universe that is highly coherent and thus true even though it is a complete fiction invented by a mastermind.[125] The only way to avoid this misleading trick seems to be correspondence with facts. But again, this is not as easy as we would like it to be because correspondence has shown itself to be difficult to apply to reality. This is because although the world may contain mind-independent reality, what we have access to is still only reality's appearances.[126] The world is always *für mich* even though I am aware that reality is not dependent

---

find the critique of his position convincing, for example in Ladyman, *Understanding Philosophy of Science*, 185–93.

121 "[A]ccording to which a given item (sentence, proposition, etc.) is true if and only if it agrees with or corresponds to whatever aspect of reality it purports to be about." Puntel, *Structure and Being*, 144.

122 Usually accounted for in terms of Tarski's famous definition: "a true sentence is one which says that the state of affairs is so and so, and the state of affairs indeed is so and so." Alfred Tarski, 'The Concept of Truth in Formalized Language,' in *Logic, Semantics, Metamathematics: Papers from 1923 to 1938*, ed. John Corcoran, Second Edition (Indianapolis: Hackett, 1983), 155. Puntel adds an important interpretation, saying: "The little word 'indeed' is the decisive factor in this characterization, because without the 'indeed,' what the true sentence is supposed to 'say' would be a senseless tautology or repetition of the same formulation." Puntel, *Structure and Being*, 226.

123 If one theory should be named most widely accepted, the only contender would be *correspondence* theory of truth. Cf. Rescher, *The Coherence Theory of Truth*, 5. See also Kirkham, *Theories of Truth*, chap. 4.

124 Not that "truth" is the criterion, though: "But truth is not suitable as a criterion for the (self-)determination of this philosophy, because a criterion must be available; truth itself is the goal of the endeavor, not the criterion." Puntel, *Structure and Being*, 464.

125 An example might be the *Lord of the Rings* series by J.R.R. Tolkien with its fully described background mythology, including geography, languages, history, etc. This gives a coherent account of a fictional world, yet hardly anyone would say it is a true world.

126 Rescher, *Reality and Its Appearance*, 4–19.

on or created by me, which is seen when I compare the degree of coherence of my understanding of the world with those of other people – I can be mistaken. Thus, to follow Rescher, we can say that "correspondence theory is doubtless best construed as attempting to answer the question of the definition of truth: as a criterion of truth it suffers from difficulties of the sort just enumerated."[127] Rescher presents five critical remarks about correspondence theory that seem devastating. Abbreviated, they go as follows: It will not be workable (1) for genuinely universal propositions, (2) for propositions regarding the past where the 'facts of the matter' are simply not available for comparison, (3) for propositions that assert probabilities, (4) for modalized propositions of necessity and possibility, (5) for hypothetical and conditional propositions. Especially (1) seems to point in a good direction for coherence, as will be obvious in the following account.[128]

In the following, I assume the variant of coherence theory that seeks "coherence with *data*"[129] and thus tries to integrate the most valuable – and intuitive – insights from correspondence theory (and thereby avoid "the problem of fiction"). Data are not regarded as truths but only as truth-candidates (3.4.6). We have a very large pool of truth-candidates that *in toto* is incoherent, and the strategy is to select the largest possible coherent set of truth-candidates for the strongest account of the truth. Coherence is thus also a tool to select candidates from the vast amount of data that reality presents us with (including what is created by humans).[130] The concept of "data" in the work of Rescher is very broad. This is an important point for systematic theology, because if we wish to compare ontologies in terms of coherence, then the amount of data we must work with in systematic theology becomes very large indeed. Scripture, church tradition, philosophy, scientific facts, religious experiences, other religions, everyday life, cultural contexts etc., must all be considered. Not everything constitutes data, though. There must be "*some* logico-epistemic bite" to any datum,[131] and there must be a distinction between

---

127 Rescher, *The Coherence Theory of Truth*, 9.
128 Rescher, *The Coherence Theory of Truth*, 8.
129 Rescher, *The Coherence Theory of Truth*, 65. See also the introduction to this in 3.4.6.
130 But this does not entail that we can identify truth by coherence. Also, the problem is that we can systematize the optimal amount of data in different ways that are equally coherent. Thus, an important point is that "the truth-value of every theological [or philosophical] claim is relative to the theoretical framework in and through which it is presented." Asle Eikrem, *God as Sacrificial Love: A Systematic Exploration of a Controversial Notion*, T&T Clark Studies in systematic theology (London and New York: Bloomsbury T&T Clark, 2018), 2–3. Here it is important to note that Puntel distinguishes between two kinds of relativity, a *basal* and an *immanent* one, respectively. The point stated here is of the basal kind, of which he writes, "every theory [...] involves an intelligibility and coherence *exclusively relative to the theoretical framework*." Puntel, *Structure and Being*, 466. Original italics.
131 Rescher, *The Coherence Theory of Truth*, 56.

what can be reasonably presented as a truth-candidate and what is merely possible. This requirement is made in an attempt to avoid the hijacking of the theoretical work by obscure and diffuse data. All data should be seen as relevant, and yet there are some data that it is most obvious to interpret as mere human ideas or inventions (relevance is context-dependent and comes in degrees). To give an example, it is possible that creatures like trolls and unicorns – and alleged experiences involving these – must be building blocks in our description of reality, but they will soon appear clearly to fit best in the large picture as inventions or misunderstanding and not as actual beings. It would be clearly less coherent to take them as actual beings because there is no logico-epistemic bite to the claim of their existence.

How do we then proceed if not all data are equally useful? We know we have a surplus of data, here called truth-candidates, and we want to find the most coherent account possible. To do this, we need relevant criteria for selecting among the data, and Rescher suggest three criteria for selecting data for a theory: *consistency*, *comprehensiveness*, and *cohesiveness*.[132] I explicate these terms in the following because they are central to the remainder of the present book.

First, we can determine whether the theory is logically coherent.[133] The various aspects of the theory cannot contradict one another in any regard. Thus, consistency is a purely *negative* concept.[134] This means that a theory has to follow basic logical principles such as the Law of Contradiction (not both P and -P about the same thing at the same time), the Law of Bivalence in a weakened form (a proposition is either true or false, relative to its theoretical framework), the Law of Negation (maximally either P or -P), and the Law of Excluded Middle in a weakened form (either P or -P will be true, relative to its theoretical framework).[135] This seems obvious and non-controversial on a small scale, but when we handle a large amount of data, it becomes complicated and demanding. One reason is that Puntelian relativism is also implied here so that consistency is relative to the theoretical framework. This means that consistency is not necessarily a static concept because concepts evolve and what is inconsistent at one time may be consistent at another time. This is why

---

132 Rescher, *The Coherence Theory of Truth*, 169. This points to the important emphasis that coherentism is not so much a "finished theory as a programme for theory-construction." (page 334) I briefly mentioned these terms in 1.3.

133 This is what many understand coherence to be, and some are very critical towards this concept. See, e. g., Erik J. Olsson, *Against Coherence. Truth, Probability, and Justification* (Oxford: Clarendon, 2005).

134 Puntel, *Structure and Being*, 464.

135 Rescher describes these logical laws in *The Coherence Theory of Truth*, page 42–43, but I have combined his descriptions with the Puntelian notion of a theoretical framework. However, this is not a foreign notion for Rescher, who can write the following: "A coherentist theory of knowledge views the founding of knowledge on its data in terms of the determination of truths relative to families of (not necessarily consistent) premises by means of a coherence analysis." (page 316).

it needs to be emphasized that consistency involves two statements about the same thing at the same time.

Second, we can determine not only whether the theory is logically consistent, but also whether the amount of data incorporated is optimal. The theory must embrace the optimal amount of relevant data.[136] Lack of comprehensiveness is – among other things – what makes correspondence theory insufficient and this parameter is thus all the more important for coherence theory: "The general idea of *comprehensiveness* that underlies and unites all of these various considerations is absolutely fundamental to the traditional conception of a coherence theory of truth,"[137] as Rescher puts it.

Third, we can determine whether the theory has organized the available data as cohesively as possible, which means to relate the data with as many relevant connections as possible. The more connections it is possible to make, the more difficult it is to assume that one string of data could be left out. Cohesiveness thus means robustness. Of course, the connections cannot be arbitrary, but must be argued for so that a part of the argument is to show the connections between data and determine their relative strengths compared to other connections.[138] In this manner, we are able to assess particular theories *and* to compare their relative strengths. If a theory is clearly less coherent, that theory can be said to have been falsified.

To sum up the threefold criterion for selecting data, I take Puntel's poignant remark to be enlightening: "The concept of coherence is a *positive* one that presupposes consistency, but involves beyond that a certain interrelatedness among concepts, sentences, theories, etc. Coherence is thus an eminently *contentual* concept, and involves interrelations in all contentual contexts."[139] The three-fold criterion aims to create the best theories and in this way work both critically (falsifying less coherent theories) and heuristically (developing the best theories based on precise criteria). With these criteria at hand, I can go deeper into how Puntel develops his theory of

---

136 Note, however, that Rescher can also speak of coherence in an idealized perspective: "as *optimal* coherence with a *perfected* data base." Nicholas Rescher, 'Truth as Ideal Coherence,' *The Review of Metaphysics* 38, no. 4 (June 1985): 796. Original italics. Comprehensiveness in this regard is thus also idealized. This idealized version is less interesting in my opinion because what we aim to understand is reality as such and not a smoothened version of it. It is exactly his acceptance of reality's messiness that makes Rescher so interesting.
137 Rescher, *The Coherence Theory of Truth*, 171. Original italics.
138 Rescher's account of cohesiveness is given in two propositions: "(I) The truth of a proposition is to be determined in terms of its relationships to other propositions in its logico-epistemic environment. And consequently, (II) The true propositions form one tightly knit unit, a set each element of which stands in logical interlinkage with others so that the whole forms a comprehensively connected and unified network." Rescher, *The Coherence Theory of Truth*, 173.
139 Rescher, *Structure and Being*, 464. Original italics.

coherence. But before doing so, I elaborate on the notion of the truth-candidate, which is closely connected to the selection of data.

Rescher uses the notion of truth-candidates as a synonym for relevant data, as I explained earlier (3.4.6), but we could also use the term to refer to the final theories. Because we do not have a God's-eye view of reality, we can never be absolutely certain that our theories are true (which is a reason to adhere to *fallibilism*). I suggest a continuum for coherent theories, ranging from *potential* truth-candidates to *qualified* truth-candidates. If a theory is coherent in Rescher's understanding of the term, it is a potential truth candidate. But because we know that even fictions can be characterized by such coherence, we prefer theories that have elements corresponding with reality. A theory that says that Donald Duck and Duckburg are fictions is more coherent than a theory that says that they are really to be found somewhere on earth, because the former theory coheres with the weekly publication of Donald Duck stories published by Disney, who are known for publishing fictional stories, and the latter theory would cohere very badly with our understanding of evolution, our lack of experiences of talking ducks, our knowledge of American geography, and so on. Thus, the greater the number of elements that correspond with reality, the better the theory is.

With this said, it is time to go deeper into Puntel's understanding of coherence. Puntel has worked with theories of truth for many years, and he is an ardent supporter of coherence theory. He has also worked with Nicholas Rescher over the last three decades, and their influence upon each other is reciprocal. Puntel's own theory of coherence is an expanded and elaborated account of a general coherence theory. Puntel's work centres on the development of theoretical frameworks, and he seeks to present the most central building blocks for substantiated frameworks.[140] A strength of his program is that he enables us to assess and compare different theoretical, including ontological, frameworks. For this purpose, he introduces three conceptual parameters: (1) surface structures versus deep structures. (2) fine-

---

140 This is also the reason for his support of coherentism: "[…] the project pursued here is not foundationalist, but instead coherentist, which means that there is no reliance on putatively fundamental truths that are presented at the outset as true, that hold throughout, and that, in conjunction with logical procedures of one sort or another, would establish as true, as they emerged, all of the additional theses or theories that were components of the ultimate system." Puntel, *Structure and Being*, 51. His argument against foundationalism is rather classic but still forceful. He lists three common apologies for foundationalism and then three objections: 1. You perpetuate the demand for grounding, but this leads to an infinite regress. 2. You appeal to statements that are called self-grounding, but this is logically circular. 3. You simply stop the procedure at some point, but this is arbitrary (pages 55–56). However, grounding is still a focal point for Puntel, but as a final step of the theoretical undertaking rather than as the initial point. Inside the coherent system, a grounding is achieved. See ibid. 68.

grained versus coarse-grained structures. (3) different degrees of coherence.[141] These three parameters all define structural continuums. As for (1), there is a continuum between surface structures and deep ones. According to Puntel, these terms can be translated to the classic distinction between particularistic and universalistic perspectives. Puntel defines the terms as follows: "*Surface* structures (or surface levels or aspects of structures) are those that are articulated on the basis of *particularistic* perspectives or of *particularistic* theoretical frameworks […] *Deep* structures are those that develop within increasingly universal theoretical frameworks."[142] There is no sharp distinction between these two kinds of structures because they have to be seen as forming a continuum, as stated above, but the point is that the world manifests itself ever more universally in its own structuration and thus less and less in a particularistic manner.

As for (2), this is in continuation of (1), because (2) determines a different and more precise account of the relationship between surface and deep structures. If structures can show differentiation, detail, and specificity, then they are fine-grained structures (or more finely grained).[143] Correspondingly, if there is a relative lack of differentiation among data, a lack of detail and specificity, then the data are more coarse-grained.

The third form of structural continuum for Puntel is between greater and lesser coherence. Greater coherence is determined by two factors: "first, by a greater number of aspects or structural moments (this is the 'material' aspect), and second, by the totality of the relations by means of which what may be termed the 'material elements' are interconnected."[144] This is the decisive criterion for comparing theoretical frameworks. Puntel also names this "*greater* or *relatively maximal coherence*."[145] This is a very useful criterion because it allows different frameworks to strengthen through wider work as well as providing an intersubjective criterion for comparison and falsification: "a theory (a sentence, a system …) has a greater intelligibility than another (and thereby a greater coherence) if it develops and articulates a more detailed structuration of the subject matter (the issue, the domain, etc.) that is in question."[146]

---

141 Puntel, *Structure and Being*, 408.
142 Puntel, *Structure and Being*, 408.
143 Puntel, *Structure and Being*, 409.
144 Puntel, *Structure and Being*, 410. Note that Puntel here explicitly refers to Rescher's *The Coherence Theory of Truth*.
145 Puntel, *Structure and Being*, 69. Original italics.
146 Puntel, *Structure and Being*, 70.

These three steps are very demanding to follow because it is difficult for a researcher to demonstrate that a theory gets a high score on all of the above criteria.[147] But coherence is still a very useful tool in at least two regards: First, it works with fallibilism.[148] It is possible to organize the data differently and thus to adjust or even discard a theory if a better version emerges – or new data are provided that fit better within a different system.[149] This points to the fact that coherence is a matter of degree and new evidence can strengthen or weaken a theory's degree of coherence. Second, coherence is regulative.[150] We have an idea of where we are heading: towards the most coherent theory of the relevant subject matter. This makes the endeavour intersubjective and rational, as becomes yet clearer in chapter six below.

In the next section, I discuss the notion of systematization, which is crucial for the proposed understanding of how to explicate coherent theories that can be compared and assessed and possibly falsified.

5.2.8.2 Systematization

An important component of coherence theory is the notion of systematization. Determining whether something is coherent presupposes a system that can be evaluated. Thus, according to Rescher, a well-performed systematization is the mark of coherence: "The coherentist sees knowledge as a *system* and takes the view that the mind itself makes an essential and formative contribution to this

---

[147] Puntel, *Structure and Being*, 245. As Puntel writes: "They articulate truths *relative to this framework*. The genuine – and extremely difficult – task, in this case, is to compare this theoretical framework with other theoretical frameworks and quite particularly with the successor theoretical framework in order to determine *what sorts of truths* the corresponding theories articulate." Original italics.

[148] Rescher, *The Coherence Theory of Truth*, 189: "[T]he coherence approach is *inherently fallibilistic*. Its considered position is that a changing context can always force a reclassification of the truth-status of a proposition. Coherence theorists have always stressed the provisional character of man's knowledge of the truth." (Italics added). This is a basic pragmatist insight from Charles Sanders Peirce, duly credited by Rescher (pages 318–319). See Peirce's essay, "Questions Concerning Certain Faculties Claimed for Man," *Journal of Speculative Philosophy*, 2 (1868), 103–114.

[149] The history of science – and of philosophy as well – also exhibits this type of development: "the history of science shows that our 'discoveries' about how things work in the world secured through scientific coherentism constantly require adjustment, correction, replacement. We cannot say that our coherence-grounded inductive inquiries provide us with the real (definitive) truth, but just that they provide us with *the best estimate* of the truth that we can achieve in the circumstances at hand." Rescher, 'Truth as Ideal Coherence,' 805. Original italics.

[150] "The coherentist's *regulative* conception of truth accords this concept a place in the epistemic scheme no less important than the *descriptive* role it plays in other theories." Rescher, *The Coherence Theory of Truth*, 183.

systematization."[151] With the vast amount of data we have at hand, the human mind must organize the data in systems in order to assess what can be regarded as an aspect of ideal truth. But because systematicity can be defined in more than one way, it seems constructive to introduce some defining characteristics. Rescher himself has enumerated ten factors that characterize systematicity, and I list them all here including Rescher's original comments with my own comments in the first paragraph after the list.

1. *Wholeness*: unity and integrity as a genuine whole that embraces and integrates its constituent parts;
2. *Completeness*: comprehensiveness, avoidance of gaps or missing components, inclusiveness with nothing needful left out;
3. *Self-sufficiency*: independence, self-containment, autonomy;
4. *Cohesiveness*: connectedness, interrelationship, interlinkage, coherence (in one of its senses), a conjoining of the component parts, rules, laws, linking principles; if some components are changed or modified, then others will react to this alteration;
5. *Consonance*: consistency and compatibility, coherence (in another of its senses), absence of internal discord or dissonance; harmonious mutual collaboration or coordination of components "having all the pieces fall into place";
6. *Architectonic*: a well-integrated structure of arrangement of duly ordered component parts; generally in an hierarchic ordering of subordination and superordination;
7. *Functional unity*: purposive interrelationship, a unifying rationale or telos that finds its expression in some synthetizing principle of functional purport;
8. *Functional regularity*: rules and lawfulness, orderliness of operation, uniformity, normality (conformity to "the usual course of things");
9. *Functional simplicity*: elegance, harmony and balance, structural economy, tidiness in the collaboration or coordination of components;
10. *Mutual supportiveness*: the components of a system are so combined under the aegis of a common purpose or principle as to conspire together in mutual collaboration for its realization; interrelatedness.[152]

The point of all this is well put by the title of Rescher's chapter on systematization, that is, "inference to the best systematization."[153] If we accept coherence as a criterion for truth – that it is a criterion for something to be true that it be coherent

---

151 Rescher, *The Coherence Theory of Truth*, 323. Original italics.
152 Rescher, *Philosophical Reasoning*, 191.
153 Rescher, *Philosophical Reasoning*, chapter 10. See also 4.2.3.2.

in the way described in 5.2.8.1 – we then seek to develop and arrive at the best systematization we can possibly articulate. When we have done so, it is a part of the job to compare our best systematization with relevant alternatives, and if a theory is clearly less coherent than the others, the former is to be regarded as falsified.

Note that Rescher's list is from a phase when he emphasized a more pragmatic notion of truth compared to his 1973 book on coherence as truth. This is seen, for example, in point 9 above where "functional simplicity" becomes relevant if we systematize for pragmatic reasons to comprehend being as we perceive it. Puntel – and I – would disagree and maintain that coherence provides both a criterion for and a definition of truth, which implies that simplicity is a relevant criterion only when we have to select between two equally coherent theories. Beforehand, we have no reason to think that reality is simple or that a simpler systematization is truer than a complex one.

To do systematization is to make coherence work in practice. But this work is always executed within a theoretical framework that sets the terms for it. The notion of the theoretical framework needs to be investigated further to see how it affects systematization.

5.2.8.3 Theoretical Framework

If Puntel is correct in proposing that every truth is relative to some theoretical framework, a thorough understanding of the concept is needed (see 3.4.5.1.1). According to Puntel, the notion is a development of Rudolf Carnap's concept of a "linguistic framework."[154] Puntel explains the fundamentality of theoretical frameworks as follows: "The account proceeds from the fundamental insight that every theoretical questioning, every theoretical sentence, argument, every theory, etc., is intelligible and evaluable only if understood as situated within a theoretical framework."[155] This is what above I called the relativity to a theoretical framework.[156]

---

[154] Carnap presents this theory in Carnap, 'Empiricism, Semantics, and Ontology,' 206. Puntel comments further on Carnap on pages 22–23 of *Structure and Being*.

[155] Puntel, *Structure and Being*, 9.

[156] Again, this claim reflects Puntel's rejection of foundationalism in any sense. But he claims a relativity that is "moderate" and "non-contradictory," thus addressing the obvious problems with a more classic notion of relativity. An example of the relativity is given in the language of the framework: "Sentences are true only relative to their theoretical frameworks" (page 9). Later, he gives a clarifying example through a distinction between philosophical and scientific language. When a cosmologist speaks of the beginning of the universe, she does so by presupposing a specific natural-scientific framework. Here the term "beginning" has a very specific and determinate meaning. A philosopher can also speak of a beginning but does so in a metaphysical sense. The philosopher's job is to carefully explicate the differences between these languages. The border between languages is not fixed but always negotiable. See Puntel, *Structure and Being*, 13.

The basic constitutive elements of a theoretical framework are described by concepts such as a language, a logic, and a conceptuality that govern the development of the framework itself. Puntel's project is to develop a *systematic* philosophy explicating the most fundamental "structures" of reality[157] – formal, semantic, and ontological structures. The formal structures are subdivided into logical and mathematical structures,[158] and the semantic and ontological structures are subdivisions of contentual structures.

The formal structures differ in comprehensiveness and in the status of language, so that, for example, mathematics does not thematize its own language, which is precisely the role of logic. What is more important to consider is how these structures relate to each other, especially the semantic and ontological structures. According to Puntel, the concept of truth provides the answer: "It can now be said and shown that the function of the truth operator is that of fully determining the status of the interconnections of the three types of fundamental structures."[159] Truth connects syntactic, semantic, and ontological structures into a coherent whole, and this tripartite structure forms the comprehensive truth claim of Puntel's theory. It is important to notice that the development of a theory cannot be complete without a critical examination of all its presuppositions, even the ontological ones: "any truth-theory that accords truth an ontological import must remain vague and unconvincing until the ontology it maintains or presupposes is made explicit and investigated critically."[160] The notion of a framework is obviously very comprehensive – and complex – aiming at the integration of all the basic structures into a coherent whole (including linguistic, semantic, conceptual, and ontological structures). But this is what makes articulations of theoretical content possible, which is the core of theoretical work.[161] When we seek to develop coherent systematization we can assess, compare, and possibly falsify, we need to be aware that all our work is done within theoretical frameworks. This does not make our work strongly relativistic because we can also explicate the structures in other frameworks and compare these with each other.

---

157 Puntel, *Structure and Being*, 11. Later, he expands the definition as follows: "a structure is a differentiated and ordered interconnection or interrelation of elements or parts or aspects of an entity, a domain, a process, etc." (page 27). Chapter three of *Structure and Being* is devoted to a comprehensive description of structures (pages 155–245).

158 "Logical and mathematical structures are the fundamental formal structures that play, within the structural-systematic philosophy, a central and therefore indispensable role." Puntel, *Structure and Being*, 173.

159 Puntel, *Structure and Being*, 222–223.

160 Puntel, *Structure and Being*, 235–36. Italics removed.

161 "Philosophical (and scientific) theoretical frameworks are instead instruments that make possible the articulation, conceptualization, and explanation of theoretical contents or subject matters." Puntel, *Structure and Being*, 23–24.

With this in mind, I end this elaboration of a revised account of falsification as comparing degrees of coherence by discussing a critical point, namely that scientific theories must be falsifiable as a whole but not actually falsified.

5.2.8.4 Scientific Theories must be Falsifiable but not Actually Falsified

I have a concern that this way of thinking as presented in 5.2.8 may allow for theories that are not only falsifiable but actually falsified to be applied in research, which would be problematic. But I argue that it is possible to draw a distinction between falsifiable theories and falsified theories. If we take a classic example such as astrology, supporters may say that astrological theories are falsifiable and therefore should be viewed as scientific. But astrology is generally considered to be falsified already and is therefore classified as a pseudoscience.[162] In scientific practice, it is usually the case that a theory is falsified when a better, more coherent theory replaces it. This is also what I have argued for with the suggestion that falsification should be seen in relation to coherence theory. Astrology was replaced by astronomy, which makes much more precise predictions and provides superior explanations, and this is one example of how falsification works in practice. Falsifiability is thus a relevant criterion only for theories that are not already falsified.

5.2.9 Conclusion on Premise 1

The investigation of Premise 1 has shown that there are good reasons for accepting the premise. I qualified the discussion of falsification by emphasizing that falsification should be seen not only as concerning individual statements but also, and more importantly, as achieved through the testing of whole theories. To be scientific, the theory as a whole must be falsifiable but not already falsified. A theory is a truth candidate as long as there are no clearly more coherent alternatives available, but if such a theory is systematized, the old theory is to be seen as falsified. In sum, the analysis of Premise 1 has shown that falsifiability in a qualified (non-empirical) way regarding whole theories is a good criterion for science and that systematic

---

162 Paul R. Thagard, 'Why Astrology is a Pseudoscience,' *PSA. Proceedings of the Biennial Meeting of the Philosophy of Science Association* Vol. 1: Contributed Papers (1978): 223–34. Note, however, that Thagard rejects falsification as a valid criterion and rests his case on other arguments. The point, though, that astrology is a failed discipline is still defended (cf. page 226). Thagard introduces two principles for distinguishing between science and pseudoscience. These are interesting: "(1) [a scientific theory now regarded as pseudo-scientific] has been less progressive than alternative theories over a long period of time, and faces many unresolved problems; but (2) the community of practitioners makes little attempt to develop the theory towards solutions of the problems, shows no concern for attempts to evaluate the theory in relation to others, and is selective in considering confirmations and disconfirmations." (page 228)

theology theories must thus be falsifiable in order to be regarded as scientific. How systematic theology meets this criterion is the topic for the following discussion (5.3).

5.3 Premise 2

When I discuss whether the theories of systematic theology can be falsified, I mean theistic ontologies as such. As demonstrated in 5.2, falsification primarily concerns whole theories because we never test single statements or propositions. For this reason, it is not of much interest here to discuss whether single statements in theology can be falsified (see 5.3.3 though), and I shall ask instead whether standard theories about God can be falsified or even whether they have been falsified (as has astrology).

As stated above, an ontology consists of many elements, and there is no single theistic ontology but a variety thereof due to the various possibilities of organizing data and the possibility of organizing data in various frameworks within theology. But no matter how many variations there may be, some notion of God must be present in any theistic ontology. Thus, much of the debate about falsification within systematic theology has focused on the very notion of God but also on the question *when* (now or in the eschaton) such a falsification can be demanded.

The following discussion of Premise 2 consists of five parts. First, two examples of how falsification within theology has been discussed is presented (5.3.1), then, second, I discuss a version of falsification within theology that has been popular, namely the concept of eschatological verification (5.3.2). In the third part, I discuss how to understand falsification in relation to the individual loci of dogmatics (systematic theology 2), in other words, whether falsification has anything to say here if it primarily concerns whole theories (5.3.3). Fourth, I discuss more recent attempts to understand how falsification can work with systematic theology (5.3.4), before I end with a subconclusion concerning the discussion of Premise 2 (5.3.5).

5.3.1 Examples of Uses of Falsification

In 1950, philosopher Antony Flew posed a simple but hard question to his symposiasts, Richard M. Hare and Basil Mitchell: "What would have to occur or to have occurred to constitute for you a disproof of the love of, or of the existence of God?"[163] Flew's question ends a short line of thought, articulated around his

---

163 Anthony Flew, R.M. Hare, and Basil Mitchell, 'Theology and Falsification. The University Discussion,' in *New Essays in Philosophical Theology* (London: SCM Press, 1955), 99.

frustration that theologians seem to guard their beliefs behind endless qualifications. When sceptics pose hard questions to theological assertions, theologians seem always to be able to qualify their statements even though they presumably end up compromising their original views. But a "hypothesis may thus be killed by inches, the death by a thousand qualifications."[164]

I next look at three different responses to Flew's criticism; the discussion should make it clear that no consensus reigns among theologians concerning how to respond to this criticism. The reason is obvious: because a response rests on the overall theoretical framework that a theologian adheres to and because no single ontology is *the* theistic one, we are bound to see different responses. I discuss the responses by Stephen Davis, Schubert Ogden, and John Hick – the last one found in the next section in relation to the concept of eschatological verification.

Twenty years after the initial debate between Flew, Hare, and Mitchell, the American philosopher Stephen T. Davis wrote an article discussing Flew's view.[165] Davis helpfully encircles two types of "limits" that Flew seems to be looking for, that is, a *psychological* and an *evidential* limit, respectively. According to Davis, a psychological limit is reached "if there is a limit to the contrary evidence which a believer will allow before he modifies his beliefs, the statement he believes is an assertion; if there is no such limit, it is not an assertion."[166] But what Flew is actually looking for is an evidential limit, which is "a limit of contrary evidence which actually falsifies a statement, a circumstance which, when it obtains, makes it irrational to believe the statement."[167] Davis seems to suggest that the history of Christianity shows a covetable ability to learn from new evidence such that "many dogmas" have been reframed; even though I am suspicious about the validity of this claim, his two mentioned examples are interesting: (1) the doctrine of indulgences, which was questioned by Luther (we might call this an *internal* critique), and (2) Bishop James

---

164 Flew, Hare, and Mitchell, 'Theology and Falsification,' 97. Some have argued against Flew's view and said that theologians do not make endless qualification but are restricted to only two very precise qualifications that they keep coming back to: first, that the theologian cannot prove the existence of an omnipotent and good God (at least to such a degree that an atheist is satisfied), and second, that the theologian cannot give an adequate answer to the problem of evil. Cf. Stephen T. Davis, 'Theology, Verification, and Falsification,' *International Journal for Philosophy of Religion* 6, no. 1 (Spring 1975): 29.
165 Davis, 'Theology, Verification, and Falsification,' 23–39.
166 Davis, 'Theology, Verification, and Falsification,' 25. Even though I find this attempt interesting, it also seems very difficult to handle in principle. If a philosopher like Flew would challenge a devoted believer to find out where the psychological limit to his belief might be found, the conversation would inevitably move to a discussion of evidence and thus a discussion of where the evidential limit might be. Moreover, I agree with Davis when he says that it seems obvious that people can have strong beliefs and yet change their views over time (page 27).
167 Davis, 'Theology, Verification, and Falsification,' 25.

Ussher's chronology, dating the creation to 4004 B.C., which was refuted by modern science (we might call this an *external* critique). It could be objected that neither of these examples refers to theories or views that had doctrinal status, but according to Davis they can be seen as examples of "a healthy open-mindedness" on the part of religious believers and a willingness to scrutinize, adjust, or discard certain doctrines.[168] Davis then sharpens Flew's argument with a helpful distinction. Flew says that some religious believers stick to their faith even though many anti-theistic arguments had been presented to them, but "this does not entail what Flew seems to believe it entails – that the faith of these believers would remain steady in the face of any anti-theistic evidence *that could conceivably be pointed out to them*."[169]

I regard the notion of a psychological limit as vague and find it more fruitful to discuss the evidential limit. I agree with Davis that it is mandatory to explicate what is meant by "falsifying a statement," or – stated differently in Flew's jargon – "what is an evidential limit after all?" Davis says that an evidential limit can be understood either as (1) "an amount or quality of contrary evidence so overwhelming in its weight that it would convince anyone beyond a shadow of doubt that the statement in question is false," or (2) if the evidential limit cannot sustain itself, "Flew would be running the risk of collapsing the notion of an evidential limit into that of a psychological limit."[170] The limit, then, is the convention agreed upon by the community of rational agents, but the problem is obvious: there is no agreed-upon convention among rational agents in the area of theology.

As for (1), the philosophy of science has shown that no evidence is so strong that the possibility of future revision can be ruled out. Thus, Davis has a good argument when he writes, "[r]eligious believers cannot be criticized for failing to specify evidential limits to their faith, for on this definition no statement (outside logic and mathematics) can have an evidential limit."[171] As for (2), Davis suggests an adjustment where "evidential limit" is understood in terms of propositions that on closer scrutinization turn out to be false.[172] What Davis intends to point to here is his understanding of (2): theological statements *do* have an evidential limit, but the verdict can only be announced in an unknown future. I return to this notion of "eschatological verification" in the next section.

---

[168] Davis, 'Theology, Verification, and Falsification,' 27–28.
[169] Davis, 'Theology, Verification, and Falsification,' 30. Original italics.
[170] Davis, 'Theology, Verification, and Falsification,' 31.
[171] Davis, 'Theology, Verification, and Falsification,' 31.
[172] Davis, 'Theology, Verification, and Falsification,' 32. Davis's own account is clear enough, but it is unclear how this differs from Flew's understanding of the evidential limit. They say basically the same thing.

In 1974, the year before Davis's, theologian Schubert M. Ogden also discussed the notion of falsification in theology in an article.[173] The article is not a response to Flew but to Alastair McKinnon's short book *Falsification and Belief* (1970), yet it is still interesting today because Ogden also makes general arguments for the compatibility of falsification and theology. The debate is about the differences and/or similarities between science and religion. Two solutions are offered, according to Ogden: First, there is no possibility of a conflict because science and religion each cover their own distinct domain.[174] Second, science and religion are in fact similar, and any apparent disagreement should thus be overcome.[175]

McKinnon presents two central views that are prevalent in modern critiques of religion, namely that religious claims are "unfalsifiable and vacuous"[176] and that the foundations of religion are "undemonstrated and indemonstrable."[177] To counter this, he says that even though the charges are important, they "reflect both a failure to do justice to the nature and complexity of religious belief and an easy acceptance of certain familiar but doubtful theories about how language actually functions."[178] McKinnon seems to mean that because both science and Christianity are "interpretive activities" they are "fundamentally similar,"[179] and he thus supports the second point above. Ogden, on the other hand, defends the first point above and states his "own belief that what is striking about Christianity when it is considered without question-begging assumptions is not its similarity to science but its radical difference."[180] Thus, according to Ogden, it is not possible to falsify Christian claims because they are located at a fundamental level that resists this kind of investigation: "Thus, whereas the cognitive claims of science proper, as distinct from such 'meta-claims' as it presupposes, are all merely factual, and hence factually falsifiable, the foundational claims of religion are quite beyond factual falsification, being the nonfactual or strictly metaphysical type of cognitive claims."[181] You may "*challenge*" a dogma, but that is something completely different from "*disproving*" one.[182] The reason is that all of Christianity's foundational assertions are strictly metaphysical and thereby evade the possibility of factional falsification: "Because

---

173 Schubert M. Ogden, 'Falsification and Belief', *Religious Studies* 10, no. 1 (March 1974): 21–43.
174 This is similar to what evolutionary biologist Stephen Jay Gould has called NOMA, i. e., "non-overlapping magisterial," e. g., in the book *Rock of Ages* from 1999.
175 Ogden, 'Falsification and Belief', 21.
176 Alastair McKinnon, *Falsification and Belief* (The Hague: Mouton, 1970), 47–69.
177 McKinnon, *Falsification and Belief*, 70–91.
178 McKinnon, *Falsification and Belief*, 5. Quoted from Ogden, 'Falsification and Belief', 23.
179 McKinnon, *Falsification and Belief*, 21.
180 Ogden, 'Falsification and Belief', 31.
181 Ogden, 'Falsification and Belief', 38.
182 Ogden, 'Falsification and Belief', 38.

he [the Christian], above all, knows that his foundational assertions, at least, are strictly metaphysical, he also knows that they cannot be factually falsified, not even in their determinate form, *since no evidence can count against them unless all evidence does*."[183] Even though to a large degree I agree with Ogden's view that faith is an existential category, I find it problematic to say that Christianity – or religion in general – does not make factual claims, because in explicating a coherent ontology, Christianity cannot avoid doing this. Ogden, thus, unintentionally becomes an example of the "death by thousand qualifications" that Flew famously articulated, which illustrates that even a distinct kind of existential theology such as Ogden's cannot protect theology from Flew's objection. Because Premise 1 is valid, and because theology necessarily presents factual claims, it is not a viable solution for theology to seek shelter from falsification in this particular approach. In the next subsection, I discuss a third option, namely the notion of eschatological verification.

5.3.2   The Concept of Eschatological Verification

The concept of eschatological verification is traditionally associated with philosopher John Hick's response to the challenge from verificationism. The idea is to accept the challenge and then contribute a *temporal* aspect to the understanding of verification, thereby defending the claim that theological propositions are "genuinely factual assertions"[184] that are also "cognitively meaningful."[185] The idea rests on the view that because verification and falsification are not symmetrically related, "the statement 'God exists' may not be falsifiable, but it is an assertion because it can be verified by means of an eschatological experience."[186] What kind of experience? To Hick, what is involved is an afterlife experience of the reign of Christ in the Kingdom of God.[187] Or, differently stated, an experience such that the lofty claims of the NT about the nature of Jesus Christ are irrefutably convincing to anyone who

---

183 Ogden, 'Falsification and Belief,' 40. Italics added.
184 John Hick, *The Existence of God*, Problems of Philosophy Series (New York: Macmillan, 1964), 262. I do not discuss here the extensive feedback and criticisms that Hick received as a response to his concept. Replies were given by philosophers such as Basil Mitchell, Kai Nielsen and D.R. Duff-Forbes (see ibid. for bibliography).
185 Davis, 'Theology, Verification, and Falsification,' 32.
186 Davis, 'Theology, Verification, and Falsification,' 32. Cf. Hick, *The Existence of God*, 257–59.
187 Hick speaks of a "development of our experience" resulting in the removal of rational doubt about the existence of God. The two developments are "first, an experience of the fulfillment of God's purpose for ourselves, as this has been disclosed in the Christian revelation; in conjunction, second, with an experience of communion with God as he has revealed himself in the person of Christ." Hick, 269. Italics removed.

has the experience. This means that statements like "God exists" or "Jesus speaks the truth" will be verified – or falsified – in the eschaton.[188]

It seems to be true that many theological issues cannot be settled before the end of time, which also constitutes an argument for unrestricted openness in our quest for the most coherent theory of reality. Yet I am still uneasy with an argument according to which falsification in systematic theology is restricted to the concept of eschatological verification (or falsification). The main reason for hesitation is that religious belief concerns many things – e. g., values, ethics, meaning, rituals, etc. – but also truth-claims about reality, and it is unsatisfying for our everyday lives but also for our truth-seeking endeavour in science to postpone the verdict about theological statements and theories until the afterlife. We are entitled to ask how to discern among the many worldviews presented to us and also to demand evidence from anyone who tries to convince us to accept a specific position. Or, stated differently: Even though a final verification – or falsification – can only be given in the afterlife (if there is such a thing), we are driven towards other criteria that work already here and now, and the notion of falsification is still the most useful criterion for comparing ontologies by looking to their degrees of coherence. To emphasize that our investigation of reality is unrestrictedly open is to emphasize that we will possibly learn more about many things at the end of time, from concrete objects to the largest theories about everything. But at the same time, we have to ask what is most well-founded theory now because it is here and now that we have to believe something (on both a small and a large scale). For example, it is possible that we will have to think very differently about Christ when/if he appears, but until then, we have to ask which theory about Christ is the most well-founded as of now. When we seek to discover the most coherent theory about reality, we should note that future data – i. e., data that will appear in the future – are weak since they are only very loosely connected to currently available data and therefore score very low on a scale for meeting the criterion of coherence. Theology can point to the future and/or the eschaton with some right because the meaning of all things cannot be settled until the end of time. But we need to make decisions here and now, and the criterion of falsifiability calls for a more refined understanding of the theories of

---

188 Davis mentions two types of critiques of Hick: (1) That he needs theological terms to explicate theological terms but that the former are themselves open to question (see, e. g., Kai Nielsen, 'On Fixing the Reference Range of God,' *Religious Studies* 2, no. 1 (October 1966): 15.); (2) that afterlife experiences must be private experiences and thus cannot be used as objective verification. Davis, 'Theology, Verification, and Falsification,' 33. I find these arguments unconvincing because the theological terms appear within a cluster of coherent arguments that receive their cognitively meaningful content from the possibility of verification *as a whole*. (This seems to be a part of Hick's argument as well, cf. Hick, *The Existence of God*, 259). And if we follow the Biblical and the traditional expectation of the coming of Christ as a public event recognizable even to those who do not expect it, we *are* dealing with a public event even in the terms of Flew.

systematic theology, which the notion of coherence gives us. Thus, falsification in relation to the theories of systematic theology is a reasonable criterion even here and now because we can develop, assess, and compare theories in terms of their degrees of coherence.[189]

In this part of the chapter, I focus on the falsification of whole theories because the discussion of Premise 1 showed that falsification is problematic in relation to individual propositions. But in the following section, I nevertheless focus on individual propositions in theology in order to argue that falsification is also possible in relation to specific doctrines but also that systematic theology as such is not compromised by possibly falsified theories in systematic theology 2. Only the falsification of a general theistic ontology (systematic theology 3) could compromise theology irrevocably.

5.3.3   Excursus: Falsification at the Level of Systematic Theology 2

In discussing the notion of falsification in relation to systematic theology, we usually refer to the existence of God (as the few examples from the history of the discussion of falsification in theology showed). Is it possible to falsify the God hypothesis? But as a theologian I am *also* interested in discussing the scientific status of the different *loci* within Christian dogmatics (systematic theology 2). As the discussion of Premise 1 showed, it is not unproblematic to have falsifiability as a criterion for individual propositions, but in this short excursus I am occupied with the question of the possibility of falsifying particular propositions within theology.

At first, falsification seems to work unpersuasively at the level of systematic theology 2 given the many different views on almost every topic here. There is no consensus among theologians about the understanding of the Eucharist, what it means to be born again, the nature of Scripture, the nature of life after death, and so on. This is often counted as evidence against the truthfulness of the Christian faith.[190] But is this any different from what we find in almost all other scientific

---

189 Note that an objection here could be that claims of existence can never be falsified but only verified, and thus the falsification of a theistic ontology with the conclusion that God does not exist cannot be convincing. The reply to this is that any coherent theory is always a work in progress, and thus the conclusion can never be that God *cannot* exist, but it could be the conclusion that the theories of theistic ontology that we have at hand are falsified by comparison with relevant alternatives (in other words: other theistic ontologies could be developed in the future which could change our assessment).

190 In informal conversations with peers from other disciplines, this point is often heralded as prime evidence against Christianity. Some also claim that this is a direct result of the fact that theology can only (ever) deepen its claims but not widen its scope. When we constantly dig deeper, we have a plurality of interpretations as an inevitable result. I value the criticism but often respond by pointing to the conceptual problem-solving nature of systematic theology (cf. Laudan) and the

disciplines? Take history as an example. There are multiple theories about the causes for every major historical event, and still we take historical studies to be a valuable academic discipline. We know that historians are influenced by their specific interests, and yet we do not reject academic work in history.[191] Events such as the fall of Rome, the French Revolution, the presidency of Abraham Lincoln, the invasion of Iraq – to name crucial events throughout Western history – are discussed without any overall consensus among modern Historians.[192]

But the difficulties of other disciplines should not be an argument for the acceptance of systemtic theology's own problems; instead, the comparison is only mentioned by way of perspective. What is crucial here is that the relation between the whole theory and its individual propositions implies that it is acceptable to have unfalsifiable statements at the propositional level if the general ontology is deemed satisfactory. A certain complexity arises from the fact that the ontology informs the development of the individual statements – and in some cases this relationship is reciprocal between theory and proposition – so that, for example, systematic theology 3 constitutes systematic theology 2, and in some cases *vice versa*. The point is that if the ontology is carefully explicated, there can be an openness to the tentative exploration of its implications. If a theistic ontology is a truth-candidate that could be falsified by comparison, we can allow unfalsifiable statements at the level of systematic theology 2, such as those concerning life after death or the presence of the Holy Spirit in the heart of a believer.

That said, in this proposal it must be emphasized that statements at the level of systematic theology 2 must also be coherent relative to the relevant framework (the larger dogmatics), and there is thus also a possibility of holist testing at the level of systematic theology 2. But due to the existence of systematic theology 3, we may allow for unfalsifiable theories at the level of systematic theology 2 if they do not introduce internal inconsistencies. Even though the doctrine that mankind is sinful seems to be unfalsifiable, theologians still seek to develop coherent theories of the relation between notions such as sin, baptism, faith, conversion, repentance, guilt etc., in relation to the data of theology (Bible, tradition, reason, and experience).

After this brief excursus about falsification at the level of systematic theology 2, I return to the focus on falsification of theories (systematic theology 3) and discuss two recent attempts in the works of Alasdair MacIntyre and Graham Oppy to render ontologies comparable. They contribute to the discussion with very sophisticated accounts of how this comparison can be done, and an interesting point is that

---

constant exchange with other sciences in interdisciplinary reflection and investigation as examples of the widening of the scope that also takes place within systematic theology.
191 See, e. g., Herman Paul, *Key Issues in Historical Theory* (New York and London: Routledge, 2015).
192 If pluralism is granted as evidence against the scientific nature of a discipline, then almost all disciplines are in trouble, as I also pointed out in the discussion of Kuhn above.

they come from directly opposite frameworks but both insists on the possibility of falsifying large theories through comparison. This also points forward to the discussion in the next chapter of intersubjectivity.

5.3.4   Recent Attempts at Rendering Ontologies Comparable

Much of the discussion of falsification in the 20th century concerned the debate between Popper and Kuhn and their heirs.[193] In an attempt to drive this discussion further, Alasdair MacIntyre has pointed anew to the relationship between the philosophy of science and the history of science: "The theory of scientific rationality has to be embedded in a philosophy of history."[194] Thus, he seeks a middle road between a Cartesianism that focuses too narrowly on the individual researcher and a Kuhnianism that is in danger of becoming irrational. According to MacIntyre, the middle road amounts to realizing that all rationality is inevitably embedded in a context, which is always understood through a narrative. In this light, Descartes' scepticism is naïve and cannot be followed. Descartes claimed that his doubt was a contextless and all-inclusive one,[195] but no one starts with a *tabula rasa*. Like everybody else, Descartes inherited his epistemological ideals, not to mention his use of the Latin and French languages, which he never questioned, and thus he was not without a tradition after all. The point is that we do not doubt and test hypotheses synchronically, as though there was no diachronic reason for our suspicion – the inverse is true: we inherit knowledge that we begin to doubt and then question *according to our inherited epistemological ideals*. Thus, neither Kuhn nor Popper is correct in their accounts of scientific work. The correct account, according to MacIntyre, is a refined balance between the two. Two central quotes from MacIntyre express this contention:

> The criterion of a successful theory is that it enable us to understand its predecessors in a newly intelligible way. It, at one and the same time, enables us to understand precisely why its predecessors have to be rejected or modified and also why, without and before its illumination, past theory could have remained credible.[196]

And

---

193 Cf. Fuller, *Kuhn vs. Popper*.
194 MacIntyre, 'Epistemological Crises, Dramatic Narrative and the Philosophy of Science,' 467.
195 "But of course someone who really believed that he knew nothing would not even know how to begin on a course of radical doubt." MacIntyre, 'Epistemological Crises, Dramatic Narrative and the Philosophy of Science,' 458.
196 MacIntyre, 'Epistemological Crises, Dramatic Narrative and the Philosophy of Science,' 460.

It is more rational to accept one theory or paradigm and to reject its predecessor when the later theory or paradigm provides a standpoint from which the acceptance, the life-story, and the rejection of the previous theory or paradigm can be recounted in more intelligible historical narrative than previously.[197]

What MacIntyre offers here is a criterion for the falsification of a theory by comparing two theories, but he does so in a way different from what I have proposed. Instead of looking for coherence as the decisive aspect, MacIntyre points to a *temporal* aspect as the most important one. The *locus* for knowledge is (always) in a tradition, and even scientific knowledge can *only* be understood as an integrated part of a narrative: "Scientific reason turns out to be subordinate to, and intelligible only in terms of, historical reason. And if this is true of the natural sciences, *a fortiori* it will be true also of the social sciences."[198] This is what Nancey Murphy labels MacIntyre's "holist epistemology" (pointing to the tradition of Lakatos and Quine).[199] For the purpose here, it is especially relevant that MacIntyre (as well as Murphy) seeks to develop a method for comparing traditions.[200] This is helpful even though I downplay the role of tradition in contrast to an emphasis on a synchronic evaluation of the coherence of an ontology.[201] This is not because I am blind to embeddedness in context and tradition but because I emphasize the trans-traditional possibilities of focusing on coherence. This proposal is close to MacIntyre's because I use the Puntelian notion of theoretical frameworks, which is close to a MacIntyrian notion of tradition, but I believe the tool for comparison between two such frameworks or traditions can be made more analytical than MacIntyre suggests.

In Murphy's words, what MacIntyre argues is that a tradition proves superior to another when they both explain the world equally well, but one of the traditions can also give an account of the successes and failures – strengths and weaknesses – of the other.[202] The comparison thus does not concern merely of the number of data integrated and the degree of cohesiveness among them but also the explanatory power of the other view. How this suggestion is elaborated is better understood if we know more about what a tradition is. According to MacIntyre, a tradition is a shared

---

197 MacIntyre, 'Epistemological Crises, Dramatic Narrative and the Philosophy of Science,' 467.
198 MacIntyre, 'Epistemological Crises, Dramatic Narrative and the Philosophy of Science,' 464.
199 Murphy, *A Philosophy of the Christian Religion*, 79.
200 Murphy calls these "large-scale traditions," but I do not see why this qualification is important and, after all, she does not use it systematically in her text. Murphy, *A Philosophy of the Christian Religion*, 80.
201 As stated above, this is a way of reasoning that MacIntyre would not accept in any regard.
202 Murphy, *A Philosophy of the Christian Religion*, 85. "Both may explain *the world* equally well, but *one can also explain the other's successes and failures in a way that the other cannot.*" (Original italics)

culture that operates on the basis of common "schemata."[203] This "make[s] our behavior intelligible and relatively predictable to one another."[204] This may sound abstract, but it works in everyday life as that which makes our actions intelligible to others. In science, these schemata tell us what facts are, what counts as good evidence for something, what is relevant to investigate and by which methods, etc.

MacIntyre discusses as an example the debate between Galileo's science and the Aristotelian-Ptolemaic science in the late Middle Ages. Galileo prevailed not just because he could point to certain facts, but also because he could integrate his results into the new conception of science that was arising – an understanding that problematized the old categories of the Ptolemaic system, which was "inconsistent not only with empirical observations but also with widely accepted Platonic standards for true science, and with some aspects of Aristotle's physics."[205] The point is that facts cannot be assessed in isolation because the theories are not static but change over time and are always a part of a cluster of theories. If I have understood MacIntyre correctly, his proposal is very similar to mine, but he emphasizes the historical development more than I do, because I focus more analytically on the possibility of comparing degrees of coherence across theories. MacIntyre's historical view contributes important nuances to the present proposal and he is interesting because he has an eye for the importance of traditions, including theistic ones.

Another recent example from a different standpoint is Graham Oppy's comparison of the strengths and weaknesses of atheism, agnosticism, and theism in his short book in the Cambridge Elements series.[206] Oppy is an atheistic philosopher who has written extensively on themes in the philosophy of religion and especially the discussion of arguments for and against the existence of God.[207] He is relevant here because he presents a view of how to compare theories from a naturalistic

---

203 The term "schemata" plays a decisive role in Kant's philosophy where it represents the possibility of objective science as such, because schemata mediate between reason's notions and the modes of perception in time and space. Thus, the schemata solve the problem of detached rationalism/dogmatism and detached empiricism. Kant, *Kritik der reinen Vernunft. Erster Teil*, 3:189–190 [B179–180]. Cf. Frederik Stjernfelt, 'Symbol og skema i Neo-Kantiansk semiotik,' *Psyke & Logos* 16, no. 1 (1995): 76–98. Neither MacIntyre nor Murphy refers to Kant but both seem none the less to draw on his work here.
204 Murphy, *A Philosophy of the Christian Religion*, 83. A bit more condensed, in the words of MacIntyre himself: "[To share a culture] is to share schemata which are at one and the same time constitutive of and normative for intelligible action by myself and are also means for my interpretations of the actions of others." MacIntyre, 'Epistemological Crises, Dramatic Narrative and the Philosophy of Science,' 453.
205 Murphy, *A Philosophy of the Christian Religion*, 83.
206 Oppy, *Atheism and Agnosticism*.
207 See, e. g., Graham Oppy, *Arguing about Gods* (New York: Cambridge University Press, 2006).

framework.[208] This approach is important as an example of someone sharing the overall aim of this book but working within a non-theistic framework.

Oppy uses notions like "isms," "theories of everything," "worldviews," or "big pictures" to discuss the notion of ontology.[209] In a section called "Theoretical Background for Assessment," he lays out a method for comparing these big pictures. First, he notes that our best big pictures are "radically incomplete" and that all big pictures thus need refinement and can therefore be revised in numerous ways.[210] Because this is the case, Oppy says, we inevitably ask what the prospects are for comparing ontologies: "Given that our big pictures are radically incomplete, it might seem puzzling that we can form views about the comparative merits of best big pictures."[211] And indeed it does. But as I have also emphasized, from the perspective of this book the quest for truth is unrestrictedly open and has to be so because the amount of data we seek to understand is growing every day. But not everything changes, fortunately. Some things are more static so that we can be confident that we understand them to a very high degree. This gives us reason to accept a large amount of evidence so that we can expect that our best *big pictures* will not prove entirely wrong even though they will inevitably develop.[212]

Oppy accepts that there is more than one viable big picture available today. Thus, the intriguing question is what the method for the comparison is according to Oppy. He states that "[i]n principle, the method is straightforward. First, we articulate the various big pictures: we write them out in exhaustive detail. Second, we provide an internal review of each big picture, looking for inconsistencies; where big pictures are inconsistent, we can safely set them aside. Third, we compare the virtues of those big pictures that survive internal review: more virtuous big pictures are better than less virtuous big pictures."[213] This is very close to the proposal of this book, but there are some differences. First, Oppy problematizes the possibility of writing an exhaustive account of a big picture,[214] but I say that this depends on the criterion

---

208 See further in the elaborated study on this subject: Graham Oppy, *Naturalism and Religion: A Contemporary Philosophical Investigation* (London and New York: Routledge, 2018).
209 E. g., Oppy, *Atheism and Agnosticism*, 6. See further pages 22–24.
210 Oppy, *Atheism and Agnosticism*, 23. This, of course, implies fallibilism, which must be accepted as a presupposition for working with these questions. It would be helpful if Oppy had commented on the possibility that a big picture may contain anomalies for some time before it either solves these anomalies or dissolves as a whole.
211 Oppy, *Atheism and Agnosticism*, 23.
212 Oppy, *Atheism and Agnosticism*, 23.
213 Oppy, *Atheism and Agnosticism*, 24.
214 In addition, some argues that if we understand the world as radically open (stratified, structural, emergent etc.), as in critical realism, then the task of an exhaustive description is an impossibility. See, e. g., Roy Bhaskar, *A Realist Theory of Science*, 113–18; Andrew Collier, *Critical Realism. An Introduction to Roy Bhaskar's Philosophy* (London and New York: Verso, 1994), 43; Roy Bhaskar, *The*

for success. The explication that I have taken from Puntel shows that we can use less than complete descriptions/definitions. Second, Oppy says that we cannot finish the task of looking for inconsistencies because there is always more work to do, and even though this is surely correct we can also accept less than that. We can start the comparison before we have assurance that we have a perfect theory. Third, the notion of a virtuous big picture is more easily understandable if we compare for coherence understood as consistency, cohesiveness, and comprehensiveness. These three criteria can be explicated and compared to a more fine-grained degree than Oppy's account presents.

I agree with Oppy that big pictures – or ontologies – are working hypotheses.[215] This assertion resembles the understanding of the aim of coherence theory presented here, where we also take the world to be radically open and thus need to refine our theories along the way either due to the emergence of new data or due to a refinement of our theoretical framework. This is exactly what makes falsification a valuable tool for comparing ontologies. As we continuously work on our ontologies, various kinds of difficulties may appear, and after comparing the solutions proposed by different ontologies, we can regard one of them as falsified.

Thus, the very helpful accounts of MacIntyre and Oppy are instructive and fruitful to engage with. They have different aims and conceptualities, but they both emphasize the possibility of comparing large-scale traditions or big pictures, and this lends credence to the proposal I present. I argue that they also have minor shortcomings, and that it is helpful to focus more analytically on the task of comparison than MacIntyre suggests, and to accept less perfect explications of individual ontologies than Oppy allows for. But they both point to the possibility of comparing ontologies and agree that falsification in relation to whole theories is possible and desirable as a criterion for scientific work.

5.3.5 Conclusion on Premise 2

Premise 2 stated that the theories of systematic theology are not falsifiable. I can now conclude that this premise is false. Theological theories are falsifiable when we compare ontologies. There is no single theistic ontology, and we thus also make these comparisons internally, but the argument here is that systematic theology 3 is capable of explicating a fine-grained ontology that can work as a truth-candidate in comparison with relevant alternatives. It is not necessary to postpone such assessment to the eschaton because we are able to make these comparisons now, and

---

Order of Natural Necessity. A Kind of Introduction to Critical Realism, ed. Gary Hawke (Unspecified: Unspecified, 2017).
215 Oppy, *Atheism and Agnosticism*, 25.

we have some well-developed tools for this purpose as I showed with reference to MacIntyre and Oppy. The account of coherence theory proposes a methodologically clear and epistemologically pragmatic trajectory that makes it ideal for this kind of work. Premise 2 is thus false because theories at the level of systematic theology 3 can be developed and compared with the same degree of precision as their alternatives. Falsification is thus a good criterion for science, also in relation to systematic theology.

The understanding of the division of labour between systematic theology 2 and systematic theology 3 may cause some to wonder if philosophy does not gain the last word if systematic theology 3 is separated too much from dogmatics. But as I have emphasized a couple of times above, the division should not be overstated so that information cannot flow between the strata. What I intend to say is that the theistic framework that systematic theology 3 explores, deepens, and defends is not the *last* word but the *first*. It cannot stand alone but calls for more explication, more integration of data, and more development of relations between the data. For this reason, to say that falsification primarily works towards theistic ontology at the third level, systematic theology 3, does not compromise systematic theology 2 but rather makes its scientific aspirations tenable.

5.4 Conclusion

The notion of falsification cannot be upheld in the natural sciences without qualification, for several reasons. The underdetermination of theories, the complex relation between theory and observation, the complex relation between language and perceptions, and the historical and social factors involved in scientific work are among the most important insights that nuance falsification. In general, it cannot be the only criterion in relation to individual statements or propositions. But falsifiability is a good criterion in relation to whole theories. If we integrate the concept of falsification as one of the central factors in the comparison of different theories (here ontologies), then it is useful and constructive. Thus, I affirm that scientific theories should be falsifiable in this nuanced way – including the theories of systematic theology – and that the theories of systematic theology are indeed falsifiable when we take the approach of comparing ontologies for coherence.

In the next chapter, I discuss the third objection to the proposed understanding of systematic theology. Even though I have shown in chapter four that the theories of systematic theology can be tested, and in the present chapter that the best method for testing, i. e., falsification, works fine in systematic theology, there might be a problem with the criterion of intersubjectivity, so that systematic theology would get a lower score on this criterion because there is no agreement on the status of data, methods, presuppositions, and results.

Chapter Six: Objection 3—Intersubjectivity

Premise 1.   If systematic theology is a science, then systematic theology works (sufficiently) intersubjectively.
Premise 2.   Systematic theology does not work (sufficiently) intersubjectively.
Conclusion.   Therefore, systematic theology is not a science.

6.1   Introduction

In this chapter the criterion of "intersubjectivity" is investigated as grounds for a possible objection to the understanding of systematic theology presented in chapter three. After discussing the objection concerning testability in chapter four, which objection said that systematic theology does not have a workable standard at all for testing theological theories, and the discussion of falsification in chapter five, with the objection stating that the most commonly used standard cannot work to a satisfying degree, I next discuss a third objection, which says that systematic theology has no agreement on what the standard says. In other words, an objection can be stated because even though we might agree on the possibility of a standard and even of the most common standard, we might still disagree on what the standard says to a degree that makes the standard inapplicable. In other words, we might agree on testability and falsification, but we might nevertheless still disagree on (a) which data are important, (b) how to understand the data, (c) what the data imply, and (d) which conclusion to draw regarding the data.

In this chapter, "intersubjectivity" is understood in close affinity with "objectivity."[1] I have chosen "intersubjectivity" as the label because the notion of objectivity has been so heavily discussed and criticized in recent philosophy of science.[2] Even though objectivity can be understood in several ways – and hence should not be discarded right away – I have chosen the less contested notion of intersubjectivity in order not to get stuck in clarifications of the more controversial term.

Thus, I need a chapter on intersubjectivity in addition to chapters four and five to discuss the possible problem that even though systematic theology is testable

---

1   See the discussion of the use of the term "objectivity" in science in Godfrey-Smith, *Theory and Reality*, 228–30.
2   E. g., "'Objectivity' in this context obviously cannot mean a complete independence of interpretation from the interpreter's position, but only that for every such position, the thing to be interpreted must be distinguishable from the subjectivity of the interpreter, and that its distinctness must be given full weight." Pannenberg, *Theology and the Philosophy of Science*, 167.

and falsifiable by comparing degrees of coherence among two or more theories, it may not be intersubjective to a sufficient degree, and this would be a problem if intersubjectivity is a valid criterion. The problem is discussed with reference to the notion of coherence that is the key term in the present book. Because no one can integrate every datum into the system, the intersubjective challenge is to decide which data are most important and which connections between these data are weak or strong. The problem seems to be to decide which connections are good and important for coherence in relation to science and especially systematic theology.

It is central to determine the relevant scope of intersubjectivity in scientific research, so what exactly does the term refer to? Is it that two researchers should agree on something? Is it the legitimacy of theoretical frameworks so that two researchers working in two different theoretical frameworks can acknowledge each other's work? Is it agreement on the relevance of the data that are used in research? Philosopher of science Helen Longino discusses these questions in relation to the notion of objectivity and says that two views are commonly stated. The *first* relates objectivity to the question of truth, stating that truth is the result of the research which is independent of the subjectivity of the individual researcher. The *second* relates objectivity to method, maintaining that the method used in scientific inquiry should be evaluated by nonarbitrary and non-subjective criteria. The first concerns the status of scientific knowledge, the second the status of scientific method.[3]

For the present book, standards such as realism, aiming for truth, and fallibilism are assumed. Hence, it is important to emphasize that there are other ways to understand and frame the notion of intersubjectivity, which create their own possibilities and problems. One alternative is to emphasize the social aspect of scientific practice, which would result in a view that sees intersubjectivity as obvious, as in "there is no alternative to intersubjectivity."[4] This goes for theory choice, choice of methods, sources, problems, questions, possible answers, etc. Another alternative would be sceptical, because a distrust in rationality leads to the opinion that universality is not possible, as in "a common and shared standard is not possible."[5] These are prevalent positions, but I shall not discuss them here.[6] Instead, I proceed from

---

3 Helen E. Longino, 'Values and Objectivity,' in *Philosophy of Science: The Central Issues*, ed. Martin Curd and J.A. Cover (New York: W.W. Norton & Company, 1998), 170–71. See also the critical comments on the article by the book's editors, pages 239–245.

4 See, e. g., Bruno Latour, 'When Things Strike Back: A Possible Contribution of "Science Studies" to the Social Sciences,' *British Journal of Sociology* 51, no. 1 (2000): 107–23.

5 See, e. g., Michel Foucault, 'The Order of Discourse,' in *Untying the Text. A Post-Structuralist Reader*, ed. R. Young (Boston: Routledge and Kegan Paul, 1981), 51–78.

6 Besides the primary texts, almost every introduction to philosophy of science discusses these themes. See the reference list for various suggestions.

the discussion in the previous two chapters and investigate the notion of intersubjectivity, especially in relation to the proposed understanding of systematic theology.

With the presuppositions in mind, the relevance of the objection presented in the syllogism becomes obvious. The claim is that because I have showed that testability is a valid criterion for scientific research and because falsification is a workable type of scientific test, we can now add a third aspect: the scientific test must not be a private test. That a person may be able to reproduce her own results or falsify her own assumptions is helpful for that person's *private* knowledge.[7] But it will not be *scientific* knowledge. To be scientific knowledge, it must be testable and/or reproducible for others beside the researcher herself. That is, the methods and the results cannot be dependent on the individual researcher. This is the argument in essence, and I discuss its different aspects at length in this chapter.

To give intersubjectivity its own chapter is not a given. The objections discussed in chapters four, five, and seven all touches upon relevant aspects of intersubjectivity. Intersubjectivity could thus be treated en route in the text when different concerns demanded it. But as this chapter shows there are sufficient critical aspects with intersubjectivity in research to give it its own chapter. Arguably, the challenge is instead to treat a multifaceted problem in a cohesive way. I have decided to cover several topics to give an impression of the many concerns here, but this leaves me a number of opens ends in the different sections. Nevertheless, the argument of the chapter is clear and coherent and thus weighty enough for careful discussion.

This chapter follows the construction principle from chapters four and five: I discuss the two premises in order and draw subconclusions from the two discussions before I draw an overall conclusion concerning the objection. To anticipate the conclusion, I find Premise 1 to be sustained in a qualified way, while Premise 2 fails in an ultimate sense but has more bite to it than we saw in objections 1 and 2. Systematic theology arguably scores a little lower on the scale of intersubjectivity than many other disciplines because it is difficult to get researchers to agree on which data, tests, and results should be used and how good these data, tests, and results are.

6.2 Premise 1

The premise I investigate in this first part is, "If systematic theology is a science, then systematic theology works (sufficiently) intersubjectively." In the following, I first

---

[7] It is questionable, however, whether falsification can work in practice if there is no intersubjectivity involved. Cf. Ladyman, *Understanding Philosophy of Science*, 80.

present a definition of intersubjectivity and see how it has been understood in two important philosophical traditions (6.2.1); second, I suggest another understanding of the criterion of intersubjectivity that I argue works better for scientific discourse (6.2.2). After this, I present what is gained from intersubjectivity in science (6.2.3) before I discuss various difficulties for intersubjectivity in science (6.2.4). After these four sections I conclude on Premise 1 (6.2.5).

6.2.1 What is Intersubjectivity?

In this first part, I briefly clarify what is meant by "intersubjectivity" in the context of scientific research. The word has a broad use and can be treated in numerous ways. Intersubjectivity can refer to what is shared by two or more individuals; it can refer to what is shared by at least two consciousnesses; it can refer to what is universal and thus testable and/or reproducible. In this book I am concerned with themes relating to the latter understanding, which means that I take the criterion of intersubjectivity to be the requirement that data, methods, and results cannot be dependent on the individual researcher.

Etymologically, "intersubjectivity" concerns the relationship "between subjects." In a scientific context, intersubjectivity concerns how the presuppositions, methods, and results of one researcher become *available* and *accessible* to another researcher. This is not a very precise definition, but instead the first step in an explication of what intersubjectivity is. The notion of intersubjectivity is probably one of those areas in philosophy where it is easier to agree on what counts as a contribution to the discussion than on what counts as *the* definition of something.[8] One approach forward could be to carefully map how intersubjectivity has been understood and discussed in the past in order to track important nuances.[9] But even though this would be fruitful, it is not the aim here. I do not go into an extensive discussion of the historical positions, but instead briefly present two major positions – empiricism and phenomenology – that have engaged with the notion of intersubjectivity in important ways. They have both been dominant in the understanding of intersubjectivity, and it is still standard procedure to discuss a given understanding of intersubjectivity in relation to at least one of these positions. I follow this procedure here before I proceed to suggest a revised account of intersubjectivity in science.

---

8 Cf. Darrell P. Rowbottom, 'Scientific Realism: What it is, the Contemporary Debate, and New Directions', *Synthese* 196 (2019): 451, fn. 1.

9 I have not succeeded in finding a reference that does this job; thus, if I am correct that such a mapping is not available, it could be a topic for another researcher at another time.

6.2.1.1 Two Major Positions

In the following subsection, I begin with a presentation of the understanding of intersubjectivity in relation to empiricism (6.2.1.1.1) before I present a phenomenological take on intersubjectivity (6.2.1.1.2). The task here is not to undertake elaborate discussions of either of these approaches but instead to point to the characteristics that can be used in further elaboration of the criterion.

6.2.1.1.1 *Empiricism*

The relationship between empiricism and intersubjectivity is interesting because it was a focal point in the internal debate among empiricists – between phenomenalists and physicalists – especially among the members of the Vienna School. This debate is situated in the discussion of the distinction between observational and theoretical terms (O-terms and T-terms, respectively). For Moritz Schlick, a phenomenalist, only those terms that directly referred to sensations were observational, but for Otto Neurath, a physicalist, this was too restrictive because it made science a private matter if only sensations and not physical objects were placed under the umbrella of O-terms. Instead, Neurath argued that science must also include as O-terms propositions about physical matter and subject these to intersubjective testing.[10] Here, he was in agreement with Carnap, who also held that states of affairs in science should be intersubjectively observable.[11] In order to be so, the subject-object relations should be expressed in physicalist language, in what philosophers like Neurath and Carnap called "protocol statements."[12] Protocol statements are statements that are directly involved in the verification process, because they articulate what the scientist observes and what is being put to test by experiments.[13] The ontological premise for protocol statements is a distinction between subject and object that can be expressed in physicalist language and therefore be put to test intersubjectively. For this reason, protocol statements also rest on a presupposed anthropological concept of individualism, where individuals are able to make observations based on sensations and then describe them in a clear manner that is accessible to others. As we will see now, this has been challenged by another major stream of thought, namely phenomenology.

---

10 Godfrey-Smith, *Theory and Reality*, 28.
11 Rudolf Carnap, 'Testability and Meaning,' *Philosophy of Science* 3, no. 4 (1936): 419–71; Rudolf Carnap, 'Testability and Meaning—Continued,' *Philosophy of Science* 4, no. 1 (1937): 1–40.
12 Jordi Cat, 'Otto Neurath,' in *The Stanford Encyclopedia of Philosophy*, ed. Edward N. Zalta (Metaphysics Research Lab, Stanford University, 2021).
13 Zhenming Zhai, 'The Problem of Protocol Statements and Schlick's Concept of "Konstatierungen",' *PSA: Proceedings of the Biennial Meeting of the Philosophy of Science Association* Volume One: Contributed Papers (1990): 16.

6.2.1.1.2   Phenomenology

As with empiricism, the aim is to point to phenomenology's emphasis on the importance of intersubjectivity in scientific research. Phenomenology can be described in numerous ways, and the different entrances to phenomenology may be contradictory – also in relation to intersubjectivity. Still, to my knowledge many phenomenologists would agree that intersubjectivity is necessary for objective scientific cognition and knowledge.[14] This may be surprising due to phenomenologists' emphasis on subjectivity, but it seems to rest on a mistaken interpretation of the concept of subjectivity.[15] In brief, more recent phenomenologists argue – especially in light of neuroscientific studies – that subjects are *persons in communion*, that is, that the particularity of the subject and the commonality of humans as a kind are equi-primordial.[16] The subject and the community are intertwined such that the one cannot exist without the other. Hence, there is no valid subject-object schema; this is one of the basic insights in this tradition.[17] But the distinctive point of view of phenomenology is that intersubjectivity is not an existing structure in the world that can be described and assessed from a third-person perspective. Instead, intersubjectivity is always a relation *between* subjects from a first-person perspective, as the etymology indicates.[18]

But what does this mean for scientific research? First, when we understand how little the individual subject can comprehend, we become aware of the omnipresence of intersubjectivity. *Only* in intersubjectively is scientific research possible.[19] In Husserl's sophisticated terminology, this is "transcendental intersubjectivity" – the absolute and self-sufficient ontological foundation – which is the premise for both objectivity and truth.[20] Second, it calls for a tentative consensus at the end of the investigation. That is, phenomenologists point to the move from a first-person investigation by an individual subject to a third-person agreement on evidence; in other words, from subjectivity to intersubjectivity.

---

14 Phenomenology can be understood in a number of ways, but in the following I draw on Husserl's understanding through Dan Zahavi's interpretation. Zahavi writes that Husserl himself was the first to discuss *intersubjectivity* in a "systematic and extensive" way. Dan Zahavi, *Phenomenology: The Basics*, (London and New York: Routledge, 2019), 87.

15 This is sometimes referred to as the accusation of (methodological) solipsism. See Dan Zahavi, *Husserl's Phenomenology*, (Stanford: Stanford University Press, 2003), 109–110.

16 See, e. g., Dan Zahavi, 'Self and Other: From Pure Ego to Co-Constituted We,' *Continental Philosophy Review* 48, no. 2 (2015): 143–60.

17 Zahavi says that the relation is triple among the Subject, the Other, and the World. Zahavi, *Phenomenology*, 88.

18 Zahavi, *Phenomenology*, 88.

19 Zahavi, *Husserl's Phenomenology*, 110–11.

20 Zahavi, *Husserl's Phenomenology*, 111.

These two major positions are different attempts to reveal the fact that scientific research is not done in isolation. No matter the perspective – and empiricism and phenomenology are radically different views – the emphasis on intersubjectivity is strong. This indicates that extraordinarily reasons should be provided if we are to accept a rejection of the criterion of intersubjectivity. Hence, even though the precise explication of what intersubjectivity is may differ, I can say at this stage that the basic criterion is mandatory: Without intersubjective testing, we are not engaged in science, and this is in itself a strong claim.

Before digging deeper into what I argue is the best version of intersubjectivity for science (6.2.2), I discuss the question of what the notion of intersubjectivity presupposes. As briefly hinted at already, there are various difficult categories that are assumed or presupposed when we refer to intersubjectivity.

6.2.1.2 What Does Intersubjectivity Presuppose?

By this question, "What does intersubjectivity presuppose?" I refer to the version of intersubjectivity that is directly relevant for testing scientific hypotheses, because this is the subject of the present book. I mention three important notions that are presupposed by the concept of intersubjectivity articulated in this book.

First, *objectivity*. As said in the introduction (6.1), objectivity and intersubjectivity are concepts that can to a large degree be used synonymously. "Objectivity" is sometimes used ontologically as a synonym for "realism" as in the view that something exists mind-independently,[21] but here I am referring to the epistemological view that the results of a transparent method are subject-independent in that they can be tested and reproduced by another subject if this second subject follows the premise(s) and method(s) of the first.[22] This is compatible with Puntel's notion of theoretical frameworks, which makes every proposition and theory relative to the theoretical framework it is expressed within.[23] This is relativity in a weak sense rather than a strong one.[24] Thus, objectivity here only refers to the

---

21 Godfrey-Smith, *Theory and Reality*, 238. See also the clarification in chapter one above.
22 It is debatable whether the epistemological version of objectivity entails the ontological version. Collier notes that realism and intersubjective testing go hand in hand and that scientific fallibilism requires both. See Collier, *Critical Realism*, 12–14.
23 Puntel, *Structure and Being*, 9 et passim.
24 By "strong" relativism I refer to philosophers such as Paul Feyerabend and Richard Rorty. Cf. Maria Baghramian and J. Adam Carter, 'Relativism,' in *The Stanford Encyclopedia of Philosophy*, ed. Edward N. Zalta (Metaphysics Research Lab, Stanford University, 2021), sec. 1.4.2. "Strong relativism is the claim that one and the same belief or judgment may be true in one context (e. g., culture or framework or assessment) and false in another."

point that subject 2 can test and reproduce the work of subject 1, if subject 2 follows the presuppositions of the theoretical framework of subject 1.

Second, *universality as intelligibility*. This is also a contested term because it is sometimes understood as a naïve ignoring of the cultural, historical, and linguistic conditions for our being in the world, and also because it seems impossible to verify that we have shared standards across the globe and across time – instead it seems easier to argue for the counter-perspective that epistemology and hermeneutics are relative to something (what this something is, is discussed intensively).[25] But in relation to intersubjectivity in scientific testing, the concept is less ambitious. I take universality to mean merely that the scientific methods, presuppositions, and theoretical framework should be made transparent and that for this reason they are not bound to a specific context but can be assessed, adopted, or discarded by colleagues everywhere.[26] It is possible for modern physicists to assess Newton's three laws because he made his presuppositions, his methods, and his results transparent and therefore open to intersubjective criticism.[27] Universality does not mean uniformity, and because of the complexity of reality and the large amount of unknowns in contemporary reflection, a great variety of theories should be expected. But this is no problem for the notion of universality employed here, because the emphasis is on the possibility of making one's data, methods, and results intelligible for someone in another theoretical framework, which seems possible.

Third, *rationality*. Science in general seeks to present rationally justified public discourse, and for this reason the presupposition of "rationality" is not surprising. In relation to intersubjective tests in science, it refers to an anthropological notion that goes back to ancient stoicism,[28] sometimes described by the term *homo humanitatis*.[29] It is an anthropology that follows from the notion of universality, because it points to the general constitution of human beings. It states that humans share a number of epistemological, moral, and political competences that make,

---

25 Michael N. Forster, 'Hermeneutics: Francophone Approaches,' in *The Cambridge Companion to Hermeneutics*, ed. Michael N. Forster and Kristin Gjesdal (New York: Cambridge University Press, 2019), 260–62.
26 A reference to universality will, of course, always be referred. It cannot be observed by contingent beings, thus our perspectives will always be particular. The claim here is that transparency of methods, presuppositions, and frameworks is a possibility and it is therefore legitimate to talk about universality in this qualified sense.
27 Tim Maudlin, *Philosophy of Physics: Space and Time*, Princeton Foundations of Contemporary Philosophy (Princeton and Oxford: Princeton University Press, 2012), 1–46.
28 Ernst Cassirer, *The Myth of the State* (New Haven: Yale University Press, 2009), 163–75.
29 Frederik Stjernfelt, 'Homo humanitatis,' in *Kampen om mennesket: Forskellige menneskebilleder og deres grænsestrid*, ed. David Budtz Pedersen, Finn Collin, and Frederik Stjernfelt (København: Hans Reitzels Forlag, 2018), 227–48.

e. g., scientific discussions fruitful.[30] Hence, the results of science are not bounded by culture, class, gender, nationality, religion, etc. (they are probably coloured by these factors but that is something different). As philosopher of science Frederik Stjernfelt argues:

> On the contrary, the scientific norms – open presentation, objective accounts of subjects, evidence, data, experiments, arguments, references, 'organized scepticism,' etc. – presuppose that all well-informed persons in principle, irrespective of their background, can test arguments, check data and sources, repeat experiments, etc. […] That humans should be able – in cooperation, over many generations and in widely different countries, cultures, and languages – to develop and refine an increasing number of insights in a scientific institution that is not the product of single groups or nations but of human rationality as such, presupposes some variety of *Homo humanitatis*.[31]

It is not necessary to claim that rationality leads to frictionless harmony. As Alasdair MacIntyre has shown, the notion of rationality in practical (e. g., moral) discourse is situated within a tradition with certain conceptual schemes that organize how morality is understood and argued about.[32] But this does not undermine the notion of rationality as I understand it here, because MacIntyre describes the possibility of comparing and assessing other traditions, and he thus appeals to the kind of rationality in intersubjective criticism that I aim at.[33]

It is also important to clarify that even though I presuppose these contested terms in a precise way regarding intersubjectivity, I am not presupposing foundationalism, a view I take to be invalid as an epistemological position. As Wolterstorff says,

---

30 This relates to Puntel's notion of "the absolutely essential primary facts" that are necessary in constituting a human being. Puntel, *Structure and Being*, 274. Here Puntel mentions three: "thinking," "willing," and "being-conscious." It is curious that "being-embodied" is not mentioned here, because it is difficult to understand how to constitute humanity distinctively apart from embodiment. If Puntel's three words are taken without the notion of the body, an artificial intelligence can be understood as a human being.
31 "Tværtimod forudsætter de videnskabelige normer – åben fremlæggelse, objektiv sagfremstilling, evidens, data, eksperimenter, argumenter, referencer, 'organiseret skepsis', osv. – at i princippet alle kyndige personer, uanset baggrund, kan efterprøve argumenter, tjekke data og kilder, gentage eksperimenter osv. […] At mennesker skulle være i stand til i fællesskab, over mange generationer og i vidt forskellige lande, kulturer og sprog, at udvikle og forfine en voksende mængde indsigter i en videnskabelig institution, der er produkt ikke af enkelte grupper eller nationer, men af den menneskelige fornuft som sådan, forudsætter en variant af *Homo humanitatis*." Stjernfelt, 'Homo humanitatis', 246. Translation MAM.
32 See also Alasdair MacIntyre, *Whose Justice? Which Rationality?* (Notre Dame: University of Notre Dame Press, 1988).
33 MacIntyre, *Whose Justice?*, 361–62. See further in 6.3.2.2.

"theorizing is without the foundation of indubitables,"[34] which is a way of saying that, even though objectivity, universality, and rationality are presupposed, so is fallibilism.[35]

One last question to be briefly touched upon is that of the "friendly outsider." Especially in relation to theology, it is critical to emphasize that a personal ontological commitment to theism is not required. For this reason, it is possible to take the position of a friendly outsider. I discuss this more closely in the next chapter in relation to the concept of normativity, and the present brief discussion is thus more general. Stated in other words: Can we have a criterion – intersubjectivity – that depends on the psychological ability to make oneself conversant with a rival perspective? I see two reasons to provide a positive answer to this question. First, it would imply an unacceptable scepticism if "outsiders" could not assess, test, criticize, adopt, refine, etc., proposed hypotheses. Stjernfelt's argument for a shared rationality seems correct, and the alternative would be bleak because it would reduce scientific work to ideological scaffolds. Second, the three presuppositions introduced above can easily incorporate insights from a mild scepticism in hermeneutics. To point to objectivity, universality, and rationality in the way I do here is optimistic but not naïvely so.[36] In section 6.2.4 I return to these questions and discuss the difficulties they entail for a clear concept of intersubjectivity in research.

In the following section, I discuss more closely what the best understanding of the criterion of intersubjectivity in research is. I point to public accessibility (6.2.2.1), independence (6.2.2.2), and criticism (6.2.2.3) as key terms for how methods, presuppositions, data, and results can be understood intersubjectively.

6.2.2 What is the Best Understanding of the Criterion of Intersubjectivity in Research?

In the following sections I outline what I argue to be the best understanding of the criterion of intersubjectivity for research. It is not very fruitful to get stuck in delicate anthropological technicalities, so instead I point to two demands and then a general virtue (criticism). This is because the term "intersubjective" can easily become either too vague or too restrictive. I only aim to provide the necessary arguments for clarifying the already accepted concept (6.2.1.2).

---

34 Nicholas Wolterstorff, *Reason within the Bounds of Religion*, Second Edition (Grand Rapids: Eerdmans, 1984), 57.
35 Also included in the notion of fallibilism is some version of realism, I would argue, because it is the belief of scientists in a mind-independent reality that enables theories to make claims about reality that could be wrong. Cf. Collier, *Critical Realism*, 16.
36 The legitimacy of optimism in science, even in research fields beset by great difficulties, is intriguingly defended in Currie, *Rock, Bone, and Ruin*.

6.2.2.1   Methods, Presuppositions, Data, and Results must be Publicly Accessible

Scientists seek to present rationally justified public discourse, and accordingly, theologians seek to present rationally justified public discourse about God. The qualifier "public" demands intersubjectivity with regard to methods, data, presuppositions, and results. These parameters must be clearly known – often stated – in a transparent and accessible manner. A central reason for this is that definitions are slippery.[37] It is always possible to argue for different definitions, because definitions are relative to the theoretical frameworks they are explicated within.[38] Hence the definitions that structure a given work must be clearly stated. If not, it is simply impossible for others to understand what is said, which is necessary in order to assess it. If a full definition cannot be given, we should explicate the structures of the theory as carefully and in as much detail as possible, which is often the best we can do in metaphysics.

6.2.2.2   Methods, Data, and Results must be Independent from the Researcher

Methods, data, and results must be independent from the individual researcher, as I have already mentioned a couple of times. It is, for example, not a good argument in a theological discussion at the level of systematic theology 2 to say that God revealed to one privately what the correct view of the Eucharist is.[39] A private revelation is not a public datum and there is no shared method for testing the validity of the claim. It does not make the claim of revelation untrue, but it makes it irrelevant for the public discourse about the Eucharist because it is entirely bound to the subject.

The demand for the independency of the methods, data, and results is not to be understood in a naïve empiricist way where observations are pure. Instead, it is to be understood such that methods are tools that can be used by anyone who accepts the presuppositions that these methods rely on, and such that the results are not dependent on the individual researcher conducting the experiment or making the argument. This is not an easy criterion to handle because there may be more or less agreement, as measurably on a scale, about what counts as data, tests, and

---

37 For a stimulating account of "rigorous" definitions, see Nuel Belnap, 'On Rigorous Definitions,' *Philosophical Studies: An International Journal for Philosophy in the Analytic Tradition* 72, no. 2/3 (1993): 115–46. See also Hughes and Lavery, *Critical Thinking. An Introduction to the Basic Skills*, 31–39.

38 Puntel, *Structure and Being*, 26.

39 This is not an imagined example; Zwingli argued this way once in his debate with Luther in the text *Subsidium sive coronis de eucharistia*, cf. Francis Pieper, *Christian Dogmatics*, vol. 3 (Saint Louis: Concordia, 1953), 333–34.

results, and how good or in-depth the data, tests, and results are. But the minimum requirement is transparency in the explication of what is investigated (data), from which perspective (presupposition), how it is done (method), and with what result.

This shows why the context of justification is such a valuable concept. Introspection, opinions, beliefs, revelations, feelings, values, etc., are important, valuable, and welcomed in the context of discovery, but not sufficient in the context of justification.[40] There may be epistemic warrant for believing in a personal experience of God communicating information about some future events. But the validity of this prediction in science cannot rest on the personal experience or conviction but must instead be tested independently from researcher 1 by researcher 2 (moving from the first- to the third-person perspective). The claim is not that experiences are irrelevant, but only that science is a definite activity that has a deliberately hesitant attitude concerning specific claims, i. e., claims that are not publicly/intersubjectively testable. To make science the yardstick of everything would be counter-productive, but within its own borders it is still our best tool for attaining genuine knowledge, and this is – among other things – because there is a distinction between the context of discovery and the context of justification.[41]

For this reason, transparency is needed so that theoretical frameworks can be understood and assessed in their own rights. A lot of misunderstanding and talk at cross-purposes can be avoided if methods, data, and results are clearly stated, e. g., situated clearly within the theoretical framework.

In the next section I discuss a related theme, namely how and why the notion of criticism is so important in relation to intersubjectivity. Intersubjectivity is not just a mechanical repetition of already executed research but is instead a critical endeavour to scrutinize the work of colleagues.

6.2.2.3   The Importance of Criticism for Intersubjectivity

In this section, I discuss the importance of criticism in relation to the concept of intersubjectivity. Most will probably agree that activities must include criticism in order to be scientific, e. g., institutionalized in the work of committees, peer reviews, doctoral defences, book reviews, etc., so the following section is not so much a defence of criticism as it is an investigation of how to understand it more precisely.

"Intersubjectivity" is not synonymous with "criticism," however, because intersubjectivity can find expression in a more "mechanical" activity (e. g., reproducing

---

40   Ladyman, *Understanding Philosophy of Science*, 76.
41   Gillian Barker and Philip Kitcher, *Philosophy of Science: A New Introduction*, Fundamentals of Philosophy Series (New York: Oxford University Press, 2014), 13–15.

results from well-described methods) without a deeper examination of the theory or the experiment (as, e. g., in laboratory training in chemistry or calculation exercises in mathematics), but many will take this to be insufficient in relation to research where we need *critical* examinations of theories and hypotheses. When worked out in this way, I argue, intersubjectivity lends credence to theories because in this way – through criticism – they are tested in the most vigorous way. When skilful and sceptical colleagues examine a work and find it robust, this "organized scepticism"[42] supports the theory in question.

But how to do proper criticism? This is an enormous issue, and instead of pretending to provide a comprehensive answer, I point to the Norwegian philosopher Arne Næss's six standards for criticism or norms for sober discussion. These are: (1) avoid tendentious irrelevant talk, (2) avoid tendentious renderings, (3) avoid tendentious ambiguity, (4) avoid tendentious use of straw men, (5) avoid tendentious representations, (6) avoid tendentious preparation of responses.[43] The first of these states what scientists ought to do (i. e., include only relevant talk), while 2 through 6 state what they ought *not* to do. There are numerous other things to avoid and, for this reason, the list is incomplete. But anyway, the decisive factor is the first statement because we have here a very clear and useful prescription for criticism, even though it is unnecessary for Næss to add the adjective "tendentious" to the standard. It refers to irrelevant talk that supports one side of the argument, but the standard should be that all irrelevant talk be kept out of the debate. But the point is that Næss states positively that the only things you should bring forward in a reasoned debate are elucidating clarifications and supplementary arguments that are valid and relevant. Everything else is irrelevant for proper criticism in research and theoretical discourse.[44]

In relation to theology, I find it important to discuss the relevance and possibility of criticism as intersubjectivity in relation to textual studies, because texts are often the main data (or sources) in systematic theology. In textual studies, the main concern is the possibility of doing a multi-faceted critical inquiry in relation to the relevant text. I suggest that a combination of a "hermeneutics of faith" that seeks to *restore* the meaning of the texts with a "hermeneutics of suspicion" that

---

[42] Robert K. Merton, 'The Normative Structure of Science,' in *The Sociology of Science. Theoretical and Empirical Investigations*, ed. Norman W. Storer (Chicago: The University of Chicago Press, 1973), 267–78. See further in 7.2.2.2.
[43] Arne Næss, *En del elementære logiske emner*, Eleventh Edition (Oslo: Universitetsforlaget, 1975), 108–28.
[44] Hughes and Lavery, *Critical Thinking. An Introduction to the Basic Skills*, 127–40.

seeks to *decode* the meanings of the texts could be fruitful.[45] The first tradition is often associated with names such as Ricœur or Gadamer and can be understood as a more faithful attempt to engage with the viewpoints of authors.[46] The second tradition is the one from Nietzsche, Marx, and Freud that seeks out patterns of power, ideology, irregularities, etc.[47] Both approaches are relevant in the context of criticism as intersubjectivity because, on the one hand, we need to be aware that textual interpretation – as a science – is practiced by fallible humans, that all sorts of external factors (aside from the search for truth) are present and fighting for attention, and that in research, these are regulative factors in competition with the aim for truth. In order to identify problematic aspects such as abuse of texts to suppress or marginalize people, biased interpretations to promote power structures, rejection of arguments to uphold the status quo, etc., we need critical and sceptical interpretations of texts. But on the other hand, we need faithful engagement with texts in order to criticize the right things, and in order not to misunderstand struggles of previous generations for understanding. We should avoid what historian Dominic Erdozain has called the "intellectual fallacy," which is "a tendency to privilege the clean logic of ideas above the raw fuel of human experience among the forces of historical change."[48] Hence, both suspicious and faithful hermeneutics are needed in textual studies.

Good criticism includes self-criticism, which is also very important and thus needs to be explicitly articulated in a theory of theoretical criticism. In relation to intersubjectivity, the relevant aspect is the awareness of the fact that I do not know what I do not know and hence I need criticism from peers.[49] As a scholar, I can miss all sorts of things that would be necessary, helpful, fruitful, etc., to know when conducting an experiment, making an argument, testing a hypothesis, etc. This also points to the important insight that criticism from peers can be relevant at different stages of research and can take different forms.[50]

---

45 The order between these two kinds of hermeneutics must be seen as circular or spiral. They continually develop in light of the findings of the other. However, an intensive use of the hermeneutics of suspicion could compromise the fruitfulness of the hermeneutics of faith.

46 See, e. g., David Jasper, *A Short Introduction to Hermeneutics* (Louisville and London: Westminster John Knox Press, 2004), 106.

47 This iconoclastic line of thought was famously analyzed by Paul Ricœur in *De l'interprétation. Essai sur Freud* from 1965.

48 Dominic Erdozain, *The Soul of Doubt: The Religious Roots of Unbelief from Luther to Marx* (Oxford and New York: Oxford University Press, 2015), 5. This is a comment on the intellectual history of the development of secularization presented in Taylor, *A Secular Age*.

49 As former US Secretary of Defense Donald Rumsfeld famously said, there are "unknown unknowns," and this goes for scientific reasoning as well.

50 Jacalyn Kelly, Tara Sadeghieh, and Khosrow Adeli, 'Peer Review in Scientific Publications: Benefits, Critiques, & A Survival Guide,' *EJIFCC* 25, no. 3 (2014): 227–43.

What is added in this section is that intersubjectivity is not something mechanical but a critical feature of scientific work. Science is done by fallible humans, and thus much of science is impure, imperfect, and in need of careful scrutinization by other researchers. I have emphasized that elucidating clarifications and supplementary arguments are valid and relevant in scientific debate but also that self-criticism and openness towards criticism from others are necessary in scientific work because a single researcher cannot have a comprehensive view of everything and therefore needs the criticism of other researchers.

In the next section I discuss what is gained from the criterion of intersubjectivity before I end the treatment of Premise 1 with a discussion of possible difficulties for the proposed understanding of intersubjectivity.

6.2.3   What is Gained from Intersubjectivity?

It is now relevant to clarify what is gained from intersubjectivity. This should not be a truism for philosophy of science but must be explicated precisely. In 6.2.4, I discuss various difficulties for a clear concept of intersubjectivity, of which there are several that are crucial. But in advance, it is helpful to know some of the gains of this concept because they in themselves point to why widely different philosophical positions continue to treat this concept as necessary for scientific research and evaluation (6.2.1.2).

First, intersubjectivity is important because it helps us to integrate the most perspectives in our comprehensive theory of reality. Science aims for truth, and truth is the sum of correct perspectives (i. e., ideal coherence), so the perspectives must be stated clearly in order to be integrated within the most coherent theory possible. If they are stated clearly, it is possible for the researcher to determine whether A and B can be connected in a more comprehensive theory or whether they instead fundamentally contradict each other and therefore cannot both be parts of the most coherent theory of reality. Researcher A can thus check whether researcher B has understood A's theory and whether their integration of A's theory is solid. Every human has a limited perspective and a limited amount of data in their frame of understanding, and each thus needs confirmation and/or critique from others to develop even more coherent theories and to approach truth even closer.

Second, intersubjectivity is the best tool against complacency (cf. criticism, 6.2.2.3). A related word for "complacency" could be "consensus," and because consensus is not a good criterion for the truth that is the aim of science (because the majority can be wrong), intersubjective criticism is very important. Through intersubjective criticism we can expose flaws and weaknesses in arguments and approach truth.[51] History shows many examples of wrong consensus and bad complacency, and intersubjectivity helps researchers to push their boundaries and stay attentive to potential weaknesses or flaws in their argumentation or their theoretical framework so they can avoid repeating historical mistakes. As pointed out in 6.2.2.3, a researcher cannot know what she does not know, and intersubjectivity is therefore an important criterion to safeguard science against complacency, mistakes, flaws, weak coherence, etc.

Third, intersubjectivity is the best safeguard against the illegitimate practice of *ad hoc* reasoning (5.2.2). This malpractice covers the theoretical attempt to save a certain theory by adding premises or propositions with the sole purpose of rescuing the theory.[52] It is sometimes discussed whether *ad hoc* reasoning is a proper logical fallacy or just a rhetorical strategy, but in either case it is insufficient as a scientific practice because researchers aim for truth and not for protecting their own theories.[53] But because we want to be right and want to protect our own results, we are hostile against corrections, counterevidence, etc., and hence we need our peers' criticism to avoid falling prey to the temptation of *ad hoc* reasoning. I take this point to be important in theology as well, because for many people – and also many researchers – there is a lot at stake in research with much to lose existentially if you are wrong and therefore more pressing reasons to protect your theory. This point is also one of the reasons why I think Laudan's proposal is better than Lakatos's; the temptation of *ad hoc* reasoning is stronger if your protection belt is intended to guard the fixed core of your theory.[54] Fallibilism should count higher in scientific research than a solid core because the history of science has taught us that even our most coherent theories can be revised due to of new evidence. Usually, simplicity is seen as a very helpful pragmatic bulwark against *ad hoc* auxiliary hypotheses (even though simplicity is not a criterion for truth), but I add that the criterion of intersubjectivity is a more valuable instrument for researchers.[55] Sometimes *ad hoc* reasoning is talked about as an intentional malpractice, as a way to save a theory in a period of cognitive dissonance. But it is also important to remember that science is a creative practice conducted by fallible agents and that for this reason, what

---

51 The best argument against the notion of consensus I have come across is Rescher, *Pluralism. Against the Demand for Consensus*.
52 See, e. g., Laudan, *Progress and Its Problems*, 114–16. Note that Laudan here gives a defense of the usefulness of *ad hoc* reasoning in the problem-solving activity of science.
53 Popper, *The Logic of Scientific Discovery*, 19–20.
54 But Lakatos's distinction between *progressive* and *degenerating* research programs may account for this, so that he can ascribe all instances of bad *ad hoc* reasoning to degenerating research programs. See Nancey Murphy, 'Review of "Philip Clayton, Explanation from Physics to Theology. An Essay in Rationality and Religion", *Faith and Philosophy: Journal of the Society of Christian Philosophers* 9, no. 1 (1992): 125.
55 Cf. with Popper, *The Logic of Scientific Discovery*, 130–131.

appears to be a deliberate *ad hoc* solution to a problem could be a case of an honest mistake. Here, too, I argue that intersubjective criticism is the best criterion to enable us to avoid these unintentional instances of *ad hoc* reasoning.

Fourth, intersubjectivity is the best safeguard against *automatic* scepticism. In a way, this is the other side of the coin from *ad hoc* reasoning. As explained above, "organized scepticism" is a characteristic of scientific practice, but scepticism can also be mobilized in an unhelpful way because it is possible to be sceptical about anything in principle. Intersubjectivity is helpful because it helps us to be sceptical about the right things, i. e., where a given theory is weak or in need of clarification, elaboration, or adjustment (6.2.2.3). As a fallibilist, I welcome all kinds of qualified criticism, and the scientific community has the responsibility to develop what "qualified" covers because this is not an obvious concept but something relative to the subject of research.

These four points make clear that much is gained from the criterion of intersubjectivity even though it is a complex term to handle. In the next section, I discuss difficulties for a clear concept of intersubjectivity. I first discuss relevant cognitive biases (6.2.4.1). Then I discuss whether insights from hermeneutics and history of science compromise the criterion (6.2.4.1). Thirdly, I discuss whether it compromises the criterion that all humans have most of their knowledge from testimonies (6.2.4.3) before I end the section with a discussion of how the holistic relationship between ontology and epistemology might challenge the criterion developed (6.2.4.4).

6.2.4 Difficulties for a Clear Concept of Intersubjectivity

After these arguments in favour of intersubjectivity as an inevitable condition for scientific reasoning, I now discuss instances of difficulties that give reasons to think that a clear concept of intersubjectivity is unattainable. These are numerous, and I have chosen some the most critical ones in relation to the understanding of intersubjectivity within the larger theoretical framework presented here. The ambition is not to develop these difficulties at length since they are well-described in the literature but to organize them as a joint argument against intersubjectivity that needs to be addressed. First, I discuss seven varieties of cognitive biases (6.2.4.1). Then I discuss a problem that may arise from the more recent hermeneutical insight that we make interpretations (create meaning) in specific communities that are bounded by their paradigms (6.2.4.2). Thirdly, I discuss a new and fast-growing field of "epistemology of testimonies" that essentially says that almost all of our knowledge rests on the testimonies of others, which problematizes the relevance of intersubjectivity as I use the term (6.2.4.3). Lastly, I briefly discuss what effects the entanglement of ontology and epistemology has for the possibility of assessing a peer's work (6.2.4.4). These four themes are indirectly related to the present understanding of intersubjectivity as possible problems and should thus be discussed here.

6.2.4.1 Cognitive Biases in Relation to Intersubjective Criticism

There are numerous types of cognitive biases documented in the psychological literature.[56] There are a number of these that are important to be aware of because they cause possible obstacles for intersubjectivity in science.

- *Confirmation bias.* This type of bias refers to the tendency to seek information and stick to results that confirm one's views. In relation to intersubjectivity, the problem could be that if a scientist looks for confirmation of (or protection for) his own theory, he could therefore be unconsciously disposed towards a specific assessment of his peer's theory. Further, it is possible to imagine both a *positive* and a *negative* version of the confirmation bias. *Positively* that a peer confirms a theory wrongly because he thinks the results support his own view of the matter. *Negatively* that a peer rejects a theory because he thinks the results problematize his own view of the matter. Both instances would be unintentional or unconscious, as biases are, but nonetheless problematic for intersubjective criticism.
- *Bandwagon effect.* This refers to the tendency to do, believe or claim something because the majority does, believes or claims something. *Positively* we can have wrong confirmation of a peer's theory because it is taken to support the consensus. *Negatively* we can have a wrong rejection of a peer's theory because it is thought to challenge the consensus. In both cases, the work of the peer is reduced to a conservative guard post for the status quo. Again, this may be unintentional or unconscious but still problematic for intersubjective criticism.
- *Courtesy bias.* This term is closely related to the bandwagon effect because it refers to the tendency to claim something because it is thought to be socially correct and thus mimic correct social opinions. The practice of double blinded peer review processes is one attempt to try to overcome the negative effects of this bias. But the practice is not possible to execute in all settings, and there could be many different instances where names, institutions, research groups, networks

---

56 Jonathan Howard writes that almost 200 different biases have been identified, though no official list exists. Jonathan Howard, *Cognitive Errors and Diagnostic Mistakes: A Case-Based Guide to Critical Thinking in Medicine* (Cham. Switzerland: Springer, 2018), 4. See the illustration made by John Manoogian: *Cognitive Bias Codex*, 5 September 2016, https://commons.wikimedia.org/wiki/File:Cognitive_Bias_Codex_-_180%2B_biases,_designed_by_John_Manoogian_III_(jm3).jpg. (Accessed 13.12.2021).

and so on affect intersubjective criticism through the courtesy bias.[57] What is "socially correct" is of course quite dynamic and not very easy to control. It is also questionable whether researchers will be willing to admit their disposition for courtesy biases, and such a disposition may also change according to context. In one context, a researcher may be a proud outsider and, in another context, simply jump on the bandwagon as a matter of courtesy.

- *Continued influence effect.* This term refers to the tendency to stick to a view, position or some piece of information even after it has been proved unwarranted. Such information can then function problematically in many contexts because it can affect the inferences we make despite having been disproved as misinformation. As we will see in 6.2.4.3, the testimony of peers is inevitable in knowledge acquisition. However, this creates a lot of problems because we cannot control everything we hear and learn and thus easily fall prey to misinformation. Ideally, the scientific community *in toto* adjusts the information due to its testability, but there may be a naturally transferring time when new knowledge is transmitted. Anomalies may also be unpopular and thus subject to attempted suppression for a while, which is another factor of the continued influence effect (also called *the Semmelweis reflex*, which is the automatic reaction of discarding new evidence that goes against your point of view). I see this bias in continuation of the first three, because the temptation to stick with wrong information probably comes from the wish to be right.
- *Dunning-Kruger effect.* This effect is somewhat bizarre, because it involves the tendency for unskilled people to overstate their competences and knowledge *and* for skilled people to underestimate their competences and knowledge. The Dunning-Kruger effect is very well-described in the literature. In this context, the relevance is related to the question of "How to know if a peer is qualified for intersubjective criticism?" It could be the case that researcher A thinks she is able to judge the work of researcher B, but even though the presuppositions, the data, the methods, and the theoretical framework is clearly articulated, she is not able to follow the steps. The crucial point is not the probability of this scenario but the possibility. For if it is possible by a factor 1:100.000 (+/-), how can we trust intersubjective criticism in general? Most researchers are likely to be honest about their own shortcomings and do not take on tasks of criticism outside their area of expertise. But some might. And it is equally problematic for the totality of science if peers have a tendency to underestimate their abilities because it makes the collective sum of expertise more narrow than necessary.

---

57 Philosopher Peter Singer attempts something new here with the Journal of Controversial Ideas, a peer-reviewed journal where authors can publish under a pseudonym in order to make it less dangerous to publish material that goes against public opinion. https://journalofcontroversialideas.org/ (accessed 13.12.2021).

This bias is also closely related to the previous ones. If a reader of a review article seeks arguments against a theory she has read in a book, she will be inclined to believe the criticism of the critic despite its not having been made by an expert in the given field. Or she might think she is able to judge in favour of the critic even though she read the book and did not have the ability to counter its arguments on her own.

- *Selective perception.* This is another way of talking about theory-laden observations because it covers the tendency for our expectations to influence our observations and perceptions. This is broadly accepted in philosophy of science, and it is therefore relevant to reflect upon the problems it creates for intersubjective criticism. I take it to be obvious that it creates possible problems but not insurmountable ones. As per the Dunning-Kruger effect, we cannot know if a scientist fully understands the presuppositions, the data, the methods, and the theoretical framework that are needed to test the validity of someone's theory. But even when they do, we could have a possible problem with the lack of neutrality in observation. Every observation is theory-laden and thus a matter of interpretation.[58] But interpretation also rests on several presuppositions, and even though it is the intention of the peer to follow the colleague's process objectively, this may be more or less impossible.
- *Implicit bias*: This label refers to the tendency to act on prejudices and preconceptions without *intending* to do so.[59] Therefore, the name of this bias seems to be pleonastic because a bias is often defined as an implicit cognitive pattern.[60] But the content is crucial. A researcher may herald scientific virtues and intend to engage in intersubjective criticism in the described way and still make his judgment based on prejudice. The virtue of being open to new hypotheses can be compromised by this bias.

The question is of course how deeply these biases affect the possibility of intersubjectivity and, more profoundly, the scientific work as such. To the best of my knowledge, this is still an open question because the well-documented insights from psychology have not been integrated in any common way into the scientific fields and the biases are not discussed thoroughly in the literature of philosophy

---

[58] The reproduction of an experiment also rests on interpretation; another argument for the view that no pure data exist.

[59] Michael Brownstein, 'Implicit Bias,' in *The Stanford Encyclopedia of Philosophy*, ed. Edward N. Zalta (Metaphysics Research Lab, Stanford University, 2019).

[60] Howard, *Cognitive Errors and Diagnostic Mistakes*, 4–5.

of science.[61] Some of the biases have been a theme in the discussions related to Popper and Kuhn, but it is not a common theme in introductory books. Some might choose to be passive and just reject the relevance of these insights, others might turn sceptical and conclude that genuine knowledge is impossible. I argue that a more fruitful way forward is to approach the biases as points of alertness that could cause faulty judgment and premature conclusions. This also calls for a strong concept of fallibilism, albeit not necessarily one that would compromise the pragmatic argument that intersubjective science is still our best tool for attaining genuine knowledge despite all the difficult obstacles arising from, e. g., cognitive biases.

In addition, it is relevant to nuance the discussion because I have focused narrowly on the work of criticism by one subject in relation to the work of another. However, there is ideally not only one peer available to test a theory but several, participating in the ongoing refinement of a theory, and for this reason, the biases may be overcome through the triangulation of the different perspectives of the researchers. Collaborative research *and* collaborative assessment increase the strength of the results and the quality of judgment even though several of the mentioned biases also work at the level of the collective. In the next subsection, I look more deeply into the collective aspect with special reference to hermeneutics.

6.2.4.2 Interpretive Communities and Paradigmatic Thinking as Possible Problems for Intersubjective Criticism

The second difficulty for the present understanding of intersubjectivity springs from arguments in the fields of hermeneutics and the sociology of science. The key question is whether the understanding proposed in 6.2.2 is compromised if these views are taken into account.

The field of hermeneutics is immense, its history spanning the period from Antiquity until today and the literature expanding daily. For this reason, there are many different approaches to hermeneutics and its possibilities and problems, and the following is obviously no deep assessment.[62] The aim here is only to point to the difficulties of assessing theories in other frameworks than one's own, in other words the problem of how hermeneutics is related to the notion of intersubjectivity in science. I frame the discussion around two key thinkers, i. e., Stanley Fish and Thomas Kuhn. Both have been and still are influential in many disciplines, and

---

61 The only instance I have found is Barker's and Kitcher's rejection of the term and their use of "situated knowledge" as a more positive account of some of the related issues. Barker and Kitcher, *Philosophy of Science*, 107–12.
62 A new useful companion is Michael N. Forster and Kristin Gjesdal, eds., *The Cambridge Companion to Hermeneutics* (New York: Cambridge University Press, 2019).

both have written a substantial work that deals with these questions. First, I discuss Fish and his notion of interpretive communities. Next, I deal Kuhn and his idea of paradigmatic thinking in normal science.

Fish published his book *Is There a Text in This Class?* in 1980.[63] It is a collection of previously published essays (part one) and a written argument in favour of his view of hermeneutics, which he calls interpretive communities (part two). Fish's book is a part of a larger shift of focus in literary theory from the text to the reader – often called reader-response theory[64] – as evident in the work of scholars such as Roland Barthes, Normann Holland, and Wolfgang Iser, among many others.[65] Fish's main point is that there is no meaning[66] in the text before it is interpreted by a reader. Any reading is always located in a social context that influences the reading, but on the other hand it also limits the interpretative possibilities so that an infinite pluralism cannot arise.[67] Kevin Vanhoozer nicely sums up Fish's position with the formulation "[c]ontext […] is everything,"[68] which points to the double importance of contexts, which both influence and constrain the possible interpretations. In Fish's view, the context is always present, even when it is not articulated or invoked, and if someone claims that a sentence is self-evident regardless of context, we immediately, mentally, supply the most common context we can think of for the sentence.[69] But Fish does not simply reverse the order, so that context comes first and then the meaning of the sentence can be deduced automatically. The relationship is more closely enmeshed and intuitive.[70] Fish has taken an example from a classroom where a former student asks a colleague of Fish if there is a text in the class he is conducting. The colleague understands this as a question about the curriculum, but the student was actually asking the theoretical question of whether his professor believes in the primacy of the text (as opposed to Fish). Fish sums up his understanding of the entanglements

---

63 Stanley Fish, *Is There a Text in This Class? The Authority of Interpretive Communities* (Cambridge: Harvard University Press, 1980).

64 For a helpful introduction with critical essays see Jane P. Tompkins, ed., *Reader-Response Criticism: From Formalism to Post-Structuralism* (Baltimore: The Johns Hopkins University Press, 1980).

65 This is not a monolithic school because there are a great many different understandings of exactly how the reader is responsible for the text, and there is also a dynamic evolution within the thought and works of individual scholars throughout their careers, e. g., Stanley Fish's. Cf. Lois Tyson, *Critical Theory Today: A User-Friendly Guide*, Third Edition (New York: Routledge, 2014). See also Marjorie Godlin Roemer, 'Which Reader's Response?', *College English* 49, no. 8 (December 1987): 911–21.

66 It is not clear precisely what Fish understands by meaning. Maybe it is equal to interpretation so that no meaning in a text means no stability in the interpretation? But this is not clear either. Cf. Fish, *Is There a Text in This Class*, 307 and 312.

67 Fish, *Is There a Text in This Class?*, 307.

68 Vanhoozer, *Is There a Meaning in This Text?*, 169.

69 Fish, *Is There a Text in This Class?*, 310.

70 Fish, *Is There a Text in This Class?*, 313.

of contexts in relation to this story as follows: "In both cases the words that are uttered are immediately heard within a set of assumptions about the direction from which they could possibly be coming, and in both cases, what is required is that the hearing occur within another set of assumptions in relation to which the same words ('Is there a text in this class?') will no longer be the same."[71] The colleague is able to switch contexts in the conversation because he has talked to Fish so many times that he recognizes the intention of the question. But in the classroom, he first had a more intuitive understanding that set the frame for his understanding.[72]

Of course, there is much more to say about Fish's sophisticated understanding of language and interpretation, but for the purposes here it is sufficient to discuss the implication for intersubjectivity in science. Before I do so, I briefly introduce Kuhn's idea of paradigmatic thinking. After this, I assess the implications of both positions for intersubjectivity.

I have already engaged at length with Kuhn (5.2.3), but it is relevant to bring him into the discussion once again, because the topic of intersubjectivity is closely related to his central idea of the paradigm. Kuhn's idea is that most science is a puzzle-solving activity taking place within a well-defined paradigm with its own peculiar understanding of methods and possible solutions. This is "normal" science, which is conservative, aiming simply at the increased precision of the paradigm.[73] When anomalies occur, they are normally rejected or explained away, but over time they accumulate and destabilize the paradigm. Often, younger scientists are the ones who dare to suggest new proposals for solving the anomalies, and when they do so convincingly, a new paradigm can replace the former one. The most controversial aspect of Kuhn's theory – and the one most relevant here – is his notion of scientific revolutions as changes of worldview.[74] He writes that, "when paradigms change, the world itself changes with them."[75] The radical implication is that to Kuhn, there is a fundamental incommensurability between the two paradigms.[76] And if there is such an incommensurability, we are, obviously, unable to compare them and therefore unable to weigh their strengths and weaknesses against each other. Kuhn hesitates to articulate exactly what constitutes a paradigm,[77] and he does

---

71 Fish, *Is There a Text in This Class?*, 316.
72 As he writes, "[t]he change from one structure of understanding to another is not a rupture but a modification of the interests and concerns that are already in place; and because they are already in place, they constrain the direction of their own modification." Fish, *Is There a Text in This Class?*, 316.
73 Kuhn, *The Structure of Scientific Revolutions*, 35–42.
74 Kuhn, *The Structure of Scientific Revolutions*, 111–35.
75 Kuhn, *The Structure of Scientific Revolutions*, 111.
76 Kuhn, *The Structure of Scientific Revolutions*, 112.
77 As said above, Kuhn himself identifies two usages in his postscript from 1970 (ibid. 175), but critics see many more. See references in section 5.2.3, footnote 32.

not explicate how researchers could do intersubjective evaluations across different paradigms. One reason might be that he often uses physics as his example and there has perhaps been less plurality – or messiness – in this discipline than in many other disciplines, which makes the notion of a single paradigm as "normal" more intuitive. There is hardly any other field – maybe except the overarching evolutionary framework in biology, even though there are discussion about the details of how to understand the mechanism of natural selection, etc. – that has one dominating paradigm with an opponent paradigm unsuccessfully striving to undermine it. But I argue that we can see the implications for intersubjectivity implicit in Kuhn's writings. Kuhn is most interested in showing that how scientists make theory-choices is partly a biographical matter because it rests on subjective persuasion and not on pure arguments.[78] This implies that it is virtually impossible for researcher A from paradigm 1 to understand the methods, data, presuppositions, and results of researcher B from paradigm 2 in such a way that A can evaluate B through intersubjective criticism (and it implies the danger of internal confirmation bias in a given paradigm). Kuhn addresses different questions in his attack on the linear understanding of scientific accumulation, but analogically it is useful to consider the implications.

Now, I bring the above observations together. Both Fish's and Kuhn's views challenge the notion of intersubjectivity in science (intentionally or not); the question is just how they do so. One way to assess the implication – assuming their views are convincing – is to ask whether Fish's hermeneutics and Kuhn's sociology challenge the understanding of intersubjectivity that I outlined in 6.2.2. Another way is to ask whether their views could force us to give a negative answer to the question that organizes this third objection to theology, that is, "can we agree on methods, presuppositions, data, and results?", even though we have a robust criterion for testing and the best standard tool for testing, namely falsification. I engage the questions in order. First, do Fish's and Kuhn's arguments challenge the understanding presented in 6.2.2? Let me assess their views against the subpoints presented in 6.2.2.1–3.

- *Methods, data, presuppositions, and results must be publicly accessible.* I think both Fish and Kuhn would agree, because the problem for both would not be the accessibility of these four things but the possibility of arguing for a definite understanding of these notions. For this reason, Fish, for example, would probably be sceptical of the understanding of the "clearly explicated definitions" that are to structure a work. When his colleague finally understands the student's question, it is *not* because of additional words or clarifications, Fish says, but

---

78 Kuhn, *The Structure of Scientific Revolutions*, 199–200.

through a different conception of the context.[79] Such re-conception may occasionally be necessary in informal oral conversation, but because science works much more slowly and carefully, explications of the structures that guide the researcher's work can be made much finer-grained and therefore less confusing. Again, intersubjectivity is only about following a researcher's process from a research question to a well-tested answer through a set of clearly explicated presuppositions, and I think neither Fish nor Kuhn gives reasons to discard this conception.

- *Methods, data, and results must be independent of the researcher.* As I wrote in 6.2.2.2, methods, data, and results must be independent of the researcher but "not independent as in naïve empiricism where observations are pure, but in that methods are tools that can be used by anyone who accepts the presuppositions that these methods work upon." If I had meant the naïve or strong version of independence, Fish and Kuhn would have a valid point, but I cannot see how their standpoints can challenge a qualified notion of intersubjectivity in any critical way. The problem for a modern physicist is not to understand Newtonian physics or follow Newton's clearly stated procedure to get specific results, and for this reason their new paradigm of special relativity does not make intersubjective testing impossible.[80] In the same way, it is not impossible for a conservative Old Testament scholar to understand the methods, data, presuppositions, and results of a minimalist Old Testament scholar, and for this reason their sticking to an old paradigm does not make intersubjective testing impossible.[81] Given the presuppositions, we can follow the method all the way to a result. We should expect disagreement about overall assessments because no one has a comprehensive overview of all data and disagreement here is thus unproblematic. In both cases, there are many other difficulties but the proposed understanding of intersubjectivity is not compromised by Fish's and Kuhn's ideas.

- *The importance of criticism for intersubjectivity.* In 6.2.2.3, I argued for an understanding of criticism as "avoiding tendentious irrelevant talk," which I took to mean that the only relevant contributions to a discussion are (a) elucidating clarifications and (b) supplementary arguments. There would be no scientific work without such criticism, and it should be as organized as possible. Both Fish and Kuhn can be read as critics of this position, even though their own works

---

79 Fish, *Is There a Text in This Class*, 311.
80 See the works by Maudlin, Carroll or Greene as examples.
81 See, e. g., Jens Bruun Kofoed, *Text and History: Historiography and the Study of the Biblical Text* (Winona Lake: Eisenbrauns, 2005); James K. Hoffmeier and Dennis R. Magary, eds., *Do Historical Matters Matter to Faith? A Critical Appraisal of Modern and Postmodern Approaches to Scripture* (Wheaton: Crossway, 2012).

can also be read as good examples of criticism.[82] In this way, their work and its reception strengthen the proposed argument for the importance of criticism despite what they write about difficulties with making elucidating clarifications and supplementary arguments.

Second, is it possible, then, to understand and comprehend others' data, methods, presuppositions, and results if Fish's and Kuhn's views are convincing? I do not think so. Even though both reject the label of relativism[83] that many critics have associated with them, it is difficult not to read them as claiming that the historical and social contexts are so influential that neither data nor results are understandable across paradigms or interpretive communities. It follows from such a claim that a scholar from paradigm A cannot assess results from a paradigm B scholar. That is the central point of Fish's and Kuhn's theories. But the respective scholars of paradigms A and B cannot even agree on data because data are theory-laden in a very strong sense. A way forward is to nuance the sharp demarcations between the paradigms and to point to how actual science is not the confrontation of paradigm A versus paradigm B but the negotiation among numerous paradigms that struggle and strive concerning all sorts of minor and larger differences.[84] Some paradigms may be incommensurable, but often paradigms share a lot of data, interpretations, methods, and results and then differ from each other in some very specific details. This could be understood in terms of scientific theories in each discipline often being closely aligned through family resemblances, to use Wittgenstein's term. This view could be exemplified by the following schematization:

1. A-B-C-D-E-F
2. B-C-D-E-F-G
3. C-D-E-F-G-H
4. …
5. G-H-I-J-K-L.[85]

---

82 In that both their works are full of examples and references to other researchers' work and their interpretations are often insightful and engaging.
83 See Fish, *Is There a Text in this Class?*, 320–321 and Kuhn, *The Structure of Scientific Revolutions*, 174–210.
84 Simo Køppe, Frederik Stjernfelt, and David Budtz Pedersen, eds., *Kampen om disciplinerne: viden og videnskabelighed i humanistisk forskning* (København: Hans Reitzels Forlag, 2015), 13. See especially footnote 5.
85 Here, I have altered a figure found in Eikrem, *God as Sacrificial Love*, 4. Eikrem's figure is altered from a figure in Lars Haikola, *Religion as Language-Game: A Critical Study with Special Regard to D.Z. Phillips* (Lund: Gleerup, 1977), 71.

This is a very simple example of the idea: (1) and (5) do not share anything in common; they are completely demarcated from each other. For this reason, their approaches to a specific field are incommensurable, but through (2)–(4), there are family resemblances even between (1) and (5), and for this reason they can be (tentatively) compared, even though it is a difficult business to conduct such comparison. Family resemblance is a helpful tool when essentialism is discarded. For many disciplines where foundational discussions are prevalent and unresolved, it will be difficult to isolate an essence, but this does not render intersubjectivity in the qualified sense impossible.

There might be cause to worry that the more recent hermeneutics leave us in a communicative echo chamber that is impossible to escape. I have suggested that there are steps to be taken that make conversation among different theoretical frameworks theoretically possible, and on this basis, I can conclude that hermeneutics at the present stage of history is no threat to the criterion of intersubjectivity. I also think that our experiences and our reasoning suggest in principle that we can expand our horizons of understanding by including new evidence, new data, and even new paradigms, that we can wander among these, and that researchers within other paradigms can confirm that we understand their views and arguments. It therefore seems to be possible to overcome the difficulties indicated by Fish and Kuhn.

6.2.4.3 The Epistemology of Testimony

The third possible difficulty for the understanding of intersubjectivity that I have chosen is constituted by a relatively new field in epistemology called "the epistemology of testimony."[86] The idea is simple: We all believe and know many things about the world, but most of it is received through the testimonies of others, either because we lack the skills required to gain the knowledge on our own or because we simply do not have the time to collect all the relevant knowledge for our lives. For example, I seem to know many things about Brazil, even though I have never been there, do not speak Portuguese, and have never met a native Brazilian. I also do not believe the earth is flat even though I cannot understand the arguments *for* a flat earth that conspiracists claim and lack the ability to disprove them – but I trust that others can.[87] Philosopher C.A.J. Coady has written an influential introduction to the epistemology of testimony where he gives a two-fold argument for the warrant of testimonies: first, that we are naturally *disposed* to believe the testimonies of

---

86 See especially the landmark study, C. A. J. Coady, *Testimony: A Philosophical Study* (Oxford and New York: Clarendon, 1992).
87 Alec Ryrie, *Unbelievers: An Emotional History of Doubt* (London: William Collins, 2019), 52.

others, and, secondly, that we are *justified* in doing so.[88] If this is so, it is possible to connect the insights from the epistemology of testimony with coherence theory so that the testimonies are seen as *data* that serve as truth candidates, and for this reason they take part in the ever-increasing refinement of our web of beliefs. The more coarse-grained the information is, the less likely we should be to believe something. For example, my ability to access the respective testimonies for the historical existence of Martin Luther King and experiences of UFOs are basically the same, but the connectedness of the data regarding King's existence are much more fine-grained than the data regarding the UFO experiences. There are many, strong, and fine-grained connections among data relating to King, and there are no coherent alternatives, but there are fewer, weaker, and coarser-grained data related to UFOs plus contradictions among descriptions and alternative coherent explanations. For this reason, for the time being, the former but not the latter set of testimonies should be integrated into my web of beliefs.

For science, there is at first no exception. Almost all our knowledge comes from others, and when we test a theory, we accept something beforehand and not necessarily the same as others. Both confirmations and deviations in results may be underdetermined. Wolterstorff points to the implications for modern epistemology: "Epistemology of the modern period has been shaped by the image of human beings as solitary individuals forming beliefs by perception, introspection, rational intuition, inference, memory, and so on. But testimony, and the acceptance of testimony, are inherently communal in character."[89] Or *intersubjective*, I might add.

Coady focuses especially on what he calls "reporting" i. e., perceptual or observational reports received about objects outside someone's vicinity.[90] But science has higher standards for testimony than we do in mundane life. It is a truism that the researcher who seeks to do the critical intersubjective work should have the skills to do so – but how does a third party know if this is the case?[91] When a committee is selected for assessing a doctoral thesis, how do we know they are capable of doing so? Because the institution that has invited them says they are – often on the background of information given by other colleagues, including their merits

---

88 Coady argument is summarized like this in Peter J. Graham, 'The Reliability of Testimony,' *Philosophy and Phenomenological Research* 61, no. 3 (November 2000): 696. Coady organized his argument in a discussion of Hume's rejection of testimonies, especially the one explicated in section 10 of *An Enquiry Concerning Human Understanding* on miracles. For this reason, it is already in close affinity with the theological theme of this book.
89 Wolterstorff, *Religion in the University*, 82.
90 It is not the only kind of evidence, of course, but the one of the four categories he investigates. The other three are observation, deductive inference, and inductive inference; see C.A.J. Coady, 'Testimony and Observation,' *American Philosophical Quarterly* 10, no. 2 (April 1973): 149.
91 As I also discussed in relation to the biases, 6.2.4.1.

and publication lists (which are of course also awarded or published by approval of colleagues.)[92]

A nuance to be added here is what Wolterstorff calls "data-background beliefs." He writes, "there will always be a large set of beliefs such that one's holding them is a condition of one's accepting as data that which one does. Let us call these *data-background beliefs*."[93] The argument is against epistemological foundationalism, but it is easy to see how this challenges the possibility of intersubjectivity. When I ask whether we can agree on methods, presuppositions, data, and results even though we have accepted both the criterion of testability and the specific subcategory of falsification, the answer is very complex given the ever-present data-background beliefs.

6.2.4.4   Epistemology and Ontology are Related Holistically

The last possible difficulty for a clear understanding of intersubjectivity in science that I address here is the holistic relatedness of epistemology and ontology.[94] In a way, this point integrates the discussions in 6.2.4.1 through 6.2.4.3. I presuppose realism in this book, which I take to be the view that a part of reality is mind-independent. But what reality is, how it is described, understood, organized, etc., is not given *a priori* but is language-infused (theory, conceptuality, etc.).[95] For example, I make an observation that there is something outside my window. But even though this reality is a fact (according to realism) whether I believe it or not, whether I observe it or not, the distinction between inside and outside, the difference between a tree and a flower, between a ball and a trampoline are distinctions that we make with language.[96] In other words, a realist presupposes the existence of something, but accepts that *what* it is (its essence) is not a given without linguistic distinctions.

To be a realist here is to assume that reality is such that not all distinctions, classifications, taxonomies, etc., are equal, but that some are more precise in the description of reality. Puntel argues well that because the world is structured, it is non-arbitrarily expressible through language, with the help of distinctions, cate-

---

92 See Coady, 'Testimony and Observation,' 151.
93 Wolterstorff, *Reason within the Bounds of Religion*, 67. Original italics. And theology is no exception to this condition; see ibid. 85.
94 Cf. Jan-Olav Henriksen, *Life, Love, and Hope: God and Human Experience* (Grand Rapids: Eerdmans, 2014), 39.
95 Puntel, *Structure and Being*, 363.
96 Cf. Ingolf U. Dalferth, 'On Distinctions,' *International Journal for Philosophy of Religion* 79 (2016): 171–83.

gories, theories, etc.[97] The most coherent description of reality will be the most convincing one, but because it is possible to organize reality in numerous ways – and it will not always be immediately clear which one is the most coherent one – there is no way around the hard work of testing different descriptions against one another by comparison.[98]

No observation is neutral, because there can be no observation that is not dependent on language and thus on interpretation.[99] This could undermine the criterion of intersubjectivity, as I have discussed in 6.2.4.2, but I argue instead that scientific interpretations are not arbitrary and that not every interpretation is convincing. Coherence as a criterion makes us capable as humans of assessing each other's proposals, interpretations, theories, ideas, etc. The possibility of failure is always present, and the complexity of testimonies, traditions, contexts, and much more makes a naïve intersubjectivism impossible. But according to a more nuanced understanding, where the best version of intersubjectivity (described in 6.2.2) is taken as the frame for the criterion, intersubjectivism is still a needed criterion for making scientific testing reliable.

6.2.5 Conclusion on Premise 1

The third objection against systematic theology rests on the premise that intersubjectivity is a valid criterion for scientific work. I have defined intersubjectivity in a qualified way as the notion that methods, data, presuppositions, and results cannot be dependent on the researcher but must be testable and reproducible by others if they follow the clearly stated theoretical framework and the methods, etc. I discussed different difficulties for a clear concept of intersubjectivity such as cognitive biases, hermeneutical and historical relativization, the epistemology of testimony, and the holistic relatedness of epistemology and ontology. But even though these are difficult challenges, they do not compromise the criterion to such a degree that we have to reject it. For this reason, the criterion is valid, and the first premise is accepted. If a field of study is to be counted as a science, it must work intersubjectively in this qualified way.

---

97 Puntel, *Structure and Being*, 17.
98 Puntel, *Structure and Being*, 245.
99 Godfrey-Smith, *Theory and Reality*, 160. See also Henriksen, *Life, Love, and Hope*, 37–40.

6.3. Premise 2

6.3.1 Stating the Problem

The first premise was investigated above, and the conclusion sustained the premise; it is a good criterion for science that it must be intersubjective. Hence, in this section, I look into the second premise, which says that "Systematic theology does not work (sufficiently) intersubjectively," where the parenthesis is now explained as "meeting the qualified definition of intersubjectivity developed in the discussion of Premise 1."

The relevance of this third objection to the discussion of systematic theology (i. e., how testability and falsification are not sufficient and convincing objections against systematic theology) is poignantly stated by philosopher John Worrall: "The claim that 'God exists' fails to be scientific, not because it cannot be proved from evidence, not because it can never be falsified by evidence, but because it can never be confirmed (and therefore can never be disconfirmed either) by any possible – intersubjectively agreed – evidence."[100] Worrall does not say that the criteria discussed in chapters four and five of this book are met by theology, but that the real problem for theology is the criterion of intersubjectivity discussed in this chapter. The problem is not with testing in itself but with agreement on what counts as relevant data, testing, and results, and on how good these are. The aim of this part of the chapter is to investigate this claim in depth.

To some, it might be hard to take Premise 2 seriously. Theology is, of course, intersubjective, as it is (often) done collaboratively, has widespread and high-level structures of peer review in academic journals and publishers, is done in doctoral programs in the most esteemed universities, etc. But the criticism pertains not to intersubjectivity as such but to intersubjectivity *to a sufficient* degree.[101] As Worrall says, the problem is that we do not agree on how to test – confirm or disconfirm – the hypothesis of God. Another way to state the issue is to say that even though we do, in general, agree that testability is a good criterion for science and that falsification, in general, is the highest standard for testability, we might agree neither on the interpretation of the data that enter into the test nor on the results of

---

[100] John Worrall, 'Philosophy of Science: Classic Debates, Standard Problems, Future Prospects,' in *The Blackwell Guide to the Philosophy of Science*, ed. Peter K. Machamer and Michael Silberstein, Blackwell Philosophy Guides 7 (Malden: Blackwell, 2002), 22.

[101] The ambition is not to just be a tolerated part of academia because it proves to be impossible to demarcate precisely between science and pseudoscience, but to be a part of research institutions because systematic theology qualifies to be a member in a convincing way on accepted criteria. See also 3.1.

the test. As I take truth as the aim of science and coherence to be the best understanding of truth, another way to say this is that determining which connections are good and important in relation to coherence may be the important challenge for intersubjectivity.[102] Coherence as understood in the present book is something that comes in degrees, and I would therefore initially say that intersubjectivity should be understood as a continuum where different practices of intersubjectivity score differently on a broad scale. I look more into this at the end of the discussion.

In the next section I investigate different models for intersubjectivity in systematic theology. This is a construction of mine because it is not an established discussion in its own right within systematic theology. But I argue that it is possible to identify three major models of intersubjectivity in systematic theology that I call *demarcated* intersubjectivity (6.3.2.1), *paradigmatic* intersubjectivity (6.3.2.2), and *critical* intersubjectivity (6.3.2.3). They are all sophisticated approaches that are built on several presuppositions, and for this reason they deserve more extensive assessment than I provide here. But for the purpose of mapping a field that is more background than frontline in most discussions, I still take this initial work to be helpful.

6.3.2 Models for Intersubjectivity in Systematic Theology

The aim and challenge for systematic theology is to present something that qualifies as a rationally justified *public* discourse about God – that is, rational *and* public *and* about God. To meet the criteria for proper science is to be rationally justified, but it is still an open question whether systematic theology can meet these criteria in a public way and still talk about God responsively.

In the following section, I discuss different models for intersubjectivity in systematic theology. The organizing of these models needs an explanation, and for this reason I provide one now before I investigate the respective models. In this book, I work on Puntel's understanding of the theoretical framework, which is mildly relativistic.[103] To recapitulate, this means that the relativism is not related to the subject but to the framework, and for this reason it is to be distinguished from the stronger relativism that I reject.[104] I see an influential example of the stronger relativism, which is related to the subject, in Kuhn's paradigmatic thinking, which

---

[102] This is a theme that has my attention but escapes Puntel's because he is explicitly not very interested in the problems concerning intersubjectivity. Cf. Puntel, *Structure and Being*, 32.
[103] Puntel's own word for it is "moderate relativism." Puntel, *Structure and Being*, 241–45.
[104] Puntel, *Structure and Being*, 18.

I investigated in 6.2.4.2.[105] In the following sections, I have used the distinction between mild and strong relativism as a heuristic tool when encircling different approaches to the topic of intersubjectivity in systematic theology. They are idealized types of models (especially the middle one), and they should not be understood as separate boxes but more as forming a continuum; however, it is still helpful to have three distinct categories to inform us of different possible understandings of intersubjectivity in systematic theology. Let me briefly introduce the three views here before I elaborate at length in the following:

- *Demarcated* intersubjectivity is a narrow understanding of intersubjectivity and is critical of the possibilities for any transcommunal criterion. It implies that different traditions/worldviews/paradigms are segregated with very little interchange or even possibility for reflexive understanding.
- *Paradigmatic* intersubjectivity is more positive towards a transcommunal criterion but is preoccupied with a defence of the relevance of tradition-specific criteria for feasibility and justification, especially in relation to religious explanations for any given phenomenon.[106]
- *Critical* intersubjectivity is positive towards a transcommunal criterion to such a degree that it implies the attempt to comprehend, assess, discuss, and compare different theories that are developed in different frameworks.

In the following, I discuss these types in the listed order before I argue for the perspective of critical intersubjectivity.

6.3.2.1   Demarcated Intersubjectivity

For the discussion of demarcated intersubjectivity in theology, I have chosen a group of thinkers from American theology that emphasize the demarcation between different presuppositions. This group is mainly represented in reformed American theology, and their view is called "presuppositional apologetics," a view that has gained increased attention in the last fifty years or so. Through the resurgence of

---

105 Kuhn was a complex thinker and a nuanced and careful reading of his relativistic legacy can be found in Alexander Bird, 'Thomas Kuhn's Relativistic Legacy,' in *Blackwell Companion to Relativism*, ed. Steven D. Hales (Oxford: Wiley-Blackwell, 2011), 456–74.
106 What Nancy Murphy has called "communal discernment." See Murphy, *Theology in the Age of Scientific Reasoning*, 163. "The point of arguing for participant descriptions of the results of discernment is that such descriptions can then provide data for theology *that already contain reference to God.*" Original italics.

the work of theologians Cornelius Van Til[107] and Gordon H. Clark, seen, e. g., in the work of theologians Greg L. Bahnsen[108] and John M. Frame,[109] there has been renewed discussion about the presuppositions and possibilities of Christian apologetics in a pluralized society.[110] The discussion here concerns intersubjectivity, and thus I do not focus on many intricate details within this position. I read Frame as a contemporary example and focus on how he rejects the possibility of critical intersubjectivity in theology as I use the term in the present book.

Frame typically builds his case around three points: (1) Presupposing God in apologetics, (2) a distinction between legitimate and illegitimate circularity in argumentation, and (3) a transcendental argument that says that the Christian God is needed for the possibility of knowledge as such.

As for (1), according to Frame, to presuppose God is *also* to presuppose the supernatural revelation of God in the Scriptures, but neither of these presuppositions is shared by non-Christians: "If his argument presupposes the truths of Scripture, then his conclusions will be the same as his presuppositions. He will argue from Christian presuppositions to Christian conclusions. But because the unbeliever will not grant the Christian presuppositions, he will not find the argument persuasive. But if the apologist presents an argument that does not presuppose the truths of Scripture, how can he be faithful to his Lord? And how can he produce an intelligible argument unless he presupposes those conditions that are necessary for intelligibility?"[111] This provides us with the returning questions that become a *crux* for this model: if the process is "from Christian presuppositions to Christian conclusions," how can it be followed by non-Christians? It cannot, says Frame. He emphasizes that Christians as well as non-Christians engage the world and then make corrections and adjustments to their understanding based on observation, thinking, testing, etc. But the *Merkmal* of presuppositional apologetics is that there are several non-negotiables for a Christian, a limit for possible rectifications: "May

---

107 Cornelius Van Til, *Christian Apologetics*, ed. William Edgar, Second Edition (Phillipsburg: P & R Publishing, 2003).

108 Greg L. Bahnsen, *Presuppositional Apologetics: Stated and Defended*, ed. Joel McDurmon (Powder Springs: American Vision Press, 2010); Greg L. Bahnsen, *Van Til's Apologetic* (Phillipsburg: P & R Publishing, 1998).

109 John M. Frame, *Apologetics: A Justification of Christian Belief*, ed. Joseph E. Torres (Phillipsburg: P & R Publishing, 2015); John M. Frame, 'Presuppositional Apologetics,' in *Five Views on Apologetics*, ed. Steven B. Cowan (Grand Rapids: Zondervan Academic, 2000), 207–64.

110 There have, of course, also been many critics, also among conservative theologians, see, e. g., the critique in section 3 of John H. Gerstner, Arthur W. Lindsley, and R. C. Sproul, *Classical Apologetics*, (Grand Rapids: Zondervan Academic, 1984).

111 John M. Frame, 'Presuppositional Apologetics,' Frame-Poythress.org, 23 May 2012, https://frame-poythress.org/presuppositional-apologetics/. (Accessed 13.12.2021)

a Christian revise those presuppositions in the course of an inquiry? He may certainly revise his *understanding* of those presuppositions by inquiring further into God's revelation in Scripture and nature. But he may not abandon the authority of Scripture itself, as long as he believes that Scripture is God's Word. God must prove true, though every man a liar (Rom. 3.4). Nor may he abandon the most fundamental truths of Scripture, such as the existence of God, the deity of Christ, and salvation by the shed blood of Jesus, without denying Christ himself."[112] That this has huge consequences for the possibility of critical intersubjectivity, which I defend at the end of this section, should be obvious.

As for (2), this is central to the present discussion. Frame's argument is that everybody relies on non-provable axioms. Taken in a narrow sense, this is very unconvincing; as Frame says: "*Narrowly* circular arguments, like 'the Bible is God's Word, because it is God's Word' can hardly be persuasive. But more *broadly* circular arguments can be. An example of a more broadly circular argument might be 'The Bible is God's Word, because it makes the following claims…, makes the following predictions that have been fulfilled…, presents these credible accounts of miracles…, is supported by these archaeological discoveries…, etc.'"[113] This is a valid argument and I think Frame is correct here. Bad circularity arises when the number of data is very small and the interrelations are few, such as A because of A, or A because of B and B because of A. But more complex relations such as A because of B and C, and C because of A and D, etc., are legitimate because this is a manifestation of good coherence and this kind of reasoning is the basis for all knowledge. For this reason, Frame regards the axiom of the inerrancy of the Bible as adequately defended and non-negotiable. All thoughts proceed in a circular fashion, and it is not possible to switch from the non-Christian circle to the Christian circle without the supernatural grace of God.[114] This is important, because no matter how committed the apologist is to her work, and no matter how obligated she is to present the case for Christianity in a convincing way, at the end of the day, the work is fruitless without divine intervention, according to this model. I assume that some will argue that there is a large gap between Christianity as conceived by Frame and the non-belief that he excludes, but because the aim here is to present and discuss the notion of intersubjectivity, I do not pursue this issue further here.

---

112 John M. Frame, 'Presuppositional Apologetics.' The article originally appeared in W. C. Campbell-Jack, Gavin J. McGrath, and C. Stephen Evans, eds., *New Dictionary of Christian Apologetics* (Downers Grove: IVP Academic, 2006).
113 Frame, 'Presuppositional Apologetics,' 23 May 2012.
114 This resembles the controversial notion of "conversion" in Kuhn's theory when an individual changes her paradigm as in a scientific revolution, see Kuhn, *The Structure of Scientific Revolutions*, 111–35.

As for (3), the transcendental argument concerns the point that the Christian God is not a fact to be discovered but the presupposition that makes everything else intelligible. The point is that with God, everything makes sense but without God, nothing makes sense. The task of the apologist is to show this convincingly. As Steven Cowen says, "[t]hey argue that all meaning and thought – indeed, every fact – logically presupposes the God of the scriptures."[115]

This demarcated intersubjectivity – where arguments are seen as so closely connected to their presuppositions that meaningful dialogue dissolves – works on its own premises, especially that of the noetic effects of sin being so severe that humans in general are incapable of assessing evidence in favour of the Christian faith; this makes them epistemically biased in their judgments. But judged against the framework of the present book, this approach fails to be public to a satisfying degree.

Another problem is that in practice this view is not followed. For example, I am able to understand the view of demarcated intersubjectivity even though I disagree; I can describe it, understand it, present the arguments for and against, and I can see where the presuppositions are headed – and Frame and the rest do the same all the time when they assess and engage in a wide variety of positions and views.[116] Maybe the case is that presuppositional apologetics focuses primarily on the acquisition of salvific faith and the threshold between "lost" and "saved" cannot possibly be crossed by nonbelievers voluntarily, but as a theory of intersubjectivity, it falls short.

6.3.2.2   Paradigmatic Intersubjectivity

I have termed the next model "paradigmatic intersubjectivity," and although, like "demarcated intersubjectivity," it fails to be public to a sufficient degree, it does come closer than the model discussed above. I could mention many scholars associated with the model of paradigmatic intersubjectivity, but among them is Nancey Murphy, with whom I have already engaged in the above, and so I return to this thinker here as well as engaging with the Dutch theologian Gijsbert van den Brink. I only provide a relatively brief and crude description of their sophisticated positions, and there is a danger of simplifying their arguments too much. But the aim here is only to exemplify a model of intersubjectivity that works better than the demarcated view, but still needs improvements in order to work sufficiently as a criterion. As said above, the identified positions are not isolated boxes but form a continuum,

---

115 Steven B. Cowan, 'Introduction,' in *Five Views on Apologetics*, ed. Steven B. Cowan (Grand Rapids: Zondervan Academic, 2000), 19.
116 Many of Frame's numerous book reviews start with comprehensive and detailed summaries that are often reliable and loyal to the original accounts. See his website, which records his many writings, for further examples: https://frame-poythress.org/ (accessed 13.12.2021).

and hence this middle position is the most difficult one to isolate. A critical question is whether it is possible to identify exclusively with paradigmatic intersubjectivity or whether a perspective will always emphasize either demarcated or the critical intersubjectivity. The following short discussion reveals that the latter is the case. I start with van den Brink before I proceed to Murphy.

van den Brink's interest is in the scientific status of theology, and it is thus unavoidable that the discussion of positivism takes up a lot of space in his account.[117] Logical Positivism lost support rather quickly, but the request for "confirmation" stuck with us; as van den Brink writes: "According to confirmationism, strict verification is not necessary for a proposition to be scientifically warranted; it suffices if we find enough confirmation for it."[118] If this is so, van den Brink argues, the millions of testimonies from believers all over the globe and across time should be more than enough confirmation for the existence of God: "In short, the statement that God exists has a particularly high degree of confirmation, and can within a confirmationist framework therefore be considered as scientifically tested (and therefore as true)."[119] Then why is this not convincing for many in a scientific context? First, because existential propositions are much easier to confirm than non-existential. Like astrology, which I discussed briefly in the context of falsification (see 5.2.2 and 5.2.7.4), confirmations of all sorts happen all the time. Second, because there is also an underdetermination of data here, because there could be other reasons for the constant confirmation of the God hypothesis, such as some kind of evolutionary neural side-effect[120] or confirmation bias in general (6.2.4.1).[121] Like texts, experiences are not "pure," they must be interpreted, and in general this leaves a certain ambiguity to this argument.[122] Third, there are too many inconsistent linkages between data that are included in diverse religious experiences so that one informant may experience the risen Christ while others experience Shiva, djinns, metempsychosis, or something else. But fourth, and most importantly, it is also critical that science be subject to a criterion of intersubjectivity. We cannot have

---

117 E. g., Brink, *Philosophy of Science for Theologians*, 29–42 and 159–70.
118 Brink, *Philosophy of Science for Theologians*, 162.
119 Brink, *Philosophy of Science for Theologians*, 162.
120 See, e. g., Pascal Boyer, *Religion Explained: The Evolutionary Origins of Religious Thought* (New York: Basic Books, 2002).
121 In his long comparison of "perceptual practice" and "Christian practice," Alston writes similar things, even though he ends with a defense of the rationality of private religious experiences. Cf. William P. Alston, 'Christian Experience and Christian Belief,' in *Faith and Rationality: Reason and Belief in God*, ed. Alvin Plantinga and Nicholas Wolterstorff (Notre Dame: University of Notre Dame Press, 1983), 122–23. See also page 129, where Alston connects some of the conditions normally accepted by religious believers for religious experiences with a rejection of a demand for universality.
122 See, e. g., Henriksen, *Life, Love, and Hope*, 31–35 et passim.

only rationally justified *private* discourse about God; we need to have a *public* discourse based on arguments and testability, and it is still debatable how private experiences can count as confirmations in intersubjective discourse.

Murphy has provided many reflections on the similarities and differences between natural science and theology, especially in relation to the philosophical work of Imre Lakatos and Alasdair MacIntyre. In her classic book *Theology in the Age of Scientific Reasoning*, she argued that theology engages data, e. g., religious experiences, in a way that is similar to the data of the natural sciences. In this sense, Murphy "considers religious experiences (along with historical events, Scriptural texts, etc.) to be important *data*. From a structural point of view, she argues, there is no difference, in this regard, between natural-scientific programs and theological ones."[123] In Lakatosian manner she sees theological doctrines to resemble natural scientific theories in consisting of a hard core, a protective belt, and a heuristic,[124] and in MacIntyrian manner she sees the rationality of these doctrines to have their own internal logic developed and protected through their tradition.[125] Murphy is making a big claim here because the religious data used in theology are normally seen as less robust and more coarse-grained than the data used in the natural sciences.[126] But the aim here is not to challenge her view of data but only to explicate her view of intersubjectivity, and I thus leave this criticism for another time.

Murphy and van den Brink both have sophisticated accounts of scientific work. But the question here is how to judge paradigmatic intersubjectivity after this introduction? As said, as the middle position on a continuum it is more flexible and dynamic. What makes it hard to find in pure form is that if a researcher is able to do intersubjective criticism to a satisfying degree, she is not working paradigmatically but critically (see next section), and if she works paradigmatically, she is not doing intersubjective criticism to a satisfying degree but instead leans toward the demarcated perspective. But still the perspective of paradigmatic intersubjectivity is needed because otherwise we would have two distinctly separated approaches that would be too crude to capture the complex field. This is why especially the paradigmatic approach is an ideal type and not restricted to the discussed figures.

---

123 Brink, *Philosophy of Science for Theologians*, 186. This is a helpful summary of a long argument in *Theology in the Age of Scientific Reasoning*, pp. 157–173.
124 Murphy, *Theology in an Age of Scientific Reasoning*, 183–191.
125 Murphy, *Theology in an Age of Scientific Reasoning*, 162–163.
126 In a way, she also admits this when she says: "Although we have found agreement on the possibility of discernment and great overlap in lists of signs and criteria to be used, there is a diversity in views about the kinds of events and phenomena that are appropriately to be so judged." Murphy, *Theology in an Age of Scientific Reasoning*, 158. This points forward to the conclusion I make in 6.4.

6.3.2.3 Critical Intersubjectivity

A third, and last, model is "critical intersubjectivity," with representatives such as Philip Clayton and Wentzel van Huyssteen. They emphasize what van Huyssteen calls "transcommunal and intersubjective explanations," a concept implying that the criteria for testing must not be bound to a specific tradition or faith but should also provide insights and evidence for external communities.[127] This is applicable to systematic theology because the death of foundationalism has put fallibilism at the centre of research and thus also included theological prolegomena as parts of an ongoing trial-and-error process where questions are not answered in advance but adjusted as the practice unfolds.[128] Clayton presents a four-fold methodological program for systematic theology that explicates the model of critical intersubjectivity

1. [Theories of systematic theology] must be open to intersubjective examination and criticism.
2. No *a priori* limits can be set on who can participate in this examination, even though some may qualify more as experts than others.
3. No solution can be grounded by privileged premises.
4. *All* beliefs in a discursive context must ultimately be treated as *hypotheses*.[129]

I add to (3) that there can be an extra set of data for the believer, viz., what it is like to be a believer and have religious experiences, but even if these data are interesting, they cannot avoid or remove the requirement of making the solutions intersubjectively testable. As for (4), I take Clayton's notion of "hypothesis" to equal the notion of "truth-candidate."

The reason for Clayton's broad scope of criticism is an insistence on a similarly broad thematic scope. systematic theology is not concerned with Christian practices and beliefs in isolation, but according to Clayton seeks to "explain broad areas of human experience" and hence cannot argue in a paradigmatic way that guards its theories from outside criticism.[130] This argument is very convincing as a response to the problems that are shared by the demarcated intersubjectivity of John Frame.

But, from a theological point of view, it is relevant to ask if this approach qualifies, to a satisfying degree, as a public discourse *about the Christian God* and the lives

---

127 J. Wentzel van Huyssteen, *Essays in Postfoundationalist Theology* (Grand Rapids: Eerdmans, 1997), 97. See also the interpretation in Brink, *Philosophy of Science for Theologians*, 191.
128 Philip Clayton, *Explanation from Physics to Theology: An Essay in Rationality and Religion* (New Haven: Yale University Press, 1989), 152.
129 Clayton, *Explanation*, 161.
130 Clayton, *Explanation*, 162.

of Christian believers. In other words, we should not claim intersubjectivity to be mandatory in a way that compromises the relevant tasks of systematic theology 1 and systematic theology 2, which is to explicate coherent theories about the Christian faith and the lives of Christian believers. If systematic theology 3 succeeds in its task, the work in systematic theology 1 and systematic theology 2 is legitimate even though some parts of the work might work intersubjectively to a lesser degree than systematic theology 3 and other disciplines. Clayton agrees, and to avoid such compromising, he subscribes to Ian Barbour's five requirements for theological reflection, which are set up as requirements of distinction from what I call demarcated and paradigmatic intersubjectivity, but which prove to provide an implicit argument for the requirements of distinct theological content in research: "systematic consistency, criticizability, trueness to one's religious tradition as well as current thought and practice, coherence with paradigm beliefs, and correlation with paradigm-external disciplines."[131] Points 3 and 4 show that systematic theology 1 and systematic theology 2 are included in Clayton's critical intersubjectivity but in a transcommunal way that makes criticism *and* engagement among traditions and disciplines possible. The best way to approach this criticism and engagement, according to Clayton, is through a notion of truth that is understood as coherence, which is further understood as an umbrella term for different truth theories that are integrated: correspondence, consensus, semantic, scope, consistency, etc.[132] Fallibilism demands openness in theories, and theological hypotheses are, therefore, viable possibilities if they can meet the same standards as other disciplines. As Clayton concludes: "In summary: if the arguments given in this section for an objective referential function of assertorical language are valid, we are justified, more sceptical positions in the philosophy of language notwithstanding, in continuing to speak of the possible objective truth of a given belief system."[133] The arguments are convincing and for this reason, the model of critical intersubjectivity can work as the framework within which systematic theology can meet the requirements of intersubjectivity for rationally justified *public* discourse.

To sum up the brief introduction of three models of intersubjectivity in systematic theology: These three models are deliberately idealized and should not be understood as isolated boxes but more as a continuum. The individual researcher will usually be more dynamic than static, and what the three models articulate is an awareness of different possible emphases rather than a schematic way of thinking, and the same goes for the figures I have chosen and only engaged with very briefly. All three models take intersubjectivity to be important; the question

---

131 Clayton, *Explanation*, 166. Clayton takes these requirements from Ian G. Barbour, *Myths, Models and Paradigms: The Nature of Scientific and Religious Language* (London: S.C.M. Press, 1974).
132 Clayton, *Explanation*, 110.
133 Clayton, *Explanation*, 177.

is rather one of how broadly intersubjectivity is to be understood and what its possibilities – and challenges – are. To recapitulate what I wrote in the introduction (6.3.2): *Demarcated* intersubjectivity implies a narrow understanding of intersubjectivity and a critical view of the possibilities for a transcommunal criterion. It means that the different traditions/worldviews/paradigms are segregated with very little interchange or even possibility for reflexive understanding. *Paradigmatic* intersubjectivity implies a more positive stance towards a transcommunal criterion but also a preoccupation with defending of the relevance of tradition-specific criteria for feasibility and justification, especially in relation to religious explanations for a given phenomenon. *Critical* intersubjectivity implies a positive stance towards a transcommunal criterion, even entailing a demand to try to comprehend, assess, discuss, and compare different theories that are developed in different frameworks. I have argued in favour of critical intersubjectivity, but I am aware of possible problems that this concept may create for the stratification of systematic theology. The difficulty might be that the operating space of systematic theology 1 and systematic theology 2 is confined so narrowly that the distinct marks of theology are compromised, but if coherence is the criterion to test theological theories against, then internal coherence, semantic consistency, etc., are all parts of the research program. Furthermore, as I have emphasized a couple of times there is an ongoing exchange between the strata. As such, the operating space for, e. g., systematic theology 2 in relation to systematic theology 3 is not too confined. To make it clear, systematic theology 2 is primarily the realm for internal coherence, but it cannot be restricted to this, because it is where the meaning and the reference of the concepts used in theology has to be clarified. Some of these (especially the notion of God) are the concepts which have to be used at the level of systematic theology 3 at some point.

The argument here in 6.3.2 is that even though good cases can be made for all three types of intersubjectivity, critical intersubjectivity is best suited for operationalizing the criterion of intersubjectivity in science.

In the next two sections, I discuss two critical questions in relation to intersubjectivity in systematic theology, namely, how to deal with complexities (6.3.3) and how to deal with insecurities (6.3.4). After these discussions, I conclude on Premise 2 (6.3.5).

6.3.3 Complexities in systematic theology in Relation to Intersubjectivity

In this section, I discuss a question that concerns a general problem but a problem that is also of special interest for theology: How to deal with thematic complexities in relation to intersubjectivity. It is a characteristic of ontological theories that they are enormously complex, and it is possible that this affects their prospects for intersubjective testing. The problem is that the pool of data that exists is so large that no one can include everything in a complete theory. And if this is true, how can we then discriminate between the alternatives, let alone assess the degree of coherence between two theories that integrate (very) different sets of data? Coherence theory is, nevertheless, a helpful tool at least because (1) it is analytically productive as a heuristic tool and (2) it is a critical authority because the results can form a kind of "no-miracle" argument that is convincing. As for (1), it is a positive heuristic because the pool of data is already available, and coherence is a useful tool to organize the data. In this sense, it is very pragmatic because it accepts that data can be provided from many different sources and be of many different kinds, but also that the internal relations among the data are important because no datum in isolation can be taken as true in anything other than a trivial way.[134]

As for (2), coherence is a critical authority because it forms a "no miracle" argument. The most coherent theory will not just integrate a vast number of data (*comprehensiveness*) but also have many fine-grained connections among the data (*cohesiveness*), and that would be almost impossible if the theory was not true – or at least truth-indicating.[135] So generally, the notion of *no-miracle* arguments should be understood as an argument for coherency, so that the more coherent a theory is, the more well-founded it is. To take an example, modern physics is a complicated activity if only because the pool of data is so vast. A physical theory, however, in which all calculations agree down to the decimals is hardly coincidental, even though it is beset by various kinds of insecurities in observation, calculation, organizing of data, etc. There is still a real risk of self-confirmation because the instruments that scientists use are often based on the theories they are testing (both science and technology/engineering are complex fields, and it is often the case that those who make the instruments and those who use them do not understand each other's work, and there is therefore a real risk of error or self-confirmation here). Still, even though there will always be a risk of incorrectness, as the history of science has taught us (fallibilism is mandatory), a theory in physics can – for the moment – be convincing because a high degree of coherence works as a no-miracle argument. But theology seems to have difficulties producing theories that work as no-miracle arguments. For example, there is a long theological tradition for trying to understand the hiddenness of God.[136] It is legitimate to investigate the coherence of this notion

---

134 Puntel, *Wahrheitstheorien in der neueren Philosophie*, 191–96.
135 For this reason, I understand this version of coherence as evidence for a theory. And evidence is in my understanding *truth indicators*, a term I have taken from Francis Jonbäck, *The God Who Seeks but Seems to Hide*, Ph.D. Dissertation (Uppsala: Uppsala Universitet, 2016), 11.
136 Especially in the Lutheran tradition – that is strong in my own Nordic context – the concept of *Deus absconditus* is influential. See, e. g., Marius Timmann Mjaaland, *The Hidden God. Luther, Philosophy, and Political Theology* (Bloomington and Indianapolis: Indiana University Press, 2016), chap. 9 (especially). The prevalence of this argument is especially due to Luther's famous response

in relation to other *loci* at the level of systematic theology 2, but it is problematic to use the notion as an excuse for not (trying to) providing an explanation. On the other hand, if the notion of the hiddenness of God is used as an explanation for various phenomena – such as why an omnipotent God seems so hesitant to prevent pointless evils or why the existence of an omnipresent God is not more obvious to humans[137] – it would not be a fine-grained theory that could work as a no-miracle argument. A certain hiddenness may be necessary, if not, all events would be revelations. But this is coarse, because it does not explain why God is not revealed *more* to us.[138]

Maybe it is too demanding to claim that theological theories must work as no-miracle arguments because the data are more coarse-grained than the data in the natural sciences. This is similar to related fields such as history. It is true that physics can identify universal laws (generalizations) and precise micro-data, and still it is more interesting and useful to hear a historian argue for an interpretation of why the Second World War began than what a physicist might say to explain the event.[139] Some disciplines cannot but work at coarser-grained levels with data on a macro-level, but still the reference to coherence is our best tool to assess theories, which work as *no-miracle* arguments if they are coherent to a high degree.

To put the matter a bit differently, it is simply easier to say something fine-grained about water than about God or life after death.[140] This is a condition following from the scope of the questions, the comprehensiveness of the data, the integration of different aspects such as time, space, consciousness, etc., but it is also a difficulty for the theological theories with regard to the possibility of intersubjective testing. Other disciplines can also have coarse-grained connections among fine-grained data, but these connections are often many and uncontested, while theology may

---

to Erasmus in *De Servo Arbitrio* from 1525 (WA 18). Of course, other sources from the history of theology are relevant and important, but Luther's solution to understanding the role of faith in relation to grasping the *opus alienum Dei* in the cross of Christ has been found useful by many. When God hides (*Deus absconditus*), a room for faith is created, and faith is the goal of God's actions and as such *opus proprium Dei*. See Alister E. McGrath, *Luther's Theology of the Cross: Martin Luther's Theological Breakthrough* (Oxford: Blackwell, 1985), 148–51.

137 See, e. g., Søvik, *The Problem of Evil and the Power of God*, 109–10 and 206–7.
138 This is not the place for a longer treatment of this difficult case. See the essays in Paul K. Moser and Daniel Howard-Snyder, eds., *Divine Hiddenness. New Essays* (Cambridge: Cambridge University Press, 2002) for interesting perspectives.
139 A reductionist like Sean Carroll agrees even though he says that it would be possible for a physicist to explain historical events. See Sean Carroll, *The Big Picture*.
140 A difference is that much of physics can proceed without solving complicated metaphysical questions even though metaphysics is a central part of physics (cf. Maudlin, *Philosophy of Physics. Space and Time*, xiv). The same is of course not the case with systematic theology, in which nothing can be solved without an explicated metaphysic.

have few connections, and both the connections and the data are coarse-grained and contested by alternative explanations and alternative data. A historian might have a weak basis for saying that Caesar crossed the Rubicon, but it fits well with other data, and there are no relevant alternative explanations or internal inconsistencies, while theological theories such as that of God raising Christ from the dead or working in the Eucharist are thinner, more open to alternatives, more contested by alternative data, etc. In sum, theology has difficulty presenting no-miracle arguments because its theories are often coarse-grained, have few connections, and use contested data. This also reveals that theology scores a little lower on the spectrum of intersubjectivity, which I will argue for in the conclusion (6.4).

So, the problem with dealing with complexities in relation to intersubjectivity is general and not reserved for theology, but theology is challenged by its many coarse-grained theories, which is evident from the great variety of theories at the level of systematic theology 2 in relation to the traditional *loci*.[141] In other words, we begin to see that this third objection to the stratified notion of systematic theology is more critical for theology than objections 1 and 2. The individual sciences also have many coarse-grained explanations, and they are also often left with vague statements,[142] but theology seems to have this vagueness more or less as a working condition.

In the next section I discuss another question that challenges the notion of intersubjectivity in relation to the proposed understanding of systematic theology, namely, how to deal with insecurities in relation to data and theories that systematic theology makes use of.

6.3.4 Insecurities in systematic theology in Relation to Intersubjectivity

In this section, I discuss a topic related to 6.3.3, namely how to deal with insecurities in systematic theology in relation to intersubjectivity. Insecurity here simply means that it is uncertain whether a theory is true. Due to the complexity that is an inevitable part of holistic ontological theories – theistic ones included – our theories will be insecure, so how can we assess the relative strengths of two theories? I first discuss how ontology as a field of investigation has insecurity as a premise (6.3.4.1), and then I discuss which insecurities can be accepted in an ontological theory (6.3.4.2).

---

141 A survey of these can be found in many textbooks, e. g., McGrath, *Christian Theology. An Introduction*.
142 "Vague" here refers to imprecise or coarse-grained. When the relations between the data are indistinct the statements can only be vague, imprecise or coarse-grained.

6.3.4.1. Ontology Deals with Comprehensiveness, Which Often Creates Insecurity

How is it possible that so acclaimed a philosopher as van Inwagen would state that metaphysics is totally open, we might ask?[143] Why is it that metaphysics is so diverse, so vague, so controversial that even the best minds in the field seem to disagree about almost everything? These questions are topics for multiple dissertations, but an initial answer might be that, in general, when we raise the degree of comprehensiveness and the depth of the matter (embrace the fundamental organization of reality), we also raise the degree of insecurity. When we raise the degree of comprehensiveness and depth of the matter, we almost always raise the degree of complexity (as we saw in the previous section). And with complexity comes insecurity. In physics, both the general theory of relativity and quantum mechanics are complex theories that very few humans understand.[144] Still, most experts agree that these complex theories are largely correct descriptions of reality.[145] But they are inconsistent, and for this reason there is an insecurity among physicists about how to integrate these two well-documented theories into a more comprehensive theory.[146]

With this in mind, I argue for two points in this section: (1) that insecurity comes in degrees from less to more insecure, and (2) that the status of alternative theories is important as well because they can also be more or less secure than the first theory. A comparison between theories is thus critical.

As for (1), I think it is very important but also obvious. As a fallibilist, I take insecurity to be inevitable because final verification is not possible. But at the same time, this does not imply that theories do not differ as to their degrees of insecurity. Some theories are very vague or insecure, e. g., the theory of multiple universes,[147] that some gigantic sauropods had pneumatized skeletal structures (i. e., "hollow"

---

143 Cf. 3.4.1. van Inwagen, *Metaphysics*, 9–15.
144 Nobel Laureate Richard Feynman once said that "I think I can safely say that nobody understands quantum mechanics" and Sean Carroll notes that "the sentiment is equally applicable today." Carroll, *The Big Picture*, 159. Of course, we can understand quantum mechanics in the sense that we can predict accurately the outcome of experiments. But if we ask what quantum mechanics tells about the world, i. e., the truth of quantum mechanics, then it is very diffuse and we have a lot of competing ideas.
145 See, e. g., Greene, *Until the End of Time* or Carroll, *The Big Picture*.
146 See, e. g., Norma G. Sanchez, 'Unifying Quantum Mechanics with Einstein's General Relativity,' *Research Outreach* (blog), 19 December 2019, https://researchoutreach.org/articles/unifying-quantum-mechanics-einstein-general-relativity/ and Norma G. Sanchez, 'New Quantum Structure of Space-Time,' *Gravitation and Cosmology* 25, no. 2 (1 April 2019): 91–102. Sean Carroll gives it a try in *The Big Picture*, see especially the technical appendix, pages 435–441.
147 Peter Byrne, 'The Many Worlds of Hugh Everett,' *Scientific American* 297, no. 6 (December 2007): 98–105.

bones),[148] or that humans have a soul,[149] and so on. Some are very strong theories with almost no insecurity even though they are difficult to test, e. g., the theory of plate tectonics,[150] that climate change is man-made,[151] that space and time are related,[152] and so on and so forth.

The question here in relation to systematic theology is to what degree theories such as the universe as a contingent-created entity, the resurrection of Christ, or the universality of basic moral intuition are insecure. This seems to depend on the theoretical frameworks they are understood within, but there is also the possibility of assessing them according to (2), i. e., if alternative theories are clearly less secure (or in other words more unconvincing), then we have greater confidence in our own theory. Thus, as for (2), we see the difficulty of aligning insecurity and intersubjectivity because it is very difficult to assess the relative strength of two insecure theories. To assess and compare the degrees of coherence seem to be the best tool at hand but this is of course not an easy short cut to a solution. Coherence emphasizes fallibilism and especially in relation to insecurities our judgments must be tentative.

In the next section I discuss more deeply which insecurities can be accepted in the organization of coherent ontological theories.

6.3.4.2 Accepted Insecurities in an Ontological Theory

The question for this section – which insecurities can be accepted in an ontological theory – is so vast that, in the context of this book, it can only be addressed according to coherence theory. So, the more particular version of the question would be, which insecurities, if any, can be accepted in such a way that the coherence of a given theory is not unacceptably compromised? The qualifier "if any" could be seen as a reflection on a possible problem for coherence, that is sometimes called "the antinomy of negation."[153] The idea here is that the basic criteria in Puntel's understanding of coherence cannot be accepted because incompleteness seems to

---

148 Currie, *Rock, Bone, and Ruin*, 33–53, esp. 51.
149 Murphy, 'Nonreductive Physicalism.'
150 Robert J. Stern, 'The Evolution of Plate Tectonics,' *Philosophical Transactions of the Royal Society A: Mathematical, Physical and Engineering Sciences* 376, no. 2132 (13 November 2018).
151 See, e.g., the sixth report from FN's Climate Panel from 2021: IPCC, 'Sixth Assessment Report,' accessed 1 September 2021, https://www.ipcc.ch/assessment-report/ar6/.
152 Tim Maudlin, *Philosophy of Physics: Space and Time*, Princeton Foundations of Contemporary Philosophy (Princeton and Oxford: Princeton University Press, 2012).
153 Mühling, *Post-Systematic Theology I*, 350–55. See also Patrick Grim, *The Incomplete Universe: Totality, Knowledge, and Truth*, (Cambridge: Bradford, 1991). Cf. Puntel, *Structure and Being*, 424–430.

be an inevitable part of every large system.[154] Theologian Markus Mühling writes, "[i]n a basic way, the antinomy of negation ensures that the cohesion of what is real cannot be a system, a network, transport, but wayfaring in the mesh – on all levels, on the level of primary stories as well as on the level of secondary stories. At the same time, it ensures that universal coherence is incomprehensible and that there is no totality of truth."[155] In other words, if the antinomy of negation is valid, Puntel's systematicity seems to fall apart. If inconsistency and lack of cohesiveness cannot be excluded from a comprehensive and intelligible theory of reality and truth, then incompleteness seems to be an inevitable part of reality.

What is the best response to this possible problem? Puntel deals with the problem several times, and he basically accepts Gödel's proof.[156] Puntel emphasizes openness and incompleteness as conditions for theoreticity,[157] so that "the structural-systematic philosophy is an open system (i. e., that it is essentially *incomplete*)."[158] Puntel's philosophy thus explicitly addresses the unrestricted openness of theoreticity, and this is in itself an argument for the use of coherence in philosophical work because we do not know in advance if there will be an answer to a research question, so we should strive for more coherence in order to be able to choose the best possible answer. We never have good reasons for choosing the less coherent solution even though we do not have a complete overview of reality. For this reason, the notion of incompleteness is not an argument *against* but rather *for* Puntel's understanding of a "coherent system." Rescher would agree, I assume, because he is aware of the fact that it is not possible to integrate all data into one theory. What he seeks to do instead is to develop theoretical tools to choose between the data. For this reason, there are ways around the implications of the antinomy of negation.[159]

And what about theology? As stated above, when we raise the degree of complexity and depth, we raise the degree of insecurity and therefore it seems to be a condition for systematic theology that insecurity is a central part of the work. But in relation to the criterion of intersubjectivity it creates a difficulty that seems insurmountable. Take a case from systematic theology 2, the Lord's supper. There are various explications of this doctrine that are based on Scriptural interpretation,

---

154 Gödel's "incompleteness theorem" from 1931 is the famous proof for this claim. Kurt Gödel, 'Über Formal unentscheidbare Sätze der Principia Mathematica und verwandter Systeme,' *Monatshefte für Mathematik und Physik* 38 (1931): 173–98.
155 Mühling, *Post-Systematic Theology I*, 353.
156 Puntel, *Structure and Being*, 117.
157 Puntel, *Structure and Being*, 243.
158 Puntel, *Structure and Being*, 20. Original italics.
159 See Rescher, *The Coherence Theory of Truth*.

metaphysics, traditions, and societal/church structures, etc.[160] For example, there are many things that must be the case in order to sustain the Lutheran doctrine, and many of these are controversial.[161] This makes the doctrine questionable, but is it then legitimate for a Lutheran theologian in a research context to point to insecurity as a result? Or is reference to insecurity a strategy that guards the doctrine from legitimate critique? In general, we should not settle for an incoherent view of reality because that would open a gateway to all sorts of false views. Reality is intelligible and that what is intelligible is coherent. Reality is the sum of all there is, and therefore we can say that truth is the most coherent description of reality. The Lutheran view might therefore be challenged by the notion of coherence, but only more careful explication and discussion will enable us to determine whether it ultimately fails.

I shall not try to solve all these matters here, but the issue is now stated to show that underdetermination in the theological data creates insecurities in the theoretical work, and this could call for new reconstructions by more precise theoretical and philosophical criteria.[162] Science aims for truth, and accordingly so does theology, which means that theological theories should be judged by their degrees of coherence in comparison with relevant alternatives, even though theology's data are partly coarse and vague (and therefore has an uncertain truth-status).

6.3.5   Conclusion on Premise 2

Systematic theology deals with complex theories systematized from a large reservoir of data. systematic theology must therefore make a lot of subtheories and draw many subconclusions and these must be coherent with the large theory presented at the level of systematic theology 3. This process from data through subtheories to theory must be explicated carefully so that it can be tested intersubjectively and compared with alternatives. That is the ideal, but there are difficulties in practice. Due to the enormous amount of data that constitutes reality it is not possible for humans to integrate them all into one perfect system. This is a condition and not necessarily a weakness concerning the ideal of coherence.[163] Coherence can be seen as a regulative idea to strive towards, and then we can keep on working on,

---

160 See, e. g., Pannenberg, *Systematic Theology*, 3:283–369; McGrath, *Christian Theology. An Introduction*, 400–420.

161 I am thinking of notions such as Christ's real presence in the elements, the consubstantiation of the elements, the purifying and salvific efficacy of the Eucharist, the union of the believers in Christ through corporate participation in the meal, etc.

162 Eikrem, *God as Sacrificial Love*, 6–7.

163 Cf. Nicholas Rescher, 'Truth as Ideal Coherence', *The Review of Metaphysics* 38, no. 4 (June 1985): 795–806.

updating, adjusting, and refining our theories because we should always choose the most coherent theory that is available. Coherence is not without its own problems, but it is the best tool available for assessing and comparing theories, also within systematic theology.

When it comes to intersubjectivity in relation to coherence and systematic theology, I have argued that intersubjectivity comes in degrees. It is not an either-or, but a continuum on a broad scale. Due to what I have previously discussed as conditions of complexity (6.3.3) and insecurity (6.3.4), I argue that systematic theology can and should be done intersubjectively while at the same time admitting that it scores a little lower on a scale of intersubjectivity than most of the natural sciences and probably also the social sciences.[164] This is because much of the data in theology are coarse-grained with few strong connections among them and often with competing explanations. Still, if the proposed understanding of the best understanding of the criterion for intersubjectivity in research (6.2.2) is accepted, I think systematic theology can work intersubjectively to an acceptable degree as critical intersubjectivity (6.3.2.3). It is possible to explicate the presupposition and the methods, and to make the results transparent and publicly accessible, which are the minimal demands for any scientific theory.[165]

6.4 Conclusion

Let me recapitulate the discussion of the objections so far. The first objection said that it was not possible to test systematic theology, and the second objection said that it was not possible to test systematic theology in the most critical way, i. e., to falsify its theories. This third objection then says that even though objections 1 and 2 do not hold, it is not possible to agree on methods, data, presuppositions, and results, and thus systematic theology cannot work intersubjectively in a sufficient way but only internally in systematic theology's own discourse. This gave me the syllogism presented at the beginning of this chapter, where the conclusion deducted from the premises was that systematic theology is not a science. After the above extensive discussion of these premises, the question is, is the conclusion correct?

In 6.2.5, I concluded that Premise 1 is sustained. The criterion of intersubjectivity in research is legitimate and helpful when it is understood as requiring the

---

[164] It is also possible that the reason for a challenged notion of intersubjectivity in systematic theology is not the cause of coarse data, but the result of a higher claim for ultimate coherence. If we work with more traffic between the strata of systematic theology and thus makes systematic theology 1–3 into one meta-theological theory, we have an enormous claim for universal coherence that, of course, would be challenged in all sorts of way, not least on its critical intersubjectivity.

[165] Gravem, *KRL – et fag for alle?*, 5.

explication of data, presuppositions, and methods and the transparency and public accessibility of results. In this way, the development from data over method and theory to results must be exposed to public critique to be scientific.

In 6.3.5, I concluded that we have a bigger problem for systematic theology in relation to the objection of intersubjectivity than in relation to objections 1 and 2. The enormous reservoir of data and the impossibility of integrating everything into one system complicates the task of comparing different systems. It makes it very difficult to agree on the right methods, data, and presuppositions and therefore on acceptable and convincing results. This is not an isolated problem for systematic theology because at least the neighbouring discipline of philosophy faces the same problems. But relative to the possibility of intersubjectivity in the natural sciences and several of the social sciences (even though these are more complex to handle), I can conclude that systematic theology scores a little lower on a scale of intersubjectivity. However, because intersubjectivity comes in degrees, I also conclude that systematic theology is intersubjective to a sufficient degree to be counted as a science – as is philosophy.

What creates the problems for systematic theology, philosophy, and possibly the rest of the humanities is that the hermeneutical factor is much more central, understood as the particularity of the researcher. The scope of the data in systematic theology and philosophy is so vast that it might entail a weaker intersubjectivity, but this only emphasizes the importance of seeing intersubjectivity as scalar, not as a wholesale disqualification of these fields of study. I have also discussed the problem of personal biases in relation to intersubjectivity (6.2.4.1), and because these seem to be inevitable, the most I can conclude is that everyone should be aware of them, and because you do not know your own biases because you do not know what you do not know, you need competent and careful criticism from peers.

To agree on data in systematic theology and philosophy is much harder than in the natural sciences, and this creates a fundamental challenge.[166] This is because the data of systematic theology are often more coarse-grained and less cohesive than are those of other sciences. But as I have argued, we still want to research and discuss even weak and coarse-grained data scientifically because that is our best way to assess these data, and hence theology should not be discarded for doing the job, especially when systematic theology's presuppositions, methods, and results are made publicly accessible and therefore open to criticism and mutual reflection. The problem would be critical if naturalism were clearly more coherent than theism – like astronomy is much more coherent than astrology – but this is

---

166 But as Maudlin writes, this is only because much of (e. g.) physics can be executed without a clear understanding of the metaphysics behind the work. When the metaphysics is explicated, much controversy is exposed.

not the case at the moment.[167] As long as relevant alternatives are also insecure, we can accept the insecurity of systematic theology while we work on better, that is, more coherent, theories.

In the next chapter, I investigate a fourth objection to the present understanding of systematic theology. To recapitulate, I have addressed the objection that systematic theology fails to be testable (objection 1), the objection that systematic theology fails to be testable in the best way, i. e., falsifiable (objection 2), and the objection that systematic theology fails to be intersubjective because there is no agreement on data and results (objection 3). Even if all these objections are met – though objection 3 is a bit stronger than are 1 and 2 – there is a fourth objection that is critical. This objection says that even though a case for a sufficient degree of intersubjectivity in systematic theology can be made, there is still an imbalance in the choice and acceptance of specific data, methods, presuppositions, etc., that makes systematic theology problematic. In other words, the objection is that systematic theology is normative to an illegitimate degree and should for this reason be discarded as a science. This is the theme for the next chapter.

---

167 See further in 3.4.5 and 5.3.4.

Chapter Seven: Objection 4—Normativity

Premise 1. Sciences cannot be normative in a strong sense.
Premise 2. Systematic theology is normative in a strong sense.
Conclusion. Therefore, systematic theology is not a science.[1]

7.1   Introduction

At this stage of the book, it might be relevant to ask how new objections could problematize the status of systematic theology as a legitimate field of research. I have argued that the theories of systematic theology can be tested by their degrees of coherence (chapter four) and that it is possible to test them according to the most common standard for testing (falsification) by comparing the degrees of coherence of relevant alternatives (chapter five). I have also argued that in a qualified way, intersubjectivity works with theories of systematic theology although to a lesser degree than other disciplines (chapter six), and these three chapters suggest a robust answer to the research question about how systematic theology is best construed as a scientific discipline. Yet there are still other objections to consider, and in this and the following chapter I discuss two of the most important objections that could create problems for the present understanding of systematic theology as science.

In the present chapter, I discuss the objection that systematic theology is a normative discipline in such a problematic way that it must be rejected as a proper science. The objection maintains that even though we might accept the answer to the third objection and accept that systematic theology can work intersubjectively in a critical way, there is still an imbalance in the selection of data, methods, presuppositions, etc. that results from the discipline's concern with supernatural entities. Related to this objection, I discuss a final objection in the next chapter (chapter eight), namely the claim that systematic theology is only a legitimate research field when it gives up its characteristics and peculiarities and becomes a special kind of philosophy or a part of religious studies; at the moment it becomes a distinct discipline, it dissolves as a science.

---

1 The correct *modus tollens*-argument says: Premise 1: If systematic theology is a science, systematic theology cannot be normative in a strong sense. Premise 2: Systematic theology is normative in a strong sense. Conclusion: Systematic theology is not a science.

The construction principle for this chapter is the same as for the previous three. After an introduction that describes the crucial point of the objection, I address the two premises of the syllogism before I draw a conclusion.

The objection that systematic theology is problematically normative is often heralded by colleagues in religious studies.[2] A standard claim would be that theologians *make* religion while religious scholars *describe* religion.[3] Some would even say that this is the whole point of the discipline of religious studies: to do distanced, detached, balanced, critical, etc., studies of religion(s) means not participating in the ideological production of the theologians.[4] Taken as a caricature, the objection would be irrelevant, but because these views are expressed within academia and in serious channels of publication, I take them seriously. The objection that systematic theology is problematically normative could be understood as *the* central objection from some of the closest colleagues in academia, i. e., the scholars of religion.[5]

What normativity is and how it is best understood are thoroughly discussed in 7.2. Before I engage with these questions, I explicate an understanding of the relationship between normativity and the other criteria I have discussed so far. As has become evident, I see the objections as successive and closely related, tracing a common thread throughout the present book.[6] Two Puntelian notions have organized the study so far: "theoretical framework" and "coherency." In chapters four through six, I showed how these notions answer the objections in satisfying ways. Preliminarily, the same goes for the objection considered in this chapter. Normativity can be understood as what characterizes the conclusion a researcher draws when she has developed the most coherent theory within her theoretical framework, clarified the degree of coherence of the theory, and compared it to other relevant theories. If her theory proves to be superior, it is normative in that we should count it as true because it is best substantiated. This also includes theories that refer to supernatural entities. This claim is explained, discussed, and defended throughout this chapter.

---

[2] E. g., Donald Wiebe, *The Politics of Religious Studies. The Continuing Conflict with Theology in the Academy* (New York: systematic theology. Martin's Press, 1999).

[3] Ninian Smart, *The Science of Religion and the Sociology of Knowledge* (Princeton: Princeton University Press, 1973), 6–7; Jens-André P. Herbener, 'The Study and Making of Christian Religion in Danish Academic Theology,' in *Contemporary Views on Comparative Religion: In Celebration of Tim Jensen's 65th Birthday*, ed. Peter Antes, Armin W. Geertz, and Mikael Rothstein (Sheffield: Equinox, 2016), 210.

[4] The sources in the previous footnote are representative examples.

[5] As Jens-André P. Herbener says, the conclusion drawn by religious-studies scholars is that academic theology should be "excluded from academia." Herbener, 'The Study and Making of Christian Religion in Danish Academic Theology,' 211.

[6] See also the overview in the introduction to part three and the summary in chapter nine.

I can also describe the relationship between the objections *negatively* by saying that normativity becomes problematic – or even illegitimate – when a theory is assessed as incoherent but still not abandoned.[7] Despite its being comparatively inferior to other theories, no consequence is drawn. All sorts of reasons for such misbehaviour could be conceived of such as sloppy thinking, laziness, lack of self-criticism, abuse of power, submissiveness towards authorities, consensus-seeking, etc.[8] In this way, problematical normativity arises when for various reasons a researcher does not follow the evidence but accepts a problematic position for other (external) reasons.

Such normativity is related to the objections treated above through the notions of the theoretical framework and coherency, but it does not imply that I underestimate the complexity of the field. It is only a necessary limitation of the field. Normativity in its broadest conception is a complicated topic with many ramifications and involving many positions, and it applies to various concerns within ethics, moral psychology, qualitative studies/empirical research, etc.[9] And in all fields there are bound to be discussions of choice of theory, choice of sources, choice of methods, perspectives, conversation partners, criteria for good research, presuppositions, etc.[10] It is not possible to address all these issues here, but this is not a problem because I can focus on a narrower discussion related to the conflict between systematic theology and religious studies, which is the context for and the core of the objection.

There are two hypotheses for this chapter. The first says that normativity can be either problematic or unproblematic. A problematic kind of normativity is at play when a theory is found incoherent but is still argued for as a norm. An unproblematic kind of normativity is evident when a theory is found coherent and therefore is argued for as a norm. The second hypothesis relates to the first distinction and says that both a weak and a strong version of normativity can be unproblematic. I explain the distinction between weak and strong normativity in the following.

---

7 Theories that are falsified and abandoned could be revitalized in the future due to new data. This is an implication of the fallibility of all our theories, and our ignorance of the future. Still, we have to make theoretical decisions here and now and we do not have good reasons to accept clearly less coherent theories or incoherent theories.

8 These misbehaviors follow several of the problematic aspects of the biases discussed in the previous chapter.

9 See, e. g., Jonathan Dancy, ed., *Normativity* (Oxford: Blackwell, 2000); Stephen Darwall, 'Normativity,' in *Routledge Encyclopedia of Philosophy*, (London: Routledge, 2016); Maria Olson and Tatjana Zimenkova, '(Hidden) Normativity in Social Science Education and History Education,' *Journal of Social Science Education* 14, no. 1 (Spring 2005): 2–5; Christine M. Korsgaard, *The Sources of Normativity*, ed. Onora O'Neill (Cambridge: Cambridge University Press, 1996).

10 As I quoted MacIntyre in 4.3.5, all traditions – including scientific research – need and have a specific set of standards for excellence, which is also another word for normativity.

This chapter and the next are shorter than the previous three, which in itself indicates that these objections are less critical to theology than the first three. The following chapters are also relatively shorter because they build on the work I have done in the previous three chapters, and the book thus exhibits an organic systematic progression.

In the next section I consider Premise 1. I start by providing a working definition (a preliminary explication) of normativity (7.2.1.1) before I discuss a couple of major positions that are relevant as background for the discussion (7.2.1.2). Here I also address the question whether normativity is inevitable and, if so, how (7.2.1.3). I end this section by discussing normativity in closer relation to the presuppositions of the present book, emphasizing the legitimacy of strong normativity (7.2.2). The conclusion concerning Premise 1 is that it is false because strong normativity is a legitimate part of all scientific research (7.2.3).

7.2 Premise 1

Premise 1 states, "Sciences cannot be normative in a strong sense." In other words, the premise claims that there is an incompatibility between "science" and "strong normativity" such that strong normativity cannot be a part of science. In the context of this book (so far), for a theory to be scientific means that it is testable and falsifiable in sufficiently intersubjective ways (chapters four through six). Premise 1 says that these three criteria are incompatible with strong normativity, i. e., that one cannot test by falsification in an intersubjective way and be strongly normative while doing so. Clearly, this premise calls for an explication of what strong normativity is because the reasonableness of the premise rests on the persuasiveness of the concept. But it is necessary to start broader and discuss the notion of normativity generally because this is often in itself assumed to be a problematic concept in science.

7.2.1 What is Normativity?

This section includes several subsections that contribute to an explication of what normativity is in the context of the present book. The first subsection gives a short definition of normativity (a preliminary explication) (7.2.1.1); the next subsection presents two major positions in the debate, especially between theology and religious studies. Even though the first premise concerns general philosophy of science, there is no reason to postpone this crucial discussion because it is still related to the basic discussion of the topic and its keeps our focus on systematic theology alive (7.2.1.2). The third subsection discusses the inevitability of normativity exposed in the previous subsection and begin to engage in the discussion on strong normativity, and for this reason it ends by problematizing the short definition from the first subsection (7.2.1.3). These three subsections organize the discussion of Premise 1, and following them, I determine whether Premise 1 stands. As already stated above, it does not. The following discussion should demonstrate why.

7.2.1.1 Short Working Definition of Normativity

"Normativity" is a substantivized adjective from "normative," a word that refers to the quality of something as the "norm," i. e., as the prescriptive standard within a sphere. "Normativity" is then the state of being a norm within a given context. "Normativity" within science is then the prescriptive standard of a way to do research.[11] But it is common for scholars to distinguish between descriptive and normative approaches to a topic in scientific research. Understood this way, a normative approach does not only *describe* a phenomenon in great detail but *prescribes* the norm for how the phenomenon should be understood.[12] In this sense, the present book's continuous emphasis on coherence theory is an example of normativity. Coherence is here understood as a prescribed norm for how to understand and assess phenomena in science. Coherence is prescribed as what it takes to be a theoretical truth-candidate and as a criterion for what relevant data are and for how to assess them, organize them, and integrate them, etc. This is a normative practice and not reduced to descriptions or explications. Parts of the work in coherence theory can work descriptively, e. g., the comparison of different theories, but the conclusions are always normative – and aim to be so.[13]

The short definition then is that "normativity" refers to something as the norm of a given field, and especially to the practice of claiming something to be the right, correct, true interpretation or understanding of something. For this reason, normativity is an inevitable part of every field and therefore unproblematic. But the objection could instead be that there are more specific forms of normativity that are problematic, for example, that descriptions of religious behaviour can be correct and thus normative relative to a naturalistic framework but that normative claims about which religious interpretation of reality is correct are beyond the scope of human epistemological conditions and therefore impossible to make. For this reason, the objection could be that *strong* normativity – normativity about supernatural

---

11 Compare with MacIntyre: "A practice involves standards of excellence and obedience to rules as well as the achievement of goods. To enter into a practice is to accept the authority of those standards and the inadequacy of my own performance as judged by them. It is to subject my own attitudes, choices, preferences and tastes to the standards which currently and partially define the practice." MacIntyre, *After Virtue*, 190.
12 See, e. g., Godfrey-Smith, *Theory and Reality*, 6.
13 See, e. g., Puntel, *Structure and Being*, 69–71.

entities – is problematic because there are other more neutral, objective ways to engage with a field, i. e., *weak* normativity – a kind of normativity that is only normative about natural entities.

Given this distinction, I discuss two major positions in the debate about normativity in science in the next section. Because the discussion between religious studies and theology is of great importance to the present book and because it anticipates the next chapter on distinct research, I have chosen this debate as a relevant case of a more general debate about normativity in science. The first position argues that it is possible to separate descriptive and normative practices and that only the first are scientific (7.2.1.2.1). The second position argues instead that it is not possible to separate descriptive and normative practices and that the demarcation between science and pseudoscience is located instead in the degree of awareness of normativity, the self-critical reflections, the explication of presuppositions, etc. (7.2.1.2.2). As with previous discussions the aim is not to isolate two "boxes." The different researchers are distributed along a continuum but isolating only two positions is beneficial for later discussions, and I have therefore contented myself with these two. The aim is not to provide a conceptual genealogy of these positions because their relevance in this context, for the purpose of a systematic study, lies in providing representative examples of how such positions might understand themselves.

7.2.1.2   Major Positions

7.2.1.2.1   It Is Possible to Separate the Descriptive from the Normative

By now, there is a prevalent train of thought saying that it is possible to separate descriptive and normative approaches and that only the first kind is scientific. In the following, I present how three representative authors[14] – Ninian Smart, Donald Wiebe, and Russell T. McCutcheon – describe this position before I identify a number of main concerns with this position. I end this section by answering the question of what the characteristics of the descriptive practice are (that is, what religious studies does and what systematic theology does not do) according to this position.

In an article from 1997, historian of religions Ninian Smart distinguished theology from religious studies categorically.[15] Theology he saw as "expressing faith, not so much describing it," while religious studies "is much wider, intentionally

---

14 There are many examples of this position in public debate, and it would be helpful to map the different uses of this position in the public debate, especially in a contemporary context where systematic theology is under pressure in many ways. Still, I have chosen to focus on how researchers discuss this more technically because the context here is fundamental philosophy of science.
15 Ninian Smart was a key figure in the first department of religious studies in Britain after the foundation of the new university in Lancaster. The vision is presented briefly in Robert A. Segal, 'Ninian

descriptive, hopefully impartial and infused with informed empathy."[16] Christian theology "is basically a denominational activity: it is not a secular activity. It is imperfectly scholarship."[17] On the other hand, religious studies is "impartial and given to informed empathy. It is in this way the purest of the social sciences and indeed an example to the social sciences, because it takes *epoché* so seriously."[18] Of course, Smart is well aware of the complexity of the field and the growing muddle between systematic theology and religious studies when the level of detail is raised, however, he sticks to two fundamental differences. (1) "Religious Studies' main thrust is descriptive and explanatory" i. e., "methodologically agnostic" [...] and (2) religious studies is "cross-cultural, and indeed trans-religious."[19] Theology on the other hand is "community based" and for this reason "it is [essentially] preaching."[20] Smart's view is emphatically dualistic, but the schematic opposition clarifies the question helpfully at this stage.

Philosopher of religion Donald Wiebe is one of the scholars who have written most extensively about the difference between religious studies and systematic theology, or more precisely, between the scientific study of religion and the study of religion that is religiously coloured.[21] As he says, "[b]y 'scientific' I mean essentially that the study of religion in the context of the modern research university aims at achieving what we might call 'public knowledge of public faiths,' mediated through intersubjectively testable sets of statements, whether at the descriptive level of history, ethnography, and phenomenology, or at the explanatory level of law-like generalizations and theory."[22] According to Wiebe, this approach is "disinterested"

Smart and Religious Studies,' *The Council of Societies for the Study of Religion Bulletin* 30, no. 2 (2001): 27–29.
16   Ninian Smart, 'Religious Studies and Theology,' *The Council of Societies for the Study of Religion Bulletin* 26, no. 3 (1997): 66.
17   Smart, 'Religious Studies and Theology,' 67.
18   Smart, 'Religious Studies and Theology,' 67. "Epoché" means to bracket – at least for a while – one's judgment on a given topic. It has a long history, but is often, in contemporary philosophy, associated with Edmund Husserl and phenomenology. Christian Beyer, 'Edmund Husserl,' in *The Stanford Encyclopedia of Philosophy*, ed. Edward N. Zalta (Metaphysics Research Lab, Stanford University, 2020), See point 6.
19   Smart, 'Religious Studies and Theology,' 67–68.
20   Smart, 'Religious Studies and Theology,' 68.
21   This is seen for example in his evaluations of the presidential addresses at the American Academy of Religion (AAR) and the development within the North American Association for the Study of Religion (NAASR). See, e. g., Donald Wiebe, 'An Eternal Return All Over Again: The Religious Conversation Endures,' *Journal of the American Academy of Religion* 74, no. 3 (2006): 674–96 or Donald Wiebe, 'Change the Name! On the Importance of Reclaiming NAASR's Original Objectives for the Twenty-First Century,' *Method & Theory in the Study of Religion* 25, no. 4/5 (2013): 350–61.
22   Wiebe, 'An Eternal Return All Over Again,' 691.

and "neutral" instead of following "religio-theological" agendas that are "idiosyncratic subjective."[23] This scientific approach will seek "to explain 'the supernatural' naturalistically."[24] It is surprising that Wiebe seems to be unaware that naturalism is also a metaphysical position with a number of chosen presuppositions that are not obvious, but this is how he presents his view.

It is not the case that Wiebe rejects the notion of scientific theology as such;[25] he merely claims that the scientific study of theology results in something that is detrimental to "fundamental religious aspirations."[26] And this is also evident in the writings of professional theologians, says Wiebe. Through close readings of the prolegomenal studies of Andrew Louth, Sallie McFague, and Amos Wilder, he intends to show that they unsuccessfully seek to combine academic rigor with religious aspirations, because – unintentionally – they end up with texts that are scientific when they are not theology and theology when they are not scientific.[27] Stated poignantly, scientific theology separates "thought about God" from "commitment to God" but this is exactly what the three authors seek to overcome.[28] In this sense they seek to be normative instead of descriptive, or then engage in "reproducing" life instead of "describing and explaining" it.[29] The sharp dualism of Ninian Smart is thus continued and developed by Wiebe.

Of interest is that even within a naturalist camp there is a growing tension concerning how to understand the distinction between normative and descriptive elements. Scholar of religion Russell T. McCutcheon, for example, is a contemporary writer who is a central figure in the methodological debate in religious studies today.[30] He is an anti-realist[31] and fundamentally critical towards the categorical

---

23 Wiebe, 'An Eternal Return All Over Again,' 691.
24 Wiebe, 'An Eternal Return All Over Again,' 692.
25 He writes that "academic theology" in his terminology is "a scientific discipline of the same order as the other disciplines to be found in the university curriculum." Donald Wiebe, *The Irony of Theology and the Nature of Religious Thought* (Montreal & Kingston: McGill-Queen's University Press, 1991), 12. See also the categorial distinction between scientific and religious theology on page 15, fn. 24, which he elaborates on page 30.
26 Wiebe, *The Irony of Theology*, 7, 11, 44 and 175. To quote the last reference: "not all forms of theology are detrimental to or in conflict with religion; that not all theology is incompatible or incommensurable with religion, but only the theology that emerges as an academic/scientific discipline is so." This is the quintessence of the fundamental distinction – and critique – in Wiebe's book.
27 Wiebe, *The Irony of Theology*, 16–28.
28 Wiebe, *The Irony of Theology*, 17.
29 Wiebe, *The Irony of Theology*, 28.
30 See, e. g., Russell T. McCutcheon, *Critics Not Caretakers: Redescribing the Public Study of Religion* (Albany: State University of New York Press, 2001).
31 E. g., Russell T. McCutcheon, *Fabricating Religion: Fanfare for the Common e. g.* (Berlin and Boston: De Gruyter, 2019). Compare with the summary of McCutcheon's position and a response from a

notion of religion.[32] These views make him different from Smart and Wiebe, and at first sight we might intuitively think that he therefore – and furthermore because of his strong social constructivism – regards all scientific work as inevitably normative, but this does not seem to be the case. His "theory-as-critique" – that is, the study of the concepts used in academic discourse (who invented them and how are they used?) – is intrinsically different from Wiebe's "theory-as-explanation" – that is, the naturalistic study of how and why religious believers do and think as they do and think – but where Wiebe sees the critique-position as religious production, McCutcheon sees it as the rational approach to the study of religion.[33]

Of special interest for the purpose here is McCutcheon's view on the "insider/outsider problem" in the study of religion.[34] His basic point is that emic (insider) and etic (outsider) perspectives are entangled and can only be understood as a complex continuum. The reason is that without outsiders there would be no insiders and vice versa; the insiders learn to self-reflect through the curiosity of the outsiders, and the outsiders get their questions from the self-articulation of the insiders.[35] A problem for the outsider is whose viewpoints are to be authorized as authentic descriptions of the insiders' outlook and by which criteria.[36] But this does not imply that McCutcheon abandons the etic perspective: "scholars of religion seek to develop criteria from outside each of these particular social systems [religious views, MAM] so as to compare them or their elements, and then to develop a theory capable of explaining the possible reasons for the similarities and differences that their comparisons bring to light. Etic scholarship therefore ought not to be constrained by the way in which the people one studies say they act or think. Instead, it should be constrained by the rules that govern all rational, comparative, scientific

---

  critical realist in Kevin Schilbrack, 'A Metaphysics for the Study of Religion: A Critical Reading of Russell McCutcheon,' *Critical Research on Religion* 8, no. 1 (2020): 87–100.
32 See, e. g., chapter one "What's in a Name" in Russell T. McCutcheon, *Studying Religion: An Introduction*, Second Edition (London and New York: Routledge, 2018), 7–14. Problematizing the notion of religion in religious studies had attracted increased attention in recent decades, for example in influential works by Talal Asad and J.Z. Smith. See, e. g., Talal Asad, 'The Construction of Religion as an Anthropological Category,' in *Genealogies of Religion: Discipline and Reasons of Power in Christianity and Islam* (Baltimore: Johns Hopkins University Press, 1993), 27–54; Jonathan Z. Smith, 'Religion, Religions, Religious,' in *Critical Terms for Religious Studies*, ed. Mark C. Taylor, Second Edition (Chicago: The University of Chicago Press, 1998), 269–84.
33 At least according to Wiebe. See Wiebe, 'Change the Name! On the Importance of Reclaiming NAASR's Original Objectives for the Twenty-First Century,' 354–55.
34 As McCutcheon says, the insider/outsider problem is not limited to religion but is present in other fields such as linguistics and anthropology. McCutcheon, *Studying Religion*, 50.
35 McCutcheon, *Studying Religion*, 52–53.
36 McCutcheon, *Studying Religion*, 53.

analyses that are found throughout the modern university."[37] That this clearly is a normative position should be evident from McCutcheon's own words – even though he would maybe not use this word himself – but the question is whether this kind of normativity legitimizes stronger forms of normativity. After discussing a case of theodicy, McCutcheon introduces a distinction between (a) the descriptive level where participants and non-participants of religious discourses might overlap to a large degree, and (b) the explanatory or analytical level where an immense variety between these will appear because they will disagree about whether there is a problem in the first place.[38] If an omnipotent and good God is not assumed, can there be a problem of evil?

These short introductions to Smart, Wiebe, and McCutcheon point to a growing diversity within the field, but I shall not follow this trajectory further here. Instead, to sum up, they see their own field of religious studies as distinct from systematic theology and other religious discourses. Whereas religious studies is more or less a descriptive activity and a critical activity based on a naturalistic framework, systematic theology and other religious discourses are normative and producers of religion.

I now raise two questions. First, what are the main concerns behind discarding normativity for scholars such as Smart and Wiebe? In short, it is to protect the scientific study of religion from religious intervention. From the initial stage of the discipline, it has portrayed itself as an alternative to the religious approaches to the study of religion seen for example in Christian theology. The problem with this religious approach is in essence that it does not *investigate* the data scientifically, but instead *produces* the data that the religious studies scholars critically analyse. Instead of studying religion, it produces religion.[39] The problem seems to be that by producing religion instead of studying it, theology becomes normative and thereby lacks testability and intersubjectivity (thus falls on objections 1–3 in this book). But the problem also seems to be that theologians argue for what the data of theology should be instead of merely describing the religious data that are available (in the present terminology, at the level of systematic theology 1). In other words, the theologians argue for what Christianity should be; they do not just track how it is understood. But the problem with this objection is that related disciplines have the same ambition, e. g., when philosophers argue how free will should be understood – or even whether free will exists at all. This is comparable with the theologians who argue about how God is to be understood – and whether God exists at all. We see this kind of work in other fields as well. For example, in physics

---

37 McCutcheon, *Studying Religion*, 54.
38 McCutcheon, *Studying Religion*, 57.
39 Herbener, 'The Study and Making of Christian Religion in Danish Academic Theology,' 210.

where the physicists discuss whether particles, fields, forces, etc., exist or not and thus how physicists should understand their data; or the historian of religion who discusses what religion is, what counts as religion, what its functions are, etc.

This also shows the close connection between objections 3 and 4 in the present book; to be normative is to problematize the legitimate demand for intersubjectivity, because the objection says that it is not possible to reproduce the production of religion in a scientific way and that the selection of data is problematic. Normativity is thus seen as one way to compromise the criterion of intersubjectivity, but the question is whether this objection is convincing. Given the understanding of science in chapters four through six, it seems not. A clear and transparent description of methods, data, presuppositions, and results makes it possible even for a researcher using a different theoretical framework to test and reproduce the work. If all one's presuppositions are stated, the criterion of intersubjectivity is not compromised even by a strong normativity. An atheist can contribute to the development of systematic theology at all strata just as a Christian theologian can contribute to the development of Islamic theology by suggesting, assessing, comparing, and criticizing the degrees of coherence of different theories. The first objection of scholars like Wiebe and Smart therefore seems unwarranted.

Second, what are the "descriptive" characteristics that mark religious studies and that systematic theology lacks? Somewhat surprisingly, it is rare to find careful explications of key words like "disinterested," "neutral," "objective," and "dispassionate" which as we have seen are common designators. They seem to be taken as truisms, which they evidently are not.[40] A more explicated term that could be seen as the most common designator is *methodological atheism/agnosticism/naturalism* in the tradition of Peter L. Berger's sociology of religion.[41] His apt description of this understanding and practice is that "[n]eedless to say, it is impossible within the frame of reference of scientific theorizing to make any affirmations, positive *or* negative, about the ultimate ontological status of this alleged reality. Within this frame of reference, the religious projections can be dealt with only in this way, as products of human activity and human consciousness, and rigorous brackets have to be placed around the question as to whether these projections may not *also*

---

40 Cf. Godfrey-Smith, *Theory and Reality*, 6.
41 See Peter L. Berger, *The Sacred Canopy: Elements of a Sociological Theory of Religion* (New York: Anchor, 1990), 121. In footnote 36, Berger says that he has taken the term from Anton Zijderveld. In *Appendix II*, Berger discusses the term at length (pages 204–214). Berger's own version has been discussed and criticized for decades, but his central point of bracketing ontological commitments is still prevalent. Cf. Douglas V. Porpora, 'Methodological Atheism, Methodological Agnosticism and Religious Experience,' *Journal for the Theory of Social Behaviour* 36, no. 1 (2006): 57–75. See also Michael A. Cantrell, 'Must a Scholar of Religion Be Methodologically Atheistic or Agnostic?', *Journal of the American Academy of Religion* 84, no. 2 (June 2016): 373–400.

be something else than that (or, more accurately, *refer to* something else than the human world in which they empirically originate)."[42] Husserl's phenomenological idea of "bracketing" the truth question (*"epoché"*) is thus seen as the definitive characteristic of religious studies – a bracketing that distances it from systematic theology and a bracketing that makes religious studies scientific, according to the view that it is possible to separate the descriptive and the normative in the field of religion.

To conclude on this, if a scholar of religion made a distinction between what she can and cannot do as a scholar of religion as opposed to a theologian but still counted both religious studies and theology as sciences, hardly any discussion would be needed. But the claim of the position described in this subsection is that the distinction between what a scholar of religion can and cannot do as opposed to a theologian coincides with the criteria of distinction between science and pseudoscience, and this is a more polemical claim. But with this summary, I am about to anticipate the discussion of the next chapter on distinct science, so I postpone a more thorough assessment of this view (see especially 8.3.3.1).

In the next subsection, I discuss the opposite view, which says that it is not possible to separate descriptive and normative elements and features in scientific work.

7.2.1.2.2 It Is Not possible to Separate the Descriptive from the Normative

The next position claims the diametrical opposite from the previous one by saying that it is not possible to separate the descriptive from the normative. As in 7.2.1.2.1, I first investigate three representative examples – here Thomas A. Lewis, Gavin D'Costa, and Jan-Olav Henriksen – and then try to answer the key question of what the main concerns are for this position. Why reject the old dichotomy? Lastly, I differentiate two challenges for the old view that give rise to two different focal points for these researchers, namely empirical and hermeneutical challenges, respectively.

Scholar of religion Thomas A. Lewis contrasts his position with the one considered in the previous section. Though primarily on the basis of informal conversation, he recognizes a widespread assumption that theology is normative while religious studies is not (or at least should not be).[43] But according to Lewis there is an obvious problem here: normativity is essential to disciplines like philosophy and political science but there is no fundamental criticism of these disciplines for their normativity, and they are not seriously contested in modern universities.[44] What kinds of

---

42 Berger, *The Sacred Canopy*, 121. Original italics.
43 Thomas A. Lewis, 'The Inevitability of Normativity in the Study of Religion. Theology in Religious Studies', in *Theology and Religious Studies in Higher Education. Global Perspectives*, ed. D.L. Bird and Simon G. Smith (London: Continuum, 2009), 87.
44 Lewis, 'The Inevitability of Normativity', 87.

normativity Lewis is talking about is not made clear, and it would be helpful to have a more precise explication of the term. It is correct that philosophy is occupied with truth but also with ethical normativity, which is something else. Political science is normative as well, concerned with questions of what a good society is or what justice is (and the like), and the answers to such questions are more contingent than the philosophical ones and thus contribute to a weaker normativity. Other disciplines are normative as well, such as pedagogics or economics (Why educate? How to organize the finances in the society?) but they are also descriptive (How do teachers teach? Which consequences do a financial policy have?). But all these examples could be seen as examples of weak normativity – with the possible exception of philosophy – and this could problematize Lewis's argument.

Nonetheless, Lewis' view is that the distinction between religious studies and systematic theology in much religious studies discourse is due to an implicit understanding of religion as something that cannot be argued for, because it is "reason's other."[45] He sums up the consensus in two key points: "first, of those writing on religion, only the theologians make normative claims, and, second, normative claims related to religion are fundamentally a matter of faith, where faith is juxtaposed with reason."[46] It is not clear whether Lewis describes the critics of religion as distinguishing between weak and strong normativity, in the present terminology, or instead as making the more dualistic distinction I considered in the previous section. Nevertheless, what is Lewis's response? Instead of excluding normative claims – which according to Lewis is impossible because there are normative claims in all disciplines – a researcher should be willing to offer a justification for her normative claims.[47] So when a religious studies scholar claims something to be "delusional," "fabricated," "constructed,"[48] and so on and so forth, these are normative claims about the nature of reality.[49] This reductionistic approach is widespread in religious studies, according to Lewis, because it is the logical implication of the naturalistic methodology inherent in many theoretical frameworks.[50] The critical edge here for Lewis is that it is actually disciplines like theology that represent the

---

45 Lewis, 'The Inevitability of Normativity', 88.
46 Lewis, 'The Inevitability of Normativity', 88.
47 Lewis, 'The Inevitability of Normativity', 88, 92 and 94. Lewis points to George Lindbeck and Alasdair MacIntyre as examples of thinkers who are normative in a good way: "Lindbeck and MacIntyre represent two different models of making arguments for their normative claims that neither appeal to self-evident foundations of which so many are suspicious nor simply take for granted the authority of any particular claim or canon." (page 93).
48 The first two terms are Lewis' while the last is mine with reference to McCutcheon's constructivism.
49 Lewis, 'The Inevitability of Normativity', 90. And I could add – with reference to McCutcheon – that even to say something is "religion" is a normative claim. McCutcheon, *Studying Religion*, 54–57.
50 See, e. g., Boyer, *Religion Explained*. Cf. Anil Mundra, 'Naturalism, Normativity, and the Study of Religion,' *Religions* 8, no. 10 (2017).

more honest approach because they openly declare their normative judgments. Descriptive work is also normative, according to Lewis, but this is often tacit or implicit and thus remains unjustified.[51] Basically, Lewis wants a more inclusive understanding of religious studies, such that theology is a part of the discipline if theologians argue for their normative claims – as the religious studies scholars should do as well: "Focusing on normativity and the willingness to offer justification for normative claims redirects the debate towards the substantive issues at stake," Lewis says, and adds that "[u]ltimately, then, one of the most important reasons for including theological elements in the study of religion in the secular university is that it educates people to think more critically about religious claims."[52] Lewis does not distinguish between different kinds of normativity, but his overall goal is to argue for the legitimacy and inevitability of (weak) normativity in all religious research.

The next example is theologian Gavin D'Costa, who has specialized in the relationship among the religions viewed from a trinitarian perspective. He brings another perspective to the discussion here because he sees a fundamental problem in the different paradigms, among both religious-studies scholars and theologians. In an article, D'Costa criticizes common approaches to assessing a religion other than one's own. His examples are theologians Keith Ward and Harold Netland, who are examples of diametrically opposite positions in the field of theology of religions. Each represents an axiom of D'Costa's that he describes as follows: "The first [axiom] is that *in relation to the increased specificity of an alleged neutral proposal its neutrality diminishes* [represented by Netland, MAM]. The second [axiom] is that *in relation to the decreased specificity of an alleged neutral proposal its usefulness diminishes* [represented by Ward, MAM]."[53] The problem is that the more fine-grained your explication of another religion is, the less neutral your explication will be. It dissolves in the details. If you then decide to explicate another religion in a coarse-grained way, your neutrality may be maintained, but your study becomes unconvincing and uninteresting because you claim too little. D'Costa gives an example from moral reasoning. In Christian apologetics it is common to claim that there are universal moral standards that everyone adheres to – consciously or not – for example that it is morally evil and therefore wrong to sacrifice children. But this abstract viewpoint dissolves, according to D'Costa, when it becomes more specific. As a Roman Catholic, he sees abortion as a modern version of "child sacrifice," and the moral view is thus context dependent: "There are no sets of basic moral values which are neutral and acceptable to all people, and as soon as one tries to specify

---

51 Lewis, 'The Inevitability of Normativity,' 90.
52 Lewis, 'The Inevitability of Normativity,' 95.
53 Gavin D'Costa, 'Whose Objectivity? Which Neutrality? The Doomed Quest for a Neutral Vantage Point from Which to Judge Religions,' *Religious Studies* 29 (1993): 81. Original italics.

some [of] them their historical and tradition-specific nature becomes evident."[54] For this reason, D'Costa's argument is – in line with MacIntyre – that one cannot but start from a clearly "tradition-specific starting point" and thus neutrality in all research, including religious studies and theology, is an illusion.[55] The implication is that theology should not fall prey to secularization within universities but instead be theologized and allowed to be tradition-specific.[56] For this reason, D'Costa seems to defend strong normativity even though his notion of normativity is not entirely clear. He comments directly on Ninian Smart's epistemology, which intends to be neutral: "It is not an objective and dispassionate methodology by which to approach 'religions,' but a highly biased and historically and philosophically situated enterprise."[57] According to D'Costa, the solution is that a pluralization of starting points be allowed, where proponents label them clearly and allow the positions to interact through conversation and criticism.[58] So his argument seems to be that weak normativity is an inevitable part of all science and this should lend credence to the strong normativity of theological theories.

The third example is theologian Jan-Olav Henriksen, who has worked intensely with religion and values in contemporary society for about three decades. Besides philosophical and theological studies he has worked with empirical studies in different contexts. This gives him a third important voice in this discussion. Henriksen says that theological researchers are often closely connected to their object of study and therefore should try to "alienate" themselves from the religious lifeworld: "Precisely because religion and theology have such a tremendous impact on the formation of people's (and often researcher's) life-world, it is important to establish a reflexive distance towards this life-world."[59] And here is the intrinsic problem. For many, to research theological issues is to research the familiar and hence there is a possibility of becoming blind to the "internalized normativities." For this reason, normativity becomes problematic when it prevents us from seeing

---

54 D'Costa, 'Whose Objectivity? Which Neutrality?' 87.
55 D'Costa, 'Whose Objectivity? Which Neutrality?' 95. I have discussed MacIntyre several times already; D'Costa refers to *After Virtue* as a source for his view. *Three Rival Versions*, chapter ten could also be a reference – as it is elsewhere for him: Gavin D'Costa, 'On Theologising Theology within the Secular University,' *Transformation* 22, no. 3 (2005): 154–55.
56 This is one of the main theses of his book D'Costa, *Theology in the Public Square. Church, Academy and Nation*.
57 D'Costa, 'On Theologising Theology within the Secular University,' 155.
58 D'Costa, 'On Theologising Theology within the Secular University,' 156.
59 Jan-Olav Henriksen, 'Researching Theological Normativity. Some Critical and Constructive Suggestions,' *Studia Theologica. Nordic Journal of Theology* 60, no. 2 (2006): 208. This resembles Bertolt Brecht's famous *Verfremdungseffekt* that he described in the essay "Alienation Effects in Chinese Acting" from 1936.

interesting or critical features in our research topics or objects.[60] This goes for any field where gender, race, age, political or ideological views, etc., can be blinding factors. The solution is to allow a "theoretical pluralism" that can destabilize our perspectives and open the discussions anew.[61] Henriksen emphasizes that questions about normativity have two focal points: towards the material and towards the researcher herself.[62] Of interest in relation to the framework of this book is that Henriksen deals with the distinction between foundationalism and coherentism. Note that normativity plays a crucial role in both approaches but in different ways: "A coherentist approach is one in which we constantly have to articulate the regulating normativities and ask for their implications and relation to other elements of knowledge, while this is not the same case in a foundationalist approach, that more easily assumes the basic normativities as the foundation from which to depart in the ongoing reflections."[63] Theology *can* be illegitimately – or at least unconstructively – normative, but *need not* be so. The solution is to see theology as a part of a larger conversation that negotiates the insights of different perspectives – both past and present.[64] Here the discussion moves to include hermeneutical insights, which are also important points for those who seek to dissolve the demarcation between descriptive and normative features. To establish – and I add, to negotiate – normativity is "a *hermeneutical* enterprise," according to Henriksen.[65] It is not clear whether Henriksen would accept strong normativity as a part of the conversation or only weak normativity, but as representing the position here in 7.2.1.2.2, his vision is clear and understandable.

The issues that Lewis, D'Costa, and Henriksen address differ, but the three have a shared concern with dissolving the alleged distinction between descriptive and normative features. In essence, their view is captured by saying that the claim to be free of normativity is a claim to a fake neutrality. Normativity can be explicit or implicit, but it is always present, and the fruitful way forward is to demand that the normativity be articulated and argued for and then leave it to the ongoing

---

60 Henriksen, 'Researching Theological Normativity', 209.
61 Henriksen, 'Researching Theological Normativity', 209. Henriksen gives the example of "comparative studies," known for example from social anthropology (p. 210).
62 Henriksen, 'Researching Theological Normativity', 212.
63 Henriksen, 'Researching Theological Normativity', 214. Henriksen refers to Van Huyssteen's work here. See also endnote 10 where Henriksen explains his own position in relation to postfoundationalism (p. 219).
64 Henriksen, 'Researching Theological Normativity', 215: "Theological work scrutinizes, probes and gives reasons for what is held to be normative, and suggests (new) proposals and reasons for why a position should be formulated in such and such a way, in order that it consequently can be recognised as normative."
65 Henriksen, 'Researching Theological Normativity', 217, original italics. As he says, "normativity and rationality in theological discourse presuppose and justify each other reciprocally."

negotiation to determine which views are most convincing. Normativity is inevitable and should not be regarded as problematic per se; it is often difficult to handle in a good way, but this merely calls for critical discussion and explication. The question is once again whether these arguments include all kinds of normativity or only the weak normativity that is inevitably a part of all scientific disciplines. Because the figures considered in this section do not make this distinction, I restrain from guessing because what I have aimed at is to identify a view of the entanglement of descriptive and normative features that can open up the discussion in relation to the objection that this chapter is addressing. An assessment is given in the following section (7.2.1.3).

Additionally, as seen from these three representatives – most clearly from Henriksen's text – there are both empirical and hermeneutical challenges associated with a claim of being free of normativity. In relation to systematic theology, it varies which of these are most challenging because it depends on what the topic is, but normativity is a unifying challenge for all science because not even empirical data are pure, since they need interpretation. For this reason, according to the view considered in this section, the heralded epoché of religious-studies' phenomenology – e. g., in the work of Smart – is an illusion. Choice of material/data, of method, of presuppositions, of conversation partners, of research questions, etc., are not pregiven but instead the result of deliberate choices made by the researcher and therefore dependent on normative decisions by the researcher, according to this position.

Basically, I share the point of view expressed in this position and want to articulate it more precisely in the next section. I aim to add some extra perspective to this position in relation to the theoretical framework used in the present book and argue for the legitimacy of strong as well as weak normativity.

7.2.1.3 The Inevitability of Normativity

In this section, I give two reasons why the short definition of normativity given in 7.2.1.1 breaks down. The reason for the construction principle of this chapter is that there is a standard apprehension of the difference between descriptive and normative features in research, which is seen in the figures chosen for 7.2.1.2.1 and 7.2.1.2.2. For this reason, it is reasonable to begin with the standard apprehension before I suggest a more precise explication of what normativity is in research and where the problems for systematic theology might be. Thus, in the following I first present the two objections to the standard view and then propose a more precise understanding of normativity in scientific research.

The first reason for the breakdown of the standard apprehension is that all research implies the normative view that certain types of knowledge are valuable.[66] If we could have something like pure descriptions and these were the ideal scientific practice, it is hard to see good arguments for choosing, for example, life-saving activities over life-damaging activities.[67] Instead of developing new vaccines we could develop new viruses for biochemical warfare. Both would be scientific tasks developed through standard scientific procedures (e. g., the criteria considered in chapters four through six). Instead of developing psychological tools to help people recover from depression, we could develop new tools for breaking them down, which might be useful when interrogating captured terrorists. Without inherent values, both would be uncontroversial scientific tasks. But it seems intuitively right to do life-saving research, and our feelings and values support it.[68]

There are also external factors that guide the research – e. g., private or public funding, and public demand for certain knowledge – but the point is that we often have internal normative reasons for choosing research questions and methods. Even a *"le-savoir-pour-le-savoir"* argument, which is intrinsic for many researchers, is a normative claim for the inherent value of knowledge. Additionally, what are usually called scientific "values" are held up as guiding lights, and these are clearly normative concepts.[69] For this reason, research cannot work in any fruitful way if normativity is not a part of its framework. Scientific values are not central to the discussion here, but it is worth noticing that they lend even more support to the claim of the inevitability of normativity.[70]

The second reason is that there can be no evaluation of research if there is no norm functioning as a standard. When a peer tests a colleague's work, she is looking for consistency, coherence among presuppositions, methods, and results, clarity in style, honest presentation of facts and rendering of deviant positions, and the

---

66 Barker and Kitcher, *Philosophy of Science*, 136–41.
67 See, e. g., Damasio, *The Strange Order of Things*, chapters 1 and 8. This is also seen in many "mission statements" in the scientific community. A representative example is the British Royal Society who in their mission statement writes that their mission is "to recognise, promote, and support excellence in science and to encourage the development and use of science *for the benefit of humanity*." https://royalsociety.org/about-us/mission-priorities/. Italics added.
68 Why is this the case? Neuroscientist Antonio Damasio has developed a model that seeks to explain this that he calls "The Somatic-Marker Hypothesis." This hypothesis explains how cognitive and emotional processes are combined in human activity. "In short, *somatic markers are a special instance of feelings generated from secondary emotions.* Those emotions and feelings *have been connected, by learning, to predicted future outcomes of certain scenarios*." Antonio Damasio, *Descartes' Error*, Revised Edition (London: Vintage, 2006), 174. Original italics.
69 McGrath, *The Territories of Human Reason*, 101–21.
70 See, e. g., Barker and Kitcher, *Philosophy of Science*, 47 and 100.

like. But these are all normative standards for research.[71] And when we talk about "excellence" in research, we do so because we know that science is also scalar and you can do trustworthy and robust science that is boring or paradigmatic, but you can also do science that is though-provoking and ground-breaking. We aim for the second – e. g., as made evident by the prizes and awards that we hand to the most excellent researchers – but why is this so? This is again not intrinsic to science but a norm we rely on.

Both these reasons show that normativity is inevitable in research and that the old apprehension cannot be sustained. John Dewey captures this by saying, "all deliberate, all planned human conduct, personal and collective, seems to be influenced, if not controlled, by estimates of value or worth of ends to be attained […] Human behavior *seems* to be influenced, if not controlled, by considerations such as are expressed in the words 'good-bad', 'right-wrong' 'admirable-hideous', etc."[72] As the discussion of this chapter shows so far, there are good arguments in support of Dewey's view, also in contemporary debates about normativity in research. It is still to be discussed if this only includes weak normativity, but that the old apprehension is compromised has been shown. Before I investigate strong normativity, I briefly consider another philosophical debate that has influenced the discussion of normativity.

In the history of philosophy, normativity has been discussed – implicitly or explicitly – in relation to the so-called "fact/value distinction," for example in the writings of David Hume and Hilary Putnam. The distinction concerns "what is" (fact) versus "what ought to be" (value), which is an ontological distinction often related to ethics.[73] A way to make this distinction is to say that facts come from the senses and values come from private opinions. Hume said that it is fallacious to argue that something *ought* to be the case merely based on the premises of what *is* the case.[74] The debates about these key texts and thinkers are vast and not the topic here, but it is important to notice that much newer philosophy has left this

---

71 Putnam mentions "coherence" and "simplicity" as prevalent "values" that work as "action guiding terms." Cf. Hilary Putnam, 'Beyond the Fact-Value Dichotomy', *Crítica: Revista Hispanoamericana de Filosofía* 14, no. 41 (1982): 7.

72 John Dewey, 'Theory of Valuation', in *The Later Works of John Dewey, 1925–1953*, ed. Jo Ann Boydston, vol. 13: 1938–1939, Collected Works of John Dewey (Carbondale: Southern Illinois University Press, 2008), 192–93.

73 In ethics, G.E. Moore's *Principia Ethica* is the primary text. He called it a "naturalistic fallacy" when someone argues from "what is" to "what ought to be." G.E. Moore, *Principia Ethica* (Cambridge: Cambridge University Press, 1965), 9–10 et passim.

74 David Hume, *A Treatise of Human Nature*, ed. David Fate Norton and Mary J. Norton, A Critical Edition, vol. 1: Texts (Oxford: Clarendon Press, 2007), 293–306.

distinction behind and many have accepted the entanglement of facts and values.[75] This is an example showing that a distinction between the descriptive and the normative cannot be clearly made and that normativity is inevitable in all types of research. As Putnam writes: "without the cognitive values of coherence, simplicity, and instrumental efficacy we have no world and no facts, not even facts about what is so *relative to* what."[76] The question concerns instead what *good* normativity is – in the terminology of this book, whether both weak and strong normativity can be accepted. This I address in the next section in relation to the elaborated articulation of normativity. But before I proceed, I explicate more carefully the distinction between weak and strong normativity that I take to be the real issue between religious studies and systematic theology, and the suggestion is that if these terms – or at least the concern – could be integrated into the debate, we would get a more precise discussion of how to understand, debate, and criticize normativity in research.

Let me begin by clarifying the question. Normativity is an inevitable part of all research if only because of the two arguments just given. A weak normativity can therefore be nothing but unproblematic, because it only accepts that we all have to make choices with regard to research questions, data, methods, etc., and if we seek to avoid this, we cannot even begin our research. All research is executed in some theoretical framework with presuppositions and standards that are weakly normative. The question, then, is whether there is a stronger kind of normativity that is not included with the acceptance of the weak. A methodological naturalist could accept that hers is not a more neutral framework than its alternatives and yet argue that her presuppositions are more easily shared by others than are the presuppositions of the alternatives (e. g., theistic ones). She could say that all she presupposes is that physical and natural entities exist – which probably everybody will accept – but nothing more (as some suggest). A stronger notion of normativity thus entails that we can argue normatively for what is true about supernatural entities,[77] while a

---

[75] See, e. g., Putnam, 'Beyond the Fact-Value Dichotomy', 11. "we should recognize that *all* values, including the cognitive ones, derive their authority from our idea of human flourishing and our idea of reason." The expression "entanglement of fact and value" is taken from Hilary Putnam, *The Collapse of the Fact/Value Dichotomy and Other Essays* (Cambridge: Harvard University Press, 2004), 8.

[76] Putnam, 'Beyond the Fact-Value Dichotomy', 8. Original italics. For a longer treatment, see Hilary Putnam, *Reason, Truth and History* (Cambridge and New York: Cambridge University Press, 1981), chap. 6.

[77] To recapitulate on the terminology here (see 1.2.1). "Supernatural" only refers to entities that are not confined by natural laws (generalizations). "Entity" is here not a synonym for "thing." An entity is a structure that can be distinguished from another structure. A "supernatural entity" is thus a structure that can be distinguished from other structures and is not confined by the natural laws. On "structures," see 3.4.5.1.1.2.

weak normativity only entails arguing for the truth of propositions and theories about natural entities. With this distinction at hand, I can understand religious studies as a discipline that studies religion through the lens of weak normativity while criticizing theology for arguing for religious truths while relying on strong normativity. Systematic theology on the other hand could accept this distinction but seek to argue for the scientific legitimacy of research characterized by strong normativity. The key question here is therefore the following: should strong normative claims about the truth of supernatural entities be excluded from religious studies but accepted in science in general (thus making systematic theology a legitimate scientific discipline), or should strong normative claims be excluded from all kinds of scientific research?

In the next section (7.2.2), I give an argument for the inclusion of strong normativity in research; the argument is in line with the argument presented in chapters four through six, that is, that coherence theory gives us a rational and critical tool for developing and assessing theories that include supernatural entities.

7.2.2 What is Normativity Given the Presuppositions of this Book?

The discussion in this chapter is developed, like the rest of the book, on the basis of the presuppositions introduced in chapter one. With other presuppositions, the question of normativity might not be relevant at all, but here it is focal. In this section, I argue for an integration of strong normativity into scientific work based on the discussion hitherto in this chapter. I argue through three themes: I first discuss the relationship between normativity and truth (7.2.2.1), then I consider whether the concept of strong normativity compromises what Robert Merton called the normative structure of science, often referred to under the acronym "CUDOS" (7.2.2.2), and lastly, I consider whether normativity makes presuppositions and premises immune to revision (7.2.2.3). These three themes touch upon different aspects of what weighs for or against strong normativity, but the argument is that we benefit mostly from accepting – or even embracing – strong normativity in research if our alleged aim for truth is to be more than words.

7.2.2.1 Normativity and Truth

That science aims for truth is a presupposition of this book. But now the question is whether arguments for strong normativity can be included in this scientific quest for truth. According to the old dichotomy discussed in the previous section, the answer seems to be no. Facts are what is, which makes them true (often understood as a correspondence between language and phenomenon), whereas values are subjective opinions that are only personally true (relative to the individual). But much of this traditional way of thinking is contested, also in the present book (7.2.1.2.3). As

Putnam showed, we must move beyond the dichotomy, and as Puntel has shown, we need a more sophisticated account of truth which he explicates under the headline of coherence.[78]

For this reason, strong normativity is not a hindrance to attaining truth. The opposite is the case if we understand normativity as the assertion of what is to be counted as the best theory after a comparison of coherence of the relevant candidates, which must include metaphysical theories about supernatural entities.[79] As William Alston said, to be justified epistemologically means "not being in violation of the norms."[80] For this reason, to follow the norms of a given discipline is to develop a normative theory, and when the theory turns out to be comparatively better than alternatives, that theory is considered the best yet available. And if we have reasons to believe that a theory is momentarily coherent to a large degree and comparatively the strongest, we can consider it true, even if this theory includes reference to supernatural entities.[81]

7.2.2.2 Normativity and CUDOS

In 1942, the sociologist of science, Robert Merton, isolated a (weak) normative structure of science that has since been known under the acronym "CUDOS," which stands for *communism, universalism, disinterestedness, and organized scepticism*.[82] This is the modern "ethos of science": "The ethos of science is that affectively toned complex of values and norms which is held to be binding on the man of science."[83] As the adjective indicates, Merton takes these to be normative, and the point is thus not that there is a conflict between Merton's theory and an insistence on the inevitability of normativity. Rather, the point is to determine whether the account of strong normativity conflicts with Merton's understanding of the normative structure of science. I argue in the negative by saying that even though Merton's labels seem to contradict the explication of strong normativity, Merton's own description of the concept shows that there is no conflict. For *universalism*, he says that

---

78 Puntel, *Wahrheitstheorien in der neueren Philosophie*, 172–204.
79 See, e. g., Puntel, *Structure and Being*, 410.
80 William P. Alston, 'Christian Experience and Christian Belief,' in *Faith and Rationality: Reason and Belief in God*, ed. Alvin Plantinga and Nicholas Wolterstorff (Notre Dame: University of Notre Dame Press, 1983), 114.
81 Nicholas Rescher, 'Truth as Ideal Coherence,' *The Review of Metaphysics* 38, no. 4 (June 1985): 795–806.
82 Robert K. Merton, 'The Normative Structure of Science,' in *The Sociology of Science. Theoretical and Empirical Investigations*, ed. Norman W. Storer (Chicago: The University of Chicago Press, 1973), 267–78.
83 Merton, 'The Normative Structure of Science,' 268–269.

"truth-claims [...] are to be subjected to *preestablished impersonal criteria*," which is closely related to the present book's explication of the criteria for intersubjectivity.[84]

Communism is simply "the nontechnical and extended sense of common ownership of goods [...] The substantive findings of science are a product of social collaboration and are assigned to the community."[85] From this also follows "the imperative for communication of findings."[86]

Disinterestedness is therefore not a psychological state but "a basic institutional element." This means that personal commitments, interests, passions, motives, etc., are legitimate, but as institutions, universities cannot show specific interests. This implies that institutions encourage exact "scrutiny of fellow experts."[87]

The fourth norm, *organized scepticism*, is entangled with the first three. It is both "a methodological and an institutional mandate."[88] The first term (organized) refers to the attitude that no beliefs or opinions are guarded against scrutinization and that every subject is in itself open to investigation: "The scientific investigator does not preserve the cleavage between the sacred and the profane, between that which requires uncritical respect and that which can be objectively analyzed."[89] What this means is that we must not block the way of inquiring – as Charles Peirce said[90] – in such a way that specific questions, themes, or issues are protected from investigation. The second term (scepticism) concerns the possible conflict with other institutions, e. g., religious or political ones, and how science ideally does not descend into ideological interests or power plays.

Merton's four norms are useful guidelines for research, and they also show that weak normativity is a part of all research for good reasons. The question is whether these norms can include strong normativity, and immediately there seems to be no conflict between strong normativity and Merton's own explication of these terms. Strong normativity can accept all of these norms for scientific research. But strong normativity needs to show that revisions can be accepted as parts of strong normative research; this is very important to emphasize given the tentative and fallibilistic nature of the human work we call science. This is the topic of the next section.

---

84 Merton, 'The Normative Structure of Science,' 270.
85 Merton, 'The Normative Structure of Science,' 273.
86 Merton, 'The Normative Structure of Science,' 274.
87 Merton, 'The Normative Structure of Science,' 276.
88 Merton, 'The Normative Structure of Science,' 277.
89 Merton, 'The Normative Structure of Science,' 277–278.
90 Charles Sanders Peirce, '§4. The First Rule of Reason,' in *The Collected Papers, Vol. 1: Principles of Philosophy*, 1931.

7.2.2.3   Normativity and Revision

One concern about embracing strong normativity could be that it makes intersubjective criticism more blurry and it thus becomes more difficult to challenge and revise the presuppositions and premises of research. To give up a sharp dichotomy between descriptive and normative features could be seen as an attempt to provide research with immunity because criticism could be avoided by referring to differences in values or perspectives. It would be very critical if revisions were ruled out, because fallibilism is the proper attitude in research, as I have argued several times. In order for presuppositions and premises not to be subject to invalid immunity, they need to be made explicit and be open to intersubjective criticism. For this reason, I argue that weak normativity is inevitable but at the same time emphasize that normativity can only work properly in close relation with a strong account of intersubjectivity. The same goes for a strong account of normativity. It is more difficult to agree on data, methods, and results here, but it is not impossible, and often it will even be fruitful to integrate discussion between theoretical frameworks, also in fields with strong normativity. The final criterion of coherence, which integrates all the other relevant criteria, can thus work critically also with theories that refer to or explicate supernatural entities. I deepen the defence of a strong account of normativity in the discussion of the second premise (7.3).

7.2.3   Conclusion of Premise 1

To recapitulate: the first premise said that "science cannot be normative in a strong sense." I first discussed the standard apprehension among many religious studies scholars that it is possible to distinguish between descriptive and normative features in research, and this discussion has shown that weak normativity is inevitable in research. And not just inevitable, but a good and necessary condition for doing high-quality research on relevant topics. I then proposed a distinction between weak and strong normativity and engaged in the more open discussion of whether strong normativity should be excluded only from religious studies or from science as such. This clarification of the question shows why the premise is an objection stated against strong normativity and not against weak varieties. I have defended a strong version of normativity as a legitimate part of science and argued that coherence theory is the critical tool that makes it possible to accept strong normativity because it makes it an open, intersubjective, and fallibilistic research program. Thus, Premise 1 fails.

7.3 Premise 2

In this second part of the chapter, I investigate the second premise, which says that "Systematic theology is normative in a strong sense." After the discussion in 7.2, the reader might have the impression that this premise has become irrelevant. But the task still remains to determine whether the strong normativity of systematic theology is problematic or not because even though normativity is inevitable and even a good thing, it does not follow that all kinds of normativity are good or desirable, as I mentioned in 7.2.2.

In this part of the chapter, I therefore deepen the argument for the acceptance of strong normativity in research, and the procedure is as follows: first, I discuss possible problems for strong normativity in systematic theology stated in three claims (7.3.1). Then I map different models for normativity in systematic theology that are parts of the contemporary conversation (7.3.2). This mapping is heuristic in the sense that I isolate various positions to get an overview of a problem that is not in itself the topic of an established discussion (as I also did in chapter six on intersubjectivity, see 6.3.1).[91] Lastly, I discuss how to understand strong normativity in relation to coherence, which is the main theoretical tool of this book (7.3.3), before I draw a conclusion with regard to Premise 2 (7.3.4).

7.3.1 Stating the Problem of Strong Normativity in Three Claims

As argued above, the notion of strong normativity is questionable to many, but I need to investigate more closely what the problem consists in. In the following, I discuss possible problems for a strong normativity stated in three claims. The first claim is that strong normativity becomes a problem when it rests on questionable foundations, especially problematic data (7.3.1.1). The second claim is that strong normativity becomes a problem when there is a claim of truth about supernatural entities (7.3.1.2), which is related to the discussion in 7.2 because truth-claims are a part of all scientific disciplines but claims of truth related to supernatural entities may be questionable. The third claim is that strong normativity becomes a problem when it is based on limited data (7.3.1.3); this is a claim that is related to the selection, interpretation, and assessment of data (as I also discussed in chapter six).

---

[91] Normativity is, of course, discussed widely, but – to my knowledge – not in the sense that it has been the theme of a journal volume or been a part of a "three-views-on-normativity" series or something like that.

7.3.1.1 Strong Normativity Becomes a Problem when it Rests on Questionable Foundations

The issue in this section is to determine whether strong normativity becomes a problem when it rests on questionable foundations, especially related to problematic data. As discussed earlier (3.4.5), systematic theology has a wide variety of sources and there is an open discussion of the relationships among these sources. Which sources are deemed most relevant and which ones have most authority change over time. Since the rise of higher criticism, even many Protestants will say that a doctrine of *sola scriptura* is unhelpful.[92] Others will say that the church tradition seen as a unified entity is not a convincing source because it is so diverse and self-contradictory.[93] Others again will be critical of a too-uncritical reference to reason because they argue that the Enlightenment promotion of pure reason has turned out to be an illusion.[94] And so on. In this context – where I try to isolate general characteristics – I argue that our guide should again be coherence. We must keep updating our theories through critical discussions and compare the strengths of the different proposals with regard to integrating as much data as possible and establishing as many relevant connections among the data as possible.[95]

In addition to the point that strong normativity can become problematic if it rests on questionable foundations, it is critical to see that the question of strong normativity should be asked after the test or the argument has been executed, not as the point of departure (see also 7.2.2.3). As a point of departure, we all share some notions of weak normativity (as Dewey, Damasio, Lewis, etc., argued for), but the strong notion of normativity is so closely related to the notion of truth that it should be seen as pertaining to a goal or a conclusion. Science is also a pragmatic work, and there may be a more organic entanglement of weak and strong normativity in some disciplines, but as a rule of thumb we should restrict strong normativity to conclusions. In relation to systematic theology, it could be a concern that a specific view of the Bible or of church tradition or confessional affiliation assigns a strong normativity (i. e., fixes the conclusion) before the research has begun. It is therefore important to emphasize that research cannot work properly with fixed

---

[92] See, e. g., Wolfhart Pannenberg, *Basic Questions in Theology. Collected Essays, Volume One* (Philadelphia: Fortress, 1968), 1–14 or Pannenberg, *Systematic Theology*, 1:241–43.

[93] Niels Henrik Gregersen, 'Den generøse ortodoksi,' in *Den generøse ortodoksi. Konflikt og kontinuitet i kristendommen* (København: Eksistensen, 2016), 7–49. See also Gregersen, *Teologi og kultur*, 230.

[94] E. g., in the Radical Orthodoxy movement, see especially John Milbank, *Theology and Social Theory: Beyond Secular Reason*, Second Edition (Oxford: Blackwell, 2006) and John Milbank, Catherine Pickstock, and Graham Ward, eds., *Radical Orthodoxy: A New Theology* (London and New York: Routledge, 1998).

[95] Puntel, *Structure and Being*, 408–11.

conclusions, but there has to be an unrestricted openness to research because there will always be more to know plus we can be wrong about what we assume to be established knowledge (the argument for fallibilism). To do research on the basis of coherence is thus to see normativity as pertaining to the goal and not to the point of departure. This distinction can be compared to what I have earlier discussed as the difference between coherence and consensus. Consensus can be an invalid position that impedes critical engagement with established facts because there are social reasons to protect certain views, or it can be a regulative ideal, something we strive for, such that the most coherent theory convinces most researchers and such that there will be an established – but not fixed – consensus after the debate.[96] This can work properly in systematic theology, and it seemingly does in many contexts.[97]

To sum up, questionable foundations, especially related to problematic data, are always important to be aware of and discuss critically, and the best tool for this is to keep revising our theories by upgrading their degrees of coherence. This goes for theories with strong normativity as well.

7.3.1.2 Strong Normativity Becomes a Problem When There is a Claim of Truth concerning Supernatural Entities

The second concern could be that strong normativity in research on religion equals attributing a universal truth value to specific religious content, e. g., a dogmatic system (such as systematic theology 2). If we confine this to systematic theology, a criticism might be to say that systematic theology is primarily concerned with truth but has a static notion of what truth *can* be.[98] For this reason, if normativity is analogous to making truth-claims, research seems to stagnate in inflexible positions. But because it is a presupposition for the present book that science aims for truth, it cannot be the preoccupation with truth in itself that is the problem. So how is truth understood here, and how is "static" as an adjective to be understood?

As I have argued, normativity broadly understood is the claim that the best theory is approximately true (7.1). This refers to the assessment after the hypothesis has been proposed, tested, and compared to relevant alternatives. Such assessment is fallible and open to new scrutinization, but for the time being it is acceptable to claim it as true. Hence, truth in research is the goal and it has been productive to have this goal throughout the history of science. As realism is also a presupposition in the present book, I add that the increasing fine-grainedness of our best theories also raises the degree of the miraculous if they turn out to be wrong (see also 6.3.4).

---

96 See the careful discussion in Puntel, *Wahrheitstheorien in der neueren Philosophie*, 144–64. See also Rescher's excellent account in Rescher, *Pluralism. Against the Demand for Consensus*.
97 Cf. Clayton, *Explanation from Physics to Theology*, 110–11.
98 Schaffalitzky, 'Findes teologisk forskning?', 168–69.

The point is that a theory that is well-proposed, -tested, and -compared and has proven to be superior compared to relevant alternatives needs very convincing arguments against it to alter it. Convincing arguments would here consist either in indicating errors or presenting a more coherent alternative.

It is a central task for systematic theology to explore the truth-claims of Christianity, which include references to supernatural entities.[99] To explore the truth-claims of Christianity is a task that unites systematic theology 1–3. In the context of pluralistic modernity, this task cannot and should not proceed without recognition of the insights and arguments of religious critics.[100] But on the other hand, the pool of data that is the material for systematic theology is also relevant in a human quest for truth. Systematic theology aims for truth, as all science does, and systematic theology 2 is no exception. systematic theology 2 deals with internal questions related to the maximal internal coherency of the Christian faith, and this endeavour borrows its academic validity from the status of systematic theology 3.[101] But the theories developed at the level of systematic theology 2 are also truth-candidates in themselves and should be assessed as such. The exploration of truth that unites systematic theology 1–3 makes systematic theology a more complicated discipline than its critics often note, hence the arguments that say that systematic theology has a specific problem with a fixed notion of truth are not convincing. I discuss this further in the next chapter (see 8.3.3).

That theistic theories include references to supernatural entities, and hence do not fit with naturalistic presuppositions, cannot make them problematic. They become problematic if a naturalistic alternative is clearly more coherent.[102] If this is not the case, to argue for the truth of a coherent theory that includes supernatural entities is not problematic but necessary in order to assess all relevant truth-candidates.

---

99 Pannenberg, *Systematic Theology*, 1:48–61.
100 Pannenberg, *Systematic Theology*, 1:152.
101 This means that if a theistic ontology is a viable truth-candidate we are entitled to work with intra-systematic coherence too.
102 See also the discussion in 4.3.5 and 5.3.4. Note, however, that the problem of a comparison between theism and naturalism appears *not only* in regarding coherence, but also in what counts as data in-between which coherence reigns. Naturalism does exclude a lot of phenomena as data, e. g., the concept of revelation or the notion of God that explains many things in a theistic ontology, so the problem is but also related to comprehensiveness. Naturalism rests on limited data since a specific kind of phenomena are excluded from the beginning on. But this only emphasizes the importance of the work at systematic theology 3 for the development of theories at systematic theology 1 and systematic theology 2.

7.3.1.3 Strong Normativity Becomes a Problem When it is Based on Limited Data

Related to the problem in 7.3.1.2, a critique might be to say that strong normativity becomes a problem when results are based on limited data, i. e., on a narrow selection of sources.[103] If science aims for truth, and systematic theology does so in the religious sphere, why is it that the Bible, the church tradition, the religious experiences of believers, and so on are taken to be of special importance? How do we know that this particular selection of sources will bring us closer to truth? As I have argued earlier, the discussion of relevant sources is important, and it should be an ongoing discussion what status they have. But at the same time, it is important to remember that no one can integrate all relevant data into a unified theory, so every researcher must make selections of data.[104] Thus, it cannot be the selection in itself that is problematic but only a selection that is not argued for or not argued for in a convincing way. Systematic theology does have a presupposition that says that the sources of the Christian tradition are relevant to engage with, but this is not dissimilar from presuppositions about data in other disciplines. Presuppositions are necessary. They should be open to criticism, refinement, and revision, but they are legitimate as a part of a necessary theoretical framework that is indispensable and vital for doing research. This topic is also developed at greater length in the next chapter, on distinct research.

To sum up, the alleged problems of a strong notion of normativity in systematic theology are not convincing, and there are good reasons for accepting theories that include reference to supernatural entities as long as alternatives are not clearly more coherent.

In the next section I investigate three models of normativity for systematic theology that in various ways emphasize aspects of normativity.

7.3.2 Models of normativity for Systematic Theology

In this section, I briefly discuss three models for how normativity is conceived in modern systematic theology, three models that I have constructed through reading the literature. As explained above, it is a mapping that should be seen as heuristic for the conversation and nothing more than that. I have grouped the different approaches and not adopted any known typologies. I have identified three models or approaches, and I discuss them in the following order: first, the

---

103 Schaffalitzky, 'Findes teologisk forskning?', 168–69.
104 See also Henriksen, 'Researching Theological Normativity. Some Critical and Constructive Suggestions,' 217–18.

model that takes normativity in systematic theology to be like the normativity in religious studies (7.3.2.1); second, the model that takes normativity in systematic theology to resemble orthodoxy (7.3.2.2); third, the model that takes normativity in systematic theology to be an impossibility because all theology is contextual and thus relativistic (7.3.2.3). As is clear, these models are ideal types in the Weberian sense so that the chosen figures are exemplifications rather than prototypes.

7.3.2.1 As in Religious Studies

The main thesis here is that systematic theology and religious studies have similar notions of normativity. As I showed in 7.2.1.2.2, it is imperative for several scholars to emphasize the inevitability of weak normativity in the study of religions, theology included. As I understand those scholars, weak normativity is thus neither good nor problematic but simply there as an inevitable part of every theoretical framework and every executed research project. What is important is to transparently declare the presupposed point of view, and when this is done, weak normative claims should be embraced. What the status of strong normativity is according to this position is not easy to identify. This model is seen in the writings of Thomas A. Lewis and Gavin D'Costa, both already examined (7.2.1.2.2).

7.3.2.2 Orthodoxy

The notion of orthodoxy has a long and complicated history.[105] Of course, it is not the goal here to analyse the relationship between normativity and orthodoxy in depth. What I aim to do is point to a criterion for systematic theology that can be understood as a criterion for normativity, i. e., the "criterion of authenticity."[106] If systematic theology is an open investigation of the truth-claims of the Christian faith, how can any results be fixed in advance by symbols or creeds? This model turns the table and says that no systematic theology is done in a historical vacuum, and contemporary theology must compare new findings with results from theological history, so authenticity is seen as a regulative principle and not as a control mechanism. For this reason, only those claims that can be integrated convincingly as parts of authentic Christian faith will be candidates for normative Christian

---

[105] Jörg Baur, 'Orthodoxie, Genese und Struktur,' De Gruyter, accessed 28 June 2021, http://www.degruyter.com/document/database/TRE/entry/tre.25_498_1/html.

[106] Gregersen, *Teologi og kultur*, 236–38. "Here the point of departure must be that theology recognize that new theological propositions that deviate from those of the tradition incur a special burden of legitimation as regards their Christian authenticity." ("Udgangspunktet må her være, at teologien anerkender, at nye teologiske udsagn, der afviger fra traditionen, pådrager sig en særlig legitimationsbyrde, hvad angår deres kristne autenticitet." (Translation MAM)).

theology. This model is seen in conservative theological positions such as evangelicalism, conservative charismatics, classic Eastern orthodoxy, etc., but also in more mainstream modern theology, e. g., that of Niels Henrik Gregersen.[107] I take this model to include both weak and strong forms of normativity.

A challenge, if not a problem, is what Peter L. Berger has called "the heretical imperative."[108] The history of theology is very diverse, and it is not possible to be coherent and to be in alignment with all the main figures. Thus, an additional norm is needed, a criterion for the criterion, which seems to result in an endless regress.[109] Here it is helpful to distinguish between two kinds of authenticity that are at work in systematic theology. (1) There is an unproblematic account of authenticity that we can call "authenticity of meaning." This kind of authenticity is a part of all research because it refers to the definition of the field: what counts as relevant data for the study of theology, physics, biology, or sociology? What should count as relevant data is discussed in all fields, but this is a consequence of the vast amount of data that we seek to investigate, and the consequence is that we need multiple disciplines to make science work in a comprehensive investigation of reality. (2) But there is also a more contested account of authenticity, which we can call "authenticity of truth," which argues for something as *the* true version of Christianity or what is revealed by God. Related to this kind of authenticity, we immediately get the problem of the heretical imperative introduced by Berger. It is not the aim here to discuss the notions of "authenticity of truth" or of the "heretical imperative" but only to identify a second understanding of normativity in systematic theology and a possible problem connected with it. The authenticity of meaning will often resemble weak normativity, while the authenticity of truth will resemble strong normativity.

7.3.2.3   No Normativity—All Theology Is Contextual

A third model that integrates a diverse collection of views and authors claims that strong normativity is an impasse, because all theology is contextual and thus relative in a way that makes strong normative claims impossible (I take them to accept weak normativity). There are many different ways to express this, e. g., in the map of contextual theology described by Stephen Bevans.[110] It is also a focal point for

---

107 See the last footnote, fn. 106.
108 Peter L. Berger, *The Heretical Imperative: Contemporary Possibilities of Religious Affirmation* (New York: Anchor, 1979).
109 John Kaufman, 'Historical Relativism and the Essence of Christianity,' *Studia Theologica. Nordic Journal of Theology* 70, no. 1 (2016): 4–21.
110 Stephen B. Bevans, *Models of Contextual Theology* (Maryknoll: Orbis, 2002).

much newer constructive theology, which includes disparate streams of thought.[111] What is shared is a willingness to deconstruct central elements of the Christian faith, but there is no agreement on what to construct instead. It might, however, be fair to say that the constructions generally have a pragmatic agenda, which is to seek to develop theologies that support the flourishing of human lives.[112] For this reason, the normative element understood as a "criterion of authenticity" is not central because this kind of normativity will be seen as a closed position that cannot embrace the diversity of lived lives and lived religion. Therefore, this position is of course also normative, often with a deliberately activistic touch.[113] It is an open discussion whether this kind of normativity is weak or strong.

These three models for addressing normativity show in sum that a unified model is not at hand in contemporary theology and that any unambiguous dismissal of *the* normative in systematic theology is a hoax. Much more precision is needed if the discussion is to be fruitful. I am interested in developing an account of strong normativity that can be accepted in scientific research, and in the following I therefore explicate strong normativity in relation to coherence, which is presented as the proposal for a solution (7.3.3).

7.3.3 Strong Normativity in Relation to Coherence in Systematic Theology

In this book, coherence is both a tool/a method and a goal/an ideal, and I argue that normativity is also both for systematic theology. Weak normativity is a part of the tool/method as in all other disciplines, and strong normativity is a part of the goal/ideal with systematic theology's aim of developing a coherent theistic ontology.

As a tool, coherence is a heuristic device so that the most comprehensive theory with maximal relevant connectivity between the data in a way that is consistent is counted as the best theory available, and we can use this understanding to keep trying to organize our data in new ways and compare the results in terms of coherency. For this reason, coherence is also the norm, i. e., the most coherent theory is also the best theory available and should be taken as the norm for the field.

Normativity is also a matter of degree from weak to strong, and normativity can be seen as based on the degree of coherence. The more coherent a theory is in comparison with relevant alternatives, the more normative we are allowed to be, which is to say the following: this theory *should* be accepted as (approximately) true.

---

111 Jason A. Wyman Jr., *Constructing Constructive Theology: An Introductory Sketch* (Philadelphia: Fortress, 2017); Marion Grau and Jason Wyman, eds., *What is Constructive Theology? Histories, Methodologies, and Perspectives*, Paperback Edition (London: T&T Clark, 2022).
112 This is a vague and abstract ambition because human flourishing is not an obvious category.
113 See, e. g., Cornel West, *Prophesy Deliverance!* (Louisville: Westminster John Knox Press, 2002).

This should be seen only as a muted conclusion that is relative to future discoveries or better theoretical explications. The point is that because science aims for truth, it is appropriate to classify as true a theory that is shown to be comparatively much better than alternatives. This is a part of the process whereby unconvincing theories are discarded.[114] As I said above, coherence theory does not discriminate between weak and strong normativity so science, too, should not.

But, on the other hand, I do not take normativity to be present to the same degree in all aspects of systematic theology. That means that some aspects of systematic theology may be more or less normative than others, just as falsification works differently in relation to single statements and to whole theories. Systematic theology covers such a large amount of data that normativity can work differently in the different strata of systematic theology. For this reason, it is possible to see a difference in degrees of normativity among systematic theology 1, 2, and 3. And the same goes internally for the different strata. In general, I understand normativity to be strongest in systematic theology 3 and then to be loosened from systematic theology 3 to systematic theology 2 and again from systematic theology 2 to systematic theology 1. But this can only be a very general rule if it is correct that differences can occur among topics in the same stratum.[115] Different theories in systematic theology will be normatively strong in the sense described above, e. g., arguing for truths about supernatural entities. But all kinds of theories in systematic theology are related to one overall supernatural entity (i. e., God) and these theories should not be understood as equally persuasive, i. e., they need not be equally cohesive or equally focal to systematic theology in general. The theory of creation and the theory of eternal (post-mortem) life are not equally cohesive and not equally focal to systematic theology.[116]

Understanding normativity as scalar makes it possible to have a flexible yet useful understanding of the issue. It applies to different materials in different ways, and it allows for fine-grained distinctions at local levels in a discipline. This goes for all scientific disciplines, and systematic theology is not excluded from this. Systematic theology is dependent on the acceptance of strong normativity, but with a robust

---

114 This "survival of the fittest" aspect of scientific progress has been argued for by many, and in a moderate sense I see it as a truism. See, e. g., Popper, *The Logic of Scientific Discovery*, 20.
115 This is applied to systematic theology in the present discussion, but it could be applied to all scientific disciplines because all disciplines have different strata and many different theories at each level with more or less coherence and thus also more or less normativity.
116 Since systematic theology 2 aims at internal coherence and therefore is a kind of holism that matter is tricky.Often, it will be the case that an alteration in one *loci* will effect all the others. What I argue here is therefore only that some girders are more important in the building of systematic theology. God is more important than angels, Jesus is more important than David, Easter is more important than Lent and so on.

account of coherence as the final criterion for truth, this is acceptable as long as theories of systematic theology are open to scrutinization and revision.

7.3.4 Conclusion concerning Premise 2

Premise 2 stated that "Systematic theology is normative in a strong sense," and the investigation of this premise has confirmed it. But because Premise 1 is false (7.2.3), the task for the investigation has been to investigate more precisely what the strong normativity of systematic theology consists in. I have argued that strong normativity is acceptable in research because it works with coherence theory, and I take coherence to be the final criterion for truth. This conclusion is further nuanced by the discussion that differentiated between different applications of normativity at different strata of systematic theology – and also differentiated between topics at the different levels. For this reason, the general conclusion "Systematic theology is normative in a strong sense" has to be qualified in individual instances, and the assessments are not fixed but dynamic, changing as the discussion progresses and new data, new theories, new methods, and new perspectives are brought to the conversation.

7.4 Conclusion

A conclusion follows from the premises, thus the conclusion originally said that "Systematic theology is not a science." But because Premise 1 turned out to be false, the conclusion is false too. Systematic theology cannot be discarded as a scientific discipline just because it is normative, because all sciences are weakly normative, and indeed should be, when we understand weak normativity to mean living up to the standards of some theoretical framework: of following premises, presuppositions, methods, etc., and drawing conclusions from these. And when the conclusions turn out to be comparatively more coherent than relevant alternatives, scientists should count them as true even though this judgment is temporary, relative, and fallible.

The notion of strong normativity is more controversial, but I have argued for the relevance and legitimacy of strong normativity in relation to coherence theory. Further, I have argued that normativity comes in degrees, and for this reason it is applicable to different strata of systematic theology, and at the different strata, it is applicable to different topics in different ways. And this pluralization of the notion is the same in all scientific fields. Systematic theology is *weakly* normative, and should be so, as is the case with other scientific disciplines. Systematic theology is also *strongly* normative and should be so because this is necessary for the investigation of the truth-candidates that this field seeks to assess.

Chapter Eight: Objection 5—Distinct Discipline with Distinct Research

Premise 1. If systematic theology is a distinct scientific discipline, it must do *distinct research* that no other discipline could conduct equally well.
Premise 2. Systematic theology does not do *distinct research* that no other discipline could conduct equally well.
Conclusion. Systematic theology is not a distinct scientific discipline.

8.1 Introduction

As previously, I start this chapter by outlining why it is relevant to discuss the objection expressed by the syllogism above. By now, I have discussed four objections to the present explication of systematic theology, and in all four instances, I have concluded that the objections should be rejected. Let me briefly recapitulate the arguments:

- It is not a good objection that systematic theology has no standard for testing at all because coherence theory is a relevant tool for testing (chapter four).
- Nor is it a good objection that the most common standard for testing – falsification – cannot apply to systematic theology because comparisons of degrees of coherency can work as falsifications (chapter five).
- It is a better objection against systematic theology to claim that there is no agreement on what the testing standard says and that there is thus no proper intersubjectivity. For this reason, there seem to be more problematic aspects connected with this objection than with the previous ones. But because intersubjectivity is (mainly) about clearly stating presuppositions, methods, data, and results – which can then be tested by others even if they do not share the same theoretical framework – the objection is not enough to rule systematic theology out as a scientific discipline (chapter six).
- And as I discussed in the previous chapter, it is not a good objection to say that systematic theology uses a problematic standard of strong normativity because strong normativity, rightly conceived, can be coherent with the central criteria of science (chapter seven).

To sum up: the progress in chapters four through seven has shown that systematic theology is testable, also by falsification, in an intersubjective way, and even when this includes strong normativity. What remains to discuss now is whether what is really defended in chapters four through seven is a systematic theology that is a distinct scientific discipline or whether it is something else such as philosophy or religious studies.

Thus, what I investigate in this chapter, which concerns the last objection to the present understanding of systematic theology that I bring to the scene in this book, is the objection that nothing distinguishes the discipline of systematic theology from other closely related fields. What is implied here is that *either* systematic theology is swallowed up by other disciplines when it does proper science (it is scientific, but not theology) *or* it is illegitimately singular in the sense that its characteristics compromise its scientific status (it is theology, but not science). This fifth objection thus relies on a specific approach to the problem of demarcation,[1] where I seek to determine whether systematic theology is a genuine scientific field in itself or whether its scientific credibility is instead borrowed from neighbouring disciplines. Or, stated in an aphorism: when systematic theology works scientifically, it is not theology, and when systematic theology works theologically, it is not scientific.[2] Against this background, then, the aim and task of this chapter is to determine whether systematic theology is a distinct scientific discipline with distinct research of its own or whether instead we must relocate it within either religious studies or philosophy in order to grant it scientific status.

In the following, I discuss the first premise. The focus is on "distinct research" and a clarification of this expression because this is the central aspect of a "distinct discipline." Thus, I begin with a discussion of what characterizes distinct research (8.2.1), and then I discuss why this criterion is important (8.2.2). The discussion of Premise 1 is short but poignant because the hard questions arise in relation to Premise 2, hence the focus of the discussion is located here, which makes the treatment of Premise 2 comparatively longer. This also implicates that contrary to previous chapters – with chapter seven as a partial exception – I include systematic theology in the discussion of both premises. This choice is also legitimate because the objection discussed here is so closely related to systematic theology since it is not often – to my knowledge – discussed in relation to other university disciplines.[3]

---

[1] As I said in 5.2.2 "the problem of demarcation" is closely related to the name of Karl Popper, who – after his rejection of inductive logic – sought new ways to distinguish between empirical sciences and metaphysical systems.

[2] Cf. Schaffalitzky, 'Findes teologisk forskning?', 164. See also page 174: "Therefore, the philosophical conclusion is for now that theological research exists, but that which is research is not specifically theological and that which is specifically theological is not research." ("Den filosofiske konklusion er derfor for nuværende, at der findes forskning i teologien, men at det, der er forskning, ikke er specifikt teologisk, og det, der er specifikt teologisk, ikke er forskning." (Translation MAM)).

[3] Artistic disciplines might be an exception. In some countries, topics like "creative writing," "musical composition," or "choreography" are parts of university programs even though they are more oriented

8.2 Premise 1

The first premise of the objection says, "If systematic theology is a distinct scientific discipline, it must do *distinct research* that no other discipline could conduct equally well." If this premise is to have any bite to it, the notion of "distinct research" must be explicated precisely. This is the topic of the next section.

8.2.1 What is Distinct Research?

By "distinct research" I refer to something that marks a discipline in contrast to related disciplines. Many disciplines are characterized either by their problem-solving activities – empirical or conceptual – within a specific area[4] or by foundational questions within some defined regional ontology.[5] This taxonomy of disciplines is dynamic, and new disciplines may show up when a new set of problems appears or new discoveries – empirical or theoretical – make new questions urgent.

It is important to note that the concept of "distinct research" does not imply that systematic theology has to be fully distinct in all its aspects and thus could not overlap with other sciences at all. That would be a preposterous requirement for two reasons. First, it would eliminate systematic theology as a field because its theme is not a delimited regional ontology but instead a universal ontology and for this reason it integrates data from many disciplines into its systematizations.[6] To protest the overlapping of such an aim with other disciplines is senseless. But, second, it would also make a specific demand on systematic theology that is not met by other disciplines, because there is much overlap between, e. g., biology and medicine or between sociology and social anthropology (to name just two examples) even though the fields are kept separate for a reason. Hence, potential

---

toward practice than study/research. For this reason, it could be discussed whether these disciplines are situated in the right context. But what I discuss here is the criterion of "distinct research," and to my knowledge, these artistic disciplines do not claim to practice this, and thus they are irrelevant here.

4 Laudan, *Progress and Its Problems*, 11–69.
5 Frederik Stjernfelt, *Diagrammatology. An Investigation on the Borderlines of Phenomenology, Ontology, and Semiotics*, vol. 336, Synthese Library. Studies in Epistemology, Logic, Methodology, and Philosophy of Science (Dordrecht: Springer, 2007), 175–79. The notion of "regional ontology" is taken from Edmund Husserl's *Ideen zu einer reinen Phänomenologie und Phänomenologischen Philosophie, drittes Buch*. In *Diagrammatology*, Stjernfelt combines Husserl's idea with the idea of fallibilistic a priori in the tradition of the Austrian logicians. Cf. Barry Smith, 'In Defense of Extreme (Fallibilistic) Apriorism,' 12, no. 1 (Spring 1996): 179–92.
6 See, e. g., Pannenberg, *Theology and the Philosophy of Science*, 301–26. A Barthian like John Webster has said similar things. See, e. g., his article John Webster, 'What Makes Theology Theological?', *Journal of Analytic Theology* 3 (May 2015): 17–28.

or real overlap should be accepted to some degree. Thus, the point here is instead that there must be *so much* and *so much good* and *enough specific differences* as to legitimize a discipline as its own science. This is the case for biology and sociology as for medicine and social anthropology and should also be the case for systematic theology. This is the reason why the first premise says that (a) a discipline has to do *something* distinct but *not* necessarily *only* something distinct and (b) do this "something" better than other disciplines could do (if they should try to treat the data) and not just equally well. In other words, scientific disciplines refer to clusters of data and because the amount of data is so comprehensive there will inevitably always be overlaps between the disciplines. But every discipline needs a distinct pivot that marks that discipline from the others. Otherwise, it is nothing but a subbranch of other disciplines.

In relation to systematic theology, there are huge overlaps with certain disciplines such as religious studies, philosophy of religion, and general metaphysics (philosophy), and there is no problem with that. The pool of data is so vast that all scientists benefit from a plurality of discourses that can bring forward the best hypotheses and theories for the comparison of their degrees of coherence.[7] And yet, overall, there must be a sufficient number of elements that mark systematic theology as its own discipline (the pivot of the cluster of data). The boundaries may be dynamic and overlapping, but something distinctly theological that is still good research must be identified.[8]

In chapter two, I presented the historical background for this book, and the theme of objection 5 was a central concern for several of the authors discussed there. The context for systematic theology, as I have argued throughout this book, is *public* discourse. In this context, theologians aim to speak about God in a way that is rationally justified; in other words, to do Christian theology as a legitimate scientific discipline (that meets common criteria). An example from chapter two, where this was the main concern, was Anders Nygren from the Lundensian school, who opted for the identification of the "specifically Christian."[9] What he aimed to show was how the structures ("motifs") of Christianity have evolved through history. Hence, Nygren identified his research object to be Christianity as a historical configuration and his task as charting the development of this religion. He rejected normative theology and sought instead to present rigorous objective descriptions. A critical question for this approach is, is this sufficient for showing systematic theology to be a distinct research discipline? I think not. It is not enough to identify how

---

7 Puntel, *Structure and Being*, 43. See also Jan-Olav Henriksen, 'Researching Theological Normativity. Some Critical and Constructive Suggestions,' *Studia Theologica. Nordic Journal of Theology* 60, no. 2 (2006): 210.

8 Gregersen, *Teologi og kultur*, 236–38.

9 Nygren, *Meaning and Method*, 11–12.

different religions have formulated answers to basic questions about life because this is already the task of parts of religious studies. The amount of data in the Christian tradition makes it economical to isolate this religion, and the cultural heritage in the West makes it intuitive to choose Christianity if the curriculum only makes room for the study of one religion. But these external reasons are not the object of discussion here because I look for internal reasons. And as I show in 8.3.3.1, there is an intrinsic difference between systematic theology and religious studies that cannot be ignored if systematic theology is to meet the criterion of distinct research that I investigate here.

In the next section I discuss why the criterion of distinct research is important. It is not usually as clearly thematized in discussions about religious studies and systematic theology and philosophy and systematic theology as I do it here, and I thus need to clarify why I find it important.

8.2.2 Why is the Criterion of Distinct Research Important?

The question of this section, why the criterion of "distinct research" is important, was briefly touched upon in the introduction (8.1). But the remarks there did not fully address the question, and it therefore needs to be addressed more thoroughly now. I divide the response to the question into two subquestions: What is the contribution of this criterion? And which concerns does it answer?

The contribution is mainly – as said in 8.1 – that it works as a demarcation criterion in a qualified sense. I shall now amplify the argument for this view. To know what disciplines (and all that comes along with them such as presuppositions, methods, perspectives, implications, etc.) are genuinely scientific is very important. It is important, for example, because the sciences have a focal democratic role to play in our societies, and because enormous amounts of money go to research, and we need to know what in the various fields provide us value for money. But it is also intrinsically important because science aims for truth and if a discipline is not genuine, we have no good reason to think that it contributes to this aim of science. It should be noted that demarcation lines are not static but dynamic because convincing arguments for or against any discipline's questions, methods, presuppositions, relevance, etc., can change the status of the discipline. These concepts must be explicated precisely to have meaning, but the idea should be clear: demarcation is a useful and necessary tool for the organization of scientific research.

As for the concerns, it should be said that there are institutional questions that play a significant role in the contemporary discussion, but even though these questions are relevant and urgent, I shall not address them here. These questions concern for example (a) whether theology should have its own faculty (as is still the case in many places in Western Europe even though the arrangement is in decline); (b) if theology is not to have its own faculty, how should it be organized in relation to religious studies? There are many questions concerning matriculation and the job market. These are closely connected, but there are political possibilities for supporting even small disciplines and making the relevant job market more attractive. Systematic theology aims at being a scientific discipline, but the main job market is still the church, and it is an open question what influence the church should have on the curriculum of theology.[10]

Another concern of this criterion is that most people want an efficient and relevant university and hence we need promising fields of study. For this reason, if systematic theology wants to be a part of the modern research university, it should be a distinct scientific discipline – at least in distinctive parts – so that it cannot be relocated into departments of religious studies or philosophy. What does this mean? A field is adequately distinct when there is a sufficient amount of data that marks it off. It is thus the data – not the methods – that designate a discipline. It is the amount of *relevant* data that establishes the legitimacy of each distinct field of research so that the pivot of the cluster of data is clarified and thematized. "Relevant" is a slippery term and not easy to make more precise, but it indicates that even though my garden, for example, represents a vast amount of data and would be very demanding to investigate in depth, there are not enough *relevant* data to create the discipline of "Mike's garden studies" because there is nothing *distinctive* in my garden that marks it off and if someone found it important to investigate my garden, it should be a part of some already established discipline. But the question is not, however, whether it is possible to reduce one field of study to another; this is always possible because we can call everything "philosophy." The question is instead whether there are sufficiently distinct relevant data to make it a research area in its own right. Because we see an accumulation of relevant data every day, we could end up with a plethora of disciplines – but this will of course be regulated by external factors such as financing/funding, matriculation, job markets, demand for certain knowledge, etc. But the point is that the external-regulating factors are secondary when it comes to the assessment of the discipline's scientific status and the possibility in principle of establishing a relevant discipline. This is established with reference to the amount of relevant data.

---

10 I will not engage in this important discussion here, but I refer to the growing amount of secondary literature, which presents a qualified discussion. See, e. g., Volf and Croasmun, *For the Life of the World* for an engaging discussion of these topics. David H. Kelsey, *To Understand God Truly. What's Theological About A Theological School* (Louisville: Westminster John Knox Press, 1992) and David H. Kelsey, *Between Athens and Berlin. The Theological Education Debate* (Eugene: Wipf & Stock, 1993) are older but also relevant. For newer studies see, e. g., Higton, *A Theology of Higher Education*; D'Costa, *Theology in the Public Square. Church, Academy and Nation*; Ford, *The Future of Christian Theology*; David Ford et al., eds., *Fields of Faith: Theology and Religious Studies for the Twenty-First Century* (Cambridge and New York: Cambridge University Press, 2005).

I will then ask in relation to this, is the criterion of distinct research still important? Is it still important to ask for the distinctive marks of a discipline and to know what "distinct research" a discipline conducts? I argue it is, and the reason is that science develops, and promising fields of studies can turn out to degenerate and cease to exist. What counts as "distinct research" today may be discarded tomorrow, and there thus needs to be a continuous reflection concerning which disciplines are robust and promising.

In the case of systematic theology, it is possible that the accumulation of results within the study of religion – e. g., from critics of religion – makes it difficult for systematic theology to have enough distinct *relevant* data to be a discipline on its own. For example, if Kant's distinction between *für uns* and *an sich* is applied, theology is only a description of human responses to the divine and not a direct engagement with the object of faith itself, i. e., God.[11] It then becomes more difficult to see how it is a discipline distinct from religious studies.[12] The notion of "distinct relevant" data is of course controversial because relevance comes in degrees and is closely connected to contexts. But the point here would be that systematic theology cannot exclusively point to ecclesiastical relevance but must have scientific relevance, and be able to identify what its scientific relevance is. The overall argument of the present book – from the development of an understanding of systematic theology as stratified to a response to the most critical objections – is in itself an identification of what the scientific relevance of systematic theology could be understood to be.

8.2.3   Conclusion on Premise 1

"Distinct research" is the distinctive marks that distinguish a discipline from other disciplines in relation to specific data. Distinct research must be robust and promising research concerning these data with the goal of contributing to the overall aim of science, which is to uncover truth. For both external and internal reasons it is important to be able to mark what makes a specific discipline distinct, because this criterion works as a demarcation line between legitimate and illegitimate research. Thus, Premise 1 is upheld.

---

11 Compare the different visions of, e. g., Pannenberg and Webster: Pannenberg, *Systematic Theology*, 1:63–73; Webster, 'What Makes Theology Theological?' For a seminal study of this Kantian problem, see Clayton, *The Problem of God in Modern Thought*.
12 Cf. Ford, *The Future of Christian Theology*, 148–67.

8.3 Premise 2

The second premise says, "Systematic theology does not do *distinct research* that no other discipline could conduct equally well." In other words, the premise claims that either systematic theology is not distinct, or it is not scientific.

On the one hand it should be said that if systematic theology is *not distinct*, that does not entail that what theologians do is unscientific but only that their work could be fully integrated into other fields of study. If that were the case, there would only be external reasons to preserve theology as its own discipline, e. g., historical, cultural, or job-related reasons. Even though these are legitimate – maybe even necessary – reasons, they are not sufficient to establish the scientific status of theology, which cannot be jettisoned as a focal part of arguing for the existence of theology in a research university.[13] On the other hand it goes without saying that if theology is *not scientific*, it is not a legitimate part of any research university.[14] If theology is not scientific, that is because it includes sufficiently many topics, methods, presuppositions, etc., that cannot meet the standard criteria for science. The notion "sufficiently many" is deliberately flexible because it is still unclarified in contemporary discourse how much is sufficient, and maybe it is impossible to generalize. Systematic theology is a complicated case because many would recognize that theology is methodologically eclectic with an enormous variation of addressed topics and data – organized, assessed, and discussed on the basis of specific presuppositions.[15] Thus, it is not easy to determine whether there are sufficient deviations from standard approaches to make it unscientific.

I start this investigation of Premise 2 by briefly outlining what the general problem of this premise is (8.3.1). In 8.3.2, I discuss four supposed problems for systematic theology as a distinct yet scientific field: that systematic theology cannot demarcate its object of study (8.3.2.1); that systematic theology cannot identify its methods because of the first problem (8.3.2.2); that systematic theology cannot explain, only

---

13 This way of arguing has been important at least since Schleiermacher's influential book *Kurze Darstellung des Theologischen Studiums/Brief Outline of the Study of Theology* from 1811/1830. In more recent debate, it is a key part of, e. g., Gijsbert van den Brink's defense of theology (though his argument is broader than Schleiermacher's). See Gijsbert van den Brink, 'How Theology Stopped Being Regina Scientiarum – and How Its Story Continues,' *Studies in Christian Ethics* 32, no. 4 (2019): 442–54.

14 Which, of course, does not make it unvaluable, only unscientific, which is not the same thing, as I said in the introduction.

15 This is not unique to systematic theology. A huge mapping of humanistic research in Denmark has documented a widespread eclecticism in methods and concerns. My impression is that this is shared in almost all Western European academic contexts. See David Budtz Pedersen and Frederik Stjernfelt, eds., *Kortlægning af dansk humanistisk forskning* (Copenhagen: Hans Reitzels Forlag, 2016), 90.

describe (8.3.2.3); and that systematic theology builds on a weak foundation of evidence (8.3.2.4). After these problems have been addressed, I can proceed to discuss what the distinctive marks of systematic theology are (8.3.3). This is best done in comparison with other fields of study, so I compare systematic theology with religious studies (8.3.3.1) and philosophy (8.3.3.2). The conclusion is that systematic theology can identify the marks that make it a distinctive discipline, and that systematic theology is able to show that the investigation of this distinct area meets standard criteria for research. Premise 2 thus fails (8.4).

8.3.1 What is the General Problem?

The objection that theology does not do distinct research is not new but has been recurrent in academic history. At least since Schleiermacher's defence of academic theology, it has been crucial for systematic theology to argue for its distinct yet scientific character.[16] I chapter two, I gave the historical background for this book and much of the Swedish debate discussed there hovered around the accusation that theology could not be distinct and still scientific. In the debate book *Tro och vetande* [Faith and Knowledge], philosopher Ingemar Hedenius accused theology of being an ideology that postulated many things without a shred of evidence.[17] Hedenius argued that theologians hid their empty claims behind various postulates and were incapable of doing scientific research on intersubjective ground. When theologians did something scientific, it was not theology. In newer debates, the objection from lack of distinct research has also been pointed to. Philosopher Caroline Schaffalitzky, for example, addresses the question whether *distinct* theological research exists, and then says, "[i]t should be mentioned right away that most of the research conducted at the theological departments in the university escape these objections – namely the research that might as well be conducted by other disciplines [...] The question is therefore not just if there exist areas inside theology where good research takes place; it can be further specified to whether *specific theological* good research can exist – i. e., good research that might not just as well be conducted outside theology."[18] The same critique is articulated by Jens-André

---

16 The context shifted with the foundation of the University of Berlin around 1810. systematic theology was already discussed as a scientific discipline when the University of Paris was founded around 1200, but then it was an ecclesiastical critique. From 1200 to 1810 the main critics of academic theology came from inside the church. Cf. introduction to chapter two.
17 Ingemar Hedenius, *Tro och vetande* (Stockholm: Albert Bonniers Förlag, 1950), 53.
18 Schaffalitzky, 'Findes teologisk forskning?', 164. "Det skal dog med det samme nævnes, at store dele af den forskning som produceres ved universiteternes teologiske afdelinger, uden videre går fri af disse indvendinger – nemlig den forskning, der lige så vel kunne være udført ved andre fagområder [...] Spørgsmålet her er derfor ikke kun, om der findes områder inden for teologien, hvor der foregår god forskning, men kan præciseres yderligere til, hvorvidt der kan findes *specifik teologisk* god forskning

P. Herbener. After criticizing Danish academic theologians for being normative, faith-producing, and religious agents, he writes, "[f]urthermore, several academic theologians work along the same lines as humanists in general and there are numerous examples of splendid research and teaching within Danish academic theology past and present. Obviously, my criticism does not concern this line of work, which is important to point out."[19] According to Herbener, the only legitimate approach is a naturalistic one that treats all aspects of religion as human activities (see further in 7.2.1.2.1). The personal convictions of the researcher are unimportant: "In other words, when most scholars of religions study religion as a human phenomenon, it is not necessarily because they deny the existence of a metaphysical phenomenology, but because it cannot be subjected to academic examination whether it is in terms of verification or falsification."[20] In this way, Herbener's critique explicitly points to legitimate and illegitimate presuppositions for studying religion, a discussion that Schaffalitzky does not address.

The different formulations of the objection have been articulated in specific contexts of critical debate. Their polemical nature is therefore intentionally uncompromising and pushed to the extreme, and the scattered softening of the critique can be seen as academic nuances to a one-sided critique. But still, the general problem with systematic theology for the critics is clear: Theologians do research, but this is not theological, and when they do something else, that "something" is not research but theology (ideology, preaching, religious production, moralizing, etc.). The general critique needs further explication before I can determine whether Premise 2 stands. In the following, I therefore isolate more specific problems from these general criticisms and then discuss possible answers to these supposed problems.

8.3.2 Supposed Problems for systematic theology as Distinct Research

Because systematic theology is a very large field with a long history, it contains a vast amount of data, and it is therefore possible to think of all sorts of problems for defending systematic theology as distinct research. Nevertheless, I have identified four problems that supposedly could compromise the notion of systematic theology as distinct research, and I argue that these four problems more than anything else are the tender spots for systematic theology. I discuss them one by one in the following, starting with the problem that systematic theology cannot identify its object of study (8.3.2.1), proceeding to the problem that systematic theology cannot identify its methods because of the first problem (8.3.2.2), before I come to the third problem,

---

– dvs. god forskning som ikke lige så godt kunne finde sted uden for teologien" (translation MAM, original italics).

19 Herbener, 'The Study and Making of Christian Religion in Danish Academic Theology,' 215.
20 Herbener, 'The Study and Making of Christian Religion in Danish Academic Theology,' 211.

which is that systematic theology cannot explain, only describe, which is a specific objection against systematic theology 1 (8.3.2.3), and end with the problem that systematic theology builds on a weak foundation of evidence (8.3.2.4). If systematic theology can adequately deal with these supposed problems, it has made a solid case for itself as distinct research. What is left then is to identify precisely what distinguishes systematic theology from religious studies and philosophy; this task will be confronted in 8.3.3.

8.3.2.1 Systematic Theology Cannot Identify its Object of Study

The first supposed problem is that systematic theology is unable to identify its object of study, which includes the notion of God. More than any other theme in systematic theology, the notion of God has become problematic since the time of Kant.[21] Today, of course, there is no "*the* notion of God" but several such notions, and this can often be helpful to clarify because critics of systematic theology can sometimes oversimplify when they talk about the notion of God.[22] When they do so, a more careful and precise explication of the term can raise the level of discussion.[23] When I read the literature against systematic theology as an academic discipline, authors do not take great pains to clarify what precisely they mean when they talk of "God," but roughly they seem to refer to something like classical theism, which they argue cannot discuss God in a scientific way.[24] But what is, more precisely, the problem with "God" in scientific terms? Why is it supposed to be a problem to do distinct research here?

---

21 Cf. Clayton, *The Problem of God in Modern Thought*, 25. "The Kantian challenge to God-language represents the most serious threat to theology in the modern era." Clayton embraces Kant's philosophy while others try to criticize it. Valuable attempts are, for example, Andrew Chignell, '"As Kant Has Shown." Analytic Theology and the Critical Philosophy,' in *Analytic Theology: New Essays in the Philosophy of Theology*, ed. Oliver Crisp and Michael C. Rea (Oxford: Oxford University Press, 2011); Nicholas Wolterstorff, 'Is It Possible and Desirable for Theologians to Recover from Kant?', in *Inquiring about God*, ed. Terence Cuneo (Cambridge: Cambridge University Press, 2010), 35–55.

22 This is, for example, a central counterargument against the "New Atheism" of Richard Dawkins, Sam Harris, Christopher Hitchens and the like. See, e. g., Alvin Plantinga, 'The Dawkins Confusion: Naturalism "Ad Absurdum" A Review of Richard Dawkins's The God Delusion,' in *God Is Great, God Is Good. Why Believing in God Is Reasonable and Responsible*, ed. William Lane Craig and Chad Meister (Downers Grove: IVP, 2009), 247–58.

23 E. g., attempted in James Porter Moreland and William Lane Craig, *Philosophical Foundations for a Christian Worldview*, Second Edition (Downers Grove: IVP Academic, 2017), 510–39 or by Richard Swinburne in Swinburne, *The Coherence of Theism*.

24 Herbener is a representative example here, cf. Herbener, 'The Study and Making of Christian Religion in Danish Academic Theology.'

Chapter Eight: Objection 5—Distinct Discipline with Distinct Research

First, many theologians agree that we cannot talk directly about God. Rudolf Bultmann famously refused to talk *about* God,[25] and there are many heirs to this point of view. The Danish theologian and historian of religion Anders Klostergaard Petersen says, "[i]n recognition of its university status, a future theological education must abandon any claim to speak about God in an ontological way. Within the limits of human experience – and they, after all, define the university – there is no ontological access to talking about God. As an academic discipline theology must be content to talk about Christian religion and its epistemic and social consequences."[26] This view is also expressed in Niels Henrik Gregersen's post-doctoral thesis (habilitation): "First, theology has to abandon its pretention to talk directly about God himself."[27] Instead, theology must talk indirectly about God through the interpretations of human existence and experience.[28] These are just two examples of a prevalent tendency among theologians to discard direct God-talk and replace it with something else. That this is done to save theology as a reliable research discipline is often explicit.

Second, if I compare the notion of God with other data in science, we may get a better impression of the problem. As said above in the introduction, the method has to match the data, but there seems to be an inherent problem with the notion of God that does not exclusively emerge from God's non-empirical nature but also from the character of God's nature. This becomes evident when we compare God with two other types of research objects.

- (A) Sometimes the research object is free observable agents (e. g., humans). Humans are complicated research objects because they are undetermined and not bounded by lawlike behaviour. But because they are material entities, we can observe their behaviour and suggest theories, models, concepts, etc., for

---

25 "If you understand talk 'of God' as talk '*about God*' then that kind of talk makes no sense at all." ("Versteht man unter 'von Gott' reden '*über Gott*' reden, so hat solches Reden überhaupt keinen Sinn" (translation MAM)). Bultmann, *Glauben und Verstehen*, 1:26.
26 Anders Klostergaard Petersen, 'Teologi 2010,' *Fønix* 23, no. 3 (1999): 138–43. Quoted from Herbener, 'The Study and Making of Christian Religion in Danish Academic Theology,' 214. Herbener's article, from which I have quoted several times, is a shorted version of a Danish article that contains multiple interesting examples of the "production of Christianity" ["kristendomsproduktion"] by Danish university theologians. See Jens-André P. Herbener, 'Eksempler på kristendomsproduktion og sandhedsspørgsmål i dansk universitetsteologi,' *Chaos: Skandinavisk Tidsskrift for Religionshistoriske Studier* 53 (2010): 49–78.
27 Gregersen, *Teologi og kultur*, 234. "For det første må teologien opgive sin prætention om at tale direkte om Gud selv." (Translation MAM, italics removed)
28 Gregersen, *Teologi og kultur*, 234. This is similar to how Pannenberg describes the task in his *Systematic Theology*, 1:63–73.

their individual and collective behaviour. Humans can also articulate their experiences, feelings, and thoughts in written or oral records, and these productions can be studied in various ways. This is the complex topic for disciplines like sociology, psychology, ethnography, linguistics, and different kinds of "studies" (gender, cultural, migrant, etc.) among many others.

- (B) Sometimes the research object is unobservable but has regular effects. This is often the case in the natural sciences. Gravity, other forces, atoms, some evolutionary mechanisms, and so on are all established topics in physics and biology even though they are unobserved. Yet their effects have been recognized so often and with so much precision that their effects has been called "regular" or even "lawlike."[29]
- (C) The question is now whether a research object can be a *free unobservable agent*, given that *free* and *unobservable* are two necessary concepts in relation to the notion of God in Christianity. God is free and therefore undetermined and cannot be predicted, but at the same time unobservable by humans.

The possibility of research in relation to (A) is that these agents can be observed but not predicted (because they are free). In relation to the second group, (B) are not observables, but can be predicted (because of regular effects) and for this reason they can be studied by means of well-described observations. But with the third (C), we have neither observability nor prediction and this seems to leave us with a problematic research object.

As discussed earlier (chapter five), Pannenberg's solution to this problem has been very influential. His idea is to agree that God can be neither observed nor predicted, but also that it is possible to detect God's influences on reality through the effects of God's actions.[30] These detections are of course no more than plausibilities and cannot be definitively falsified or verified before the eschatological consummation.[31]

---

[29] The question of natural "laws" is complicated and much debated. See section 4.2.3.1, footnote 53 for considerations on terminology.

[30] Niels Henrik Gregersen, 'Introduction. Wolfhart Pannenberg's Contributions to Theology and Science,' in *The Historicity of Nature. Essays on Science and Theology* (West Conshohocken: Templeton Foundation Press, 2008), xiv.

[31] Pannenberg, *Systematic Theology*, 1:55. Cf. Paul O'Callaghan, 'Whose Future? Pannenberg's Eschatological Verification of Theological Truth,' *Irish Theological Quarterly* 66 (2001): 34. Pannenberg's view seems to be adopted from Søren Kierkegaard, who argued against Hegel's holism by pointing to the unfinished history of the world. Only after history has ended will we be able to judge our philosophical systems. A difference is that Pannenberg acknowledges the need for a provisional decision between the views of the ultimate, a view with which I concur. See Pannenberg, *Theology and the Philosophy of Science*, 343, "Nevertheless, since assumptions about reality as a whole are unavoidable for the lives of men in the present, it is necessary here and now to work out criteria which will make possible at least a provisional decision between them."

But Pannenberg's point is that if God exists, this is the best way to treat the hypothesis scientifically, and there are no good convincing arguments against this endeavour.[32]

A different suggestion would be on the one hand to recognize the difficulties a free unobservable agent entails for research, but on the other hand to suggest a preliminary understanding of "God" as nothing more and nothing less than a way to structure totality.[33] Different theoretical proposals could explicate the coherence of such understandings and assess the possible scope of more precise articulations of theology.[34] This is another way to talk of the trajectory from systematic theology 3 to systematic theology 2. A demarcation of the absolute is not possible as a delimitation (of a regional ontology) but is possible as a thematization through the research questions of systematic theology 3.

8.3.2.2 Systematic Theology Cannot Identify its Methods Because of the First Problem

This second problem is closely related to the problem of identifying God as a research object. If God is a free unobservable agent, there seem to be no good methods for studying God. In 8.3.2.1, I pointed to the view, which sees God as a possible term for the structuring of totality and hereby the relationship between the absolute and the contingent. But more needs to be said about method, and that is the aim here. It is important to be able to identify applied methods for the sake of transparency and intersubjective criticism, and systematic theology is not exempted from this demand. But maybe the supposed problem of this subsection rests on a too-narrow understanding of methods and experimentation. I give four arguments that invert the problem and make a case for the study of God even as a free unobservable agent: that research is the investigation of hypotheses (8.3.2.2.1), that research can make use of thought experiments (8.3.2.2.2), that research reflects upon practices (8.3.2.2.3), and that research uses conceptual analysis and hypothetico-deductive methods as methods in ontology (8.3.2.2.4).

8.3.2.2.1 Research Is the Investigation of Hypotheses

A short but poignant definition of research is that it is the systematic investigation of hypotheses. The hypotheses must be stated clearly and transparently, and the investigation must be done with clearly stated methods so other researchers can repeat the investigation afterwards. When, e. g., Wolfhart Pannenberg states that for systematic theology the statements about the Christian God are hypotheses, is this

---

32 Pannenberg, *The Historicity of Nature. Essays on Science and Theology*, 21.
33 Cf. Puntel, *Structure and Being*, 441–60; Puntel, *Being and God*, 145–282.
34 What Puntel calls "the metaphysical basis for a theory of God," *Structure and Being*, 447 (italics removed).

then a convincing claim?[35] I argue that it is. Pannenberg's hypothesis is that God is "the all-determining reality," and he presents the methodology to test this claim as follows: "It follows that assertions about God and his actions or revelation cannot be directly verified against their object. This does not, however, mean that they cannot be verified at all. It is, after all, possible to test assertions by their implications."[36] This is not unique to theology, as Pannenberg notes, because historical science and parts of the natural sciences also study implications.[37] Studying the implications is necessary if God is to be more than a useful fiction. Under the auspices of Kantian philosophy (the distinction between *Ding an sich* and *Erscheinungen*), Gordon D. Kaufman has presented a theology that is stripped of empirical implications because God is reduced to a useful fiction in human imagination.[38] If we want to avoid this approach as the only legitimate one for systematic theology, studying the possible implications of the doctrines is a useful and relevant way to assess the truth-candidates of Christian theology.[39] In this way, systematic theology has (at least) a double method that is relevant for studying a free unobservable agent: coherence theory and observation of empirical implications. This is enough to provide a solution to the supposed problem of this subsection.

8.3.2.2.2   Research Can Use Thought Experiments

As I have discussed above (3.4.4.1), thought experiments are valid and useful in research.[40] Often, they bring about new insights and new pathways for research.[41] In systematic theology, thought experiments are useful tools to discuss possible articulations of statements concerning a free unobservable agent. Coherence theory is a helpful tool to organize the results from these thought experiments, and it is an instrument to falsify failed suggestions. Those theories that pass the coherence test should be seen as truth-candidates for further investigation. Because I have already

---

35 Pannenberg, *Systematic Theology*, 1:56.
36 Pannenberg, *Theology and the Philosophy of Science*, 332.
37 Pannenberg, *Theology and the Philosophy of Science*, 332.
38 See, e. g., Kaufman, *An Essay on Theological Method* or Gordon D. Kaufman, *God the Problem* (Cambridge: Harvard University Press, 1972).
39 I agree with Pannenberg here, when he writes, "[r]eligious language can be regarded as cognitive in practice only if the reality it asserts is accessible independently of it." Pannenberg, *Theology and the Philosophy of Science*, 328. For this reason, the religious semantics of Kaufman is insufficient for systematic theology.
40 See further, Chris Daly, *Introduction to Philosophical Methods* (Peterborough: Broadview Press, 2010), 101–30.
41 As I have mentioned before, Gijsbert van den Brink's *Reformed Theology and Evolutionary Theory* is a book-length attempt to solve the following thought experiment: What are the implications for classical reformed theology if evolutionary theory is correct? Often, the thought experiments are not so explicitly stated, but this is a clear and helpful example of the relevance of this approach.

given a case for the use of thought experiments as sources in systematic theology, I shall not repeat the arguments here. What is important is only to draw attention to this resource once again to remind us that systematic theology has sources and tools to compensate for a difficult research object.

8.3.2.2.3 Research Reflects Upon Practices

When scholars of religion take a deliberative naturalistic stance and an etic perspective on religious experiences – with the ambition of not favour the believer's own interpretation – some theologians will argue that it is legitimate and relevant to reflect upon the question, "What if these experiences are genuine?" We have literally millions of testimonies of encounters with the divine, and it is a demanding task to clarify how to investigate these testimonies.[42] What some have called the "practice turn" of systematic theology with scholars such as Natalie Wigg-Stevenson, Nancy Ammerman, Jeff Astley, and Meredith B. McGuire[43] is an attempt to take these experiences as systematic data that should influence the theoretical suggestions in systematic theology. This is a way of making the data of systematic theology 1 relevant to systematic theology 2(and possibly also systematic theology 3) , and there are well-described methods for this practice in the literature. The idea here is that this is all well and good if the scientific status of systematic theology 3 is established. If I presuppose this status here, there is a legitimate, clear, and transparent relation between data and method regarding religious experiences in systematic theology.

8.3.2.2.4 Research Uses Conceptual Analysis and the Hypothetico-Deductive Method

Hardly any theologians refer to God as an empirical object (see also 8.3.2.4).[44] Instead they use other tools to investigate God as a free unobservable agent. I have already pointed to the study of indirect implications as an influential procedure in the tradition of Pannenberg. There are two other notions prevalent in general research that are usefully applied in systematic theology as well.

---

42 Brink, *Philosophy of Science for Theologians*, 162.
43 For a recent overview of this emerging field, see Geir Afdal, 'Two Concepts of Practice and Theology,' *Studia Theologica. Nordic Journal of Theology* 75, no. 1 (2021): 6–29.
44 It would even contradict the notion of God in the Christian tradition to claim otherwise, cf. Pannenberg, *Theology and the Philosophy of Science*, 331–32. Mormons do, of course, but then we have the question of authenticity once again, because it would be controversial for some to say that Mormons are authentic Christians (see further 3.2.1).

The first is conceptual analysis,[45] which concerns the explication of a concept with the highest attainable level of detail and precision.[46] It is a demanding and complex task, but to clarify the concepts used in systematic theology is a central activity, an activity that is shared with much work done in analytic philosophy.[47]

The second is the hypothetico-deductive method that I assessed in 5.2.7. There are different versions of this method, but the general idea is closely related to Pannenberg's rendering: Formulate a hypothesis and deduce the expected implications and then determine whether the observed phenomena match the prediction. After this, we know whether the hypothesis is falsified or still a viable option, i.e., a truth-candidate.

The point here is that both approaches – conceptual analysis and the hypothetico-deductive method – are prevalent and accepted methods in general scientific discourse and they both work well with systematic theology and the notion of God as a free, unobservable agent.

8.3.2.3 Systematic Theology Cannot Explain, Only Describe (Systematic Theology 1)

A supposed problem for systematic theology in relation to the objection that it cannot conduct distinct research is that systematic theology cannot *explain* the religious behaviours of believers but only *describe* what they do and what they believe and assess the logical strength of these practices and beliefs (systematic theology 1). This is somewhat surprising considering the inverted accusation in relation to the normative/descriptive debate. But what is intended here is to criticize systematic theology for being too motivated for presenting theological interpretations to consider alternative (more critical) explanations – e.g., economic, psychological, cognitive – therefore leaving these perspectives more or less out.[48] In other words, the more critical or negative explanations of religious behaviour are left out, and for this reason the theological explications are regarded as selective, biased, and uncritical.

I have three responses to this criticism: (1) Irrespective of the validity of this criticism, it is legitimate to demand more than mere descriptions. It is essential that the work at systematic theology 1 not only state but also argue for the concerns, motives, interests, etc., that believers might have in connection with different beliefs

---

45 Of course, this is an umbrella term covering different approaches. For a useful overview, see Milos Kosterec, 'Methods of Conceptual Analysis,' *Filozofia* 71, no. 3 (2016): 220–30.
46 See Puntel, *Grundlagen einer Theorie der Wahrheit*, 67–74.
47 Daly, *Introduction to Philosophical Methods*, 41–100.
48 McCutcheon, *Studying Religion*, 54–57.

and/or practices. That should be seen as a part of the work that needs to be done in explicating the data at the level of systematic theology 1(cf. 3.2).

(2) Even though we need to argue and not just make assertions, it is also an important theoretical task to assess the degree and strength of the internal coherence. This is both valid and useful. It might be deficient, but it is still legitimate. Thus, the alternative/critical explanations are relevant but not the only relevant ideas to consider.

(3) Because internal coherence is insufficient, we need external comparisons of degrees of coherence. These comparisons are legitimate, and they are more than mere descriptions. They are a central, critical task for researchers, functioning as arguments because they show the comparative strengths or weaknesses of ontological theories. Thus, work at the different strata of systematic theology should not be judged in isolation but seen as one part of a larger theoretical approach to a complex field of research. I have emphasized a distinct division of labour among the different strata but also emphasized that there are continuous exchanges among the strata and that the propositions and theories at the different strata inform one another reciprocally.

In sum, if the problem is valid, the criticism is appropriate because systematic theology 1 needs to do more than just describe practices. Still, assessments of internal and external coherences are helpful and valuable tools that are more than mere descriptions.

8.3.2.4 Systematic Theology Builds on a Weak Foundation of Evidence

The last supposed problem for distinct research that I address is the objection that systematic theology builds on a weak foundation of evidence, including the claim that its selection of sources is predefined in a problematic way (8.3.2.4.1).[49] The problem with a weak foundation of evidence for systematic theology can be briefly stated as follows: even if we recognize the often intricate and sophisticated distinctions, definitions, systematizations, and theoretical explorations, there still remains an unacceptable lack of empirical evidence in systematic theology. The ghosts of abstract scholasticism and unrestrained speculation seem to linger around the body of systematic theology. This is closely related to 8.3.2.1, because the critics will say that there is a lack of evidence for God's existence but also weak evidence for many of the central doctrines in systematic theology 2.

---

49 Cf. Schaffalitzky, 'Findes teologisk forskning?', 172.

Another way to discuss this is through the distinction between *private* and *public* knowledge, which I have addressed several times.[50] In other words: what is epistemologically warranted are legitimate styles of cognition, and this includes private knowledge.[51] But science is a public enterprise with a specific set of standards where intersubjective testing is central (chapter six). The point is that the conditions for evidence are stronger in the public sphere. Thus, for example, it might be sufficient evidence for a person to believe in God that he felt a response to his evening prayer, and his belief is epistemically warranted as demonstrated by reformed epistemology's valid argument. But this will not suffice in public discourse, where the conditions for rational justification are different. And the objection is that systematic theology builds on a weak foundation of evidence understood as evidence that is certified in the public discourse of science.

This problem is very important. But – maybe surprisingly to some critics – many theologians agree that the problem is important, as I showed in chapter two. They have agreed for decades, and they still agree today – the present book is also an example of a project that accepts the problem and seeks to address it. The solutions to this problem are of course numerous, but the point is that the recognition of the problem is prevalent in academic theology.

The suggestion here is that the problem of the weak foundation of evidence is best addressed through a distinction between systematic theology 2 and systematic theology 3 (see further in chapter three). Much of what theologians do takes place in systematic theology 2, but this is legitimate if a strong case for the scientific status of systematic theology 3 can be given, which seems to be the case. Speculations, theoretical clarifications, model production, etc., are not reserved for theology but are central theoretical practices in many disciplines. Even though we might say that two wrongs don't make a right, it is significant that robust disciplines like physics, biology, psychology, palaeontology, etc., also accept theoretical speculation and seek to develop good tools for assessing hypotheses and theories. Systematic theology might be more vulnerable to the objection because the weak empirical foundation concerns the kernels of many of the discipline's themes, but there is a widespread self-awareness of this challenge, and there are good processes for dealing with it, as the discussion of 8.3 so far has shown. I have argued throughout for coherence theory as the best tool for this kind of scientific work, and the arguments are not repeated here (see 5.2.8.1).

---

50 Schaffalitzky mentions the same distinction and says her criticism only regards the question of whether theology is publicly or scientifically warranted. Schaffalitzky, 'Findes teologisk forskning?', 172–173.
51 E. g., Alston, *Perceiving God* and Alvin Plantinga, *Warranted Christian Belief* (Oxford: Oxford University Press, 2000).

The upshot of all this is that systematic theology is aware of the possible problem of the weak foundation of evidence it is working on and has therefore developed tools and resources to compensate for this, tools and resources that are refined and developed all the time. I end this discussion of the supposed problems for systematic theology as distinct research with a discussion of the problem that the sources of systematic theology and ideals are predefined. I take this to be a subproblem of the problem of weak foundation of evidence. After this discussion I conclude on 8.3.2.

8.3.2.4.1 The Problem That the Selection of Sources and Ideals Is Predefined

The subproblem of predefined sources and ideals does not concern a central notion or theme in theology but is related to the question of normativity (chapter seven). The problem seems to be that systematic theology not only has a very specific set of sources (Bible, tradition, reason, and experience), but also predefined ideals related to the sources, e. g., that religion/Christianity is valuable, that prayer is good, that church attendance is a positive sociological phenomenon, that the Christian tradition has something of value to bring to the democratic discussion, that the investigation of Christian doctrine is a fruitful endeavour, and much more.[52]

This is relevant criticism, for, as I showed in chapter three, the question of sources is important to contemporary systematic theology. On the one hand, the bundle of sources is not fixed and settled because revisions could occur if the arguments against an existing source or for a new source were sufficiently strong. On the other hand, the theological tradition is so long, broad, and varied that it is impossible to treat it as a monolith. Revisions that argue against one source as a whole, e. g., against tradition, seem impossible, but more precise arguments against parts of a source – e. g., against a specific Biblical text or theme or against themes in the theological tradition[53] – could be relevant. This is of course both complex and controversial in real-life debates because it is possible to understand the different theological traditions as variations of priority and emphasis concerning these sources, and suggestions for revision will therefore be one part of a broader argument that includes personal and communal interests, power structures, political interests, etc. It is also worth noticing that possibly every revision will create new problems along with new possibilities. The argument that systematic theology has

---

[52] Schaffalitzky, 'Findes teologisk forskning?,' 168–71. Not everyone sees this as a problem, of course, Gregersen for example points to these sources as parts of the criteria of authenticity and tradition. Cf. Gregersen, *Teologi og kultur*, 236–38.

[53] Hardly any text in the Bible is protected against criticism, and the validity, authenticity, value, relevance, etc., of all the texts are continuously up for discussion. The same goes for all the major streams of Christian tradition, with a prevalent discussion and negotiation of what should count as Christianity today.

a problem with legitimacy because the selection of sources is fixed is thus not convincing because systematic theology can maintain an ongoing conversation about what the relevant sources are.

There are historical and cultural reasons to prefer the conventional selection of sources in systematic theology. But the accusation that this is a fixed and settled list is not convincing because the list is up for revision if good arguments are provided. The sources are so broad and include such a large amount of data that much work in systematic theology is about trying to organize them coherently, and this will lead to many disparate results that call for further scrutiny. To agree on sources is not to agree on results. And the normative status is also up for discussion, as the enormous amount of literature in this field discloses. Because it is not possible to agree with everything and everyone in the theological tradition and because new voices keep coming into the conversation, the notion of *truth-candidate* is helpful and relevant because it allows for a diversity of data to be tried and assessed in attempts to create coherent systems (see 3.4.6–7).

As is evident from the discussion of these four supposed problems, there are various arguments against the distinct yet scientific character of systematic theology, but all of the objections can be met with examples of actual research in theology. The criticism is helpful because it sharpens the methods and perspectives of theology, but at the moment, it does not make systematic theology as a rationally justified public discourse about God illegitimate.

8.3.3 What Are the Distinctive Marks of Systematic Theology 3?

In the last part of this chapter, I focus on the distinctive marks of systematic theology in relation to religious studies and philosophy, which I see as the closest neighbouring disciplines. I first discuss systematic theology in distinction from religious studies (8.3.3.1) which is the easiest distinction to make, before I discuss systematic theology in distinction from philosophy (8.3.3.2), which is a harder distinction to draw, but I suggest that because of systematic theology's data and its commitment to a theistic ontology it is possible to distinguish it from philosophy.

8.3.3.1 Contra Religious Studies

As chapter seven clarified, it is a presupposition of religious studies that the truth question is bracketed, and that judgments of the truth-claims of the different religions are not engaged with (7.2.1.2.1). This does not mean that religious studies is not engaged with truth claims at all, because science aims for truth and religious studies as a scientific discipline is a part of this endeavour (as the discussion of normativity showed, cf. 7.2). Thus, it is a specific set of truth-claims that religious studies brackets, such as claims about the ultimate, the absolute, the totality, or whatever name we give it. Systematic theology 3, on the other hand, has this ultimate, absolute, totality as the central theme of its investigations and therefore does not fall under religious studies. The critical question is whether the truth-aim of systematic theology can be achieved, i. e., whether the "epistemological interests" of academic theologians "match their epistemological possibilities."[54] A negative answer to this question is given in Kantian philosophy with its emphasis on the gap between ultimate ontological reality and human epistemology.[55] This "gap" can be made more or less radical. A less radical approach is given by the later Rescher, whose pragmatic philosophy admits a distinction between reality and its appearances to humans.[56] Puntel on the other hand would answer in the affirmative. In his discussion of "Being as a whole" he discusses "the modalities" and says that these are a part of the human ability to ask about "anything and everything" (see 3.4.5.1.4).[57] And because Puntel's philosophy argues for the universal expressibility of Being, which includes the linguistic and the conceptual, there cannot be any gap between semantics and ontology.[58]

The point here is only that the theme of truth related to the absolute or the ultimate is a distinctive mark of systematic theology in relation to religious studies. And even though it is a controversial question whether humans have the cognitive capacity to deal with this question, the work of philosophers such as Puntel makes it worthwhile to assess and discuss further. His philosophy is one example of not only a legitimation of the research but also a positive contribution to actual research in this area.

8.3.3.2 Contra Philosophy

The distinction between systematic theology and religious studies is relatively easy to outline, probably due, not least, to the fact that this has been addressed for more than a century and is central to the self-understanding of both disciplines. But the distinction between systematic theology 3 and philosophy is much harder to clarify. This is probably because every field to some extent is a form of philosophy – or has

---

54 Herbener, 'The Study and Making of Christian Religion in Danish Academic Theology,' 214.
55 E. g., seen in the response to Martin Heidegger from the neo-Kantian philosopher Ernst Cassirer in their famous dispute in Davos in 1929. Cassirer's argument is that because we have no direct access to infinity, we have instead to follow the finite in every possible direction. See "Davoser Disputation zwischen Ernst Cassirer und Martin Heidegger," in: Martin Heidegger, *Gesamtausgabe. 3: Abt. 1, Veröffentlichte Schriften 1910 - 1976: Kant und das Problem der Metaphysik*, 2. Auflage (Frankfurt am Main: Vittorio Klostermann, 2010), especially p. 286.
56 Rescher, *Reality and Its Appearance*.
57 Puntel, *Structure and Being*, 444.
58 Puntel, *Structure and Being*, 359–371, especially pp. 369–371 where Puntel briefly presents "four theses" against the "putative gap" between ontology and epistemology/semantics.

clear philosophical implications and presuppositions – and thus to draw a sharp distinction between any given field and philosophy is ultimately futile.[59] In Puntel's words, every discipline is a *topic* for philosophy (including logic and mathematics), but philosophy should not and cannot contribute to these disciplines.[60] As he later clarifies: "One must note at the outset that *in one specific respect* there is and can be no metadimension for systematic philosophy. The reason for this is that every 'thing,' every domain, theoretical or non-theoretical (every discipline, every activity, every phenomenon of whatever sort) can and indeed must be considered to be a topic that in principle is a possible topic *for* systematic philosophy."[61]

But this is not all there is to say. There is, of course, a specific discipline called "philosophy," with certain methods, data, and aims – no matter how diverse the field is in practice. The question is whether systematic theology can distinguish itself from this discipline to such an extent that it becomes its own discipline, because contrary to all the other disciplines that work with regional ontologies, systematic theology thematizes the absolute and this is a distinct approach that is only shared with philosophy.[62] But I suggest that instead of looking at aims or themes, we look at the data that the two disciplines work with. If we do so, a clearer demarcation between them appears. The data of systematic theology have been addressed several times already, but in sum, I can say that the Biblical and historical data create a natural reference point for systematic theology and make its focus very precise.[63] For this reason, there is a natural delimitation to its thematization of the absolute. This is not a natural way for philosophy to operate because its scope is much wider. Philosophy is thus a necessary tool for systematic theology, but systematic theology is not a necessary tool for philosophy. In this way, systematic theology aligns with the other disciplines.

In science, the criterion of intersubjectivity is critical (chapter six) and in the discussion of this criterion, I argued that systematic theology as a whole has a weakness in comparison with other disciplines. But systematic theology 3 does

---

59 The different series of "Philosophy of …" books is a clear indication of this. Just to point to one example among many, see the Princeton Foundations of Contemporary Philosophy series with books on the philosophy of physics, law, mathematics, biology, etc. https://press.princeton.edu/series/princeton-foundations-of-contemporary-philosophy (accessed 13.12.2021).
60 Puntel, *Structure and Being*, 172. An obvious example is philosophy of science, which does not contribute to the development of the individual sciences but investigates and clarifies the presuppositions for the work.
61 Puntel, *Structure and Being*, 470. Original italics. He gives an additional reason on page 477: "articulating the most general or universal structures of the unrestricted universe of discourse is clearly not the task of any natural or empirical science, nor that of any formal science; for this reason, the natural or empirical sciences can all be termed *particular* sciences."
62 Cf. Pannenberg, *Theology and the Philosophy of Science*, 336.
63 This especially includes the difficult concept of revelation as I briefly suggested at the end of 3.4.5.1.7.2.

not have this weakness because the work at this level can unproblematically be executed by everyone. Some might find it challenging to embrace this claim because systematic theology 3 – according to the argument here – legitimates systematic theology 1 and systematic theology 2. Therefore, it is crucial to emphasize that it is not mandatory to go from systematic theology 3 to systematic theology 2 or systematic theology 1 (even though it seems very obvious to do so). The work of Lorenz Puntel himself is an example of a philosophy that stops its investigation at the level of systematic theology 3.[64] For both systematic theology 3 and parts of philosophy, the specific question of research can be said to be that of "the ultimate." At the level of systematic theology 3, we seek to explicate the relations between different notions at a fundamental level, e. g., between God and humans (the ultimate and (a part of) the contingent dimension of being), and this can also be a theme of philosophical reflection, even though such studies may be rare in contemporary philosophical research in Western Europe. However, the argument should not be assessed by current thematic concerns but by theoretical possibilities, and here systematic theology 3 and philosophy share a common possibility for investigating these fundamental relations. The point, then, is that even though methodological naturalism may be prevalent in contemporary Western philosophy, it is not a necessary condition for something to be philosophical or the only legitimate approach to thematizing the ultimate.[65]

But if this is convincing, if both philosophy and systematic theology 3 are investigations of the basic structures of reality and the relations between different fundamental entities, what is the difference? Is it only systematic theology 1 and systematic theology 2 that guarantee the distinctness of systematic theology, two strata that derive their scientific nature from the sustainability of systematic theology 3? Is systematic theology 3 in fact no more than a narrower version of philosophy? One answer would be affirmative and say that systematic theology 3 is a kind of philosophy but with special obligations and responsibilities (a philosophical theology). Another answer would be more hesitant and say that systematic theology 3 does distinct research, not because its thematic field is distinct but because it has a certain perspective or emphasis on this thematic field that marks it out.[66] In other words,

---

[64] Puntel, *Being and God*, 260–82; Puntel, *Structure and Being*, 458–60. Note, though, that Puntel does not call his work systematic "theology."

[65] In the US, we see a growing percentage of Christian philosophers in the most esteemed philosophical societies, which some atheistic philosophers see as problem. See, e. g., Quentin Smith, 'The Metaphilosophy of Naturalism,' *Philo* 4, no. 2 (2001): 195–215.

[66] Cf. Pannenberg, *Theology and the Philosophy of Science*, 337: "Like historical and hermeneutical hypotheses, theological statements relate to a body of data connected with their particular subject-matter which has to be given a coherent explanation in terms of that subject-matter. Theology is concerned with how the data have been mediated by the historic nature of religious experience." See also Pannenberg's distinctions between philosophy and systematic theology on pages 340–341, where

systematic theology has a deliberately narrower focus than philosophy. In a way, this makes it more focused; in another way it makes it more vulnerable. Systematic theology 3 puts all its eggs in one basket: If God does not exist, a very large part of systematic theology – past and present – will be uninteresting and wrong. At the moment, there is no agreement that the hypothesis of God is clearly less coherent than relevant alternatives, and for this reason, it is still a lively truth-candidate.[67] We do not know whether future studies will eventually falsify the hypothesis of God through comparison, but if so, systematic theology 3 will lose most of its relevance. It is important to note, however, that the same goes for much of philosophy – and other sciences too. There is a hypothetical possibility that reality is radically different from what we commonly agree on – for example, that reality as we perceive it is determined by or is a production of data simulation – and if either of these possibilities is shown to be true, then much of the work in contemporary philosophy will become uninteresting. This is always a possible threat and thus not restricted to systematic theology.

Systematic theology 3 has a deliberately narrow focus with an explicit ontological commitment to the investigation of the God hypothesis in relation to everything else. This foundation is fragile, because "God" might turn out to be an unfruitful hypothesis and then systematic theology 3 will be unfruitful. But most – if not all – of research consists in critical exploration of hypotheses (8.3.2.2.1) and often – if not always – this exploration comes with a great danger of failure. Systematic theology 3 is not exempted from this, but nor does it stand alone. Because every scientific endeavour rest on specific – though maybe implicit – ontological commitments, a careful scrutinization of any field's metaphysical elements is required and valuable, and likewise for systematic theology 3. The critical question is still whether this work can be done in an equally *good* way by other disciplines such as philosophy or religious studies. The present discussion seems to deny this, because the ontology systematic theology commits itself to is the investigation of a theistic ontology, a limitation neither philosophy nor religious studies will accept, often explicitly refusing it. Systematic theology also commits itself to a specific (though revisable) set of data, and this set of data does not overlap with those of either religious studies or philosophy. There is thus a positive need for the work of systematic theology 3 in the collective quest for truth that is the aim of science.

As I said above, the work at the level of systematic theology 3 can be done in isolation, and this kind of research does not imply the acceptance of the Christian

---

he emphasizes the relation between history and theology much more than I do in my explication of systematic theology.

67 As even atheistic, agnostic, or naturalistic philosophers often admit. They argue against the notion of God for various reasons but not often because they find the hypothesis illegitimate. See, e. g., Oppy, *Atheism and Agnosticism*; Draper, 'Seeking but Not Believing: Confessions of a Practicing Agnostic.'

faith or a commitment to investigating the internal coherence of the Christian faith at the level of systematic theology 2.[68] But nor is there a prohibition against such investigation. In fact, if the investigation of the ontological commitments has convinced the researcher that it is possible to present rationally justified public discourse about God, following the lead of the argument and beginning a careful study of the internal coherence of the Christian faith is a natural step to take. But this is the subject of a different book project.[69]

8.3.4 Conclusion on Premise 2

The second premise is "Systematic theology does not do *distinct research* that no other discipline could conduct equally well." The investigation of this premise and the discussion of it has shown that systematic theology is able to identify the features that make it a distinct discipline. It is able to argue against the supposed problems (8.3.2), and it is able to point to its distinguishing marks in relation to its closest academic allies (8.3.3). Therefore, the conclusion about Premise 2 is that it fails.

8.4 Conclusion

The logical conclusion of the syllogism was that "Systematic theology is not a distinct scientific discipline" because of Premise 1 and Premise 2. The investigation showed that Premise 1 is sustained, but Premise 2 fails. As for Premise 1, it is important to be able to mark what makes a specific scientific discipline distinct, for both external and internal reasons. The distinct-research criterion is thus a legitimate one. As for Premise 2, systematic theology is able to identify the marks that make it a distinct scientific discipline, and thus it does meet the criterion articulated by Premise 1. Systematic theology is to be counted as a distinct scientific discipline because it does distinct research in as comparatively strong a sense as related disciplines.

In the last chapter, I conclude the book and sum up by answering the research question: how can systematic theology best be construed as a scientific discipline?

---

68 Puntel, *Being and God*, 271–82. Cf. Gregersen, *Teologi og kultur*, 228. "Theology demands no personal conviction, only an engagement with theology's proper theme: the possibility of formulating current Christian interpretations inside a contemporary cultural context." ("Teologien kræver ingen personlig bekendelse, kun et engagement for selve teologiens tema: muligheden for at formulere aktuelle kristne tydninger inden for en nutidig kulturel kontekst" (Translation MAM)).

69 I have used Pannenberg as a main source in this book. He took this step with a lengthy exploration of the Christian faith in this three-volume systematic theology. Hence, he integrated the three levels of systematic theology (even though he did not use these terms, instead he seems to use first-, second-, and third-order hypotheses, cf. Pannenberg, *Theology and the Philosophy of Science*, 333) so that the different strata are arguments for one another.

Part Four: Conclusion

Chapter Nine

In this final chapter, I have three remaining tasks: first, to give a summary of the central findings in this book (9.1); second, to give a global answer to the research question (9.2); third, to summarize the findings and the conclusion in ten theses (9.3).

9.1 Summary of the Findings

Relying on the construction principle identified in the introduction, I have had three foci: to present the best understanding of systematic theology I have found and criticize this with the best objections I have found and lastly to try to answer the objections in the best way I could think of. In the following, I present the findings of the book in their essentials. I do not recapitulate the content of the different chapters; for this, I refer to the detailed outline presented in the introduction (1.4.1).

Part one included the introduction in chapter one and the historical background in chapter two. These two chapters presented the framework and the background for the work and thus do not postulate any discoveries. Nevertheless, it is reasonable to see the framework as a part of the findings because there is no such thing as theoretical work detached from a theoretical framework with its language, logic, presuppositions, etc. I stated two important presuppositions: realism and truth. Realism refers to the thesis that there is a mind-independent reality that we can access through language and describe precisely, though fallibilistically. Truth is presupposed as the aim of science, conceived not just as a pragmatic endeavour seeking instrumental results but instead as aiming at fine-grained descriptions of reality. I have worked from this presupposition because it is important for the understanding of systematic theology's relevance that humans aim at truth with our metaphysical theories and that we have proper tools for assessing truth-claims. The final criterion for truth, I have argued, is coherence, which is also a robust and fine-grained tool for developing, comparing, and assessing theories. With these presuppositions at hand, I was able to outline a procedure for answering the research question of how systematic theology can best be construed as a scientific discipline. The second chapter, about the historical background, introduced four debates from the 20th century about the scientific status of theology. With these four examples I showed how the research question has been discussed in the immediate past, and I also used them to point to the relevance of a wide debate that does not isolate the discipline of theology from common criteria for science.

Part two included chapter three, on the proposed understanding of systematic theology as a stratified discipline, which is the core of the book because it is the notion that is examined in the rest of the work. I followed Niels Henrik Gregersen's suggestion of dividing the work of systematic theology into three distinct strata as a way of capturing the multi-faceted work that is systematic theology. But contrary to Gregersen, I argued that systematic theology 3 is the scientific core of systematic theology and that systematic theology 1 and systematic theology 2 are scientific only by derivation from systematic theology 3. The reason is that if a theistic ontology is not convincing in comparison with relevant alternatives – for the time being, the competitor seems to be naturalism – the explication of any believer's religious expression should be nothing more than mere sociology of religion (instead of systematic theology 1), and the coherent development of Christian theories would be only instrumental or therapeutic, if not futile (systematic theology 2). If systematic theology 3 succeeds in explicating a coherent ontology that is better or at least not clearly poorer than its alternatives, then the work of systematic theology 1 and systematic theology 2 is fruitful. I have argued that systematic theology 3 meets the most common criteria for science, and thus the stratification is the best way to sustain systematic theology as a scientific discipline that is both critical and constructive. I argued that even though many of the sources of systematic theology are historical, a synchronic constitution of the field of systematic theology is possible, as seen in the work of Puntel. The reason for this long treatment of a superficial field of study was to show that systematic theology is not relevant only for historical or cultural reasons but for contemporary metaphysical and philosophical reasons as well.

Part three included chapters four through eight and treated the five objections against the proposed understanding of systematic theology and the responses to the objections. In sum, the study showed that none of the objections could be sustained when scrutinized – in other words, systematic theology could meet the objections and sustain itself as a scientific discipline. The key was to integrate coherence into the concepts of testability, falsification, intersubjectivity, and normativity – specifically in relation to the objections as well as more broadly as the key to understanding science's aim for truth.

The first objection was that systematic theology cannot be tested scientifically. But the dissolving in the general philosophy of science of testability as concerned with single propositions, which has been replaced by the notion of testing whole theories, has implications for systematic theology, too. I argued that testability can best be understood in terms of testing for the coherence of whole theories. Testability is thus a criterion for scientific work as such, and ontologies – including systematic theology theories – can be tested by following an explicated and transparent methodology, the results of which can be assessed for their coherence.

The second objection was that theories of systematic theology cannot be tested by the most common tool, falsification. I argued that this turns out to be unfounded when we consider that the notion of falsification can best be conceived as the comparison of two theories with the (clearly) less coherent theory then being regarded as falsified. Falsification (properly understood) is a criterion for scientific work, and it is possible to falsify ontologies – including theories of systematic theology – by comparing degrees of coherence.

The third objection was that theories of systematic theology cannot be tested intersubjectively to a satisfying degree, but I argued against this understanding even though I also argued that systematic theology gets a lower score on the spectrum of intersubjectivity than do most other disciplines. This is because it is harder to achieve agreement on what the standard actually says, also regarding fundamental notions in the field. In relation to intersubjectivity, too, I argued that the notion of coherence is useful because it allows us to know exactly what to look for when we assess theories in other frameworks with different presuppositions. Intersubjectivity is a criterion for scientific work, which means that conclusions must not be dependent on the researcher drawing them.

The fourth objection was that systematic theology is normative in a problematic way. I argued that all science is weakly normative, but because systematic theology is also strongly normative – arguing for the truthfulness of claims concerning supernatural entities – the critical focus was on strong normativity. I argued that systematic theology's strong normativity can be sustained with reference to coherence because we have different ontologies that argue differently for the fundamental constitution of reality and the comparison between the best theories is best executed with coherence as the final criterion. There is no reason to presuppose that the fundamental constitution of reality cannot include supernatural entities, and therefore should theories of systematic theology not be discredited prior to testing by comparison. In sum, I therefore argued that normativity is a scalar notion and if assessed for coherence, both weak and strong normativity can have scientific legitimacy.

The fifth and final objection was that a discipline must be distinct yet scientific and with distinct research, and that systematic theology cannot meet this double demand. When systematic theology is distinct, it is not scientific, and when it is scientific, it is not systematic theology. I argued against this objection by showing that systematic theology is different from religious studies exactly because of its strong normativity, i. e., the truth pretention of the theories of systematic theology about supernatural entities. And that systematic theology is different from philosophy in its commitment to a theistic ontology that makes systematic theology both narrower in its focus but also more fragile than philosophy. I argued that the ideal of distinct research – research that is distinct yet scientific – is a good criterion for a scientific discipline, but also that systematic theology meets this criterion with its commitment to a theistic ontology, its specific data and hypotheses, and its strong normativity that can all be assessed, compared, criticized, and developed through reliance on the final criterion of coherence.

9.2 Conclusion

The research question was, "How can systematic theology best be construed as a scientific discipline?" and as the introduction made clear, the answer rests on the understanding of what "systematic theology," "scientific," and "discipline" mean. With the proposed understanding of systematic theology as a stratified discipline and the understanding of science based on the criteria I formulated as objections against systematic theology, I have given a fine-grained answer to the question: systematic theology is best construed according to a stratification where systematic theology 3 develops and compares a theistic ontology with relevant alternatives, and if this comparison does not compromise systematic theology 3, then the work of systematic theology 1 and systematic theology 2 is derivatively scientific and legitimized. As assessed via coherence theory, systematic theology is sustained as a scientific discipline with the same robustness as neighbouring disciplines like religious studies and philosophy, because its theories can be tested, falsified, and criticized intersubjectively. I criticized the objection that strong normativity is scientifically problematic by pointing to coherence, and I furthermore encircled how systematic theology distinguishes itself from religious studies and philosophy by focusing on strong normativity and on its commitment to a theistic ontology.

9.3 Theses of the Book

1. Science aims for truth, and the criterion for truth is here taken to be coherence. Coherence comes in degrees, so the most coherent theory we are able to present at the moment we will take as true. This holistic theory is fallible and thus only approximately true, but it is the best tool we have at hand.
2. Systematic theology is a complex and diversified field that should be organized into different strata, here called systematic theology 1, systematic theology 2, and systematic theology 3. Only systematic theology 3, which is the work of explicating a theistic ontology and comparing it with relevant alternative ontologies, should be counted as scientific in itself.
3. Systematic theology 1 and systematic theology 2 are only derivatively scientific. If systematic theology 3 is rejected, systematic theology 1 and systematic theology 2 would be something other than science, but maybe relevant activities in other contexts.

4. Systematic theology 3 can explicate a robust theoretical framework in which it can present a coherent ontology, and it thus has a scientific theory to present as a truth-candidate.
5. Testability is a criterion for scientific work, and ontologies can be tested by following an explicated and transparent methodology and assessed for their coherence.
6. Falsification (properly understood) is a criterion for scientific work, and it is possible to falsify ontologies by comparing degrees of coherence.
7. Intersubjectivity is a criterion for scientific work, which means that conclusions must not be dependent on the researcher drawing them.
8. Normativity is a scalar notion, and if assessed for coherence, both weak and strong normativity can have scientific legitimacy.
9. The ideal of *distinct research* – research that is distinct to a given discipline yet scientific – is a criterion for a scientific discipline. Systematic theology 3 meets this criterion given its commitment to a theistic ontology, its specific data and hypotheses, and its reference to strong normativity.
10. In light of points 1–9, systematic theology 3 should be counted as scientific and as a legitimate field of research that lends credence to systematic theology 1 and systematic theology 2, and through this stratification, systematic theology is thus sustained as a scientific discipline.

Bibliography

Afdal, Geir. 'Two Concepts of Practice and Theology'. *Studia Theologica. Nordic Journal of Theology* 75, no. 1 (2021): 6–29.

Agazzi, Evandro, ed. *Varieties of Scientific Realism. Objectivity and Truth in Science*. New York: Springer, 2017.

Allen, Paul L. 'Is There Verification in Theology?' *Open Theology* 3 (2017): 417–33.

Alston, William P. 'Christian Experience and Christian Belief'. In *Faith and Rationality: Reason and Belief in God*, edited by Alvin Plantinga and Nicholas Wolterstorff, 103–34. Notre Dame: University of Notre Dame Press, 1983.

Alston, William P. *Perceiving God. The Epistemology of Religious Experience*. Ithaca: Cornell University Press, 1993.

Aquinas, Thomas. 'Quaestiones Disputatae de Potentia 7'. https://isidore.co/aquinas/QDdePotentia7.htm#7:5. Accessed 20 December 2021.

Asad, Talal. 'The Construction of Religion as an Anthropological Category'. In *Genealogies of Religion. Discipline and Reasons of Power in Christianity and Islam*, 27–54. Baltimore: Johns Hopkins University Press, 1993.

Asztalos, Monika. 'The Faculty of Theology'. In *A History of the University in Europe. Universities in the Middle Ages*, edited by Hilde de Ridder-Symoens, 1:409–41. Cambridge: Cambridge University Press, 1992.

Atkins, Peter William. *Conjuring the Universe. The Origins of the Laws of Nature*. Oxford: Oxford University Press, 2018.

Ayer, Alfred J. *Language, Truth and Logic*. Harmondsworth: Penguin, 1983 [1936].

Bacon, Francis. *Novum Organum*. Frederiksberg: Anis, 2007.

Baggini, Julian. *Atheism. A Very Short Introduction*. Second Edition. New York: Oxford University Press, 2021.

Baghramian, Maria, and J. Adam Carter. 'Relativism'. In *The Stanford Encyclopedia of Philosophy*, edited by Edward N. Zalta. Metaphysics Research Lab, Stanford University, 2021. https://plato.stanford.edu/archives/spr2021/entries/relativism/. Accessed 20 December 2021.

Bahnsen, Greg L. *Presuppositional Apologetics. Stated and Defended*. Edited by Joel McDurmon. Powder Springs: American Vision Press, 2010.

Bahnsen, Greg L. *Van Til's Apologetic*. Phillipsburg: P & R Publishing, 1998.

Barbour, Ian G. *Myths, Models and Paradigms. The Nature of Scientific and Religious Language*. London: S.C.M. Press, 1974.

Barker, Gillian, and Philip Kitcher. *Philosophy of Science. A New Introduction*. Fundamentals of Philosophy Series. New York: Oxford University Press, 2014.

Barth, Karl. *Church Dogmatics. The Doctrine of the Word of God. §1-7*. Edited by Geoffrey William Bromiley, Thomas F. Torrance, and Frank McCombie. Study Edition. Vol. I1. London and New York: T & T Clark, 2010.

Barth, Karl. *Dogmatik im Grundriß*. Eleventh Edition. Zürich: TVZ, Theologischer Verlag, 2013.

Baur, Jörg. 'Orthodoxie, Genese Und Struktur'. De Gruyter. http://www.degruyter.com/document/database/TRE/entry/tre.25_498_1/html.Accessed20December2021.

Beauchamp, Tom L., and Thomas A. Mappes. 'Is Hume Really A Sceptic About Induction?' *American Philosophical Quarterly* 12, no. 2 (April 1975): 119–29.

Belnap, Nuel. 'On Rigorous Definitions'. *Philosophical Studies. An International Journal for Philosophy in the Analytic Tradition* 72, no. 2/3 (1993): 115–46.

Berger, Peter L. *The Heretical Imperative. Contemporary Possibilities of Religious Affirmation*. New York: Anchor, 1979.

Berger, Peter L. *The Sacred Canopy. Elements of a Sociological Theory of Religion*. New York: Anchor, 1990.

Bevans, Stephen B. *Models of Contextual Theology*. Maryknoll: Orbis, 2002.

Beyer, Christian. 'Edmund Husserl'. In *The Stanford Encyclopedia of Philosophy*, edited by Edward N. Zalta. Metaphysics Research Lab, Stanford University, 2020. https://plato.stanford.edu/archives/win2020/entries/husserl/. Accessed 20 December 2021.

Bhaskar, Roy. *A Realist Theory of Science*. Radical Thinkers 29. London and New York: Verso, 2008.

Bhaskar, Roy. *The Order of Natural Necessity. A Kind of Introduction to Critical Realism*. Edited by Gary Hawke. Unspecified: Unspecified, 2017.

Bird, Alexander. 'Thomas Kuhn's Relativistic Legacy'. In *Blackwell Companion to Relativism*, edited by Steven D. Hales, 456–74. Oxford: Wiley-Blackwell, 2011.

Bonhoeffer, Dietrich. *The Cost of Discipleship*. Unabridged Edition. New York: Macmillan, 1980.

Boyer, Pascal. *Religion Explained. The Evolutionary Origins of Religious Thought*. New York: Basic Books, 2002.

Brink, Gijsbert van den. 'How Theology Stopped Being Regina Scientiarum – and How Its Story Continues'. *Studies in Christian Ethics* 32, no. 4 (2019): 442–54.

Brink, Gijsbert van den. *Philosophy of Science for Theologians. An Introduction*. Contributions to Philosophical Theology 12. Frankfurt am Main and New York: Peter Lang, 2009.

Brink, Gijsbert van den. *Reformed Theology and Evolutionary Theory*. Grand Rapids: Eerdmans, 2020.

Brink, Gijsbert van den. 'Social Trinitarianism. A Discussion of Some Recent Theological Criticisms'. *International Journal of Systematic Theology* 16, no. 3 (2014): 331–50.

Bromberger, Sylvain. 'Why-Questions'. In *Mind and Cosmos. Essays in Contemporary Science and Philosophy*, edited by R.G. Colodny, 86–111. Pittsburgh: University of Pittsburgh Press, 1966.

Brown, James Robert, and Yiftach Fehige. 'Thought Experiments'. In *The Stanford Encyclopedia of Philosophy*, edited by Edward N. Zalta. Metaphysics Research Lab, Stanford University, 2019. https://plato.stanford.edu/archives/win2019/entrieshought-experiment/. Accessed 20 December 2021

Brownstein, Michael. 'Implicit Bias'. In *The Stanford Encyclopedia of Philosophy*, edited by Edward N. Zalta. Metaphysics Research Lab, Stanford University, 2019. https://plato.stanford.edu/archives/fall2019/entries/implicit-bias/. Accessed 20 December 2021.

Budtz Pedersen, David, and Frederik Stjernfelt, eds. *Kortlægning af dansk humanistisk forskning*. København: Hans Reitzels Forlag, 2016.

Bultmann, Rudolf. *Glauben und Verstehen*. Vol. 1. Gesammelte Aufsätze. Tübingen: J.C.B. Mohr (Paul Siebeck), 1966.

Byrne, Peter. 'The Many Worlds of Hugh Everett'. *Scientific American* 297, no. 6 (December 2007): 98–105.

Campbell-Jack, W. C., Gavin J. McGrath, and C. Stephen Evans, eds. *New Dictionary of Christian Apologetics*. Downers Grove: IVP Academic, 2006.

Cantrell, Michael A. 'Must a Scholar of Religion Be Methodologically Atheistic or Agnostic?' *Journal of the American Academy of Religion* 84, no. 2 (June 2016): 373–400.

Carnap, Rudolf. 'Empiricism, Semantics, and Ontology'. *Revue Internationale de Philosophie* 4 (1950): 20–40.

Carnap, Rudolf. 'Testability and Meaning'. *Philosophy of Science* 3, no. 4 (1936): 419–71.

Carnap, Rudolf. 'Testability and Meaning—Continued'. *Philosophy of Science* 4, no. 1 (1937): 1–40.

Carroll, Sean. *The Big Picture. On the Origins of Life, Meaning and the Universe Itself*. London: Oneworld, 2016.

Carroll, Sean. 'Why (Almost All) Cosmologists Are Atheists'. Notre Dame, 2003. https://www.preposterousuniverse.com/writings/nd-paper/. Accessed 20 December 2021.

Cartwright, Nancy. 'Do the Laws of Physics State the Facts?' In *Philosophy of Science: The Central Issues*, edited by Martin Curd and J.A. Cover, 865–77. New York: W.W. Norton & Company, 1998.

Cassirer, Ernst. *The Myth of the State*. New Haven: Yale University Press, 2009.

Cassirer, Ernst. *The Problem of Knowledge. Philosophy, Science, and History since Hegel*. Translated by William H. Woglom and Charles W. Hendel. New Haven: Yale University Press, 1950.

Cat, Jordi. 'Otto Neurath'. In *The Stanford Encyclopedia of Philosophy*, edited by Edward N. Zalta. Metaphysics Research Lab, Stanford University, 2021. https://plato.stanford.edu/archives/spr2021/entries/neurath/. Accessed 20 December 2021.

Chakravartty, Anjan. *A Metaphysics for Scientific Realism. Knowing the Unobservable*. Cambridge: Cambridge University Press, 2007.

Chakravartty, Anjan. 'Scientific Realism'. In *The Stanford Encyclopedia of Philosophy*, edited by Edward N. Zalta. Metaphysics Research Lab, Stanford University, 2017. https://plato.stanford.edu/archives/sum2017/entries/scientific-realism/. Accessed 20 December 2021.

Chignell, Andrew. '"As Kant Has Shown". Analytic Theology and the Critical Philosophy'. In *Analytic Theology. New Essays in the Philosophy of Theology*, edited by Oliver Crisp and Michael C. Rea. Oxford: Oxford University Press, 2011.

Clayton, Philip. *Explanation from Physics to Theology. An Essay in Rationality and Religion*. New Haven: Yale University Press, 1989.

Clayton, Philip. *The Problem of God in Modern Thought*. Grand Rapids: Eerdmans, 2000.

Clayton, Philip, and A. R. Peacocke, eds. *In Whom We Live and Move and Have Our Being. Panentheistic Reflections on God's Presence in a Scientific World*. Grand Rapids: Eerdmans, 2004.

Coady, C. A. J. *Testimony. A Philosophical Study*. Oxford and New York: Clarendon, 1992.

Coady, C.A.J. 'Testimony and Observation'. *American Philosophical Quarterly* 10, no. 2 (April 1973): 149–55.

Cobban, Alan Balfour. *The Medieval English Universities. Oxford and Cambridge to c. 1500*. Aldershot: Scolar Press, 1988.

Cohnitz, Daniel, and Marcus Rossberg. 'Nelson Goodman'. In *The Stanford Encyclopedia of Philosophy*, edited by Edward N. Zalta. Metaphysics Research Lab, Stanford University, 2019. https://plato.stanford.edu/archives/sum2019/entries/goodman/. Accessed 20 December 2021.

Collier, Andrew. *Critical Realism. An Introduction to Roy Bhaskar's Philosophy*. London and New York: Verso, 1994.

Cowan, Steven B. 'Introduction'. In *Five Views on Apologetics*, edited by Steven B. Cowan, 7–20. Grand Rapids: Zondervan Academic, 2000.

Craig, William Lane. *Reasonable Faith. Christian Truth and Apologetics*. Third Edition. Wheaton: Crossway, 2008.

Craig, William Lane, and J.P. Moreland, eds. *The Blackwell Companion to Natural Theology*. Oxford: Wiley-Blackwell, 2012.

Curd, Martin, and J.A. Cover, eds. *Philosophy of Science. The Central Issues*. New York: W.W. Norton & Company, 1998.

Currie, Adrian. *Rock, Bone, and Ruin. An Optimist's Guide to the Historical Sciences*. Cambridge: The MIT Press, 2018.

Dalferth, Ingolf U., ed. *Eine Wissenschaft oder viele? Die Einheit evangelischer Theologie in der Sicht ihrer Disziplinen*. Leipzig: Evangelische Verlagsanstalt, 2006.

Dalferth, Ingolf U. 'On Distinctions'. *International Journal for Philosophy of Religion* 79 (2016): 171–83.

Dalferth, Ingolf U. 'The Historical Roots of Theism'. In *Traditional Theism and Its Modern Alternatives*, edited by Svend Andersen, 18:15–41. Acta Jutlandica LXX:1 Theological Series. Aarhus: Aarhus University Press, 1994.

Daly, Chris. *Introduction to Philosophical Methods*. Peterborough: Broadview Press, 2010.

Damasio, Antonio. *Descartes' Error*. Revised Edition. London: Vintage, 2006.

Damasio, Antonio. *The Strange Order of Things. Life, Feeling, and the Making of Cultures*. New York: Vintage, 2017.

Dancy, Jonathan. *An Introduction to Contemporary Epistemology*. Oxford: Blackwell, 1986.

Dancy, Jonathan., ed. *Normativity*. Oxford: Blackwell, 2000.

Darwall, Stephen. 'Normativity'. In *Routledge Encyclopedia of Philosophy*. London: Routledge, 2016.

Davis, Stephen T. 'Theology, Verification, and Falsification'. *International Journal for Philosophy of Religion* 6, no. 1 (Spring 1975): 23–39.

D'Costa, Gavin. 'On Theologising Theology within the Secular University'. *Transformation* 22, no. 3 (2005): 148–57.

D'Costa, Gavin. *Theology in the Public Square. Church, Academy and Nation*. Oxford: Blackwell, 2005.

D'Costa, Gavin. 'Whose Objectivity? Which Neutrality? The Doomed Quest for a Neutral Vantage Point from Which to Judge Religions'. *Religious Studies* 29 (1993): 79–95.

Dewey, John. 'Theory of Valuation'. In *The Later Works of John Dewey, 1925–1953*, edited by Jo Ann Boydston, vol. 13, 1938–1939:191–251. Collected Works of John Dewey. Carbondale: Southern Illinois University Press, 2008.

Diem, Hermann. *Theologie Als Kirchliche Wissenschaft*. Vol. 1. 3 vols. Munich: Chr. Kaiser Verlag, 1951.

Dilthey, Wilhelm. *Einleitung in die Geisteswissenschaften. Versuch einer Grundlegung für das Studium der Gesellschaft und der Geschichte*. Ninth Unchanged Edition. Gesammelte Schriften 1. Stuttgart: Teubner, 1990.

Douven, Igor. 'Abduction'. In *The Stanford Encyclopedia of Philosophy*, edited by Edward N. Zalta, Summer 2017. Metaphysics Research Lab, Stanford University, 2017. https://plato.stanford.edu/archives/sum2017/entries/abduction/. Accessed 20 December 2021.

Douven, Igor. 'Abduction > Peirce on Abduction (Stanford Encyclopedia of Philosophy)'. https://plato.stanford.edu/entries/abduction/peirce.html. Accessed 20 December 2021.

Draper, Paul. 'Atheism and Agnosticism'. In *The Stanford Encyclopedia of Philosophy*, edited by Edward N. Zalta. Metaphysics Research Lab, Stanford University, 2017. https://plato.stanford.edu/archives/fall2017/entries/atheism-agnosticism/. Accessed 20 December 2021.

Draper, Paul. 'Seeking but Not Believing. Confessions of a Practicing Agnostic'. In *Divine Hiddenness. New Essays*, edited by Paul K. Moser and Daniel Howard-Snyder, 197–214. Cambridge: Cambridge University Press, 2002.

Eikrem, Asle. 'Dogmatikk som samtidsteologi'. *Dansk Teologisk Tidsskrift* 74. årg., no. 2 (2011): 152–66.

Eikrem, Asle. *God as Sacrificial Love. A Systematic Exploration of a Controversial Notion*. T&T Clark Studies in Systematic Theology . London and New York: Bloomsbury T&T Clark, 2018.

Eikrem, Asle. 'Korsets gåte?' *Teologisk tidsskrift* 8, no. 3 (2019): 198–204.

Eikrem, Asle. 'Mer korsteologi – Ny replikk til Hegstad'. *Teologisk tidsskrift* 9, no. 1 (2020): 52–58.

Elgin, Catherine Z, ed. *The Philosophy of Nelson Goodman. Selected Essays*. New York: Garland, 1997.

England, Jeremy. *Every Life Is on Fire. How Thermodynamics Explains the Origins of Living Things*. New York: Basic Books, 2020.

Erdozain, Dominic. *The Soul of Doubt. The Religious Roots of Unbelief from Luther to Marx*. Oxford and New York: Oxford University Press, 2015.

Evans, G. R. *Old Arts and New Theology. The Beginnings of Theology as an Academic Discipline*. Oxford: Clarendon, 1980.

Fehige, Yiftach. 'Theology and Thought Experiments'. In *The Routledge Companion to Thought Experiments*, edited by Michael T. Stuart, Yiftach Fehige, and James Robert Brown, 183–94. Routledge Philosophy Companions. London and New York: Routledge/Taylor & Francis Group, 2018.

Ferruolo, Stephen C. *The Origins of the University. The Schools of Paris and Their Critics, 1100–1215*. Stanford: Stanford University Press, 1985.

Feyerabend, Paul. *Against Method*. Third Edition. London and New York: Verso, 2010.

Feyerabend, Paul. 'Consolations for the Specialist'. In *Criticism and the Growth of Knowledge*, edited by Alan Musgrave and Imre Lakatos, 197–230. Cambridge: Cambridge University Press, 1970.

Fish, Stanley. *Is There a Text in This Class? The Authority of Interpretive Communities*. Cambridge: Harvard University Press, 1980.

Flew, Anthony, R.M. Hare, and Basil Mitchell. 'Theology and Falsification. The University Discussion'. In *New Essays in Philosophical Theology*, 96–130. London: SCM Press, 1955.

Ford, David F. 'On Being Christologically Hospitable to Jesus Christ. Hans Frei's Achievement'. *The Journal of Theological Studies* 46, no. 2 (October 1995): 532–46.

Ford, David F. *The Future of Christian Theology*. Oxford: Wiley-Blackwell, 2011.

Ford, David F. *Theology. A Very Short Introduction*. Second Edition. Oxford: Oxford University Press, 2013.

Ford, David, Ben Quash, Janet Martin Soskice, and Michael J. Buckley S.J., eds. *Fields of Faith. Theology and Religious Studies for the Twenty-First Century*. Cambridge and New York: Cambridge University Press, 2005.

Forster, Michael N. 'Hermeneutics. Francophone Approaches'. In *The Cambridge Companion to Hermeneutics*, edited by Michael N. Forster and Kristin Gjesdal, 260–85. New York: Cambridge University Press, 2019.

Forster, Michael N., and Kristin Gjesdal, eds. *The Cambridge Companion to Hermeneutics*. New York: Cambridge University Press, 2019.

Foucault, Michel. 'The Order of Discourse'. In *Untying the Text. A Post-Structuralist Reader*, edited by R. Young, 51–78. Boston: Routledge and Kegan Paul, 1981.

Frame, John M. *Apologetics. A Justification of Christian Belief*. Edited by Joseph E. Torres. Phillipsburg: P & R Publishing, 2015.

Frame, John M. 'Presuppositional Apologetics'. In *Five Views on Apologetics*, edited by Steven B. Cowan, 207–64. Grand Rapids: Zondervan Academic, 2000.

Frame, John M. '"Presuppositional Apologetics"'. Frame-Poythress.org, 23 May 2012. https://frame-poythress.org/presuppositional-apologetics/. Accessed 20 December 2021.

Frege, Gottlob. *The Foundations of Arithmetic. A Logico-Mathematical Enquiry into the Concept of Number*. Translated by J.L. Austin. Second Revised Edition. New York: Harper & Brothers, 1960.

Frei, Hans W. *The Eclipse of Biblical Narrative. A Study in Eighteenth and Nineteenth Century Hermeneutics*. Revised Edition. New Haven: Yale University Press, 1980.

Frei, Hans W. *Theology and Narrative. Selected Essays*. Edited by George Hunsinger and William C. Placher. New York: Oxford University Press, 1993.

Frei, Hans W. *Types of Christian Theology*. New Haven and London: Yale University Press, 1992.

Fuller, Steve. *Kuhn vs. Popper. The Struggle for the Soul of Science*. Cambridge: Icon, 2003.

Gauch, Hugh G. *Scientific Method in Practice*. New York: Cambridge University Press, 2003.

Geertz, Clifford. 'Thick Description. Toward an Interpretive Theory of Culture'. In *The Interpretation of Cultures. Selected Essays*, 3–30. New York: Basic Books, 1973.

Gerstner, John H., Arthur W. Lindsley, and R. C. Sproul. *Classical Apologetics*. Grand Rapids: Zondervan Academic, 1984.

Gettier, Edmund L. 'Is Justified True Belief Knowledge?' *Analysis* 23, no. 6 (June 1963): 121–23.

Giere, Ronald N. *Scientific Perspectivism*. Chicago: The University of Chicago Press, 2006.

Göcke, Benedikt Paul, ed. *Die Wissenschaftlichkeit der Theologie. Volume 1. Historische und systematische Perspektiven*. Studien zur systematischen Theologie, Ethik und Philosophie, 13/1. Münster: Aschendorff Verlag, 2018.

Gödel, Kurt. 'Über Formal unentscheidbare Sätze der Principia Mathematica und verwandter Systeme'. *Monatshefte für Mathematik und Physik* 38 (1931): 173–98.

Godfrey-Smith, Peter. *Theory and Reality. An Introduction to the Philosophy of Science*. Chicago: University of Chicago Press, 2003.

Godin, Benoıt, and Yves Gingras. 'The Experimenters' Regress. From Skepticism to Argumentation'. *Studies in History and Philosophy of Science. Part A* 33, no. 1 (1 March 2002): 133–48.

Goodman, Nelson. *Fact, Fiction, and Forecast*. Fourth Edition. Cambridge: Harvard University Press, 1983.

Graham, Peter J. 'The Reliability of Testimony'. *Philosophy and Phenomenological Research* 61, no. 3 (November 2000): 695–709.

Grau, Marion, and Jason Wyman, eds. *What Is Constructive Theology? Histories, Methodologies, and Perspectives*. Paperback Edition. London: T&T Clark, 2022.

Gravem, Peder. *KRL – et fag for alle? KRL-faget som svar på utfordringer i en flerkulturell enhetsskole*. Vallset: Oplandske bokforlag, 2004.

Greene, Brian. *Until the End of Time. Mind, Matter, and Our Search for Meaning in an Evolving Universe*. New York: Alfred A. Knopf Books, 2020.

Gregersen, Niels Henrik. 'Den Generøse Ortodoksi'. In *Den Generøse Ortodoksi. Konflikt Og Kontinuitet i Kristendommen*, 17–49. København: Eksistensen, 2016.

Gregersen, Niels Henrik. 'Dogmatik som samtidsteologi'. *Dansk Teologisk Tidsskrift* 71 (2008): 290–310.
Gregersen, Niels Henrik. 'Introduction. Wolfhart Pannenberg's Contributions to Theology and Science'. In *The Historicity of Nature. Essays on Science and Theology*, vii–xxiv. West Conshohocken: Templeton Foundation Press, 2008.
Gregersen, Niels Henrik. 'Samtidsteologiens horisont og fokus'. *Dansk Teologisk Tidsskrift* 74. årg., no. 2 (2011): 167–72.
Gregersen, Niels Henrik. *Teologi og kultur. Protestantismen mellem isolation og assimilation i det 19. og 20. århundrede*. Acta Jutlandica, LXV:1. Aarhus: Aarhus Universitetsforlag, 1988.
Gregersen, Niels Henrik. 'The Role of Thought Experiments in Science and Religion'. In *The Science and Religion Dialogue. Past and Future*, edited by Michael Welker, 129–40. New York: Peter Lang Edition, 2014.
Grim, Patrick. *The Incomplete Universe. Totality, Knowledge, and Truth*. Cambridge: Bradford, 1991.
Grosse, Sven. *Theologie und Wissenschaftstheorie*. Paderborn: Verlag Ferdinand Schöningh, 2019.
Grube, Dirk-Martin. 'Justification Rather than Truth. Gotthold Ephraim Lessing's Defense of Positive Religion in the Ring-Parable'. *International Journal for Philosophy and Theology* 66, no. 4 (2005): 357–78.
Haack, Susan, and Konstantin Kolenda. 'Two Fallibilists in Search of the Truth'. *Aristotelian Society Supplementary Volume* 51, no. 1 (10 July 1977): 63–104.
Hägglund, Bengt. 'Skandinavische Beiträge zur Methodenfrage der Systematische Theologie'. *Theologische Rundschau* 50, no. 4 (November 1985): 364–78.
Hansson, Sven Ove. 'Science and Pseudo-Science'. In *The Stanford Encyclopedia of Philosophy*, edited by Edward N. Zalta. Metaphysics Research Lab, Stanford University, 2017. https://plato.stanford.edu/archives/sum2017/entries/pseudo-science/. Accessed 20 December 2021.
Harman, Gilbert. 'The Inference to the Best Explanation'. *Philosophical Review* 74, no. 1 (1965): 88–95.
Harrison, Peter. *The Territories of Science and Religion*. Chicago: The University of Chicago Press, 2017.
Hauerwas, Stanley. *The State of the University. Academic Knowledges and the Knowledge of God*. Oxford: Blackwell, 2007.
Hauerwas, Stanley. 'Why the "'Sectarian Temptation'" Is a Misrepresentation. A Response to James Gustafson (1988)'. In *The Hauerwas Reader*, edited by John Berkman and Michael Cartwright, 90–110. Durham and London: Duke University Press, 2001.
Hedenius, Ingemar. *Tro och vetande*. Stockholm: Albert Bonniers Förlag, 1950.
Hegstad, Harald. 'Koherent uten å være autentisk?' *Teologisk tidsskrift* 8, no. 3 (2019): 205–9.
Hegstad, Harald. 'Korset som uttrykk for Guds kjærlighet – Sluttreplikk til Asle Eikrem'. *Teologisk tidsskrift* 9, no. 1 (2020): 59–62.

Hegstad, Harald. 'Var korset nødvendig?' *Teologisk tidsskrift* 8, no. 1 (2019): 41–54.
Heidegger, Martin. *Gesamtausgabe. 3: Abt. 1, Veröffentlichte Schriften 1910 - 1976: Kant und das Problem der Metaphysik*. Second Edition. Frankfurt am Main: Vittorio Klostermann, 2010.
Heidegger, Martin. *Sein und Zeit*. Tübingen: Max Niemeyer Verlag, 1967.
Hempel, Carl Gustav. *Philosophy of Natural Science*. Foundations of Philosophy Series. Englewood Cliffs: Prentice-Hall, 1966.
Hempel, Carl Gustav, and Paul Oppenheim. 'Studies in the Logic of Explanation'. *Philosophy of Science* 15, no. 2 (April 1948): 135–75.
Henderson, Leah. 'The Problem of Induction'. In *The Stanford Encyclopedia of Philosophy*, edited by Edward N. Zalta. Metaphysics Research Lab, Stanford University, 2019. https://plato.stanford.edu/archives/win2019/entries/induction-problem/. Accessed 20 December.
Henriksen, Jan-Olav. *Life, Love, and Hope. God and Human Experience*. Grand Rapids: Eerdmans, 2014.
Henriksen, Jan-Olav. 'Researching Theological Normativity. Some Critical and Constructive Suggestions'. *Studia Theologica. Nordic Journal of Theology* 60, no. 2 (2006): 207–20.
Herbener, Jens-André P. 'Eksempler på kristendomsproduktion og sandhedsspørgsmål i dansk universitetsteologi'. *Chaos. Skandinavisk tidsskrift for religionshistoriske studier* 53 (2010): 49–78.
Herbener, Jens-André P. 'The Study and Making of Christian Religion in Danish Academic Theology'. In *Contemporary Views on Comparative Religion. In Celebration of Tim Jensen's 65th Birthday*, edited by Peter Antes, Armin W. Geertz, and Mikael Rothstein, 207–18. Sheffield: Equinox, 2016.
Hick, John. *Philosophy of Religion*. Second Edition. Foundations of Philosophy Series. Englewood Cliffs: Prentice-Hall, 1973.
Hick, John. *The Existence of God*. Problems of Philosophy Series. New York: Macmillan, 1964.
Higton, Mike. *A Theology of Higher Education*. Oxford: Oxford University Press, 2012.
Hoffmeier, James K., and Dennis R. Magary, eds. *Do Historical Matters Matter to Faith? A Critical Appraisal of Modern and Postmodern Approaches to Scripture*. Wheaton: Crossway, 2012.
Holmer, Paul L. *The Grammar of Faith*. San Francisco: Harper & Row, 1978.
Howard, Jonathan. *Cognitive Errors and Diagnostic Mistakes: A Case-Based Guide to Critical Thinking in Medicine*. Cham. Switzerland: Springer, 2018.
Howard, Thomas Albert. *Protestant Theology and the Making of the Modern German University*. Oxford and New York: Oxford University Press, 2006.
Howson, Colin. 'Theories of Probability'. *The British Journal for the Philosophy of Science* 46, no. 1 (1995): 1–32.
Hughes, William, and Jonathan Lavery. *Critical Thinking. An Introduction to the Basic Skills*. Canadian Edition, Seventh Edition. Peterborough: Broadview Press, 2015.

Humboldt, Wilhelm von. 'Über die innere und äussere Organisation höheren wissenschaftlichen Anstalten in Berlin'. In *Schriften zur Politik und Zum Bildungswesen. Werke in Fünf Bänden*, Vol. 4. Darmstadt: Hermann Gentner Verlag, 1993.

Hume, David. *A Treatise of Human Nature*. Edited by David Fate Norton and Mary J. Norton. A Critical Edition. Vol. 1: Texts. 2 vols. Oxford: Clarendon Press, 2007.

Hume, David. *An Enquiry Concerning Human Understanding*. Edited by Peter Millican. Oxford's World Classics. Oxford: Oxford University Press, 2007.

Huyssteen, J. Wentzel van. *Essays in Postfoundationalist Theology*. Grand Rapids: Eerdmans, 1997.

IPCC. 'Sixth Assessment Report'. https://www.ipcc.ch/assessment-report/ar6/. Accessed 20 December 2021.

Israel, Jonathan I. *Democratic Enlightenment. Philosophy, Revolution, and Human Rights, 1750–1790*. Illustrated Edition. Oxford: Oxford University Press, 2013.

Israel, Jonathan I. *Radical Enlightenment. Philosophy and the Making of Modernity 1650–1750*. Illustrated Edition. Oxford: Oxford University Press, 2002.

Israel, Jonathan I. *The Enlightenment That Failed. Ideas, Revolution, and Democratic Defeat, 1748–1830*. New York: Oxford University Press, 2020.

Jasper, David. *A Short Introduction to Hermeneutics*. Louisville and London: Westminster John Knox Press, 2004.

Jeanrond, Werner. 'Correlation Theology and the Chicago School'. In *Introduction to Christian Theology. Contemporary North American Perspectives*, edited by Roger A. Badham, 137–53. Louisville: Westminster John Knox, 1998.

Jeanrond, Werner. *Theological Hermeneutics. Development and Significance*. New York: Crossroad, 1991.

Jeffner, Anders. *Kriterien christlicher Glaubenslehre. Eine prinzipielle Untersuchung heutiger protestantischer Dogmatik im deutschen Sprachbereich*. Studia doctrinae Christianae Upsaliensia 15. Uppsala: Almqvist & Wiksell, 1977.

Jonbäck, Francis. *The God Who Seeks but Seems to Hide*. Ph.D. Dissertation. Uppsala: Uppsala Universitet, 2016.

Joyce, James. 'Bayes' Theorem'. In *The Stanford Encyclopedia of Philosophy*, edited by Edward N. Zalta. Metaphysics Research Lab, Stanford University, 2021. https://plato.stanford.edu/archives/fall2021/entries/bayes-theorem/. Accessed 20 December 2021.

Kant, Immanuel. *Kritik der reinen Vernunft. Erster Teil*. Vol. 3. 10 vols. Kant Werke. Darmstadt: Wissenschaftliche Buchgesellschaft, 1968.

Kant, Immanuel. *Kritik der reinen Vernunft. Zweiter Teil*. Vol. 4. 10 vols. Kant Werke. Darmstadt: Wissenschaftliche Buchgesellschaft, 1968.

Kant, Immanuel. *Prolegomena to Any Future Metaphysics*. Translated by James W. Ellington. Second Edition. Indianapolis: Hackett, 2001.

Kaufman, Gordon D. *An Essay on Theological Method*. Missoula: Scholars Press, 1975.

Kaufman, Gordon D. *God the Problem*. Cambridge: Harvard University Press, 1972.

Kaufman, John. 'Historical Relativism and the Essence of Christianity'. *Studia Theologica. Nordic Journal of Theology* 70, no. 1 (2016): 4–21.

Kelly, Jacalyn, Tara Sadeghieh, and Khosrow Adeli. 'Peer Review in Scientific Publications: Benefits, Critiques, & A Survival Guide'. *EJIFCC* 25, no. 3 (2014): 227–43.

Kelsey, David H. *Between Athens and Berlin. The Theological Education Debate*. Eugene: Wipf & Stock, 1993.

Kelsey, David H. *To Understand God Truly. What's Theological About A Theological School*. Louisville: Westminister John Knox Press, 1992.

Kirkham, Richard L. *Theories of Truth. A Critical Introduction*. Cambridge: MIT Press, 1997.

Knauer, Peter. 'Ist Theologie Eine Wissenschaft?' *Theologie Und Philosophie* 93, no. 1 (2018): 81–96.

Kofoed, Jens Bruun. *Text and History. Historiography and the Study of the Biblical Text*. Winona Lake: Eisenbrauns, 2005.

Køppe, Simo, Frederik Stjernfelt, and David Budtz Pedersen, eds. *Kampen om disciplinerne. viden og videnskabelighed i humanistisk forskning*. København: Hans Reitzels Forlag, 2015.

Korsgaard, Christine M. *The Sources of Normativity*. Edited by Onora O'Neill. Cambridge: Cambridge University Press, 1996.

Kosterec, Milos. 'Methods of Conceptual Analysis'. *Filozofia* 71, no. 3 (2016): 220–30.

Kraschl, Dominikus. 'Christiche Theologie als paradigmebasierte Wissenschaft. Ein Plädoyer in wissenschaftstheoretischer Perspektive'. In *Die Wissenschaftlichkeit der Theologie. Vol. 1. Historische und systematische Perspektiven*, edited by Benedikt Paul Göcke, 277–314. Studien zur systematischen Theologie, Ethik und Philosophie, 13/1. Münster: Aschendorff Verlag, 2018.

Krauss, Lawrence M. *A Universe from Nothing. Why There Is Something Rather than Nothing*. London: Simon & Schuster, 2012.

Kuhn, Thomas S. *The Structure of Scientific Revolutions*. Second Edition, Enlarged. Chicago: Chicago University Press, 1970.

LaCugna, Catherine Mowry. *God for Us. The Trinity and Christian Life*. New York: HarperSanFrancisco, 2006.

Ladyman, James. *Understanding Philosophy of Science*. New York: Routledge, 2001.

Ladyman, James, Don Ross, David Spurrett, and John G. Collier. *Every Thing Must Go. Metaphysics Naturalized*. Oxford: Oxford University Press, 2007.

Lakatos, Imre. *The Methodology of Scientific Research Programmes*. Philosophical Papers 1. Cambridge: Cambridge University Press, 1999.

Lakatos, Imre, and Paul Feyerabend. *For and Against Method. Including Lakatos's Lectures on Scientific Method and the Lakatos-Feyerabend Correspondence*. Edited by Matteo Motterlini. Chicago: University of Chicago Press, 2000.

Lantin, Robert. 'Hume and the Problem of Induction'. *Philosophia* 26 (March 1998): 105–17.

Latour, Bruno. 'When Things Strike Back. A Possible Contribution of "Science Studies" to the Social Sciences'. *British Journal of Sociology* 51, no. 1 (2000): 107–23.

Laudan, Larry. 'A Confutation of Convergent Realism'. *Philosophy of Science* 48, no. 1 (March 1981): 19–49.

Laudan, Larry. *Progress and Its Problems. Towards a Theory of Scientific Growth*. Berkeley: University of California Press, 1978.

Lewis, Thomas A. 'The Inevitability of Normativity in the Study of Religion. Theology in Religious Studies'. In *Theology and Religious Studies in Higher Education. Global Perspectives*, edited by D.L. Bird and Simon G. Smith, 87–98. London: Continuum, 2009.

Lindbeck, George A. *The Nature of Doctrine. Religion and Theology in a Postliberal Age*. Philadelphia: Westminster Press, 1984.

Lipton, Peter. *Inference to the Best Explanation*. New York: Routledge, 2004.

Liston, Michael. 'Scientific Realism and Antirealism'. Internet Encyclopedia of Philosophy, (Year not specified). https://www.iep.utm.edu/sci-real/. Accessed 20 December 2021.

Lonergan, Bernard. *Method in Theology*. Toronto: University of Toronto Press, 1971.

Longino, Helen E. 'Values and Objectivity'. In *Philosophy of Science. The Central Issues*, edited by Martin Curd and J.A. Cover, 170–86. New York: W.W. Norton & Company, 1998.

Machamer, Peter K., and Michael Silberstein, eds. *The Blackwell Guide to the Philosophy of Science*. Blackwell Philosophy Guides 7. Malden: Blackwell, 2002.

MacIntyre, Alasdair. *After Virtue. A Study in Moral Theory*. Second Edition. London: Duckworth, 1985.

MacIntyre, Alasdair. 'Epistemological Crises, Dramatic Narrative and the Philosophy of Science'. *The Monist* 60, no. 4 (October 1977): 453–72.

MacIntyre, Alasdair. *Whose Justice? Which Rationality?* Notre Dame: University of Notre Dame Press, 1988.

Manoogian. *Cognitive Bias Codex*. 5 September 2016. https://commons.wikimedia.org/wiki/File:Cognitive_Bias_Codex_-_180%2B_biases,_designed_by_John_Manoogian_III_(jm3).jpg. Accessed 20 December 2021.

Martinson, Mattias. *Perseverance without Doctrine. Adorno, Self-Critique, and the Ends of Academic Theology*. European University Studies. Series XXIII, Theology. Frankfurt am Main and New York: Peter Lang, 2000.

Masterman, Margaret. 'The Nature of a Paradigm'. In *Criticism and the Growth of Knowledge*, edited by Alan Musgrave and Imre Lakatos, 59–89. Cambridge: Cambridge University Press, 1970.

Maudlin, Tim. *Philosophy of Physics. Space and Time*. Princeton Foundations of Contemporary Philosophy. Princeton and Oxford: Princeton University Press, 2012.

McCutcheon, Russell T. *Critics Not Caretakers. Redescribing the Public Study of Religion*. Albany: State University of New York Press, 2001.

McCutcheon, Russell T. *Fabricating Religion. Fanfare for the Common e. g.* Berlin and Boston: De Gruyter, 2019.

McCutcheon, Russell T. *Studying Religion. An Introduction*. Second Edition. London and New York: Routledge, 2018.

McGrath, Alister E. *A Scientific Theology. Nature*. Vol. 1. 3 vols. Grand Rapids: Eerdmans, 2001.
McGrath, Alister E. *A Scientific Theology. Reality*. Vol. 2. 3 vols. London and New York: T&T Clark, 2006.
McGrath, Alister E. *A Scientific Theology. Theory*. Vol. 3. 3 vols. Grand Rapids: Eerdmans, 2003.
McGrath, Alister E. *Christian Theology. An Introduction*. Fifth Edition. Oxford: Wiley-Blackwell, 2011.
McGrath, Alister E. *Luther's Theology of the Cross. Martin Luther's Theological Breakthrough*. Oxford: Blackwell, 1985.
McGrath, Alister E. *The Territories of Human Reason. Science and Theology in an Age of Multiple Rationalities*. New York: Oxford University Press, 2019.
McKinnon, Alastair. *Falsification and Belief*. The Hague: Mouton, 1970.
Merton, Robert K. 'The Normative Structure of Science'. In *The Sociology of Science. Theoretical and Empirical Investigations*, edited by Norman W. Storer, 267–78. Chicago: The University of Chicago Press, 1973.
Milbank, John. *Theology and Social Theory. Beyond Secular Reason*. Second Edition. Oxford: Blackwell, 2006.
Milbank, John, Catherine Pickstock, and Graham Ward, eds. *Radical Orthodoxy. A New Theology*. London and New York: Routledge, 1998.
Mjaaland, Marius Timmann. *The Hidden God. Luther, Philosophy, and Political Theology*. Bloomington and Indianapolis: Indiana University Press, 2016.
Molendijk, Arie L. *Aus dem Dunklen ins Helle. Wissenschaft und Theologie im Denken von Heinrich Scholz*. Amsterdam: Editions Rodopi, 1991.
Moore, G.E. *Principia Ethica*. Cambridge: Cambridge University Press, 1965.
Mørch, Michael Agerbo, ed. *En plads blandt de lærde. Teologiens videnskabelighed til debat*. Frederiksberg: Eksistensen, 2019.
Moreland, James Porter, and William Lane Craig. *Philosophical Foundations for a Christian Worldview*. Second Edition. Downers Grove: IVP Academic, 2017.
Moser, Paul K., and Daniel Howard-Snyder, eds. *Divine Hiddenness. New Essays*. Cambridge: Cambridge University Press, 2002.
Moustakas, Ulrich. *Theologie im Kontext von Wissenschaftstheorie und Hermeneutik*. Hamburg: Kovac, Dr. Verlag, 2017.
Mühling, Markus. *Post-Systematic Theology I. Ways of Thinking - A Theological Philosophy*. Paderborn: Wilhelm Fink at Brill, 2020.
Munchin, David. '"Is Theology a Science?" Paul Feyerabend's Anarchic Epistemology as Challenge Test to T.F. Torrance's Scientific Theology'. *Scottish Journal of Theology* 64, no. 4 (2011): 439–55.
Munchin, David. *Is Theology a Science? The Nature of the Scientific Enterprise in the Scientific Theology of Thomas Forsyth Torrance and the Anarchic Epistemology of Paul Feyerabend*. Leiden and Boston: Brill, 2011.

Mundra, Anil. 'Naturalism, Normativity, and the Study of Religion'. *Religions* 8, no. 10 (2017).
Murphy, Nancey C. 'Nonreductive Physicalism'. In *Personal Identity in Theological Perspective*, edited by Richard Lints, Michael Scott Horton, and Mark R. Talbot. Grand Rapids: Eerdmans, 2006.
Murphy, Nancey C. 'Review of "Philip Clayton, Explanation from Physics to Theology. An Essay in Rationality and Religion."' *Faith and Philosophy. Journal of the Society of Christian Philosophers* 9, no. 1 (1992): 124–26.
Murphy, Nancey C. *A Philosophy of the Christian Religion for the Twenty-First Century*. London: SPCK, 2018.
Murphy, Nancey C. *Theology in the Age of Scientific Reasoning*. Ithaca: Cornell University Press, 1993.
Musgrave, Alan. 'Method or Madness?' In *Essays in Memory of Imre Lakatos*, edited by R. S. Cohen, Paul Feyerabend, and Marx W. Wartofsky, 457–91. Boston Studies in the Philosophy of Science 39. Dordrecht and Boston: Springer, 1976.
Næss, Arne. *En del elementære logiske emner*. Eleventh Edition. Oslo: Universitetsforlaget, 1975.
Niederbacher, Bruno, and Gerhard Leibold, eds. *Theologie als Wissenschaft im Mittelalter. Texte, Übersetzungen, Kommentare*. Münster: Aschendorff, 2006.
Nielsen, Kai. 'On Fixing the Reference Range of God'. *Religious Studies* 2, no. 1 (October 1966): 13–36.
Norton, John. 'Are Thought Experiments Just What You Thought?' *Canadian Journal of Philosophy* 26 (1996): 333–66.
Nygren, Anders. *Meaning and Method*. Translated by Philip S. Watson. London: Epworth Press, 1972.
O'Callaghan, Paul. 'Whose Future? Pannenberg's Eschatological Verification of Theological Truth'. *Irish Theological Quarterly* 66 (2001): 19–49.
Ogden, Schubert M. 'Falsification and Belief'. *Religious Studies* 10, no. 1 (March 1974): 21–43.
Ohly, Lukas. *Theologie als Wissenschaft. Eine Fundamentaltheologie aus phänomenologischer Leitperspektive*. Frankfurt am Main: Peter Lang, 2017.
Okasha, Samir. *Evolution and the Levels of Selection*. Oxford and New York: Clarendon and Oxford University Press, 2006.
Okasha, Samir. *Philosophy of Science. A Very Short Introduction*. Second Edition. A Very Short Introduction 67. Oxford: Oxford University Press, 2016.
Okasha, Samir. 'What Did Hume Really Show About Induction?' *The Philosophical Quarterly* 51, no. 204 (July 2001): 307–27.
Olson, Maria, and Tatjana Zimenkova. '(Hidden) Normativity in Social Science Education and History Education'. *Journal of Social Science Education* 14, no. 1 (Spring 2005): 2–5.
Olsson, Erik J. *Against Coherence. Truth, Probability, and Justification*. Oxford: Clarendon, 2005.
Oppy, Graham. *Arguing about Gods*. New York: Cambridge University Press, 2006.

Oppy, Graham. *Atheism and Agnosticism*. Cambridge Elements. Elements in the Philosophy of Religion. Cambridge: Cambridge University Press, 2018.

Oppy, Graham. *Naturalism and Religion. A Contemporary Philosophical Investigation*. London and New York: Routledge, 2018.

Pannenberg, Wolfhart. *Basic Questions in Theology. Collected Essays, Volume One*. Philadelphia: Fortress, 1968.

Pannenberg, Wolfhart. *Systematic Theology*. Translated by Geoffrey W. Bromiley. Vol. 1. 3 vols. Grand Rapids: Eerdmans, 1991.

Pannenberg, Wolfhart. *Systematic Theology*. Translated by Geoffrey W. Bromiley. Vol. 2. 3 vols. London and New York: T&T Clark International, 2004.

Pannenberg, Wolfhart. *Systematic Theology*. Translated by Geoffrey W. Bromiley. Vol. 3. 3 vols. London and New York: T&T Clark International, 2004.

Pannenberg, Wolfhart. *The Historicity of Nature. Essays on Science and Theology*. West Conshohocken: Templeton Foundation Press, 2008.

Pannenberg, Wolfhart. ed. 'The Task of Systematic Theology in the Contemporary University'. In *Theology and the University. Essays In Honor Of John B. Cobb, Jr.*, 81–93. Albany: State University of New York Press, 1991.

Pannenberg, Wolfhart. *Theology and the Philosophy of Science*. Philadelphia: The Westminster Press, 1976.

Paul, Herman. *Key Issues in Historical Theory*. New York and London: Routledge, 2015.

Pearl, Judea, and Dana Mackenzie. *The Book of Why. The New Science of Cause and Effect*. London: Penguin Books, 2019.

Peirce, Charles Sanders. '§4. The First Rule of Reason'. In *The Collected Papers, Vol. 1: Principles of Philosophy*, 1931. http://www.textlog.de/4249.html. Accessed 20 December 2021.

Petersen, Anders Klostergaard. 'Teologi 2010'. *Fønix* 23, no. 3 (1999): 138–43.

Pieper, Francis. *Christian Dogmatics*. Vol. 3. 4 vols. Saint Louis: Concordia, 1953.

Plantinga, Alvin. 'The Dawkins Confusion. Naturalism "Ad Absurdum" A Review of Richard Dawkins's The God Delusion'. In *God Is Great, God Is Good. Why Believing in God Is Reasonable and Responsible*, edited by William Lane Craig and Chad Meister, 247–58. Downers Grove: IVP, 2009.

Plantinga, Alvin. *Warranted Christian Belief*. Oxford: Oxford University Press, 2000.

Plantinga, Alvin. *Where the Conflict Really Lies. Science, Religion, and Naturalism*. New York: Oxford University Press, 2011.

Plantinga, Alvin, and Nicholas Wolterstorff, eds. *Faith and Rationality. Reason and Belief in God*. Notre Dame: University of Notre Dame Press, 1983.

Plato. 'Euthyphron'. In *Werke*, 1:351–97. Darmstadt: Wissenschaftliche Buchgesellschaft, 1977.

Popper, Karl R. *Conjectures and Refutations. The Growth of Scientific Knowledge*. Third Edition. London: Routledge, 2002.

Popper, Karl R. *The Logic of Scientific Discovery*. New York: Routledge, 2002.

Porpora, Douglas V. 'Methodological Atheism, Methodological Agnosticism and Religious Experience'. *Journal for the Theory of Social Behaviour* 36, no. 1 (2006): 57–75.

Potter, Garry, and José López. 'After Postmodernism. The New Millennium'. In *After Postmodernism. An Introduction to Critical Realism*, edited by Garry Potter and José López, 3–16. London and New York: Bloomsbury Academic, 2005.

Psillos, Stathis. *Scientific Realism. How Science Tracks Truth*. Philosophical Issues in Science. London: Routledge, 1999.

Psillos, Stathis, and Martin Curd, eds. *The Routledge Companion to Philosophy of Science*. Routledge Philosophy Companions. London: Routledge, 2010.

Puntel, Lorenz B. *Being and God. A Systematic Approach in Confrontation with Martin Heidegger, Emmanuel Levinas, and Jean-Luc Marion*. Translated by and in collaboration with Alan White. Evanston: Northwestern University Press, 2011.

Puntel, Lorenz B. 'Der Wahrheitsbegriff in Philosophie und Theologie'. *Zeitschrift für Theologie und Kirche*, no. Beiheft 9: Theologie als gegenwärtige Schriftauslegung (June 1995): 16–45.

Puntel, Lorenz B. *Grundlagen einer Theorie der Wahrheit*. Grundlagen der Kommunikation und Kognition. Berlin: de Gruyter, 1990.

Puntel, Lorenz B. *Structure and Being. A Theoretical Framework for a Systematic Philosophy*. Translated by and in collaboration with Alan White. Pennsylvania: The Pennsylvania State University Press, 2008.

Puntel, Lorenz B. *Wahrheitstheorien in der neueren Philosophie. Eine kritisch-systematische Darstellung*. Third Edition. Vol. 83. Erträge Der Forschung. Darmstadt: Wissenschaftliche Buchgesellschaft, 1993.

Puntel, Lorenz B. *Sein und Nichts. Das ursprüngliche Thema der Philosophie*. Tübingen: Mohr Siebeck, 2021.

Purvis, Zachary. *Theology and the University in Nineteenth-Century Germany*. Oxford Theology and Religion Monographs. Oxford: Oxford University Press, 2016.

Putnam, Hilary. 'Beyond the Fact-Value Dichotomy'. *Crítica. Revista Hispanoamericana de Filosofía* 14, no. 41 (1982): 3–12.

Putnam, Hilary. *Mathematics, Matter, and Method*. Second Edition. Philosophical Papers, vol. 1. Cambridge and New York: Cambridge University Press, 1979.

Putnam, Hilary. *Reason, Truth and History*. Cambridge and New York: Cambridge University Press, 1981.

Putnam, Hilary. *The Collapse of the Fact/Value Dichotomy and Other Essays*. Cambridge: Harvard University Press, 2004.

Quine, W.V. *Philosophy of Logic*. Foundations of Philosophy Series. Englewood Cliffs: Prentice-Hall, 1970.

Quine, W.V. 'Two Dogmas of Empiricism'. *The Philosophical Review* 60, no. 1 (January) (1951): 20–43.

Rahner, Karl. *The Trinity*. Translated by Joseph Donceel. London: Burns and Oates, 1970.

Rasmusson, Arne. 'A Century of Swedish Theology'. *Lutheran Quaterly* XXI (2007): 125–62.

Rescher, Nicholas. *Cognitive Systematization. A Systems-Theoretic Approach to a Coherentist Theory of Knowledge*. Totowa: Rowman and Littlefield, 1979.
Rescher, Nicholas. 'Fallibilism'. In *Routledge Encyclopedia of Philosophy*. London: Routledge, 2016.
Rescher, Nicholas. *Philosophical Reasoning. A Study in the Methodology of Philosophizing*. Malden: Blackwell Publishers, 2001.
Rescher, Nicholas. *Pluralism. Against the Demand for Consensus*. Oxford: Oxford University Press, 1993.
Rescher, Nicholas. *Reality and Its Appearance*. Continuum Studies in American Philosophy. London and New York: Continuum, 2010.
Rescher, Nicholas. *Scientific Realism. A Critical Reappraisal*. Dordrecht: Reidel, 1989.
Rescher, Nicholas. *The Coherence Theory of Truth*. Oxford: Oxford University Press, 1973.
Rescher, Nicholas. *The Strife of Systems. An Essay on the Grounds and Implications of Philosophical Diversity*. Pittsburgh: University of Pittsburgh Press, 1985.
Rescher, Nicholas. 'Truth as Ideal Coherence'. *The Review of Metaphysics* 38, no. 4 (June 1985): 795–806.
Rescher, Nicholas. *What If? Thought Experimentation in Philosophy*. New Brunswick: Transaction Publishers, 2005.
Riekert, Heinrich. *Kulturwissenschaft und Naturwissenschaft*. Tübingen: J.C.B. Mohr, 1921.
Roemer, Marjorie Godlin. 'Which Reader's Response?' *College English* 49, no. 8 (December 1987): 911–21.
Rosenberg, Alexander. *Philosophy of Science. A Contemporary Introduction*. Third Edition. New York: Routledge, 2012.
Rowbottom, Darrell P. 'Scientific Realism. What It Is, the Contemporary Debate, and New Directions'. *Synthese* 196 (2019): 451–84.
Rüegg, Walter. 'Theology and the Arts'. In *Universities in the Nineteenth and Early Twentieth Centuries (1800–1945)*, edited by Walter Rüegg, 393–458. A History of the University in Europe 3. Cambridge: Cambridge University Press, 2004.
Russell, Robert John, and Nancey Murphy, eds. *Quantum Cosmology Laws of Nature. Scientific Perspectives on Divine Action*. Berkeley: University of Notre Dame Press, 1993.
Ryrie, Alec. *Unbelievers. An Emotional History of Doubt*. London: William Collins, 2019.
Salmon, Wesley C. *The Foundations of Scientific Inference*. 50th Anniversary Edition. Pittsburgh: University of Pittsburgh Press, 2017.
Sanchez, Norma G. 'New Quantum Structure of Space-Time'. *Gravitation and Cosmology* 25, no. 2 (1 April 2019): 91–102.
Sanchez, Norma G. 'Unifying Quantum Mechanics with Einstein's General Relativity'. *Research Outreach* (blog), 19 December 2019. https://researchoutreach.org/articles/unifying-quantum-mechanics-einstein-general-relativity/. Accessed 20 December 2021.
Sandbeck, Lars. *Den gudløse verden. Ateisme og antireligion i en postkristen æra*. Frederiksberg: Eksistensen, 2020.

Sanders, Fred. *The Image of the Immanent Trinity. Rahner's Rule and the Theological Interpretation of Scripture.* Vol. 12. Issues in Systematic Theology. New York: Peter Lang, 2005.

Sauter, Gerhard. *Theologie als Wissenschaft. Aufsätze und Thesen.* München: Chr. Kaiser, 1971.

Sauter, Gerhard. *Wissenschaftstheoretische Kritik der Theologie. Die Theologie und die neuere wissenschaftstheoretische Diskussion. Materialien, Analysen, Entwürfe.* München: Chr. Kaiser, 1973.

Schaffalitzky, Caroline. 'Findes teologisk forskning?' In *En plads blandt de lærde. Teologiens videnskabelighed til debat*, edited by Michael Agerbo Mørch, 163–76. Frederiksberg: Eksistensen, 2019.

Schellenberg, J. L. *Divine Hiddenness and Human Reason.* Ithaca: Cornell University Press, 1993.

Schilbrack, Kevin. 'A Metaphysics for the Study of Religion. A Critical Reading of Russell McCutcheon'. *Critical Research on Religion* 8, no. 1 (2020): 87–100.

Schleiermacher, Friedrich. *Brief Outline of the Study of Theology.* Translated by William Farrer. Eugene: Wipf & Stock, 2007.

Schneider, Christina. '"Gott" als theoretischer Term?' In *Die Wissenschaftlichkeit der Theologie. Vol. 1. Historische und systematische Perspektiven*, edited by Benedikt Paul Göcke, 315–36. Studien zur systematischen Theologie, Ethik und Philosophie, 13/1. Münster: Aschendorff Verlag, 2018.

Schneider, Ruben. 'Struktural-systematische Theologie. Theologie als Wissenschaft vor dem Hintergrund der transzendentalen und der linguistischen Wende'. In *Die Wissenschaftlichkeit der Theologie. Vol. 1. Historische und systematische Perspektiven*, edited by Benedikt Paul Göcke, 33–83. Studien zur systematischen Theologie, Ethik und Philosophie, 13/1. Münster: Aschendorff Verlag, 2018.

Scholz, Heinrich. 'Was ist unter einer theologischen Aussage zu verstehen?' In *Theologie als Wissenschaft. Aufsätze Und Thesen*, edited by Gerhard Sauter, 265–77. München: C. Kaiser, 1971.

Scholz, Heinrich. 'Wie ist eine evangelische Theologie als Wissenschaft Möglich?' *Zwischen den Zeiten* Vol. 9 (1931): 8–53.

Schurz, Gerhard. *Philosophy of Science. A Unified Approach.* New York: Routledge, 2014.

Searle, John R. 'The Classical Model of Rationality and Its Weaknesses'. In *Rationality and Irrationality. Proceedings of the 23rd International Wittgenstein-Symposion*, edited by Berit Brogaard and Barry Smith, 311–24. Schriftenreihe Der Wittgenstein-Gesellschaft 29. Vienna: ÖBV & HPT, 2001.

Segal, Robert A. 'Ninian Smart and Religious Studies'. *The Council of Societies for the Study of Religion Bulletin* 30, no. 2 (2001): 27–29.

Shapere, Dudley. 'The Structure of Scientific Revolutions'. *The Philosophical Review* 73, no. 3 (July 1964): 383–94.

Shermer, Michael Brant. 'God's Number Is Up'. Michael Shermer, 1 July 2004. https://michaelshermer.com/sciam-columns/gods-number-is-up/. Accessed 20 December 2021.

Slingerland, Edward G. *What Science Offers the Humanities. Integrating Body and Culture*. Cambridge: Cambridge University Press, 2008.

Smart, Ninian. 'Religious Studies and Theology'. *The Council of Societies for the Study of Religion Bulletin* 26, no. 3 (1997): 66–68.

Smart, Ninian. *The Science of Religion and the Sociology of Knowledge*. Princeton: Princeton University Press, 1973.

Smith, Barry. 'In Defense of Extreme (Fallibilistic) Apriorism' 12, no. 1 (Spring 1996): 179–92.

Smith, Jonathan Z. 'Religion, Religions, Religious'. In *Critical Terms for Religious Studies*, edited by Mark C. Taylor, Second Edition., 269–84. Chicago: The University of Chicago Press, 1998.

Smith, Quentin. 'The Metaphilosophy of Naturalism'. *Philo* 4, no. 2 (2001): 195–215.

Snow, C.P. *The Two Cultures*. Canto Edition. Cambridge: Cambridge University Press, 1998.

Søvik, Atle O. 'A Theoretical Framework for Talking Seriously about God'. In *Talking Seriously About God. Philosophy of Religion in the Dispute between Theism and Atheism*, 4:55–76. Nordic Studies in Theology. Zürich: Lit Verlag, 2016.

Søvik, Atle O. *The Problem of Evil and the Power of God*. Studies in Systematic Theology 8. Leiden and Boston: Brill, 2011.

Stalker, Douglas, ed. *Grue! New Riddle of Induction*. Chicago: Open Court, 1992.

Stenmark, Mikael. 'Science and a Personal Conception of God: A Critical Response to Gordon D. Kaufman'. *Journal of the American Academy of Religion* 71, no. 1 (March 2003): 175–81.

Stern, Robert J. 'The Evolution of Plate Tectonics'. *Philosophical Transactions of the Royal Society A. Mathematical, Physical and Engineering Sciences* 376, no. 2132 (13 November 2018): 20170406.

Stjernfelt, Frederik. *Diagrammatology. An Investigation on the Borderlines of Phenomenology, Ontology, and Semiotics*. Vol. Vol. 336. Synthese Library. Studies in Epistemology, Logic, Methodology, and Philosophy of Science. Dordrecht: Springer, 2007.

Stjernfelt, Frederik. 'Homo humanitatis'. In *Kampen om mennesket. Forskellige menneskebilleder og deres grænsestrid*, edited by David Budtz Pedersen, Finn Collin, and Frederik Stjernfelt, 227–48. København: Hans Reitzels Forlag, 2018.

Stjernfelt, Frederik. *Natural Propositions. The Actuality of Peirce's Doctrine of Dicisigns*. Boston: Docent Press, 2014.

Stjernfelt, Frederik. 'Symbol Og Skema i Neo-Kantiansk Semiotik'. *Psyke & Logos* 16, no. 1 (1995): 76–98.

Swinburne, Richard. *Epistemic Justification*. Oxford and New York: Clarendon Press, 2001.

Swinburne, Richard. *Faith and Reason*. Second Edition. Oxford and New York: Clarendon, 2005.

Swinburne, Richard. *The Coherence of Theism*. Oxford: Clarendon Press, 1977.

Swinburne, Richard. *The Existence of God*. Second Edition. Oxford & New York: Clarendon & Oxford University Press, 2004.

Tillich, Paul. *Systematic Theology*. Vol. 1. 3 vols. Chicago: University of Chicago Press, 1973.

Tarski, Alfred. 'The Concept of Truth in Formalized Language'. In *Logic, Semantics, Metamathematics. Papers from 1923 to 1938*, edited by John Corcoran, Second Edition. Indianapolis: Hackett, 1983.

Taylor, Charles. *A Secular Age*. Cambridge: Belknap, 2007.

Taylor, Charles. 'The Meaning of Secularism'. *The Hedgehog Review* 12, no. 3 (Fall 2010): 23–34.

Thagard, Paul R. 'Why Astrology Is A Pseudoscience'. *PSA. Proceedings of the Biennial Meeting of the Philosophy of Science Association* Vol. 1. Contributed Papers (1978): 223–34.

Thiemann, Ronald F. *Revelation and Theology. The Gospel as Narrated Promise*. Notre Dame: University of Notre Dame Press, 1985.

Thomsen, Søren Ulrik. 'Pro Ecclesia'. In *Kritik af den negative opbyggelighed*, by Frederik Stjernfelt and Søren Ulrik Thomsen, 151–97. Valby: Vindrose, 2005.

Til, Cornelius Van. *Christian Apologetics*. Edited by William Edgar. Second Edition. Phillipsburg: P & R Publishing, 2003.

Tompkins, Jane P., ed. *Reader-Response Criticism. From Formalism to Post-Structuralism*. Baltimore: The Johns Hopkins University Press, 1980.

Toulmin, Stephen. *The Uses of Argument*. Cambridge: Cambridge University Press, 1958.

Tracy, David. *The Analogical Imagination. Christian Theology and the Culture of Pluralism*. New York: Crossroad, 1981.

Tyson, Lois. *Critical Theory Today. A User-Friendly Guide*. Third Edition. New York: Routledge, 2014.

Unwin, Stephen D. *The Probability of God. A Simple Calculation That Proves the Ultimate Truth*. New York: Crown Forum, 2004.

van Fraassen, Bas C. *The Scientific Image*. Clarendon Library of Logic and Philosophy. Oxford and New York: Clarendon Press, 1980.

van Inwagen, Peter. *Metaphysics*. Second Edition. Dimensions of Philosophy Series. Cambridge: Westview Press, 2002.

Vanhoozer, Kevin J. *Biblical Authority after Babel. Retrieving the Solas in the Spirit of Mere Protestant Christianity*. Grand Rapids: Brazos Press, 2016.

Vanhoozer, Kevin J. *Is There a Meaning in This Text? The Bible, The Reader, and the Morality of Literary Knowledge*. Grand Rapids: Zondervan, 1998.

Veeneman, Mary M. *Introducing Theological Method. A Survey of Contemporary Theologians and Approaches*. Grand Rapids: Baker Academic, 2017.

Volf, Miroslav, and Matthew Croasmun. *For the Life of the World. Theology That Makes a Difference*. Grand Rapids: Brazos Press, 2018.

Webster, John. 'What Makes Theology Theological?' *Journal of Analytic Theology* 3 (May 2015): 17–28.

Weinberg, Steven. *The First Three Minutes. A Modern View of the Origin of the Universe*. Updated Edition. New York: Basic Books, 1993.

West, Cornel. *Prophesy Deliverance!* Louisville: Westminster John Knox Press, 2002.

White, Alan. *Toward a Philosophical Theory of Everything. Contributions to the Structural-Systematic Philosophy*. New York: Bloomsbury, 2014.

Wiebe, Donald. 'An Eternal Return All Over Again. The Religious Conversation Endures'. *Journal of the American Academy of Religion* 74, no. 3 (2006): 674–96.

Wiebe, Donald. 'Change the Name! On the Importance of Reclaiming NAASR's Original Objectives for the Twenty-First Century'. *Method & Theory in the Study of Religion* 25, no. 4/5 (2013): 350–61.

Wiebe, Donald. *The Irony of Theology and the Nature of Religious Thought*. Montreal & Kingston: McGill-Queen's University Press, 1991.

Wiebe, Donald. *The Politics of Religious Studies. The Continuing Conflict with Theology in the Academy*. New York: St. Martin's Press, 1999.

Wittgenstein, Ludwig. *On Certainty*. Edited by G.E.M. Anscombe and G.H. von Wright. Translated by Denis Paul and G.E.M. Anscombe. Oxford: Basil Blackwell, 1969.

Wittgenstein, Ludwig. *Philosophische Untersuchungen. Philosophical Investigations*. Edited by G. E. M. Anscombe, P. M. S. Hacker, and Joachim Schulte. Revised Fourth Edition. Malden: Wiley-Blackwell, 2009.

Wittgenstein, Ludwig. *Tractatus Logico-Philosophicus*. Translated by C.K. Ogden. London: Kegan Paul, Trench, Trubner & Co., 1922.

Wolterstorff, Nicholas. 'Is It Possible and Desirable for Theologians to Recover from Kant?' In *Inquiring about God*, edited by Terence Cuneo, 35–55. Cambridge: Cambridge University Press, 2010.

Wolterstorff, Nicholas. *Reason within the Bounds of Religion*. Second Edition. Grand Rapids: Eerdmans, 1984.

Wolterstorff, Nicholas. *Religion in the University*. New Haven: Yale University Press, 2019.

Wood, James. 'Child of Evangelism'. *London Review of Books*, 3 October 1996. https://www.lrb.co.uk/the-paper/v18/n19/james-wood/child-of-evangelism. Accessed 20 December 2021.

Worrall, John. 'Philosophy of Science. Classic Debates, Standard Problems, Future Prospects'. In *The Blackwell Guide to the Philosophy of Science*, edited by Peter K. Machamer and Michael Silberstein, 18–36. Blackwell Philosophy Guides 7. Malden: Blackwell, 2002.

Wright, G. H. von. *Explanation and Understanding*. London: Routledge and K. Paul, 2012.

Wyman Jr., Jason A. *Constructing Constructive Theology. An Introductory Sketch*. Philadelphia: Fortress, 2017.

Zachhuber, Johannes. *Theology as Science in Nineteenth-Century Germany. From F.C. Baur to Ernst Troeltsch*. Oxford: Oxford University Press, 2013.

Zahavi, Dan. *Husserl's Phenomenology*. Stanford: Stanford University Press, 2003.

Zahavi, Dan. *Phenomenology: The Basics*. London and New York: Routledge, 2019.

Zahavi, Dan. 'Self and Other: From Pure Ego to Co-Constituted We'. *Continental Philosophy Review* 48, no. 2 (2015): 143–60.

Zhai, Zhenming. 'The Problem of Protocol Statements and Schlick's Concept of "Konstatierungen"'. *PSA. Proceedings of the Biennial Meeting of the Philosophy of Science Association* Volume One: Contributed Papers (1990): 15–23.

Index

Index of Person

A

Adler, Alfred   209, 210
Alston, William   328
Ammerman, Nancy   356
Aquinas, Thomas   121–123
Aristotle   250
Aspect, Alain   224
Astley, Jeff   356
Ayer, Alfred   147, 183

B

Bacon, Francis   153
Bahnsen, Greg   288
Barbour, Ian   202, 294
Barth, Karl   30, 32, 43, 44, 46–48, 63
Barthes, Roland   276
Bayes, Thomas   162
Berger, Peter   61, 317, 337
Bevans, Stephen   337
Bohr, Niels   91
Bostrom, Nick   90
Brown, James   91
Bultmann, Rudolf   352

C

Carnap, Rudolf   145, 146, 149, 150, 152, 237, 259
Chakravartty, Anjan   167, 168
Chomsky, Noam   152
Clark, Gordon   144, 288
Clayton, Philip   83, 96, 103, 293, 294
Coady, C.A.J.   281, 282
Cover, Jan   176

Cowen, Steven   290
Curd, Martin   176

D

Damasio, Antonio   332
Darwin, Charles   177
Davis, Stephen   241–243
Descartes, René   248
Diem, Hermann   32, 43, 48–50, 52, 63
Duhem, Pierre   222, 224, 225
D'Costa, Gavin   39, 318, 320–322, 336

E

Ebeling, Gerhard   60
Eikrem, Asle   72–74, 77, 81, 82
Einstein, Albert   90, 91, 224
Erdozain, Dominic   268

F

Fehige, Yiftach   91
Feyerabend, Paul   34, 210, 212, 215–217, 224, 225
Fichte, Johann   42
Fish, Stanley   275–281
Flew, Antony   91, 240–244
Frame, John   288–290, 293
Frege, Gottlob   151
Frei, Hans   32, 43, 61, 62, 64
Freud, Sigmund   209, 268

G

Gadamer, Hans-Georg   268
Galilei, Galileo   90, 250
Gauch, Hugh   128, 129

Geertz, Clifford   61, 73
Giere, Ronald   143, 178
Gilkey, Langdon   60
Gödel, Kurt   301
Godfrey-Smith, Peter   148, 171, 221, 223
Goodman, Nelson   154, 155, 157
Gravem, Peder   170
Greene, Brian   183
Gregersen, Niels Henrik   32, 39, 67, 68, 72–82, 90, 337, 352, 370

H

Hägglund, Bengt   54
Hare, Richard   240, 241
Harman, Gilbert   90, 158
Harvey, Van   60
Hauerwas, Stanley   25, 39
Hedenius, Ingemar   349
Heidegger, Martin   95, 109, 120, 121
Heisenberg, Werner   91
Hemberg, Jarl   55
Hempel, Carl Gustav   220, 221
Henriksen, Jan-Olav   318, 321–323
Herbener, Jens-André   350
Hick, John   91, 241, 244
Hilbert, David   90
Holland, Normann   276
Holte, Ragnar   55
Humboldt, Wilhelm   41
Hume, David   142, 146, 153–157, 191, 198, 207, 325
Husserl, Edmund   75, 260, 318

I

Irenaeus   122
Iser, Wolfgang   276

J

Jeanrond, Werner   63
Jeffner, Anders   32, 43, 53–57, 63, 64

K

Kant, Immanuel   42, 44, 83, 84, 97, 98, 149, 150, 347, 351
Kaufman, Gordon   60, 355
Kuhn, Thomas   34, 178, 192, 210–213, 217, 219, 224, 225, 248, 275–281, 286
Küng, Hans   60

L

Ladyman, James   148, 153–157
Lakatos, Imre   34, 147, 190, 210, 212–215, 217–219, 224, 225, 249, 270, 292
Latour, Bruno   143
Laudan, Larry   34, 168, 210, 217–219, 224–228, 270
Lewis, Thomas   318–320, 322, 332, 336
Lindbeck, George   32, 43, 61–64
Lipton, Peter   158, 159
Lonergan, Bernard   61
Longino, Helen   256
López, Jose   172
Louth, Andrew   314
Luther, Martin   175, 241

M

Mach, Ernst   146
MacIntyre, Alasdair   25, 34, 61, 192–195, 199, 247–250, 252, 253, 263, 292, 321
Marx, Karl   268
McCutcheon, Russell   312, 314–316
McFague, Sallie   314
McGrath, Alister   33, 61, 160, 179, 180, 186–189, 192, 193, 195, 200, 201, 203
McGuire, Meredith   356
McKinnon, Alastair   243
Merton, Robert   327–329
Metz, Johann   60
Mitchell, Basil   240, 241
Mühling, Markus   301
Murphy, Nancey   33, 179, 180, 186, 189–203, 249, 290–292

N
Næss, Arne   267
Netland, Harold   320
Neurath, Otto   259
Newton, Isaac   262, 279
Nietzsche, Friedrich   198, 268
Nygren, Anders   32, 43, 53, 54, 57, 59, 60, 63, 64, 344

O
Ogden, Schubert   60, 241, 243, 244
Okasha, Samir   159, 221
Oppy, Graham   34, 247, 250–253

P
Pannenberg, David   191
Pannenberg, Wolfhart   28, 29, 32, 33, 37, 43, 48–50, 52, 56, 59, 60, 63, 173, 179–186, 189–192, 200–203, 353–357
Pascal, Blaise   96
Peirce, Charles   329
Petersen, Anders Klostergaard   352
Phillips, Dewi   160
Plantinga, Alvin   194
Plato   113, 195, 250
Popper, Karl   34, 142, 152, 176, 182, 205–210, 212–214, 216–218, 224, 225, 248, 275
Potter, Gary   172
Puntel, Lorenz   23, 28, 29, 33, 74, 79, 84, 93, 96–127, 132–134, 178, 179, 181, 185, 202, 203, 224, 229, 232–234, 237, 238, 249, 252, 261, 283, 286, 300, 301, 328, 362–364, 370
Putnam, Hilary   22, 152, 325, 326, 328

Q
Quine, Willard   33, 145, 148–152, 175, 224, 225, 249

R
Rasmusson, Arne   54
Rescher, Nicholas   23, 28, 29, 84, 115, 127–132, 142, 160, 161, 167, 191, 202, 203, 224, 229–233, 235–237, 301, 362
Ricœur, Paul   268
Rosenberg, Alex   148
Russell, Bertrand   90, 151
Russell, Robert John   197
Ryle, Gilbert   73

S
Salmon, Wesley   143
Sauter, Gerhard   32, 43, 48, 50–52, 63
Schaffalitzky, Caroline   69, 70, 349, 350
Schleiermacher, Friedrich   42, 349
Schlick, Moritz   146, 259
Scholz, Heinrich   32, 43–48, 51, 56, 63
Schrofner, Erich   48
Schurz, Gerhard   174
Siemer, Helge   48
Smart, Ninian   312–317, 321, 323
Söderblom, Nathan   54
Søvik, Atle   80
Stjernfelt, Frederik   263, 264
Swinburne, Richard   164–166

T
Taylor, Charles   25
Thiemann, Ronald   96
Tillich, Paul   32, 43, 58, 59, 64
Torrance, Thomas   43
Toulmin, Stephen   60
Tracy, David   32, 43, 58–61, 64

U
Ussher, James   242

V
van den Brink, Gijsbert   92, 201, 290–292
van Huyssteen, Wentzel   293

van Inwagen, Peter   83–85, 299
Van Til, Cornelius   288
Vanhoozer, Kevin   276

W
Ward, Keith   320
Weber, Max   336
White, Alan   108, 110
Wiebe, Donald   312–317

Wigg-Stevenson, Natalie   356
Wilder, Amos   314
Wittgenstein, Ludwig   61, 104, 160, 280
Wolff, Christian   98
Wolterstorff, Nicholas   263, 282, 283
Worrall, John   285

Y
Yale school   32, 61

Index of Subjects

A

aboslute necessary personal Being   124
absolute dimension of Being   111
absolute nothingness   117, 118
absolutely necessary Being   118–122
absolutely necessary dimension of Being   123
absolutely necessary minded Being   121, 122, 126
absolutely necessary minded free creating Being   126
absolutely necessary personal Being   124
academic discipline   351
academic theology   63, 64
academy   59
ad hoc   129, 159, 210, 213, 270, 271
aesthetic experience   57
afterlife   92, 183, 244–247, 297
Agent-Network-Theory   143
agnosticism   250, 317
all-determining reality   50, 85, 182, 185, 201, 355
an sich   114, 347, 355
analogy   102, 118, 121–124, 211
analytic philosophy   57, 357
analyticity   150
antinomy of negation   300, 301
antirealism   23, 71, 168, 314
anything goes   215
apologetics   164, 288, 320
astrology   88, 193, 208, 209, 239, 240, 291, 304
astronomy   193, 200, 239, 304
asymptotic approximation   134
atheism   96, 250, 317
atomistic   151, 191
authenticity   72, 74–77, 315, 336, 337
authenticity of meaning   337
authenticity of truth   337

B

background knowledge   222
baptism   86, 176, 247
basic structure   238
Bayes, Thomas   163
Bayesian Inference   142, 152, 157, 159, 161, 162, 164, 166, 167
 – background knowledge   162, 164–166
 – probability theory   142, 161
Being   95, 96, 98, 109–111, 113–127, 180, 362
 – the analogy-answer   118
 – the bottom-up-answer   118
being   98, 110, 113, 114, 116, 120, 121, 182, 184, 190, 237, 364
Being as a whole   101, 102, 109, 114, 116, 119, 122, 362
Being as such   109–111, 113, 114, 116, 117, 119, 176
Being as such and as a whole   81, 85, 98, 109–111, 117–120, 176
Being as such and as whole   109
Bible   18, 57, 75, 76, 90, 94, 159, 170, 247, 289, 332, 335, 360
 – Scripture   41, 89, 94, 193, 230, 246, 288, 289
Big Bang   177, 183
big picture   251, 252
biology   69, 200, 201, 278, 337, 343, 344, 353, 359
biophysics   166
blindness thesis   97
boundary question   200, 202
brute fact   151, 166, 189
bundle   222

C

caloric theory of heat 177
causality 122, 165
causation 121
cause and effect 153, 154, 171
Chicago school 58, 61–64
Christ 46, 49, 54, 75, 80, 86, 92, 159, 185, 189, 244, 245, 289, 291, 298, 300
Christian practices 72, 293
Christian tradition 26, 69, 78, 188, 189, 194, 196, 197, 199, 335, 345, 360
Christianity 35, 50, 54, 57, 59, 62, 63, 68, 72–76, 79, 81, 127, 185, 195–197, 199, 200, 202, 243, 244, 289, 316, 334, 337, 344, 345, 353, 360
Christology 184
church 24, 25, 31, 32, 46, 51, 52, 59, 63, 72, 75, 77, 87, 94, 125, 126, 193, 197, 225, 335, 346
church history 27, 69
climate change 300
coarse-grained 26, 195, 199, 234, 282, 292, 297, 298, 303, 304, 320
coextensiveness 113, 118–120
cognitive bias 34, 271, 272, 275, 284
　– bandwagon effect 272
　– confirmation bias 272, 291
　– continued influence effect 273
　– courtesy bias 272
　– Dunning-Kruger effect 273, 274
　– implicit bias 274
　– selective perception 274
　– Semmelweis reflex 273
cognitive science of religion 198, 199
coherence 22, 23, 28, 29, 32–34, 37, 39, 45, 68, 73, 74, 76–80, 82, 85, 88–90, 100, 103, 114–116, 128–134, 157, 159–161, 169, 172–174, 176, 179–181, 185, 187–189, 193, 199, 201–203, 205, 206, 217, 219, 223, 224, 228–230, 232–237, 239, 245, 246, 249, 250, 252, 253, 256, 269, 270, 284, 286, 289, 294–297, 300–303, 307–309, 311, 317, 324, 326, 328, 330–334, 338, 340, 341, 344, 354, 355, 358, 366, 369–373
　– coherent 20, 29, 35, 68, 69, 71, 72, 74, 78–81, 84–88, 91, 94, 98–101, 104, 106, 115, 119, 123, 124, 126, 129, 130, 132–134, 161, 172, 176, 178, 182, 185, 191–193, 199, 201, 202, 206, 216, 224, 228–233, 235–239, 244, 245, 247, 257, 270, 282, 284, 294, 296, 297, 300–305, 308, 309, 328, 333–335, 337, 338, 340, 341, 361, 365, 370–373
　– cohesiveness 28, 109, 131, 180, 185, 202, 231, 232, 249, 252, 296, 301
　– comprehensiveness 28, 109, 176, 180, 202, 231, 232, 236, 238, 252, 296, 297, 299
　– consistency 28, 76, 114, 132, 180, 202, 231, 232, 236, 252, 294, 295, 324
　– external coherence 68, 81, 180, 202, 358
　– internal coherence 68, 77–79, 85, 86, 180, 358
coherence theory 29, 33–35, 43, 79, 84, 90, 92, 109, 111, 115, 127, 129–131, 141, 167, 173, 200–203, 228–230, 232, 233, 235, 239, 252, 253, 282, 296, 300, 311, 327, 330, 339–341, 355, 359, 372
coherentism 134, 219, 322
common criterion 20, 23, 30, 37, 39, 50, 52, 54, 60, 135, 344, 369, 370
comparison 81, 206, 219, 228, 252, 315, 341, 358
comprehensive systematics 98
computer science 69
conceptual analysis 155, 354, 357
conceptual problem 92, 224–228
　– external conceptual problem 226
　– internal conceptual problem 226

configuration   71, 109, 113–115, 123, 127, 224, 344
 – positive interlinkings   114
confirmation theory   147
confirmationism   207
conjecture   209
consciousness   27, 113, 120, 144, 297, 317
consensus   77, 96, 197, 201, 241, 246, 247, 260, 269, 270, 272, 294, 309, 319, 333
consensus theory   229
constitution of reality   22, 85, 95, 371
constitutional conditions   95
construction   78, 81, 185, 286, 338
construction principle   30, 205, 257, 308, 323, 369
context of discovery   30, 207, 222, 266
context of justification   30, 186, 207, 222, 223, 266
context principle   100
contextual   35, 131, 200, 336, 337
contingent beings   98, 110, 117–122, 124
conversion   86, 247
correlation method   64
correspondence theory   107, 128, 129, 177, 219, 229, 230, 232, 294
corroborate   207, 209
cosmology   83, 177, 200
counseling   67
creation   80, 120–124, 126, 172, 175, 182–184, 230, 242, 300, 339
creeds   75, 76, 336
 – the Apostles' creed   76
criterion   23, 24, 26–39, 43, 44, 46, 47, 52, 55–58, 61–64, 68–72, 74–79, 81, 89, 103, 104, 108, 128–130, 134, 139–146, 148, 158, 161, 164, 167–175, 178–180, 188, 193, 201, 203, 205, 206, 208, 209, 212, 214, 217, 220, 229–232, 234–237, 239, 240, 245, 246, 248, 249, 251–253, 255–259, 261, 264, 265, 269–271, 278, 281, 283–287, 290, 291, 293, 295, 300–303, 308–311, 315, 317, 318, 324, 329, 330, 336, 337, 340–342, 345–349, 363, 366, 369–373
criterion of authenticity   338
critical intersubjectivity   35, 286, 287, 289, 293, 295
critical rationalism   207, 216
critical realism   114, 187
crucial experiment   90, 222
CUDOS   327, 328
cultural proximity   33, 69
culture   57, 59

D

data   27–30, 34–36, 42, 69, 77, 80, 84, 85, 87, 89, 92–94, 101–103, 107–109, 126–130, 132, 134, 135, 139, 140, 151, 158–161, 164, 170, 172, 173, 176, 177, 179, 188, 190, 191, 193, 201, 202, 207, 220, 222, 224, 227, 230–236, 240, 245, 247, 249, 251–253, 255–258, 262–267, 269, 273, 274, 278–285, 289, 291–293, 295–298, 301–305, 307, 311, 316, 317, 323, 326, 330–335, 337–341, 343–348, 350, 352, 356, 358, 361, 363, 365, 372, 373
data-background beliefs   283
datum   101, 230, 256, 265, 296
death of god-theology   43
deduction   33, 90, 141, 156, 220, 224
 – deductive-nomological model   220, 221
deductive-nomological model   220
 – the covering law model   220
deep metaphysics   98
deep structure   233, 234
definition   23, 27, 30, 37, 46, 62, 70, 79, 84, 112, 113, 129, 139, 155, 156, 158, 161, 176, 192, 210, 229, 230, 237, 242, 258, 265, 285, 310, 311, 323, 337, 354

demarcated intersubjectivity 35, 286, 287, 290, 292, 293, 295
demarcation 342, 345, 363
demarcation problem 208, 214
determinism 182, 183, 197
Dewey, John 325, 332
discipline 17–20, 27, 36, 37, 39, 51, 53, 59, 60, 63, 68–70, 72, 86–88, 95, 96, 103, 108, 125, 127, 140, 144, 173, 175–177, 180, 190, 200–202, 223, 247, 278, 280, 304, 307, 308, 316, 320, 327, 328, 334, 339, 341–349, 352, 359, 363, 366, 369, 371–373
discourse 20, 24, 25, 28, 35, 37, 41, 42, 44, 46–49, 54, 57–59, 61–63, 67, 73, 76, 85, 86, 89, 95, 96, 98, 100–103, 110, 111, 126, 131, 135, 169, 174, 178, 179, 262, 263, 265, 267, 286, 292–294, 303, 315, 319, 344, 348, 357, 359, 366
dissipative adaptation 165, 184
distinct research 36, 37, 139, 140, 312, 335, 341–351, 357, 358, 360, 364, 366, 371, 373
distinct science 318
divine action 182, 195–197
 – quantum divine action 196
divine agency 126
divine attributes 123
divine reality 182
doctrine 31, 77, 79, 80, 86, 92, 124, 125, 135, 182, 185, 241, 247, 301, 302, 332, 360
dogma of analyticity 149, 150
dogma of reductionism 149, 150
dogmatics 46, 67, 77–80, 92, 126, 240, 246, 247, 253
Donald Duck 233
Duckburg 233

E
eclecticism 173
ecology 200

economics 69, 201, 319
eidetic variation 75
emic 315
empiricism 33, 34, 145, 146, 148–151, 197, 220, 258–261, 265, 279
Enlightenment 18, 57, 61, 187, 332
 – universal knowledge 61
 – universal rationality 64
epistemic crisis 194
epistemology 24, 32, 71, 90, 96, 104, 146, 191–193, 196, 199, 253, 261–263, 271, 281–284, 321, 328, 359, 362
epistemology of testimony 34, 271, 281, 282, 284
epoché 313, 318, 323
 – bracket 36
 – bracketing 318
 – brackets 317, 361
eschatological verification 34, 91, 240–242, 244, 245
eschatology 50
eschaton 240, 245, 252
eternal conscious punishment 172
eternal, the 32, 54, 64
eternity 92
ethics 64, 67, 200, 227, 245, 309, 325
ethnography 313, 353
ethos of science 328
etic 315, 356
Eucharist
 – holy communion 126
eucharist 86, 246, 265, 298
 – Last Supper 194
 – Lord's supper 301
Euthyphro Dilemma 195
evidence 29, 36, 61, 82, 84, 85, 152, 155, 163–166, 189, 190, 193, 194, 198, 201, 202, 209, 213, 215, 219, 235, 241, 242, 244–246, 250, 251, 260, 263, 270, 273, 281, 285, 290, 293, 309, 349, 351, 358–360

evidential limit   241, 242
evolution   57, 120, 219, 233
evolutionary biology   76, 93, 224, 227
evolutionary theory   18, 92, 120, 122, 177, 278, 291, 353
– genetics   177
exegesis   27, 69
existence   19, 22, 49, 58, 59, 87, 88, 91, 96, 110, 121, 122, 160, 164–166, 175, 183, 184, 188, 194, 197, 225, 231, 240, 246, 247, 250, 282, 283, 289, 291, 297, 348, 350, 352, 358
existential proposition   291
experience   50, 55, 57, 89, 115, 129, 146, 148, 150, 151, 154, 165, 182, 189, 192, 244, 245, 247, 266, 268, 291, 293, 352, 360
experiment   34, 83, 93, 146, 220, 223, 265, 267, 268
explanation   25, 42, 53, 121, 122, 158–161, 163, 165, 166, 171, 183, 184, 186, 187, 189, 196–199, 220, 221, 286, 297, 315
explication   20, 24–27, 31, 33, 37, 39, 45, 51, 62, 63, 68, 70–74, 76, 80–82, 84–87, 91, 96, 99–103, 107, 110–113, 116, 118–123, 125–127, 129, 134, 135, 145, 175, 178, 182, 184, 185, 187, 188, 198, 201, 205, 228, 231, 235, 238, 242, 244, 247, 252, 253, 258, 261, 265, 266, 269, 278, 279, 292, 294, 302–304, 308, 310, 312, 317, 319, 320, 323, 326, 328–330, 338, 341, 343, 345, 350, 351, 354, 357, 358, 364, 370, 372, 373
expressibility   115, 116

F

fact/value distinction   325
faith   17, 33, 55–57, 60, 63, 64, 68, 72, 74, 75, 77, 78, 81, 86, 94, 172, 242, 244, 246, 247, 290, 294, 319, 334, 336, 338, 347, 366

fallibilism   22, 31, 37, 46, 82, 89, 94, 128, 143, 157, 163, 173, 192, 207, 233, 235, 256, 264, 268–271, 275, 293, 294, 296, 299, 300, 329, 330, 333, 340, 369, 372
falsifiability   27, 139, 141, 203, 205, 208, 209, 239, 245, 246, 253
falsification   34, 36, 39, 103, 108, 139, 141, 170, 203, 205–210, 212, 215–220, 222–225, 228, 234, 239, 240, 243–249, 252, 253, 255–257, 278, 283, 285, 291, 307, 310, 339, 341, 350, 370, 371, 373
– anti-confirmation   208
family resemblance   280, 281
feminist theology   76
fideistic   87
final verification   84, 143, 207, 214, 245, 299
fine-grained   40, 79, 85, 92, 134, 178, 183, 189, 196, 202, 203, 228, 229, 234, 252, 282, 296, 297, 320, 333, 339, 369, 372
fine-tuning   92, 166, 183
foundationalism   71, 134, 194, 263, 283, 293, 322
four-stage method   102, 108, 109, 132
freudian psychology   208
– psychoanalysis   209
friendly outsider   264
fundamental motif   32, 53, 54, 63
– Agape motif   54
– motif analysis   54
– motif research   54
fundamental structures   116, 118
für mich
– Erscheinungen   114, 355
für uns   347

G

general hermeneutics   51
general metaphysics   98, 344
general theory of relativity   299

God   19–21, 24–26, 32, 37, 41–44, 46–50, 54, 57–59, 61–63, 67, 76, 80, 85–89, 92, 95–102, 110, 111, 118, 120–124, 126, 127, 131, 135, 164–166, 169, 172–176, 178–185, 194–199, 201, 233, 240, 244–246, 250, 265, 266, 285, 286, 288–293, 295, 297, 298, 314, 316, 337, 339, 344, 347, 351–359, 361, 364–366
- Absolute   21
- absolute   361
- abstract entity   21
- ground of Being   21, 59
- minded absolutely necessary Being   120
- minded Being   118, 120
- the Absolute   176
- totality   361
- totality of existence   21
- ultimate   317, 361, 362, 364
- ultimate concern   59
- Ultimate Reality   200
- ultimate reality   50
God of the gaps   183
good research   309, 344, 349
ground of Being   176
guilt   247

H

heretical imperative   337
hermeneutics   50, 104, 170, 175, 185, 262, 264, 271, 275, 278, 281, 284, 304, 318, 322, 323
hermeneutics of faith   267, 268, 288
hermeneutics of suspicion   267, 268
hiddenness of God   76, 296, 297
higher criticism   196, 332
history   17, 44, 50, 51, 67, 69, 85, 87, 92, 94, 96, 125–127, 130, 148, 169, 175, 180, 182, 185, 186, 189, 191–193, 197, 205, 213, 229, 246–248, 275, 281, 297, 313, 336, 344, 349, 350

history of Christianity   241
history of philosophy   34, 41, 325
history of philosophy of science   144
history of physics   211
history of religion   54, 185
history of science   22, 31, 217, 222, 227, 248, 270, 271, 296, 333
history of theology   33, 41, 95, 123, 172, 191, 337
holism   45, 134, 148, 150, 175, 223
holist epistemology   249
holistic   64, 79, 133, 150, 151, 175, 191, 271, 283, 284, 298, 372
holistic account of testability   151
holistic relatedness of epistemology and ontology   34
holistic theories   145, 161, 172
holistic theory   109
Holy Spirit   247
homiletics   67
human flourishing   88, 174
human mind   113, 118–120, 187, 236
human rationality   263
human science   26, 29, 144, 169, 200
- humanities   38
hypothetico-deductive method   34, 84, 87, 205, 206, 219–224, 227, 354, 357

I

identity theory   107
identity thesis   102, 107
imago Dei   172
immanence   124, 127, 184
induction   33, 141, 142, 148, 152–158, 161, 166, 167, 173, 207, 213, 220
inductive   90, 146, 147, 156, 159, 160, 222, 224
inductive inference   155, 157
inference   33, 122, 141, 142, 152, 153, 156–158, 161, 166, 167, 173, 174, 205, 220, 223, 273, 282

Inference to the Best Explanation   84, 115, 142, 152, 156–160, 162, 167, 186, 203
- abduction   158, 186, 188–190
Inference to the Best Systematization   115, 142, 160, 167, 236
insider/outsider problem   315
instrumentalism   168, 219
intellectual fallacy   268
intentional coextensiveness   119, 120
interpretations of reality   50
interpretive community   34, 276, 280
intersection of reason   38, 39
intersubjectivity   24, 27, 31, 34–37, 39, 40, 49, 55, 57, 62, 86, 89, 91, 95, 135, 139, 166, 169, 170, 172, 223, 234, 235, 248, 253, 255–275, 277–279, 281–295, 297, 298, 300–305, 307, 310, 313, 316, 317, 329–331, 341, 349, 354, 359, 363, 370–372
intrasystemic   62

J

Jesus of Nazareth   49, 126, 160
- Jesus   50, 54, 159, 184, 185, 189, 244, 245, 289

K

Kantian philosophy   362
kerygma   59
kingdom of God   244
knowledge   22, 31, 38, 42, 45, 47, 49, 50, 57, 68, 82, 84–86, 92, 94, 97, 115, 147, 151, 153, 156, 157, 162–168, 173, 174, 177, 178, 180, 184, 191, 192, 195, 198, 199, 207, 211, 212, 220, 224, 233, 235, 248, 249, 256, 257, 260, 266, 271, 273–275, 281, 282, 288, 289, 313, 322, 324, 333, 346, 359

L

language   22, 25, 31, 61, 72–74, 78, 85, 96, 99, 104–108, 113–115, 122, 129, 145, 146, 150–152, 154, 188, 211, 225, 238, 243, 253, 259, 277, 283, 284, 294, 327, 369
large-scale tradition   194, 199, 203, 252
Law of Bivalence   131, 231
Law of Contradiction   231
Law of Excluded Middle   231
Law of Negation   231
Law of the Excluded Middle   131
laws of nature   154, 184, 214, 297
- natural laws   26, 166
linguistic framework   237
linguistics   101, 353
literary studies   69
literary theory   276
liturgical elements   72
logic   25, 71, 72, 96, 99–102, 104, 107, 114, 116, 119, 131, 133, 140, 145, 153, 207, 216, 226, 231, 238, 242, 268, 270, 292, 319, 357, 363, 366, 369
Logical Positivism   84, 145–152, 168, 175, 181, 207, 291
- Vienna Circle   146, 152
logico-epistemic bite   128, 230, 231

M

Martin Luther King   282
marxist theory   208, 209
mathematics   46, 69, 201, 238, 242, 267, 363
maximally consistent subsets   132
meaning   50, 51, 53, 54, 63, 73, 79, 84, 95, 104, 115, 146, 149, 151, 152, 168, 174, 185, 191, 226, 245, 267, 271, 276, 290, 295, 345
medicine   69, 343, 344
metaphysica generalis   98
metaphysical proposition   181
metaphysical theory   83, 84, 171, 328, 369

metaphysics 17, 18, 44, 45, 53, 83–85, 103, 116, 120–122, 145, 168, 203, 227, 265, 299, 302
method 17, 20, 22, 27, 31, 32, 34, 36, 42, 43, 47, 48, 52–54, 56, 59, 64, 67, 68, 71–74, 76, 78, 81, 82, 89, 95, 102, 103, 111, 112, 125, 132, 135, 143, 144, 149, 152, 155, 158, 161, 169, 170, 172–175, 184, 193, 196, 198, 201, 203, 207, 213, 215–217, 221, 224, 225, 249–251, 253, 256–258, 261, 262, 264–267, 273, 274, 277–280, 283, 284, 303–305, 307, 309, 317, 323, 324, 326, 330, 338, 340, 341, 345, 346, 348, 350, 352, 354–357, 361, 363, 370, 373
– methodology 63, 71, 217, 319, 321
method of correlation 58
methodological agnosticism 38
minded Being 120, 121
mind-independent 22, 229, 261, 283, 369
missiology 67
modality 362
modern cosmology 76
moral authority 199, 200
moral psychology 309

N

naïve inductivism 153
natural entity 35, 312, 326, 327
natural science 18, 26, 27, 42, 45, 46, 60, 80, 90, 93, 94, 120, 144, 172, 179, 189, 198, 200, 201, 205, 222, 224, 227, 249, 253, 292, 297, 303, 304, 353, 355
natural theology 183
naturalism 38, 194–200, 202, 250, 304, 311, 314–317, 319, 326, 334, 350, 356, 364, 370
New Riddle of Induction 154
– grue 155
no-miracle argument 22, 157, 296–298
non-being 121

non-deductive inference 158
non-existence 165, 166
non-observable entity 84, 156
normal science 211, 212, 276, 277
– puzzle-solving 211, 212, 277
normative ontology 68, 82, 85
normativity 27, 35–37, 39, 53, 60, 69, 82, 85, 139, 140, 219, 227, 264, 305, 307–312, 314–328, 330, 331, 333, 335–340, 344, 350, 357, 360, 361, 370, 371, 373

O

objectivity 144, 255, 256, 260, 261, 264
observation 129, 145–148, 151, 153–155, 157, 164, 179, 208, 210, 214, 220, 222, 224, 274, 283, 284, 288, 296, 355
ontological structures 116
ontological theories 85, 89, 180, 201
ontological theory 201–203, 295, 298, 300, 358
ontology 22, 26, 33, 34, 73, 80, 81, 83–86, 88, 89, 96, 98–100, 102, 105–107, 115–117, 119, 131, 132, 135, 161, 175, 176, 180, 189, 202, 206, 228, 230, 238, 240, 241, 244–247, 249, 251–253, 261, 264, 271, 283, 284, 298, 317, 325, 338, 352, 354, 362, 365, 366, 370–373
onto-theology 120, 122
optical theory of luminiferous ether 177
organized scepticism 267, 271
orthodoxy 35, 336, 337
overdetermination of data 191

P

palaeontology 224, 359
panentheism 124, 127
pantheism 124
paradigmatic intersubjectivity 292
paradigm 62, 178, 179, 188, 200, 201, 211–213, 217, 249, 271, 277–281, 287, 294, 295, 320

paradigmatic intersubjectivity   35, 286, 287, 290–292, 295
paradigmatic thinking   34, 276, 277, 286
Paul   184
pedagogics   319
perspectivism   178
pessimistic meta-induction   219, 224
phenomenology   34, 75, 258–261, 313, 318, 323, 350
philology   69
philosophical theology   91, 120, 177
philosophy   24, 36, 41, 43, 49, 53, 60, 62, 67, 79, 93, 97, 98, 101, 102, 106–108, 111, 116, 118, 125–127, 132, 134, 146, 147, 149, 150, 157, 176, 190–192, 206, 209, 213, 215, 219, 228, 230, 238, 253, 258, 294, 301, 304, 307, 318, 319, 325, 342, 344–346, 349, 351, 355, 361–365, 371, 372
philosophy of language   61
philosophy of physics   176
philosophy of religion   53, 67, 91, 164, 192, 250, 344
philosophy of science   18, 20, 21, 23, 28, 29, 31, 34, 37, 39, 48, 95, 135, 141, 146, 148, 152, 154, 161, 164, 168, 169, 177, 178, 186, 188, 190, 192, 193, 199, 200, 205, 206, 208, 210, 215–217, 219, 220, 227, 242, 248, 255, 269, 274, 275, 310, 370
physicalism   198
physics   45, 144, 180, 200, 201, 215, 226, 250, 278, 279, 296, 297, 299, 316, 337, 353, 359
plate tectonics   300
pluralism   29, 30, 59, 64, 95, 99, 100, 171, 196, 197, 276, 322
political science   69, 144, 206, 319
posit   121, 122, 124
positivism   219
post-metaphysical   76

practical theology   67
practice   23, 29, 35, 40, 71, 78, 90, 167, 168, 171, 172, 192, 200, 212, 213, 215, 218, 223, 237, 239, 270, 272, 290, 293, 294, 302, 311, 312, 317, 356, 363
practice turn   356
pragmatic   23, 69, 73, 81, 98, 105–107, 171, 218, 224, 275, 338, 369
pragmatic theory   229
pragmatism   129, 168, 171, 173, 225, 237, 253, 270, 296, 332, 362
prayer   72, 183, 359, 360
prediction   22, 154, 157, 172, 223, 266, 353, 357
presupposition   20–24, 30, 34, 38, 43, 45, 46, 51, 61, 70, 76, 87, 89, 95, 135, 150, 173, 175, 188, 199, 203, 228, 238, 253, 257, 258, 262, 264–266, 273, 274, 278–280, 283, 284, 286–290, 303–305, 307, 309, 310, 312, 314, 317, 323, 324, 326, 327, 330, 333–335, 340, 341, 345, 348, 350, 361, 363, 369, 371
presuppositional apologetics   287, 288, 290
prime fact   102
prime proposition   102
prime sentence   104
primodial dimension of Being   104
principle of ontological rank   118–120
privat discourse   24
probability   87, 90, 156, 157, 159, 161–163, 165, 166, 184, 190, 213, 219, 273
problem of evil   76, 228
problem of irrelevance   221
problem of symmetry   221
problem-solving activity   224, 225
progress   22, 29, 54, 85, 163, 199, 201, 211, 214, 223
prolegomena   25, 43, 55, 293, 314
proleptic eschatology   92
properly basic   194

proposition   44, 45, 47, 50, 100, 101, 107, 109, 128, 130, 131, 141, 145, 147, 149, 151, 157, 159, 168, 173, 176, 179, 181, 182, 184–186, 203, 206, 210, 230, 240, 242, 244, 246, 247, 253, 259, 270, 327, 358
protocol statements   259
pseudoscience   171, 207–210, 213, 214, 239, 312, 318
psychology   52, 60, 200, 206, 226, 274, 353, 359
public   19, 20, 24, 25, 29, 37, 38, 41, 42, 44, 46, 47, 49, 52, 57–63, 86, 95, 96, 98, 100–102, 110, 126, 130, 131, 135, 169, 174, 178, 179, 186, 262, 264, 265, 286, 290, 292–294, 304, 313, 324, 344, 359, 361, 366

Q

quadrilateral, the   89
quantum mechanics   91, 224, 299

R

rationality   20, 47, 51, 58, 61, 63, 134, 144, 182, 187, 188, 196, 207, 215, 248, 256, 262–264, 292
rationally justified   20, 24, 25, 36, 37, 41, 42, 44, 46, 47, 49, 52, 57–59, 61–63, 67, 86, 89, 95, 96, 98, 100–102, 110, 125–127, 131, 135, 169, 174, 178, 179, 262, 265, 286, 292, 294, 344, 361, 366
rationally justified public discourse   52
reader-response theory   276
realism   21–24, 71, 114, 168, 172, 177, 178, 189, 219, 256, 261, 283, 333, 369
 – critical realism   160
 – scientific realism   160
reality   22–24, 38, 45, 49–51, 79, 84–86, 92, 93, 96, 101, 107, 108, 114, 125, 128–130, 135, 146, 147, 151, 160, 166, 173, 176, 178, 181, 182, 184–187, 189, 229–231, 233, 237, 238, 245, 262, 269, 283, 284, 299, 301, 302, 311, 317, 319, 337, 353, 362, 364, 365, 369
reason   17, 41, 88–90, 173, 233, 243, 247, 249, 253, 286, 294, 319, 332, 336, 360, 370
reconstruction   74, 170, 172, 173
re-description   78
reductionism   93, 150, 151, 215
reformed epistemology   24, 359
refutation   147, 209
regional ontology   45, 343, 354, 363
relativism   85, 100, 178, 219, 231, 280, 286, 287, 336
religion   32, 33, 50, 52–54, 62, 69, 81, 91, 160, 185, 198, 199, 230, 243, 244, 263, 308, 313, 315–321, 327, 333, 336, 338, 344, 345, 347, 350, 352, 356, 360, 361
 – hellenistic religion   54
 – judaic religion   54
religious discourse   72
religious experience   57, 61, 87, 126, 130, 189, 193, 197, 230, 291–293, 335, 356
religious expression   33, 72, 135
religious studies   19, 32, 35, 36, 38, 43, 52, 55, 82, 307–310, 312–314, 316–321, 326, 327, 330, 336, 342, 344–347, 349, 351, 361, 362, 365, 371, 372
repentance   247
research discipline   352
research program   190, 199, 214, 217, 295, 330
 – auxiliary belt   218
 – auxiliary hypotheses   213
 – hard core   190, 199, 213, 215, 218, 292
 – positive heuristic   190, 214, 215, 292, 296
 – protection belt   214, 215, 270
 – protective belt   213, 292
research tradition   217–219

research university 19, 31, 37–39, 313, 346, 348
restricted universe of discourse 108
resurrection 50, 159, 189, 300
revelation 32, 43, 46, 47, 51, 63, 80, 126, 185, 186, 188, 189, 197, 265, 288, 289, 355

S

sacraments 72
sauropods 299
scepticism 42, 71, 76, 96, 215, 248, 263, 264, 329
science 19–23, 26–30, 33, 34, 37–39, 42, 44–47, 49–55, 57, 64, 67, 69, 71, 84, 94, 129, 135, 141, 142, 144–150, 153, 156, 167–174, 177, 180, 184, 186, 188, 192, 194, 197–202, 205–208, 211–213, 215, 216, 218, 224–228, 239, 242, 243, 245, 250, 253, 255–259, 261–263, 266, 268–270, 272, 273, 275, 277–280, 282–286, 291, 295, 296, 302–305, 307, 310–312, 317, 318, 321, 323, 325, 327–330, 332–335, 337, 339–342, 344, 345, 347, 348, 352, 355, 359, 361, 363, 365, 369–372
 – scientific 18–21, 25–29, 31–38, 41–43, 46–48, 50–54, 56, 63, 68–71, 82, 86–88, 101, 135, 139, 140, 144, 146, 156, 170–172, 174, 175, 177, 179–181, 190, 193, 194, 197–199, 201, 205–210, 213–218, 220, 223–225, 227, 228, 230, 239, 240, 246, 248, 253, 256, 258, 260, 263, 266, 271, 273, 274, 277, 278, 284, 285, 291, 292, 304, 310, 312–318, 323, 324, 327, 329, 331, 339, 340, 342, 344–349, 351, 356, 357, 359, 361, 364, 365, 369–373
 – scientifically 21, 44, 198, 291, 304, 316, 354, 370, 372
scientific credibility 68, 70, 342
scientific criteria 17, 47, 49, 70

scientific discipline 17, 19–21, 25, 30, 33, 36, 37, 40, 43, 44, 56, 69–71, 88, 89, 96, 174, 180, 201, 214, 307, 327, 340–344, 346, 361, 366, 369–373
scientific discourse 169, 258
scientific hypothesis 261
scientific inference 143
scientific knowledge 57, 157, 172, 249, 257
scientific method 262
scientific practice 167, 239, 256, 270, 271, 324
scientific progress 172
scientific realism 187
scientific reasoning 157, 192, 271
scientific research 37, 69, 71, 95, 146, 256–258, 260, 261, 269, 270, 310, 311, 323, 327, 329, 338, 345, 349
scientific test 186, 257, 262
scientific theology 31, 38, 49, 63, 64, 126, 186, 189, 190, 203, 314
scientific theories 22, 33–35, 120, 129, 141, 144, 151, 173, 208, 219, 239, 253, 280
scientific theory 143, 144, 157, 169, 190, 193, 203, 207, 213, 218, 222, 292, 303
scientific work 24, 27, 31, 43, 59, 60, 71, 89, 108, 135, 139, 144, 145, 147, 148, 170, 171, 174, 175, 178, 185, 188, 208, 211, 215–217, 219, 224, 225, 248, 252, 253, 264, 269, 274, 279, 284, 292, 315, 318, 327, 359, 370, 371, 373
secularism 38
secularization 19, 31, 38, 41, 180
 – secular 39, 49, 53, 313, 320
semantic 68, 73, 81, 106, 150, 294, 295
semantic structure 68, 73, 77, 102, 107, 108, 116
semantic theory 229
semantic traditions 68
semantics 22, 33, 68, 72–74, 76, 78–81, 99–102, 104, 106, 107, 116, 362
 – Christian semantics 72

set theory   132, 133
sin   197, 247, 290
social anthropology   343, 344
social science   26, 27, 175, 200, 201, 249, 303, 304, 313
society   24, 51, 59
sociology   52, 60, 69, 278, 337, 343, 344, 353
sociology of religion   61, 67, 73, 317, 370
sociology of science   275
soul   92, 183, 300
source   17, 48, 51, 80, 89, 90, 94, 95, 101, 160, 175, 185, 256, 263, 267, 296, 309, 332, 335, 356, 358, 360, 361, 370
strata   32, 33, 67, 68, 71, 72, 74, 80–82, 85, 86, 88, 126, 135, 206, 253, 295, 317, 339, 340, 358, 364, 370, 372
 – level   68, 71, 72, 75, 77, 80, 81, 86, 96, 103, 106, 126, 135, 160, 161, 172, 173, 176, 178, 180, 194, 202, 206, 225, 243, 246, 247, 253, 265, 275, 285, 295, 297, 298, 301, 302, 313, 316, 334, 351, 357, 358, 364–366
 – levels   67, 68, 71, 81, 82, 102, 107, 135, 173, 182, 188, 194, 225, 234, 297, 301, 339, 340
stratification   37, 39, 67, 82, 135, 178, 206, 295, 370, 372, 373
stratified discipline   370, 372
string theory   179
strong normativity   31, 35, 36, 307, 309–311, 317, 319, 321–323, 325–333, 335–342, 359, 371–373
strong verification   147, 148
structure   24, 26, 30, 36, 53, 71, 75, 84, 101, 102, 104, 107, 108, 115, 116, 118, 126, 132–134, 171, 178, 182, 225, 234, 236, 238, 260, 265, 278, 279, 328, 344, 354, 364
 – conceptual structure   238
 – formal structure   238
 – fundamental structure   238
 – linguistic structure   238
 – logical structure   238
 – mathematical structure   238
 – ontological structure   101, 102, 106, 107, 238
 – ontological structures   102
 – semantic structure   238
 – semantic structures   238
 – syntactic structure   238
subjective leftovers   83
substance ontology   105
supernatural entity   26, 35, 307, 308, 312, 326–328, 330, 331, 334, 335, 339, 371
surface structure   233, 234
synchronic constitution   33, 96, 98, 99, 102, 126, 127, 178, 185, 370
systematic philosophy   103, 105, 108, 109, 111, 116–118, 121, 123, 124, 126, 127, 134, 363
systematic reconstruction   80, 170, 172, 175
systematic theology   17, 20, 21, 23–25, 27, 29–41, 54, 67–71, 76, 78, 79, 82, 85–87, 89, 92, 93, 96, 98, 99, 102, 114, 118, 127, 135, 139–142, 160, 169, 172, 174–182, 185, 187, 190, 201, 203, 205, 206, 217, 219, 224, 230, 240, 245–247, 253, 255–257, 267, 284–287, 293–295, 298, 300–305, 307–310, 312, 313, 316–319, 323, 326, 327, 331–351, 354–366, 369–373
 – academic theology   55
 – Christian theology   17, 26, 29, 31, 58, 62, 77, 92, 122, 125, 135, 160, 226, 313, 316, 337, 344, 355
 – theology   17–21, 24, 26, 27, 29–32, 35, 37–39, 41–64, 67–70, 76, 78, 82, 87, 91–96, 98, 101, 120, 123, 125–127, 135, 147, 158–160, 162, 174, 175, 178, 180, 183–186, 189–191, 194, 196, 197,

200–203, 206, 212, 218, 225, 227, 228, 240, 242–244, 246, 247, 264, 267, 270, 278, 285, 287, 288, 291, 292, 295–298, 301–304, 310, 312, 314, 316–322, 327, 336–338, 342, 344–350, 352, 354, 355, 359–361, 364, 369
systematic theology 1   33, 68, 69, 71–76, 80, 81, 85–88, 126, 135, 140, 194, 225, 294, 295, 316, 339, 351, 356–358, 364, 370, 372
– first-order theology   68, 194
systematic theology 2   33, 34, 68, 69, 71, 74, 77–81, 85–89, 92, 123, 126, 135, 140, 161, 176, 180, 194, 202, 225, 246, 247, 253, 265, 294, 295, 297, 298, 301, 333, 334, 339, 354, 356, 358, 359, 364, 366, 370, 372, 373
– second-order theology   68, 194
systematic theology 3   33, 68, 71, 72, 79–82, 85–92, 94, 95, 98, 123, 125–127, 130, 131, 135, 140, 161, 172, 173, 176, 178, 180, 182, 194, 201, 206, 225, 228, 247, 252, 253, 294, 295, 302, 334, 339, 354, 356, 359, 362–365, 370, 372, 373
systematization   68, 78, 129, 131, 133–135, 161, 177, 216, 235–238
system-constituting method   134

T

testability   27, 33, 39, 45, 95, 103, 108, 139, 141–145, 147, 149, 151, 152, 167–181, 184–186, 201, 203, 205, 209, 210, 220, 221, 255, 257, 273, 283, 285, 292, 316, 370, 373
– holistic view   141, 152
– single propositions   33, 141, 143, 144, 148, 151, 166, 167, 170, 175, 176, 203, 370

– single statements   212, 217, 219, 240, 339
– whole theories   33, 141–143, 148, 149, 151, 152, 160, 161, 167, 168, 170, 173, 176, 203, 217, 219, 224, 225, 228, 239, 240, 246, 252, 253, 339, 370
textual studies   267, 268
theism   26, 135, 160, 194, 250, 264, 304, 351
– theistic   26, 76, 96, 135, 190, 200, 241, 242, 246, 250, 253, 298, 326, 334, 338, 370, 372
theistic ontology   26, 36, 126, 135, 240, 247, 252, 253, 361, 365, 371–373
theological method   61
theological scope   79
theology   46, 60, 62, 69, 245, 285, 312, 313, 322
– scientific theology   71
theology of religion   320
theoretical framework   25, 27–29, 45, 67, 70, 71, 75, 87–89, 94, 96, 97, 99–101, 104, 106–109, 125–127, 130, 134, 135, 166, 168, 170, 176, 178, 185, 188, 189, 193, 202, 203, 210, 211, 219, 231, 233, 234, 237, 238, 241, 247–249, 251–253, 256, 261, 262, 265, 266, 270, 271, 273, 274, 278, 281, 284, 286, 290, 291, 294, 300, 308, 309, 311, 316, 317, 319, 322–324, 326, 330, 335, 336, 340, 341, 369, 373
theoretical operator   102–106, 238
theoretical physics   93, 179
theory   20, 28, 29, 31, 34, 35, 57, 77, 80, 85, 86, 91, 92, 96, 98, 99, 102, 103, 105, 107, 109, 110, 115, 119, 123, 128, 130–133, 135, 142–145, 150, 151, 154–156, 158, 161, 164, 167, 170, 172–174, 176, 177, 179, 180, 183, 190–193, 196, 198, 199, 201, 202, 206–215, 217–220, 222–226, 228, 229, 231–235, 237–239, 245, 247–249, 252, 253, 261, 265, 267–272,

274, 275, 277, 282, 283, 290, 296–304, 308–310, 313, 315, 328, 333–335, 338, 339, 371–373
theory-laden   151, 164, 175, 188, 253, 274, 280
thermodynamics   165, 227
thick description   73, 87, 126
thought experiment   78, 90–93, 147, 154, 354–356
  – accelerating elevator   90
  – Brain in a Vat   90
  – Gettier Problem, the   90
  – hammer and feather experiment   90
  – Hilbert's Hotel   90
  – Russell's Paradox   90
  – Simulation Hypothesis   90
tradition   26, 27, 57, 59, 61–63, 69, 75, 76, 78, 80, 87, 89, 90, 94, 95, 98, 109, 115, 116, 142, 146, 151, 177, 187–190, 192–196, 198–200, 218, 230, 247–249, 260, 263, 268, 292–294, 296, 317, 321, 335, 356, 360, 361
tradition ethics   61
tradition-constituted rationality   203
transcendence   123, 124, 126, 127, 184
transcendental intersubjectivity   260
trial-and-error   147, 206, 223, 293
trinity   77
truth   18, 21, 23, 24, 28, 31, 35, 37, 38, 45, 48–50, 59, 62, 63, 77, 79, 84, 85, 94, 95, 102, 104, 106, 107, 115, 127–131, 134, 150, 151, 159–161, 167, 173, 179–181, 185, 186, 197, 201, 206, 207, 218, 219, 224, 228–230, 232, 233, 236–238, 245, 251, 256, 260, 268–270, 286, 294, 301, 302, 318, 319, 327, 328, 331–335, 339, 340, 345, 347, 361, 362, 365, 369–372
truth-candidate   29, 30, 33, 78–80, 86, 88, 95, 101, 127, 128, 130, 132, 133, 191, 201, 202, 206, 230, 231, 233, 239, 247, 252, 282, 293, 311, 334, 340, 355, 357, 361, 365, 373
truth-claim   78, 80, 181, 185, 186, 245, 329, 331, 333, 334, 336, 361, 369
truth-indicating   296
two dimensions of Being   118

U

UFO   282
uncertainty principle   91
underdetermination of data   291
underdetermination of theory   106, 147, 151, 160, 164, 175, 185, 188, 202, 216, 253, 282
  – underdetermined   76
universal expressibility   120
universal ontology   343
universal rationality   187, 188
universal science   127
universality   256, 262, 264, 300
universally expressible   119
university   17, 19, 24, 38, 39, 41, 42, 52, 60, 71, 96, 175, 180, 316, 320, 342, 346, 349, 352
unobservable entity   22
unrestricted universe of discourse   108, 109, 111, 116
unscientific   71, 348

V

verification   259
verification principle   145–149
verificationism   210, 214
Vienna School   259
  – phenomenalists   259
  – physicalists   259

W

weak normativity 35, 309, 312, 319–323, 325–330, 332, 336–340, 371, 373
weak verification 34, 147, 148, 167, 173, 176, 182, 224
web of belief 282
world 22, 37, 50, 74, 75, 87, 93, 107, 110, 114, 115, 126, 142, 149, 153, 157, 159, 160, 166, 168, 171, 172, 176, 179, 182, 183, 187, 195, 196, 198, 225, 229, 230, 234, 249, 252, 260, 262, 277, 281, 283, 288, 318, 326
worldview 38, 61, 74, 94, 173, 190, 211, 227, 228, 251, 277
worship 46, 72, 188

Y

Yale school 58, 61–64
 – postliberal 59, 61–63